CALIFORNIA REAL ESTATE

PRINCIPLES

SIXTH EDITION

CHARLES O. STAPLETON III
MARTHA R. WILLIAMS

JOE NEWTON, CONTRIBUTING EDITOR

Dearborn™
Real Estate Education

This publication is designed to provide accurate and authoritative information in regard to the subject matter covered. It is sold with the understanding that the publisher is not engaged in rendering legal, accounting, or other professional service. If legal advice or other expert assistance is required, the services of a competent professional person should be sought.

President: Roy Lipner
Publisher: Evan Butterfield
Associate Publisher: Louise Benzer
Managing Editor, Production: Daniel Frey
Quality Assurance Editor: David Shaw
Typesetter: Todd Bowman
Creative Director: Lucy Jenkins

Published by Dearborn™ Real Estate Education,
a division of Dearborn Financial Publishing, Inc.®
30 South Wacker Drive, Suite 2500
Chicago, IL 60606-7481
(312) 836-4400
http://www.dearbornRE.com

Printed in the United States of America.

05 06 07 10 9 8 7 6 5 4 3 2 1

Library of Congress Cataloging-in-Publication Data

Stapleton, Charles O.
  California real estate principles / Charles O. Stapleton III, Martha R. Williams.–6th ed.
    p. cm.
  Includes index.
  ISBN 0-7931-8802-4
  1. Real estate business—California. 2. Real property—California. I. Williams, Martha R.
  II. Title.
HD266.C2S73 2004
333.33'09794—dc22

2004016300

CONTENTS

PREFACE

California Real Estate Principles is an introduction to the many interesting aspects of the real estate business. This book has been written primarily for the prospective real estate broker or salesperson, but it will also be of interest to the consumer or investor.

It is difficult to overestimate the growing importance of the Internet to the real estate industry. The resources available there have brought together the interests of agents, consumers, and investors. Throughout this book you will find addresses on the World Wide Web. We encourage you to explore the Internet resources mentioned in this book to expand on what you read here. To make it easy to find site references, they are highlighted in the margins of the text. There is also a complete list of all site references in the Internet Appendix at the back of the book. As with any resource, you are cautioned to use good judgment when considering the validity of the information you find on the Internet.

The purpose of the sixth edition is to provide accurate and timely information. The California Department of Real Estate made changes to the salesperson and broker licensing exams last spring. This new edition addresses those changes to the extent possible in a limited amount of space. Additional information is available at *www.dearbornRE.com.* Click on the link under "Real Estate Educators" that takes you to the Instructor Resources page.

■ HOW TO USE THIS BOOK

Each chapter in this book is divided into **sections.** Usually, each section has one or more **examples** of how the material covered may be applied to real-life situations.

Throughout each chapter are **exercises** that will require you to use what you have learned to solve problems involving practical applications of the topics covered. After you complete an exercise, you can check your answers by turning to the Answer Key at the back of the book.

The text of each chapter concludes with a **summary** of the material covered, with the most important terms highlighted in **bold type. Important terms** also appear in a list that follows the chapter summary. If you are familiar with those

viii   California Real Estate Principles

terms you should have no problem successfully completing the **achievement** examination at the end of the chapter. Another way to gauge your progress is to attempt to answer the achievement exam questions *before* you begin the chapter text. When you have finished the chapter, you should find the achievement exam much easier to work through a second time.

■ MONITORING YOUR PROGRESS

You should not be discouraged if at first you do poorly on the examinations despite your best efforts. Part of learning how to succeed at an examination is learning how to take a test. This skill may require some practice, particularly if you have been out of school for some time. If you are using this book to prepare for a licensing exam, you should restudy any material you are unsure of and retake each exam until you can answer 90 percent of the questions correctly.

Don't forget that the Answer Key at the back of the book provides an answer for every exercise and examination question that you encounter as you proceed through the text. Check your work as often as necessary to make sure you understand what you have read. By doing so, you will be more likely to retain what you have learned as well.

■ ACKNOWLEDGMENTS

The authors wish to thank the real estate educators and professionals who contributed their very helpful criticism of earlier editions of this book. Reviewers of the first edition include George H. Miller, West Valley College; Larry Copeland, Coastline Community College; Kathleen Monaco, Mesa College; Lois Kadosh, REALTOR®; Dr. Alan R. Klofkorn, Irvine Valley College; Don Names, Mt. San Antonio College; and Fred Weber, Saddleback College. Reviewers of the second edition were: Faz Elahi, Los Angeles Community Colleges; Richard Gonzalez, College of Marin; Dr. Alan R. Klofkorn, Irvine Valley College; Arthur L. Olderich, Chaffey College; William H. Pivar, College of the Desert; and Sherry Shindler, Fullerton College.

Reviewers of the third edition were: Ray Benningson, College of Marin; Mark R. Chamberlin, Chamberlin Real Estate School, Inc.; Thomas E. Duffy, Jr., Los Angeles City College; Dr. Joan M. Harrison, Harrison Seminars, Laguna Beach; Ernie Hubert, 2000 School of Real Estate; Judith Meadows; James R. Overton, Yuba Community College; and J. D. Ryan, Irvine Valley College.

Reviewers of the fourth edition were: Thurza B. Andrew, GRI, Butte Community College; Fax Elahi, West Los Angeles College; Meldy Langager, Diablo Valley College; Russell H. Gatlin, Television Education, Inc.; Ignacio Gonzalez, Mendocino

Community College; James R. Gromley, Prudential California Realty School of Real Estate; Don Kalal, GRI, California Brokers Institute; Larry Scheer, Anthony Schools of San Diego; and Jason K. Wolins, Anthony Schools.

Reviewers of the fifth edition were: Professor Olivia Vasquez Anderson, East Los Angeles College; Frank Diaz, Mission College, Santa Clara; Ignacio Gonzalez, Mendocino College, Ukiah; Professor Donna Grogan, MBA, GRI, CPM, CRS, El Camino College; Don Kalal, GRI, California Brokers Institute; Minnie Lush, GRI, Lush Enterprises.

The authors would like to offer a special thanks to the following reviewers whose expertise has been invaluable:

> C. Anthony Phillips, CPA, Down Stream Exchange
>
> Llewellyn Chin, Senior Counsel, California Association of REALTORS®
>
> Yin Bihr, Century 21® Masters, San Marino
>
> Dennie L. Rowland, President, First American Title Company, Los Angeles
>
> Gordon Peterson, Account Executive, First American Title Company, Los Angeles
>
> Juliana Tu, Certified Escrow Officer, Arch Escrow, San Marino
>
> George Lawrence, American Capitol Loans, Torrance
>
> Jennifer Dodge, California Association of REALTORS®, Director, Profession and Promotional Products
>
> Minnie Lush, GRI, Lush Enterprises

The authors especially thank the following reviewers for their valuable assistance in the development of *California Real Estate Principles*, Sixth Edition:

> Leonel A. Bello, MBA, real estate broker, City College of San Francisco
>
> Mark L. Chamberlin, President, Chamberlin Real Estate School
>
> Ignacio Gonzalez, Mendocino Community College
>
> Bud Zeller, broker, GRI, CRS, RECS, SRES, CREA, RIM, IREI, SierraProperties.com

No real estate text is complete without contracts, documents, and other forms. The California Department of Real Estate, California Association of REALTORS®, Professional Publishing Corporation, First American Title Company, Los Angeles, and others noted throughout the text generously allowed material from their publications to be reprinted.

> Charles O. Stapleton III
>
> Martha R. Williams, J.D.

1

THE BUSINESS OF REAL ESTATE

■ THE REAL ESTATE LAW

Less than a century ago, buyers had few protections from unscrupulous sellers and real estate agents. Instead, the common-law doctrine of *caveat emptor* (a Latin phrase meaning "Let the buyer beware") prevailed.

In 1917, California became the first state to legislate licensing requirements for real estate brokers and salespersons. Although that initial legislation was declared unconstitutional, it was quickly amended, and the California Supreme Court upheld the **Real Estate Act of 1919.** Now, all 50 states and the District of Columbia license real estate agents. This means that to conduct business as a real estate agent in any state, you must be licensed by that state. In California there are currently more than 380,000 real estate licensees. About one third are licensed as brokers and the rest are salepersons.

> The state's police power allows it to license real estate agents.

The state's licensing ability is an exercise of its **police power** to enact laws within constitutional limits to promote the public health, safety, and general welfare.

Major Provisions of the Law

California legislation has been compiled in a series of books called **codes.** What is commonly referred to as the **Real Estate Law** is actually Division 4 of the **Business and Professions Code.** The Real Estate Law has two parts:

■ Part 1 covers licensing.

■ Part 2 covers transactions and includes the **Subdivided Lands Law.**

www.leginfo.ca.gov

The complete text of all 29 volumes of the California codes, as well as information on bills pending before the California legislature, can be found at *www.leginfo.ca.gov.*

Real estate licensees are also subject to the **Regulations of the Real Estate Commissioner,** which are enforceable as law. These serve to clarify and interpret the Real Estate Law.

The primary purpose of both the Real Estate Law and the Regulations of the Real Estate Commissioner is to protect the members of the public with whom real estate licensees come into contact in their business activities.

Department of Real Estate

www.dre.ca.gov

The **Department of Real Estate,** headed by the **Real Estate Commissioner,** administers the Real Estate Law in California. Every state has a similar department or agency responsible for enforcing laws concerning real estate licensees.

Information about California's Department of Real Estate (DRE), including the current status of all real estate licensees, can be found at the Department's Web site, *www.dre.ca.gov.*

California Department of Real Estate Office Locations

Sacramento (Main Office)	San Diego
2201 Broadway	1350 Front Street, Suite 3064
Sacramento, CA 95818	San Diego, CA 92101-3687
(916) 227-0931	(619) 525-4192
Los Angeles	Fresno
320 W. 4th St., Suite 350	2550 Mariposa Mall, Room 3070
Los Angeles, CA 90013-1105	Fresno, CA 93721-2273
(213) 620-2072	(559) 445-5009
Oakland	
1515 Clay St., Suite 702	
Oakland, CA 94612-1402	
(510) 622-2552	

All offices are open 8–5 weekdays.

Real Estate Commissioner. The Real Estate Commissioner is appointed by the governor and serves at the governor's discretion. The person selected as commissioner is required to have been a practicing real estate broker in California for five years or engaged in some form of real estate activity for five of the past ten years.

The Real Estate Commissioner

Assisted by Department of Real Estate staff members, the Real Estate Commissioner

- screens candidates for licensing;
- prepares subdivision public reports;
- conducts licensee disciplinary action;
- investigates nonlicensees performing activities for which a license is required; and
- regulates nonexempt franchises and real property securities.

The Real Estate Commissioner determines administrative policy and enforces that policy in the best interests of those dealing with real estate licensees. The responsibilities of the Real Estate Commissioner are highlighted in the box above.

Real Estate Advisory Commission. The **Real Estate Advisory Commission** makes recommendations to the Real Estate Commissioner on matters involving the Department of Real Estate.

The ten members of the Real Estate Advisory Commission are appointed by the commissioner, who presides over their meetings. Six commission members must be licensed California real estate brokers. Four commission members must be nonlicensed members of the public. Unlike the commissioner, commission members serve without compensation, although they are reimbursed for some expenses.

The commissioner must call meetings of the commission at least four times a year. At those meetings, which are open to the public, commission members express their views of department policy and function and make recommendations to the commissioner.

■ REAL ESTATE BROKERAGE

Anyone handling a real estate transaction in California for compensation must be licensed by the Department of Real Estate as a **real estate broker** or **real estate salesperson**. A real estate salesperson (often referred to as a **sales associate** or **associate licensee**) can act only under the control and supervision of the real estate broker by whom the salesperson is employed.

A **real estate brokerage** is a business in which real estate license–related activities are performed under the supervision of a real estate broker. A real estate brokerage may consist of only one broker of record and no employees. But a brokerage may be large enough to have specialized departments with many salespeople, a support staff that includes administrative and clerical workers, and a number of branch offices.

No matter how large a real estate office is or how its ownership is structured, there must always be at least one broker under whose license the real estate activities of the firm are carried out.

Sole proprietorship. A real estate brokerage that is a sole proprietorship must be owned by a licensed real estate broker, a salesperson, or a nonlicensee. Real estate activities can only be carried out by or under the authority of a licensed real estate broker, however. No separate formalities are required to start a business as a sole proprietor. For business liability and tax purposes, however, most brokerages choose to incorporate.

Corporation. A brokerage may be set up as a corporation, provided that at least one officer of the corporation is a licensed broker and is designated the responsible **broker-officer.** The corporation must submit to the Department of Real Estate

- the corporation license application and fee;
- a **Certificate of Status** issued by the Secretary of State within 30 days prior to submission of the application; *or* the Articles of Incorporation filed with the Secretary of State if a California stock corporation originally filed the articles within six months of the application; and
- a statement of officers as filed with the Secretary of State.

Partnership. A brokerage can be established as a partnership. Every partner who performs activities that require a real estate license must be individually licensed as a real estate broker. At least one broker partner must obtain an additional license for each branch office location. The partnership itself needs no separate license.

Use of a Fictitious Business Name

> A fictitious name is any name other than that of a real estate licensee.

A brokerage, whether a sole proprietorship, corporation, or partnership, can do business under a fictitious name. A **fictitious business name statement** must be filed with the county clerk in the county of the broker's principal business address. The statement is effective for five years from December 31 of the year filed and is commonly referred to as a *DBA* (doing business as). A copy of the fictitious business name statement must be sent to the Real Estate Commissioner. The business cards of a real estate licensee should use exactly the same name that appears on the license. Note: The filing requirements for fictitious business names also apply to Internet domains used to identify a real estate brokerage or licensee.

License Inspection

The broker's license must be available for inspection by the commissioner (or the commissioner's representative) at the broker's principal place of business. If a broker maintains more than one place of business, each branch office must be separately licensed and the license must be available for inspection there. The license of any salesperson(s) working for the broker must also be available for inspection at the broker's main office.

The Broker/Salesperson Relationship

For purposes of the Real Estate Law, a salesperson is always considered the *employee* of the broker. This means that the broker is held accountable for the salesperson's conduct in performing business activities. For compensation, tax, and other purposes, a salesperson can be treated as either an employee or an independent contractor, as discussed in Chapter 6, "The Law of Agency."

A salesperson's license is activated only after the name of the employing broker is provided to the Department of Real Estate. The broker and salesperson are required by the Real Estate Law to have a **written agreement.** Regulation 2726 of the Real Estate Commissioner states: "The agreement shall be dated and signed by the parties and shall cover material aspects of the relationship between the parties, including supervision of licensed activities, duties and compensation."

www.dre.ca.gov

When a Salesperson Changes Brokers

The following steps must be taken when a salesperson changes employment from one broker to another. Detailed information and printable forms are available at the DRE Web site, *www.dre.ca.gov.*

1. The former employing broker must notify the Department of Real Estate's Sacramento headquarters immediately, in writing.

2. The former employer must return the salesperson's license certificate within three days of termination of employment and sign the Salesperson Change Application, R/E Form 214.

3. R/E Form 214 must be completed by the salesperson and new employer within five days and sent to:

Department of Real Estate
P.O. Box 187003
Sacramento, CA 95818-7003

When a Salesperson Is Discharged

If an employing broker discharges a salesperson for a violation of the Real Estate Law, the broker must immediately file a certified, written statement of the facts with the Real Estate Commissioner.

A sample broker-salesperson contract, with the salesperson treated as independent contractor, appears on the next three pages as Figure 1.1.

This is the first of many forms that appear in this book. You should be alert to the differences in the types of forms that you will see.

- The content of some forms is *proprietary,* which means that the form is unique to the entity that created it. You will see a copyright notice on such forms, which indicates that you are not allowed to copy the form without permission of the copyright holder.
- Other forms consist of wording that is dictated by state law—what we refer to as *statutory language.* Even though the wording of the form is mandated (and even the style and size of the type used may be dictated by state law), the overall design of the form may still be copyrighted.
- Last, some forms combine state requirements and those of an association or company. Most of these customized forms also are copyrighted.

www.car.org
www.profpub.com

With the rapid changes in both California and federal law, form updates are an ongoing process. By the time you see them, the forms in this book may have already been revised. To keep up with the pace of change, the two largest forms publishers in the state have Web sites where form updates can be ordered and even downloaded for immediate use. The California Association of REALTORS® is headquartered in Los Angeles and found at *www.car.org.* Professional Publishing, Inc., is located in Novato and found at *www.profpub.com.*

Exercise 1-1   May a broker-salesperson agreement transfer responsibility for all brokerage activities to the salesperson?

■ ACTIVITIES OF A REAL ESTATE BROKER

The Real Estate Law sets out the activities that require a real estate broker's license. Those activities also may be performed by a licensed real estate salesperson. The law defines a real estate salesperson as someone who is employed for compensation (salary or commissions) by a licensed real estate broker to perform acts that require a real estate license. The salesperson can only conduct business as the employee of the broker. All of the salesperson's contracts with clients and customers will be executed in the broker's name.

FIGURE 1.1

Independent Contractor Agreement

CALIFORNIA
ASSOCIATION
OF REALTORS®

INDEPENDENT CONTRACTOR AGREEMENT
(Between Broker and Associate-Licensee)

This Agreement, dated _____ is made between _____
_____ ("Broker") and
_____ ("Associate-Licensee").

In consideration of the covenants and representations contained in this Agreement, Broker and Associate-Licensee agree as follows:

1. **BROKER:** Broker represents that Broker is duly licensed as a real estate broker by the State of California, ☐ doing business as _____
   _____ (firm name), ☐ a sole proprietorship, ☐ a partnership, ☐ a corporation.
   Broker is a member of the _____
   Association(s) of REALTORS ®, and a subscriber to the _____
   listing service(s). Broker shall keep Broker's license current during the term of this Agreement. _____ multiple

2. **ASSOCIATE-LICENSEE:** Associate-Licensee represents that, (a) he/she is duly licensed by the State of California as a ☐ real estate broker,
   ☐ real estate salesperson, and (b) he/she has not used any other names within the past five years, except _____
   _____. Associate-Licensee shall keep his/her license current during
   the term of this Agreement, including satisfying all applicable continuing education and provisional license requirements.

3. **INDEPENDENT CONTRACTOR RELATIONSHIP:**

   A. Broker and Associate-Licensee intend that, to the maximum extent permissible by law: **(i)** This Agreement does not constitute an employment agreement by either party; **(ii)** Broker and Associate-Licensee are independent contracting parties with respect to all services rendered under this Agreement; **(iii)** This Agreement shall not be construed as a partnership.

   B. Broker shall not: **(i)** restrict Associate-Licensee's activities to particular geographical areas or, **(ii)** dictate Associate-Licensee's activities with regard to hours, leads, open houses, opportunity or floor time, production, prospects, sales meetings, schedule, inventory, time off, vacation, or similar activities, except to the extent required by law.

   C. Associate-Licensee shall not be required to accept an assignment by Broker to service any particular current or prospective listing or parties.

   D. Except as required by law: **(i)** Associate-Licensee retains sole and absolute discretion and judgment in the methods, techniques, and procedures to be used in soliciting and obtaining listings, sales, exchanges, leases, rentals, or other transactions, and in carrying out Associate-Licensee's selling and soliciting activities, **(ii)** Associate-Licensee is under the control of Broker as to the results of Associate-Licensee's work only, and not as to the means by which those results are accomplished, **(iii)** Associate-Licensee has no authority to bind Broker by any promise or representation and **(iv)** Broker shall not be liable for any obligation or liability incurred by Associate-Licensee.

   E. Associate-Licensee's only remuneration shall be the compensation specified in paragraph 8.

   F. Associate-Licensee shall not be treated as an employee with respect to services performed as a real estate agent, for state and federal tax purposes.

   G. The fact the Broker may carry worker compensation insurance for Broker's own benefit and for the mutual benefit of Broker and licensees associated with Broker, including Associate-Licensee, shall not create an inference of employment.

4. **LICENSED ACTIVITY:** All listings of property, and all agreements, acts or actions for performance of licensed acts, which are taken or performed in connection with this Agreement, shall be taken and performed in the name of Broker. Associate-Licensee agrees to and does hereby contribute all right and title to such listings to Broker for the benefit and use of Broker, Associate-Licensee, and other licensees associated with Broker. Broker shall make available to Associate-Licensee, equally with other licensees associated with Broker, all current listings in Broker's office, except any listing which Broker may choose to place in the exclusive servicing of Associate-Licensee or one or more other specific licensees associated with Broker. Associate-Licensee shall provide and pay for all professional licenses, supplies, services, and other items required in connection with Associate-Licensee's activities under this Agreement, or any listing or transaction, without reimbursement from Broker except as required by law. Associate-Licensee shall work diligently and with his/her best efforts: **(a)** To sell, exchange, lease, or rent properties listed with Broker or other cooperating Brokers; **(b)** To solicit additional listings, clients, and customers; and **(c)** To otherwise promote the business of serving the public in real estate transactions to the end that Broker and Associate-Licensee may derive the greatest benefit possible in accordance with law. Associate-Licensee shall not commit any unlawful act under federal, state or local law or regulation while conducting licensed activity. Associate-Licensee shall at all times be familiar, and comply, with all applicable federal, state and local laws, including, but not limited to, anti-discrimination laws and restrictions against the giving or accepting a fee, or other thing of value, for the referral of business to title companies, escrow companies, home inspection companies, pest control companies and other settlement service providers pursuant to the California Business and Professions Code and the Real Estate Settlement Procedures Acts (RESPA). Broker shall make available for Associate-Licensee's use, along with other licensees associated with Broker, the facilities of the real estate office operated by Broker at _____
   _____ and the facilities of any other office
   locations made available by Broker pursuant to this Agreement.

   Broker and Associate-Licensee acknowledge receipt of copy of this page, which constitutes Page 1 of _____ Pages.
   Broker's Initials (_____) (_____)   Associate-Licensee's Initials (_____) (_____)

Published and Distributed by:
REAL ESTATE BUSINESS SERVICES, INC.
a subsidiary of the CALIFORNIA ASSOCIATION OF REALTORS®
525 South Virgil Avenue, Los Angeles, California 90020
PRINT DATE

REVISED 10/98

OFFICE USE ONLY
Reviewed by Broker
or Designee _____
Date _____

EQUAL HOUSING OPPORTUNITY

INDEPENDENT CONTRACTOR AGREEMENT (ICA-11 PAGE 1 OF 3)

Source: Reprinted with permission, California Association of REALTORS®. Endorsement not implied.

FIGURE 1.1

Independent Contractor Agreement (Continued)

5. PROPRIETARY INFORMATION AND FILES: (a) All files and documents pertaining to listings, leads and transactions are the property of Broker and shall be delivered to Broker by Associate-Licensee immediately upon request or termination of their relationship under this Agreement. **(b)** Associate-Licensee acknowledges that Broker's method of conducting business is a protected trade secret. **(c)** Associate-Licensee shall not use to his/her own advantage, or the advantage of any other person, business, or entity, except as specifically agreed in writing, either during Associate-Licensee's association with Broker, or thereafter, any information gained for or from the business, or files of Broker.

6. SUPERVISION: Associate-Licensee, within 24 hours (or ☐ _____) after preparing, signing, or receiving same, shall submit to Broker, or Broker's designated licensee: **(a)** All documents which may have a material effect upon the rights and duties of principals in a transaction, **(b)** Any documents or other items connected with a transaction pursuant to this Agreement in the possession of or available to Associate-Licensee and, **(c)** All documents associated with any real estate transaction in which Associate-Licensee is a principal.

7. TRUST FUNDS: All trust funds shall be handled in compliance with the Business and Professions Code, and other applicable laws.

8. COMPENSATION:

  A. TO BROKER: Compensation shall be charged to parties who enter into listing or other agreements for services requiring a real estate license:
  ☐ as shown in "Exhibit A" attached, which is incorporated as a part of this Agreement by reference, or
  ☐ as follows: _____
  _____
  _____

  Any deviation which is not approved in writing in advance by Broker, shall be (1) deducted from Associate-Licensee's compensation, if lower than the amount or rate approved above; and, (2) subject to Broker approval, if higher than the amount approved above. Any permanent change in commission schedule shall be disseminated by Broker to Associate-Licensee.

  B. TO ASSOCIATE-LICENSEE: Associate-Licensee shall receive a share of compensation actually collected by Broker, on listings or other agreements for services requiring a real estate license, which are solicited and obtained by Associate-Licensee, and on transactions of which Associate-Licensee's activities are the procuring cause, as follows:
  ☐ as shown in "Exhibit B" attached, which is incorporated as a part of this Agreement by reference, or
  ☐ other: _____
  _____
  _____

  C. PARTNERS, TEAMS, AND AGREEMENTS WITH OTHER ASSOCIATE-LICENSEES IN OFFICE: If Associate-Licensee and one or more other Associate-Licensees affiliated with Broker participate on the same side (either listing or selling) of a transaction, the commission allocated to their combined activities shall be divided by Broker and paid to them according to their written agreement. Broker shall have the right to withhold total compensation if there is a dispute between associate-licensees, or if there is no written agreement, or if no written agreement has been provided to Broker.

  D. EXPENSES AND OFFSETS: If Broker elects to advance funds to pay expenses or liabilities of Associate-Licensee, or for an advance payment of, or draw upon, future compensation, Broker may deduct the full amount advanced from compensation payable to Associate-Licensee on any transaction without notice. If Associate-Licensee's compensation is subject to a lien, garnishment or other restriction on payment, Broker shall charge Associate-Licensee a fee for complying with such restriction.

  E. PAYMENT: (1) All compensation collected by Broker and due to Associate-Licensee shall be paid to Associate-Licensee, after deduction of expenses and offsets, immediately or as soon thereafter as practicable, except as otherwise provided in this Agreement, or a separate written agreement between Broker and Associate-Licensee. **(2)** Compensation shall not be paid to Associate-Licensee until both the transaction and file are complete. **(3)** Broker is under no obligation to pursue collection of compensation from any person or entity responsible for payment. Associate-Licensee does not have the independent right to pursue collection of compensation for activities which require a real estate license which were done in the name of Broker. **(4)** Expenses which are incurred in the attempt to collect compensation shall be paid by Broker and Associate-Licensee in the same proportion as set forth for the division of compensation (paragraph 8(B)). **(5)** If there is a known or pending claim against Broker or Associate-Licensee on transactions for which Associate-Licensee has not yet been paid, Broker may withhold from compensation due Associate-Licensee on that transaction amounts for which Associate-Licensee could be responsible under paragraph 14, until such claim is resolved. **(6)** Associate-Licensee shall not be entitled to any advance payment from Broker upon future compensation.

  F. UPON OR AFTER TERMINATION: If this Agreement is terminated while Associate-Licensee has listings or pending transactions that require further work normally rendered by Associate-Licensee, Broker shall make arrangements with another associate-licensee to perform the required work, or Broker shall perform the work him/herself. The licensee performing the work shall be reasonably compensated for completing work on those listings or transactions, and such reasonable compensation shall be deducted from Associate-Licensee's share of compensation. Except for such offset, Associate-Licensee shall receive the compensation due as specified above.

9. TERMINATION OF RELATIONSHIP: Broker or Associate-Licensee may terminate their relationship under this Agreement at any time, with or without cause. After termination, Associate-Licensee shall not solicit **(a)** prospective or existing clients or customers based upon company-generated leads obtained during the time Associate-Licensee was affiliated with Broker, or **(b)** any principal with existing contractual obligations to Broker, or **(c)** any principal with a contractual transactional obligation for which Broker is entitled to be compensated. Even after termination, this Agreement shall govern all disputes and claims between Broker and Associate-Licensee connected with their relationship under this Agreement, including obligations and liabilities arising from existing and completed listings, transactions, and services.

Broker and Associate-Licensee acknowledge receipt of copy of this page, which constitutes Page 2 of _____ Pages.
Broker's Initials (_____) (_____)   Associate-Licensee's Initials (_____) (_____)

REVISED 10/98

Page 2 of ___ Pages.

OFFICE USE ONLY
Reviewed by Broker
or Designee _____
Date _____

EQUAL HOUSING OPPORTUNITY

PRINT DATE

INDEPENDENT CONTRACTOR AGREEMENT (ICA-11 PAGE 2 OF 3)

FIGURE 1.1

Independent Contractor Agreement (Continued)

10. **DISPUTE RESOLUTION:**
    A. **Mediation:** Mediation is recommended as a method of resolving disputes arising out of this Agreement between Broker and Associate-Licensee.
    B. **Arbitration:** All disputes or claims between Associate-Licensee and other licensee(s) associated with Broker, or between Associate-Licensee and Broker, arising from or connected in any way with this Agreement, which cannot be adjusted between the parties involved, shall be submitted to the Association of REALTORS® of which all such disputing parties are members for arbitration pursuant to the provisions of its Bylaws, as may be amended from time to time, which are incorporated as a part of this Agreement by reference. If the Bylaws of the Association do not cover arbitration of the dispute, or if the Association declines jurisdiction over the dispute, then arbitration shall be pursuant to the rules of California law. The Federal Arbitration Act, Title 9, U.S. Code, Section 1, et seq., shall govern this Agreement.

11. **AUTOMOBILE:** Associate-Licensee shall maintain automobile insurance coverage for liability and property damage in the following amounts $_____/$_____. Broker shall be named as an additional insured party on Associate-Licensee's policies. A copy of the endorsement showing Broker as an additional insured shall be provided to Broker.

12. **PERSONAL ASSISTANTS:** Associate-Licensee may make use of a personal assistant, provided the following requirements are satisfied. Associate-Licensee shall have a written agreement with the personal assistant which establishes the terms and responsibilities of the parties to the employment agreement, including, but not limited to, compensation, supervision and compliance with applicable law. The agreement shall be subject to Broker's review and approval. Unless otherwise agreed, if the personal assistant has a real estate license, that license must be provided to the Broker. Both Associate-Licensee and personal assistant must sign any agreement that Broker has established for such purposes.

13. **OFFICE POLICY MANUAL:** If Broker's office policy manual, now or as modified in the future, conflicts with or differs from the terms of this Agreement, the terms of the office policy manual shall govern the relationship between Broker and Associate-Licensee.

14. **INDEMNITY AND HOLD HARMLESS:** Associate-Licensee agrees to indemnify, defend and hold Broker harmless from all claims, disputes, litigation, judgments, awards, costs and attorney's fees, arising from any action taken or omitted by Associate-Licensee, or others working through, or on behalf of Associate-Licensee in connection with services rendered. Any such claims or costs payable pursuant to this Agreement, are due as follows:
    ☐ Paid in full by Associate-Licensee, who hereby agrees to indemnify and hold harmless Broker for all such sums, or
    ☐ In the same ratio as the compensation split as it existed at the time the compensation was earned by Associate-Licensee
    ☐ Other: _____
    _____
    _____
    Payment from Associate-Licensee is due at the time Broker makes such payment and can be offset from any compensation due Associate-Licensee as above. Broker retains the authority to settle claims or disputes, whether or not Associate-Licensee consents to such settlement.

15. **ADDITIONAL PROVISIONS:** _____
    _____
    _____

16. **DEFINITIONS:** As used in this Agreement, the following terms have the meanings indicated:
    (A) "Listing" means an agreement with a property owner or other party to locate a buyer, exchange party, lessee, or other party to a transaction involving real property, a mobile home, or other property or transaction which may be brokered by a real estate licensee, or an agreement with a party to locate or negotiate for any such property or transaction.
    (B) "Compensation means compensation for acts requiring a real estate license, regardless of whether calculated as a percentage of transaction price, flat fee, hourly rate, or in any other manner.
    (C) "Transaction" means a sale, exchange, lease, or rental of real property, a business opportunity, or a manufactured home, which may lawfully be brokered by a real estate licensee.

17. **ATTORNEY FEES:** In any action, proceeding, or arbitration between Broker and Associate-Licensee arising from or related to this Agreement, the prevailing Broker or Associate-Licensee shall be entitled to reasonable attorney fees and costs.

18. **ENTIRE AGREEMENT; MODIFICATION:** All prior agreements between the parties concerning their relationship as Broker and Associate-Licensee are incorporated in this Agreement, which constitutes the entire contract. Its terms are intended by the parties as a final and complete expression of their agreement with respect to its subject matter, and may not be contradicted by evidence of any prior agreement or contemporaneous oral agreement. This Agreement may not be amended, modified, altered, or changed except by a further agreement in writing executed by Broker and Associate-Licensee.

Broker:

_____
(Brokerage firm name)

By _____
Its Broker/Office manager (circle one)

_____
(Print name)

_____
(Address)

_____
(City, State, Zip)

_____
(Telephone)   (Fax)

Associate-Licensee:

_____
(Signature)

_____
(Print name)

_____
(Address)

_____
(City, State, Zip)

_____
(Telephone)   (Fax)

This form is available for use by the entire real estate industry. It is not intended to identify the user as a REALTOR®. REALTOR® is a registered collective membership mark which may be used only by members of the NATIONAL ASSOCIATION OF REALTORS® who subscribe to its Code of Ethics.

PRINT DATE

REVISED 10/98

Page 3 of ___ Pages.

OFFICE USE ONLY
Reviewed by Broker
or Designee _____
Date _____

EQUAL HOUSING
OPPORTUNITY

INDEPENDENT CONTRACTOR AGREEMENT (ICA-11 PAGE 3 OF 3)

Source: Reprinted with permission, California Association of REALTORS®. Endorsement not implied.

Real Property Transactions

The Real Estate Law permits a real estate licensee (broker or salesperson) to represent someone else in any of the following transactions involving real property or a business opportunity:

- Selling or offering to sell, including soliciting prospective sellers
- Purchasing or offering to purchase, including soliciting prospective purchasers
- Exchanging
- Soliciting or obtaining property listings for sale or exchange
- Leasing, renting, or offering to lease or rent
- Selling, purchasing, or exchanging leases
- Filing an application for purchase or lease involving land owned by the state or federal governments

The Real Estate Law does *not* require licensing for the resident manager of an apartment building or complex; the manager (or employees of the manager) of a hotel, motel, auto or trailer park; an employee of a property management company who merely opens vacant units to prospective tenants; a real estate assistant who does not perform acts that require a real estate license.

Manufactured/ Mobile Homes

The Real Estate Law permits a real estate agent to handle transactions involving a **mobile home** (termed a **manufactured home** in federal regulations discussed in Chapter 14). The home must be registered in compliance with the Health and Safety Code. If it is, the agent can perform the following activities:

- Sell
- Purchase
- Exchange

If the real estate agent displays or offers for sale two or more registered mobile homes at the agent's place of business, the agent must also be licensed as a **mobile home dealer.** The requirements for that license, which is obtained from the Department of Housing and Community Development (HCD) are in the Health and Safety Code. Information also can be found at the HCD Web site, *www.housing.hcd.ca.gov.*

www.housing.hcd.ca.gov

Mortgage Loan Transactions

In California, a real estate brokerage can also act as a **mortgage loan brokerage.** A real estate agent can represent someone else in any of the following acts involving loans secured by real property or a business opportunity:

- Soliciting borrowers or lenders for loans
- Negotiating loans

- Servicing loans (collecting payments or performing other services for borrowers or lenders)

In addition, a real estate agent can act as a principal (party to the transaction) in a transaction involving a sales contract or promissory note secured by real estate in the following cases:

- Purchase, sale, or exchange of such an obligation with a member of the public (consumer)
- Servicing of such an obligation by agreement with a member of the public

Mineral, Oil, and Gas Transactions

A real estate brokerage is permitted to handle the following activities involving mineral, oil, and gas property for others:

- Sell or offer for sale
- Purchase or offer for purchase
- Solicit prospective sellers or purchasers
- Solicit or obtain listings
- Lease or offer to lease
- Collect rent or royalties from such property or its improvements
- Exchange
- Assist or offer to assist in filing an application for the purchase or lease of such property owned by the state or federal government (An exception is made for an officer or employee of the state or federal government.)

A real estate agent can also act as the principal in a transaction involving one of the following:

- Buying or leasing, or taking an option on mineral, oil, or gas property for the purpose of sale, exchange, lease, sublease, or assignment of a lease of all or part of the property.
- Offering mining claims for sale or assignment.

There is no longer a separate **mineral, oil, and gas (MOG) broker license.** Anyone (individual or corporation) who still has an MOG license is entitled to continue to perform the listed activities, but no new MOG licenses are being issued. Existing MOG licenses must be renewed and renewal fees paid, but there is no continuing education requirement for MOG licensees.

■ BUSINESS OPPORTUNITY BROKERAGE

As noted earlier, the Real Estate Law allows a licensed real estate broker to represent others in the purchase or sale of a business. A transaction involving a **business opportunity** includes business assets that are personal property, such as inventory, trade fixtures, and the business's **goodwill** (the benefit derived from the business's favorable relationship with its customers). A business opportunity may also include or take the form of a **franchise** agreement. When real property is sold at the same time, the sales usually are treated as separate, concurrent transactions.

Franchises

A **franchise** is defined in California's Franchise Investment Law as a contract or agreement, either expressed or implied, whether oral or written, between two or more persons by which

1. a franchisee is granted the right to engage in the business of offering, selling, or distributing goods or services under a marketing plan or system prescribed in substantial part by a franchisor; and

2. the operation of the franchisee's business pursuant to such plan or system is substantially associated with the franchisor's trademark, service mark, trade name, logotype, advertising, or other commercial symbol designating the franchisor or its affiliate; and

3. the franchisee is required to pay, directly or indirectly, a franchise fee.

A business opportunity transaction may involve transfer of stock. Ordinarily, a stock transfer requires a securities license, as set out in the Corporations Code. But a stock transfer that is part of a transaction involving a business opportunity can be handled by a licensed real estate brokerage.

www.sba.gov

Business brokerage is a growing area of real estate practice. In many areas, retail stores, restaurants, manufacturing, and other businesses make up a significant number of transactions every year. The Small Business Administration (SBA), a federal agency found at *www.sba.gov*, defines a small business as one with no more than $1 million in annual sales or, if a manufacturer, with no more than 250 employees. In fact, 95 percent of U.S. businesses qualify as small businesses, and most of them change ownership every five to eight years. Some brokers specialize in business transactions, even limiting their activities to a particular type or size of business, such as retail stores of a certain square footage or annual gross income, gas stations, or warehouse storage facilities.

Taking and Handling the Business Opportunity Listing

The agent should evaluate carefully the business's location and operation, as well as the seller's records and financial statements.

Ideally, the business owner should provide profit-and-loss statements, or at least business tax reports, for the past three years, for review by the buyer's accountant. These documents also are important because the business's income stream and assets will determine the selling price. The agent should be aware of all factors that might influence the soundness of the business as an investment.

Uniform Commercial Code Requirements

California has adopted the **Uniform Commercial Code.** The Uniform Commercial Code governs the sale or transfer of goods ordinarily held for sale in the course of business. Goods held for sale by a business probably were obtained on credit from a supplier or manufacturer.

A **bulk transfer of goods** is any transfer of a substantial part of the materials, supplies, merchandise, equipment, or other inventory that is not in the ordinary course of the transferrer's business. The Uniform Commercial Code protects creditors of the seller in such a transfer by requiring that notice of the transfer be given to the transferrer's creditors. The notice is made once, at least 12 business days before the transfer is to take place. Notice is given by recordation with the county recorder, publication in a newspaper, and registered or certified mail to the County Tax Collector. Other requirements also may apply.

The prospective buyer may be an experienced businessperson, but often the business buyer will be young or inexperienced. The agent should be able to alert the buyer to federal, state, and local government requirements that must be met to obtain the necessary business permits, licenses, and clearances. In addition to federal withholding taxes, the buyer may be liable for sales tax, state payroll tax withholding, and workers' compensation insurance. The box above highlights concerns that arise under the Uniform Commercial Code. In an effort to streamline the permitting process, the California Environmental Protection Agency has created Permit Assistance Centers that can be contacted by calling (800) GOV-1-STOP or by visiting *www.calgold.ca.gov*, which lists permit requirements by city.

www.calgold.ca.gov

In short, a business opportunity listing should not be taken unless the agent is fully informed of the business's assets and liabilities and is able to convey that information to purchasers. Because of the complexities involved in the sale of a business opportunity, some brokers will not allow an associate to handle this type of transaction.

■ PREPAID RENTAL LISTING SERVICE LICENSE

A **Prepaid Rental Listing Service (PRLS)** is a business that supplies prospective tenants with listings of residential real property on payment of a fee collected at the same time or in advance of when the listings are supplied. Anyone licensed as a real estate broker may conduct a PRLS business without obtaining a separate PRLS license. The real estate broker must use a contract with the tenant/client that is approved in advance by the Department of Real Estate. Either the broker or a salesperson in the employ of the broker must be designated to supervise the PRLS activities.

An individual or a corporation may obtain a separate two-year license to conduct PRLS activities. Applicants must submit

- an application form;
- a properly completed fingerprint card;
- security in the form of a $10,000 surety bond or cash deposit for each location; and
- the appropriate license fees.

The security requirement does not apply to a PRLS operated by a tax-exempt entity; an agency of the federal, state, or local government; or a real estate broker conducting a PRLS under a real estate license.

Application requirements must be met for every location to be operated by the PRLS licensee. Before issuance of the PRLS license, the applicant must submit a copy of the contract to be entered into with prospective tenants/clients to the Department of Real Estate for approval. No examination is required.

Further information on the PRLS license may be obtained by mail from the Department of Real Estate, Original Licenses, P.O. Box 187002, Sacramento, CA 95818-7002, or by phoning (916) 227-0904.

■ EXEMPTIONS FROM REAL ESTATE LICENSING REQUIREMENTS

A real estate license is *not* needed by the people listed below:

- A person who deals only with his or her own property
- A corporation that performs any of the specified activities through one of its regular officers, who receives no special compensation for doing so
- A licensed securities broker or dealer involved in the sale, lease, or exchange of a business opportunity in that capacity

- Anyone holding a duly executed power of attorney from the owner of property
- An attorney-at-law rendering services in the performance of his or her duties as attorney
- Any receiver, trustee in bankruptcy, or person acting under order of any court
- Any trustee selling under a deed of trust
- Employees of lending institutions, pension trusts, credit unions, or insurance companies, in connection with loans secured by liens on real property or a business opportunity
- Escrow agents collecting funds in connection with loans secured by liens on real property, when the funds are deposited in the escrow agent's trust account

Other examples include cemetery authorities and persons making ten or fewer collections (in amounts of $40,000 or less in a calendar year) on notes secured by liens on real property.

To provide more time for client and customer contact, many real estate licensees are hiring one or more assistants to help with administrative and other tasks that do not require a real estate license. Activities that can be performed by an unlicensed real estate assistant include

- record filing, such as rent receipts, loan payments, or escrow sheets;
- meeting nonprincipals, such as the appraiser, home inspector, pest control, or fire inspector;
- computer data entry or retrieval, such as maintaining a client database or gathering title company records for the licensee's client record files; and
- word processing, such as downloading digital photos and graphics for flyer composition or distribution.

It is important to note that unlicensed assistants cannot perform any of the activities that require a real estate license. Those activities are listed in the Business and Professions Code starting in Section 10130. The employing broker has ultimate responsibility for complying with the law, making adequate supervision of the activities of unlicensed assistants imperative. The office policy manual should cover the use of unlicensed assistants.

■ REAL ESTATE LICENSING REQUIREMENTS

www.dre.ca.gov

An application for a real estate licensing examination can be obtained from any office of the Department of Real Estate. Forms, instructions, and licensing information are also available at the Department's Web site, *www.dre.ca.gov*. Instructions are included with the application. A license application is sent to an examinee who has successfully completed the licensing exam.

A completed license application, together with the required fingerprints and processing fee, may be taken to a department office or mailed to the Department of Real Estate, P.O. Box 187001, Sacramento, CA 95818-7001.

An applicant for a real estate license must be honest and truthful. Conviction of a crime that is either a felony or involves moral turpitude may result in the denial of a license. Failure to reveal a criminal conviction on an original license application may also result in denial of a license.

Any fraud, misrepresentation, deceit, or material misstatement of fact in a licensing application can result in a suspension of the license without hearing within 90 days of issuance.

A license or renewal applicant must provide a **Social Security number** to the Department of Real Estate. This requirement does not apply to corporations with federal tax identification numbers.

The Department of Real Estate cannot issue or renew a license if the applicant is on a list of persons who are delinquent in making court-ordered child support payments. The list is compiled by the Department of Child Support Services from information provided by the local child support agencies in California.

■ The Department of Real Estate will issue a 150-day license to a listed license applicant, if the applicant fulfills all other requirements. A regular license will not be issued unless a release is obtained from the appropriate District Attorney's office within the 150 days.

■ A currently licensed individual who is placed on the list will be notified by the Department of Real Estate that, if the obligation is not cleared within 150 days, the license will be suspended.

Real Estate Broker's License

An applicant for a real estate broker's license must be at least 18 years old at the time the license is issued. The applicant must pass a qualifying examination and meet the following requirements for experience and education:

1. The applicant must have been actively engaged as a real estate salesperson for at least two of the five years preceding the application or provide satisfactory proof to the commissioner of other experience equivalent to two years of full-time experience as a real estate salesperson. An applicant with a four-year degree from an accredited college is exempt from the experience requirement. An applicant with a two-year AA degree needs only one year of experience as a licensed salesperson.

2. The applicant must have successfully completed eight three-semester-unit (or equivalent) college-level courses taken at an accredited institution of higher learning or a private vocational school approved by the commissioner. The courses include:

- Real Estate Practice
- Legal Aspects of Real Estate
- Real Estate Finance
- Real Estate Appraisal
- Real Estate Economics (or General Accounting)

The applicant also must have taken any three of the following:

- Real Estate Principles
- Business Law
- Property Management
- Real Estate Office Administration
- Escrows
- Mortgage Loan Brokering and Lending
- Advanced Legal Aspects of Real Estate
- Advanced Real Estate Finance
- Advanced Real Estate Appraisal
- Computer Applications in Real Estate
- Common Interest Developments

If both Real Estate Economics and General Accounting are taken, only two courses from the second group are required.

Attorneys who are members of the bar of any State in the United States generally are exempt from both education and experience requirements.

Real Estate Salesperson's License

An applicant for a real estate salesperson's license must be at least 18 years old at the time the license is issued. The applicant must pass a qualifying examination and meet educational requirements.

Before taking the licensing examination, the applicant must successfully complete a college-level course in Real Estate Principles. Two additional courses also must be completed: Real Estate Practice and one of the following courses:

- Real Estate Appraisal
- Property Management
- Real Estate Finance
- Real Estate Economics
- Legal Aspects of Real Estate

- Real Estate Office Administration
- Mortgage Loan Brokering and Lending
- General Accounting
- Business Law
- Escrows
- Computer Applications in Real Estate
- Common Interest Developments

If the two additional courses are completed before application is made for a salesperson's license, the license will be issued for a full four years. If the two additional courses are *not* completed before the salesperson's license is issued, the salesperson receives a **conditional license.** If the salesperson has not completed the two courses within 18 months of issuance of the conditional license, the license is suspended automatically.

Proof of Legal Presence in the United States

The **Personal Responsibility and Work Opportunity Act** took effect August 1, 1998. This federal law requires that certain public benefits be withheld from illegal immigrants. These benefits include professional and occupational licenses issued by state agencies.

To comply with the law, the DRE adopted Regulation 2718 requiring proof of legal presence in the United States from all

- applicants for a license;
- license renewal applicants; and
- applicants for payment from the Real Estate Recovery Account.

Existing licensees must submit the required proof at the next renewal. The requirement must be met within the statutory deadline for renewal (including the statutory grace period).

For U.S. citizens and permanent resident aliens, the proof must be submitted only once. Resident aliens without permanent status must submit the proof with each license renewal.

U.S. citizenship can be established by such proof as a birth certificate, U.S. passport, certificate of naturalization, and so on. Proof of legal alien status can be established by an **Alien Registration Receipt Card** ("green card") or other specified document.

Contact the DRE or visit its Web site for the complete list of acceptable documents to meet the requirement.

FIGURE 1.2

Breakdown of Examination Topics

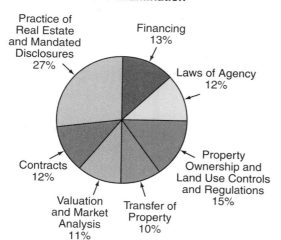

Broker's Examination

Salesperson's Examination

License Examinations

The licensing examinations consist of multiple-choice questions that are similar in format to the achievement examinations in this book, but much more complex. The topics covered on the examinations are distributed as shown in Figure 1.2.

The salesperson's exam contains 150 questions, and at least 70 percent (105 questions) must be answered correctly to pass. Salesperson applicants have one 3¼-hour session to complete the exam.

The broker's exam contains 200 questions, and at least 75 percent (150) must be answered correctly to pass. Broker applicants have a 2½-hour morning and 2½-hour afternoon session to complete the exam.

The written license examination is intended to show whether the applicant has sufficient knowledge of the required topics. It also indicates whether the applicant has the ability to read and comprehend the English language. In addition, the applicant must perform arithmetic computations common to real estate.

Interactive Voice Response System

The Department of Real Estate has an Interactive Voice Response (IVR) system, available 24 hours a day and seven days a week. Call 916-227-0900 to

■ confirm a licensing examination date, time, and location;

■ confirm examination results;

■ verify that an original salesperson or broker license number has been issued; and

■ verify that an 18-month conditional transcript has been processed and learn the date the license was mailed.

These verifications are also available at *www.dre.ca.gov*.

License Term and Renewal

The full term for a broker's or salesperson's license is four years. In general, to renew the license for an additional four years, the licensee must successfully complete 45 course hours of continuing education (CE). All courses must be approved by the Department of Real Estate. The courses taken must include three hours each of Ethics, Agency, Trust Fund Handling, and Fair Housing (a total of 12 course hours). In addition, renewal requires at least 18 hours of courses related to consumer protection. The remaining 15 hours can be in courses that fall under the categories of Consumer Service or Consumer Protection.

After the first renewal period in which all four of the mandatory courses have been taken, subsequent license renewals require a 6-hour survey course covering all of these topics, at least 18 hours of courses in the Consumer Protection category, and the remaining 21 hours in Consumer Protection or Consumer Service.

An exception to the 45-hour CE requirement is made for the first renewal of a salesperson's license. Salespersons renewing for the first time must complete 12 clock hours of courses, including three-hour courses in Ethics, Agency, Trust Fund Handling, and Fair Housing.

Expiration and late renewal.   If a license is not renewed before it expires, the licensee's real estate activities must cease immediately. If the license of an employing broker expires, the consequences can be profound. Expiration of the employing broker's license will place all licensees (whether salespersons or brokers) who work for the employing broker on nonworking status.

A license that is not renewed before it expires may be renewed at any time up to two years from the expiration date. A late renewal fee will be required. After the two-year period, the licensee must qualify for and successfully pass the appropriate real estate examination.

eLicensing

The Department of Real Estate provides a paperless, interactive, online eLicensing system at *www.dre.ca.gov* for expedited processing of license renewal and change transactions. Licensees can use eLicensing

- to renew broker and salesperson licenses;
- to request duplicate licenses;
- for salesperson requests to change employing broker;
- for broker certification of salesperson employment;
- for mailing address changes;
- for broker main office address changes; and
- to receive the *Real Estate Bulletin* publication for licensees electronically.

■ ENFORCEMENT OF THE REAL ESTATE LAW

The Real Estate Commissioner investigates complaints regarding the activities of real estate licensees. A complaint may come from a member of the public or from a private group, such as a local association of REALTORS®. The commissioner is allowed to initiate an investigation and must do so if a verified complaint is made in writing by someone who believes he or she was wronged by a licensee acting in that capacity.

The DRE investigation may include a statement by the licensee and examination of the licensee's records, bank records, title company records, and public records. An informal conference including the parties may be held to determine the necessity for a formal hearing.

If a formal hearing is held, it will be presided over by an administrative law judge. At that point, the commissioner becomes the complainant, and the licensee is the respondent. The licensee may appear with or without an attorney. The person who initiated the complaint is a witness. Other evidence also may be presented. Testimony is taken under oath.

Outcome of the hearing.   Charges not proven by the evidence are dismissed. If the charges are proven, the licensee is subject to license **suspension** or **revocation,** depending on the seriousness of the charges. If the license is revoked, an application for reinstatement cannot be made for one year.

Restricted license.   In certain circumstances, such as a violation of the Real Estate Law, the Real Estate Commissioner may decide to issue a **restricted license.** The restriction imposed could

- limit the length of the license term;
- require (for a salesperson) employment by a particular real estate broker; or
- contain some other condition, such as the filing of surety bonds for the protection of persons with whom the licensee does business.

The holder of a restricted license cannot renew the license unless and until the restriction is lifted. The commissioner has the right to suspend a restricted license without a hearing, pending a final determination after a formal hearing.

Other penalties.   The Real Estate Commissioner also has the discretion to order one or more of the following penalties for violation of the Real Estate Law:

- Education—requiring the offender to successfully complete one or more courses, such as a course in Ethics
- Payment of a fine

■ Return of documents or other materials

■ Reimbursement to the Real Estate Recovery Account of any amounts paid to victims of the violation on the offender's behalf, as explained on page 25.

Types of Violations

The Real Estate Law specifies many activities that can result in a suspension or revocation of a real estate license. Most of the ones listed below, which are found in Business and Professions Code Section 10176, are discussed in Chapters 6 and 7 of this book.

■ *Misrepresentation.* A statement or act of deception on a matter of significance to the transaction, such as the condition of the property. Failure to disclose a property defect is probably the most common form of misrepresentation.

■ *False promise.* Making any false promises of a character likely to influence, persuade, or induce. An offer of a rebate or gift to a prospective client is acceptable, as long as the terms of the offer are expressed and fulfilled.

■ *Continued misrepresentation.* A continued and flagrant course of misrepresentation or making of false promises through real estate agents or salespersons.

■ *Undisclosed dual agency.* Acting for more than one party in a transaction without the knowledge and consent of all parties.

■ *Commingling.* Placing the licensee's own money in the same account with the money of others. (The licensee can place up to $200 in an account to cover account fees.)

■ *Not specifying listing termination date.* Any exclusive listing or other agreement authorized by the Real Estate Law must specify a definite ending date.

■ *Making a secret profit.* No compensation of any form may be received by the licensee without the knowledge of the licensee's client. This can happen when the licensee purchases property through a "dummy" buyer, then resells it at a higher price.

■ *Combining listing with option without informed consent of seller.* No option to purchase combined with a listing agreement is allowed unless the licensee's profit is stated when the option is exercised and agreed to by the seller in writing.

■ *Dishonest dealing.* Any other conduct that constitutes fraud or dishonest dealing.

■ *Obtaining signature of prospective purchaser of a business opportunity without owner's authority.* No agreement to represent someone or receive compensation for the purchase, lease, rent, or exchange of a business opportunity can be obtained without prior authorization of the business owner.

■ *Willfully or repeatedly violating any provision of the Civil Code regarding real property transfer disclosures.*

A real estate license may be suspended or revoked or issuance of a license may be denied if the licensee or applicant (or person owning or controlling more than 10 percent of a corporate applicant's stock) has engaged in any of the following activities, which appear in Business and Professions Code Section 10177.

- *Obtaining license by fraud.* Obtaining a real estate license or license renewal by fraud, misrepresentation, or deceit, or making any material misstatement of fact in an application for a real estate license, license renewal, or reinstatement.

- *Criminal activities resulting in conviction.* Suffering a conviction of a felony or a crime involving moral turpitude that is related to the qualifications or duties of a real estate licensee.

- *False advertising.* Knowingly authorizing, directing, conniving at, or aiding in the publication, advertisement, distribution, or circulation of any material false statement or representation concerning his or her business or any business opportunity or any land or subdivision offered for sale. When advertising a property, a licensee must disclose that the property is offered through a licensed real estate agent. Failure to disclose this fact and provide the name of the licensee is called **blind advertising,** and is illegal.

- *Violations of other sections.* Disregarding or violating any of the provisions of the Real Estate Law or the rules and regulations of the commissioner regarding administration and enforcement of the Real Estate Law.

- *Misuse of trade name.* Using the term "REALTOR®" or any trade name or insignia of membership (such as the term Realtist) in any real estate organization of which the licensee is not a member.

- *Conduct warranting denial.* Acting in a manner that would have resulted in denial of a real estate license, such as conviction for a felony or a crime involving moral turpitude.

- *Negligence or incompetence.* Demonstrating such carelessness or incompetence as a licensee that the interests of clients or customers are endangered.

- *Negligent supervision of salespersons.* Failing, as a broker licensee or broker-officer of a corporation, to exercise reasonable supervision over the licensed activities of salespersons or the corporation.

- *Violating government trust.* Using one's employment by a governmental agency to violate the confidential nature of government records.

- *Other dishonest conduct.* Engaging in any other conduct constituting fraud or dishonest dealing.

- *Restricted license violation.* Violating any of the terms of a restricted license.

- *Inducement of panic selling.* Soliciting or inducing the sale, lease, or listing for sale or lease of residential property on the grounds, wholly or in part, of loss of value or of increase in crime or decline of the quality of the schools, due to the present or prospective entry into the neighborhood of a person or persons of another race, color, religion, ancestry, or national origin.

Manufactured/mobile homes.   Real estate licensees handling mobile (manufactured) homes are subject to the general requirements and prohibitions applicable to all real estate transactions. In addition, the Real Estate Law imposes the following restrictions on mobile home sales:

- A mobile home may not be advertised or offered for sale unless it is in place in a mobile home park or located in a location where it can legally remain for at least one year.

- An advertisement of a mobile home for sale must be withdrawn within 48 hours after receipt of notice that the mobile home is no longer available for sale, lease, or exchange.

- License or transfer of title fees may not be prorated unless buyer and seller agree or the licensee was required to pay the fees to avoid penalties that would have been imposed for late payment.

- Only a mobile home that meets Vehicle Code requirements can be represented as transportable on a California highway. All material facts pertaining to equipment requirements must be revealed. A permit from the Department of Transportation or local agency must be obtained to authorize the moving of a mobile home.

- It may not be advertised or represented that no down payment is required if in fact the buyer will be advised to secure an additional loan for that purpose.

- The licensee is responsible for making sure that the certificate of ownership or certificate of title of the mobile home is endorsed, dated, and delivered to the purchaser.

- No later than ten days after the sale of a mobile home, a real estate broker must give written notice of the transfer to the headquarters office of the Department of Housing and Community Development.

The following are grounds for revocation or suspension of a real estate license:

- Using a false or fictitious name, knowingly making a false statement, knowingly concealing a material fact, or otherwise committing a fraud in any application for registration of a mobile home.

- Failing to provide for delivery of a properly endorsed certificate of title or ownership from seller to buyer.

- Knowingly participating in the purchase or sale of a stolen mobile home.

- Violating any requirement of the Health and Safety Code, Revenue and Taxation Code, or Civil Code regarding mobile-home registration, transfer, or taxation.

- Submitting a check, draft, or money order to the Department of Housing and Community Development for any fee or other payment due the state for which payment is refused.

■ LICENSEE CONDUCT

Every licensee should have a copy of the *Reference Book* published by the Department of Real Estate. The latest edition (2000) lists examples of unlawful conduct by real estate licensees. These are shown in Figure 1.3.

In previous editions of the *Reference Book,* the Real Estate Commissioner has issued suggestions for professional conduct—desirable actions for those engaged in licensed activities. They appear in Figure 1.4. Note especially item 12 under Recommended Conduct, which refers to the "Guidelines for Professional Conduct and the Code of Ethics of any organized real estate industry group of which the licensee is a member." This includes the Code of Ethics of the National Association of REALTORS®, which has over one million members.

Trade groups often set the standard of practice for those in the profession. Membership requirements and ethical concerns can be the most direct evidence of the manner in which all professionals should carry out their responsibilities. Unfortunately, there is not enough space in this book to reproduce the directives of all of the trade groups active in California. We encourage you to obtain the most recent versions of that information from the associations listed later in this chapter.

Exercise 1-2   Broker Bob opened his first real estate brokerage office and immediately hired Salesperson Sally. Salesperson Sally printed and circulated a newsletter throughout the neighborhood. Salesperson Sally gave a few mortgage loan statistics in her newsletter and stressed the recent rapid increase in property values in the area. She concluded with the statement, "I've never handled a listing I couldn't sell." In fact, Sally has never handled any listing. Has she violated the Code of Ethics? Has Broker Bob?

■ OTHER ACTIVITIES OF THE DEPARTMENT OF REAL ESTATE

The Department of Real Estate performs many functions in addition to regulating the business activities of brokers and salespersons.

Through the **Real Estate Education and Research Fund,** research in land use and real estate development is made possible at both public and private universities and research entities throughout the state. The fund is financed by a fixed percentage of license fees.

The **Recovery Account** is another fund financed by license fees. It is available to aid victims of licensee fraud, misrepresentation, deceit, or conversion (theft) of trust fund, who are awarded money damages by a court or as the result of a

FIGURE 1.3

Unlawful Conduct

EXAMPLES OF UNLAWFUL CONDUCT
IN SALE, LEASE, OR EXCHANGE TRANSACTIONS

1. Knowingly making a substantial misrepresentation of the likely value of real property to:

   ■ Its owner either for the purpose of securing a listing or for the purpose of acquiring an interest in the property for the licensee's own account.

   ■ A prospective buyer for the purpose of inducing the buyer to make an offer to purchase the real property.

2. Representing to an owner of real property when seeking a listing that the licensee has obtained a bona fide written offer to purchase the property, unless at the time of the representation the licensee has possession of a bona fide written offer to purchase.

3. Stating or implying to an owner of real property during listing negotiations that the licensee is precluded by law, by regulation, or by the rules of any organization, other than the broker firm seeking the listing, from charging less than the commission or fee quoted to the owner by the licensee.

4. Knowingly making substantial misrepresentations regarding the licensee's relationship with an individual broker, corporate broker, or franchised brokerage company or that entity's/person's responsibility for the licensee's activities.

5. Knowingly underestimating the probable closing costs in a communication to the prospective buyer or seller of real property in order to induce that person to make or to accept an offer to purchase the property.

6. Knowingly making a false or misleading representation to the seller of real property as to the form, amount, and/or treatment of a deposit toward the purchase of the property made by an offeror.

7. Knowingly making a false or misleading representation to a seller of real property, who has agreed to finance all or part of a purchase price by carrying back a loan, about a buyer's ability to repay the loan in accordance with its terms and conditions.

8. Making an addition to or modification of the terms of an instrument previously signed or initialed by a party to a transaction without the knowledge and consent of the party.

9. A representation made as a principal or agent to a prospective purchaser of a promissory note secured by real property about the market value of the securing property without a reasonable basis for believing the truth and accuracy of the representation.

10. Knowingly making a false or misleading representation or representing, without a reasonable basis for believing its truth, the nature and/or condition of the interior or exterior features of a property when soliciting an offer.

11. Knowingly making a false or misleading representation or representing, without a reasonable basis for believing its truth, the size of a parcel, square footage of improvements, or the location of the boundary lines of real property being offered for sale, lease, or exchange.

Source: Chapter 6, Title 10, California Administrative Code.

FIGURE 1.3

Unlawful Conduct (Continued)

12. Knowingly making a false or misleading representation or representing to a prospective buyer or lessee of real property, without a reasonable basis to believe its truth, that the property can be used for certain purposes with the intent of inducing the prospective buyer or lessee to acquire an interest in the real property.

13. When acting in the capacity of an agent in a transaction for the sale, lease, or exchange of real property, failing to disclose to a prospective purchaser or lessee facts known to the licensee materially affecting the value or desirability of the property, when the licensee has reason to believe that such facts are not known to or readily observable by a prospective purchaser or lessee.

14. Willfully failing, when acting as a listing agent, to present or cause to be presented to the owner of the property any written offer to purchase received prior to the closing of a sale, unless expressly instructed by the owner not to present such an offer, or unless the offer is patently frivolous.

15. When acting as the listing agent, presenting competing written offers to purchase real property to the owner in such a manner as to induce the owner to accept the offer that will provide the greatest compensation to the listing broker without regard to the benefits, advantages and/or disadvantages to the owner.

16. Failing to explain to the parties or prospective parties to a real estate transaction for whom the licensee is acting as an agent the meaning and probable significance of a contingency in an offer or contract that the licensee knows or reasonably believes may affect the closing date of the transaction, or the timing of the vacating of the property by the seller or its occupancy by the buyer.

17. Failing to disclose to the seller of real property in a transaction in which the licensee is an agent for the seller the nature and extent of any direct or indirect interest that the licensee expects to acquire as a result of the sale. (The licensee should disclose to the seller: prospective purchase of the property by a person related to the licensee by blood or marriage; purchase by an entity in which the licensee has an ownership interest; or purchase by any other person with whom the licensee occupies a special relationship where there is a reasonable probability that the licensee could be indirectly acquiring an interest in the property.)

18. Failing to disclose to the buyer of real property in a transaction in which the licensee is an agent for the buyer the nature and extent of a licensee's direct or indirect ownership interest in such real property: e.g., the direct or indirect ownership interest in the property by a person related to the licensee by blood or marriage; by an entity in which the licensee has an ownership interest; or by any other person with whom the licensee occupies a special relationship.

19. Failing to disclose to a principal for whom the licensee is acting as an agent any significant interest the licensee has in a particular entity when the licensee recommends the use of the services or products of such entity.

Source: Chapter 6, Title 10, California Administrative Code.

FIGURE 1.4

Desirable Conduct

**RECOMMENDED CONDUCT
IN SALE, LEASE, OR EXCHANGE TRANSACTIONS**

Real estate licensees are encouraged to adhere to the following suggestions in conducting their business activities:

1. Aspire to give a high level of competent, ethical, and quality service to buyers and sellers in real estate transactions.

2. Stay in close communication with clients or customers to ensure that questions are promptly answered and all significant events or problems in a transaction are conveyed in a timely manner.

3. Cooperate with the California Department of Real Estate's enforcement of, and report to that department evident violations of, the Real Estate Law.

4. Use care in the preparation of any advertisement to present an accurate picture or message to the reader, viewer, or listener.

5. Submit all written offers in a prompt and timely manner.

6. Keep oneself informed and current on factors affecting the real estate market in which the licensee operates as an agent.

7. Make a full, open, and sincere effort to cooperate with other licensees, unless the principal has instructed the licensee to the contrary.

8. Attempt to settle disputes with other licensees through mediation or arbitration.

9. Advertise or claim to be an expert in an area of specialization in real estate brokerage activity, e.g., appraisal, property management, industrial siting, mortgage loan, etc., only if the licensee has had special training, preparation, or experience in such area.

10. Strive to provide equal opportunity for quality housing and a high level of service to all persons regardless of race, color, sex, religion, ancestry, physical handicap, marital status, or national origin.

11. Base opinions of value, whether for the purpose of advertising or promoting real estate brokerage business, upon documented objective data.

12. Make every attempt to comply with these Guidelines for Professional Conduct and the Code of Ethics of any organized real estate industry group of which the licensee is a member.

DRE administrative proceeding that are noncollectible. A maximum of $20,000 per individual or $100,000 per incident can be paid from the Recovery Account. Reimbursement to the fund by the offender will be required as part of the disciplinary process.

■ PROFESSIONAL ASSOCIATIONS

One of the best ways for the real estate licensee to become involved in and remain enthusiastic about the profession is to become a member of a professional association. Trade associations provide sources of information, training, and contact with other professionals. Associations also help shape the law and the industry by establishing and enforcing standards of practice and also by providing an effective voice for their members.

REALTORS®

www.car.org

www.realtor.com

There have been voluntary associations of real estate professionals in California since 1887, when the San Diego Realty Board was formed. As more cities formed such groups, the California Real Estate Association was organized in 1905. On January 1, 1975, the name of that organization was changed to the California Association of REALTORS® (CAR), demonstrating its affiliation with the national organization. CAR (headquartered in Los Angeles) can be found on the Web at *www.car.org*.

The term REALTOR® is a registered trademark of the National Association of REALTORS® (NAR), and may be used only by REALTOR® members of NAR. NAR's headquarters is in Chicago, Illinois, and its Web address is *www.realtor.com*. With over one million members across the country, NAR is a powerful force in lobbying on behalf of its members. Real estate licensees who fulfill NAR membership requirements may use the REALTOR® or REALTOR-ASSOCIATE® trademark. Use of either of these registered trademarks by anyone unauthorized to do so may result in a license suspension or revocation, in addition to damages in a legal action brought by NAR. NAR also has an "affiliate" membership classification open to lenders, escrow companies, and others engaged in real estate–related activities.

Realtists

www.nareb.com

Realtist is the member designation of the National Association of Real Estate Brokers, Inc., or NAREB. NAREB's Web site is *www.nareb.com*. This group was formed in 1947 in Tampa, Florida, of predominantly African-American members, and it now has local boards nationwide. In California, they include Associated Real Property Brokers, Oakland; North Bay Board of Realtists, Richmond; and the Consolidated Realty Board, Los Angeles. Members of NAREB must belong to the local group as well as to the national organization, which is headquartered in Washington, D.C. Unauthorized use of the term Realtist is unlawful (misrepresentation) and unethical.

Local Associations

Most local real estate associations are affiliated with CAR and NAR or NAREB. Local organizations bring members together to assist in community outreach as well as charitable programs. They frequently offer continuing education and other informational seminars. In addition, the local real estate association typically conducts what may be the real estate broker and salesperson's most valuable marketing tool—the multiple listing service (MLS). All licensees benefit by sharing information on available property. The frequently updated property catalogs of the larger multiple listing services would be impossible for any one agency to duplicate. Increasingly, local and regional property listings are being made part of statewide and national databases accessible by both agents and consumers on the Internet.

www.dre.ca.gov/
links_sub.htm

Major Real Estate Trade Associations

The DRE Web site lists state and federal resources, as well as the major real estate–related trade associations in California. You will find this information at *www.dre.ca.gov/links_sub.htm*. The following are the trade and related groups that maintain Web sites.

California Association of REALTORS®	*www.car.org*
California Mortgage Association	*www.californiamortgage association.com*
California Association of Mortgage Brokers	*www.cambweb.org*
California Association of Business Brokers	*www.cabb.org*
California Mortgage Bankers Association	*www.cmba.com*
California Building Industry Association	*www.cbia.org*
California Association of Community Managers	*www.cacm.org*
California Apartment Association	*www.ca-apartment.org*
Executive Council of Homeowners	*www.echo-ca.org*

■ SUMMARY

The business of real estate entails many responsibilities for the licensee. The responsibilities begin with completing qualifying **courses** and passing a **licensing examination.** They also include the obligation to make sure that the licensee obeys both the **Real Estate Law** and the **Regulations of the Real Estate Commissioner.**

The foundation of all of the activities and requirements of the **Department of Real Estate** is the element of **fair dealing.** We have come far from the days when the concept of *caveat emptor* served as a shield for the unscrupulous. Now the **police power** of the government has brought about the Real Estate Law found in the **Business and Professions Code.** The Real Estate Commissioner and Department of Real Estate are charged with the task of supervising the education, licensing, and conduct of those who call themselves real estate professionals.

The **real estate brokerage office** always has one responsible **broker** who may have one or more **salespersons (or brokers)** working out of the office. A broker-officer enables a brokerage to be incorporated. A corporate brokerage also must file a **Certificate of Status.** A **partnership** of real estate licensees also is possible. A fictitious name for a brokerage requires the filing of a **fictitious business name statement (DBA).**

Real estate licensees may deal in business opportunities, which may involve many requirements, including those of the Uniform Commercial Code.

The Real Estate Law contains many mandates and prohibitions for the licensee. Through the **Real Estate Education and Research Fund** the Department of Real Estate makes use of part of the license fees collected to finance real estate research. It also compensates victims of licensee wrongdoing from the **Recovery Account.**

By joining a local professional organization, the licensee benefits in many ways, from use of a **multiple-listing service** to attending educational programs and contributing to various charitable events.

■ IMPORTANT TERMS

Make sure you understand the following terms before you take the achievement examination.

Alien Registration Receipt Card
associate licensee
blind advertising
broker-officer
bulk transfer of goods
Business and Professions Code
business opportunity
caveat emptor
Certificate of Status
codes
conditional license
Department of Real Estate
fictitious business name statement
franchise
mobile home dealer
mortgage loan brokerage
Personal Responsibility and
    Work Opportunity Act

Prepaid Rental Listing Service (PRLS)
Real Estate Advisory Commission
real estate broker
real estate brokerage
Real Estate Commissioner
Real Estate Education and
    Research Fund
Real Estate Law
real estate salesperson
Recovery Account
Regulations of the Real Estate
    Commissioner
restricted license
sales associate
Uniform Commercial Code

■ OPEN FOR DISCUSSION

It has been suggested that all real estate licensees be required to have at least a two-year Associate of Arts degree from a community college.

1. Make at least two arguments in favor of the idea.

2. Make at least two arguments against it.

■ ACHIEVEMENT EXAMINATION 1

1. The Real Estate Law is found in the
   a. Licensing Code.
   b. Business and Professions Code.
   c. Health and Safety Code.
   d. Corporations Code.

2. The Real Estate Commissioner reports to the
   a. Department of Real Estate.
   b. governor.
   c. Real Estate Advisory Commission.
   d. legislature.

3. Salesperson Sam owns 25 percent of the outstanding shares of Rollo Realty, Inc., and Broker Barbara Rollo owns the remaining shares. This division of ownership is
   a. acceptable.   c. discouraged.
   b. mandated.   d. prohibited.

4. Salesperson Sam is part owner of Rollo Realty, Inc. In the broker's absence, Sam frequently reviews the work of sales associates. This is
   a. acceptable.   c. discouraged.
   b. mandated.   d. prohibited.

5. A real estate business that is a partnership can have more than one office location, provided
   a. a broker partner obtains an additional license for each location.
   b. all partners are real estate licensees.
   c. there is a designated broker-officer.
   d. there is at least one partner at each location.

6. The sale or transfer of goods ordinarily held for sale in the course of business is governed in California by the
   a. Business Opportunity Code.
   b. Commercial Transfer Law.
   c. Uniform Commercial Code.
   d. Real Estate Law.

7. Todd, an officer of Ajax Corporation and not a real estate licensee, successfully negotiated the purchase of the Smith Widget Plant on behalf of Ajax. Todd received a commission on the sale in addition to his normal salary. Todd
   a. did not need a real estate license for the deal.
   b. should have had a real estate license.
   c. is exempt from licensing requirements.
   d. None of the above

8. If a real estate license is not renewed before it expires, the licensee
   a. is allowed to complete transactions in progress.
   b. is allowed to finish transactions that are substantially complete.
   c. must cease all real estate activities.
   d. may act under authority of another agent's license for a period not to exceed 60 days.

9. The full term of a real estate license is
   a. six months.   c. two years.
   b. one year.   d. four years.

10. The Browns desperately want to move to Pine Bend and they like the Smith house, which is listed with Broker Bob. The Browns tell Broker Bob they will "make it worth his while" if he can persuade the Smiths to accept the Brown offer on their house, and the Browns send an expensive food basket to Broker Bob as a sign of their good faith. Bob neglects to mention this to the Smiths. This practice is
    a. acceptable.   c. discouraged.
    b. mandated.   d. prohibited.

11. Broker Bob routinely places earnest money deposits in his personal account for overnight safekeeping. This practice is
    a. acceptable.   c. discouraged.
    b. mandated.   d. prohibited.

12. Broker Luis has an exclusive listing agreement with the Pierces. The listing will terminate "when the parties agree." This practice is
    a. acceptable.
    b. mandated.
    c. discouraged.
    d. prohibited.

13. When Broker Bob exercised his option to buy Whiteacre, he presented to the owner of Whiteacre a written statement of his expected profit in the transaction. The buyer agreed in writing to proceed with the sale. This conduct is
    a. acceptable.
    b. mandated.
    c. discouraged.
    d. prohibited.

14. Maya is broker-officer of XYZ Realty, Inc. She does not like the overly aggressive sales tactics of XYZ's salespeople but has not reprimanded them because business is so good. Maya's conduct is
    a. acceptable.
    b. mandated.
    c. discouraged.
    d. prohibited.

15. Broker Bob wants to help out his neighbor's son, Igor, who recently acquired a BA in History from Back East University. Broker Bob hires Igor to show property to prospective buyers. Because Igor has no real estate license, Broker Bob handles all of the negotiating. This practice is
    a. acceptable.
    b. mandated.
    c. discouraged.
    d. prohibited.

16. Salesperson Sally is selling the Martinez Mansion. An offer has been accepted, and the closing will take place in two weeks. While the owners are out of town, the buyer asks if the closing can be put off for one day. Sally agrees on behalf of the owners, for she is sure they will not object. Sally's conduct is
    a. acceptable.
    b. mandated.
    c. discouraged.
    d. prohibited.

17. The Anderson house is for sale following the murder of Mrs. Anderson by Mr. Anderson in the breakfast room six months earlier. Salesperson Sam, showing an out-of-town prospect through the house, decides to keep information about the murder to himself. Sam's conduct is
    a. acceptable.
    b. mandated.
    c. discouraged.
    d. prohibited.

18. Broker Luis is so busy that he never has the time to return the phone calls of his principals. He prefers to spend his time in the field, making sales, and acquiring new listings. This practice is
    a. acceptable.
    b. mandated.
    c. discouraged.
    d. prohibited.

19. After attending a get-rich-quick real estate seminar, Kim wants to buy a house "cheap." She tells Broker Bob she will offer $50,000, with seller financing and no down payment, on the Henderson house. The Henderson house has an asking price of $125,000. Broker Bob presents the offer with one of his own for $85,000, telling the Hendersons that unexpected market conditions make their asking price unrealistic. His conduct is
    a. acceptable.
    b. mandated.
    c. discouraged.
    d. prohibited.

20. Rudy opens his brokerage office and immediately places an ad in the local newspaper: *List Your House with Me and I Will Pay You $500 at Closing.* This practice is
    a. acceptable.
    b. mandated.
    c. discouraged.
    d. prohibited.

CHAPTER TWO

THE NATURE
OF REAL PROPERTY

■ HISTORICAL PERSPECTIVE

Many forces have shaped the geography of California. Nature provides an abundance of both benefits and hazards, but cultural, political, and economic forces often have brought about more changes than even the most severe earthquake or fire. The earliest settlers of the region suffered greatly at the hands of those who followed. Yet the state is now home to one of the most diverse populations in the world. In recent years, economic forces have created hardships for many workers who lost their jobs in industries that were once considered secure. Yet California once more is redefining itself as businesses and workers learn to adapt to the new technologies and demands of the marketplace. With the hard work and imagination that represent the best its citizens have to offer, the California of the future promises to be an exciting place in which to live and work.

This chapter surveys the history of California very briefly to give you some idea of the dramatic origin of our system of land ownership. Then, real property is defined and distinguished from personal property. Finally, the most common ways of describing real property are discussed.

Spanish Conquest and Settlement

In 1513 Vasco Nuñez de Balboa, at the head of an advancing army of conquistadores, claimed all lands washed by the Pacific Ocean for the King of Spain.

California became—in principle, at least—part of the Spanish Empire. But the distance from Spain of that far-flung outpost meant that it would be hundreds of years before it was fully explored.

For the most part, the Native Americans who emigrated from Asia and the great tribes of the nation's heartland had ignored the land we now call California. Still, as many as 300,000 people were living in California at the time of European exploration.

Missions and presidios.   The major impetus to Spanish settlement of California was the establishment of the *missions*. Franciscan missionaries converted some of the Native Americans to Christianity and resettled them in mission communities, where they were taught agriculture and crafts.

Of course, living in such communities made the converts easy prey to epidemic disease. By 1900, only 15,000 Native Americans were estimated to be living in California.

> During the 20th century, California's Native American population grew to 100,000, in part because of immigration to California from other states.

The missions also provided a convenient source of supplies for the *presidios*, the military posts. The first mission and the first presidio were founded at San Diego in 1769. Twenty more missions were to follow by 1823, with the northernmost in Sonoma. Additional presidios were located in Santa Barbara, Monterey, and San Francisco. U.S. Highway 101 follows the route of *El Camino Real*, the main thoroughfare of Spanish California.

FIGURE 2.1

Mission

From San Diego northward, the missions established a Spanish presence in the territory that became California.

Pueblos. During Spanish rule, ownership of all the land was held by the crown—the King of Spain—with *rancho grants* made only for limited uses, such as grazing or farming. Cities, called *pueblos*, received four square leagues of land without need for a formal grant. Because a league was 4,440 acres, city officials carried much authority. The mayor and council of the pueblo could grant house lots and farm lots to inhabitants.

Treaty of Guadalupe Hidalgo

In 1822 Mexico, a territorial possession of Spain, established its independence. California became a possession of Mexico. But the tide of settlement brought Americans to the Pacific Coast, eventually leading to war with Mexico. The war ended with the signing of the **Treaty of Guadalupe Hidalgo** in 1848.

Following the Treaty of Guadalupe Hidalgo, California became a possession of the United States. Existing property rights of Mexicans in California were to be "inviolably respected." In the 26 years of Mexican rule from 1822 to 1848, mission lands had been confiscated, private land ownership encouraged, and large tracts given out. After the Treaty of Guadalupe Hidalgo, American squatters claimed some of that land, creating much conflict.

There would have been confusion in any event, because the transfer from Spanish/Mexican rule to the status of an American colony meant a change in the entire legal system. The Spanish **civil law,** consisting of detailed legal codes, was replaced by the English **common law,** an inheritance of the United States from the period before the American Revolution. This meant that Californians were to follow the laws established by the legislature, as well as the common law customs and usages established by judicial decisions. Significantly, property could be held in absolute ownership by individuals.

A holdover from Spanish law is the concept of **community property,** which is property acquired by husband and wife during marriage. Community property is discussed in Chapter 3, "Ownership of Real Property."

Statehood

In the midst of the postwar land problems, gold was discovered at Sutter's Mill in 1848. This discovery, coming within weeks of the end of the war, gave new importance to America's westernmost frontier. In 1850 California became a state.

The federal government retained certain rights in the area known as California. The new state became owner of all lands lying under navigable streams and lakes and above the ordinary high-tide line. Tidelands are held in trust for public navigation, fishing, and recreation. Certain rights to public lands can be transferred, however, which allows the collection of income from oil and gas production.

The **Board of Land Commissioners** was formed by Congress in 1851 to settle claims to private land in California. Appeal from the commissioners was to the

United States District Court, and from there to the United States Supreme Court. Most of the Mexican land grants were upheld, to the dismay of numerous squatters. Of the more than 100 million acres of California's total area, the federal government still owns about 45 percent. Basically these federal lands include everything that was not conveyed by Spanish or Mexican grant or granted to the state for education and recreation uses. Other large federal land grants were made to railroad companies to encourage the development of transportation.

www.ca.gov

You will find more information about California's history and culture at the State of California Web site, *www.ca.gov*.

California Today

City dwellers may receive the impression that California is fully developed and generally urbanized. However, there still are vast tracts of land in the state that contradict its urban, progressive reputation.

Land ownership. California land is owned approximately in the proportions shown below. About 29 percent of the total land area is devoted to agriculture.

	Number of Acres	Percent of Total
Federal	44,904,000	45
State	2,332,000	2
Local	2,050,000	2
Private	50,785,000	51
Total Acres	100,071,000	100

Population. According to the U.S. Census Bureau, the population of California was 35.5 million in mid-2003, with a projected increase of 500,000 annually.

Coastal cities continue to dominate the state.

Almost 97 percent of Californians live in a metropolitan area. Urban development generally has been concentrated in coastal and central valley areas. Major development has occurred along the coast in San Francisco, Los Angeles, and San Diego. Eventually Los Angeles and San Diego will form one continuous urban area, or "megalopolis." The cities surrounding San Francisco Bay now have few recognizable boundaries. To a lesser extent, inland cities from Yreka to Bakersfield follow the same pattern, with development gradually expanding to the outskirts of the urban areas. Attractive housing and commercial development costs currently have made Sacramento and other central valley cities the state's fastest growing communities. At the same time, increasing market demand has resulted in home prices that have moved beyond the income level of many area residents.

www.dof.ca.gov

For updates on California's population statistics, including breakdowns by county and city, visit the California Department of Finance Web site at *www.dof.ca.gov*.

FIGURE 2.2
Bundle of Rights

Control

Exclusion

Possession

Disposition

Enjoyment

Use/Will

Give/Dedicate

Explore/Cultivate

Lease/License

Mortgage/Encumber

■ REAL PROPERTY AND PERSONAL PROPERTY

Real property is often described as a **bundle of rights** that include the legal rights of ownership shown in Figure 2.2.

The major rights are

- the right of possession;
- the right of enjoyment of the property;
- the right to control the property's use;
- the right to exclude others from the property; and
- the right to dispose of the property.

From these rights flow other privileges of ownership. A property owner usually has the power to mortgage, cultivate, explore, lease, give away, share, trade, or exchange the property owned. The Spanish rancho grants, for instance, conveyed the right to use the land for such purposes as grazing or cultivation.

California law recognizes that property may be possessed by one or more persons to the exclusion of all others. All California property can be categorized as either real property or personal property.

Real Property

In California the term **real property** is synonymous with the term **real estate.** The California Civil Code definition of *real property* includes all of these elements:

- land;
- fixtures (attachments) to land;
- anything incidental or appurtenant to land; and
- anything immovable by law.

Land. **Land** is the soil, the material that makes up what is called *earth*. Land includes the substances beneath the surface that extend to the center of the earth. These include oil, gas, and water, and they may be many times more valuable than the surface itself. Land also includes the airspace above the earth's surface for an indefinite distance upward.

FIGURE 2.3

Rights in Land

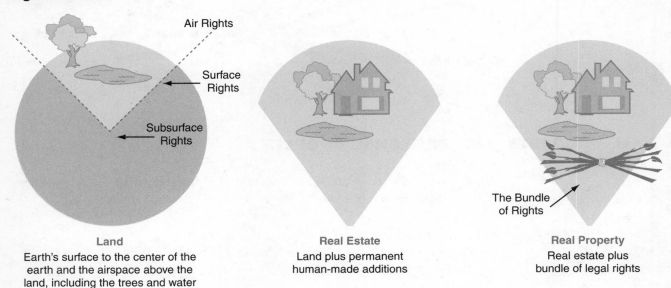

Land	Real Estate	Real Property
Earth's surface to the center of the earth and the airspace above the land, including the trees and water	Land plus permanent human-made additions	Real estate plus bundle of legal rights

In practice, use of airspace (as well as the surface and subsurface) is subject to many limitations imposed by law. These limitations will be discussed throughout this book, particularly in Chapter 15, "Government Control of Land Use." Figure 2.3 illustrates the general concept of land rights.

Mineral rights refer to the right to remove substances from the land, usually from beneath the surface. The term includes solid minerals, such as gold, coal, iron, and gravel from the soil as well as river beds.

Mineral rights also include minerals that have a "fugitive or fluid, nature, such as oil and gas." All or some of the minerals may be transferred apart from the rest of the land.

■ **FOR EXAMPLE:** Mel Muller owns 100 acres of undeveloped land in San Bernardino County. Hearing that oil might be found in the area, Mel drills a well under his property. He finds nothing, but he thinks he will be successful if he drills a well slanted to reach under his neighbor's ranch. Can Mel do so?

No, because Mel can take from the earth only what is directly under his own land. Mel can capture a fluid substance, such as oil, only when it is found within the boundaries of his property.

In California—as in other states—**water rights** are becoming increasingly important. Growing demand for commercial and residential uses must be balanced against agricultural use of both surface and underground water resources.

Water Rights

Riparian rights belong to owners of land bordering a river or other flowing stream. Owners of riparian rights do not own the water but have the right to reasonable use of it on their own property. If the stream is navigable, the state owns the land under the stream. The riparian landowner's property line is the mean high water line of the stream.

Littoral rights belong to owners of land bordering a still body of water, such as a lake. Owners of littoral rights have the right to reasonable use of the water on their own property.

Underground water rights belong to landowners, who have a right of **correlative use** of the water under their land. They may withdraw only water for which they have a beneficial use on their own property. When underground water is not confined to a defined stream, it is known as **percolating water**. The **water table** (also called **groundwater level**) is the upper limit of percolating water below the earth's surface, and may be at a depth of a few feet or hundreds of feet.

A **mutual water company** may be formed when a subdivision is created and is owned by individual lot owners, who are its stockholders. An adequate potable water supply and distribution system for domestic use and fire protection must exist, and other requirements of the Corporations Code, starting at Section 14310, must be met if the mutual water company was created on or after January 1, 1998.

The state may exercise its **right of appropriation** if there is reason to divert water for public use. Permits may be issued for use of water in an area adjoining or distant from a body of water. The California Water Project and the Central Valley Project are just two examples of the massive developments that have moved water throughout the state. Water litigation disputes may be referred by a court of law to the California State Water Resources Control Board for hearing, then returned to the court for final adjudication. For a fascinating look at the history of water usage in California, read *Cadillac Desert: The American West and Its Disappearing Water*, by San Franciscan Marc Reisner (New York: Penguin Books, 1993).

Air rights have been modified from the historic concept of infinite airspace having no limitation. Federal law (the Air Commerce Act of 1926 and the Civil Aeronautics Act of 1938) allows use of airspace by aircraft. Local laws impose building height restrictions. In central city locations, air rights may be a profitable commodity. They may be transferable from one property owner to another to allow construction of skyscrapers on limited and expensive ground area.

Fixtures. A **fixture** is anything, including improvements, that is attached ("affixed") to land. A fixture can be attached by its roots (trees or shrubs) or imbedded in the land (walls). A fixture might also be something permanently resting on the land, such as a building. A building would include all things permanently attached to it, such as siding, plaster, nails, doors, and windows.

■ **FOR EXAMPLE:** Ed's Service Station has two hydraulic lifts in place in the repair bays. If Ed decides to sell the station, will the hydraulic lifts be included?

Yes, the hydraulic lifts will be included in a sale of the property (in the absence of an agreement to the contrary). Such fixtures are ordinarily permanent installations.

Appurtenances. An **appurtenance** to land is anything used with the land for the benefit of its owners, such as a roadway or waterway. Examples of appurtenances are some easements, rights of way, and condominium parking spaces. An appurtenance is said to "run with the land" because it is transferred when the land is transferred. An appurtenance could even be a passage for light, air, or heat from or across someone else's land. Stock in a mutual water company may be appurtenant to land. If it is, it can only be transferred with the land.

■ **FOR EXAMPLE:** The Allens live at the end of a private road owned by the Baker family. The Allens own an easement over the Bakers' land; that is, they have the right to use the Bakers' roadway to enter or leave their own property. If the Allens sell their land, the new owner will have the right to use the easement.

Easements are discussed in Chapter 5, "Encumbrances."

Emblements. Cultivated crops are called **emblements.** They are considered part of the land until they are harvested. Then, they become personal property. The sale of growing crops is governed by the provisions of the Uniform Commercial Code.

Crops produced by human labor (lettuce, cotton, grapes, and so on) are also referred to by the legal term, *fructus industriales.* They are distinguished from naturally occurring plant growth (such as grasses), which are termed *fructus naturales.*

Personal Property

Personal property is every kind of property that is not real property. In general, real property (realty) is considered immovable, while personal property (personalty) is considered movable. It is possible for property to change its character as realty or personalty, depending on how it is used.

■ **FOR EXAMPLE:** Trees are real property while they are growing in the ground. When the trees are cut down, they become personal property. Tree logs may be cut into boards and used in the construction of a building that is considered part of the land. Thus, the wood from the tree that began as real property may again become real property.

Tests for a Fixture

A *fixture* is anything attached to land. This simple definition is not always simple to apply. There are times when the status of a thing as a fixture to real estate, rather than personal property, is not clear-cut.

> The listing agreement between seller and agent should identify the items the seller wants to remove.

Fixtures are personal property before being attached to the land, but what kind of attachment will convert personal property to real property? California courts use five general tests in determining whether a specific thing is a fixture—that is, considered a permanent attachment to land. The five tests for a fixture can be remembered by the name MARIA, as explained in the box below.

Tests for a Fixture

Method by which the thing is affixed. The greater the degree of permanence in the attachment, the more likely it is a fixture. A wood gazebo on a concrete foundation is attached permanently; a screened room fastened to the ground with tent stakes is not.

Adaptability of the thing for the land's ordinary use. The better adapted, the more likely it will be considered a fixture. A custom-fitted item, such as a swimming pool cover, would fall into this category.

Relationship of the parties. If a residential tenant attaches something to the premises, there will be a presumption that it is personal property and removable by the tenant. The court favors tenant over landlord, buyer over seller, and lender over borrower.

Intent in placing the item on the land. This is the most important consideration. The intent may be for reasons of health and safety rather than to improve the property, such as installation of a fire extinguisher.

Agreement of the parties. If the parties are knowledgeable, they can avoid ambiguities by specifying *in writing* whether various items are fixtures or personal property and how those items will be affected by the transaction.

■ **FOR EXAMPLE:** Mary has remodeled her family room and installed a wood-burning stove. The heavy cast-iron stove sits on a brick base, and the chimney vents through a special opening in the roof. Unexpectedly Mary is transferred by her company and decides to sell her house. The Nelsons and Mary sign a contract of sale that does not specifically mention the stove but does include "all fixtures" in the sale. Can Mary take the stove with her?

No. The installation, permanence, and use of the stove all indicate it is a fixture that should stay with the house. If Mary (or her broker) had thought of it before-hand, she could have stipulated in the contract of sale that the stove would not be included and that Mary would repair any damage caused by its removal.

Fixtures on leased premises.   Parties to a lease of real property are free to make any agreement as to fixtures. In the absence of an agreement, several laws can be applied.

If a tenant has attached personal property to the premises, the property may be removed before the end of the lease term if

- it was installed for purposes of trade, manufacture, ornament, or domestic use; and
- it can be removed without substantial damage to the premises.

A tenant may remove a fixture installed for some other purpose only if the tenant believed in good faith that the fixture could be installed and subsequently removed. To summarize, an item attached for use in a trade or business (a **trade fixture**) or for residential use may be removed. The tenant must pay for any property damage resulting from the removal.

Real Property versus Personal Property

Why bother with labeling something as either real property or personal property? There are a number of reasons.

The distinction between real and personal property is particularly important when property is sold or leased. When real estate is sold, fixtures are usually considered part of the land and go to the buyer.

> A court of another state can't decide an issue involving California real estate.

Ownership and transfer of title to *real property* are subject to the laws of the state within which the land is located. The only exceptions are for federally owned lands and land that is part of a federal proceeding, such as bankruptcy. Ownership and transfer of *personal property* are subject to the laws of the state where the property owner resides, even if the personal property is located elsewhere.

The distinction between real property and personal property also is important in the formation of a contract of sale. Most contracts involving real property must be in writing. For personal property, a written document generally is required only when the value of the property exceeds a certain amount. A written instru-ment also may be required for transactions involving personal property that fall within the rules of the Uniform Commercial Code, such as bulk sales of goods, sales of securities, and formation of security agreements.

Ownership of real property is usually transferred by an instrument called a *deed*. Ownership of personal property usually is transferred by a **bill of sale.**

As you will learn in Chapter 4, transfers of real property can be recorded with the county recorder to give notice of the transfer to other parties. Instruments conveying personal property generally cannot be recorded, and recording may not be considered notice of the conveyance.

Finally, real property and personal property are subject to separate tax laws.

Exercise 2-1   Identify each of the following as either a fixture or personal property and explain your choice.

house *real*

room air conditioner *Personal*

motor home *personal*

space heater *personal*

brick patio *real*

fireplace *real*

patio furniture *Personal*

wall-to-wall carpeting *real*

wood deck *real*

room-size rug *personal*

hot tub *person*

chandelier *real*

■ LAND DESCRIPTION

It would be impossible to own or lease land if we had no adequate way to describe or define it. Street names and numbers can be used to identify buildings. What is described by such an address is a particular parcel of real estate. Usually, all the improvements within the perimeter of a certain area of land are included. Using only a street address to identify real estate presents several problems. First, some property, such as rural, undeveloped land, cannot be identified by street address. Second, a street name may change, a driveway may be moved, or the land may be developed in a way that was not anticipated. The best practice is to use the

- ■ **legal description;**
- ■ **APN**—the tax assessor's parcel number; and
- ■ street address, when available.

Most deeds show the legal description followed by AKA (also known as) and the street address.

In the United States, most parcels of land are defined by one of three methods of **legal description.** More than one method may be used in the same property description. The three types of legal description of land (from most recent to earliest) are

1. lot and block;
2. rectangular survey system; and
3. metes and bounds.

Lot and Block

The **lot and block system** is also called the **lot, block, and tract system** or **subdivision system.** A **subdivision map** shows the boundaries of all of the parcels in the subdivision. The subdivision map is filed in the county recorder's office, usually by the developer. Each parcel in the subdivision is identified by tract, lot, and block numbers. The tract is the largest land area. The tract is divided into blocks, which are divided into lots.

The deed to each parcel of land in the subdivision refers to the tract, block, and lot numbers shown on the subdivision map. The subdivision map may also be referred to as a **plat map.** Figure 2.4 shows part of a plat map, with a block that has been divided into eight residential building lots.

In a lot and block legal description, it is usually sufficient to give the city name, county name, tract name and number, and block and lot numbers. It is a better practice to give the book and page number in the county recorder's office where the map appears, as well as the date the map was recorded.

FIGURE 2.4

Plat Map

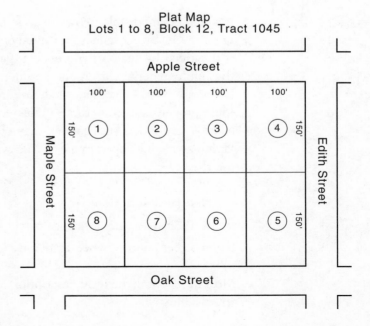

Plat Map
Lots 1 to 8, Block 12, Tract 1045

■ **FOR EXAMPLE:** Developer Richard Tice and his wife, Rose, sold Gary Hize a house located at 491 Rose Avenue, which is lot 28 of block 15 of the Tice Elms Subdivision, Walnut Creek, Contra Costa County, California. The subdivision map was recorded August 16, 1968, and can be found in book 38, on page 106. How would the property be described by the developer and in the deed to the buyer?

Richard would describe the property as 491 Rose Avenue, Tice Elms Subdivision, Walnut Creek, Lot 28, Block 15, Contra Costa County, California, as shown in Book 38, Page 106, recorded 08-16-1968. The deed Gary received described his property as Lot 28, Block 15, Tice Elms Subdivision (as recorded August 16, 1968, Book 38, Page 106 of maps), City of Walnut Creek, County of Contra Costa, State of California.

FIGURE 2.5

California Township and Range Survey System

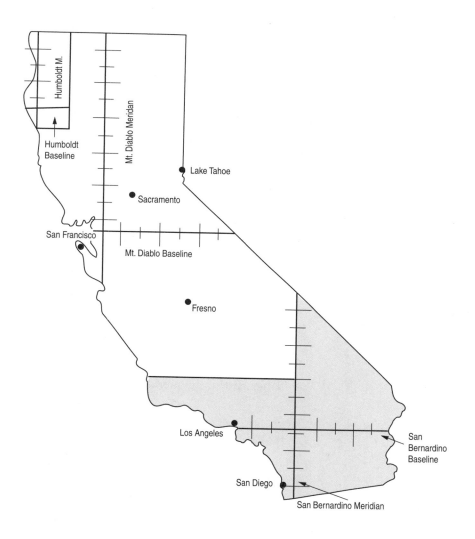

Rectangular Survey System

The **rectangular survey system** also is called the **section and township system** or **U.S. government survey system.**

This is the method used by the United States Surveyor General to survey public lands. This system bases descriptions of land on its distance from a **baseline** that runs east-west and a **meridian** that runs north-south from a reference point.

The map in Figure 2.5 shows the three principal baselines and meridians used in California land descriptions. The Humboldt Baseline and Meridian were established on Mt. Pierre in Humboldt County in 1853; the Mt. Diablo Baseline and Meridian were established on Mt. Diablo in Contra Costa County in 1851; and the San Bernardino Baseline and Meridian were established on San Bernardino Mountain in San Bernardino County in 1852. A parcel may be described using different reference points. For example, property in the City of Fresno, as shown in Figure 2.5, may be described as ____ miles South and ____ miles East of the Mt. Diablo Baseline and Meridian, or as ____ miles North and ____ miles West of the San Bernardino Baseline and Meridian.

Land division. Land area is divided into **townships** that are measured and numbered in each direction from the point of intersection of the baseline and the meridian. A township does not refer to a "town" or community. Instead, it is an area of six miles square (36 square miles).

Because of the curvature of the earth, the lines that set off each township are not perfectly parallel and there must be some way to compensate for this. Every four townships north and south of the baseline, a **correction line** is measured at the full interval (six miles) for that side of each township it borders. Every four townships east and west of the principal meridian, a **guide meridian** establishes the full interval of six miles for that side of each township it borders. This is illustrated in Figure 2.6.

Townships run north-south in **tiers** and east-west in **ranges.** The township identified as T2N, R3E is the township in the second tier north of the baseline and the third range east of the meridian. It is highlighted in Figure 2.6.

FIGURE 2.6

Townships

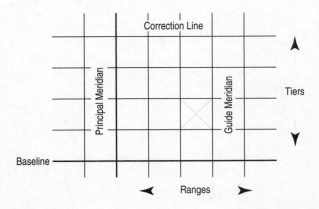

FIGURE 2.7

Divisions of a Section and Sections in a Township

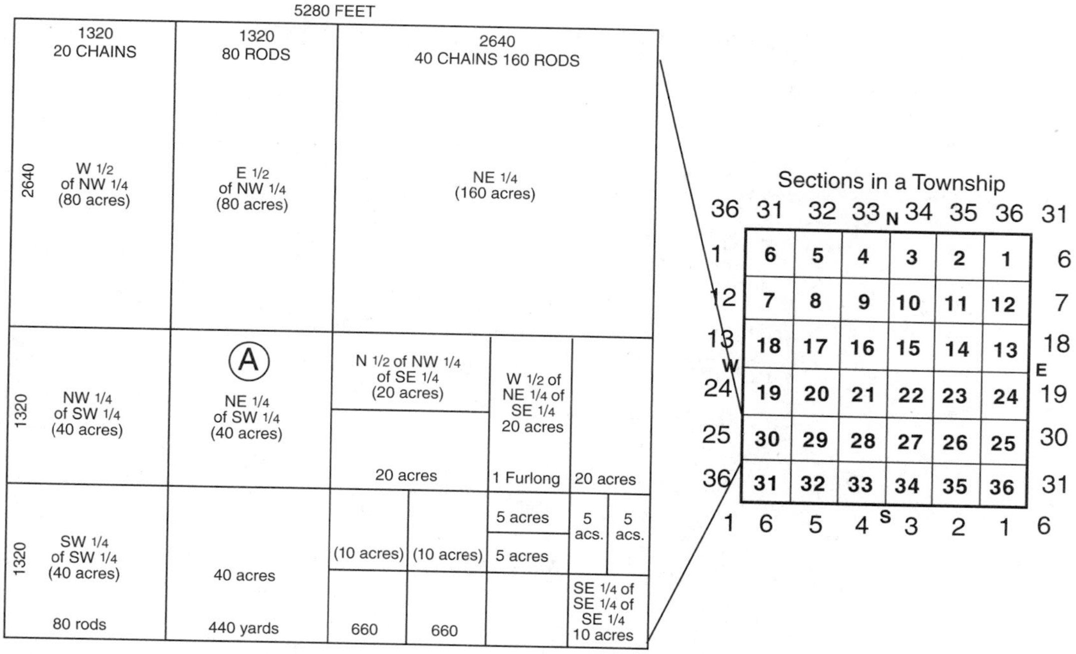

A township is composed of 36 *sections*. One standard **section** is one square mile, which contains 640 acres. A section may be further divided as shown in Figure 2.7.

The sections composing a township are numbered in a particular order, starting with section number 1 in the northeast corner of the township. The numbering system is shown in Figure 2.7.

Method of description.   The important dimensions of any rectangular survey description are the compass points: north, south, east, west. The smallest area described is given first and the largest area last, so to find a parcel, you should work backward from the largest area described.

In Figure 2.7, the parcel labeled "A" is the northeast quarter of the southwest quarter of Section 30. For greater accuracy, legal descriptions will spell out directions and fractional parts, then abbreviate them in parentheses (or vice versa).

■   **FOR EXAMPLE:**   Describe the parcel of land indicated by the shaded area of the township below.

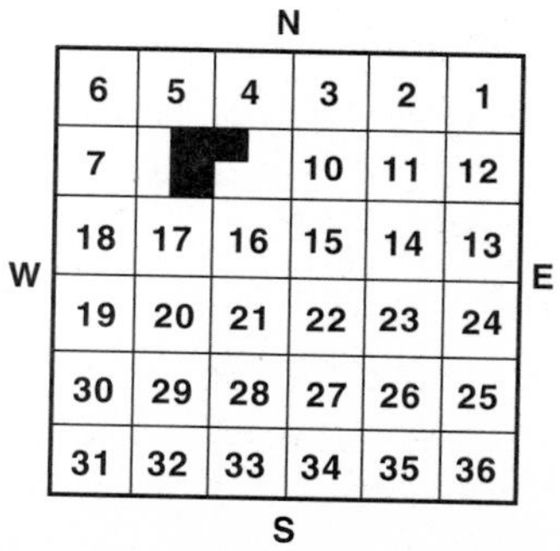

The shaded area is the east half (E½) of Section 8, and the northwest quarter (NW ¼) of Section 9.

Computing land area.   Land area is based on the following units of measurement.

Units of Measurement	
1 foot	12 inches
1 yard	3 feet or 36 inches
1 acre	43,560 square feet
1 rod	5½ yards or 16½ feet
1 furlong	40 rods
6.06 rods	100 feet
1 mile	5,280 feet, or 8 furlongs, or 320 rods, or 1,760 yards
1 league	3 miles

The area of a parcel also can be computed using the rectangular survey system. Multiply the number of acres in a section by the fractional parts of a section described.

■ **FOR EXAMPLE:**   Sue Snelling wants to buy the parcel described in the last example but doesn't want to pay more than $5,000 per acre. What is her maximum purchase price?

We know that a section has 640 acres, so we can multiply 640 acres by the fractional parts of the section that are involved.

For Section 8:

$$640 \times \tfrac{1}{2} = 320 \text{ acres}$$

For Section 9:

$$640 \times \tfrac{1}{4} = 160 \text{ acres}$$

The total acreage is 320 plus 160, or 480 acres. At $5,000 per acre, the maximum price Sue Snelling will pay is $2,400,000.

MATH CONCEPTS

There are several different ways to compute the size of a parcel of land.

Let's say you want to find the total area of a parcel described as the South ½ of the East ½ of the Northeast ¼ of the Northwest ¼ of Section 1. This could appear on a deed as the "S½ of E½ of NE¼ of NW¼ of Section 1."

Method #1

Multiply the last fraction by the number of acres in a section. Then, working backward, multiply your answer by each of the remaining fractions.

$$640 \times \tfrac{1}{4} = 160 \text{ acres}$$
$$160 \times \tfrac{1}{4} = 40 \text{ acres}$$
$$40 \times \tfrac{1}{2} = 20 \text{ acres}$$

The described parcel has 10 acres.

Method #2

This is a faster method, if you know how to multiply fractions. Multiply the fractions, then multiply that number by the number of acres in a section.

$$(\tfrac{1}{2} \times \tfrac{1}{2} \times \tfrac{1}{4} \times \tfrac{1}{4}) \times 640 \text{ acres} = \text{size of parcel}$$
$$\tfrac{1}{64} \times = 640 \text{ acres} = \text{size of parcel}$$
$$\tfrac{640}{64} \text{ acres} = 10 \text{ acres}$$

To multiply fractions, multiply their numerators (the top part of the fraction) and multiply their denominators (the bottom part of the fraction).

$$\tfrac{1}{2} \times \tfrac{1}{3} = \tfrac{1}{6}$$
$$\tfrac{2}{3} \times \tfrac{1}{4} = \tfrac{2}{12} = \tfrac{1}{6}$$

Sometimes, you will find the size of a parcel of land by adding fractional parts of one or more sections.

MATH CONCEPTS

Let's say you want to find the total area of a parcel described as the North ½ and the Southeast ¼ of Section 17.

Method #1

Multiply each fraction by the number of acres in a section. Then, add each amount to find the total number of acres.

$$640 \times \tfrac{1}{2} = 320 \text{ acres}$$
$$640 \times \tfrac{1}{4} = 160 \text{ acres}$$
$$320 \times 160 = 480 \text{ acres}$$

The described parcel has 480 acres.

Method #2

This is another method, if you know how to add fractions. To add or subtract fractions, each fraction must have the same denominator (bottom part).

$$\tfrac{1}{2} + \tfrac{1}{8} = \tfrac{4}{8} + \tfrac{1}{8} = \tfrac{5}{8}$$
$$\tfrac{1}{2} + \tfrac{1}{3} = \tfrac{3}{6} + \tfrac{2}{6} = \tfrac{5}{6}$$

In the problem above, you would go through the following steps.

$$(\tfrac{1}{2} + \tfrac{1}{4}) \times 640 \text{ acres} = (\tfrac{2}{4} + \tfrac{1}{4}) \times 640 \text{ acres}$$
$$= \tfrac{3}{4} \times 640 \text{ acres} = 480 \text{ acres}$$

Metes and Bounds

In a **metes and bounds** description a surveyor uses boundary markers and measures the distance from marker to marker to determine a property's perimeter. The term **metes** refers to distances, which may be measured in inches, feet, yards, or rods. **Bounds** are natural or artificial boundaries, such as rivers and roads. Single **monuments,** or **markers,** such as rocks, fences, iron pipes, or other natural or artificial objects also may be used. If an **angle of measurement** is given, it will be based on the degree of deviation from either north or south, as shown in Figure 2.8.

Method of description.   A metes and bounds description starts at a designated point, called the **point of beginning.** It then follows each boundary for a given distance, in a given direction, and at a precise angle from the last point. The simplest type of description using metes and bounds would be to follow the dimensions of a tract, as in the example on the following page.

FIGURE 2.8

Angles of Measurement

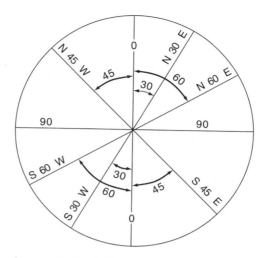

Source: California Department of Real Estate
Reference Book, 1989–90, p. 71.

■ **FOR EXAMPLE:** Using metes and bounds, describe the land below.

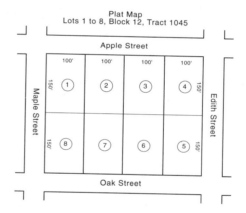

Plat Map
Lots 1 to 8, Block 12, Tract 1045

Beginning at a point on the southerly line of Apple Street, 150 feet westerly of the SW corner of the intersection of Apple and Edith Streets; running thence due south 300 feet to the northerly line of Oak Street; thence westerly along the northerly line of Oak Street, 100 feet; thence northerly and parallel to the first course, 300 feet, to the southerly line of Apple Street; thence easterly along the southerly line of Apple Street, 100 feet, to the point of beginning.

Unfortunately, rivers change their courses, and trees can burn or be cut down. Over time, bounds and markers may be impossible to locate or may simply have disappeared. Where the distance between monuments differs from that in the description, the actual distance takes precedence.

Because of the unpredictability of markers and boundaries, the metes and bounds method of land survey is not very accurate. In addition, only a professional

FIGURE 2.9

Metes and Bounds/Tract

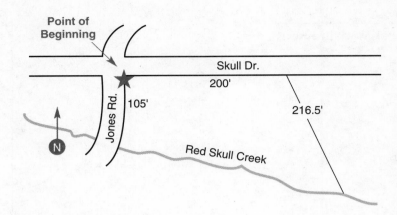

surveyor may be able to follow a complex metes and bounds description, which severely limits its usefulness. This system of land description is not often used in California, although it can be found in older documents. It is used in many other states, including Hawaii.

The following is an early example of a metes and bounds description of the land illustrated in Figure 2.9. As you read this description, consider how the boundaries specified may have changed over the past 200 years.

A tract of land located in the Village of Red Skull, described as follows: Beginning at the intersection of the East line of Jones Road and the South line of Skull Drive; thence East along the South line of Skull Drive 200 feet; thence South 15° East 216.5 feet, more or less, to the center thread of Red Skull Creek; thence Northwesterly along the center line of said Creek to its intersection with the East line of Jones Road; thence North 105 feet, more or less, along the East line of Jones Road to the place of beginning.

■ SUMMARY

The state of California has a unique history of settlement, conquest, and, ultimately, growth and prosperity. The rancho grants and the vast lands surrounding the pueblos formed the basis for private land ownership after the Treaty of Guadalupe Hidalgo in 1848. The Board of Land Commissioners solved problems of conflicting claims of property ownership. With adoption of the English **common law,** admission to the Union as a state, and the discovery of gold, California quickly assumed the importance it deserved. Even today, however, the state retains elements of its Spanish heritage, such as **community property.**

Real property is land, both at and below the surface and above the surface. **Real property** includes **mineral rights, water rights,** and **airspace.** A **fixture** is something attached or placed permanently on the land. An **appurtenance** is used with land and benefits the landowner.

Personal property is all property that is not **real property.** Something may be **personal property** but become **real property** when it is affixed to land. Five tests can be used to determine whether something is a **fixture** and thus part of the **real estate. Trade fixtures** remain the personal property of a business.

A **legal description** identifies a specific parcel of land to the exclusion of all others. The **lot and block system** uses the **subdivision map,** which shows streets and lot dimensions.

The **rectangular survey system** uses a gridlike division of land area into **townships** set in **tiers** and **ranges** along geographical dimensions called **meridians** and **baselines. Townships** are divided into **sections,** which are further divided into fractional parts.

The **metes and bounds system** uses natural or manufactured **monuments, angles of measurement,** and distances to describe a property.

■ IMPORTANT TERMS

Make sure you understand the following terms before you take the achievement examination.

air rights
appurtenance
baselines
bill of sale
bundle of rights
civil law
common law
community property
correction line
correlative use
emblements
fixture
fructus industriales
fructus naturales
guide meridian
land
legal description
littoral rights
lot and block system
markers
meridians

metes and bounds
mineral rights
monuments
personal property
plat map
point of beginning
ranges
real estate
real property
rectangular survey system
right of appropriation
riparian rights
section
section and township system
subdivision map
subdivision system
tiers
township
underground water rights
U.S. government survey system
water rights

■ OPEN FOR DISCUSSION

Population growth in California's urban areas depends upon the availability of water for both residential and nonresidential use.

1. Should growth be limited to conserve water resources?

2. Should water resources be limited to control growth?

■ ACHIEVEMENT EXAMINATION 2

1. During the days of Spanish rule, all land was owned by the
   a. missions.
   c. crown.
   b. government.
   d. conquistadores.

2. The Treaty of Guadalupe Hidalgo ended
   a. the gold rush.
   b. Spanish rule.
   c. the war with Mexico.
   d. the missions.

3. Real estate law, which relies on court decisions as well as legislation, is based on
   a. Spanish civil law.
   b. French civil law.
   c. the right of appropriation.
   d. English common law.

4. Land disputes over the Spanish and Mexican land grants were settled by
   a. the Board of Land Commissioners.
   b. the State of California.
   c. the Spanish legal code.
   d. taking all land for public use.

5. In California, the term *real estate* is synonymous with
   a. land.
   b. fixtures.
   c. real property.
   d. personal property.

6. Real property is *not*
   a. land.
   b. real estate.
   c. appurtenances to land.
   d. movable.

7. The sale of real property generally is governed by the laws of
   a. the state where the real property is located.
   b. the state where the owner of the real property resides.
   c. any of the United States.
   d. the federal government.

8. The sale of personal property generally is governed by the laws of
   a. the state where the personal property is located.
   b. the state where the owner of the property resides.
   c. any of the United States.
   d. the federal government.

9. In California, the Uniform Commercial Code governs sales transactions involving
   a. real estate.
   b. bulk sales of goods.
   c. fixtures to real estate.
   d. riparian rights.

10. For real estate to be conveyed, there must be an accurate
    a. fence line.
    b. description.
    c. soil chemical analysis.
    d. water test.

11. A subdivision map is
    a. rarely accurate.
    b. good only to describe the entire subdivision.
    c. never required.
    d. a good reference for a legal description.

12. The most useful method of describing a subdivision parcel is probably the
    a. lot and block system.
    b. rectangular survey system.
    c. metes and bounds system.
    d. U.S. government survey system.

13. The rectangular survey system is also called the
    a. U.S. government survey system.
    b. province and township system.
    c. subdivision system.
    d. California system.

14. California has how many principal baselines?
    a. One   c. Three
    b. Two   d. Four

15. A township consists of how many sections?
    a. 12   c. 4
    b. 18   d. 36

16. A section is
    a. 640 acres.
    b. six square miles.
    c. 5,000 feet by 5,000 feet.
    d. three leagues.

17. Section 6 lies in what direction from section 1 of a township?
    a. North   c. East
    b. South   d. West

18. Section 22 lies in what direction from section 17 of a township?
    a. Northeast   c. Southeast
    b. Northwest   d. Southwest

19. Land described as the South ½ of the North ½ of Section 18 contains how many acres?
    a. 80   c. 160
    b. 120   d. 320

20. The point of beginning is used in
    a. the rectangular survey system.
    b. the metes and bounds system.
    c. the lot and block system.
    d. all legal descriptions.

CHAPTER THREE

OWNERSHIP OF REAL PROPERTY

■ ESTATES IN LAND

In the previous chapter you learned that in California, the term **real property** means the same thing as **real estate.** The terms are used interchangeably to refer to

- ■ the surface of the land;
- ■ the airspace above the land;
- ■ substances below ground level; and
- ■ all improvements and fixtures to the land.

The ownership of property consists of a "bundle of rights" or interests in it. Rights of ownership include the power to possess, use, exclude others, and dispose of the property.

An **estate** is the interest of the owner of property. **Real estate (real property)** means land ownership. All property that is not **real property** is **personal property.**

The rights of land ownership that are covered in this chapter are shown in Figure 3.1.

FIGURE 3.1

Estates in Land

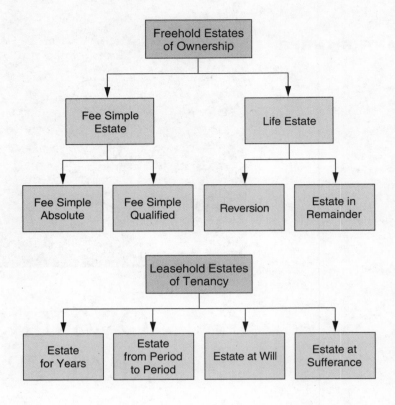

Freehold Estates

In medieval England, the **freehold estate** was the highest form of land ownership. The owner of a freehold estate in land could use the property in any way, without being subject to the demands of the overlord. Today's owner of real estate also enjoys a freehold estate. But there usually are some restraints on how the land may be used.

A freehold estate can be held for an unlimited period of time, or the period of ownership may be limited in some way.

Fee simple estate. The **fee simple estate** is what may be termed a "present, possessory interest." It carries the maximum bundle of rights. The owner of a fee simple estate has the right to use the property right now and for an indefinite period of time in the future.

The highest (most complete) form of ownership is a **fee simple absolute.** If the right of possession is restricted in some way, it is a **fee simple qualified.** A fee simple estate may be granted subject to a *limitation* on the use of the property or a *condition* that the property holder must (or must not) perform. Because the property interest can be lost or taken away, it is sometimes referred to as a **fee simple defeasible.**

With a **fee simple estate subject to a condition subsequent,** there is some action or activity that the fee simple owner must *not* perform. If the condition is broken, the former owner can retake possession of the property.

■   **FOR EXAMPLE:**   Clyde Biggs gives a 1,000-acre parcel of rural land to the church youth fellowship "on the condition that" there be no sale or manufacture of alcoholic beverages on the property. Years later, Clyde visits the retreat center established on the property by the fellowship. A reception is in progress and Clyde is surprised to find a "no host" bar at which drinks can be purchased. Clyde does not buy a drink but notices that many diners do. Upon mentioning this to the director of the fellowship, Clyde is assured that this is a rare occurrence and no abuse of alcohol is allowed. What can Clyde do?

The fellowship has broken the condition subsequent to its fee simple right of ownership. Clyde can reenter the property and claim possession.

Life estate.   The owner of a **life estate** has the right to possession and use of property, but the estate lasts only as long as the life of one or more identified persons. Usually, the **measuring life** is that of the holder of the life estate.

If the right of possession and use returns to the original owner of the property when the life estate ends, the original owner has a **reversion.** If the right of possession and use goes to a third person when the life estate ends, that person has a **remainder.** The **remainderman** holds an **estate in remainder** during the existence of the life estate.

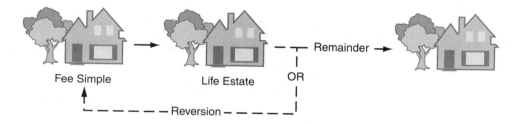

The holder of a life estate must keep up the property and pay taxes. If the holder of a life estate pays a debt, such as mortgage principal, and in so doing also benefits the reversioner or remainderman, the holder of the life estate is entitled to reimbursement.

> Mortgage interest is considered the responsibility of the life tenant.

The use of the life estate can be transferred by gift, lease, or sale, but the right to use and possession ends with the measuring life. Because there can be no guarantee that anyone will live to a certain age, the value of a life estate will be based on the life expectancy of the individual(s) against whose life the estate is measured.

A special situation arises when the measuring life is that of someone other than the holder of the life estate. The holder of the life estate may die before the person against whose life the estate is measured dies. In that case, the interest of the holder of the life estate passes to the holder's heirs and will last until the end of the measuring life. The reversioner or remainderman can give, sell, or lease that interest, but no right of possession will take effect until the termination of the life estate.

■ **FOR EXAMPLE:**   Mr. Biggs, a widower, died, leaving a life estate in his home to his sister Nell and the remainder to his only child, Ted. Nell had been living in an apartment and was very pleased to have the use of the Biggs house. Ted, upset when he found out what his father had done, insisted on being allowed to live in the house, for it was "really" his. Does Ted have that right?

No. Nell, owner of the life estate, has the sole right of use and possession of the property while she lives.

Leasehold Estates

Tenants are those who rent or lease property from **landlords.**

Tenants own nonfreehold estates called **leaseholds** or **estates of tenancy.** Instead of an ownership interest, the tenant has the right to use the property for the stated period of time. The length of the lease term determines the type of tenancy. Estates of tenancy are discussed in more detail in Chapter 12, "Landlord and Tenant."

Exercise 3-1   Identify each of the following types of ownership interest in land.

1. Dennis Holmby has sole possession of Blackacre for as long as he lives.

2. The Middle Falls School has sole possession of Whiteacre on the condition that it be used for educational purposes.

3. The town of Merry Meadows has a beautiful library building. The building is a former mansion that was donated to the town with the stipulation that it be used only as a library. What kind of estate does the town have?

4. Harvey Melman has lived at 316 Iowa Street for 15 years on a month-to-month lease term. Although his rent has been increased every few years, the landlord has never drawn up a lease agreement. What kind of estate does Harvey have in the residence on Iowa Street?

5. In her will, Mrs. Chau left her residence in Palm Springs to her nephew, Simon, for the life of Simon's sister, Annette. On Annette's death, the home is to go to Annette's daughter, Yvonne. What kind of estate does Simon have? What kind of estate does Yvonne have? What happens if Simon dies before Annette does?

■ TAKING TITLE TO REAL ESTATE

A conveyance of real estate is called a **grant.** The person conveying the property (owner) is the **grantor;** the person receiving the property is the **grantee.**

Title to real estate (its ownership) can be taken by one person or by more than one person. Advising someone on how to take title is a legal question that may have tax and other consequences. Such advice should come from an attorney. A real estate licensee is prohibited from giving legal advice.

For reasons that will become clear as we proceed with this section, individuals taking title to property should indicate their marital status as

- single (never married);
- married;
- unmarried (divorced);
- widow (if the husband has died); or
- widower (if the wife has died).

For example, title may be conveyed to "George Jones, a single man" or "Helen Trent, a widow."

Ownership in Severalty

Ownership in severalty, also called **separate ownership** or **sole ownership,** is ownership by one person. The property owner (who can be an individual or a legal entity, such as a corporation or trust) is the only person to receive the benefits of ownership. The separate owner also is the only person responsible for the burdens of ownership, such as the payment of taxes.

Concurrent Ownership

Concurrent ownership is ownership by more than one person at the same time. There are four types of concurrent ownership, as shown in Figure 3.2.

> Tenancy in common is the default form of ownership for two or more unmarried people.

Tenancy in common.   A **tenancy in common** is created when it is specified by name. It also is created when more than one person takes title, they are not married to each other, and no other method of taking title is specified.

Tenants in common may take title at different times and may own equal or unequal shares. If no distribution is specified, tenants in common are presumed to own equal shares.

Tenants in common have what is called **unity of possession,** which means that each tenant has the right to possession of the property and cannot be excluded by the cotenants. Even if they own unequal shares in the property, each has the right to use all of it. If the property is rented, tenants in common share the rent

FIGURE 3.2

Concurrent Ownership

	Tenancy in Common	Joint Tenancy	Community Property	Tenancy in Partnership
Parties	Any number	Any number	Spouses only	Any number
Time	Any time	Same time	Same time	Any time
Title	Separate titles to each interest	Only one title	Only one title	Only one title
Interest	Separate, undivided interests	Equal, undivided interests	Equal, undivided interests	Equal, undivided interests
Possession and Control of Property	Equal right for each owner	Equal right for each owner	Equal right for each owner	Equal right except for personal property
Conveyance	Yes, of each share separately	Yes, but creates tenancy in common as to that share	Only if both spouses join in the conveyance	Only if all partners join in the conveyance
Deceased's Share on Death	Passes by will or intestacy	Passes to surviving joint tenant(s)	Half to surviving spouse; half by will or intestacy	Can pass to surviving partners; heirs have right to deceased's share of profits
New Owner of Partial Interest	Tenant in common	Tenant in common	Tenant in common; no community interest	Tenant in common
Creditor Sale	Sale of individual tenant's interest	Creates tenancy in common as to that interest	Entire property available to satisfy debt	Entire property available to satisfy partnership debt

according to their individual shares. Expenses of the property, such as taxes, also are shared.

A tenant in common can give away, sell, or devise (will) his or her share of the property to someone else. The recipient(s) receives the share of the tenant in common and full right of possession.

A tenant in common may want to dissolve the shared ownership. This can be accomplished by agreement of all cotenants or, if there is a dispute, by a lawsuit known as a **partition action.** If it is possible to divide the property among the owners in equitable shares, the court will do so. Otherwise, the property will be sold. If a sale is ordered by the court, the proceeds of the sale will be distributed to the cotenants in the same shares as their ownership interests, less a proportionate part of any expenses owed.

■ **FOR EXAMPLE:** Al Pine, Sara Willow, and Jed Bush are all owners of Paradise Acres, a mountain retreat. They have a fee simple estate and hold title as tenants in common. Each has a one-third share of Paradise Acres. Gibbon Properties manages Paradise Acres. Who pays the management fee? Who gets the profits, if any?

Each of the tenants in common is responsible for one-third of the management fee. Each will take one-third of the profits, if any, after the management fee and expenses are paid.

Joint tenancy.   A **joint tenancy** is a special form of co-ownership. It requires that all co-owners take title to the property at the same time, by the same document. In addition, each must have an equal share of the property. These four unities of a joint tenancy, which can be remembered by the word **TTIP,** are

A joint tenancy requires unity of time, title, interest, and possession.

- ■ **T**—unity of **time** (each takes title at the same time);
- ■ **T**—unity of **title** (each receives title through the same deed);
- ■ **I**—unity of **interest** (each owns an equal share); and
- ■ **P**—unity of **possession** (each has the right to use all of the property).

If the joint tenancy is created properly, the joint tenants benefit from the **right of survivorship.** This means that when a cotenant dies, the survivors receive the deceased's share. If there are only two joint tenants, when one dies the other becomes sole owner of the property, and the property does not have to go through probate.

A joint tenant cannot **will** (name an heir to) his or her share of the property. As long as the joint tenancy exists, the right of survivorship in the other joint tenants takes precedence.

■ **FOR EXAMPLE:**   Jessica and Tiffany are cousins. Ten years ago they bought a house as joint tenants. Their deed did not use the words "with right of survivorship." Tiffany married Trevor and moved out of the house she shared with Jessica. Before Jessica and Tiffany could sell the house, as they had agreed, Tiffany died unexpectedly. Who owns the house?

Jessica is sole owner of the house. Jessica and Tiffany had taken title as joint tenants. Because one of the characteristics of a joint tenancy in California is the right of survivorship, those words do not need to be written into the deed transferring title to the joint tenants. Even if Tiffany had made a will leaving all of her property to Trevor, the will would be ineffective as to her share of property held in joint tenancy.

A joint tenant can terminate a joint tenancy, but the advice of an attorney should be sought to avoid problems. It is also possible for a joint tenant's share to be transferred to someone else while the joint tenant is still alive. Again, legal requirements must be followed. Such a transfer will sever the joint tenancy only as to that tenant, however. The new owner becomes a tenant in common. If there is only one other cotenant, the joint tenancy has been completely destroyed. If there is more than one cotenant, the joint tenancy remains in existence as to the other tenants. They still have the right of survivorship with respect to their interests.

Any two people can be joint tenants, including a married couple. Because spouses also can hold title to real estate as community property, they will want to consider the benefits of both forms of ownership, preferably with the advice of an attorney. As pointed out earlier, a licensed real estate agent may not give advice on how to hold title.

Community property. **Community property** is real or personal property acquired by either spouse during marriage. Each also may own *separate* (noncommunity) real or personal property, however, and acquire **separate property** during marriage.

Property that was a married person's separate property before marriage remains separate property after marriage. Property acquired during marriage may be either the separate property of one spouse or community property belonging to both spouses, depending on its source, the actions of the parties, and legal presumptions.

Separate property is property acquired

- by gift or inheritance to one spouse;
- with the proceeds of other separate property; or
- as income from separate property.

Most other property acquired during marriage is community property. Spouses are allowed to change community property to separate property by written agreement. The handling of money can change its character as separate property. If separate funds are **commingled** (placed in the same account) with community funds, they lose their status as separate property.

> Spouses can agree to change community property to separate property.

If the ownership status of property is unclear, the courts will follow the legal presumption that **real property** in California acquired during marriage and **personal property,** wherever it is located, that is acquired during marriage are community property.

Community property cannot be sold, mortgaged, or leased for one year or longer without the agreement of both spouses. Both must sign all documents.

A spouse can convey his or her interest in community property by will. The inheritor and the surviving spouse would then be tenants in common. If a spouse dies without a will, the surviving spouse is entitled to one-half of the community property as his or her own interest and also receives the deceased spouse's one-half.

Community Property with Right of Survivorship

As of July 1, 2001, husband and wife can take title to property as **community property with right of survivorship.** The document of transfer would have to stipulate that form of title, and husband and wife would accept title in that form by writing on the face of the document a statement signed or initialed by both. With the right of survivorship, title passes to the surviving spouse without probate, just as if it were held in joint tenancy. Prior to the death of either spouse, the right of survivorship may be terminated in the same way that a joint tenancy may be severed. Civil Code 682.1

■ **FOR EXAMPLE:**   Ignacio, a married man, signs a contract to sell the mountain cabin he owns as community property with his wife, Manuela. Manuela is away on a business trip at the time the contract is drawn up and isn't interested in selling the cabin anyway. Can the buyer enforce the contract?

No, because the cabin is community property. Both spouses must sign any instrument of sale.

The concept of community property is a holdover from Spanish and Mexican rule. Only California and seven other states still treat marital property in this way, and there are important differences in each state's law. In any move from state to state, the applicable laws should be determined to avoid conflict regarding property status.

Quasi-Community Property

New California residents should be aware of the concept of **quasi-community property.** Quasi-community property is

■ any California real estate acquired by an out-of-state married person that would have been considered community property if it had been acquired by a resident of California and

■ any California real estate acquired in exchange for real or personal property located anywhere, when the California real estate would have been considered community property if it had been acquired by a California resident.

Tenancy in partnership.   The members of a **partnership** can own property for partnership purposes.

A **general partnership** is established when two or more persons carry on a business for profit as co-owners. Property owned by the partnership is actually owned by the individual **partners** as a **tenancy in partnership.** All partners have the right to possession of partnership property for partnership purposes. Partnership property can be attached only by partnership creditors.

When rights to partnership property are assigned, the rights of all partners must be assigned. The death of a partner will dissolve the partnership, unless there was a prior written agreement to continue the business. If a business is dissolved, its assets are sold, creditors are paid, and the remainder is distributed to the partners. If a partner dies and the business continues, that partner's right to possession of partnership property (the business) goes to the surviving partner(s). The heirs of the deceased partner have no right to the property, although they are entitled to the deceased's share of the profits. The partners may agree in writing to a different distribution.

A partner's right in property owned by the partnership cannot be community property. For some purposes, however, a partner's interest in the partnership itself is treated as community property.

All partners are liable for debts of the partnership.

For tax purposes, all partnership income is distributed to the partners, who report that income individually. An important feature of a partnership is that each partner is liable for partnership debts. For that reason alone, the decision to form a partnership requires careful consideration.

■ **FOR EXAMPLE:**   George is a partner in Realty Agents, Inc. The partnership leases office space in four buildings. George needs storage space for some furniture he is giving his son. May he store the furniture in the partnership's office?

No. As a partner, George may not use partnership property for personal purposes.

Exercise 3-2   What form of ownership does each of the following people have in the property described?

1. Jane Newel and her brother own a farm and have a right of survivorship.

2. Fred Wells and his wife own their home as husband and wife. No form of ownership was specified in their deed, as Fred and his wife have not yet consulted an attorney.

3. Cal Murphy and Lou Erwin, both single men, bought a three-story Victorian home in Sacramento. No form of ownership was specified.

4. Helen Santiago is a partner in Real Estate Consultants, which owns a shopping center.

5. Fred Wells, a married man, inherited a cattle ranch from his uncle. Fred is the uncle's sole heir.

■ BUSINESS OWNERSHIP OF REAL ESTATE

Other types of businesses also can acquire, use, and sell real estate. This section discusses the

- sole proprietorship;
- corporation;
- general partnership;
- limited partnership;
- limited liability company; and
- trust.

Sole Proprietorship

The **sole proprietorship** is the simplest form of business ownership, because it has only one owner. The sole proprietor

- conducts business in his or her own name or under a trade name;
- reports business income on his or her individual income tax return; and
- is responsible for the business's debts.

The sole proprietor may or may not have employees, such as personal assistants.

Corporation

Every state has specific laws regulating the formation, operation, and dissolution of *corporations*. The owners of a **corporation** are called **shareholders.**

The Corporation

- Is a separate, legally recognized entity, apart from owners (shareholders)
- Must be chartered by a state
- Acts through its board of directors and officers
- May own, lease, and convey real property
- Limits liability of officers, directors, and shareholders

A corporation could be formed for a nonprofit motive. A nonprofit corporation is owned by **members** rather than shareholders. It can own, lease, and convey real estate.

Corporations are called **domestic corporations** by the state in which they are chartered (created). Corporations created in any other location are called **foreign corporations.** In California, for instance, corporations chartered by any other state are considered foreign corporations in their dealings in California.

Liability. A major benefit of doing business as a corporation is that individual officers, directors, and shareholders are usually not held personally accountable for corporate decisions and corporate debts.

S corporation. One disadvantage of a corporation is that profits are taxed twice. The corporation pays taxes on income, and income is taxed again when it is distributed to shareholders in the form of dividends. Federal tax law provides an alternative method of taxation to corporations with 35 or fewer shareholders. If the corporation is formed under the requirements of **Subchapter S of the Internal Revenue Code,** income is allowed to flow directly to shareholders, avoiding double taxation. In an **S corporation,** all shareholders must be individuals rather than other corporations.

To be treated as an S corporation, shareholders must file form 2553 with the IRS; if they do nothing, they will be taxed as a C corporation (under Subchapter C), with the double taxation mentioned above. To qualify as an S corporation, the corporation must be a domestic (U.S.) corporation with only one class of stock and no more than 35 shareholders, all of whom consent in writing to filing as an S corporation. The shareholders of an S corporation can be individuals, estates, exempt organizations, or certain trusts, but cannot be nonresident aliens. For complete information about filing as an S corporation, consult your tax adviser and the instructions for form 2553 that can be found at the Web site of the Internal Revenue Service, *www.irs.gov.*

www.irs.gov

Partnership

A **partnership** is an association of two or more persons to carry on a business as co-owners for profit. A real estate company can be established as a partnership, provided each of the partners performing activities that require a real estate license is a licensed real estate broker (Business and Professions Code Section 10137.1). In a **general partnership,** each of the partners by definition has authority to act on behalf of the partnership, and each is liable for the debts of the partnership.

Limited Partnership

To avoid the unlimited liability of being a general partner, an investor can take part in a **limited partnership.** A limited partnership can be created only in compliance with state law. In California, this includes filing certain information with the Secretary of State.

The **California limited partnership** must have one or more general partners who run the business and have unlimited liability for partnership obligations. Other investors can join as limited partners and their liability will be no more than the amount they have invested in the partnership. By law, limited partners can take no part in the management of the partnership. If they do so, they will be considered general partners and will lose their limited liability.

Real estate syndicate.   A **real estate syndicate** can take the form of a REIT, corporation, general partnership, or other entity, but is usually formed as a limited partnership. In California, real estate syndicates are popular methods of investment for both corporations and individuals. A syndicate of 100 or more participants must be approved by the Department of Corporations before syndicate interests may be offered for sale. Strict rules and regulations must be followed.

Limited Liability Company

Almost all states permit business operation and property ownership by a **limited liability company (LLC).** Although each state's law is unique, an LLC typically provides the single-level tax benefit of a partnership with a flexible organizational structure.

In California, an LLC is created by filing a one-page form with the Secretary of State. LLC members are not required to have a written operating agreement setting out their rights and responsibilities, although one is advisable. LLC members may adopt corporate formalities, such as resolutions and annual meetings, but are not required to do so.

> Taxes and fees are higher for an LLC than for a partnership.

Unlike a Subchapter S corporation, an LLC places no restriction on the number of shareholders who take part and who they are. The LLC provides something closer to the limited liability for corporate shareholders than the greater protection afforded to limited partners. Unlike limited partners, however, members of an LLC can take part in the running of the organization without incurring personal liability for business obligations. This freedom from liability does have a cost. In California, an LLC incurs higher taxes and fees than either a general or limited partnership.

> www.ss.ca.gov/business/business.htm

Information Available on the Web

The **Secretary of State Business Service Center** Web site at *www.ss.ca.gov/business/business.htm* provides information on corporations, limited liability companies, limited liability partnerships, general partnerships, and other entities, including lists of officers and directors.

Trust

A **trust** can be a form of property ownership. Title to property is conveyed by the **trustor** to the **trustee.** Title is held by the trustee on behalf of a **beneficiary.**

> Using a trust to hold title is a way to keep the true owner's identity hidden.

Who controls the property held in trust? The trustee's powers generally are defined by the document establishing the trust. If the trustor fails to define the trustee's powers, the law of the state in which the trust is created is followed. A trust can last for a short or relatively long period of time, depending on the trustor's intent. Trusts often are created by the terms of a will (a **testamentary trust**) to care for the decedent's children until they reach adulthood.

Real estate investment trust. The **real estate investment trust (REIT)** holds various forms of real estate or mortgages for the benefit of investors who own shares of the trust. REIT shares may be publicly traded. More information about REITs can be found in the box below.

REITs

In California, a Real Estate Investment Trust (REIT)

- is regulated by the Commissioner of Corporations;
- must comply with federal and state tax law;
- must be owned by at least 100 different investors;
- cannot have any five investors own more than 50 percent of the trust;
- must receive at least 95 percent of its income from investments; and
- must receive at least 75 percent of its investment income from real estate.

---

www.nareit.com

The **National Association of Real Estate Investment Trusts (NAREIT)** serves REIT owners, managers, and related companies. Information on various forms of REITs can be found at the association's Web site, *www.nareit.com.*

Living trust. The **living trust (inter vivos trust)** is an increasingly popular form of property ownership. A living trust can be used to hold title to property during the lifetime of the trustor, who is also named as the beneficiary of the trust. When the trustor dies, title to the property held in trust passes to a **contingent beneficiary** named in the trust document. In this way property can be transferred without going through an expensive probate process. A living trust also can be created by a married couple, with the property held in trust going to the contingent beneficiary on the death of the second spouse.

Properly drafted, a living trust can be an effective estate-planning tool that provides the easiest and quickest way to transfer property at death. Every living trust should be customized to the needs of the trustor by an attorney familiar with such documents.

Exercise 3-3 What form of ownership does each example below illustrate?

1. The Spice Company owns a processing plant and leases dock space for its shipments. The company is doing very well, and it paid an excellent dividend to shareholders last year.

2. Joseph Marine owns World Wide Real Estate. Joseph, a licensed real estate broker, is the only owner of World Wide and reports company income on his personal tax return.

Limited partnership

Trust

3. Mountain Properties is a real estate syndicate of 127 investors. Only five members of the syndicate are allowed to participate in investment decisions.

4. When Grandpa Peter died he left his farm to his grandson, but his grandson will not receive title to the farm until he is 25. In the meantime, Cattlemen's Bank will manage and hold title to the property.

■ SUMMARY

In California, the terms **real estate** and **real property** are synonymous. The highest form of ownership in real property is the estate in **fee simple absolute.** It is also possible to own a **life estate** to enjoy property for a time measured by one's own or another's life. A **reversion** or **remainder** is the right to possess the property after the death of the holder of the life estate. A **condition subsequent** may qualify the ownership of fee simple title, creating a **fee simple defeasible.**

Property owned by only one individual is **separate property.** Both real property and personal property can be separate property. Property acquired during marriage by gift, inheritance, or with the income or proceeds of separate property is separate property unless **commingled.** Most other property acquired during marriage is **community property.**

Two or more persons may have **concurrent ownership** of real estate as **tenants in common, joint tenants with the right of survivorship,** or **tenants in partnership.** Tenants in common share **unity of possession,** which means that each tenant has the right to use the entire property. Joint tenants share the four unities of **time, title, interest,** and **possession.** A **partition action** can be brought by a cotenant who wants to have the entire property divided or sold.

A **general partnership** can own property as a **tenancy in partnership.** All general partners have the right to use partnership property for partnership purposes. All general partners are liable for partnership debts and all share partnership income.

The **sole proprietor** may take property in his or her own name or under the business's trade name. A **corporation,** whether chartered in or out of California, may own property even if the corporation is nonprofit.

A **trust** enables a **trustee** to hold property conveyed by a **trustor** for the **beneficiary** of the trust. A **testamentary trust** is established by will. A **living trust (inter vivos trust)** an be used to convey property on death without the difficulty and expense of probate.

A real estate **syndicate** comprises a group of investors, generally organized as a **limited partnership.** The **limited partners** can benefit from the greater bargaining power of the syndicate while avoiding the liabilities of general partners. A limited partnership must comply with state law to protect the limited partners. A **limited liability company** offers the tax benefit of a partnership with the opportunity to take an active role in running the company.

■ IMPORTANT TERMS

Make sure you understand the following terms before you take the achievement examination.

beneficiary	living trust
commingled	measuring life
community property	ownership in severalty
community property with right of survivorship	partition action
	partners
concurrent ownership	partnership
contingent beneficiary	quasi-community property
corporation	real estate investment trust (REIT)
estate	real estate syndicate
estates of tenancy	remainder
fee simple absolute	reversion
fee simple defeasible	right of survivorship
fee simple estate	S corporation
fee simple qualified	separate property
freehold estate	sole proprietorship
general partnership	tenancy in common
inter vivos trust	tenancy in partnership
joint tenancy	tenants
landlords	testamentary trust
leaseholds	trust
life estate	trustee
limited liability company (LLC)	trustor
limited partnership	unity of possession

■ OPEN FOR DISCUSSION

Many countries that were formerly part of the Communist Bloc are now privatizing their system of land ownership.

1. How would you explain our system of land ownership to someone from one of those countries?

2. What arguments would you make to encourage adoption of a similar system by that country?

■ ACHIEVEMENT EXAMINATION 3

1. A fee simple estate and a life estate are
   a. freehold estates.
   b. fee simple estates.
   c. leasehold estates.
   d. estates of tenancy.

2. The highest form of ownership is the
   a. life estate.
   b. real estate syndicate.
   c. fee simple absolute.
   d. estate at will.

3. A fee simple estate that will take effect when a condition is performed is a
   a. life estate.
   b. fee simple absolute.
   c. fee simple on condition precedent.
   d. fee simple defeasible.

4. A fee simple estate that may be lost when some act is performed is a
   a. life estate.
   b. fee simple absolute.
   c. fee simple on condition precedent.
   d. fee simple on condition subsequent.

5. A fee simple estate that is conditioned upon the owner's remaining in occupancy is a
   a. life estate.
   b. fee simple absolute.
   c. fee simple on condition precedent.
   d. fee simple defeasible.

6. If Greenacre is deeded by Lou to Mary for Mary's life, Mary has
   a. a life estate.
   b. an estate in remainder.
   c. an estate in reversion.
   d. no interest.

7. If Greenacre is deeded by Lou to Mary for Mary's life, Lou has
   a. a life estate.
   b. an estate in remainder.
   c. an estate in reversion.
   d. no interest.

8. When Aunt Winifred died, she left a life estate in Whiteacre to her nephew George. When George dies, Whiteacre will go to George's daughter Elizabeth. Elizabeth is a
   a. reversioner.
   b. remainderman.
   c. holder of a life estate.
   d. joint tenant with right of survivorship.

9. If Greenacre is deeded by Lou to Mary for the life of Nancy, Nancy has
   a. a life estate.
   b. an estate in remainder.
   c. an estate in reversion.
   d. no interest.

10. The owner of a life estate can
    a. sell only the life estate.
    b. never will the life estate.
    c. sell the fee simple estate.
    d. sell both the life estate and the fee simple estate.

11. Joint tenants have unity of
    a. interest but not possession.
    b. title but not interest.
    c. possession and title only.
    d. time, title, interest, and possession.

12. Barbara and Mark own Blackacre as joint tenants. Barbara's will specifies that on her death her interest in Blackacre is to go to her sister Jacquie. When Barbara dies
    a. Jacquie will be a tenant in common of Blackacre with Mark.
    b. Jacquie will be a joint tenant of Blackacre with Mark.
    c. Mark will be sole owner of Blackacre.
    d. the probate court will have to sell Blackacre and distribute the proceeds to Mark and Jacquie.

13. Three joint tenants share interest in a property. If one joint tenant's share is sold using the proper legal formalities, the new owner will then be a
    a. joint tenant with the other joint tenants.
    b. tenant in common with the other joint tenants.
    c. tenant at sufferance.
    d. remainderman.

14. Community property is
    a. all property acquired during marriage.
    b. all property acquired by the husband during marriage.
    c. the only form of ownership during marriage.
    d. all property acquired during marriage that is not separate property.

15. One of the forms of concurrent ownership is
    a. ownership in severalty.
    b. tenancy in partnership.
    c. sole proprietorship.
    d. separate ownership.

16. A partner has
    a. an absolute right to use partnership property.
    b. the right to assign partnership property.
    c. the right to convey partnership property by will.
    d. the right to possession of partnership property for partnership purposes.

17. Absolute control, as well as absolute liability, belongs to a
    a. sole proprietor.
    b. corporate shareholder.
    c. limited partner.
    d. trustee.

18. When doing business in California, a corporation chartered in California is a
    a. domestic corporation.
    b. foreign corporation.
    c. real estate investment trust.
    d. general partnership.

19. Title to a spouse's marital property can be transferred upon death by use of a(n)
    a. oral will.
    b. tenancy in common.
    c. living trust.
    d. letter of intent.

20. A limited partner is
    a. responsible for partnership activities.
    b. a general partner in some instances.
    c. not liable for partnership debts beyond the amount invested.
    d. required to take part in partnership business.

CHAPTER FOUR

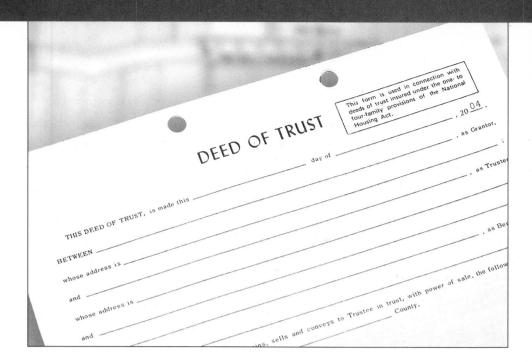

TRANSFERRING REAL ESTATE

■ HOW REAL ESTATE MAY BE ACQUIRED

Under Spanish and Mexican law, no written document was needed to transfer title to California land. A buyer could take title by taking possession at the time of sale. The seller would hand over to the buyer some part of the land (perhaps a twig or clump of dirt) to show transfer of ownership. California courts eventually decided that a written document was necessary to transfer title to land. An exception was made for a contract of sale, in which case the transfer of actual possession in the old ceremonial way was permissible. After California became a state, the legislature authorized the placing of a written document of transfer in the public records to provide evidence of a land transaction. A deed that is filed in the county recorder's office thus is the modern equivalent of the ceremonial transfer of possession.

Real estate can be acquired in one of the following ways, which are discussed in this section:

- the estate of someone who dies;
- improvements to land;
- natural forces;

- possession of someone else's property;
- transfer from a private or public owner; and
- alienation by operation of law or court action.

Will or Succession

Perhaps the least complicated way to acquire title to real estate is to receive it as part of the estate of someone who has died. The deceased can name the property's new owners in a document called a **will.** If the **decedent**—the person who died—leaves no will, the law determines the property's new owners.

Succession.   A person who dies without having made a will is said to have died **intestate.** All states make provision by law for distribution of the property of intestate persons. This legal determination of property ownership is called **intestate succession.** Figure 4.1 shows how property ownership is determined under California law. The law applies to both real and personal property. Community, quasi-community, and separate property are defined on pages 66 and 67.

- **FOR EXAMPLE:**   Hal and his wife own Sunny Acres as community property. Hal and his wife have no children. Who will have title to Sunny Acres if Hal dies without a will? If Hal and his wife have eight children and Hal dies without a will, who will receive title to Sunny Acres?

If he dies without a will specifying otherwise, Hal's one-half of the community property, including Sunny Acres, will go to his wife—regardless of the number of children. Hal's wife already owns the other half of Sunny Acres, because it is community property. When Hal dies, she will own all of Sunny Acres.

Will.   A **will** is a document made by an owner of property who is legally competent to do so, to pass title to the property to another after death. The person making a will is called the **testator** and is said to die **testate.**

The transfer of title to real estate by a will is called a **devise.** The deceased owner is the **devisor.** The person receiving property by will is a **devisee.** The transfer of property by will, particularly personal property, is also referred to as the **bequest** of a **legacy;** the recipient is a **legatee.**

A transfer of title by will takes effect on the death of the testator. During life the testator has the right to make a new will or to change a will by adding new or amended provisions through a document called a **codicil.** For this reason, until the testator's death, a devisee has no present interest in the property interest specified in a will.

> A codicil is the easiest way to change the terms of a will.

There are two types of wills currently recognized in California: the formal **witnessed will** and the **holographic** (handwritten) **will.** Oral wills are no longer considered legally valid in California.

FIGURE 4.1

Intestate Succession

CALIFORNIA LAW OF INTESTATE SUCCESSION

Community Property

If there is a surviving spouse:

- ½ already belongs to surviving spouse
- Remaining ½ goes to surviving spouse after decedent's liabilities have been paid

Community Property with Right of Survivorship

If there is a surviving spouse, surviving spouse takes entire property

Separate Property

If there is a surviving spouse and no child:

- Surviving spouse takes ½
- Surviving parent; brother or sister; or child of deceased brother or sister; or (if none of these) spouse takes ½

If there is a surviving spouse and one child:

- Surviving spouse takes ½
- Child takes ½

If there is a surviving spouse and more than one child:

- Surviving spouse takes ⅓
- Children divide ⅔ equally

If there is no surviving spouse or child:

- Property is distributed to next of kin in order prescribed by California law; if no heirs can be located, the property will escheat to the state

---

Witnessed will.   The formal **witnessed will** is a written document. It is normally prepared by an attorney and signed by the testator. The will lists all of the testator's property, specifying the desired disposition of that property on the testator's death. After the testator declares the will to be his or hers, the testator signs it in the presence of at least two witnesses, who then sign the will at the testator's request and in the testator's presence.

Holographic will.   A **holographic will** is one written by hand, dated, and signed by the testator. A holographic will does not need to be witnessed, but it must be entirely handwritten. There can be *no* printed or typewritten parts of a holographic will.

> Every word of a holographic will must be in the testator's handwriting.

Probate.   When properly drawn, a will names an **executor** to act as the decedent's representative in ensuring that the terms of the will are carried out. **Probate** is the name of the court process that determines the decedent's heirs and creditors, pays debts owed by the estate, and transfers title to any remaining property from the decedent to the decedent's heirs.

California Statutory Will

To encourage people to make a will, the California Bar Association has prepared two printed will forms that are available to the public.

1. The California Statutory Will form provides for disposition of the testator's property to the named devisees, typically the testator's spouse and/or children. Space for witnesses' signatures is included.

2. The California Statutory Will with Trust form provides for the establishment of a trust that will hold property for children of the testator until the youngest child is 21 years old. The property held in trust could be used by the named trustee (manager of the trust) for the support and education of the children before the youngest is 21.

The statutory will forms can be obtained from the State Bar of California, 555 Franklin Street, San Francisco, or 1149 South Hill Street, Los Angeles. Addresses of Bar Association offices can be found at *www.calbar.org*. Stationery supply stores also may carry statutory will forms.

---

www.calbar.org

If there is a will, the decedent's representative presents the will to the probate court and receives permission to carry out its provisions. Sometimes the deceased leaves no will, or fails to name a representative, or the named representative refuses to serve in that capacity. In any of those cases, the court may appoint an **administrator** to handle the estate.

Duties of the estate representative include

- publishing a **notice to creditors** of the decedent's death;
- conducting an **inventory** and obtaining an **appraisal** of the property in the decedent's estate;
- making a **report** to the probate court of the estate assets and liabilities; and
- **distributing the proceeds** of the estate as the court directs.

With the court's approval, estate representatives and attorneys may be paid a fee. Expenses incurred in administering the estate, federal and state estate taxes, and claims of creditors are provided for as the probate court approves. Any estate property remaining is distributed to the heirs and devisees.

> ## Probate Sales of Real Estate
>
> The **Probate Code** governs the sale of real property that is part of a probate proceeding. The **executor** or **administrator** may sell real property if it is in the best interests of the estate to do so (such as to pay debts or make specific bequests).
>
> ■ The real property may be offered for sale by the estate representative directly *or* through one or more brokers.
> ■ With court permission, the estate representative may grant an exclusive right to sell the property for up to 90 days.
> ■ The estate representative can accept an offer that is then subject to **court confirmation.**
> ■ Broker commissions are subject to statute and court approval.

Accession

> Improving land is one way to enhance its value.

Accession refers to an increase in the property owned. Man-made or natural additions to property may extend the owner's title to include those additions. These can occur by the construction of improvements, accretion, or reliction.

Improvements.   If a landowner puts up a building on the land, that man-made improvement becomes part of the owner's title to the land. If a fixture, such as a new heating system, is added to an existing building, the fixture then becomes part of the real property.

Accretion.   Land area can be increased by forces of nature. **Accretion** is the process by which land adjacent to a flowing body of water accumulates new soil. The buildup of new soil, called **alluvion** or **alluvium,** may be so gradual that it is not noticed. Buildup also can be quite dramatic and obvious, as when land is flooded.

■   **FOR EXAMPLE:**   Jack and Jill Willis own a vacation cottage on the Russian River. Over the years the river has deposited soil at the water line. The Willises' shoreline now extends one foot farther than the last recorded distance to the nearest landmark, a marker in the roadway. Has there been any increase in the square footage the Willises own?

Yes. A survey would show that the Willises' total property has increased by accretion.

But land also may be lost. The natural force of a moving body of water acting gradually or suddenly may wash away or tear land in a process called **avulsion.** You should note that avulsion is distinct from **erosion,** the process by which precipitation (rainfall) wears away only the surface of the soil.

The Unintended Improvement

Sometimes, an improvement is added to land by mistake. There may be a mistake in the address given to the builder or the lot may have an incorrect address posted on it. Sometimes the legal description in a deed is recorded incorrectly.

California law provides for what is known as a mistaken improvement. If a fixture is added to property by a person who acted innocently but on mistaken belief as to the property's owner, the fixture may be removed. The owner must be compensated for any damage to the property. The law thus protects an individual acting in good faith but under a mistake of fact (such as property location) or a mistake of law (identity of the rightful owner).

Reliction. Waters of any moving body of water may permanently recede, uncovering new land that was once under the water. This process, called **reliction,** increases the adjacent owner's property.

Occupancy

Sometimes you can acquire an ownership right to property by occupying (using) it. Your use must be without the present owner's permission, and the land cannot be publicly owned. There are three ways in which property can be acquired by occupancy:

- Adverse possession
- Prescription
- Abandonment

Adverse possession. You can acquire title to real estate by **adverse possession** if you follow the five steps listed below.

- You must occupy the property **openly** and **notoriously**—that is, without hiding the fact from anyone.
- Your occupancy must be **hostile to the true owner's interests**—in other words, without permission.
- You must **claim title** to the real estate, whether your claim of right is established by the fact of occupancy or by **color of title.** Color of title is the possession of a document erroneously appearing to convey title to the occupant. Land boundaries must be fenced or otherwise documented. If the person in possession has color of title, that document will provide a legal description of the land.
- There must be **continuous possession** for a period of **five years.** You cannot abandon the property during that time, no matter how briefly.
- You must **pay all real property taxes** during the five years of possession.

An easy way to remember the requirements for adverse possession is by using the acronym **ONCHA.** The possessor's occupancy must be

- **O**pen;
- **N**otorious;
- **C**ontinuous;
- **H**ostile; and
- **A**dverse to the interests of the real owner for five years.

Although the occupancy must be continuous for five years, successive adverse holders may add together, or **tack,** their periods of occupancy. Successive occupiers must take possession under **color of title,** which means that the new occupier receives a deed from the previous occupier. Even though the deed would not survive a challenge by the property's owner, it must appear on its face to be valid.

Title acquired by adverse possession cannot be insured and generally cannot be conveyed until it has been verified by court decree. The court decree can then be recorded in the county recorder's office.

■ **FOR EXAMPLE:**   Floyd would like to own the acreage next to Mustang Canyon. The Hendersons own the land but rarely visit it. Floyd moves onto the property, builds a shack, fences in 50 acres, and places a sign, "Floyd's Ranch," over the locked entrance gate. Whenever anyone asks about his use of the property, he tells them, "It's mine." Floyd pays the property taxes and lives only on the property.

After two years Floyd sells "all my right, title, and interest of whatever kind" in the ranch to Jud, giving Jud a deed. Floyd moves off the ranch and Jud promptly moves in, bringing his wife and six children with him. Jud pays the property taxes and proclaims to everyone that he now owns Floyd's Ranch. After about three years, Jud sells Floyd's Ranch to Sue, who in good faith records the deed Jud gives her and moves onto the land. A few months later, Harry Henderson shows up and is quite upset over what he finds. It has been more than five years since Floyd first moved onto the land. Who owns the land?

Sue owns the land. The adverse possession begun by Floyd and continued by Jud and Sue under color of title ripened into good title at the end of five years. Sue will have to bring a legal action to quiet title (discussed later in this chapter) to get the court decree she needs to give notice to the world of the validity of her title.

An individual can claim an easement by prescription.

Prescription.   The right to use or to travel over someone else's land is called an **easement.** If an easement is used without permission and the user fulfills all the other requirements for adverse possession—except for paying property taxes—an **easement by prescription** will be created. The use must be exclusive.

This means that the person claiming the easement is doing so as the assertion of a private, rather than a public, use.

■ **FOR EXAMPLE:** Marcy Morales owns a small house in La Jolla, California. Although Marcy's house is on a quiet, meandering residential street, she would prefer to have a more direct way to reach the commercial street that lies on the opposite side of the property adjacent to hers. One day, Marcy discovers that there is just enough room along the side of her neighbor's lot for her to drive her car into her backyard. She proceeds to do just that and does so at least once a day for the next six years. Marcy and her neighbor never discuss her use of what has taken on the appearance of a driveway. One day, when she drives home after work, she discovers that her neighbor has erected a chain link fence across the front of his property, blocking the entrance to the driveway she has been using. Does Marcy have the right to object?

Yes, Marcy can object to the fence her neighbor has built. By her continuing use of the driveway for more than five years, Marcy has acquired an easement by prescription to that portion of her neighbor's property. The neighbor may build a fence, but there will have to be a gate so that Marcy can have access.

In the example above, what would happen if Marcy decided to stop using the driveway across her neighbor's lot? Just as an easement by prescription can be acquired by use, it can be lost by nonuse. If the holder of an easement by prescription fails to use the easement for five years, the easement right is extinguished.

Abandonment. If leased property is abandoned by the lessee (tenant), the lessor (landlord) has the right to reacquire its possession and use. **Abandonment** is more than simple nonuse. A lessee abandons the leasehold interest by leaving the premises and acting in a way that is inconsistent with continuing possession, such as by failing to make rent payments when due, removing one's property from the premises, and filing a change of address with the post office.

Transfer

There are many ways in which title to real estate can be transferred from the present owner to someone else. They are highlighted in Figure 4.2 and explained next.

Private grant. A private grant, also called a **grant deed,** is a written instrument giving the names of both parties and a legal description of the property. The transfer of ownership may be a gift, which requires no consideration (payment) for the deed. The requirements for a deed are explained later in this chapter.

Public grant. Title to real estate that was not passed by land grant and affirmed after the war with Mexico became **public land** and part of the territory of the

FIGURE 4.2

**Ways to Transfer
Real Estate**

- Private grant
- Public grant
- Public dedication
- Alienation by operation of law or court action
- Execution sale
- Forfeiture
- Bankruptcy
- Marriage
- Escheat
- Eminent domain
- Equitable estoppel

United States. Some public land became the property of the State of California after statehood was granted. It is still possible for the federal or state government to deed public lands by public grant to private parties, as is done when old military installations are sold to developers.

■ **FOR EXAMPLE:** Fort Megan is an Air Force base that has not been used for 25 years because its runways are too short for modern aircraft. The base buildings are in disrepair, and the old landing strips have been devastated by earth movement and neglect. Nevertheless, Fort Megan is located in a densely populated urban area and could be sold for a high price per acre, for any purpose allowed by local ordinances.

Public dedication.   **Private land** can be transferred for public use or ownership by common-law dedication, statutory dedication, or deed.

A **common-law dedication** occurs when a landowner devotes land to a public use, as when a roadway is opened to public use or described as such in the deeds to adjoining parcels.

When the requirements of the Subdivision Map Act (described in Chapter 15, "Government Control of Land Use") are complied with, certain areas will be set aside for public use, such as parks, school grounds, and streets. This **statutory dedication** generally transfers an easement for the intended public use, although transfer of fee simple ownership by **deed** is becoming the preferred method of public acquisition. Fee simple title preserves the public character of the land despite the failure of the subdivision itself.

Alienation by operation of law or court action.   It is possible to bring a legal action in court for the purpose of clearing or establishing title to real estate despite the opposition of the owner of record. **Alienation** (transfer) of title may be involuntary, that is, without the original owner's consent.

An **action to quiet title** is brought to force others who have claims to the property to prove those claims or have the claims ruled invalid by the court. This is the usual method of establishing title by adverse possession and of clearing tax titles or title acquired upon a forfeited contract of sale.

A **partition action** is brought by a co-owner of property to force a severance of the co-owners' respective interests. As explained in Chapter 3, the co-owner can be a tenant in common or a joint tenant. The property is divided, if possible, or sold. After a sale, the court divides the proceeds according to the owners' respective shares.

■ **FOR EXAMPLE:**   Linda and Sheila Goa, twin sisters, own a house as tenants in common. Linda wants to sell her share but can't find a buyer, and Sheila doesn't want to sell. What can Linda do?

Linda can bring a partition action in court. The court will sell the house because the property cannot be divided into two equal parcels, and it will distribute the proceeds to the two sisters.

A **power of sale** gives the trustee under a trust deed the ability to sell the property to satisfy the unpaid debt if the debtor defaults. A mortgage or another lien document also may provide a power of sale for the mortgagee or lienholder. Trust deeds and mortgages are discussed in Chapter 8, "Financing Real Estate."

In a **judicial foreclosure action** the holder of a trust deed, a mortgage, or other lien on property requests a court-supervised sale of the property to cover the unpaid balance on the delinquent debt.

In an **action for declaratory relief** the parties petition the court for a determination of their respective rights before a controversy arises. When a deed is ambiguous, an action for declaratory relief may be brought to avoid later problems.

Execution sale.   The party who wins a legal action may receive a **judgment** from the court that includes the award of money damages against the losing party. The holder of the judgment can file the judgment in any county in the state in which the debtor owns property and then seek a writ of execution.

> If you buy real estate at an execution sale, you will receive a sheriff's deed.

A **writ of execution** is a court order directing the county sheriff or another officer to satisfy a judgment out of the debtor's property. The property available to satisfy the judgment includes any nonexempt real property owned by the debtor. The property is sold at public auction and the proceeds are used to pay the judgment. When *personal property* is sold at auction, the buyer receives a **certificate of sale.**

When *real property* is sold at auction, the buyer receives a **sheriff's deed.** The officer who conducts the sale must record a duplicate of the sheriff's deed in the office of the county recorder.

Forfeiture.   **Forfeiture** occurs if a condition subsequent in a deed is breached. The grantor (or the grantor's successor) then has the right to reacquire title.

Bankruptcy.   The U.S. Congress has sole authority to enact bankruptcy laws, and it enforces those laws through the **federal bankruptcy courts.** In a liquidation bankruptcy, a debtor's property is sold to cover debts. The **trustee in bankruptcy** carries out this function for the bankruptcy court. The buyer receives a **trustee's deed.**

Marriage.   Property acquired during marriage that is not separate property is **community property** by operation of law, as explained in Chapter 3. One spouse acting alone cannot defeat the other spouse's interest in that property.

Escheat.   California law presumes that every person who dies has an heir who could take title to the decedent's property. Sometimes, however, it is impossible to locate an heir. The Attorney General acts on behalf of the state to bring a claim against the estate and, if no claimant comes forward within five years, title to the property vests in the state. This process is called **escheat.**

Eminent domain.   The federal and state governments have the right to acquire title to property by **eminent domain.** If property is for a public purpose such as highway construction, it is first subject to **condemnation,** a process that gives notice to the property owner that the property is being taken. The property owner receives compensation based on an **appraisal,** which usually is the property's **fair market value.** Fair market value, the price a property should bring on the open market, will be explained more fully in Chapter 13, "Real Estate Appraising."

Sometimes property that has not been condemned is damaged or its use is affected by a nearby public activity. When that happens, the affected property owners may seek money damages in a legal action claiming **inverse condemnation.** For instance, if a new highway blocks off the access road to adjoining properties, those properties will lose value. The property owners will expect to be compensated for the loss in value.

Equitable estoppel.   A person may convey or appear to convey a property interest he or she does not yet own but may acquire at some future time. Such **after-acquired title** must be transferred to the new owner. The doctrine of **equitable estoppel** (a common-law theory meant to prevent unjust enrichment) prohibits a refusal to make the transfer. Equitable estoppel also prevents fraud or misrepresentation by the present owner of property. If a property owner misrepresents his or her ownership (whether by act or omission) to a person who then buys the property from another person who is the apparent owner, the true owner must convey the property to the innocent party.

■ **FOR EXAMPLE:** Max owns Blackacre but does not want Jose to know. One day, when Max, Jose, and Carlo are together, Jose asks Max and Carlo if one of them owns Blackacre. Carlo says he owns Blackacre, and Max doesn't object. Jose then pays Carlo for Blackacre. Who owns Blackacre?

Jose owns Blackacre. Max is equitably estopped from denying Joe's ownership. By his conduct Max allowed Jose to believe he was buying Blackacre from Carlo. Max will be left with an action for damages against Carlo, who has pocketed the money Jose paid for Blackacre.

Exercise 4-1

[handwritten: Helen, separate property. Both as community prop.]

1. George married Helen in January 1996. In March 1998 Helen's father died, leaving Helen his condominium in Palm Springs. Who owns the condominium and in what form of ownership?

2. George and Helen, who married in 1996, purchased a house in 1997. Who will the law presume to own the house and in what form of ownership?

[handwritten: yes, Thru eminent domain]

3. In 1998 George and Helen are notified by the city that their property is being considered as the site of a new sports arena. They protest the city's plans at a public hearing but are unsuccessful in halting the construction. Can the city take their house?

[handwritten: NO, get an appraisal]

4. George and Helen paid $246,000 for their house in 1997. In 1999, the city offers them $246,000 for the property. Do they have to accept?

[handwritten: yes.]

5. George decides to leave his half of the community property he owns with Helen to his sister Davida and has a will drawn up to that effect. When George dies, Helen is surprised when Davida claims to own half of "her" home. Can George do that?

[handwritten: NO, After 5 years squatters will WIN.]

6. Angel knows that "squatters" have moved onto the "back 40" of his ranch and have even put up a fence, but Angel is too busy to do anything about it. Even after he hears that the squatters are building a house, Angel doesn't object. He feels smug that somebody is stupid enough to build a house on his land—and pay taxes, to boot. Six years later Angel tries to sell his ranch, but the buyer says that he can't get a loan because Angel doesn't have clear title to all of the land. Angel brings an action to quiet title in court. Will he win?

[handwritten: foreclose on home]

7. Tim Brown holds a mortgage on the house of Sara Nelson, who is having financial difficulties and has missed all of her mortgage payments for the past six months. What can Tim do?

No, He died Intestate
Home now will go thru probate

Washed away!
Thru Avulsion

8. Uncle Henry died without a will. Did he die testate? What is the name of the legal process by which his property will be distributed to his heirs?

9. Lydia and Miguel own a small resort on the Colorado River with about 200 feet of lawn on a small bluff overlooking the river. Following torrential rains and flooding, Lydia and Miguel find they have only 130 feet of lawn area. What happened to the 70 feet of ground? What is this process called?

■ DEEDS

A deed is the document that transfers title to real property. There are many types of deeds that can be used to convey title to real estate. This section describes the requirements for a valid conveyance by deed and examines the different forms of deeds and their legal distinctions.

Elements of a Valid Deed

A **deed** is a written instrument that, when properly executed, delivered, and accepted, conveys title to real property. Title is conveyed by **grant** (transfer) from one person (the **grantor**) to another (the **grantee**). The words of conveyance appear in the **granting clause.** Transfer of title by deed may be the voluntary or involuntary act of the parties, as in the case of a foreclosure sale when title is transferred by operation of law.

The specific legal requirements for a valid deed are listed in Figure 4.3. If all of the requirements for a valid deed are not met, the deed may be questioned even years after the property has been conveyed.

■ **FOR EXAMPLE:**   Ted gives a deed to Nicole, telling her it will take effect on his death. Is the deed valid?

The deed is not a valid conveyance, even at Ted's death. Delivery means exactly that—the grantor holds nothing back. There can be no conditions.

It is possible to deliver a deed to a third party to be released to the grantee on the fulfillment of a condition. In that case, however, the acceptance is conditioned, not the delivery. A condition might be placed in the deed itself that would invalidate it if the grantee failed to fulfill the condition.

Note that although there is no legal requirement that a deed be dated, in practice dating a deed is preferred because delivery and acceptance will be presumed to have occurred on that date.

FIGURE 4.3

Requirements for a Valid Deed

1. The deed must be in writing.

2. There must be a description of the parties. The full name and marital status of each should be given.

3. The grantor must be legally capable of executing a written conveyance. Generally this means the grantor must be an adult of sound mind. The requirements are the same as those to create a valid contract (discussed in Chapter 7, "Contracts"). The grantee of a gift can be an incompetent or a minor, but cannot be a fictitious person.

4. There must be an adequate description of the property being conveyed, using one or more of the methods discussed in Chapter 2.

5. There must be a granting clause in which the necessary word(s) of conveyance is used, such as the word *grant* or *convey*. The words "to have and to hold" (the *habendum clause*) are not necessary.

6. The deed must be signed by the grantor(s).

7. The deed must be delivered to the grantee and accepted by the grantee. The grantor must have the present intention of conveying and the ability to convey the property.

You should remember that a deed is not a contract. A deed has different elements and is subject to different rules regarding validity. The elements of a contract are discussed in Chapter 7.

> "Love and affection" are the only consideration needed for a valid deed.

A deed, unlike a contract, does not need to be supported by consideration. That is, the grantee does not need to pay anything in return for the conveyance. If fraud is suspected, however, as when property is deeded without consideration shortly before the grantor declares bankruptcy, the deed may be set aside by a court.

There is no legal requirement that a deed be witnessed, that the grantor's signature be verified by any third person, or that the deed be recorded in the county recorder's office. Nevertheless, these steps are practical necessities to prevent future problems. Acknowledgment and recording of deeds are discussed following the exercise.

Exercise 4-2 Assuming all other requirements have been met, has a valid deed been created in each of the following cases?

1. Jared Stone is selling Greenacre, the family estate. Jared is out of the country at the time the sale is to be closed but phones the broker handling the transaction to tell her to go ahead with the sale and deliver title to the buyer. Jared intends to sign the deed when he returns.

[handwritten margin note: No Aunt Nellie still]

2. Aunt Nellie is senile and incapable of caring for herself. To help her out, her niece Roberta takes Aunt Nellie into her home. In return, Roberta asks Aunt Nellie to deed her condominium to her. Aunt Nellie does not realize what is happening, and Roberta guides her hand as she signs a deed. Who owns the condo?

[handwritten margin note: NO - Deed must be in writing]

3. Jed is a high-powered real estate investor. Over the phone he persuades Sol to sell him a 20-unit apartment building in San Diego. Jed is anxious to get the property and tells Sol to convey the property to him over the phone while his secretary takes notes. Jed tells Sol, "Your word is as good as gold."

[handwritten margin note: Yes, Needs Description of prop]

4. Angela Dell agrees to sell her farm to her friend Diego. The deed from Angela describes the property as "the old Dell place, including 100 acres, more or less." Does Diego have a problem?

[handwritten margin note: NO, Not delivered to grantee]

5. Uncle Anthony decides to make a present of his Hillsborough estate to his nephew Richard. He prepares a deed, reciting "love and affection" as the consideration, and places the deed in an envelope marked "To be opened upon my death." He then places the envelope in his safe-deposit box. Will Richard own the estate when his uncle dies?

Acknowledgment and Recording

California law requires that most written instruments affecting title to real property be acknowledged before they can be recorded in the county recorder's office. Besides deeds, those instruments include

- loan documents,
- agreements for sale,
- option agreements,
- deposit receipts,
- commission receipts, and
- any affidavits concerning one of these documents.

A document does not have to be recorded to be valid. The process of recording is important, however, because it is the primary way to give notice to the world of an interest that affects title to real estate.

Acknowledgment.   A document is **executed** when it is signed. A person who has executed a document can make a declaration, called an **acknowledgment**, that the execution is the person's own act. An acknowledgment may be made anywhere within California before an authorized official, who cannot be a party to the transaction or related to a party to the transaction. An acknowledgment may be made outside California if local laws are followed and that fact is certified by the person taking the acknowledgment.

> A notary public will verify your signature and take your thumbprint.

Persons authorized to take an acknowledgment in California include judges, court clerks, and notary publics. A notary public, in addition to signing the document, must stamp it with the seal required by the state. When notarizing a deed (including a quitclaim deed or deed of trust, discussed later in this chapter), the thumbprint of the grantor must be placed in the notary's official journal.

An acknowledgment alone, without recording the document, serves as notice of the conveyance to the parties and to persons actually knowing of it. Possession of the property involved also gives notice of ownership. The legal protection of an acknowledged but unrecorded document is not very great. The ordinary transaction does not involve many people, and only those who already know of the transaction are considered aware of it.

Recording. The safest way of ensuring that one's title to property is unquestioned is by **recording** the deed that conveys the property. The deed is brought to the office of the county recorder in the county where the property is located. As a general rule, "first in time is first in right." This means that, if more than one person claims title from the same grantor, the first to record a deed will be the successful claimant.

To be recorded, a deed must give an address of the grantee to which tax bills can be sent. A county may add up to $2 to its recording fees for a **Real Estate Fraud Prosecution Trust Fund** to help district attorneys and law enforcement agencies deter, investigate, and prosecute real property fraud crimes.

The system of making documents a part of the public record works to the advantage of the property owner as well as a prospective buyer or lessee. The property owner is able to give constructive notice to the world of the fact of his or her ownership. In theory, by inspecting the public record the prospective buyer or lessee can have the confidence of knowing that he or she is dealing with the recorded owner of the property. (The buyer or lessee still needs to verify that someone else isn't in possession of the property, of course.)

Building the Chain of Title

The recorder's office files instruments under the parties' names, so the full name of both grantor and grantee must be given. If the grantor's name is not given exactly as it appears in the conveyance to the grantor, it may not be possible to complete that "link" in the **chain of title.**

Most title searches are conducted by tracking the grantor's interest backward in time, then tracking the first recorded grantee's interest forward. To discover all the links in the chain of title, the grantor of the present conveyance should be found as the grantee of a preceding conveyance, the grantor of that conveyance should be the grantee of an earlier conveyance, and so on.

Although variance in the use of a middle name is not necessarily fatal to the validity of a deed, the better practice is to use the full name rather than an initial in place of the middle name.

A fictitious name may be used to receive title to property, provided the same name is used in any subsequent conveyance. Title cannot be conveyed to a fictitious person, however. Title can be conveyed to a corporation, because a corporation is a recognized legal entity.

Financing instruments are also recorded to give constructive notice of the lien rights of the lender, and are discussed in Chapter 8, "Financing Real Estate."

Types of Deeds

Grant deed.   A typical form of **grant deed** appears in Figure 4.4. Notice that the form actually contains the word *grant(s)*. The deed form is simple and provides for the deed to be acknowledged and recorded.

The grantor makes **implied warranties** in executing a grant deed. These are items the grantee must assume to be true, or the deed would be meaningless. Implied warranties are legally enforceable even though they are not mentioned in the deed. The grantor warrants that

- the grantor's interest in the property has not already been conveyed and
- there are no undisclosed encumbrances on the property, such as tax liens, brought about by the grantor or any person who might claim title from the grantor.

Note that the grantor does not warrant that he or she actually has a present interest in the property to convey. If the grantor attempts to convey property the grantor will acquire after the execution of the grant deed, the deed will become effective at the time such after-acquired title is actually received by the grantor. The grant deed is the only form of deed that conveys after-acquired title.

Gift deed.   Although the grant deed form leaves space for the consideration paid by the grantee, it may be used to convey property as a **gift deed** by supplying the words "love and affection" as the consideration received. As noted earlier, such a conveyance may not be made to defraud creditors of the grantor.

Quitclaim deed.   A **quitclaim deed** conveys any interest the grantor may have in the property at the time the deed is executed. No implied warranties are made by a quitclaim deed, and there is no express or implied warranty that the grantor owns any interest at all in the property. A quitclaim deed should never be used when a grant deed can be used.

FIGURE 4.4

Individual Grant Deed

RECORDING REQUESTED BY

Order No. _____ Escrow No. _____
AND WHEN RECORDED MAIL TO

Name _____

Street
Address _____

City &
State _____

———— SPACE ABOVE THIS LINE FOR RECORDER'S USE ————

INDIVIDUAL GRANT DEED   A.P.N. _____

The undersigned grantor(s) declare(s):
Documentary transfer tax is $ _____ .
(   ) computed on full value of property conveyed, or
(   ) computed on full value less value of liens and encumbrances remaining at time of sale.
(   ) Unincorporated area: (   ) City of _____ , and
FOR A VALUABLE CONSIDERATION, receipt of which is hereby acknowledged,

hereby GRANT(S) to

the following described real property in the
County of _____ , State of California:

Dated: _____   _____

STATE OF CALIFORNIA
COUNTY OF _____ } SS.   _____
On _____ before me,   _____
_____ , personally appeared   _____
_____
_____

personally known to me (or proved to me on the basis of satisfactory evidence)
to be the person(s) whose name(s) is/are subscribed to the within instrument
and acknowledged to me that he/she/they executed the same in his/her/their
authorized capacity(ies), and that by his/her/their signature(s) on the instrument the person(s), or the entity upon behalf of which the person(s) acted,
executed the instrument.

WITNESS my hand and official seal.

Signature _____   (This area for official notarial seal)

MAIL TAX
STATEMENTS TO: _____
                 NAME   ADDRESS   CITY, STATE & ZIP

Source: Reprinted by permission of First American Title Company of Los Angeles.

A quitclaim deed does ensure that whatever interest the grantor may have in the property is conveyed to the grantee. The quitclaim deed is a commonly used way of clearing a **cloud on the title** and eliminating any future claim by the grantor of the quitclaim deed. There can be no after-acquired title with a quitclaim, however.

The grantor of a quitclaim deed remains liable for any loans made using the property as security.

■ **FOR EXAMPLE:** Harvey Anderson bought Whiteacre after he married Anna, but Harvey used money from the sale of his separate property to do so. When Harvey sold Whiteacre, he signed the deed as Harvey Anderson, a married man. His wife did not sign the deed. The grantee of Whiteacre questioned the validity of that conveyance when years later a would-be purchaser was unable to acquire title insurance.

The "cloud on the title" of the present owner of Whiteacre was cleared by having Anna Anderson sign a quitclaim deed, relinquishing whatever claim she might have in the property.

Warranty deed.   A **warranty deed** expressly warrants that the grantor has good title. The grantor's warranty makes the grantor liable for a flaw in the title affecting the buyer's interest that may be discovered later, even if the grantor had no previous knowledge of it. This form of guarantee, while attractive to a property buyer, could be devastating to a property seller. It is one reason why title insurance is required (particularly by lenders) in most transactions in California. By shifting the liability to the insurer, the seller can be assured that there will be no future liability caused by an undiscovered defect in the seller's title. In turn, the buyer can rely on the resources of the title insurer if any problem covered by the title insurance should arise.

Trust deed.   The **trust deed,** also called **deed of trust** (shown in Figure 8.3 on pages 227 and 228), is used when property serves as security for a debt. The debt typically is the loan used to purchase the property, but it can be any loan using the property as collateral to guarantee payment of the amount borrowed. The requirements for creation of a security interest in real estate are in Chapter 8, "Financing Real Estate."

When the purchaser of property borrows money to finance the purchase, the borrower (new *owner*) is the **trustor** (the *grantor*) of the trust deed. The **trustee** (the *grantee*) is the party who holds title until the debt is paid. The **beneficiary,** the party on whose behalf the title is held, is the **lender.** If the underlying debt is not paid, the trustee has the power to sell the property at a foreclosure sale and pay the beneficiary the amount of the remaining indebtedness from the proceeds. Any money left over would go to the trustor. The purchaser would receive a **trustee's deed** from the trustee.

Reconveyance deed. A **reconveyance deed** executed by the trustee is the means by which the trustee returns title to the trustor when the debt is paid off. The beneficiary notifies the trustee that the debt has been cleared by sending the trustee a document called a **request for reconveyance.**

Sheriff's deed. A **sheriff's deed** is given to the purchaser at a court-ordered sale to satisfy a judgment. A sheriff's deed carries no warranties.

Tax deed. A **tax deed** is issued by the county tax collector if property is sold because of nonpayment of taxes. Tax collection procedures are discussed in Chapter 11, "Real Estate Taxation."

Exercise 4-3 What type of deed would most likely be used in each of the following situations?

1. All-cash sale of a single-family residence
2. Deed from possible former co-owner of property
3. Loan secured by deed
4. Conveyance from grandfather to grandson in consideration of grandson's "love and affection"
5. Deed to someone who has just paid off a home loan
6. Deed received after purchase of property at a court-ordered sale

[Handwritten annotations in left margin: Grant Deed / Quitclaim / Trust / gift or Grant / reconveyance / Sheriffs]

■ SUMMARY

A person who dies **testate** leaves a **will.** The **testator (decedent)** can devise his or her property to a **devisee.** By **bequest,** a **legacy** of personal property can be transferred to a **legatee.** A formal witnessed will is a written document complying with legal formalities. A **holographic** will is written entirely in the handwriting of the testator. The **law of intestate succession** provides for distribution of the property of a person who dies without leaving a valid will.

Land situated along a moving body of water may be increased by **accretion** as **alluvion (alluvium)** is deposited on the shoreline. If water recedes there may be **reliction** of land. The movement of water may diminish the land area at shoreline by **avulsion.**

By occupying land for five years, paying taxes, and claiming possession, one can acquire title by **adverse possession.** Successive owners under **color of title** can **tack** their periods of ownership. An **easement by prescription** to travel over land may be acquired in a similar fashion, but without paying taxes.

The holder of a **leasehold** interest may abandon that interest, and the landlord again may have the right of present use or possession.

Title to real estate may be transferred by **deed,** whether private or public. Land may be **dedicated** to public use, as when a developer builds streets through a subdivision.

Alienation is an involuntary transfer of title. An **action to quiet title,** a **partition action,** a **foreclosure action,** and an **action for declaratory relief** are some of the ways the courts can be called on to settle property disputes.

A **writ of execution** by the court orders the sheriff to sell a debtor's property. The buyer receives a **certificate of sale** or a **sheriff's deed.** Title could change by **forfeiture** if a **condition subsequent** were breached. A **trustee in bankruptcy** may sell real property to acquire funds for creditors. The buyer receives a **trustee's deed.** Property acquired during marriage that is not separate property is **community property.**

The **right of eminent domain** enables a governing body to **condemn,** or take, land for a public purpose. The actions of a property owner or prospective property owner may later **equitably estop,** or prevent, him or her from denying the property rights of another.

Transfer of ownership of property by **deed** must name a **grantor** and **grantee** and describe the property to be conveyed. The correct words of grant must be used, depending on the type of deed. The deed is effective once it has been delivered to the grantee and accepted. If the grantor's action is acknowledged, the deed can be **recorded** and will enter the property's **chain of title.**

Implied warranties are given in a **grant deed** by the **grantor,** who also may convey **after-acquired title.** A **quitclaim deed** gives no such warranties and cannot convey after-acquired title, but it may clear a **cloud on the title.** A **warranty deed** gives **express** (stated) **warranties.** A **trust deed** enables a **trustee** to hold title until a debt is paid to the **beneficiary** by the **trustor.** If the debt is paid, a **reconveyance deed** will put title back in the trustor. A **sheriff's deed** is given following a forced sale of real estate.

■ IMPORTANT TERMS

Make sure you understand the following terms before you take the achievement examination.

abandonment	action for declaratory relief
accession	action to quiet title
accretion	administrator
acknowledgment	adverse possession

after-acquired title
alienation
alluvion
alluvium
avulsion
bequest
certificate of sale
chain of title
codicil
color of title
common-law dedication
condemnation
decedent
deed
devise
devisee
devisor
easement
easement by prescription
eminent domain
equitable estoppel
erosion
escheat
executor
forfeiture
gift deed
grant
grant deed
grantee
granting clause
grantor

holographic will
intestate
intestate succession
judgment inverse condemnation
judicial foreclosure action
legacy
legatee
partition action
power of sale
probate
Probate Code
quitclaim deed
Real Estate Fraud Prosecution
    Trust Fund
reconveyance deed
recording
reliction
request for reconveyance
sheriff's deed
statutory dedication
tack
tax deed
testate
testator
trust deed
trustee in bankruptcy
trustee's deed
warranty deed
will
writ of execution

■ OPEN FOR DISCUSSION

A claim of title by adverse possession often is used as a fall-back position when title is challenged by legal action.

When could such a claim be made?

■ ACHIEVEMENT EXAMINATION 4

1. A person who dies without a will dies
    a. testate
    b. intestate.
    c. with an executor.
    d. in eminent domain.

2. The testator names a(n)
    a. executor or executrix.
    b. testator.
    c. devisor.
    d. administrator or administratrix.

3. Someone who receives real property by will is called a
    a. devise.   c. testator.
    b. devisee.   d. codicil.

4. A typewritten will must be
    a. made by a competent person.
    b. signed by the testator.
    c. witnessed.
    d. all of the above.

5. A statutory will is
    a. signed and witnessed.
    b. telegraphic.
    c. oral.
    d. invalid.

6. A holographic will is
    a. oral.   c. handwritten.
    b. telegraphic.   d. witnessed.

7. The probate court appoints a(n)
    a. executor or executrix.
    b. testator.
    c. devisee.
    d. administrator or administratrix.

8. When soil is deposited on a riverbank, gradually building out the land, this process is called
    a. accretion.   c. avulsion.
    b. alluvion.   d. subsidence.

9. When flood conditions cause land to be washed away, this is known as
    a. accretion.   c. avulsion.
    b. alluvion.   d. accession.

10. When water recedes, creating a new shoreline, the process is called
    a. accretion.   c. avulsion.
    b. alluvion.   d. reliction.

11. Elena moves onto J.R.'s land, builds a home, pays the property taxes, and claims she owns the property. When will she have good title, even against J.R.?
    a. After one year
    b. After three years
    c. After five years
    d. After ten years

12. Elena's friend Carl, who used to own the property in question 11, gave her a phony deed to J.R.'s land. Elena, who does not know the deed is phony, has
    a. a worthless document.
    b. color of title.
    c. a good title.
    d. to share title with J.R.

13. The right to travel over the property of someone else is
    a. an easement.
    b. equitable estoppel.
    c. a fixture.
    d. statutory dedication by deed.

14. A cotenant who wants property that is co-owned to be sold would bring a(n)
    a. foreclosure action.
    b. action for declaratory relief.
    c. action to quiet title.
    d. partition action.

15. In event of default, real property may be sold without court action if the mortgage or other lien instrument contains a
    a. trust deed.
    b. power of sale.
    c. tax deed.
    d. right of entry.

16. The court order following a judgment for money is a
    a. certificate of sale.
    b. special limitation.
    c. writ of execution.
    d. trustee in bankruptcy.

17. The power of the state to take private property for public use is called
    a. eminent domain.
    b. equitable estoppel.
    c. a public grant.
    d. abandonment.

18. To be effective, a deed must be
    a. made on a printed form.
    b. signed by the grantor.
    c. delivered to the grantee by the grantor personally.
    d. all of the above.

19. The transfer of title from grantor to grantee, and from that grantee to a subsequent grantee, and so on, is called
    a. a cloud on the title.
    b. the chain of title.
    c. delivery and acceptance.
    d. an acknowledgment.

20. Property conveyed by a deed of trust may be regained by a
    a. warranty deed.
    b. trust deed.
    c. reconveyance deed.
    d. sheriff's deed.

CHAPTER FIVE

ENCUMBRANCES

■ ENCUMBRANCES TO REAL ESTATE

An **encumbrance** is anything that has an effect on

- the fee simple title to real estate or
- the use of the property.

Some limitations on property use actually benefit property owners. Property use is often regulated by deed restrictions and other devices of control. Deeds to property in most housing subdivisions require that owners maintain property improvements for the benefit of all property owners in the subdivision. Government controls, such as zoning ordinances, also serve to regulate property use for the public good.

Because it can limit the transferability or use of property, an encumbrance may affect the property's value. A **marketable title** to real estate is one that a prudent buyer would accept. Certain encumbrances will not affect the property's marketability; others will, meaning that the property will not be worth as much as long as it has the encumbrance.

There may be a **cloud on the title.** This means that there is some reason why the owner's interest is less than perfect. With a cloud on the title, the property may not be marketable or it may be marketable only at a reduced price. A careful buyer may demand that the cloud be removed before title to the property is conveyed. The quitclaim deed (mentioned in Chapter 4) is one way in which a cloud on the title can be cleared.

This chapter examines many possible "clouds," including liens, judgments, easements, deed restrictions, and encroachments. One of the most important impediments to good title to real estate is the *lien*.

■ LIENS

A **lien** is an encumbrance that makes property security for the payment of a debt or discharge of an obligation. A lien is **general** if it applies to all property of the debtor and **specific** if it applies only to identified property, such as a parcel of real estate. Examples of liens include

- the judgment of a court (general);
- a financing instrument, such as a trust deed (specific); and
- the mechanic's lien given to someone who helps improve property (specific).

It would be much more difficult to finance land purchases and building construction if a lien on the real estate were not possible. A lien also may be used to refinance a loan, borrow additional money, or initiate a line of credit. The fact that land and improvements to land can be used as security gives lenders and builders some guarantee of payment.

A **voluntary lien** is one agreed to by the property owner. A mortgage or deed of trust that an owner of real estate gives to obtain financing is an example of a voluntary lien. Voluntary liens are covered in Chapter 8, "Financing Real Estate."

An **involuntary lien** is one that is imposed without the agreement of the property owner. Involuntary liens are made possible by laws that prescribe ways in which unpaid debts can be used by creditors or government agencies to create the burden of a lien on the property. A **tax lien,** for example, is an involuntary lien that arises from a taxpayer's obligation to pay

- real property taxes;
- state estate and income taxes; or
- federal gift, estate, and income taxes.

Tax liens will be covered in Chapter 11, "Real Estate Taxation." Some other forms of involuntary liens are mechanics' liens, judgments, and attachments, discussed in this chapter.

Mechanics' Liens

The **mechanic's lien** is used to help secure payment for any labor, service, equipment, or materials used in the construction of improvements to real estate. The mechanic's lien is an important protection rooted in the California Constitution. It is considered so important, any contract provision that purports to waive the right to a mechanic's lien has been held to be against public policy, void, and unenforceable.

A mechanic is anyone who performs such work or furnishes the material used in the work. Persons entitled to a mechanic's lien include all those who work or supply materials at the request of the property owner, or any contractor, subcontractor, sub-subcontractor, architect, builder, or other person placed in charge of all or part of a project. A mechanic's lien is available to

- material suppliers;
- contractors;
- subcontractors;
- equipment lessors;
- architects;
- registered engineers;
- licensed land surveyors;
- machinists;
- truckers; and
- laborers.

A mechanic's lien thus can be claimed by a subcontractor, such as a plumber, electrician, or roofer, even though the property's owner never dealt directly with the person claiming the lien. One way to guard against possible claims is to require that the contractor obtain a **payment bond.** The bonding company compensates the owner if the contractor defaults in the performance of contract obligations, such as the payment of workers and suppliers.

Important notice and filing requirements are specified by law for making a mechanic's lien claim. The summary shown in the box on the next page should not be used as the sole guide to when to initiate a lien. As with any form of legal action, the advice of an attorney experienced in such matters should be sought first.

The Mechanic's Lien

Preliminary Notice

Notice of the right to file a mechanic's lien should be made within 20 days of the time the work begins or the materials are furnished. A direct contract with the property owner serves this purpose. Otherwise, a **preliminary notice** is hand-delivered or sent by first-class registered or certified mail to the

- property owner
- general contractor (if any)
- construction lender (if any)

Starting Time

The **starting time** is the date the construction project begins. The starting time determines when the preliminary notice (if required) must be given.

Completion Time

The project is completed when

- work stops and the owner (or owner's agent) uses the improvement;
- the owner (or owner's agent) accepts the work;
- work has been stopped for 60 continuous days; or
- the owner has filed a **notice of cessation** after work has been stopped for 30 continuous days.

The **notice of completion** may be filed by the owner with the county recorder within ten days after the work is completed.

Filing Time

A mechanic's lien for unpaid work or materials is filed with the county recorder.

If notice of completion (or cessation) was not filed by the owner, all claimants have **90 days** after completion of the work of improvement to file the mechanic's lien.

If notice of completion (or cessation) was filed, a contractor of all or part of the job must file the mechanic's lien within **60 days** from the filing date of the notice. Everyone else has **30 days** from the filing date of the notice in which to file a mechanic's lien.

Enforcement and termination.   A mechanic's lien may be terminated by the claimant's voluntary release of the lien. A **lien release** should be filed with the county recorder to prevent a cloud on the owner's title.

A mechanic's lien must be enforced within 90 days after the filing of the lien claim. If credit is extended, notice of the extension must be filed within 90 days after filing the lien, and the extension cannot be for more than one year after completion of the work.

Enforcement of a mechanic's lien is by **foreclosure,** which will bring about a judicial sale of the property. The lienholder is paid out of the proceeds of the sale. The owner receives only what remains after all claimants have been paid.

Notice of nonresponsibility.   What protection does the owner of real estate have if unauthorized work is begun on the property? The owner can *post* a **notice of nonresponsibility** in a conspicuous place on the land and *record* a copy of the notice with the county recorder. The same procedure may be followed by anyone else having an interest in the land, such as the holder of a lease, who notices unauthorized work being done.

> If you didn't authorize work on your property, you must post-and-record within 10 days.

The notice of nonresponsibility must be posted and recorded within ten days of learning of the construction, repair, or other work. The notice of nonresponsibility must include

- a property description;
- the name, address, and property interest of the owner or other person giving notice; and
- a brief statement that the person giving notice is not responsible for any claims arising from the work.

■ **FOR EXAMPLE:**   Landlord Inosencia Rivera saw a contractor's truck outside her small apartment building on Sacramento Street. When she inquired, Inosencia was told by a man in a painter's jumpsuit, "The building is being remodeled." Inosencia never agreed to remodel the building, and she manages the building herself. What can she do?

As soon as possible, but at least within ten days, Inosencia should post a notice of nonresponsibility at the entrance to the building and file a copy of the notice in the county recorder's office.

How to Stop a Lien Foreclosure

A property owner who disputes the correctness or validity of a mechanic's lien can stop the foreclosure on the property.

The owner must file a **lien release bond** in the county recorder's office where the lien was recorded. The bond must be issued by an authorized California surety. The amount of the bond must equal 150 percent of either the entire claim or the portion of the claim allocated to the parcel(s) sought to be released. The amount of the bond will be available to cover the lien claimant's possible recovery, including costs of bringing legal action.

A lien release bond also can be filed by anyone having an interest in the property, such as the lender, or by any original contractor or subcontractor affected by the claimed lien.

Exercise 5-1   C. L. Drake is general contractor on the Bigelow Building remodeling job. C. L. signed a written agreement for the work with Busby Bigelow, the property's owner.

Busby Bigelow, a wealthy but eccentric individual, decided halfway through the project that the design was "all wrong." It has been two months since Busby stopped the project. He has not filed either a notice of completion or a notice of cessation. C. L. is owed a considerable amount for materials he furnished and wages he paid. What can he do?

Attachments and Judgments

Attachment.   The **plaintiff** is the person who files a lawsuit against a **defendant.** Sometimes the plaintiff has reason to believe that the defendant will try to sell or conceal assets that might be awarded by the court to the plaintiff if the case is decided in the plaintiff's favor. At the plaintiff's request, even before the outcome of the case is decided, the court may order that title to real or personal property of the defendant be "seized" and held by the court as security for satisfaction of the potential award to the plaintiff. This process, called **attachment,** is restricted primarily to cases involving a business, trade, or profession.

Judgment.   The **judgment** of a court is its determination of the rights of the parties to a legal action. The losing party has the right to appeal the decision to a higher court. After the time for appeal has passed (or an appellate review has taken place and the lower court's judgment is affirmed), the judgment becomes final. The judgment could take effect as it was originally made or as it was reversed or amended by the higher court. The higher court could also order a retrial and vacate the original judgment. A judgment granting money damages may come from a California or federal court.

> The court of another state cannot render a judgment affecting California real estate.

A final judgment will become a *lien* on property of the judgment debtor when it is recorded by the party to whom it was awarded. An **abstract of judgment** can be recorded in any or all of the state's 58 counties.

After it has been created by recording, a judgment lien is effective against all nonexempt real property of the debtor located in the county of filing. This includes any real property acquired within the term of the lien, which normally is ten years. Homestead property, which is covered later in this chapter, is an example of exempt real property.

Writ of execution.   Any nonexempt property (or exempt property, as the court decides) may be sold to pay a judgment debt. The lienholder requests a **writ of execution** from the court, which directs the sheriff or other officer to sell the property.

Discharge of debt.   A judgment lien may be discharged prior to the end of its term by payment of the total damages owed. This results in **satisfaction** of the debt.

Notice of satisfaction of a debt should be filed with the clerk of the court. Partial payment of money owed could result in a **release** as to some (but not all) of the property of the debtor.

■   **FOR EXAMPLE:**   Gladys Street sued Len Flimflam in a California court, claiming that Len had defrauded her of $100,000 in a real estate scam. Gladys won her lawsuit, and the judge awarded her damages of $100,000 plus interest. Len did not appeal the decision but has not volunteered any money to Gladys. Now what?

Gladys can file her judgment in any county in which Len has sufficient property to cover what she is owed. If Len persists in ignoring the judgment, Gladys can ask for a writ of execution to sell enough of his nonexempt property to cover her award.

■ BANKRUPTCY

Bankruptcy is a federal court proceeding. There are various forms of bankruptcy, identified by their chapter in the federal Bankruptcy Code. In a Chapter 11 reorganization, the court approves a plan to repay creditors. In a Chapter 7 liquidation, the court takes possession of the assets of the debtor and sells the assets to pay off creditors on a pro rata basis. Under Chapter 13, the debts of an individual who earns a regular income are reduced. A debtor may voluntarily petition for bankruptcy, or an involuntary petition may be filed by the debtor's creditors to force a liquidation and distribution of the debtor's assets.

In a liquidation, a **trustee in bankruptcy** holds title to the debtor's assets. The trustee is responsible for the sale of the assets, as necessary, and issues a **trustee's deed** to the buyer of real property. Some property is exempt from sale, and all property is subject first to the claims of lienholders.

■ EASEMENTS

The encumbrances already discussed in this chapter affect the transfer of title to real estate. Other encumbrances affect the condition or use of property. An **easement** is the right to use the land of another for a particular purpose.

Easement Appurtenant

An easement usually is the right of the owner of one parcel of land to travel over an adjoining parcel. The land over which the easement runs is called the **servient tenement.** The land benefited by the easement is the **dominant tenement.**

An **easement appurtenant** belongs to, or "runs with," the land. If the dominant tenement is sold, the new owner has the same right to use the easement that the previous owner had. If the servient tenement is sold, the new owner generally takes title subject to the easement. The fact that there is an easement will be recorded as part of the seller's deed or it will be obvious from an inspection of the property.

■ **FOR EXAMPLE:** Al owns property that he divides into two lots, lot A and lot B. Al sells lot B to Betty. Betty builds a house on lot B.

The deed to Betty conveys an easement over Al's driveway so that Betty can get to and from her land. The illustration below shows the location of lot B in relation to lot A.

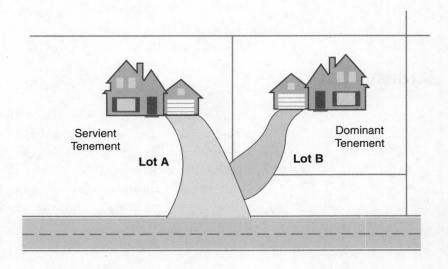

If Betty sells lot B, the new owner also will be entitled to use Al's driveway to go to and from the road. If Al sells lot A, the new owner must allow the owner of lot B to use the driveway.

Easement in Gross

Even though an easement is a real property interest, its use may be purely personal. An **easement in gross** is a personal right to use land. The right belongs to an individual (a person or business corporation) and is not appurtenant to any ownership interest in land. Because an easement in gross is a personal right, it does not "run with the land." Sometimes, a railroad's right of way is an easement in gross. The railroad does not own any adjacent land but has the right to travel over the land on which the easement lies. Pipeline and power line easements are other examples of easements in gross.

Because an easement in gross is a personal interest, it usually is not assignable by its owner and terminates on the owner's death.

How to Create an Easement

An easement may be created

- by contract;
- by express grant from the owner of the easement property;
- by reserving an easement over land that is sold;
- by implication of law;
- by long use; or
- by condemnation for a public purpose.

Creation of Easements

The owner of land may execute a contract that provides an easement right over the land. The recipient of the easement right may or may not be the owner of adjoining land, depending on the type of easement created. Other ways in which easements can arise are listed above and discussed next.

Easement by express grant or express reservation. An easement may be created by **express grant** or **express reservation** in a grant deed. The wording of the deed will depend on whether the grantor is to be the holder of the dominant or the servient tenement.

The owner of the land that will be the dominant tenement will **reserve** an easement right in the deed to the new owner of the land that will be the servient tenement.

■ **FOR EXAMPLE:** In the example illustrated on page 108, if Al had sold lot A to Betty and kept lot B for himself, he would have *reserved* an easement over Betty's driveway to get to and from lot B.

The owner of the land that will be the servient tenement will **grant** an easement right to the new owner of the land that will be the dominant tenement.

■ **FOR EXAMPLE:** In the example illustrated on page 108, Al *granted* Betty an easement when he sold lot B to her.

Only the fee owner of the servient tenement can grant an easement (whether the easement is appurtenant or in gross). Once an easement appurtenant is granted, however, the owner of the dominant tenement can convey the easement along with the land it benefits.

Easement by implication of law. In some cases the law will imply an easement to travel over someone else's land. If a subdivision plat map shows streets, an easement to use those streets is **implied by law.**

Suppose landowner A sells a parcel of land that can be reached only by traveling over another parcel of land also owned by A. It is evident from examining both parcels that landowner A has used the easement for many years. Even if landowner A doesn't specifically grant the right to use the easement, the right may be implied by law. Factors taken into account include the nature of the easement, the length of time it has been used, and whether it could be considered permanent.

Every parcel of land will be allowed some form of access.

Another form of easement by implication of law is the **easement by necessity.** A tract of land may be landlocked—that is, there may not be a road adjacent to any part of it. The owner of such a tract has an easement by necessity implied by law over any land of the seller that is adjacent and provides access to a roadway. If the seller owns no land adjacent to the landlocked parcel, there will be an implied easement over the land that provides the most efficient road access, even though that land now belongs to a "stranger" to the transaction, provided both parcels were once owned by the same person.

■ **FOR EXAMPLE:** As shown at the top of page 111, A sells B a landlocked tract. Even if A never expressly mentions an easement in the grant deed to B, B has an implied easement over the land of A to the nearest roadway.

Suppose that A, B, C, D, E, F, and G all bought their land from H. Suppose also that no easement was expressly reserved for B's land and no easement ever has been used to get to B's land for any extended period of time. B then would petition the court for an implied easement over the property that would give him the shortest reasonable access to a street. In our illustration the easement granted would most likely be over the land of *F.*

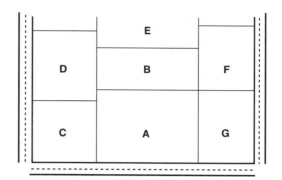

Easement by prescription.   An **easement by prescription** is acquired in much the same way that ownership of land is acquired by adverse possession. The major difference is that to acquire an easement, property taxes need not be paid. The easement use will become a legal right if it is

- open and notorious (not hidden in any way);
- continuous for five years;
- hostile to the interests of the owner (without permission);
- exclusive (a private rather than a public use, even if by more than one person); and
- under some claim of right or color of title.

Easement by condemnation.   Fee ownership of land may be acquired for a public purpose by the government's **power of eminent domain.** Rights to use land also can be acquired by eminent domain. The creation of an **easement by condemnation** begins with the condemnation of the right of use on behalf of the holder of the new easement.

Some easements benefit property owners.

The easement use (such as utility line installation and maintenance) actually may benefit the land over which the easement runs. In such a case, compensation of the landowner may not be required. Other uses, such as a railroad right-of-way or construction of major power transmission lines, are likely to require payment to the owner for the loss in value to the property caused by the easement.

Termination of an Easement

There are many ways to *terminate* an easement. They include the eight actions listed next:

1. **Express agreement of the parties.** This may be accomplished by quitclaim deed from the owner of the dominant tenement to the owner of the

servient tenement, or from the owner of an easement in gross to the owner of the land over which the easement runs.

2. **Lawsuit.** An action to quiet title can be brought against anyone claiming an easement.

3. **Abandonment of a prescriptive easement.** Although a prescriptive easement is acquired after five years of continuous use, it also can be lost if the easement is unused for five years. This is not true of an easement obtained by grant, unless the additional conditions described next are met.

4. **Estoppel.** Regardless of how it was acquired, an easement may terminate if

   ■ it is not used; *and*

   ■ the owner of the dominant tenement reasonably indicates that no further use is intended; *and*

   ■ the owner of the servient tenement makes use of the land in reasonable reliance on the representations of the owner of the dominant tenement.

   If all of these conditions are met, the owner of the dominant tenement will be prevented (estopped) from complaining of the new use.

5. **Merger of the easement with the servient tenement.** When the owner of the servient tenement acquires the right to use the easement, usually by purchase of the dominant tenement, the easement is extinguished.

6. **Destruction of the servient tenement.** Two buildings may share a common wall, called a *party wall*. The owner of each building has an easement over the other's property to the extent that the wall intrudes on that property. If the buildings are demolished and the wall destroyed, the easement terminates.

7. **Adverse possession.** If the owner of the servient tenement performs the conditions for adverse possession as to the land over which the easement lies, the easement right of the owner of the dominant tenement will terminate.

8. **Excessive use.** An easement can be terminated if the easement's use is improper or much greater than originally intended. The owner of the servient tenement could object, for instance, if land sold for residential purposes was used as a gravel pit and noisy, dusty trucks began to use the easement.

You can remember the ways to terminate an easement by the acronym **ADAM E LEE:**

■ Abandonment
■ Destruction
■ Adverse possession
■ Merger

- Express agreement
- Lawsuit
- Estoppel
- Excessive use

License to Use Land

As you learned in Chapter 3, the right to *use* land may not be an ownership right. Instead of being a *freehold* interest, it may be a *leasehold* interest. It also may be an easement, as you have learned in this chapter.

One more way in which a right to use land may be given is by a **license,** the permission given to another to come onto one's land. A license is a nonexclusive right, which means that the person to whom it is given has no right to exclude others from the owner's land. A license is personal property rather than real property and temporary rather than permanent. A license may be terminated at any time without prior notice.

An example of a license would be the permission given by an owner to neighbors to store their lawn mower in the owner's garage. The neighbors are not charged for this privilege, nor does the owner give them exclusive use of the garage but retains the right to tell them to remove their lawn mower at any time. Under this arrangement the neighbors have a license to enter the property to retrieve and return their lawn mower. They have no easement, lease, or other interest in the real estate.

Exercise 5-2   Harvey returned home to California after a six-year absence. Harvey went directly to his empty house, a palatial building on 20 acres of land.

While touring his property the next morning, Harvey was surprised to find a new power line running across the back of his land, a conspicuous and unwelcome addition. Harvey also noticed a dirt road cutting across a corner of his land to the highway from a little house just off his property.

Can the power company put up such a line? By what authority?

Yes   *Condemnation*

The little house in this exercise is located on a roadway. Can its owner create a new road across Harvey's property? How? *Yes, if has been using*

it for five years strait

■ RESTRICTIONS

Any form of **restriction** is a limitation on the use of land. The most common private restrictions are the "covenants, conditions, and restrictions" found in a deed. The most common public (government) restriction is the zoning ordinance.

Covenants, Conditions, and Restrictions

Covenants, conditions, and restrictions (CC&Rs) all serve to control land use. They are commonly found in the Declaration of Restrictions filed by a developer when a subdivision plan is recorded. The deed to each buyer of a subdivision lot will include the CC&Rs by reference to the book and page number in which they are recorded.

> A house in a subdivision probably has CC&Rs.

CC&Rs are commonly referred to simply as **restrictions.** Because they benefit the other property in the subdivision, they usually "run with the land." This means that when the property is sold, the new owner receives both the burden and benefits of the CC&Rs. Creation of a formal organization of property owners, such as a homeowners' association, usually is the most efficient and cost-effective method to enforce the CC&Rs. Even though the CC&Rs are recorded, they are useless unless they are known to property owners and have a practical method of enforcement.

CC&Rs generally can be removed only by agreement of all those who have the right to enforce them (that is, the other property owners in the subdivision). The provisions of CC&Rs also may be written so that they apply only to the original grantee, and not to subsequent owners.

Covenants.   A **covenant** is a promise

- ■ to do something or
- ■ to refrain from doing something.

■ **FOR EXAMPLE:**   Property owners in the Willow Creek subdivision covenant that they will keep buildings in good repair. They also agree to follow specific architectural guidelines for additions and design changes to buildings in the subdivision.

If a covenant is breached, the other property owners may seek an **injunction** from a court prohibiting or ordering the removal of the cause of the breach, or they may seek money damages.

A covenant also may be found in a lease. For instance, a tenant might promise to use the property only for a specified purpose.

Conditions.   A **condition** generally is enforceable by the person imposing the condition. In a sale transaction, that would be the seller. A **condition subsequent**, if performed, will enable the seller to regain title to the land. Because a condition limits the estate granted, it should appear on the face of the deed.

The remedy for breach of a condition is forfeiture of the land, a much harsher result than the money damages or injunction that can follow the breach of a covenant. Because a condition can have such a severe consequence, courts will construe any ambiguous language in a deed as a covenant, rather than a condition.

■   **FOR EXAMPLE:**   Terry deeded Greenacre to his church, to be used for church purposes. When the church used the land as a public parking lot, Terry objected, claiming the right to retake possession of the land.

The court, called on to determine the rights of the parties, found that the church *covenanted* to use the property for church purposes. Assuming that a use was not for a church purpose, Terry's remedy, the court said, would be an action for money damages or an injunction to prohibit the use.

A condition cannot require the performance of an unlawful act or an act that would be impossible to perform. There could not, for instance, be a condition that would require a crime to be committed or that would prohibit the sale of the property to a person of a certain race.

A condition also cannot impose a **restraint on alienation.** A restraint on alienation is any condition that prohibits a property owner from transferring title to the property. An example of a restraint on alienation would be a condition that the grantor's consent be obtained before the grantee could sell the property. Such a restraint is void—totally ineffective—and the grantee holds the property free of the restraint.

Deed restrictions.   A **deed restriction** is a prohibition against a property use that is imposed in the grantee's deed. Homeowners' associations frequently make use of deed restrictions to ensure that the uniform appearance of the homes in a subdivision is maintained. Some typical property maintenance standards are shown in Figure 5.1.

■   **FOR EXAMPLE:**   Anthony and Ann Rush purchased a house in Montrose Manor, which is governed by the Montrose Homeowners' Association. Anthony and Ann are aware that there are CC&Rs on their property. They have seen the latest property maintenance standards, which are the ones that appear in Figure 5.1. Anthony and Ann have decided to relandscape their property, so they are "letting it go" until next spring. They now have more weeds than plantings. Do they have a problem?

FIGURE 5.1

Property Maintenance Standards

**MONTROSE HOMEOWNERS' ASSOCIATION, INC.
PROPERTY MAINTENANCE STANDARDS**

1. Dwellings

a. Building exteriors will be maintained and painted as needed. Prior to altering an existing paint color, a written request and color samples must be reviewed and approved by the Architectural Committee.

b. Appurtenances, including but not limited to decks, overhangs, lights, attic ventilators, gutters, downspouts, and solar heating equipment, must be properly maintained and promptly repaired.

c. Broken windows, screens, garage and entry doors, and fences must be repaired or replaced within 30 days of breakage.

2. Property

a. All lots must be landscaped. Landscaping of every kind and character, including lawn, shrubs, trees, and plantings, must be trimmed, cultivated, weeded, and maintained continuously to provide a safe, clean, and groomed appearance.

b. Trees and shrubs that overhang on public sidewalks and streets must be trimmed to provide a minimum clearance of seven feet from grade. Open strips of land between fences and sidewalks are the responsibility of the property owners and should be kept neat and weeded.

c. Accumulations of rubbish, wood, or any other household or garden debris visible from other properties or the street will not be allowed for more than seven days or the next scheduled trash pickup.

d. Prolonged repair of automobiles on the street or driveway is prohibited.

3. Miscellaneous

a. Any other condition not covered above that contributes to the general appearance or disrepair of a property will be addressed by the association on an individual basis.

Yes, they do. The property standards specify that all properties must be land-scaped, "trimmed, cultivated, weeded, and maintained continuously." The Rushes can expect to hear from the homeowners' association soon.

Covenants sometimes sound like deed restrictions, and vice versa. As with a covenant, the remedy available when a deed restriction must be enforced will be an injunction or money damages. A deed restriction also may be illegal from its inception, making enforcement impossible.

Termination. Restrictions (CC&Rs) may be terminated by

- expiration of the terms of the restriction;
- voluntary cancellation;

- merger of ownership, if one individual owns both the encumbered and the benefited properties;

- government act, such as a legal prohibition against restrictions based on race or religion; or

- a change in condition that prompts a court action to remove the restriction.

Subdivision restrictions often include a provision that allows their modification on approval of the homeowners' association. That is accomplished by vote of all or a specified number of the homeowners.

■ **FOR EXAMPLE:** Clare's family has owned their home for 20 years. When it was first deeded to them by the developer, it carried a restriction that only wood shingles be used for roofing. Because of the fire hazard of a wood roof, Clare and other homeowners in her development ask the homeowners' association that the restriction be terminated.

The restriction is modified by the homeowners' association to prohibit wood shingles on new construction and to require fireproof shingles on new or replacement roofs.

Unenforceable Restrictions

Private restrictions have come under heavy legal censure when they have been used to promote racial or cultural prejudices. A deed restriction against selling property to members of a certain racial group would be in violation of both federal and state constitutional protections as well as fair housing laws. Discrimination in housing is discussed in Chapter 15, "Government Control of Land Use."

Zoning

Zoning is an act of city or county government. Zoning laws or ordinances specify the possible uses of property in a defined area. Zoning is a 20th-century invention intended to promote the public health or general public welfare. It has been the subject of many legal battles involving the extent to which public interests can take priority over private ones. We will consider zoning and other governmental controls of land use in more detail in Chapter 15, "Government Control of Land Use."

Exercise 5-3

1. Mary Miller is very concerned that her neighborhood retain its quiet, well-maintained atmosphere. Herb, her neighbor, has his house up for sale. He promises Mary that he will require anyone who buys the house to care for it properly. Can he do that? yes

2. Mary Miller has decided to move to Alaska and give her home in California to her nephew, Neil. Mary is very concerned that the neighborhood's appearance be kept up for the benefit of her old neighbors. Her deed to Neil stipulates that she must approve any future transfer of the property. Can she do that?   NO

■ ENCROACHMENTS

> An encroachment can occur on land, in airspace, or underground (a footing for a fence or building).

An **encroachment** occurs when part of an improvement extends over the boundary line between properties. Fences and buildings are typical forms of encroachment. Even the roof eave of a building can be an encroachment if it extends into the airspace of a neighboring lot.

An encroaching party who fulfills the conditions for an easement by prescription or ownership by adverse possession may earn the legal right to use the land occupied by the encroachment. If not, the owner of the occupied land can bring a legal action. The decision of the court will depend on

- the extent of the encroachment;
- the relative difficulty of removing it; and
- whether the encroaching party acted by mistake.

■ **FOR EXAMPLE:** Lester is an excellent surveyor but he has a careless office assistant. Lester neglected to note that his assistant transposed some measurements on the plans for the Skyway Office Tower. As a result, the foundation for the tower was poured 11 inches inside an adjacent vacant lot's boundary line, along the entire 200-foot width of the building. The building was completed within two years. One year after that, the owner of the vacant lot went forward with her development plans and discovered the unfortunate mistake. Can she force the owner of Skyway to demolish the 50-floor office building (or at least the 11 inches that extend onto her property)?

No. To do so would be prohibitively expensive, and courts will not require such an uneconomic outcome, particularly when the cause was inadvertent.

The Skyway owner probably will have to pay damages for the encroachment, however. The amount of damages owed could be substantial, particularly if the vacant lot owner's plans must be extensively revised.

■ HOMESTEADS

California and other states provide homeowners with special protection from creditors. Some or all of the value of the owner's equity in the **homestead** is exempt from the claims of unsecured creditors.

The homeowner's **equity** is the market value of the home less any liens and encumbrances. If the homeowner's equity is greater than the amount of the exemption, the home could be sold at the court's direction to satisfy any unpaid creditors. A sale will not be ordered if the homeowner's equity is no more than

- the remaining amount owed on the mortgage loan *plus*
- the amount of the **homestead exemption**.

If the homeowner chooses to sell the property, the amount of the exemption will be safe from creditors only if it is reinvested in a new homestead within *six months*. This could help a financially beleaguered homeowner. The **six-month rule** could allow the homeowner to move into a less costly home, for instance, and perhaps provide some equity from the sale of the former home to pay off creditors. The generous tax exclusion rules for homeowners (discussed in Chapter 11, "Real Estate Taxation") could allow the homeowner to avoid paying any tax on profit realized on the sale of the more expensive home.

Do not confuse the **homestead exemption** with the federal homesteading laws. Homesteading was discontinued after 1976, except in Alaska. Individuals may no longer homestead on public land in California as a way to acquire title.

Defining the Homestead   The homestead exemption applies only to an owner-occupied dwelling. The dwelling can be any of the following (among other forms of dwelling):

- House and land
- Mobile home and land
- Boat
- Condominium
- Planned development
- Stock cooperative
- Community apartment project

The homestead can be community property of husband and wife, the separate property of either spouse, or the separate property of an unmarried individual. If two unmarried persons share ownership, each can claim a separate homestead exemption on the dwelling they occupy.

FIGURE 5.2

Homestead Exemption

AMOUNT OF THE HOMESTEAD EXEMPTION	
Homeowner	$50,000
Homeowner who is a member of a family unit	$75,000
Homeowner, or spouse who resides with homeowner, is 65 years of age or older	$150,000
Homeowner, or spouse who resides with homeowner, is physically or mentally disabled and unable to engage in substantial gainful employment	$150,000
Homeowner is 55 years of age or older with a gross annual income of not more than $15,000 or, if the homeowner is married, with a combined gross annual income with the spouse of not more than $20,000, and the homestead is subject to an involuntary sale	$150,000

Amount of the Homestead Exemption

The amount of the homestead exemption depends on the homeowner's status, as shown in Figure 5.2.

The Family Unit

Being a member of a family unit of two or more persons qualifies a homeowner for a $75,000 exemption. At least one member of the family unit must own no interest in the property or the interest must be a community property interest with the person claiming the exemption. The various forms of family unit are listed below.

The Family Unit

The following qualify as family units for purposes of the homestead exemption:

- Homeowner and spouse, if they reside together.
- Homeowner and, if cared for and maintained in the homestead, the minor child or minor grandchild of the homeowner, spouse, or deceased or former spouse.
- Homeowner and, if cared for and maintained in the homestead, the minor brother or sister of the homeowner or homeowner's spouse or the minor child of a deceased brother or sister of either spouse.
- Homeowner and, if cared for and maintained in the homestead, the father, mother, grandfather, or grandmother of the homeowner, spouse, or deceased spouse.
- Homeowner and, if cared for and maintained in the homestead, an unmarried adult relative who is unable to care for or support himself or herself.
- Homeowner's spouse and one of the other relatives mentioned in categories 2, 3, 4, or 5 above, if that person is unable to care for or support himself or herself.

Priority of Claims

The **priority of claims** is the order in which creditors are paid. The priority of claims against a homestead has been established by law. The proceeds of a forced sale go

1. to holders of liens and encumbrances on the homestead (with any tax lien paid off first); then
2. to the homeowner in the amount of the homestead exemption only; then
3. to the levying officer for reimbursement of costs for which an advance has not been made; then
4. to judgment creditors; and finally, if anything remains,
5. to the homeowner.

Exercise 5-4

1. Harold and Cynthia Potter, husband and wife, own a houseboat docked at Lake Shasta as community property. Do they qualify for a homestead exemption? *Yes, if it is they're principal residence.*
2. Harold and Cynthia have a $95,000 mortgage on their houseboat, which has a market value of $130,000. If creditors try to force the sale of the houseboat, are they likely to succeed?

No not enough equity.

■ SUMMARY

A property owner has **marketable title** if the property is readily salable to a prudent purchaser. An **encumbrance** may create a **cloud on the title** and impede the property's marketability.

A **lien** is **voluntary** if the owner places it on the property or **involuntary** if someone else does. A **mechanic's lien** is available to anyone providing work or material for a property improvement. A **contractor's payment bond** helps minimize the risk of numerous mechanics' liens.

If a **mechanic's lien** is to be filed, **preliminary notice** must be given to the owner, the construction manager (if any), and the construction lender (if any). It is important to establish the starting time and completion time of the work or materials supply. After work has been completed, the property owner may file a **notice of completion.** An owner also can stop work and file a **notice of cessation.**

A mechanic's lien is enforced by **foreclosure.** If unsolicited work is performed, a **notice of nonresponsibility** can be filed and posted on the land.

The plaintiff in a legal action can ask to have the court retain title to the defendant's property by **attachment** even before a **judgment** is rendered. A court will make a judgment after hearing the claims that a plaintiff has against a defendant. The court may grant **money damages,** and that judgment can become a **lien** on property of the debtor if it is filed in the county where the property is located. A **writ of execution** orders the sheriff to sell the property to pay the judgment. The owner can satisfy the debt by paying it off or can pay part of the debt and have some of the property **released.**

A **debtor's** property may be taken over by a **bankruptcy court.** The **trustee in bankruptcy** holds title.

Easements allow use of another's land for a particular purpose. The owner of a **dominant tenement** has the right to use the land of the owner of a **servient tenement.** Generally an easement is conveyed with the land, but an **easement in gross** is a personal right and may not be transferable.

Easements may be created by **deed, by implication of law** or **by necessity** (if a parcel is landlocked), **by prescription** (similar to **adverse possession**), and **by condemnation** (through the **power of eminent domain**). An easement may be **terminated** by agreement, lawsuit, nonuse of a prescriptive easement, abandonment, merger of the easement and servient tenement, destruction of the servient tenement, adverse possession, or excessive use.

The **conditions, covenants, and restrictions** in a deed are private forms of limitation on land use and may bind the grantee. A court may issue an **injunction** ordering a property to refrain from activity prohibited by the **CC&Rs. CC&Rs** cannot act as a **restraint on alienation** of the property, require the performance of a crime or an impossible act, or have an illegal purpose.

Zoning is a public form of limitation on land use. An **encroachment** occurs when an improvement is placed on the wrong property.

A **homestead exemption** protects from $50,000 to $150,000 of the homeowner's equity in the dwelling from creditors.

■ IMPORTANT TERMS

Make sure you understand the following terms before you take the achievement examination.

abstract of judgment
attachment
CC&Rs
cloud on the title
condition
covenant
deed restriction
defendant
dominant tenement
easement
easement appurtenant
easement by condemnation
easement by express grant
easement by express reservation
easement by implication of law
easement by necessity
easement by prescription
easement in gross
encroachment
encumbrance
equity
general lien
homestead
homestead exemption
injunction

involuntary lien
judgment
license
lien
lien release
lien release bond
marketable title
mechanic's lien
notice of nonresponsibility
payment bond
plaintiff
power of eminent domain
preliminary notice
priority of claims
restraint on alienation
restriction
satisfaction
servient tenement
six-month rule
specific lien
starting time
tax lien
voluntary lien
writ of execution
zoning

■ OPEN FOR DISCUSSION

Deed restrictions are the most popular method of maintaining uniformity of architectural style, appearance, and upkeep of subdivision properties.

1. Do you think that deed restrictions serve a useful purpose?

2. Do you think that deed restrictions should be allowed to continue indefinitely, or should they automatically terminate after a certain period of time? If so, what should that time be?

■ ACHIEVEMENT EXAMINATION 5

1. A cloud on the title is
   a. not important.
   b. easily remedied.
   c. no impediment to a property sale.
   d. a possible impediment to a property sale.

2. A mechanic's lien can be filed by a(n)
   a. laborer.
   b. tenant.
   c. advertiser.
   d. customer.

3. Which of the following is not a mechanic?
   a. An engineer
   b. An architect
   c. An apartment lessor
   d. An equipment lessor

4. Preliminary notice of intent to file a mechanic's lien should be given
   a. 90 days after notice of completion.
   b. 60 days after notice of completion.
   c. within 10 days of the starting time.
   d. within 20 days of the starting time.

5. A notice of cessation is appropriate
   a. when the work has been stopped for 30 days.
   b. when an improvement is completed.
   c. at any time after the work is substantially finished.
   d. after work has stopped for any number of days.

6. A notice of completion should be *filed* within
   a. 20 days after completion of the work of improvement.
   b. 10 days after completion of the work of improvement.
   c. 20 days after work stops.
   d. 10 days after supplies have been received.

7. Generally, mechanic's lien claims must be *enforced* within how many days after the notice of completion is filed?
   a. 30
   b. 60
   c. 90
   d. 120

8. If unauthorized work is being done, a property owner can
   a. file a preliminary notice.
   b. file a notice of cessation.
   c. allow the job to be completed and then refuse to pay.
   d. file a notice of nonresponsibility.

9. Liens and judgments are
   a. encumbrances.
   b. encroachments.
   c. easements.
   d. void on homestead property.

10. The sheriff is directed to sell property by a
    a. writ of attachment.
    b. writ of execution.
    c. satisfaction.
    d. release.

11. The right to use adjacent land to go to and from a roadway is a(n)
    a. encroachment.
    b. easement.
    c. restriction.
    d. condition.

12. Betty's property includes an easement over Al's land. Al's property is the
    a. dominant tenement.
    b. servient tenement.
    c. easement.
    d. encroachment.

13. Betty's property includes an easement over Al's land. Betty's property is the
    a. dominant tenement.
    b. servient tenement.
    c. easement.
    d. encroachment.

14. George does not own any land but has an easement over Al's and Betty's property to go down to the river. George has an
    a. easement by necessity.
    b. easement by implication of law.
    c. easement in gross.
    d. encroachment.

15. Marilyn's 40-acre tract is landlocked, which means that she
    a. has to enter it by helicopter.
    b. has an easement in gross over any land she chooses.
    c. has an easement by implication of law over any land she chooses.
    d. can get an easement by necessity over the seller's adjoining parcel.

16. Al sold Blackacre to Betty, giving her an easement over Whiteacre. Years later Al bought Blackacre back from Betty. What effect did his purchase have on the easement?
    a. The easement stayed with Betty.
    b. The easement is dormant until Al resells Blackacre.
    c. The purchase terminated the easement.
    d. The purchase had no effect on the easement.

17. The maximum homestead exemption may be claimed by any homeowner who is
    a. a member of a family unit.
    b. older than 65 years of age.
    c. married.
    d. single.

18. A family unit is
    a. defined by law.
    b. limited in size.
    c. limited to the relatives of one's spouse.
    d. at least three people.

19. The homestead exemption for a single person is at least
    a. $150,000.   c. $50,000.
    b. $75,000.   d. $25,000.

20. The homestead exemption for a homeowner who is a member of a family unit is at least
    a. $150,000.   c. $100,000.
    b. $90,000.   d. $75,000.

CHAPTER SIX

THE LAW OF AGENCY

■ THE CONCEPT OF AGENCY

Whom does the real estate agent represent? In the traditional view of agency law, the agent most often represented the seller. This was true even when it was the buyer who first contacted the real estate agent. The buyer could be shown dozens of homes and helped through a complicated real estate purchase contract. The agent could even assist the buyer through the escrow process. Despite all that, the real estate agent was first and foremost the agent of the seller. The majority of buyers never realized that "their" agent was actually the seller's agent. It probably never occurred to the agent that the buyer should know.

The traditional view of agency law in California has changed. Recent studies, public opinion, court decisions, legislation, and the redefinition of the market-place thanks to the Internet have brought the role of the real estate agent into sharper focus. As the agency relationship is more clearly defined, it becomes easier for all agents to recognize and meet the challenges of that relationship. The real estate agent can better serve both buyers and sellers when all parties concerned know exactly whom the agent represents.

The California Civil Code provides most of the laws dealing with the formation of an agency relationship. The definitions that follow and most of the information in this chapter can be found there. To read a specific section of the law, go to *www.leginfo.ca.gov*, check "Civil Code," and enter the key words you would like

www.leginfo.ca.gov

to find. As you read through this chapter, remember that the law—no matter how well established by statute or precedent—is always subject to change.

What an Agency Is

An **agent** represents a **principal** in dealing with a third person. The act of representing someone else is called an **agency.**

California Civil Code Section 2079.13(a) defines the agent in a real estate transaction as the broker "under whose license a listing is executed or an offer to purchase is obtained." It is important to remember that all of a real estate brokerage's associate licensees (real estate salespersons or brokers who work under the supervision of the company's designated broker), including those who work in branch offices, are considered one "agent" for the purpose of agency duties and liabilities.

In the practice of real estate, there are actually many possible **agency relationships.** The listing broker acts as the agent of the seller, but the salesperson is the agent of the broker. There may be a different broker representing the buyer and that broker may have a salesperson as his or her agent.

Who May Take Part in an Agency Relationship

In every agency relationship, there is always a **principal,** an **agent,** and a **third person** with whom the agent conducts business on behalf of the principal.

The principal can be anyone who has the ability to enter into a contract. For example, a person who is mentally incompetent cannot enter into a valid agency relationship.

In California, as in all states, a real estate agent must obtain the appropriate license. All California real estate licensees must be at least 18 years old and have fulfilled the education and other requirements discussed in Chapter 1.

Special Agent versus General Agent

A **special agent** is one appointed to carry out a single act or transaction. Any other agent is called a **general agent.** The difference between a special agent and a general agent lies in the scope of authority the agent possesses.

■ **FOR EXAMPLE:**   Broker Bob is engaged by Ramon and Rosa Garcia to sell their home. Broker Bob is a special agent for that purpose. When Broker Bob sells the Garcia home, his agency relationship with the Garcias will terminate.

The Garcias employ a business manager and give that person full authority to carry out their financial affairs. What kind of agent is that person?

That person is a general agent, because of the broad authority given to the agent by the Garcias.

Delegating Authority

Some of an agent's authority may be delegated to someone else. The agent may do so without express authority of the principal when the responsibility being delegated involves a clerical or administrative act. Other activities will require the principal's agreement before they can be delegated.

■ **FOR EXAMPLE:** Broker Maya employs an administrative assistant, who performs secretarial duties, including typing sales brochures. Broker Maya's assistant performs none of the tasks that require a real estate license, such as soliciting property sellers and buyers. Broker Maya does not need the approval of her clients in order to employ her assistant.

A complete discussion of real estate listing agreements appears later in this chapter. The typical listing contract allows the listing broker to make use of the efforts of the listing broker's staff as well as the services of *cooperating brokers*.

Cooperating brokers are agents who try to sell a property that is currently listed for sale by a broker, but who work for someone other than the listing broker. Historically, it was taken for granted that the agency relationship was between the listing broker and the seller. Any agent who wrote an offer on behalf of a buyer was considered a **subagent** of the seller's broker and, with the seller's consent, the listing broker agreed to share the commission with the subagent. Unless subagency was rejected, the cooperating broker was automatically the subagent of the seller and owed all of the duties of a fiduciary to the seller.

Under the practice of subagency, the buyer was not *represented* by the cooperating broker but instead was *assisted* by the cooperating broker. The problem? Almost 70 percent of buyers believed the agent working *with* them was working *for* them. But in reality, the buyer was the third party in an agency relationship and all of the agents were loyal to the seller. In California, legislation has changed this relationship. The cooperating broker is no longer automatically the subagent of the seller, even though the cooperating broker may be entitled to a share of the commission that the listing agent receives from the seller. (The cooperating broker's share of the commission is called the **cooperating split.**) Now, a cooperating broker may be

- the agent of the listing broker,
- the subagent of the seller (with the seller's authorization, typically through use of the multiple listing service), or
- the agent of the buyer.

It is important to remember that the seller's authorization does not necessarily require a written agreement. As you will learn later in this chapter, in the section entitled "How an Agency Relationship Is Created," the conduct of the seller (the principal) also can authorize an agency relationship.

Multiple listing service. A **multiple listing service (MLS)** is an organization of real estate agents that receives information from individual members on their property listings and makes that information available to participating members. The MLS benefits sellers by making more agents aware of the availability of their property. Buyers benefit from a wide choice of properties from which an agent can present those that meet the buyers' needs.

When a real estate broker enters into a listing agreement with a property owner, the owner may authorize the agent to place the listing in the MLS. Information placed in the MLS informs other agents of the asking price, provides a property description, indicates how the property may be shown, and tells the agent representing a buyer—the cooperating broker—what the commission to the selling agent will be. The cooperating broker is entitled to the compensation offered in the MLS, regardless of agency relationships. The MLS listing will also inform other agents if subagency is optional or mandatory. A **pocket listing** is one which the listing agent markets privately before entering it in the MLS. Unless specifically authorized by the seller, this practice usually is a violation of MLS rules.

■ **FOR EXAMPLE:** Broker Bob is the exclusive agent for the O'Connors, who are selling a four-unit apartment building. The MLS has not been authorized and is not being used, although the property is being advertised for sale. If a cooperating broker brings in a buyer, what is the relationship of that broker to the O'Connors and Broker Bob?

In this case, a cooperating broker would be the subagent of Broker Bob and have no direct relationship with the O'Connors.

Employment Relationship of Principal and Agent

An agency agreement is a form of employment contract. It can be structured in several ways. The principal is the **employer,** but the agent may act as either an **employee** or an **independent contractor.** The main difference is in the type of control the principal exercises over the agent. Another difference is the form of compensation paid to the agent.

Real estate sales associates don't have a typical "9 to 5" job with evenings and weekends off.

An employee typically is under very close control as to the place where work is performed, the hours spent on the work, and the manner in which the work is carried out. An employee receives wages from which payroll taxes are deducted and may receive other employee benefits. Employee status also subjects the employer to certain liability for acts performed in the course of employment, which will be discussed later. An independent contractor, on the other hand, usually has great flexibility in accomplishing the task undertaken and will receive a commission based on completed transactions, instead of a salary, with no payroll deductions.

Real estate agents generally act as independent contractors in their dealings with clients as well as in their dealings with each other.

> ## Don't Forget
>
> A real estate salesperson can conduct business only as the agent of a broker and they must have a written employment agreement.
>
> The Real Estate License Law always considers a salesperson to be an **employee** acting under the direct supervision and control of the broker.
>
> This is true even when the salesperson is treated by the broker as an **independent contractor** for compensation, work assignment, and tax purposes.

■ **FOR EXAMPLE:**   CPU Home Loans has a staff of 12 salespeople, all of whom are assigned office time and all of whom are paid a salary plus a commission on sales. CPU deducts income taxes and Social Security from the salaries of all salespeople and also makes payments for unemployment insurance and workers' compensation. For purposes of work assignments and compensation, are the salespeople of CPU Home Loans employees or independent contractors?

The salespeople of CPU Home Loans clearly are employees.

Throughout the rest of this chapter, we will refer to the role of the real estate broker, rather than that of the real estate salesperson. (Keep in mind that a salesperson acts always as the agent of the employing broker and that someone with a broker's license may choose to be employed by another broker.) A real estate licensee employed by the broker will be referred to as an **associate licensee.**

All of the associate licensees in a real estate brokerage, including all branch offices, are considered one "agent" for the purpose of agency duties and liabilities. The designated broker is responsible for all acts of the associate licensee with regard to duties owed to the principal, third party, and other brokers. In most cases, all of the listings in a real estate company belong to the broker and not the associate licensee. If an associate licensee changes employing brokers, the listings stay with the broker under whose name they were taken, unless the broker allows the associate licensee to retain them.

FIGURE 6.1

Agency Relationships

SINGLE AGENCY

| Seller | — | Listing Broker
Associate Licensee | - - - - - - - - | Buyer/Customer |

| Seller | | | | Buyer |
| Listing Broker
Associate Licensee | - - - - - - - - | Buyer's Broker
Associate Licensee | | |

DUAL AGENCY

| Seller | — | Listing Broker
Associate Licensee | — | Buyer/Client |

Solid lines indicate agency relationships. Dotted lines indicate nonagency relationships.

Single versus Dual Agency

In a **single agency,** an agent represents only one principal. Each principal in a transaction is represented by a different broker, as shown in Figure 6.1.

In a **dual agency,** the same agent represents two principals in the same transaction. A dual agency places the agent in the precarious position of carrying out agency responsibilities to two principals whose interests are in opposition. Any agent who acts on behalf of both parties to a transaction is required by law to inform both parties and obtain their written consent to the dual representation.

The law is very specific with regard to the activities of real estate agents. A real estate broker in a dual agency relationship must make sure that both clients know of and consent to the dual representation. Otherwise, the agent faces temporary suspension or even permanent revocation of the real estate license, in addition to having to return any commission received on the transaction. The penalty may seem severe, but the chance or even the appearance of taking advantage of the special knowledge an agent possesses makes a dual agency a difficult enterprise. Not only does the broker have a real estate license to consider, but a party acting without knowledge of the dual agency could ask the court to rescind any contract that results.

Agency disclosure form.   As of January 1, 1988, the details of the agency relationship must be disclosed in any transaction involving property of one to four residential units. A written document that explains the various relationships of those involved in a residential property sale, and exactly whom the agent is representing, must be presented to both buyer and seller "as soon as practicable." The written disclosure must be made

- by the listing agent to the seller before the seller signs the listing agreement;
- by the selling agent (who may also be the listing agent) to the buyer before the buyer makes an offer to purchase; and
- by the selling agent (if different from the listing agent) to the seller before an offer to purchase is accepted.

An example of an **agency disclosure form** is shown in Figure 6.2. The wording of the form must follow the wording required by Civil Code Section 2375. In addition, the rest of the code sections dealing with the disclosure requirements must be printed on the back of the form.

The selling agent's relationship must be confirmed in writing

- in the purchase contract or
- in a separate writing executed or acknowledged by the seller, the buyer, and the selling agent before or at the same time the purchase contract is executed by buyer and seller.

The listing agent's relationship must be confirmed in writing

- in the purchase contract or
- in a separate writing executed or acknowledged by the seller and the listing agent before or at the same time the purchase contract is executed by the seller.

An example of an **agency confirmation form** is shown in Figure 6.3.

Power of Attorney

An **attorney-at-law** is someone licensed by the state to practice law.

An **attorney-in-fact** is an agent who has been granted a *power of attorney* by a principal. A **power of attorney** authorizes an agent to act in the capacity of the principal.

An attorney takes someone else's place.

A **special power of attorney** gives an agent authority to carry out a specific act or acts. A **general power of attorney** authorizes an agent to carry out all of the business dealings of the principal.

FIGURE 6.2

Disclosure Regarding Real Estate Agency Relationships

CALIFORNIA
ASSOCIATION
OF REALTORS®

**DISCLOSURE REGARDING
REAL ESTATE AGENCY RELATIONSHIPS**
(As required by the Civil Code)
(C.A.R. Form AD, Revised 10/01)

When you enter into a discussion with a real estate agent regarding a real estate transaction, you should from the outset understand what type of agency relationship or representation you wish to have with the agent in the transaction.

SELLER'S AGENT

A Seller's agent under a listing agreement with the Seller acts as the agent for the Seller only. A Seller's agent or a subagent of that agent has the following affirmative obligations:
To the Seller:
    A Fiduciary duty of utmost care, integrity, honesty, and loyalty in dealings with the Seller.
To the Buyer and the Seller:
    (a) Diligent exercise of reasonable skill and care in performance of the agent's duties.
    (b) A duty of honest and fair dealing and good faith.
    (c) A duty to disclose all facts known to the agent materially affecting the value or desirability of the property that are not known to, or within the diligent attention and observation of, the parties.

An agent is not obligated to reveal to either party any confidential information obtained from the other party that does not involve the affirmative duties set forth above.

BUYER'S AGENT

A selling agent can, with a Buyer's consent, agree to act as agent for the Buyer only. In these situations, the agent is not the Seller's agent, even if by agreement the agent may receive compensation for services rendered, either in full or in part from the Seller. An agent acting only for a Buyer has the following affirmative obligations:
To the Buyer:
    A fiduciary duty of utmost care, integrity, honesty, and loyalty in dealings with the Buyer.
To the Buyer and the Seller:
    (a) Diligent exercise of reasonable skill and care in performance of the agent's duties.
    (b) A duty of honest and fair dealing and good faith.
    (c) A duty to disclose all facts known to the agent materially affecting the value or desirability of the property that are not known to, or within the diligent attention and observation of, the parties.

An agent is not obligated to reveal to either party any confidential information obtained from the other party that does not involve the affirmative duties set forth above.

AGENT REPRESENTING BOTH SELLER AND BUYER

A real estate agent, either acting directly or through one or more associate licensees, can legally be the agent of both the Seller and the Buyer in a transaction, but only with the knowledge and consent of both the Seller and the Buyer.

In a dual agency situation, the agent has the following affirmative obligations to both the Seller and the Buyer:
    (a) A fiduciary duty of utmost care, integrity, honesty and loyalty in the dealings with either the Seller or the Buyer.
    (b) Other duties to the Seller and the Buyer as stated above in their respective sections.

In representing both Seller and Buyer, the agent may not, without the express permission of the respective party, disclose to the other party that the Seller will accept a price less than the listing price or that the Buyer will pay a price greater than the price offered.

The above duties of the agent in a real estate transaction do not relieve a Seller or Buyer from the responsibility to protect his or her own interests. You should carefully read all agreements to assure that they adequately express your understanding of the transaction. A real estate agent is a person qualified to advise about real estate. If legal or tax advice is desired, consult a competent professional.

Throughout your real property transaction you may receive more than one disclosure form, depending upon the number of agents assisting in the transaction. The law requires each agent with whom you have more than a casual relationship to present you with this disclosure form. You should read its contents each time it is presented to you, considering the relationship between you and the real estate agent in your specific transaction.

This disclosure form includes the provisions of Sections 2079.13 to 2079.24, inclusive, of the Civil Code set forth on the reverse hereof. Read it carefully.

I/WE ACKNOWLEDGE RECEIPT OF A COPY OF THIS DISCLOSURE AND CHAPTER 2 OF TITLE 9 OF PART 4 OF DIVISION 3 OF THE CIVIL CODE.

BUYER/SELLER _____ Date _____ Time _____ AM/PM

BUYER/SELLER _____ Date _____ Time _____ AM/PM

AGENT _____ By _____ Date _____
        (Please Print)   (Associate-Licensee or Broker Signature)

THIS FORM SHALL BE PROVIDED AND ACKNOWLEDGED AS FOLLOWS (Civil Code § 2079.14):
•When the listing brokerage company also represents the Buyer, the Listing Agent shall give one AD form to the Seller and one to the Buyer.
•When Buyer and Seller are represented by different brokerage companies, then the Listing Agent shall give one AD form to the Seller and the Buyer's Agent shall give one AD form to the Buyer and one AD form to the Seller.

SEE REVERSE SIDE FOR FURTHER INFORMATION

SURE TRAC
The System for Success™

Published by the
California Association of REALTORS®

EQUAL HOUSING
OPPORTUNITY

AD REVISED 10/01 (PAGE 1 OF 1)   PRINT DATE

Reviewed by _____ Date _____

DISCLOSURE REGARDING REAL ESTATE AGENCY RELATIONSHIPS (AD PAGE 1 OF 1)

Source: Reprinted with permission, California Association of REALTORS®. Endorsement not implied.

FIGURE 6.2

Disclosure Regarding Real Estate Agency Relationships (Continued)

CHAPTER 2 OF TITLE 9 OF PART 4 OF DIVISION 3 OF THE CIVIL CODE

2079.13 As used in Sections 2079.14 to 2079.24, inclusive, the following terms have the following meanings:
(a) "Agent" means a person acting under provisions of title 9 (commencing with Section 2295) in a real property transaction, and includes a person who is licensed as a real estate broker under Chapter 3 (commencing with Section 10130) of Part 1 of Division 4 of the Business and Professions Code, and under whose license a listing is executed or an offer to purchase is obtained. **(b)** "Associate licensee" means a person who is licensed as a real broker or salesperson under Chapter 3 (commencing with Section 10130) of Part 1 of Division 4 of the Business and Professions Code and who is either licensed under a broker or has entered into a written contract with a broker to act as the broker's agent in connection with acts requiring a real estate license and to function under the capacity of an associate licensee. The agent in the real property transaction bears responsibility for his or her associate licensees who perform as agents of the agent. When an associate licensee owes a duty to any principal, or to any buyer or seller who is not a principal, in a real property transaction, that duty is equivalent to the duty owed to that party by the broker for whom the associate licensee functions. **(c)** "Buyer" means a transferee in a real property transaction, and includes a person who executes an offer to purchase real property from a seller through an agent, or who seeks the services of an agent in more than a casual, transitory, or preliminary manner, with the object of entering into a real property transaction. "Buyer" includes vendee or lessee. **(d)** "Dual agent" means an agent acting, either directly or through an associate licensee, as agent for both the seller and the buyer in a real property transaction. **(e)** "Listing agreement" means a contract between an owner of real property and an agent, by which the agent has been authorized to sell the real property or to find or obtain a buyer. **(f)** "Listing agent" means a person who has obtained a listing of real property to act as an agent for compensation. **(g)** "Listing price" is the amount expressed in dollars specified in the listing for which the seller is willing to sell the real property through the listing agent. **(h)** "Offering price" is the amount expressed in dollars specified in an offer to purchase for which the buyer is willing to buy the real property. **(i)** "Offer to purchase" means a written contract executed by a buyer acting through a selling agent which becomes the contract for the sale of the real property upon acceptance by the seller. **(j)** "Real property" means any estate specified by subdivision (1) or (2) of Section 761 in property which constitutes or is improved with one to four dwelling units, any leasehold in this type of property exceeding one year's duration, and mobilehomes, when offered for sale or sold through an agent pursuant to the authority contained in Section 10131.6 of the Business and Professions Code. **(k)** "Real property transaction" means a transaction for the sale of real property in which an agent is employed by one or more of the principals to act in that transaction, and includes a listing or an offer to purchase. **(l)** "Sell," "sale," or "sold" refers to a transaction for the transfer of real property from the seller to the buyer, and includes exchanges of real property between the seller and buyer, transactions for the creation of a real property sales contract within the meaning of Section 2985, and transactions for the creation of a leasehold exceeding one year's duration. **(m)** "Seller" means the transferor in a real property transaction, and includes an owner who lists real property with an agent, whether or not a transfer results, or who receives an offer to purchase real property of which he or she is the owner from an agent on behalf of another. "Seller" includes both a vendor and a lessor. **(n)** "Selling agent" means a listing agent who acts alone, or an agent who acts in cooperation with a listing agent, and who sells or finds and obtains a buyer for the real property, or an agent who locates property for a buyer or who finds a buyer for a property for which no listing exists and presents an offer to purchase to the seller. **(o)** "Subagent" means a person to whom an agent delegates agency powers as provided in Article 5 (commencing with Section 2349) of Chapter 1 of Title 9. However, "subagent" does not include an associate licensee who is acting under the supervision of an agent in a real property transaction.

2079.14 Listing agents and selling agents shall provide the seller and buyer in a real property transaction with a copy of the disclosure form specified in Section 2079.16, and, except as provided in subdivision (c), shall obtain a signed acknowledgement of receipt from that seller or buyer, except as provided in this section or Section 2079.15, as follows: **(a)** The listing agent, if any, shall provide the disclosure form to the seller prior to entering into the listing agreement. **(b)** The selling agent shall provide the disclosure form to the seller as soon as practicable prior to presenting the seller with an offer to purchase, unless the selling agent previously provided the seller with a copy of the disclosure form pursuant to subdivision (a). **(c)** Where the selling agent does not deal on a face-to-face basis with the seller, the disclosure form prepared by the selling agent may be furnished to the seller (and acknowledgement of receipt obtained for the selling agent from the seller) by the listing agent, or the selling agent may deliver the disclosure form by certified mail addressed to the seller at his or her last known address, in which case no signed acknowledgement of receipt is required. **(d)** The selling agent shall provide the disclosure form to the buyer as soon as practicable prior to execution of the buyer's offer to purchase, except that if the offer to purchase is not prepared by the selling agent, the selling agent shall present the disclosure form to the buyer not later than the next business day after the selling agent receives the offer to purchase from the buyer.

2079.15 In any circumstance in which the seller or buyer refuses to sign an acknowledgement of receipt pursuant to Section 2079.14, the agent, or an associate licensee acting for an agent, shall set forth, sign, and date a written declaration of the facts of the refusal.

2079.17 (a) As soon as practicable, the selling agent shall disclose to the buyer and seller whether the selling agent is acting in the real property transaction exclusively as the buyer's agent, exclusively as the seller's agent, or as a dual agent representing both the buyer and seller. This relationship shall be confirmed in the contract to purchase and sell real property or in a separate writing executed or acknowledged by the seller, the buyer, and the selling agent prior to or coincident with execution of that contract by the buyer and the seller, respectively. **(b)** As soon as practicable, the listing agent shall disclose to the seller whether the listing agent is acting in the real property transaction exclusively as the seller's agent, or as a dual agent representing both the buyer and seller. This relationship shall be confirmed in the contract to purchase and sell real property or in a separate writing executed or acknowledged by the seller and the listing agent prior to or coincident with the execution of that contract by the seller.
(c) The confirmation required by subdivisions (a) and (b) shall be in the following form.

_____ is the agent of (check one): ☐ the seller exclusively; or ☐ both the buyer and seller.
(Name of Listing Agent)

_____ is the agent of (check one): ☐ the buyer exclusively; or ☐ the seller exclusively; or
(Name of Selling Agent if not the same as the Listing Agent)   ☐ both the buyer and seller.

(d) The disclosures and confirmation required by this section shall be in addition to the disclosure required by Section 2079. 14.

2079.18 No selling agent in a real property transaction may act as an agent for the buyer only, when the selling agent is also acting as the listing agent in the transaction.

2079.19 The payment of compensation or the obligation to pay compensation to an agent by the seller or buyer is not necessarily determinative of a particular agency relationship between an agent and the seller or buyer. A listing agent and a selling agent may agree to share any compensation or commission paid, or any right to any compensation or commission for which an obligation arises as the result of a real estate transaction, and the terms of any such agreement shall not necessarily be determinative of a particular relationship.

2079.20 Nothing in this article prevents an agent from selecting, as a condition of the agent's employment, a specific form of agency relationship not specifically prohibited by this article if the requirements of Section 2079.14 and Section 2079.17 are complied with.

2079.21 A dual agent shall not disclose to the buyer that the seller is willing to sell the property at a price less than the listing price, without the express written consent of the seller. A dual agent shall not disclose to the seller that the buyer is willing to pay a price greater than the offering price, without the express written consent of the buyer. This section does not alter in any way the duty or responsibility of a dual agent to any principal with respect to confidential information other than price.

2079.22 Nothing in this article precludes a listing agent from also being a selling agent, and the combination of these functions in one agent does not, of itself, make that agent a dual agent.

2079.23 A contract between the principal and agent may be modified or altered to change the agency relationship at any time before the performance of the act which is the object of the agency with the written consent of the parties to the agency relationship.

2079.24 Nothing in this article shall be construed to either diminish the duty of disclosure owed buyers and sellers by agents and their associate licensees, subagents, and employees or to relieve agents and their associate licensees, subagents, and employees from liability for their conduct in connection with acts governed by this article or for any breach of a fiduciary duty or a duty of disclosure.

(AD BACKER)

Agency Confirmation Form

CALIFORNIA ASSOCIATION OF REALTORS®

CONFIRMATION REAL ESTATE AGENCY RELATIONSHIPS
(As required by the Civil Code)

Subject Property Address _____
The following agency relationship(s) is/are hereby confirmed for this transaction:

LISTING AGENT: _____
   is the agent of (check one):
   ☐ the Seller exclusively; or
   ☐ both the Buyer and Seller

SELLING AGENT: _____
   (if not the same as Listing Agent)
   is the agent of (check one):
   ☐ the Buyer exclusively; or
   ☐ the Seller exclusively; or
   ☐ both the Buyer and Seller

I/WE ACKNOWLEDGE RECEIPT OF A COPY OF THIS CONFIRMATION.

Seller _____ Date _____   Buyer _____ Date _____

Seller _____ Date _____   Buyer _____ Date _____

Listing Agent _____ By _____ Date _____
(Please Print)   (Associate Licensee or Broker-Signature)

Selling Agent _____ By _____ Date _____
(Please Print)   (Associate Licensee or Broker-Signature)

A REAL ESTATE BROKER IS QUALIFIED TO ADVISE ON REAL ESTATE. IF YOU DESIRE LEGAL ADVICE, CONSULT YOUR ATTORNEY.

This form is available for use by the entire real estate industry. It is not intended to identify the user as a REALTOR®. REALTOR® is a registered collective membership mark which may be used only by members of the NATIONAL ASSOCIATION OF REALTORS® who subscribe to its Code of Ethics.

The copyright laws of the United States (17 U.S. Code) forbid the unauthorized reproduction of this form by any means, including facsimile or computerized formats. Copyright © 1987-1997, CALIFORNIA ASSOCIATION OF REALTORS®

Published and Distributed by:
REAL ESTATE BUSINESS SERVICES, INC.
a subsidiary of the CALIFORNIA ASSOCIATION OF REALTORS®
525 South Virgil Avenue, Los Angeles, California 90020

OFFICE USE ONLY
Reviewed by Broker
or Designee _____
Date _____

EQUAL HOUSING OPPORTUNITY

FORM AC-6 REVISED 1987

Source: Reprinted with permission, California Association of REALTORS®. Endorsement not implied.

Exercise 6-1   The following case problems illustrate some of the concepts you have just learned. Identify those concepts and answer the questions asked about them.

1. Glenda Golden is an unemancipated minor. Her grandparents, who have moved to Retirement City, transferred title to their ranch to a trust established for Glenda, their only heir. Glenda (who is not sentimental) immediately approaches Helen Silver, leading salesperson for XYZ Realty, about selling the ranch. Helen knows the property will sell quickly. Should Helen take the listing?

2. All of the salespeople at ABC Real Estate work strictly on commission. No deductions are made from their commissions, which they share with ABC. They have no office duties and are billed for any use of secretarial staff,

phones, conference rooms, and so on. They do receive referrals from ABC, which they can accept or reject. Describe the relationship between ABC Real Estate and its salespeople.

3. Salesperson Sam is a good friend of the Patels, who ask Sam to help them find a small office building for their mail-order business. The Patels tell Sam they will pay him $1,000 as a fee if within 30 days he can find a suitable building available for occupancy. The Patels and Sam sign a written agency agreement to that effect. The next day, Salesperson Sam is approached by Jim Nelson, who wishes to sell an office building that meets the Patels' specifications exactly. Can Sam sign an agency agreement on behalf of his broker with Jim Nelson? In other words, can he list the Nelson property for sale? If Sam lists the Nelson property, can he then show that property to the Patels? Should he?

■ HOW AN AGENCY RELATIONSHIP IS CREATED

The agreement between principal and agent that forms the basis of the agency may come about in one of several ways. This section discusses the creation of an agency relationship by

- express agreement;
- ratification; and
- estoppel.

Express Agreement

An **express agreement** is established by an act of the parties that both parties acknowledge. The agreement does not have to be in writing unless

- the law requires a writing or
- the agent is to perform an act on behalf of the principal that requires a writing.

This is known as the **equal dignities rule.** An agency permitting an agent to establish such a contract for the principal must itself be in writing. The **Statute of Frauds** stipulates the kinds of contracts that must be written to be enforceable. Three rules applicable to real estate are summarized below.

- The California Real Estate Law requires that the employment agreement between a real estate broker and salesperson be in writing.

■ The Statute of Frauds dictates that a contract for the sale of real estate or the lease of real estate for longer than one year must be in writing. This means that any agency agreement authorizing those actions must be written.

■ The Statute of Frauds also requires that a contract that authorizes an agent to find a purchaser or lessee (for more than one year) of real estate—a listing agreement—be written.

Ratification

An agency could also be established by a subsequent **ratification** (authorization) by either the principal or the agent of an activity of the other that held out an agency relationship.

■ **FOR EXAMPLE:** Broker Al Teller knows that his neighbor Woody is trying to sell a small lot in the downtown area that is zoned for commercial use. Because of its size, the lot is worth about $5,000. Al offers to find a buyer if he is given a 10 percent commission. Woody does not make a commitment but says he will think it over. The next day at a Chamber of Commerce luncheon, Joe Everett mentions to Al that he is looking for a small lot downtown to open a sandwich shop. Al tells Joe about his neighbor's property, and Joe is enthusiastic. Later that day Al brings Joe to see the lot, and Joe states that he is willing to offer $4,500 for it. Al brings Joe's offer to Woody. If Woody accepts Joe's offer, will he have to pay Al a commission?

If Woody accepts the offer he will ratify an agency agreement with Al, on the terms discussed earlier.

Caution: If an agency agreement for the sale of real estate is formed by ratification, the ratification must be in writing and comply with all of the other formalities that would ordinarily be required for a valid real estate contract.

Estoppel

Another way to form an agency by operation of law is by **estoppel.** Someone may represent that another person is his or her agent, and a third person may rely on that representation and deal with the "agent" accordingly. If so, the "principal" will not be able to evade the agency relationship. An agency created by estoppel is also called an **ostensible** or **implied agency.**

■ **FOR EXAMPLE:** Smith tells Jones that Broker Bob is selling the Smith home. Jones brings an offer to Broker Bob, who prepares a written offer to purchase, listing himself as the broker and stipulating a commission rate. Smith can accept the offer by signing it. If he does so, will an agency be created?

Yes, if Smith accepts the offer, which lists Broker Bob as the selling agent entitled to the sales commission. Smith's acceptance by signing the agreement would satisfy the requirement for a writing.

Exercise 6-2   Richard and Roberta Simpson have decided to sell their condominium in Long Beach. They talk to Broker Bonita, who does a market analysis for them and recommends a selling price in the $380,000 to $400,000 range. Richard and Roberta tell Broker Bonita they will think it over, but if they decide to sell, they will want to ask for $410,000 so that they will have at least $380,000 left after paying the sales commission and closing costs.

a. Is Broker Bonita the Simpsons' agent?

The next day Broker Bonita calls the Simpsons and tells them that an out-of-town buyer, anxious to close a deal on a condominium, is in her office and would like to see their home. The Simpsons allow Broker Bonita to bring the prospective buyer through their condominium.

b. Is Broker Bonita the Simpsons' agent?

The out-of-town buyer makes an offer, through Broker Bonita, of $395,000. The real estate purchase contract, signed by the buyer and Broker Bonita, lists Bonita as selling broker, to receive a 6 percent commission on the sale. After talking it over, the Simpsons decide the offer is a good one, and they accept it by signing the contract.

c. Is Broker Bonita the Simpsons' agent?

■ AGENCY AGREEMENTS

An agreement creating an agency is a form of contract. Chapter 1 included an example of an independent contractor agreement between broker and associate licensee. This section begins with a discussion of general contract requirements. Then, the types of listing agreement are explained. Finally, examples of a listing agreement and a buyer brokerage agreement are discussed.

Requirements for a Valid Contract

A real estate agency agreement must comply with all of the legal requirements necessary to create a valid contract (discussed in detail in the next chapter). The agency agreement must be made by parties who have the capacity to contract.

■ Both parties must consent to the terms of the contract.

■ The contract must have a lawful objective.

■ There must be consideration—that is, an obligation on both parties.

A real estate listing agreement generally requires the broker (the agent) to find a buyer. If a buyer is found, the seller (the principal) will be required to pay the agent a commission based on the sales price agreed on by the seller and buyer.

If all of the above requirements are met, a **bilateral contract** has been formed. Each party to the contract has a separate obligation to perform, as provided in the contract. When only one party has an obligation under the contract, a **unilateral contract** is formed. A seller of real estate, for example, is required to pay a commission if the broker finds a ready, willing, and able buyer. But the broker is not obligated to exert any effort to find such a buyer.

> **Due diligence** implies a good-faith effort to fulfill contract obligations.

For obvious reasons, unilateral contracts to sell real estate are not common in California. Listing agreements as well as other agency agreements (such as the broker-salesperson contract discussed in this chapter) require the agent to use **due diligence** in carrying out the purpose of the contract.

■ **FOR EXAMPLE:**   Salesperson Sam signs a broker-salesperson contract with Broker Bob. Sam is to use due diligence in handling the listings of Broker Bob's company. In return, Salesperson Sam will receive a percentage of the commission on every sale he makes. What is Broker Bob's obligation under the contract? What is Broker Bob's obligation if Salesperson Sam fails to sell, lease, or rent any listings?

Broker Bob will pay Salesperson Sam a share of the commission received on a completed transaction. Broker Bob has no obligation to pay Sam unless Sam actually brings about a sale or other transaction.

The Real Estate Agent's Commission

■ In California, real estate commissions are negotiable.

■ There is no predetermined commission rate.

■ Seller and broker are free to set whatever rate they agree on.

Authority of an Agent

> The role of the agent is defined in the agency agreement.

The **actual authority** of an agent is what is specified in the agency agreement. An agent can be given authority to do any lawful thing short of a personal act that only the principal can perform. A real estate agent, for example, can be authorized to conduct an open house but will not be able to order repair work done on the property. An agent's authority may be broadened in an emergency, if immediate action is required and the principal is unavailable.

A typical real estate listing agreement specifies the obligation of the broker in soliciting offers. Under a broker-salesperson contract, a salesperson is employed by a broker, for compensation or in expectation of compensation, to perform an act the broker could perform.

An agent also has **inherent authority,** depending on the nature of the agent's obligations. There always are activities the agent needs to perform that are not mentioned in the contract, no matter how detailed. In conducting an open house, for instance, a real estate licensee may advertise, distribute flyers in the neighborhood, and post signs at nearby intersections, none of which is likely to be specified in the listing agreement.

An agent may appear to have authority he or she does not actually have. This **apparent authority** places no obligation on the party the agent claims to represent, but it will make the agent liable for his or her representations.

■ **FOR EXAMPLE:** Broker Murphy meets Paula Phillips, who is looking for a house in Broker Murphy's area. Paula describes what she wants, and Broker Murphy realizes that his neighbor's house meets Paula's specifications exactly. Broker Murphy describes the house to Paula, who makes a special trip to town to see it. Broker Murphy did not tell Paula that the house he has described is not for sale. Murphy is unable to persuade his neighbor that she should put her house up for sale, and he cannot reach Paula in time to call off her trip. Does Broker Murphy have any liability to Paula?

At the least, Broker Murphy will be dealing with a disappointed customer, and he may have to pay her expenses in traveling to his area. At the worst, Paula will complain to the Real Estate Commissioner, who may discipline Broker Murphy for his misrepresentation.

Handling deposits. One of a real estate licensee's most important obligations, as expressed in standard listing agreement forms, is to receive a deposit from a prospective buyer. The form of the deposit must be clearly disclosed to the seller, and may influence the seller's decision to accept or reject the offer. For example, the offer may be accompanied by a demand note ("pay to buyer" note) or post-dated check, either of which will be less desirable than an immediately negotiable check.

Deposit funds must be placed in a neutral escrow depository or in a trust fund account set up for the specific purpose of handling client and customer monies. The offer to purchase usually provides that an agent can hold an uncashed check until the offer is accepted, but must deposit it within three business days after acceptance. A check could be held longer if the agent were given written authorization from the principal to do so.

In most cases the deposit is placed in an escrow account if the contract offer is accepted by the seller. If the offer is not accepted, the deposit is returned to the buyer.

Without express authorization in the listing agreement, the real estate agent has no authority of any kind to hold any form of payment on behalf of the seller. If unauthorized by the seller, a real estate broker or salesperson taking possession of a buyer's deposit is acting as the buyer's agent.

Above all, the real estate agent must avoid **commingling** funds. This occurs if the agent places client or customer funds in the agent's personal account. The Real Estate Commissioner can bring disciplinary action for any violation of this rule. The easiest way to avoid problems is to have the deposit check made out to the escrow (closing) agent.

Exercise 6-3

1. Frank Rice, a licensed real estate broker, lists the Marlow house for sale. If Frank becomes ill and is unable to carry out the terms of his agreement, can he delegate that responsibility to another broker?

2. Broker Frank Rice has received an offer on the Marlow house along with a deposit check for $1,000, which his agency agreement authorizes him to receive. It is early evening when Frank receives the check, and he will present the offer to the seller the next morning. What should Frank do with the check in the meantime?

3. Broker Rice has been given a deposit check for $2,000 by a buyer. Broker Rice neglected to tell the buyer to whom to make out the check, and the buyer made the check out to Broker Rice. The buyer's offer is accepted. Broker Rice deposits the check in his personal account and immediately writes out his own check to the title company that will handle the sale. Has Broker Rice acted correctly?

Listing Agreements

An agreement establishing an agency relationship between a real estate property owner and a real estate broker, for the purpose of selling or buying real estate, must be in writing. A written agreement should be signed by both parties as soon as possible after the client has indicated a willingness to list property.

The following are all forms of written real estate listing agreements. Note that all refer only to the real estate broker, because a salesperson (associate licensee) can act only on behalf of a broker. An associate licensee who acts with that authority can perform as the broker would in any of these situations.

Note also that there must be a **definite termination date** in any agreement that makes the listing broker the exclusive agent of the seller. The Business and Professions Code provides for suspension or revocation of a real estate license if the licensee claims, demands, or receives any compensation under any exclusive agreement, if the agreement "does not contain a definite, specified date of final and complete termination."

The following box summarizes the types of listing agreements.

Listing Agreements

Open Listing

Nonexclusive

Commission earned only if listing broker is procuring cause of sale

Exclusive Agency Listing

No other broker authorized

Owner may sell without owing commission

Exclusive Authorization and Right-to-Sell Listing

No other broker authorized

Cooperating broker may be brought in

Commission owed no matter who sells the property

Net Listing

No other broker authorized

Seller receives predetermined amount and broker receives excess

Option Listing

No other broker authorized

Broker has right to purchase the property

Requires full disclosure to seller of broker's profit if option exercised

---

Open listing.   An **open listing,** also called a *nonexclusive listing,* provides for a commission to the broker if the broker is the procuring cause of a sale. It provides no compensation if another broker fulfills that task or if the owner does. To be the procuring cause of a sale, the agent must be the one who brings the parties together or at least must initiate the contact that leads to a sale. Because there is no assurance that the listing broker will actually be the one to sell the listed property, this form of listing generally is avoided in residential transactions. It is often used in industrial and commercial property transactions, however.

Exclusive agency listing. With an **exclusive agency listing,** the property owner cannot list the property with another broker at the same time. The listing broker thus has the protection of getting at least a share of the commission if another broker finds a buyer. The protection is not complete, however, because the owner still may find a buyer without the broker's assistance and thus avoid paying any commission.

Exclusive authorization and right-to-sell listing. The most commonly used form of agreement is the **exclusive authorization and right-to-sell listing.** With this type of listing, the broker is entitled to a commission no matter who sells the property, even if the owner appears to find a buyer without the broker's assistance. The buyer may have found the property address on the Internet, for example, or may have seen a sign on the property and contacted the owner directly. The listing broker is the owner's agent but has the option of being a dual agent. The commission typically is shared with any cooperating broker or subagent who procures a buyer. This type of listing agreement usually contains a **safety clause** that will cover a buyer the broker is working with even after the listing expires, as long as the broker has registered that buyer with the owner. The contract will specify the length of time after the listing expires during which the broker may still be compensated.

The **multiple listing clause** that is a part of the exclusive authorization and right-to-sell listing allows the property to be made available to other brokers participating in the **multiple listing service (MLS).** The requirements of the broker's multiple listing service determine whether the broker must place every listing into the MLS and how members of the MLS will be treated.

■ **FOR EXAMPLE:** Lydia lists her residence for sale. Broker Reina has an MLS clause in her exclusive authorization and right-to-sell listing agreement with Lydia. If Broker Bob, a member of the MLS, finds a buyer, does Broker Reina deserve a commission?

Yes. Broker Reina is entitled to the listing broker's share of the commission.

Net listing. In a **net listing** the broker's compensation is whatever amount the property sells for over a previously agreed (net) amount. If the selling price is equal to or less than the agreed-on net listing amount, the broker receives no compensation.

Before it is accepted by the seller, this kind of agreement requires full disclosure of

- the selling price and
- the amount of compensation the broker will receive.

Without these disclosures the broker and associate licensee may face license revocation or suspension. Because such an arrangement is both inherently risky (the broker may earn little or no compensation) and inherently suspect (a high commission may hint at a too-low net listing price), it should be avoided.

■ **FOR EXAMPLE:**   Brad and Mary Turner are selling a buildable lot in Palm Springs, and want to receive $143,000 after the commission and all costs are paid. Broker Bob signs a net listing agreement with the Turners, specifying that they are to receive $143,000 for their property. What is Broker Bob's commission if the property is sold for $158,000? For $147,000?

$158,000	Selling Price		$147,000	Selling Price
− 143,000	Net Listing Price		− 143,000	Net Listing Price
$ 15,000			$ 4,000	
− 2,000	Costs of Sale		− 2,000	Costs of Sale
$ 13,000	Broker's Commission		$ 2,000	Broker's Commission

Option listing.   An **option listing** gives the broker the right to purchase the property. The broker thus can possibly be both a principal and agent in the same transaction. The broker must be scrupulous in fulfilling all obligations to the principal, particularly in informing the principal of all offers. If the broker exercises the option the principal must be informed of the broker's profit in the transaction and agree to it in writing.

Terms of the Listing

Figure 6.4 is a typical **exclusive authorization and right-to-sell** listing contract. This form was prepared by the California Association of REALTORS®. The features of the contract are explained below. The numbered paragraphs refer to the numbered sections of the contract.

1. Space is provided for the seller's name, the broker's name, the dates the listing will begin and end, the city and county in which the property is located, and a detailed enough description to exclude all other property. The street address may be used, but the full legal description should also be included.
2. The contract should stipulate any fixtures the owner is excluding or personal property (such as furniture) the owner is including in the sale.
3. Listing price is indicated in words and numbers. The seller's preferred purchase terms also can be indicated.
4. **The commission rate on the sale of a single-family residence is negotiable.** This fact is required by law to appear in the listing agreement for property of one to four residential units. Section 3A2 is the broker's "safety clause." The parties agree to a reasonable time after the expiration of the listing agreement during which the seller will be obliged to pay a commission if anyone brought to the seller by the broker (or a cooperating broker) during

FIGURE 6.4

Exclusive Authorization and Right-to-Sell Listing

CALIFORNIA ASSOCIATION OF REALTORS®

RESIDENTIAL LISTING AGREEMENT
(Exclusive Authorization and Right to Sell)
(C.A.R. Form LA, Revised 10/02)

1. EXCLUSIVE RIGHT TO SELL: _____ ("Seller")
hereby employs and grants _____ ("Broker")
beginning (date) _____ and ending at 11:59 P.M. on (date) _____ ("Listing Period")
the exclusive and irrevocable right to sell or exchange the real property in the City of _____,
County of _____, California, described as: _____
_____ ("Property").

2. ITEMS EXCLUDED AND INCLUDED: Unless otherwise specified in a real estate purchase agreement, all fixtures and fittings that are attached to the Property are included, and personal property items are excluded, from the purchase price.
ADDITIONAL ITEMS EXCLUDED: _____.
ADDITIONAL ITEMS INCLUDED: _____.
Seller intends that the above items be excluded or included in offering the Property for sale, but understands that: **(i)** the purchase agreement supersedes any intention expressed above and will ultimately determine which items are excluded and included in the sale; and **(ii)** Broker is not responsible for and does not guarantee that the above exclusions and/or inclusions will be in the purchase agreement.

3. LISTING PRICE AND TERMS:
   A. The listing price shall be: _____
   _____ Dollars ($ _____).
   B. Additional Terms: _____
   _____

4. COMPENSATION TO BROKER:
   Notice: The amount or rate of real estate commissions is not fixed by law. They are set by each Broker individually and may be negotiable between Seller and Broker (real estate commissions include all compensation and fees to Broker).
   A. Seller agrees to pay to Broker as compensation for services irrespective of agency relationship(s), either ☐ _____ percent of the listing price (or if a purchase agreement is entered into, of the purchase price), or ☐ $ _____,
   AND _____, as follows:
      (1) If Broker, Seller, cooperating broker, or any other person procures a buyer(s) who offers to purchase the Property on the above price and terms, or on any price and terms acceptable to Seller during the Listing Period, or any extension.
      (2) If Seller, within _____ calendar days **(a)** after the end of the Listing Period or any extension, or **(b)** after any cancellation of this Agreement, unless otherwise agreed, enters into a contract to sell, convey, lease or otherwise transfer the Property to anyone ("Prospective Buyer") or that person's related entity: **(i)** who physically entered and was shown the Property during the Listing Period or any extension by Broker or a cooperating broker; or **(ii)** for whom Broker or any cooperating broker submitted to Seller a signed, written offer to acquire, lease, exchange or obtain an option on the Property. Seller, however, shall have no obligation to Broker under paragraph 4A(2) unless, not later than **3 calendar days** after the end of the Listing Period or any extension or cancellation, Broker has given Seller a written notice of the names of such Prospective Buyers.
      (3) If, without Broker's prior written consent, the Property is withdrawn from sale, conveyed, leased, rented, otherwise transferred, or made unmarketable by a voluntary act of Seller during the Listing Period, or any extension.
   B. If completion of the sale is prevented by a party to the transaction other than Seller, then compensation due under paragraph 4A shall be payable only if and when Seller collects damages by suit, arbitration, settlement or otherwise, and then in an amount equal to the lesser of one-half of the damages recovered or the above compensation, after first deducting title and escrow expenses and the expenses of collection, if any.
   C. In addition, Seller agrees to pay Broker: _____.
   D. **(1)** Broker is authorized to cooperate with and compensate brokers participating through the multiple listing service(s) ("MLS"): **(i)** in any manner; **OR (ii)** (if checked) by offering MLS brokers: either ☐ _____ percent of the purchase price, or ☐ $ _____
      (2) Broker is authorized to cooperate with and compensate brokers operating outside the MLS in any manner.
   E. Seller hereby irrevocably assigns to Broker the above compensation from Seller's funds and proceeds in escrow. Broker may submit this agreement, as instructions to compensate Broker pursuant to paragraph 4A, to any escrow regarding the Property involving Seller and a buyer, Prospective Buyer or other transferee.
   F. **(1)** Seller represents that Seller has not previously entered into a listing agreement with another broker regarding the Property, unless specified as follows: _____.
      (2) Seller warrants that Seller has no obligation to pay compensation to any other broker regarding the Property unless the Property is transferred to any of the following individuals or entities: _____
      _____
      (3) If the Property is sold to anyone listed above during the time Seller is obligated to compensate another broker: **(i)** Broker is not entitled to compensation under this agreement; and **(ii)** Broker is not obligated to represent Seller in such transaction.

Seller acknowledges receipt of a copy of this page.
Seller's Initials (_____)(_____)

Reviewed by _____ Date _____

EQUAL HOUSING OPPORTUNITY

LA REVISED 10/02 (PAGE 1 OF 3)   Print Date

RESIDENTIAL LISTING AGREEMENT-EXCLUSIVE (LA PAGE 1 OF 3)

Source: Reprinted with permission, California Association of REALTORS®. Endorsement not implied.

FIGURE 6.4

Exclusive Authorization and Right-to-Sell Listing (Continued)

Property Address: _____   Date: _____

5. **OWNERSHIP, TITLE AND AUTHORITY:** Seller warrants that: **(i)** Seller is the owner of the Property; **(ii)** no other persons or entities have title to the Property; and **(iii)** Seller has the authority to both execute this agreement and sell the Property. Exceptions to ownership, title and authority are as follows: _____.

6. **MULTIPLE LISTING SERVICE:** Information about this listing will (or ☐ will not) be provided to the MLS of Broker's selection. All terms of the transaction, including financing, if applicable, will be provided to the selected MLS for publication, dissemination and use by persons and entities on terms approved by the MLS. Seller authorizes Broker to comply with all applicable MLS rules. MLS rules allow MLS data to be made available by the MLS to additional Internet sites unless Broker gives the MLS instructions to the contrary.

7. **SELLER REPRESENTATIONS:** Seller represents that, unless otherwise specified in writing, Seller is unaware of: **(i)** any Notice of Default recorded against the Property; **(ii)** any delinquent amounts due under any loan secured by, or other obligation affecting, the Property; **(iii)** any bankruptcy, insolvency or similar proceeding affecting the Property; **(iv)** any litigation, arbitration, administrative action, government investigation or other pending or threatened action that affects or may affect the Property or Seller's ability to transfer it; and **(v)** any current, pending or proposed special assessments affecting the Property. Seller shall promptly notify Broker in writing if Seller becomes aware of any of these items during the Listing Period or any extension thereof.

8. **BROKER'S AND SELLER'S DUTIES:** Broker agrees to exercise reasonable effort and due diligence to achieve the purposes of this agreement. Unless Seller gives Broker written instructions to the contrary, Broker is authorized to order reports and disclosures as appropriate or necessary and advertise and market the Property by any method and in any medium selected by Broker, including MLS and the Internet, and, to the extent permitted by these media, control the dissemination of the information submitted to any medium. Seller agrees to consider offers presented by Broker, and to act in good faith to accomplish the sale of the Property by, among other things, making the Property available for showing at reasonable times and referring to Broker all inquiries of any party interested in the Property. Seller is responsible for determining at what price to list and sell the Property. **Seller further agrees to indemnify, defend and hold Broker harmless from all claims, disputes, litigation, judgments and attorney fees arising from any incorrect information supplied by Seller, or from any material facts that Seller knows but fails to disclose.**

9. **DEPOSIT:** Broker is authorized to accept and hold on Seller's behalf any deposits to be applied toward the purchase price.

10. **AGENCY RELATIONSHIPS:**
    A. **Disclosure:** If the Property includes residential property with one-to-four dwelling units, Seller shall receive a "Disclosure Regarding Agency Relationships" form prior to entering into this agreement.
    B. **Seller Representation:** Broker shall represent Seller in any resulting transaction, except as specified in paragraph 4F.
    C. **Possible Dual Agency With Buyer:** Depending upon the circumstances, it may be necessary or appropriate for Broker to act as an agent for both Seller and buyer, exchange party, or one or more additional parties ("Buyer"). Broker shall, as soon as practicable, disclose to Seller any election to act as a dual agent representing both Seller and Buyer. If a Buyer is procured directly by Broker or an associate licensee in Broker's firm, Seller hereby consents to Broker acting as a dual agent for Seller and such Buyer. In the event of an exchange, Seller hereby consents to Broker collecting compensation from additional parties for services rendered, provided there is disclosure to all parties of such agency and compensation. Seller understands and agrees that: **(i)** Broker, without the prior written consent of Seller, will not disclose to Buyer that Seller is willing to sell the Property at a price less than the listing price; **(ii)** Broker, without the prior written consent of Buyer, will not disclose to Seller that Buyer is willing to pay a price greater than the offered price; and **(iii)** except for (i) and (ii) above, a dual agent is obligated to disclose known facts materially affecting the value or desirability of the Property to both parties.
    D. **Other Sellers:** Seller understands that Broker may have or obtain listings on other properties, and that potential buyers may consider, make offers on, or purchase through Broker, property the same as or similar to Seller's Property. Seller consents to Broker's representation of sellers and buyers of other properties before, during and after the end of this agreement.
    E. **Confirmation:** If the Property includes residential property with one-to-four dwelling units, Broker shall confirm the agency relationship described above, or as modified, in writing, prior to or concurrent with Seller's execution of a purchase agreement.

11. **SECURITY AND INSURANCE:** Broker is not responsible for loss of or damage to personal or real property, or person, whether attributable to use of a keysafe/lockbox, a showing of the Property, or otherwise. Third parties, including, but not limited to, appraisers, inspectors, brokers and prospective buyers, may have access to, and take videos and photographs of, the interior of the Property. Seller agrees: **(i)** to take reasonable precautions to safeguard and protect valuables that might be accessible during showings of the Property; and **(ii)** to obtain insurance to protect against these risks. Broker does not maintain insurance to protect Seller.

12. **KEYSAFE/LOCKBOX:** A keysafe/lockbox is designed to hold a key to the Property to permit access to the Property by Broker, cooperating brokers, MLS participants, their authorized licensees and representatives, authorized inspectors, and accompanied prospective buyers. Broker, cooperating brokers, MLS and Associations/Boards of REALTORS® are **not** insurers against injury, theft, loss, vandalism or damage attributed to the use of a keysafe/lockbox. Seller does (or if checked ☐ does not) authorize Broker to install a keysafe/lockbox. If Seller does not occupy the Property, Seller shall be responsible for obtaining occupant(s)' written permission for use of a keysafe/lockbox.

13. **SIGN:** Seller does (or if checked ☐ does not) authorize Broker to install a FOR SALE/SOLD sign on the Property.

14. **EQUAL HOUSING OPPORTUNITY:** The Property is offered in compliance with federal, state and local anti-discrimination laws.

15. **ATTORNEY FEES:** In any action, proceeding or arbitration between Seller and Broker regarding the obligation to pay compensation under this agreement, the prevailing Seller or Broker shall be entitled to reasonable attorney fees and costs from the non-prevailing Seller or Broker, except as provided in paragraph 19A.

16. **ADDITIONAL TERMS:** _____
    _____
    _____

17. **MANAGEMENT APPROVAL:** If an associate licensee in Broker's office (salesperson or broker-associate) enters into this agreement on Broker's behalf, and Broker or Manager does not approve of its terms, Broker or Manager has the right to cancel this agreement, in writing, within 5 days after its execution.

18. **SUCCESSORS AND ASSIGNS:** This agreement shall be binding upon Seller and Seller's successors and assigns.

Seller acknowledges receipt of a copy of this page.
Seller's Initials (_____)(_____)

Copyright © 1991-2002, CALIFORNIA ASSOCIATION OF REALTORS®, INC.

LA REVISED 10/02 (PAGE 2 OF 3)

| Reviewed by _____ Date _____ |

EQUAL HOUSING OPPORTUNITY

RESIDENTIAL LISTING AGREEMENT-EXCLUSIVE (LA PAGE 2 OF 3)

FIGURE 6.4

Exclusive Authorization and Right-to-Sell Listing (Continued)

Property Address: _____ Date: _____

19. DISPUTE RESOLUTION:

A. MEDIATION: Seller and Broker agree to mediate any dispute or claim arising between them out of this agreement, or any resulting transaction, before resorting to arbitration or court action, subject to paragraph 19B(2) below. Paragraph 19B(2) below applies whether or not the arbitration provision is initialed. Mediation fees, if any, shall be divided equally among the parties involved. If, for any dispute or claim to which this paragraph applies, any party commences an action without first attempting to resolve the matter through mediation, or refuses to mediate after a request has been made, then that party shall not be entitled to recover attorney fees, even if they would otherwise be available to that party in any such action. THIS MEDIATION PROVISION APPLIES WHETHER OR NOT THE ARBITRATION PROVISION IS INITIALED.

B. ARBITRATION OF DISPUTES: (1) Seller and Broker agree that any dispute or claim in Law or equity arising between them regarding the obligation to pay compensation under this agreement, which is not settled through mediation, shall be decided by neutral, binding arbitration, including and subject to paragraph 19B(2) below. The arbitrator shall be a retired judge or justice, or an attorney with at least 5 years of residential real estate law experience, unless the parties mutually agree to a different arbitrator, who shall render an award in accordance with substantive California Law. The parties shall have the right to discovery in accordance with Code of Civil Procedure §1283.05. In all other respects, the arbitration shall be conducted in accordance with Title 9 of Part III of the California Code of Civil Procedure. Judgment upon the award of the arbitrator(s) may be entered in any court having jurisdiction. Interpretation of this agreement to arbitrate shall be governed by the Federal Arbitration Act.
(2) EXCLUSIONS FROM MEDIATION AND ARBITRATION: The following matters are excluded from mediation and arbitration hereunder: **(i)** a judicial or non-judicial foreclosure or other action or proceeding to enforce a deed of trust, mortgage, or installment land sale contract as defined in Civil Code §2985; **(ii)** an unlawful detainer action; **(iii)** the filing or enforcement of a mechanic's lien; and **(iv)** any matter that is within the jurisdiction of a probate, small claims, or bankruptcy court. The filing of a court action to enable the recording of a notice of pending action, for order of attachment, receivership, injunction, or other provisional remedies, shall not constitute a waiver of the mediation and arbitration provisions.

"NOTICE: BY INITIALING IN THE SPACE BELOW YOU ARE AGREEING TO HAVE ANY DISPUTE ARISING OUT OF THE MATTERS INCLUDED IN THE 'ARBITRATION OF DISPUTES' PROVISION DECIDED BY NEUTRAL ARBITRATION AS PROVIDED BY CALIFORNIA LAW AND YOU ARE GIVING UP ANY RIGHTS YOU MIGHT POSSESS TO HAVE THE DISPUTE LITIGATED IN A COURT OR JURY TRIAL. BY INITIALING IN THE SPACE BELOW YOU ARE GIVING UP YOUR JUDICIAL RIGHTS TO DISCOVERY AND APPEAL, UNLESS THOSE RIGHTS ARE SPECIFICALLY INCLUDED IN THE 'ARBITRATION OF DISPUTES' PROVISION. IF YOU REFUSE TO SUBMIT TO ARBITRATION AFTER AGREEING TO THIS PROVISION, YOU MAY BE COMPELLED TO ARBITRATE UNDER THE AUTHORITY OF THE CALIFORNIA CODE OF CIVIL PROCEDURE. YOUR AGREEMENT TO THIS ARBITRATION PROVISION IS VOLUNTARY."

"WE HAVE READ AND UNDERSTAND THE FOREGOING AND AGREE TO SUBMIT DISPUTES ARISING OUT OF THE MATTERS INCLUDED IN THE 'ARBITRATION OF DISPUTES' PROVISION TO NEUTRAL ARBITRATION."

| Seller's Initials _____/_____ | Broker's Initials _____/_____ |

20. ENTIRE CONTRACT: All prior discussions, negotiations and agreements between the parties concerning the subject matter of this agreement are superseded by this agreement, which constitutes the entire contract and a complete and exclusive expression of their agreement, and may not be contradicted by evidence of any prior agreement or contemporaneous oral agreement. If any provision of this agreement is held to be ineffective or invalid, the remaining provisions will nevertheless be given full force and effect. This agreement and any supplement, addendum or modification, including any photocopy or facsimile, may be executed in counterparts.

By signing below, Seller acknowledges that Seller has read, understands, accepts and has received a copy of this agreement.

Seller _____ Date _____
Address _____ City _____ State _____ Zip _____
Telephone _____ Fax _____ E-mail _____

Seller _____ Date _____
Address _____ City _____ State _____ Zip _____
Telephone _____ Fax _____ E-mail _____

Real Estate Broker (Firm) _____
By (Agent) _____ Date _____
Address _____ City _____ State _____ Zip _____
Telephone _____ Fax _____ E-mail _____

SURE TRAC
The System for Success™
LA REVISED 10/02 (PAGE 3 OF 3)

Published by the
California Association of REALTORS®

Reviewed by _____ Date _____

EQUAL HOUSING OPPORTUNITY

RESIDENTIAL LISTING AGREEMENT-EXCLUSIVE (LA PAGE 3 OF 3)

Source: Reprinted with permission, California Association of REALTORS®. Endorsement not implied.

the listing term buys the property. The broker should give the names of such prospective buyers to the seller on termination of the contract. This provision would not apply if the seller, in good faith, signed a new listing agreement with a different broker.

Other clauses provide for the broker's compensation in the event of a property exchange, the seller's default, or the default of anyone other than the seller. In Section 4D, the broker is authorized to cooperate with other brokers through the MLS or otherwise. In Section 4E, the seller agrees to pay the broker's compensation through escrow.

5. The seller must indicate that he or she actually owns the property and any other ownership interest, if applicable.

6. The broker may be authorized to utilize the MLS.

7. Seller knows of no loan delinquency, bankruptcy, or other legal action that would affect the property or its transfer.

8. The broker promises to use reasonable effort and act with due diligence to find a buyer for the listed property. The broker is authorized to advertise and market the property. The seller promises to consider all offers presented by the broker and to act in good faith. The seller agrees to indemnify the broker (including paying the broker's legal fees) in the event of a dispute stemming from any incorrect information supplied by the seller.

9. The broker is authorized to accept a buyer's deposit.

10. The seller will receive an agency disclosure form. The broker will act as agent of the seller. Any other agency relationship requires agreement of seller and broker. Seller agrees that broker can act as a dual agent by procuring a buyer.

11. It is the seller's responsibility to insure and protect household belongings while the property is listed for sale.

12. The seller may or may not allow the use of a lockbox attached outside the house (with the house key inside, accessible to brokers).

13. The seller may or may not allow a For Sale or Sold sign on the property.

14. An antidiscrimination clause is evidence of the parties' intent to obey all applicable laws.

15. Both broker and seller are made aware that if a legal action ensues, reasonable attorney's fees and other costs will be awarded to the successful party.

16. Any other items not already covered can be mentioned here, such as repairs to be made by the seller. This is also the place to mention any potential buyers the seller has already contacted with whom the seller wishes to deal without paying the broker a commission.

17. If an associate licensee signs the contract on behalf of the broker, the broker or the broker's manager has a five-day right of cancellation.

18. The contract can be assigned.

19. The broker and seller may agree to submit any differences of opinion to mediation before going through a formal arbitration process or beginning

legal action in court. The broker and seller may agree to submit their differences, if any, to binding arbitration. If they do, neither will have the right to sue the other party in a court proceeding, except as the clause specifies.

20. The agreement incorporates any prior understanding of the broker and seller, whether written or oral.

The date of signing is given, and the seller(s) signs. If an owner is married—even if the real estate is the seller's separate property—the other spouse's signature should also be obtained, either directly or through a power of attorney. The correct address of the seller(s) and other contact information are important as well.

The broker signs and dates the contract. If an associate licensee initiates the contract, the associate signs his or her name next to the name of the broker or firm. Address, telephone, fax, and e-mail of the firm should be provided.

In completing a listing agreement, the real estate agent will be guiding the property owner through a legally binding contract. Yet the agent is not permitted to give legal advice. If the owner is confused about the meaning or ramifications of any of the contract terms, the agent should recommend in writing that the owner consult an attorney before signing.

Buyer-Broker Agreements

The real estate broker does not always represent the property seller. Increasingly, property buyers are recognizing the important advantages that can be obtained by having their own broker represent them in a transaction. As with other real estate contracts, the terms under which the buyer's broker will function must be specified in writing. Figure 6.5 is a typical form of buyer-broker agreement.

Note the following contract clauses:

- Clause 2 specifies the type of property the buyer is seeking.
- Clause 6 states the limitations on the broker in a possible dual agency representation.
- Clause 7 provides for the buyer's acceptance or rejection of the broker's representation of other buyers seeking the same or similar properties.
- Clause 8 stipulates the type of compensation to be paid to the broker. This could be a fee ("acquisition fee") to be paid to the broker, based on a stated amount or percentage of the purchase price of the property. Provision is made for compensating the broker in the event that the buyer takes an option to buy property. The terms under which compensation is to be paid are stated, as is the fact that any compensation that the buyer's broker collects from the seller through the listing broker's fee arrangement is to be credited against the fee due from the buyer. The buyer-broker agreement also includes the mandated notice that real estate commissions are negotiable.

FIGURE 6.5

Exclusive Right to Represent Buyer

FIGURE 6.5

Exclusive Right to Represent Buyer (Continued)

Buyer: _____   Date: _____

B. Buyer acknowledges and agrees that Broker: **(i)** does not decide what price Buyer should pay or Seller should accept; **(ii)** does not guarantee the condition of the Property; **(iii)** does not guarantee the performance, adequacy or completeness of Inspections, services, products or repairs provided or made by Seller or others to Buyer or Seller; **(iv)** shall not be responsible for identifying defects that are not known to Broker and either **(a)** are not visually observable in reasonably accessible areas of the Property or **(b)** are in common areas; **(v)** shall not be responsible for identifying the location of boundary lines or other items affecting title; **(vi)** shall not be responsible for verifying square footage, representations of others or information contained in Inspection reports; **(vii)** shall not be responsible for providing legal or tax advice regarding any aspect of a transaction entered into by Buyer in the course of this representation; and **(viii)** shall not be responsible for providing other advice or information that exceeds the knowledge, education and experience required to perform real estate licensed activities. Buyer agrees to seek legal, tax, insurance, title and other desired assistance from appropriate professionals.

C. Broker owes no duty to inspect for common environmental hazards, earthquake weaknesses, or geologic and seismic hazards. If Buyer receives the booklets titled "Environmental Hazards: A Guide for Homeowners, Buyers,Landlords and Tenants," "The Homeowner's Guide to Earthquake Safety," or "The Commercial Property Owner's Guide to Earthquake Safety," the booklets are deemed adequate to inform Buyer regarding the information contained in the booklets and, other than as specified in 3B above, Broker is not required to provide Buyer with additional information about the matters described in the booklets.

5. BUYER OBLIGATIONS:

A. Buyer agrees to timely view and consider properties selected by Broker and to negotiate in good faith to acquire a property. Buyer further agrees to act in good faith toward the completion of any Property Contract entered into in furtherance of this Agreement. Within **5 (or ☐ _____) calendar days** from the execution of this Agreement, Buyer shall provide relevant personal and financial information to Broker to assure Buyer's ability to acquire Property. If Buyer fails to provide such information, or if Buyer does not qualify financially to acquire Property, then Broker may cancel this Agreement in writing. Buyer has an affirmative duty to take steps to protect him/herself, including discovery of the legal, practical and technical implications of discovered or disclosed facts, and investigation of information and facts which are known to Buyer or are within the diligent attention and observation of Buyer. Buyer is obligated to and agrees to read all documents provided to Buyer. Buyer agrees to seek desired assistance from appropriate professionals, selected by Buyer, such as those referenced in the attached Buyer's Inspection Advisory.

B. Buyer shall notify Broker in writing of any material issue to Buyer, such as, but not limited to, Buyer requests for information on, or concerns regarding, any particular area of interest or importance to Buyer ("Material Consideration").

C. **Buyer agrees to (i) indemnify, defend and hold Broker harmless from all claims, disputes, litigation, judgments, costs and attorney fees arising from any incorrect information supplied by Buyer, or from any Material Consideration that Buyer fails to disclose in writing to Broker and (ii) pay for reports, Inspections and meetings arranged by Broker on Buyer's behalf.**

D. Buyer is advised to read the attached Buyer's Inspection Advisory for a list of items and other concerns that typically warrant Inspections or investigation by Buyer or other professionals.

6. TIME TO BRING LEGAL ACTION: Legal action for breach of this Agreement, or any obligation arising therefrom, shall be brought no more than two years from the expiration of the Representation Period or the date such cause of action arises, whichever occurs first.

7. OTHER TERMS AND CONDITIONS, including ATTACHED SUPPLEMENTS: ☐ Buyer's Inspection Advisory (C.A.R. Form BIA-11)
_____
_____

8. ENTIRE CONTRACT: All understandings between the parties are incorporated in this Agreement. Its terms are intended by the parties as a final, complete and exclusive expression of their agreement with respect to its subject matter, and may not be contradicted by evidence of any prior agreement or contemporaneous oral agreement. This Agreement may not be extended, amended, modified, altered or changed, except in writing signed by Buyer and Broker. In the event that any provision of this Agreement is held to be ineffective or invalid, the remaining provisions will nevertheless be given full force and effect. This Agreement and any supplement, addendum or modification, including any copy, whether by copier, facsimile, NCR or electronic, may be signed in two or more counterparts, all of which shall constitute one and the same writing.

Buyer acknowledges that Buyer has read, understands, accepts and has received a copy of this Agreement.

Buyer _____   Date _____
Address _____ City _____ State _____ Zip _____
Telephone _____ Fax _____ E-mail _____

Buyer _____   Date _____
Address _____ City _____ State _____ Zip _____
Telephone _____ Fax _____ E-mail _____

Real Estate Broker (Firm) _____
By (Agent) _____   Date _____
Address _____ City _____ State _____ Zip _____
Telephone _____ Fax _____ E-mail _____

THIS FORM HAS BEEN APPROVED BY THE CALIFORNIA ASSOCIATION OF REALTORS® (C.A.R.). NO REPRESENTATION IS MADE AS TO THE LEGAL VALIDITY OR ADEQUACY OF ANY PROVISION IN ANY SPECIFIC TRANSACTION. A REAL ESTATE BROKER IS THE PERSON QUALIFIED TO ADVISE ON REAL ESTATE TRANSACTIONS. IF YOU DESIRE LEGAL OR TAX ADVICE, CONSULT AN APPROPRIATE PROFESSIONAL.
This form is available for use by the entire real estate industry. It is not intended to identify the user as a REALTOR®. REALTOR® is a registered collective membership mark which may be used only by members of the NATIONAL ASSOCIATION OF REALTORS® who subscribe to its Code of Ethics.

Published and Distributed by:
R E B S I N C REAL ESTATE BUSINESS SERVICES, INC.
a subsidiary of the CALIFORNIA ASSOCIATION OF REALTORS®
525 South Virgil Avenue, Los Angeles, California 90020

Reviewed by _____
Broker or Designee _____ Date _____

EQUAL HOUSING OPPORTUNITY

BR-11 REVISED 4/02 (PAGE 2 OF 2) Print Date
BUYER BROKER REPRESENTATION AGREEMENT (BR-11 PAGE 2 OF 2)

Source: Reprinted with permission, California Association of REALTORS®. Endorsement not implied.

■ RIGHTS AND DUTIES OF PRINCIPAL AND AGENT

Both parties to an agency agreement have obligations. An obligation owed by one party is a corresponding right of the other party. The agent has the obligation to use **due diligence** in fulfilling the purpose of the agency agreement. This obligation may also may be expressed as the right of the principal to have the agent use such diligence. This section examines the duties each owes the other and the consequences of any failure by either to perform those duties.

Duties of Agent to Principal

One of the most important duties the agent owes the principal is the duty of **loyalty.** The agent in a real estate transaction acts as a **fiduciary,** a person to whom property or the power to act is entrusted on behalf of someone else. The agent's role in the transaction is to consider the interests of the principal first and foremost.

> The real estate agent owes the principal the duties of a fiduciary and
> ■ loyalty,
> ■ good faith,
> ■ honesty,
> ■ obedience, and
> ■ full disclosure.

The agent's fulfillment of the duties of **good faith and honesty** will allow the agent to fairly represent the principal's interests.

To the extent required by their agreement, the agent owes the principal the duty of **obedience** in relevant matters. The principal cannot obstruct the agent's activities but can direct the agent generally. For example, a real estate agent cannot insist on showing a seller's property to prospective buyers at any time, but must respect the seller's wishes. The seller, on the other hand, should comply with reasonable requests to show the property.

The agent must make **full disclosure** of all material facts concerning the transaction to the principal. This is a sensitive area for a real estate broker representing the seller in a transaction. A listing agent who brings a buyer to a seller should have qualified the buyer financially and discussed the buyer's purpose in buying real estate. Even if the listing agent legally represents only the seller, the agent inevitably is made aware of information that is useful to the seller.

For example, the agent may have learned that the buyer is an out-of-state transferee with only a limited time in which to find a house. In such a case, the seller may have a stronger bargaining position. By law, the agent must disclose such information to the client, the seller. Most real estate licensees walk a fine line in balancing their obligations to their principal against their desire to gain the confidence of the person they want to bring to a successful transaction.

The agent also must disclose to the principal any possible **conflict of interest,** such as dual representation. The agent must disclose to the principal any relationship the agent has to another party to the transaction, even if the agent or other party will derive no benefit from the relationship. At times even the appearance of impropriety is sufficient to require the agent to act. Of course, the agent can make no **secret profit** in a transaction.

■ **FOR EXAMPLE:**   XYZ Realty has listed the Rey house for sale. Mabel Perkins, an aunt of the broker who owns XYZ Realty, wants to make an offer on the Rey house. Can XYZ take the offer to the Reys?

Yes, but the relationship of Mabel Perkins to the broker must be disclosed to the sellers first, *regardless of the terms of the offer.*

The agent owes the principal the duty of **reasonable care and skill** in carrying out the tasks dictated by the agency agreement. This is true even if the relationship is gratuitous (one in which the agent receives no compensation). After the agent has performed services on behalf of the principal, whether or not for compensation, the agent owes the principal the duties of a fiduciary.

> The agent's job is to find a ready, willing, and able buyer.

The agent's primary goal in a real estate listing agreement is to find a **ready, willing, and able buyer** for the property being offered for sale. When the agent has secured an offer that is at the seller's original price and terms, and if the buyer has the cash necessary to complete the purchase or the buyer can qualify for financing by a closing date within the seller's time frame, the agent's part of the agreement has been completed. If the prospective buyer's offer and/or suggested terms are different from the owner's original stipulation, the owner can accept the different terms or make a counteroffer. When an agreement is reached, the licensee's contractual obligations have been met.

■ **FOR EXAMPLE:**   Sally and Tom Benson have listed their house at Lake Shastina for sale with Broker Luis. The asking price is $165,000, and the listing is for three months. Within two months Broker Luis procures an offer from Mary Ivers for $163,750. All other terms are as stipulated by the Bensons, and Broker Luis has determined that Ms. Ivers should qualify for the necessary loan. The Bensons accept the offer, and the sale is carried out. Has Broker Luis earned his commission?

Yes. Broker Luis has produced a ready, willing, and able buyer who made an offer that was acceptable to his clients.

Duties of Subagent to Principal and Agent

A **subagent** owes to the principal the *same* duties as the agent, and also owes those duties to the agent. The agent bears the responsibility of taking reasonable steps to ensure that the subagent acts with the required loyalty and care. Otherwise, the agent may be liable for any improper act, or failure to act, of the subagent. If the subagency was authorized by the principal, the principal shares that liability.

Duties of Principal to Agent

If the agent's contract obligations have been fulfilled, the agent is entitled to the agreed-on **compensation.** The agent must be the **procuring cause** of the sale, lease, rental, or other transaction. In other words, the agent must be the person who initiated the contact that brought the third party to the principal.

In a listing for sale, the seller usually agrees to pay the broker a commission that is a percentage of the actual sales price. In a lease or rental agreement, the agent's compensation may be a percentage of the lease or rental value, or a flat fee.

When Is a Commission Earned?

In a real estate listing agreement, the commission is earned when the real estate broker finds a buyer who is ready, willing, and able to purchase the subject property on the seller's original terms, or when the seller accepts a purchase offer at an agreed-on price and/or terms.

The principal can revoke the agency agreement but is liable for the expenses the agent has incurred and may be liable for the full amount of the agent's commission. In an open listing, if the seller accepts an offer that was not secured by the listing broker, the seller need not compensate the listing broker. If more than one acceptable buyer is brought to the seller, the listing broker will receive a commission only if his or her buyer is the first in time.

■ **FOR EXAMPLE:**   XYZ Realty has an open listing agreement with the Carters. XYZ brings to the Carters a buyer who will pay their asking price and is otherwise qualified financially. While the Carters are considering the offer, a good friend offers to buy their property for $3,000 less than the asking price. Because they will come out ahead if they do not have to pay a sales commission, the Carters accept the offer. Do the Carters owe the XYZ broker a commission?

Yes, because the first acceptable offer came through XYZ Realty. If the offer through XYZ was not at the sellers' original terms, they would be free to accept their friend's offer without obligation to pay a sales commission.

With the protection offered by an exclusive authorization and right-to-sell listing agreement, the listing broker will receive a commission regardless of who produces the buyer. A rare exception to this general rule may occur if the seller identifies a prospective buyer in the listing agreement as someone to whom the property may be sold without payment of compensation to the broker, and that person buys the property.

If a different broker sells the property, the listing broker and selling broker usually share the commission according to the terms of the purchase agreement. The commission usually is paid through escrow, an efficient and usually the safest way to distribute the commission proceeds.

A principal owes an agent a **duty of care** in that the principal may not interfere with the agent's **prospective economic advantage.** This legal term means that the principal may not sabotage the agent's business. If a seller rejects a buyer brought by a broker, the seller may not turn around and make his or her own deal with that buyer, even if the broker and seller have an open listing agreement. If the broker is the procuring cause of a transaction, the broker has earned the agreed-upon compensation.

Duties to Third Persons

A real estate agent owes to a third person a duty of **full disclosure of material facts** regarding the property that is the subject matter of their dealings. The agent bears this responsibility independent of any instruction received from the property owner. If the property owner tells the agent not to reveal certain defects, such as termite damage, the agent must inform the principal that the agent cannot hide such information. To do otherwise would make the agent liable for money damages, and place the agent's license in jeopardy.

Material Facts

A material fact can be anything that would affect the value or desirability of the subject property. Because this is such a broad definition, the legislature and courts have created their own interpretations of just what the prospective purchaser needs to know. Conspicuous physical defects must be revealed, certainly. But other factors may not be as easy to understand. It is not necessary, for instance, to reveal a death on the premises that occurred more than three years before an offer to purchase or lease is made. Nevertheless, the agent handling such a property may not make a misrepresentation if asked a direct question by the buyer. But the agent need not reveal that an occupant of the property was afflicted with, or died from, Acquired Immune Deficiency Syndrome (AIDS). This provision appears in Civil Code Section 1710.2.

Easton v. Strassburger. The decision in the California case of *Easton v. Strassburger* (1984) expanded the broker's duty of disclosure to third persons. The court held that a real estate broker has an affirmative duty to conduct a reasonably competent and diligent inspection of residential property and to disclose to prospective purchasers all facts revealed by the investigation that materially affect the value or desirability of the property. This duty was subsequently recognized by the California legislature and made a part of the Civil Code, starting at Section 2079. It applies to residential property of one to four units.

The *Easton* case involved a house built on landfill. That fact, and the fact that one of the broker's agents noticed an "uneven floor," should have acted as "red flags," warranting further investigation and disclosure to the buyer. If there is a substantial property defect the agent could have discovered by a thorough inspection of the property, even if the agent failed to notice the defect, the agent may be liable to a buyer for any resulting damages.

Easton renewed interest not only in the broker's duties to prospective purchasers of residential property but also in the seller's duties to prospective purchasers. The seller must disclose any material fact that affects the value or desirability of the property, including defects that could not be discovered from casual observation of the property.

Every seller of a residential property of one to four dwelling units is required to disclose to a potential buyer whether, during the course of the seller's ownership (or through previous knowledge), any structural additions or alterations were made to the property, and whether they were made with or without benefit of an appropriate permit.

The seller of residential property of one to four units must provide the buyer with a written **Real Estate Transfer Disclosure Statement** that details the mechanical and structural conditions of the property in a form specified by law. The disclosure requirements are subject to change. Use of a form such as the latest version prepared by the California Association of REALTORS® (shown in Figure 6.6) is the best way for the seller and broker(s) to be sure that the buyer is fully informed of the property's condition and that all legal requirements are met.

Seller disclosure is also required in a sale of a used manufactured home or mobile home if the home is classified as personal property. Wording of the disclosure form is provided in Civil Code 1102.6d.

Environmental disclosures, such as the possible presence of lead-based paint, are highlighted in the box on page 426.

Other duties.   As in dealing with the principal, a real estate agent may not make a secret profit in dealing with a third party to a transaction. To do so would make the agent liable to the third party buyer or lessee.

Exaggerating the attributes or benefits of property may subject a real estate licensee to liability if persons with whom the licensee deals accept the statements as accurate. Current concern for truth in advertising has made unacceptable what once may have been considered acceptable distortions of the literal truth. The "best school district in the state" should be exactly that by some objective standard, such as student test scores, or that representation should not be made. An agent is allowed to express an opinion, of course, but the opinion should neither be presented as fact nor misrepresent the facts.

An **agent** is liable to third persons for any tort (physical injury or property damage) or other act, such as a fraudulent misrepresentation, that the agent performs. The agent also is liable for torts or other acts committed by the principal in which the agent acquiesces, whether the agent does so by act or by omission.

FIGURE 6.6

Real Estate Transfer Disclosure Statement

CALIFORNIA ASSOCIATION OF REALTORS®

REAL ESTATE TRANSFER DISCLOSURE STATEMENT
(CALIFORNIA CIVIL CODE §1102, ET SEQ.)
(C.A.R. Form TDS, Revised 10/03)

THIS DISCLOSURE STATEMENT CONCERNS THE REAL PROPERTY SITUATED IN THE CITY OF _____
_____, COUNTY OF _____, STATE OF CALIFORNIA,
DESCRIBED AS _____.

THIS STATEMENT IS A DISCLOSURE OF THE CONDITION OF THE ABOVE DESCRIBED PROPERTY IN COMPLIANCE
WITH SECTION 1102 OF THE CIVIL CODE AS OF (date) _____. IT IS NOT A WARRANTY OF ANY
KIND BY THE SELLER(S) OR ANY AGENT(S) REPRESENTING ANY PRINCIPAL(S) IN THIS TRANSACTION, AND IS
NOT A SUBSTITUTE FOR ANY INSPECTIONS OR WARRANTIES THE PRINCIPAL(S) MAY WISH TO OBTAIN.

I. COORDINATION WITH OTHER DISCLOSURE FORMS

This Real Estate Transfer Disclosure Statement is made pursuant to Section 1102 of the Civil Code. Other statutes require disclosures, depending upon the details of the particular real estate transaction (for example: special study zone and purchase-money liens on residential property).

Substituted Disclosures: The following disclosures and other disclosures required by law, including the Natural Hazard Disclosure Report/Statement that may include airport annoyances, earthquake, fire, flood, or special assessment information, have or will be made in connection with this real estate transfer, and are intended to satisfy the disclosure obligations on this form, where the subject matter is the same:

☐   Inspection reports completed pursuant to the contract of sale or receipt for deposit.
☐   Additional inspection reports or disclosures: _____
_____

II. SELLER'S INFORMATION

The Seller discloses the following information with the knowledge that even though this is not a warranty, prospective Buyers may rely on this information in deciding whether and on what terms to purchase the subject property. Seller hereby authorizes any agent(s) representing any principal(s) in this transaction to provide a copy of this statement to any person or entity in connection with any actual or anticipated sale of the property.

THE FOLLOWING ARE REPRESENTATIONS MADE BY THE SELLER(S) AND ARE NOT THE REPRESENTATIONS OF THE AGENT(S), IF ANY. THIS INFORMATION IS A DISCLOSURE AND IS NOT INTENDED TO BE PART OF ANY CONTRACT BETWEEN THE BUYER AND SELLER.

Seller ☐ is ☐ is not occupying the property.

A. The subject property has the items checked below (read across):

☐ Range	☐ Oven	☐ Microwave
☐ Dishwasher	☐ Trash Compactor	☐ Garbage Disposal
☐ Washer/Dryer Hookups		☐ Rain Gutters
☐ Burglar Alarms	☐ Smoke Detector(s)	☐ Fire Alarm
☐ TV Antenna	☐ Satellite Dish	☐ Intercom
☐ Central Heating	☐ Central Air Conditioning	☐ Evaporator Cooler(s)
☐ Wall/Window Air Conditioning	☐ Sprinklers	☐ Public Sewer System
☐ Septic Tank	☐ Sump Pump	☐ Water Softener
☐ Patio/Decking	☐ Built-in Barbecue	☐ Gazebo
☐ Sauna		
☐ Hot Tub	☐ Pool	☐ Spa
☐ Locking Safety Cover*	☐ Child Resistant Barrier*	☐ Locking Safety Cover*
☐ Security Gate(s)	☐ Automatic Garage Door Opener(s)*	☐ Number Remote Controls ____
Garage: ☐ Attached	☐ Not Attached	☐ Carport
Pool/Spa Heater: ☐ Gas	☐ Solar	☐ Electric
Water Heater: ☐ Gas	☐ Water Heater Anchored, Braced, or Strapped*	
Water Supply: ☐ City	☐ Well	☐ Private Utility or
Gas Supply: ☐ Utility	☐ Bottled	Other _____
☐ Window Screens	☐ Window Security Bars ☐ Quick Release Mechanism on Bedroom Windows*	

Exhaust Fan(s) in _____ 220 Volt Wiring in _____ Fireplace(s) in _____
☐ Gas Starter _____ ☐ Roof(s): Type: _____ Age: _____ (approx.)
☐ Other: _____
Are there, to the best of your (Seller's) knowledge, any of the above that are not in operating condition? ☐ Yes ☐ No. If yes, then describe. (Attach additional sheets if necessary): _____

(*see footnote on page 2)

TDS REVISED 10/03 (PAGE 1 OF 3) Print Date

Buyer's Initials (_____)(_____)
Seller's Initials (_____)(_____)

Reviewed by _____ Date _____

EQUAL HOUSING OPPORTUNITY

REAL ESTATE TRANSFER DISCLOSURE STATEMENT (TDS PAGE 1 OF 3)

FIGURE 6.6

Real Estate Transfer Disclosure Statement (Continued)

Property Address: _____   Date: _____

B. Are you (Seller) aware of any significant defects/malfunctions in any of the following? ☐ Yes ☐ No. If yes, check appropriate space(s) below.

☐ Interior Walls ☐ Ceilings ☐ Floors ☐ Exterior Walls ☐ Insulation ☐ Roof(s) ☐ Windows ☐ Doors ☐ Foundation ☐ Slab(s) ☐ Driveways ☐ Sidewalks ☐ Walls/Fences ☐ Electrical Systems ☐ Plumbing/Sewers/Septics ☐ Other Structural Components

(Describe: _____

_____

_____

_____)

If any of the above is checked, explain. (Attach additional sheets if necessary.): _____

_____

_____

_____

*This garage door opener or child resistant pool barrier may not be in compliance with the safety standards relating to automatic reversing devices as set forth in Chapter 12.5 (commencing with Section 19890) of Part 3 of Division 13 of, or with the pool safety standards of Article 2.5 (commencing with Section 115920) of Chapter 5 of Part 10 of Division 104 of, the Health and Safety Code. The water heater may not be anchored, braced, or strapped in accordance with Section 19211 of the Health and Safety Code. Window security bars may not have quick release mechanisms in compliance with the 1995 edition of the California Building Standards Code.

C. Are you (Seller) aware of any of the following:

1. Substances, materials, or products which may be an environmental hazard such as, but not limited to, asbestos, formaldehyde, radon gas, lead-based paint, mold, fuel or chemical storage tanks, and contaminated soil or water on the subject property . . . . ☐ Yes ☐ No
2. Features of the property shared in common with adjoining landowners, such as walls, fences, and driveways, whose use or responsibility for maintenance may have an effect on the subject property . . . . ☐ Yes ☐ No
3. Any encroachments, easements or similar matters that may affect your interest in the subject property . . . . ☐ Yes ☐ No
4. Room additions, structural modifications, or other alterations or repairs made without necessary permits . . . . ☐ Yes ☐ No
5. Room additions, structural modifications, or other alterations or repairs not in compliance with building codes . . . ☐ Yes ☐ No
6. Fill (compacted or otherwise) on the property or any portion thereof . . . . ☐ Yes ☐ No
7. Any settling from any cause, or slippage, sliding, or other soil problems . . . . ☐ Yes ☐ No
8. Flooding, drainage or grading problems . . . . ☐ Yes ☐ No
9. Major damage to the property or any of the structures from fire, earthquake, floods, or landslides . . . . ☐ Yes ☐ No
10. Any zoning violations, nonconforming uses, violations of "setback" requirements . . . . ☐ Yes ☐ No
11. Neighborhood noise problems or other nuisances . . . . ☐ Yes ☐ No
12. CC&R's or other deed restrictions or obligations . . . . ☐ Yes ☐ No
13. Homeowners' Association which has any authority over the subject property . . . . ☐ Yes ☐ No
14. Any "common area" (facilities such as pools, tennis courts, walkways, or other areas co-owned in undivided interest with others) . . . . ☐ Yes ☐ No
15. Any notices of abatement or citations against the property . . . . ☐ Yes ☐ No
16. Any lawsuits by or against the Seller threatening to or affecting this real property, including any lawsuits alleging a defect or deficiency in this real property or "common areas" (facilities such as pools, tennis courts, walkways, or other areas co-owned in undivided interest with others) . . . . ☐ Yes ☐ No

If the answer to any of these is yes, explain. (Attach additional sheets if necessary.): _____

_____

_____

_____

_____

Seller certifies that the information herein is true and correct to the best of the Seller's knowledge as of the date signed by the Seller.

Seller_____   Date _____

Seller_____   Date _____

Buyer's Initials (_____)(_____)

Seller's Initials (_____)(_____)

Copyright © 1991-2003, CALIFORNIA ASSOCIATION OF REALTORS®, INC.

TDS REVISED 10/03 (PAGE 2 OF 3)

Reviewed by _____ Date _____

EQUAL HOUSING OPPORTUNITY

REAL ESTATE TRANSFER DISCLOSURE STATEMENT (TDS PAGE 2 OF 3)

Source: Reprinted with permission, California Association of REALTORS®. Endorsement not implied.

FIGURE 6.6

Real Estate Transfer Disclosure Statement (Continued)

Property Address: _____ Date: _____

III. AGENT'S INSPECTION DISCLOSURE
(To be completed only if the Seller is represented by an agent in this transaction.)

THE UNDERSIGNED, BASED ON THE ABOVE INQUIRY OF THE SELLER(S) AS TO THE CONDITION OF THE PROPERTY AND BASED ON A REASONABLY COMPETENT AND DILIGENT VISUAL INSPECTION OF THE ACCESSIBLE AREAS OF THE PROPERTY IN CONJUNCTION WITH THAT INQUIRY, STATES THE FOLLOWING:

☐ Agent notes no items for disclosure.

☐ Agent notes the following items: _____
_____
_____
_____
_____

Agent (Broker Representing Seller) _____ By _____ Date _____
(Please Print)   (Associate Licensee or Broker Signature)

IV. AGENT'S INSPECTION DISCLOSURE
(To be completed only if the agent who has obtained the offer is other than the agent above.)

THE UNDERSIGNED, BASED ON A REASONABLY COMPETENT AND DILIGENT VISUAL INSPECTION OF THE ACCESSIBLE AREAS OF THE PROPERTY, STATES THE FOLLOWING:

☐ Agent notes no items for disclosure.

☐ Agent notes the following items: _____
_____
_____
_____
_____

Agent (Broker Obtaining the Offer) _____ By _____ Date _____
(Please Print)   (Associate Licensee or Broker Signature)

V. BUYER(S) AND SELLER(S) MAY WISH TO OBTAIN PROFESSIONAL ADVICE AND/OR INSPECTIONS OF THE PROPERTY AND TO PROVIDE FOR APPROPRIATE PROVISIONS IN A CONTRACT BETWEEN BUYER AND SELLER(S) WITH RESPECT TO ANY ADVICE/INSPECTIONS/DEFECTS.

I/WE ACKNOWLEDGE RECEIPT OF A COPY OF THIS STATEMENT.

Seller _____ Date _____ Buyer _____ Date _____

Seller _____ Date _____ Buyer _____ Date _____

Agent (Broker Representing Seller) _____ By _____ Date _____
(Please Print)   (Associate Licensee or Broker Signature)

Agent (Broker Obtaining the Offer) _____ By _____ Date _____
(Please Print)   (Associate Licensee or Broker Signature)

SECTION 1102.3 OF THE CIVIL CODE PROVIDES A BUYER WITH THE RIGHT TO RESCIND A PURCHASE CONTRACT FOR AT LEAST THREE DAYS AFTER THE DELIVERY OF THIS DISCLOSURE IF DELIVERY OCCURS AFTER THE SIGNING OF AN OFFER TO PURCHASE. IF YOU WISH TO RESCIND THE CONTRACT, YOU MUST ACT WITHIN THE PRESCRIBED PERIOD.

A REAL ESTATE BROKER IS QUALIFIED TO ADVISE ON REAL ESTATE. IF YOU DESIRE LEGAL ADVICE, CONSULT YOUR ATTORNEY.

THIS FORM HAS BEEN APPROVED BY THE CALIFORNIA ASSOCIATION OF REALTORS® (C.A.R.). NO REPRESENTATION IS MADE AS TO THE LEGAL VALIDITY OR ADEQUACY OF ANY PROVISION IN ANY SPECIFIC TRANSACTION. A REAL ESTATE BROKER IS THE PERSON QUALIFIED TO ADVISE ON REAL ESTATE TRANSACTIONS. IF YOU DESIRE LEGAL OR TAX ADVICE, CONSULT AN APPROPRIATE PROFESSIONAL.
This form is available for use by the entire real estate industry. It is not intended to identify the user as a REALTOR®. REALTOR® is a registered collective membership mark which may be used only by members of the NATIONAL ASSOCIATION OF REALTORS® who subscribe to its Code of Ethics.

SURE TRAC
The System for Success™

Published by the
California Association of REALTORS®

TDS REVISED 10/03 (PAGE 3 OF 3)

Reviewed by _____ Date _____

EQUAL HOUSING OPPORTUNITY

REAL ESTATE TRANSFER DISCLOSURE STATEMENT (TDS PAGE 3 OF 3)

Source: Reprinted with permission, California Association of REALTORS®. Endorsement not implied.

The **principal** is liable for

- his or her own acts;

- acts of an agent or a subagent that were performed on the principal's behalf; and

- torts committed by an agent who is an employee (not an independent contractor) acting in the scope of the employment.

■ **FOR EXAMPLE:** Real estate broker Luis hires Sally and agrees to pay her a salary as well as a commission on sales she makes. When showing a house, Sally carelessly neglects to lock the back door. Before the owner returns, someone enters the house and steals a video game player. Is Broker Luis liable for the owner's loss?

Yes, because Sally was acting within the scope of her employment while showing the house.

Recovery Account

The responsibilities of real estate licensees to their clients and customers are taken seriously by the California legislature. A **Recovery Account** has been established to help compensate victims of fraud, misrepresentation, deceit, or conversion (the legal term for theft) of trust funds when they cannot collect a court-ordered judgment against a real estate licensee. The Recovery Account is funded by 5 percent of all real estate license fees collected. The amount paid out is limited to $20,000 per transaction and $100,000 per licensee, regardless of the number of victims.

If a recovery is allowed against a licensee, the real estate license of that person is automatically suspended. Reinstatement cannot be considered until the licensee has fully reimbursed the fund for the amount paid out plus interest.

Exercise 6-4 Broker Cindy Carroll of ABC Realty would like to list the Meyer estate. She offers to handle the sale at a commission of 5 percent of the selling price. Mrs. Meyer, a widow, signs a listing agreement with Broker Carroll. Broker Carroll discusses the Meyer estate with an investor she knows. Broker Carroll agrees to bring the investor's offer to Mrs. Meyer and, if the offer is accepted, to represent the investor when he resells the property, which will take place immediately after the first sale. The investor offers somewhat less than the asking price, but Broker Carroll persuades Mrs. Meyer to accept the offer. A few weeks after the sale, Broker Carroll sells the property for the investor, who makes a 20 percent profit on the transaction. Broker Carroll earns two commissions.

Comment on Broker Carroll's activities.

■ TERMINATION OF AN AGENCY

The California Civil Code lists the ways in which an agency relationship may be terminated. They are summarized below.

Ways to Terminate an Agency

- ■ Fulfillment of the agency agreement
- ■ Expiration of the term of the agreement
- ■ Destruction of the property
- ■ Death of either the principal or agent
- ■ Incapacity of the agent to act as an agent, or incapacity of the principal to enter into a contract
- ■ Agreement of the principal and agent
- ■ By operation of law, as in a bankruptcy

The principal or agent always has the power to terminate the agency unilaterally (without the other person's consent) in writing. But the person who terminates the agency may be liable for damages to the other party. An early cancellation of a listing agreement by a seller is an example of a situation in which the seller may be liable to the listing broker for expenses or a commission.

Notice of termination must be given to third parties with whom the principal and agent are dealing.

■ **FOR EXAMPLE:** Sara and Sam Schuster decided to move from Laguna Beach to Boise and listed their home for sale with Broker Bonita Fish. After an extended vacation in Boise, the Schusters decided to stay in Laguna Beach and notified Broker Fish that they were taking their house off the market. Can they cancel the listing agreement?

Yes, the Schusters can unilaterally cancel the listing agreement. Broker Fish must decide whether she wants to charge the Schusters for any expenses she incurred in marketing their property. If Broker Fish had already found a ready, willing, and able buyer for the Schuster house, she could also insist on payment of her commission on the transaction.

■ SUMMARY

The **agency relationship** establishes the authority of the **agent** as a **special agent** or **general agent** to act on behalf of a **principal** in dealing with third parties.

A **real estate listing agreement** authorizes a broker to receive a deposit on behalf of the seller, market the property, and authorize payment to **cooperating brokers.** The **multiple listing service (MLS)** is an association of real estate agents who place properties listed for sale in a network that may be accessed by other MLS members. A seller may make an offer of **subagency** through the MLS.

An agent may be an **employee** or an **independent contractor.** The **California Real Estate Law** will always treat a salesperson or another associate licensee as an employee of a broker in considering the associate's rights and responsibilities to buyers, sellers, and other parties to a real estate transaction.

A **dual agent** serves both buyer and seller in the same transaction. All transactions of residential properties of up to four units require **written disclosure** of the agent's representation. A **power of attorney** granted to an **attorney-in-fact** will enable that person to act in the capacity of the principal.

An agency may be established by **express agreement.** A principal may **ratify** conduct that establishes an agency, or an **ostensible (implied) agency** could be formed by **estoppel.**

A contract between broker and salesperson must have the same formalities as any contract, including consideration by both parties.

An agent's **authority** may be **actual, inherent,** or **apparent.** If a real estate licensee receives funds on behalf of a client or customer, those funds must not be **commingled** with the licensee's own funds.

Listing agreements, which must be written, establish the agency relationship of real estate broker and client. The parties may agree to an **open (nonexclusive) listing,** an **exclusive agency listing,** an **exclusive authorization and right-to-sell listing** (which may have a **multiple listing clause**), a **net listing,** or an **option listing.**

Buyer-broker agreements, which must also be written, provide important benefits and protections for property buyers through representation by their own real estate broker.

The real estate agent owes the duties of a **fiduciary** to the principal, whether a buyer or seller. The agent must reveal any possible **conflict of interest** and may not make a **secret profit.**

The real estate agent's main task in listing property for sale is to find a **ready, willing, and able buyer.** The principal must pay the agreed-on compensation if the agent fulfills the agreement. In a real estate transaction, that means that the agent is the **procuring cause** of a sale, a lease, a rental, or another agreement.

Both principal and agent owe certain duties to third persons. Both must **disclose all material facts and defects affecting the desirability of the property.** Both must **inspect** the property and reveal its **condition** to a potential buyer. The agent must not make a **secret profit** at the expense of a third person.

The **Recovery Account** has been formed to help compensate victims of misconduct by real estate licensees.

■ IMPORTANT TERMS

Make sure you understand the following terms before you take the achievement examination.

actual authority	implied agency
agency	independent contractor
agency confirmation form	inherent authority
agency disclosure form	loyalty
agent	multiple listing clause
apparent authority	multiple listing service (MLS)
associate licensee	net listing
attorney-in-fact	obedience
bilateral contract	open listing
commingling	option listing
compensation	ostensible agency
conflict of interest	pocket listing
cooperating brokers	power of attorney
cooperating split	principal
dual agency	procuring cause
due diligence	prospective economic advantage
duty of care	ratification
employer and employee	ready, willing, and able buyer
equal dignities rule	Real Estate Transfer Disclosure
estoppel	Statement
exclusive agency listing	reasonable care and skill
exclusive authorization and	Recovery Account
right-to-sell listing	safety clause
express agreement	secret profit
fiduciary	single agency
full disclosure	special agent
full disclosure of material facts	special power of attorney
general agent	subagent
general power of attorney	unilateral contract
good faith and honesty	

■ OPEN FOR DISCUSSION

In some large real estate offices, the broker of record manages the work of many associate licensees.

Do you think there should be a limit on the number of licensees that are supervised by any one broker? If so, what should that limit be?

■ ACHIEVEMENT EXAMINATION 6

1. Generally an agent works for the
   a. principal.
   b. third person.
   c. subagent.
   d. Department of Real Estate.

2. An emancipated minor
   a. may be a licensed real estate agent.
   b. may enter into a valid real estate contract.
   c. may be a licensed real estate salesperson.
   d. is anyone younger than 18 years of age.

3. Someone appointed to carry out a particular transaction is a
   a. general agent.   c. secret agent.
   b. special agent.   d. subagent.

4. An independent contractor is distinguished by
   a. responsibility for Social Security and other payments.
   b. no flexibility in setting work hours.
   c. little control over work methods.
   d. no legal obligation to employer.

5. The California Real Estate Law treats a real estate salesperson as a(n)
   a. independent contractor of the broker.
   b. employee of the broker.
   c. sole proprietor.
   d. partner of the broker.

6. A salesperson is a broker's
   a. principal.   c. subagent.
   b. agent.   d. third person.

7. An agency agreement to perform an act that requires a writing
   a. must itself be in writing.
   b. may be oral or written.
   c. cannot be an express agreement.
   d. violates the Statute of Frauds.

8. To be enforceable, all real estate sales contracts
   a. may be oral or written.
   b. must be in writing.
   c. must comply with the equal equities rule.
   d. must be completed within 90 days of origination.

9. As a contract, a real estate agency agreement
   a. can have any objective.
   b. needs only to be made by parties with the capacity to contract.
   c. does not need to be supported by consideration.
   d. must meet the requirements for a valid contract.

10. Real estate commission rates
    a. are established by the Department of Real Estate.
    b. should be no lower than 2 percent.
    c. should be no higher than 10 percent.
    d. are not fixed by law.

11. All real estate agency agreements must
    a. expire in 90 days.
    b. be in writing.
    c. be signed before a buyer is solicited.
    d. be approved by the Department of Real Estate.

12. The most commonly used form of real estate listing agreement is the
    a. open listing.
    b. exclusive agency listing.
    c. exclusive authorization and right-to-sell listing.
    d. net listing.

13. A real estate agent owes duties to the
    a. principal.   c. subagent.
    b. third person.   d. All of these

14. The agent owes the principal the duty of
    a. loyalty.
    b. compensation.
    c. extraordinary care and skill.
    d. dual representation.

15. A real estate agent must make full disclosure of
    a. all material facts known by the agent.
    b. all material facts revealed by the owner of the property.
    c. material facts that are known by the agent or that would be revealed by a reasonable inspection of the property.
    d. all actual or potential property defects, of whatever kind.

16. The principal owes the agent
    a. only the duty of compensation.
    b. the duty of obedience.
    c. the duty of care.
    d. the duties of a fiduciary.

17. A real estate seller must disclose
    a. only visible property defects.
    b. structural additions or repairs only if made by the seller.
    c. material facts concerning the property's value or desirability.
    d. only defects that would be revealed by a property inspection.

18. Exaggerating a property's value or desirability
    a. is permissible.
    b. is expected in the average transaction.
    c. may not be permissible if the statements are not factual.
    d. is never permitted.

19. The Recovery Account is available to
    a. brokers.
    b. salespeople.
    c. people victimized by a real estate licensee.
    d. real estate licensees victimized by their clients.

20. An agency relationship may not be terminated by
    a. completion of the agreement.
    b. expiration of the terms of the agreement.
    c. agreement of the parties.
    d. someone outside the agency relationship.

CHAPTER SEVEN

CONTRACTS

■ WHAT IS A CONTRACT?

A **contract** is a promise made by one person to another to do something *or* to refrain from doing something. A person who takes part in a contract is referred to as a **party** to the contract. The contract promise may be made by only one of the parties, or a separate promise may be made by each of the parties. The promise each party makes is called that party's **contractual obligation.** An offer to perform a contractual obligation is called a **tender.**

A contract must meet certain requirements to be legally valid. If the contract is valid, each party has the **duty to perform** the specified contractual obligations. A party who does not fulfill the promise made will be liable to the other party for **breach of contract.**

A **real estate listing agreement** and a **real estate purchase contract** are examples of the most common types of contracts used by real estate agents. Listing agreements were covered in Chapter 6. This chapter will examine a typical form of real estate purchase contract. We begin with definitions of some of the terms we will use throughout this chapter. They include

- ■ executory and executed contracts;
- ■ express and implied contracts;
- ■ bilateral and unilateral contracts; and
- ■ valid, void, voidable, and unenforceable contracts.

Executory and Executed Contracts

A contract is said to be **executory** when some future contract obligation is yet to be performed. A listing agreement is executory, because the real estate broker must find a buyer for the listed property in order to earn the compensation promised by the seller. Until the sale is closed, a real estate purchase contract also is executory. The buyer must find financing for the purchase, and other conditions must be met before title is transferred.

When all of the contract obligations have been performed, the transaction is completed and the contract has been **executed.**

Note: Don't be confused by use of the word *execute* to mean the signing of a document. For example, after the terms of a property listing agreement have been decided on and prepared in written form, both seller and broker execute the agreement by signing it.

Express and Implied Contracts

An **express contract** is a contract of words established by an oral or a written agreement in which the parties declare their intention to make a contract. An **implied contract** is established by the conduct of the parties, without a specific oral or written agreement.

■ **FOR EXAMPLE:** Wanda and William South moved to Imperial City but never notified the local waste disposal company to start service at their address. The Souths leave their trash out at the usual pickup time, and it is removed by the disposal company. Can the waste company bill them for the service?

Yes. By making use of the waste disposal company's service, the Souths made an implied contract to pay for the service.

Bilateral and Unilateral Contracts

In a **bilateral contract,** both parties make a promise to do something or to refrain from doing something and both are obligated to perform. In a **unilateral contract,** only one party promises, and only that party is obligated to perform. The promise is accepted by the performance of the other party.

■ **FOR EXAMPLE:** Hearth Homes is offering an extra incentive to agents to attract more buyers to the newest Hearth Homes subdivision. For every sale that is closed before Labor Day, the selling agent will earn an extra $1,000 commission. This offer is advertised in a flyer sent to each brokerage office. Broker Luis brings a client to the Hearth Homes subdivision and the client purchases a home. The sale is finalized on August 31. Is Broker Luis entitled to the $1,000 bonus?

Yes. Because Broker Luis met the terms of the unilateral offer, he is entitled to the extra compensation.

The typical real estate purchase contract is *bilateral*. One party promises to transfer the right of ownership or use of real estate, and the other party promises to pay some form of compensation for that right.

Valid, Void, Voidable, and Unenforceable Contracts

A **valid contract** can be created easily, if all of the required elements are present.

1. The parties must have the **legal capacity** to enter into a contract.
2. There must be an **offer** by one party and **acceptance** of that offer by the other party.
3. There must be a **lawful object** to the contract.
4. There must be some form of **consideration,** or payment, supporting the contract.
5. The contract may have to be **written.**

Each of these elements is discussed in the next section, "Elements of a Contract."

A **void contract** is one that has no legal effect from its inception. An agreement to do something that is illegal is void.

A **voidable contract** is one that may be disavowed by one or both parties, depending on the circumstances. An example of a voidable contract is one that someone signs while intoxicated.

An **unenforceable contract** is valid on its face, but its enforcement would violate some law. An example is an **oral** contract on a matter that the law requires to be **in writing.** An oral contract to purchase real estate is unenforceable, no matter what its terms, because it is oral and not written. The kinds of contracts that require a written agreement will be covered later in this chapter.

■ ELEMENTS OF A CONTRACT

1. Legal Capacity to Contract

All parties must have the **legal capacity to contract.** This means that they must have the legal ability to make a contract. If they do not, either the contract will be voidable by the person who lacks the capacity to contract, or the contract will be void from its inception.

A **minor** (in California, anyone younger than 18) generally cannot make a contract concerning real estate. Any such contract is *voidable*. A minor *can* contract as an adult, however, if he or she is an **emancipated minor.** A minor becomes emancipated by marrying, by joining the armed forces, or by petitioning the court, which may make that decision.

Spanish Language Contracts

Many California real estate transactions involve parties for whom Spanish is the first language—in some cases, the only language. As a result, contracts are frequently negotiated in Spanish. Civil Code Section 1632 imposes special requirements on any person engaged in a trade or business (such as a real estate licensee) who negotiates orally or in writing primarily in the Spanish language in the course of entering into a

- lease, sublease, or rental agreement, for a period of longer than one month, of a dwelling, apartment, mobile home, or other dwelling unit normally occupied as a residence;
- loan negotiated by a real estate broker and secured by a lien on a dwelling of one to four units—the law applies to the loan disclosure statement made by the broker;
- loan or extension of credit secured by personal property, or unsecured, for use primarily for personal, family, or household purposes;
- contract or agreement for purchase or lease of a motor vehicle;
- contract or agreement for legal services from a person licensed to practice law.

Before the English-language version of the contract is signed, the party to the contract must be given an unexecuted Spanish-language translation of the contract. A Spanish-language translation also is required for disclosures made by financial organizations under the Financial Code or the Federal Truth in Lending Act. The law does not apply if the party to the contract uses his or her own interpreter.

A Spanish-language notice of this law must be conspicuously displayed at any time and place at which an applicable contract or agreement is being executed.

Any minor may receive property as a gift or an inheritance, usually taking title without the appointment of an adult guardian. A guardian must be appointed, however, to handle any property conveyance, lease, encumbrance, or other transaction on behalf of an unemancipated minor.

If someone makes a contract while drugged or intoxicated, the contract is **voidable** by that person. He or she can let the contract stand or can disaffirm (cancel) it.

■ **FOR EXAMPLE:** Harvey Lock, feeling no pain after six margaritas, gripes at a party that he is so fed up with his job he will sell his house to the first person who offers him a motor home in trade for it so he can fulfill his lifelong dream of visiting all 50 states. Sue Wilson offers Harvey her well-used "Minnie-Winnie" in exchange for his Beverly Hills home. Harvey, amid much laughter, accepts the offer and tells Sue to get the paperwork ready to sign the next day. Sue shows up at Harvey's the next day with her attorney. Now what?

Harvey, who only vaguely remembers the "deal" of the night before, can do one of two things. He can disaffirm the contract because he was intoxicated at the time and lacked the capacity to enter an agreement. Or he can thank Sue for the terrific motor home as he signs the deed that her attorney has prepared.

A **mentally incompetent person** cannot form a valid contract. Any such contract would be **void**. A person may be determined by a court to be mentally incompetent. Even without a judicial determination, however, evidence may show that a person is without understanding and thus unable to form a contract.

The property of a **deceased person** is handled by the personal representative of the estate. This can be either an executor named in the deceased's will or an administrator appointed by the court if no executor was named by the deceased or if the named representative declined to serve. The actions of the estate representative must always have the approval of the probate court.

Contracts by Businesses

A business entity can make a contract concerning real estate.

A **sole proprietor** acts in his or her own name, or with a spouse.

A **partnership** may hold real property in the name of the partnership, the name of one of the partners, or the name of a trustee. Any authorized partner (and spouse) may contract to transfer the real estate.

A **corporation** acts through its officers, as authorized by the board of directors. The directors may be personally liable for actions taken on behalf of the corporation.

When dealing with a business entity, it is important that the authority of the person acting on behalf of the business be verified and documented.

2. Offer and Acceptance

A contract is not created until the parties show that they have given their **mutual consent** to its terms. There must be some form of a "meeting of the minds" to create a valid and enforceable contract. This normally takes place in a process called **offer and acceptance.** An *offer* by one party is *accepted* by the other party.

An offer exists only when the **offeror** (the person making the offer) has communicated its terms to the **offeree** (the person receiving the offer). The fact that an offer is being made should be clear. Because a standard, well-detailed form is used in most real estate transactions, establishing the intent of the offeror usually is not a problem.

Rejection.   The offeree can refuse to accept the offer. **Rejection** of an offer can be accomplished by simply taking no action that would indicate acceptance. An offer is also rejected if the offeree makes a change in its terms as a condition of acceptance, resulting in a counteroffer to the offeror. Then, their roles are reversed. The person making the counteroffer becomes the *offeror* and the person to whom the counteroffer is made becomes the *offeree*.

Counteroffer.   A **counteroffer** is created by any change in the terms of an offer as originally made. There may be considerable negotiation required to finalize a contract. At each step, an offer by one side may be met by a counteroffer from the other side. Any counteroffer has the effect of rejecting the offer that it counters. The previous offer, on the terms proposed, is terminated. It can no longer be accepted by the party to whom it was made.

■   **FOR EXAMPLE:**   The asking price for the Belton residence is $95,000. John and Jane Murray offer $88,600 for the house. George Belton makes a counteroffer of $92,000. John and Jane reject the counteroffer. George decides $88,600 is not such a bad offer after all and signs the original purchase contract, returning it to the Murrays. Can he do that?

No. Once George made a counteroffer, he effectively turned down the Murrays' original offer. Of course the Murrays can be invited to remake their original offer, which the owner can accept if he chooses.

Revocation of an offer.   In general, an offer may be revoked before it is accepted if the offeror communicates the **revocation** directly to the offeree. It also is revoked if the offeree learns of the revocation from a reliable source (such as the real estate agent) and observes the offeror do something that is not consistent with the offer still being considered.

■   **FOR EXAMPLE:**   Mary Burns wants to rent an apartment. She fills out a rental application at Ocean Villas and is told that she can expect to hear back in two days. The next day, Mary learns that her company is moving its office to Modesto. News of the move appears in the newspaper the same morning and the manager at Ocean Villas sees the article. He phones Mary's place of business and learns that all employees, including Mary, will be relocating to Modesto. Before Mary can get back to Ocean Villas to withdraw her rental application, the manager signs it and faxes a copy of the rental agreement to her. Does the manager have a new tenant?

No. Once he learned of Mary's change of circumstance from a reliable source and verified it with a phone call to her place of business, the manager had sufficient notice of Mary's intended revocation of the application.

The Exception to the Revocation Rule

An offer is revocable before acceptance *unless* it is supported by some form of consideration (payment). An example is an option agreement entered into by a prospective purchaser and seller. The prospective purchaser gives the seller the consideration for the option—usually money. In return the purchaser receives the right to purchase the property during the option period. During that time the seller is not allowed to revoke the buyer's right to exercise the option.

Offer made freely and voluntarily.   For a valid acceptance, the offeree must *not* be acting under

- threat of harm,
- undue influence,
- mistake, or
- as a result of a fraudulent misrepresentation by the offeror.

A contract is **voidable** if it is entered into under threat of harm to a person or thing.

No undue influence or fraud.   **Undue influence** may not be used to gain an acceptance. Most often, this happens when the parties are related or known to each other and one of them takes advantage of that position of confidence.

- **FOR EXAMPLE:**   Jim is the neighbor, good friend, and accountant of Clara, who is 82 years old and legally blind. Jim wants to buy Clara's house. He tells her that property values are going down, and she should sell her house while she has the chance. Jim then offers Clara $100,000 for her house, about $150,000 less than it is actually worth, based on what nearby houses have sold for recently. Because Clara paid $13,000 for her house in the 1957, she is very impressed with the offer and accepts. Shortly after the offer is accepted but before the sale is closed, Clara is visited by her niece. Clara's niece informs her of what a poor deal she has made. Can Clara do anything about it?

Yes. Clara should contact an attorney immediately to disaffirm the contract with Jim. She should have no problem doing so, because the offer Jim persuaded her to take is so obviously inadequate.

A fraudulent act is either affirmative or negative.

- Fraud is **affirmative** when it is a deliberate statement of a material fact that the speaker knows to be false and on which the speaker intends another person to rely, to his or her detriment.
- Fraud is **negative** when it is a deliberate concealment of something that should be revealed.

Actual fraud can be any of the following actions, as long as it is performed with the intent to deceive.

- The suggestion as a fact of that which is not true by one who knows it is not true
- The positive assertion, in a manner not warranted by the information of the person making it, of that which is not true, though the person believes it to be true (that is, the belief is not justified)
- The suppression of that which is true by one who knows of or believes the fact
- A promise made without any intention of performing it
- Any other act of deception

Constructive fraud is any misrepresentation made without fraudulent intent, that is, deliberate intent to deceive. An agent can reasonably rely on some information (such as the owner's report of the results of a termite inspection). Other information, however, such as the construction of a new school, should be verified. The agent could be guilty of constructive fraud if the information turns out to be false.

- **FOR EXAMPLE:**   Jim and Janet Day want to buy a house in Woodville. They contact Broker Charles Charton, who shows them several houses, including one near a major thoroughfare. The Days talk to the owner, who tells them that the traffic noise will be reduced considerably after the city puts up a cement block wall along the property closest to the roadway. Broker Charton, who is present, knows that such a wall has been proposed to the city council but has not yet been approved. Broker Charton does not contradict the owner, however. The Days make an offer, which is accepted. Before the close of the sale, they check with the city authorities to find out when the soundproofing wall will be erected. The Days discover the truth. Can the Days back out of their deal with the seller?

Probably, for the seller misrepresented the condition of the property—that the noise problem would be alleviated. Broker Charton knowingly went along with that misrepresentation, for he was present when it was made but did not object. Broker Charton's conduct could be reported to the Real Estate Commissioner.

Penalties for Fraud

A contract induced by fraud is **voidable** by the injured party. Action must be taken within a reasonable time after the fraud is discovered, as specified by the Statute of Limitations.

The injured party may also seek **money damages,** including punitive damages.

A **criminal prosecution** may be brought against the person who committed the fraud, resulting in a fine and/or imprisonment.

A **real estate agent** who takes part in fraud may suffer loss or suspension of the real estate license, in addition to the penalties mentioned above.

Note that a **fraudulent misrepresentation** is different from a **negligent misrepresentation.** A negligent misrepresentation is not made with criminal intent to deceive. It is the result of carelessness. Although negligent misrepresentation carries no criminal penalties, it can result in a voidable contract, civil damages, and disciplinary action against the licensee.

Definite terms.   The subject matter of the contract must be clearly expressed in **definite terms.**

- If the subject matter is real estate, there must be an adequate **description** of the property.
- **All parties** must be identified unambiguously. The full name and address of each are preferred.
- The **price** must be specified in a real estate contract, unlike contracts for other types of property in which a reasonable (market) price may be inferred. It would be sufficient in a real estate contract to state the manner in which the price is to be determined, such as the valuation reached by an identified licensed appraiser as of a specified date.
- The terms that specify the **nature** of the transaction and any **conditions** to its performance must be clear.
- The **time of performance** is important. Particularly in real estate purchase contracts, deadlines for certain activities, such as qualifying for and obtaining a loan, should be given.

■   **FOR EXAMPLE:**   John and Jane Murray offer to purchase the Belton residence. Their offer to purchase describes the property as the George Belton residence on Gray Street, Meadowville, Washington County. Is this description adequate? Is it advisable?

The description could be adequate if George Belton owns only one house on Gray Street. It is not advisable, however. Not only could George Belton own more than one house on Gray Street—there is no description of the land involved.

3. Lawful Object

One cannot make a valid contract to perform an **illegal activity.** An example is an agreement to use real estate for an unlawful purpose, such as the manufacture of illegal drugs. If the contract has a lawful as well as an unlawful objective, it will be valid only to the extent that the lawful object alone can be carried out.

4. Consideration

A contract must be supported by **consideration**—an obligation or a payment on the part of each party—to be enforceable. The fact that each party supplies consideration is referred to as **mutuality of contract.** The consideration can be a promise to do something (or refrain from doing something) in the future.

As noted earlier, if consideration has been given to create a valid **option,** the option agreement cannot be revoked by the person giving the option before the end of the option period.

■ **FOR EXAMPLE:** Harvey gives Cecilia a one-year lease and an option to buy his house, in exchange for $5,000 and monthly lease payments of $1,000. Before the year is up, Harvey decides to give the house to his son Hal. Harvey notifies Cecilia by certified mail, enclosing a money order for $5,000. Does Cecilia still have an option to buy the house? What can Cecilia do?

Cecilia still has a valid option contract but will have to return the $5,000 to Harvey. If she delays she may be understood as approving his revocation of the agreement. If Cecilia had already decided—or decides when she gets the $5,000—that she will not exercise the option, she is $5,000 richer than she would have been had Harvey not returned her money. Either way, Cecilia should talk to her attorney.

5. Writing

Certain agreements are *enforceable* only if they are **in writing.** A "handshake deal" may work perfectly well as long as the parties have no problems. But if something goes wrong and one party backs out, the other party won't be able to enforce the agreement.

A summary of the types of agreements involving real estate that *must* be in writing appears in the box on the next page.

■ **FOR EXAMPLE:** Jim and Janet Day make an offer, through Broker Luis, to purchase the Castle estate. The Days love the furniture in the family room and want to purchase that as well. Their offer is countered by the Castles, and after considerable negotiation a purchase price of $347,000 is agreed on. Somewhere along the line the request for the family room furnishings is omitted, and the signed purchase offer does not include them. What can the Days do?

If the omission was inadvertent (a mistake) the Days may be able to reform the contract to conform to the understanding of the parties. A separate agreement and bill of sale for personal property, stating at least a nominal consideration (such as $10), is preferable.

The Statute of Frauds

The **Statute of Frauds** is a part of the California Civil Code that originated in the English common law. The Statute of Frauds lists the types of contract that are required to be **in writing.** They include the following:

1. An agreement that will not be completed within a year

2. An agreement for the sale of real property or an interest in real property, or the lease of real property for more than one year (and an agent making such an agreement on behalf of a principal must be authorized to do so by a written agreement)

3. An agreement that employs an agent, a broker, or any other person to

   ■ purchase or sell real property;

   ■ lease real property for a period longer than one year; or

   ■ find a purchaser or seller of real property or a lessee or lessor of real property where the lease period is for longer than one year

4. An agreement by a purchaser of real property to pay a debt secured by a mortgage or deed of trust on the property purchased, unless the purchaser is to assume the debt

---

Exercise 7-1

1. Homeowner Clive Lentil is trying to sell his house without the assistance of a real estate agent. After four months in which he receives no offers on the house, Clive places an ad in the newspaper that states, "Three percent commission paid to buyer's agent at closing." Salesperson Sally phones Clive, identifies herself as a real estate agent, and makes an appointment to show Clive's house to one of her clients. Do Sally and Clive have an agreement? If Clive accepts the offer made by Sally's client, and the offer does not mention any commission for Sally, do Sally and Clive have an agreement? At closing, is Clive obliged to pay Sally the 3 percent commission? If the purchase offer that Clive accepted stipulated that Sally would receive a 3 percent commission on the transaction, would Clive and Sally have had an agreement at that point?

2. Jerry Kramer decides to make an all-cash offer on the Hardecker house. He fills out a standard offer to purchase, giving the street address of the property, and notes that the selling price is to be "agreed to by the parties." If Hardecker signs the contract, can Kramer enforce it?

3. When Jerry Kramer is shown the Hardecker house in Pasadena, the listing broker tells him the house was designed by Frank Lloyd Wright. Kramer immediately decides to buy the house. He questions Mr. Hardecker on the house's designer, and Hardecker also tells him the designer was Frank Lloyd Wright. Kramer makes an offer that is accepted by Hardecker. Before the sale closes, Kramer checks the city records and learns that Floyd White designed the house. Does Jerry have to go ahead with the sale?

4. On Monday, January 6, Sally Berman agreed to a one-year lease on an apartment at Shady Acres. The lease term began on Monday, January 13. Is the oral lease contract valid? Can the management of Shady Acres enforce the oral contract if Sally moves out before the end of the lease term?

■ DISCHARGING A CONTRACT

A **discharged contract** is one that is terminated. As discussed next, there are many ways to terminate a contract or change one or more of its terms, including the following:

- ■ Performance
- ■ Rescission
- ■ Release
- ■ Novation
- ■ Reformation
- ■ Assignment
- ■ Breach

Performance

Performance of its terms discharges a contract.

A contract may be discharged if some intervening cause creates an **impossibility of performance,** such as when the property that is the subject matter of the contract is destroyed. If a buyer of real estate suffers an unexpected disability and job loss, making it impossible to go through with the purchase, the buyer's performance will be excused.

Performance may be excused in the event of **impracticability of performance,** also called **commercial frustration.** If changed circumstances make a purchase uneconomic, there may be an excuse for nonperformance. This might be the case if a buyer's financial condition were to take a downturn (say, a sudden, extreme drop in market value of the buyer's company's stock), so that the purchase, although not impossible, would impose an extreme financial hardship. There also could be other reasons that were not known at the time the contract was formed.

Rescission

If both parties agree, they may take back (rescind) the contract in the process called **rescission.**

Release

A party to whom an obligation is owed may sign a written **release,** possibly for further consideration. The contract is then discharged, and the other party no longer has an obligation to perform.

Novation

By a **novation** the parties may substitute a new agreement for the original one, discharging the original agreement. If the new agreement falls within the Statute of Frauds, it must be written.

■ **FOR EXAMPLE:**   Jim and Janet Day make an offer to purchase the Castle estate. The offer is accepted, and the closing of the sale is to take place in two months. Before the closing date, Jim and Janet decide to dissolve their marriage and live apart. Alone, neither can qualify for a loan to purchase the Castle estate. What can Jim and Janet do to get out of their offer of purchase?

The Days should immediately inform the Castles, who may agree to rescind the contract. If not, the Days could refuse to perform on the grounds of impracticability but should consult an attorney first.

Reformation

At some point during the life of the contract, one of the parties may determine that a mistake has been made in the contract terms or that certain information should be made a part of the contract. There may be an inaccurate description of the subject property, the financing terms may need to be clarified, or new information may be discovered about the true condition of the property, particularly following an appraisal or property inspection. In any of those instances, it may be possible to bring about a **reformation** of the contract.

If all parties agree to the reformation, it is simply a matter of redrafting the contract or amending the escrow instructions. If one party objects, it is possible to bring a legal action to reform a contract, although the time and expense of a legal action usually make this alternative undesirable.

Assignment

Unless the contract requires a personal service or specifically prohibits an **assignment,** it probably can be assigned. In an assignment, the **assignee** is the new party who takes on the duties of the **assignor,** the party who makes the assignment. In return the assignee receives the compensation that would have gone to the assignor.

Breach

A contract also may be discharged by a **breach of contract.** A breach occurs when one of the parties fails to perform all or part of the obligations required by the contract. The nonbreaching party who is injured by the breach is entitled to legal relief.

> No two parcels of real estate are exactly alike.

An injury due to breach of contract entitles the injured party to ask for **money damages.** With some forms of contracts, **specific performance** of the contract also may be sought. If a court grants specific performance, the breaching party must fulfill the terms of the contract. Specific performance will be ordered only if the subject of the contract is considered unique and not readily replaceable. By definition, no parcel of real estate is exactly like any other parcel of real estate.

A court will not order specific performance unless the contract is supported by adequate consideration. This requires an offer (tender) of the entire purchase price by the offeror. Specific performance also will not be granted if the contract involves a personal service of the breaching party or if the agreement involves securing the consent or conduct of a third party.

Specific performance can only be obtained by bringing a lawsuit, which is expensive and time-consuming. As a result, this remedy is not sought very often. Most buyers of residential real estate have neither the ability nor the inclination to litigate a claim to a particular parcel of real estate.

The injured party in the breach of a real estate contract can ask for either money damages or specific performance. In some cases both may be sought. Damages may include the return of any consideration already given to the breaching party (if specific performance is not being sought) and payment of any expenses incurred because of the breach.

■ **FOR EXAMPLE:** A week before closing, Jim and Janet Day, who have reconciled their differences, decide against buying the Castle estate. What recourse do the Castles have when informed of the Days' decision?

The Castles can agree to rescind their contract and either keep or return the Days' earnest-money deposit. If the Castles keep the deposit, the Days could sue for its return. The Castles could agree to release the Days from their contractual obligation, but retain the security deposit as consideration for the release.

Or the Castles could sue the Days for specific performance. Most likely the Castles will sell the property as soon as possible to someone else and sue the Days for any loss in value that might result.

The injured party also could decide to **waive** the matter breached and enforce the contract on its remaining terms. Another use of a waiver is to remove a condition that a party has the right to enforce.

■ **FOR EXAMPLE:**   The Yees' offer to buy the King residence is conditioned on the Yees selling their home within the next 30 days. The Kings receive another offer that has no contingencies. The Kings ask the Yees to remove the home sale contingency from their offer to purchase within 48 hours, as is permitted by the contract. The Yees decide to go forward with the purchase, even though they have not yet sold their old home. To do so, the Yees sign a waiver of the home sale contingency in their contract with the Kings.

Often, the facts of a case may support more than one remedy. In any situation potentially involving a lawsuit, the advice of a real estate attorney should be sought as early as possible to ensure that no legal rights are lost.

Statute of Limitations

A legal action (lawsuit) must be brought within a specific period of time after the act that gives rise to it. The **Statute of Limitations** prescribes time limits for various lawsuits. You can remember the deadlines below by remembering the numbers 5-4-3-2-10.

- A lawsuit to recover **title** to real property must be brought within **five years.**
- An action based on a **written instrument** (such as a real estate sales contract) must be brought within **four years.**
- An action based on **fraud** must be brought within **three years** of the discovery of the fraud.
- An action based on an **oral agreement** (such as a lease for only a few months) must be brought within **two years.**
- An action based on a **judgment** must be brought within **ten years** of the awarding of the judgment.

Exercise 7-2

1. Brad and Mary Turner want to buy a house. They make an offer to purchase the Markham house for $365,000. Ted Markham, who is single, accepts. Before the sale is closed, Brad Turner is seriously injured on the job. The

Turners can no longer expect to comfortably make the house payments. What can they do?

2. The Wilsons are in the process of buying the Mulholland farm. Their offer was accepted, and they have received a loan commitment from a lender. Before the closing, however, the Mulhollands inform the Wilsons that they no longer wish to sell their property, "for sentimental reasons." What recourse do the Wilsons have?

■ REAL ESTATE CONTRACTS

This section examines one of the forms of real estate purchase contract and receipt for deposit currently used in California.

Real Estate Purchase Contracts

When someone is ready to make a purchase offer, the next step is the preparation of a **purchase contract.** The offer to purchase usually includes a **deposit** on the purchase price, so the purchase contract will also serve to acknowledge receipt of the deposit, if the offer is accepted.

As with any contract, a **real estate purchase contract and receipt for deposit** must be made by parties who have the **legal capacity** to do so. There must be an **offer** made on **definite terms** and with a **lawful objective.** There must be acceptance of those terms by all parties, and the contract must be supported by some form of payment, or **consideration.**

Use of a printed form. Figure 7.1, shown on pages 185–192 is a typical form of purchase contract and receipt for deposit that also serves as escrow instructions. It is followed by Figure 7.2, a two-page Buyer's Inspection Advisory form. This form adds information that the buyer should know.

Remember, until the purchase contract is signed by the seller, it is an offer only and can be withdrawn by the buyer at any time prior to acceptance. Because such a contract is long and quite detailed, it is likely to contain corrections and written additions. The general rule regarding preprinted forms is that

- **typed** insertions take precedence over **preprinted** material,
- **handwritten** insertions take precedence over both **typed** and **preprinted** material, and
- **specific information** takes precedence over **general information.**

Duties of the broker. A real estate broker (or associate licensee) may guide the buyer through the contract provisions and fill in the required information. Then the broker will present the offer to the seller in the presence of the listing broker, if that is a different person from the selling broker.

FIGURE 7.1

Residential Purchase Agreement

CALIFORNIA
RESIDENTIAL PURCHASE AGREEMENT
AND JOINT ESCROW INSTRUCTIONS
For Use With Single Family Residential Property — Attached or Detached
(C.A.R. Form RPA-CA, Revised 10/02)

Date _____, at _____, California.

1.   OFFER:
A.   THIS IS AN OFFER FROM _____
B.   THE REAL PROPERTY TO BE ACQUIRED is described as _____ ("Buyer").
_____, Assessor's Parcel No. _____, situated in
_____, County of _____, California, ("Property").
C.   THE PURCHASE PRICE offered is _____
_____ Dollars $ _____
D.   CLOSE OF ESCROW shall occur on _____ (date)(or ☐ _____ **Days** After Acceptance).

2.   FINANCE TERMS: Obtaining the loans below **is a contingency** of this Agreement unless: **(i)** either 2K or 2L is checked below; or **(ii)** otherwise agreed in writing. Buyer shall act diligently and in good faith to obtain the designated loans. Obtaining deposit, down payment and closing costs **is not a contingency.** Buyer represents that funds will be good when deposited with Escrow Holder.
A.   INITIAL DEPOSIT: Buyer has given a deposit in the amount of . . . .$ _____
to the agent submitting the offer (or to ☐ _____),
(or ☐ _____), made payable to _____), by personal check
which shall be held uncashed until Acceptance and then deposited within **3** business days after
Acceptance (or ☐ _____), with
Escrow Holder, (or ☐ into Broker's trust account).
B.   INCREASED DEPOSIT: Buyer shall deposit with Escrow Holder an increased deposit in the amount of . .$ _____
within _____ **Days** After Acceptance, or ☐ _____
C.   FIRST LOAN IN THE AMOUNT OF . . . .$ _____
(1) NEW First Deed of Trust in favor of lender, encumbering the Property, securing a note payable at
maximum interest of _____% fixed rate, or _____% initial adjustable rate with a maximum
interest rate of _____%, balance due in _____ years, amortized over _____ years. Buyer
shall pay loan fees/points not to exceed _____. (These terms apply whether the designated loan
is conventional, FHA or VA.)
(2) ☐ FHA ☐ VA: (The following terms only apply to the FHA or VA loan that is checked.)
Seller shall pay _____% discount points. Seller shall pay other fees not allowed to be paid by
Buyer, ☐ not to exceed $_____. Seller shall pay the cost of lender required Repairs
(including those for wood destroying pest) not otherwise provided for in this Agreement, ☐ not to
exceed $ _____. (Actual loan amount may increase if mortgage insurance premiums,
funding fees or closing costs are financed.)
D.   ADDITIONAL FINANCING TERMS: ☐ Seller financing, (C.A.R. Form SFA); ☐ secondary financing, ...$ _____
(C.A.R. Form PAA, paragraph 4A); ☐ assumed financing (C.A.R. Form PAA, paragraph 4B)
_____
_____
E.   BALANCE OF PURCHASE PRICE (not including costs of obtaining loans and other closing costs) in the amount of . . .$ _____
to be deposited with Escrow Holder within sufficient time to close escrow.
F.   PURCHASE PRICE (TOTAL): . . . .$ _____
G.   LOAN APPLICATIONS: Within **7** (or ☐ _____) **Days** After Acceptance, Buyer shall provide Seller a letter from lender or
mortgage loan broker stating that, based on a review of Buyer's written application and credit report, Buyer is prequalified or
preapproved for the NEW loan specified in 2C above.
H.   VERIFICATION OF DOWN PAYMENT AND CLOSING COSTS: Buyer (or Buyer's lender or loan broker pursuant to 2G) shall, within
7 (or ☐ _____) **Days** After Acceptance, provide Seller written verification of Buyer's down payment and closing costs.
I.   LOAN CONTINGENCY REMOVAL: **(i)** Within **17** (or ☐ _____) **Days** After Acceptance, Buyer shall, as specified in paragraph
14, remove the loan contingency or cancel this Agreement; **OR (ii)** (if checked) ☐ the loan contingency shall remain in effect
until the designated loans are funded.
J.   APPRAISAL CONTINGENCY AND REMOVAL: This Agreement is (OR, if checked, ☐ is NOT) contingent upon the Property
appraising at no less than the specified purchase price. If there is a loan contingency, at the time the loan contingency is
removed (or, if checked, ☐ within **17** (or _____) **Days** After Acceptance), Buyer shall, as specified in paragraph 14B(3), remove
the appraisal contingency or cancel this Agreement. If there is no loan contingency, Buyer shall, as specified in paragraph
14B(3), remove the appraisal contingency within **17** (or _____) **Days** After Acceptance.
K.   ☐ NO LOAN CONTINGENCY (If checked): Obtaining any loan in paragraphs 2C, 2D or elsewhere in this Agreement is NOT
a contingency of this Agreement. If Buyer does not obtain the loan and as a result Buyer does not purchase the Property, Seller
may be entitled to Buyer's deposit or other legal remedies.
L.   ☐ ALL CASH OFFER (If checked): No loan is needed to purchase the Property. Buyer shall, within **7** (or ☐ _____) **Days** After Acceptance,
provide Seller written verification of sufficient funds to close this transaction.

3.   CLOSING AND OCCUPANCY:
A.   Buyer intends (or ☐ does not intend) to occupy the Property as Buyer's primary residence.
B.   Seller-occupied or vacant property: Occupancy shall be delivered to Buyer at _____ AM/PM, ☐ on the date of Close Of
Escrow; ☐ on _____; or ☐ no later than _____ **Days** After Close Of Escrow. (C.A.R. Form PAA, paragraph 2.) If
transfer of title and occupancy do not occur at the same time, Buyer and Seller are advised to: **(i)** enter into a written occupancy
agreement; and **(ii)** consult with their insurance and legal advisors.

RPA-CA REVISED 10/02 (PAGE 1 OF 8)   Print Date

Buyer's Initials (_____)(_____)
Seller's Initials (_____)(_____)

Reviewed by _____ Date _____

EQUAL HOUSING
OPPORTUNITY

CALIFORNIA RESIDENTIAL PURCHASE AGREEMENT (RPA-CA PAGE 1 OF 8)

FIGURE 7.1

Residential Purchase Agreement (Continued)

Property Address: _____ Date: _____

C. **Tenant-occupied property: (i) Property shall be vacant** at least **5 (or ☐ _____) Days** Prior to Close Of Escrow, unless otherwise agreed in writing. **Note to Seller: If you are unable to deliver Property vacant in accordance with rent control and other applicable Law, you may be in breach of this Agreement.**

OR **(ii)** (if checked) ☐ **Tenant to remain in possession.** The attached addendum is incorporated into this Agreement (C.A.R. Form PAA, paragraph 3.);

OR **(iii)** (if checked) ☐ **This Agreement is contingent** upon Buyer and Seller entering into a written agreement regarding occupancy of the Property within the time specified in paragraph 14B(1). If no written agreement is reached within this time, either Buyer or Seller may cancel this Agreement in writing.

D. At Close Of Escrow, Seller assigns to Buyer any assignable warranty rights for items included in the sale and shall provide any available Copies of such warranties. Brokers cannot and will not determine the assignability of any warranties.

E. At Close Of Escrow, unless otherwise agreed in writing, Seller shall provide keys and/or means to operate all locks, mailboxes, security systems, alarms and garage door openers. If Property is a condominium or located in a common interest subdivision, Buyer may be required to pay a deposit to the Homeowners' Association ("HOA") to obtain keys to accessible HOA facilities.

4. **ALLOCATION OF COSTS (If checked):** Unless otherwise specified here, this paragraph only determines who is to pay for the report, inspection, test or service mentioned. If not specified here or elsewhere in this Agreement, the determination of who is to pay for any work recommended or identified by any such report, inspection, test or service shall be by the method specified in paragraph 14B(2).

A. **WOOD DESTROYING PEST INSPECTION:**
(1) ☐ Buyer ☐ Seller shall pay for an inspection and report for wood destroying pests and organisms ("Report") which shall be prepared by _____, a registered structural pest control company. The Report shall cover the accessible areas of the main building and attached structures and, if checked: ☐ detached garages and carports, ☐ detached decks, ☐ the following other structures or areas _____ _____. The Report shall not include roof coverings. If Property is a condominium or located in a common interest subdivision, the Report shall include only the separate interest and any exclusive-use areas being transferred and shall not include common areas, unless otherwise agreed. Water tests of shower pans on upper level units may not be performed without consent of the owners of property below the shower.

OR **(2)** ☐ **(If checked)** The attached addendum (C.A.R. Form WPA) regarding wood destroying pest inspection and allocation of cost is incorporated into this Agreement.

B. **OTHER INSPECTIONS AND REPORTS:**
(1) ☐ Buyer ☐ Seller shall pay to have septic or private sewage disposal systems inspected _____.
(2) ☐ Buyer ☐ Seller shall pay to have domestic wells tested for water potability and productivity _____.
(3) ☐ Buyer ☐ Seller shall pay for a natural hazard zone disclosure report prepared by _____.
(4) ☐ Buyer ☐ Seller shall pay for the following inspection or report _____.
(5) ☐ Buyer ☐ Seller shall pay for the following inspection or report _____.

C. **GOVERNMENT REQUIREMENTS AND RETROFIT:**
(1) ☐ Buyer ☐ Seller shall pay for smoke detector installation and/or water heater bracing, if required by Law. Prior to Close Of Escrow, Seller shall provide Buyer a written statement of compliance in accordance with state and local Law, unless exempt.
(2) ☐ Buyer ☐ Seller shall pay the cost of compliance with any other minimum mandatory government retrofit standards, inspections and reports if required as a condition of closing escrow under any Law. _____.

D. **ESCROW AND TITLE:**
(1) ☐ Buyer ☐ Seller shall pay escrow fee _____. Escrow Holder shall be _____.
(2) ☐ Buyer ☐ Seller shall pay for **owner's** title insurance policy specified in paragraph 12E _____. Owner's title policy to be issued by _____. (Buyer shall pay for any title insurance policy insuring Buyer's **lender**, unless otherwise agreed in writing.)

E. **OTHER COSTS:**
(1) ☐ Buyer ☐ Seller shall pay County transfer tax or transfer fee _____.
(2) ☐ Buyer ☐ Seller shall pay City transfer tax or transfer fee _____.
(3) ☐ Buyer ☐ Seller shall pay HOA transfer fee _____.
(4) ☐ Buyer ☐ Seller shall pay HOA document preparation fees _____.
(5) ☐ Buyer ☐ Seller shall pay the cost, not to exceed $ _____, of a one-year home warranty plan, issued by _____, with the following optional coverage: _____.
(6) ☐ Buyer ☐ Seller shall pay for_____.
(7) ☐ Buyer ☐ Seller shall pay for_____.

5. **STATUTORY DISCLOSURES (INCLUDING LEAD-BASED PAINT HAZARD DISCLOSURES) AND CANCELLATION RIGHTS:**
A. **(1)** Seller shall, within the time specified in paragraph 14A, deliver to Buyer, if required by Law: **(i)** Federal Lead-Based Paint Disclosures and pamphlet ("Lead Disclosures"); and **(ii)** disclosures or notices required by sections 1102 et. seq. and 1103 et. seq. of the California Civil Code ("Statutory Disclosures"). Statutory Disclosures include, but are not limited to, a Real Estate Transfer Disclosure Statement ("TDS"), Natural Hazard Disclosure Statement ("NHD"), notice or actual knowledge of release of illegal controlled substance, notice of special tax and/or assessments (or, if allowed, substantially equivalent notice regarding the Mello-Roos Community Facilities Act and Improvement Bond Act of 1915) and, if Seller has actual knowledge, an industrial use and military ordnance location disclosure (C.A.R. Form SSD).
(2) Buyer shall, within the time specified in paragraph 14B(1), return Signed Copies of the Statutory and Lead Disclosures to Seller.
(3) In the event Seller, prior to Close Of Escrow, becomes aware of adverse conditions materially affecting the Property, or any material inaccuracy in disclosures, information or representations previously provided to Buyer of which Buyer is otherwise unaware, Seller shall promptly provide a subsequent or amended disclosure or notice, in writing, covering those items. **However, a subsequent or amended disclosure shall not be required for conditions and material inaccuracies disclosed in reports ordered and paid for by Buyer.**

Buyer's Initials (_____)(_____)
Seller's Initials (_____)(_____)

RPA-CA REVISED 10/02 (PAGE 2 OF 8)

Reviewed by _____ Date _____

CALIFORNIA RESIDENTIAL PURCHASE AGREEMENT (RPA-CA PAGE 2 OF 8)

Source: Reprinted with permission, California Association of REALTORS®. Endorsement not implied.

FIGURE 7.1

Residential Purchase Agreement (Continued)

Property Address: _____   Date: _____

(4) If any disclosure or notice specified in 5A(1), or subsequent or amended disclosure or notice is delivered to Buyer after the offer is Signed, Buyer shall have the right to cancel this Agreement within **3 Days** After delivery in person, or **5 Days** After delivery by deposit in the mail, by giving written notice of cancellation to Seller or Seller's agent. (Lead Disclosures sent by mail must be sent certified mail or better.)

(5) Note to Buyer and Seller: Waiver of Statutory and Lead Disclosures is prohibited by Law.

B.   NATURAL AND ENVIRONMENTAL HAZARDS: Within the time specified in paragraph 14A, Seller shall, if required by Law: **(i)** deliver to Buyer earthquake guides (and questionnaire) and environmental hazards booklet; **(ii)** even if exempt from the obligation to provide a NHD, disclose if the Property is located in a Special Flood Hazard Area; Potential Flooding (Inundation) Area; Very High Fire Hazard Zone; State Fire Responsibility Area; Earthquake Fault Zone; Seismic Hazard Zone; and **(iii)** disclose any other zone as required by Law and provide any other information required for those zones.

C.   DATA BASE DISCLOSURE: NOTICE: The California Department of Justice, sheriff's departments, police departments serving jurisdictions of 200,000 or more and many other local law enforcement authorities maintain for public access a data base of the locations of persons required to register pursuant to paragraph (1) of subdivision (a) of Section 290.4 of the Penal Code. The data base is updated on a quarterly basis and a source of information about the presence of these individuals in any neighborhood. The Department of Justice also maintains a Sex Offender Identification Line through which inquiries about individuals may be made. This is a "900" telephone service. Callers must have specific information about individuals they are checking. Information regarding neighborhoods is not available through the "900" telephone service.

6.   CONDOMINIUM/PLANNED UNIT DEVELOPMENT DISCLOSURES:
   A.   SELLER HAS: 7 (or ☐ _____) Days After Acceptance to disclose to Buyer whether the Property is a condominium, or is located in a planned unit development or other common interest subdivision (C.A.R. Form SSD).
   B.   If the Property is a condominium or is located in a planned unit development or other common interest subdivision, Seller has **3 (or ☐ _____) Days** After Acceptance to request from the HOA (C.A.R. Form HOA): **(i)** Copies of any documents required by Law; **(ii)** disclosure of any pending or anticipated claim or litigation by or against the HOA; **(iii)** a statement containing the location and number of designated parking and storage spaces; **(iv)** Copies of the most recent 12 months of HOA minutes for regular and special meetings; and **(v)** the names and contact information of all HOAs governing the Property (collectively, "CI Disclosures"). Seller shall itemize and deliver to Buyer all CI Disclosures received from the HOA and any CI Disclosures in Seller's possession. Buyer's approval of CI Disclosures is a contingency of this Agreement as specified in paragraph 14B(3).

7.   CONDITIONS AFFECTING PROPERTY:
   A.   Unless otherwise agreed: **(i) the Property is sold (a) in its PRESENT physical condition as of the date of Acceptance and (b) subject to Buyer's Investigation rights; (ii)** the Property, including pool, spa, landscaping and grounds, is to be maintained in substantially the same condition as on the date of Acceptance; and **(iii)** all debris and personal property not included in the sale shall be removed by Close Of Escrow.
   B.   SELLER SHALL, within the time specified in paragraph 14A, DISCLOSE KNOWN MATERIAL FACTS AND DEFECTS affecting the Property, including known insurance claims within the past five years, **AND MAKE OTHER DISCLOSURES REQUIRED BY LAW (C.A.R. Form SSD).**
   C.   NOTE TO BUYER: You are strongly advised to conduct investigations of the entire Property in order to determine its present condition since Seller may not be aware of all defects affecting the Property or other factors that you consider important. Property improvements may not be built according to code, in compliance with current Law, or have had permits issued.
   D.   NOTE TO SELLER: Buyer has the right to inspect the Property and, as specified in paragraph 14B, based upon information discovered in those inspections: **(i)** cancel this Agreement; or **(ii)** request that you make Repairs or take other action.

8.   ITEMS INCLUDED AND EXCLUDED:
   A.   NOTE TO BUYER AND SELLER: Items listed as included or excluded in the MLS, flyers or marketing materials are **not** included in the purchase price or excluded from the sale unless specified in 8B or C.
   B.   ITEMS INCLUDED IN SALE:
      (1) All EXISTING fixtures and fittings that are attached to the Property;
      (2) Existing electrical, mechanical, lighting, plumbing and heating fixtures, ceiling fans, fireplace inserts, gas logs and grates, solar systems, built-in appliances, window and door screens, awnings, shutters, window coverings, attached floor coverings, television antennas, satellite dishes, private integrated telephone systems, air coolers/conditioners, pool/spa equipment, garage door openers/remote controls, mailbox, in-ground landscaping, trees/shrubs, water softeners, water purifiers, security systems/alarms; and
      (3) The following items: _____
      _____
      (4) Seller represents that all items included in the purchase price, unless otherwise specified, are owned by Seller.
      (5) All items included shall be transferred free of liens and without Seller warranty.
   C.   ITEMS EXCLUDED FROM SALE: _____
      _____

9.   BUYER'S INVESTIGATION OF PROPERTY AND MATTERS AFFECTING PROPERTY:
   A.   Buyer's acceptance of the condition of, and any other matter affecting the Property, is a contingency of this Agreement as specified in this paragraph and paragraph 14B. Within the time specified in paragraph 14B(1), Buyer shall have the right, at Buyer's expense unless otherwise agreed, to conduct inspections, investigations, tests, surveys and other studies ("Buyer Investigations"), including, but not limited to, the right to: **(i)** inspect for lead-based paint and other lead-based paint hazards; **(ii)** inspect for wood destroying pests and organisms; **(iii)** review the registered sex offender database; **(iv)** confirm the insurability of Buyer and the Property; and **(v)** satisfy Buyer as to any matter specified in the attached Buyer's Inspection Advisory (C.A.R. Form BIA). Without Seller's prior written consent, Buyer shall neither make nor cause to be made: **(i)** invasive or destructive Buyer Investigations; or **(ii)** inspections by any governmental building or zoning inspector or government employee, unless required by Law.
   B.   Buyer shall complete Buyer Investigations and, as specified in paragraph 14B, remove the contingency or cancel this Agreement. Buyer shall give Seller, at no cost, complete Copies of all Buyer Investigation reports obtained by Buyer. Seller shall make the Property available for all Buyer Investigations. Seller shall have water, gas, electricity and all operable pilot lights on for Buyer's Investigations and through the date possession is made available to Buyer.

Buyer's Initials (_____)(_____)
Seller's Initials (_____)(_____)

RPA-CA REVISED 10/02 (PAGE 3 OF 8)

Reviewed by _____ Date _____

CALIFORNIA RESIDENTIAL PURCHASE AGREEMENT (RPA-CA PAGE 3 OF 8)

FIGURE 7.1

Residential Purchase Agreement (Continued)

Property Address: _____ Date: _____

10. **REPAIRS:** Repairs shall be completed prior to final verification of condition unless otherwise agreed in writing. Repairs to be performed at Seller's expense may be performed by Seller or through others, provided that the work complies with applicable Law, including governmental permit, inspection and approval requirements. Repairs shall be performed in a good, skillful manner with materials of quality and appearance comparable to existing materials. It is understood that exact restoration of appearance or cosmetic items following all Repairs may not be possible. Seller shall: **(i)** obtain receipts for Repairs performed by others; **(ii)** prepare a written statement indicating the Repairs performed by Seller and the date of such Repairs; and **(iii)** provide Copies of receipts and statements to Buyer prior to final verification of condition.

11. **BUYER INDEMNITY AND SELLER PROTECTION FOR ENTRY UPON PROPERTY:** Buyer shall: **(i)** keep the Property free and clear of liens; **(ii)** Repair all damage arising from Buyer Investigations; and **(iii)** indemnify and hold Seller harmless from all resulting liability, claims, demands, damages and costs. Buyer shall carry, or Buyer shall require anyone acting on Buyer's behalf to carry, policies of liability, workers' compensation and other applicable insurance, defending and protecting Seller from liability for any injuries to persons or property occurring during any Buyer Investigations or work done on the Property at Buyer's direction prior to Close Of Escrow. Seller is advised that certain protections may be afforded Seller by recording a "Notice of Non-responsibility" (C.A.R. Form NNR) for Buyer Investigations and work done on the Property at Buyer's direction. Buyer's obligations under this paragraph shall survive the termination of this Agreement.

12. **TITLE AND VESTING:**
    A. Within the time specified in paragraph 14, Buyer shall be provided a current preliminary (title) report, which is only an offer by the title insurer to issue a policy of title insurance and may not contain every item affecting title. Buyer's review of the preliminary report and any other matters which may affect title are a contingency of this Agreement as specified in paragraph 14B.
    B. Title is taken in its present condition subject to all encumbrances, easements, covenants, conditions, restrictions, rights and other matters, whether of record or not, as of the date of Acceptance except: **(i)** monetary liens of record unless Buyer is assuming those obligations or taking the Property subject to those obligations; and **(ii)** those matters which Seller has agreed to remove in writing.
    C. Within the time specified in paragraph 14A, Seller has a duty to disclose to Buyer all matters known to Seller affecting title, whether of record or not.
    D. At Close Of Escrow, Buyer shall receive a grant deed conveying title (or, for stock cooperative or long-term lease, an assignment of stock certificate or of Seller's leasehold interest), including oil, mineral and water rights if currently owned by Seller. Title shall vest as designated in Buyer's supplemental escrow instructions. THE MANNER OF TAKING TITLE MAY HAVE SIGNIFICANT LEGAL AND TAX CONSEQUENCES. CONSULT AN APPROPRIATE PROFESSIONAL.
    E. Buyer shall receive a CLTA/ALTA Homeowner's Policy of Title Insurance. A title company, at Buyer's request, can provide information about the availability, desirability, coverage, and cost of various title insurance coverages and endorsements. If Buyer desires title coverage other than that required by this paragraph, Buyer shall instruct Escrow Holder in writing and pay any increase in cost.

13. **SALE OF BUYER'S PROPERTY:**
    A. This Agreement is NOT contingent upon the sale of any property owned by Buyer.
    OR B. ☐ (If checked): The attached addendum (C.A.R. Form COP) regarding the contingency for the sale of property owned by Buyer is incorporated into this Agreement.

14. **TIME PERIODS; REMOVAL OF CONTINGENCIES; CANCELLATION RIGHTS: The following time periods may only be extended, altered, modified or changed by mutual written agreement. Any removal of contingencies or cancellation under this paragraph must be in writing (C.A.R. Form CR).**
    A. SELLER HAS: 7 (or ☐ **_____) Days** After Acceptance to deliver to Buyer all reports, disclosures and information for which Seller is responsible under paragraphs 4, 5A and B, 6A, 7B and 12.
    B. (1) BUYER HAS: 17 (or ☐ **_____) Days** After Acceptance, unless otherwise agreed in writing, to:
        (i) complete all Buyer Investigations; approve all disclosures, reports and other applicable information, which Buyer receives from Seller; and approve all matters affecting the Property (including lead-based paint and lead-based paint hazards as well as other information specified in paragraph 5 and insurability of Buyer and the Property); and
        (ii) return to Seller Signed Copies of Statutory and Lead Disclosures delivered by Seller in accordance with paragraph 5A.
    (2) Within the time specified in 14B(1), Buyer may request that Seller make repairs or take any other action regarding the Property (C.A.R. Form RR). Seller has no obligation to agree to or respond to Buyer's requests.
    (3) By the end of the time specified in 14B(1) (or 2I for loan contingency or 2J for appraisal contingency), Buyer shall, in writing, remove the applicable contingency (C.A.R. Form CR) or cancel this Agreement. However, if the following inspections, reports or disclosures are not made within the time specified in 14A, then Buyer has **5 (or** ☐ **_____) Days** after receipt of any such items, or the time specified in 14B(1), whichever is later, to remove the applicable contingency or cancel this Agreement in writing: **(i)** government-mandated inspections or reports required as a condition of closing; or **(ii)** Common Interest Disclosures pursuant to paragraph 6B.
    C. CONTINUATION OF CONTINGENCY OR CONTRACTUAL OBLIGATION; SELLER RIGHT TO CANCEL:
        (1) Seller right to Cancel; Buyer Contingencies: Seller, after first giving Buyer a Notice to Buyer to Perform (as specified below), may cancel this Agreement in writing and authorize return of Buyer's deposit if, by the time specified in this Agreement, Buyer does not remove in writing the applicable contingency or cancel this Agreement. Once all contingencies have been removed, failure of either Buyer or Seller to close escrow on time may be a breach of this Agreement.
        (2) Continuation of Contingency: Even after the expiration of the time specified in 14B(1), Buyer retains the right to make requests to Seller, remove in writing the applicable contingency or cancel this Agreement until Seller cancels pursuant to 14C(1). Once Seller receives Buyer's written removal of all contingencies, Seller may not cancel this Agreement pursuant to 14C(1).
        (3) Seller right to Cancel; Buyer Contract Obligations: Seller, after first giving Buyer a Notice to Buyer to Perform (as specified below), may cancel this Agreement in writing and authorize return of Buyer's deposit for any of the following reasons: **(i)** if Buyer fails to deposit funds as required by 2A or 2B; **(ii)** if the funds deposited pursuant to 2A or 2B are not good when deposited; **(iii)** if Buyer fails to provide a letter as required by 2G; **(iv)** if Buyer fails to provide verification as required by 2H or 2L; **(v)** if Seller reasonably disapproves of the verification provided by 2H or 2L; **(vi)** if Buyer fails to return Statutory and Lead Disclosures as required by paragraph 5A(2); or **(vii)** if Buyer fails to sign or initial a separate liquidated damage form for an increased deposit as required by paragraph 16. **Seller is not required to give Buyer a Notice to Perform regarding Close of Escrow.**
        (4) Notice To Buyer To Perform: The Notice to Buyer to Perform (C.A.R. Form NBP) shall: **(i)** be in writing; **(ii)** be signed by Seller; and **(iii)** give Buyer at least **24 (or** ☐ **_____) hours** (or until the time specified in the applicable paragraph, whichever occurs last) to take the applicable action. A Notice to Buyer to Perform may not be given any earlier than **2 Days** Prior to the expiration of the applicable time for Buyer to remove a contingency or cancel this Agreement or meet a 14C(3) obligation.

Buyer's Initials (_____)(_____)
Seller's Initials (_____)(_____)

RPA-CA REVISED 10/02 (PAGE 4 OF 8)

Reviewed by _____ Date _____

CALIFORNIA RESIDENTIAL PURCHASE AGREEMENT (RPA-CA PAGE 4 OF 8)

FIGURE 7.1

Residential Purchase Agreement (Continued)

Property Address: _____   Date: _____

D. EFFECT OF BUYER'S REMOVAL OF CONTINGENCIES : If Buyer removes, in writing, any contingency or cancellation rights, unless otherwise specified in a separate written agreement between Buyer and Seller, Buyer shall conclusively be deemed to have: **(i)** completed all Buyer Investigations, and review of reports and other applicable information and disclosures pertaining to that contingency or cancellation right; **(ii)** elected to proceed with the transaction; and **(iii)** assumed all liability, responsibility and expense for Repairs or corrections pertaining to that contingency or cancellation right, or for inability to obtain financing.

E. EFFECT OF CANCELLATION ON DEPOSITS: If Buyer or Seller gives written notice of cancellation pursuant to rights duly exercised under the terms of this Agreement, Buyer and Seller agree to Sign mutual instructions to cancel the sale and escrow and release deposits, less fees and costs, to the party entitled to the funds. Fees and costs may be payable to service providers and vendors for services and products provided during escrow. **Release of funds will require mutual Signed release instructions from Buyer and Seller, judicial decision or arbitration award. A party may be subject to a civil penalty of up to $1,000 for refusal to sign such instructions if no good faith dispute exists as to who is entitled to the deposited funds (Civil Code §1057.3).**

15. FINAL VERIFICATION OF CONDITION: Buyer shall have the right to make a final inspection of the Property within **5 (or _____) Days** Prior to Close Of Escrow, NOT AS A CONTINGENCY OF THE SALE, but solely to confirm: **(i)** the Property is maintained pursuant to paragraph 7A; **(ii)** Repairs have been completed as agreed; and **(iii)** Seller has complied with Seller's other obligations under this Agreement.

16. LIQUIDATED DAMAGES: If Buyer fails to complete this purchase because of Buyer's default, Seller shall retain, as liquidated damages, the deposit actually paid. If the Property is a dwelling with no more than four units, one of which Buyer intends to occupy, then the amount retained shall be no more than 3% of the purchase price. Any excess shall be returned to Buyer. Release of funds will require mutual, Signed release instructions from both Buyer and Seller, judicial decision or arbitration award. BUYER AND SELLER SHALL SIGN A SEPARATE LIQUIDATED DAMAGES PROVISION FOR ANY INCREASED DEPOSIT. (C.A.R. FORM RID)

Buyer's Initials _____/_____	Seller's Initials _____/_____

17. DISPUTE RESOLUTION:

A. MEDIATION: Buyer and Seller agree to mediate any dispute or claim arising between them out of this Agreement, or any resulting transaction, before resorting to arbitration or court action. Paragraphs 17B(2) and (3) below apply whether or not the Arbitration provision is initialed. Mediation fees, if any, shall be divided equally among the parties involved. If, for any dispute or claim to which this paragraph applies, any party commences an action without first attempting to resolve the matter through mediation, or refuses to mediate after a request has been made, then that party shall not be entitled to recover attorney fees, even if they would otherwise be available to that party in any such action. THIS MEDIATION PROVISION APPLIES WHETHER OR NOT THE ARBITRATION PROVISION IS INITIALED.

B. ARBITRATION OF DISPUTES: (1) Buyer and Seller agree that any dispute or claim in Law or equity arising between them out of this Agreement or any resulting transaction, which is not settled through mediation, shall be decided by neutral, binding arbitration, including and subject to paragraphs 17B(2) and (3) below. The arbitrator shall be a retired judge or justice, or an attorney with at least 5 years of residential real estate Law experience, unless the parties mutually agree to a different arbitrator, who shall render an award in accordance with substantive California Law. The parties shall have the right to discovery in accordance with California Code of Civil Procedure §1283.05. In all other respects, the arbitration shall be conducted in accordance with Title 9 of Part III of the California Code of Civil Procedure. Judgment upon the award of the arbitrator(s) may be entered into any court having jurisdiction. Interpretation of this agreement to arbitrate shall be governed by the Federal Arbitration Act.

(2) EXCLUSIONS FROM MEDIATION AND ARBITRATION: The following matters are excluded from mediation and arbitration: (i) a judicial or non-judicial foreclosure or other action or proceeding to enforce a deed of trust, mortgage or installment land sale contract as defined in California Civil Code §2985; (ii) an unlawful detainer action; (iii) the filing or enforcement of a mechanic's lien; and (iv) any matter that is within the jurisdiction of a probate, small claims or bankruptcy court. The filing of a court action to enable the recording of a notice of pending action, for order of attachment, receivership, injunction, or other provisional remedies, shall not constitute a waiver of the mediation and arbitration provisions.

(3) BROKERS: Buyer and Seller agree to mediate and arbitrate disputes or claims involving either or both Brokers, consistent with 17A and B, provided either or both Brokers shall have agreed to such mediation or arbitration prior to, or within a reasonable time after, the dispute or claim is presented to Brokers. Any election by either or both Brokers to participate in mediation or arbitration shall not result in Brokers being deemed parties to the Agreement.

"NOTICE: BY INITIALING IN THE SPACE BELOW YOU ARE AGREEING TO HAVE ANY DISPUTE ARISING OUT OF THE MATTERS INCLUDED IN THE 'ARBITRATION OF DISPUTES' PROVISION DECIDED BY NEUTRAL ARBITRATION AS PROVIDED BY CALIFORNIA LAW AND YOU ARE GIVING UP ANY RIGHTS YOU MIGHT POSSESS TO HAVE THE DISPUTE LITIGATED IN A COURT OR JURY TRIAL. BY INITIALING IN THE SPACE BELOW YOU ARE GIVING UP YOUR JUDICIAL RIGHTS TO DISCOVERY AND APPEAL, UNLESS THOSE RIGHTS ARE SPECIFICALLY INCLUDED IN THE 'ARBITRATION OF DISPUTES' PROVISION. IF YOU REFUSE TO SUBMIT TO ARBITRATION AFTER AGREEING TO THIS PROVISION, YOU MAY BE COMPELLED TO ARBITRATE UNDER THE AUTHORITY OF THE CALIFORNIA CODE OF CIVIL PROCEDURE. YOUR AGREEMENT TO THIS ARBITRATION PROVISION IS VOLUNTARY."

"WE HAVE READ AND UNDERSTAND THE FOREGOING AND AGREE TO SUBMIT DISPUTES ARISING OUT OF THE MATTERS INCLUDED IN THE 'ARBITRATION OF DISPUTES' PROVISION TO NEUTRAL ARBITRATION."

Buyer's Initials _____/_____	Seller's Initials _____/_____

Buyer's Initials (_____)(_____)
Seller's Initials (_____)(_____)

Copyright © 1991-2003, CALIFORNIA ASSOCIATION OF REALTORS®, INC.
RPA-CA REVISED 10/02 (PAGE 5 OF 8)

Reviewed by _____ Date _____

EQUAL HOUSING OPPORTUNITY

CALIFORNIA RESIDENTIAL PURCHASE AGREEMENT (RPA-CA PAGE 5 OF 8)

FIGURE 7.1

Residential Purchase Agreement (Continued)

Property Address: _____ Date: _____

18. **PRORATIONS OF PROPERTY TAXES AND OTHER ITEMS:** Unless otherwise agreed in writing, the following items shall be PAID CURRENT and prorated between Buyer and Seller as of Close Of Escrow: real property taxes and assessments, interest, rents, HOA regular, special, and emergency dues and assessments imposed prior to Close Of Escrow, premiums on insurance assumed by Buyer, payments on bonds and assessments assumed by Buyer, and payments on Mello-Roos and other Special Assessment District bonds and assessments that are now a lien. The following items shall be assumed by Buyer WITHOUT CREDIT toward the purchase price: prorated payments on Mello-Roos and other Special Assessment District bonds and assessments and HOA special assessments that are now a lien but not yet due. Property will be reassessed upon change of ownership. Any supplemental tax bills shall be paid as follows: **(i)** for periods after Close Of Escrow, by Buyer; and **(ii)** for periods prior to Close Of Escrow, by Seller. TAX BILLS ISSUED AFTER CLOSE OF ESCROW SHALL BE HANDLED DIRECTLY BETWEEN BUYER AND SELLER. Prorations shall be made based on a 30-day month.

19. **WITHHOLDING TAXES:** Seller and Buyer agree to execute any instrument, affidavit, statement or instruction reasonably necessary to comply with federal (FIRPTA) and California withholding Law, if required (C.A.R. Forms AS and AB).

20. **MULTIPLE LISTING SERVICE ("MLS"):** Brokers are authorized to report to the MLS a pending sale and, upon Close Of Escrow, the terms of this transaction to be published and disseminated to persons and entities authorized to use the information on terms approved by the MLS.

21. **EQUAL HOUSING OPPORTUNITY:** The Property is sold in compliance with federal, state and local anti-discrimination Laws.

22. **ATTORNEY FEES:** In any action, proceeding, or arbitration between Buyer and Seller arising out of this Agreement, the prevailing Buyer or Seller shall be entitled to reasonable attorney fees and costs from the non-prevailing Buyer or Seller, except as provided in paragraph 17A.

23. **SELECTION OF SERVICE PROVIDERS:** If Brokers refer Buyer or Seller to persons, vendors, or service or product providers ("Providers"), Brokers do not guarantee the performance of any Providers. Buyer and Seller may select ANY Providers of their own choosing.

24. **TIME OF ESSENCE; ENTIRE CONTRACT; CHANGES:** Time is of the essence. All understandings between the parties are incorporated in this Agreement. Its terms are intended by the parties as a final, complete and exclusive expression of their Agreement with respect to its subject matter, and may not be contradicted by evidence of any prior agreement or contemporaneous oral agreement. If any provision of this Agreement is held to be ineffective or invalid, the remaining provisions will nevertheless be given full force and effect. **Neither this Agreement nor any provision in it may be extended, amended, modified, altered or changed, except in writing Signed by Buyer and Seller.**

25. **OTHER TERMS AND CONDITIONS,** including attached supplements:
    A. ☑ Buyer's Inspection Advisory (C.A.R. Form BIA) _____
    B. ☐ Purchase Agreement Addendum (C.A.R. Form PAA paragraph numbers:)
    C. _____
    _____
    _____

26. **DEFINITIONS:** As used in this Agreement:
    A. **"Acceptance"** means the time the offer or final counter offer is accepted in writing by a party and is delivered to and personally received by the other party or that party's authorized agent in accordance with the terms of this offer or a final counter offer.
    B. **"Agreement"** means the terms and conditions of this accepted California Residential Purchase Agreement and any accepted counter offers and addenda.
    C. **"C.A.R. Form"** means the specific form referenced or another comparable form agreed to by the parties.
    D. **"Close Of Escrow"** means the date the grant deed, or other evidence of transfer of title, is recorded. If the scheduled close of escrow falls on a Saturday, Sunday or legal holiday, then close of escrow shall be the next business day after the scheduled close of escrow date.
    E. **"Copy"** means copy by any means including photocopy, NCR, facsimile and electronic.
    F. **"Days"** means calendar days, unless otherwise required by Law.
    G. **"Days After"** means the specified number of calendar days after the occurrence of the event specified, not counting the calendar date on which the specified event occurs, and ending at 11:59PM on the final day.
    H. **"Days Prior"** means the specified number of calendar days before the occurrence of the event specified, not counting the calendar date on which the specified event is scheduled to occur.
    I. **"Electronic Copy" or "Electronic Signature"** means, as applicable, an electronic copy or signature complying with California Law. Buyer and Seller agree that electronic means will not be used by either party to modify or alter the content or integrity of this Agreement without the knowledge and consent of the other.
    J. **"Law"** means any law, code, statute, ordinance, regulation, rule or order, which is adopted by a controlling city, county, state or federal legislative, judicial or executive body or agency.
    K. **"Notice to Buyer to Perform"** means a document (C.A.R. Form NBP), which shall be in writing and Signed by Seller and shall give Buyer at least 24 hours **(or as otherwise specified in paragraph 14C(4))** to remove a contingency or perform as applicable.
    L. **"Repairs"** means any repairs (including pest control), alterations, replacements, modifications or retrofitting of the Property provided for under this Agreement.
    M. **"Signed"** means either a handwritten or electronic signature on an original document, Copy or any counterpart.
    N. **Singular and Plural** terms each include the other, when appropriate.

Buyer's Initials (_____)(_____)
Seller's Initials (_____)(_____)

RPA-CA REVISED 10/02 (PAGE 6 OF 8)

Reviewed by _____ Date _____

EQUAL HOUSING OPPORTUNITY

CALIFORNIA RESIDENTIAL PURCHASE AGREEMENT (RPA-CA PAGE 6 OF 8)

FIGURE 7.1

Residential Purchase Agreement (Continued)

Property Address: _____   Date: _____

27. AGENCY:

    A. DISCLOSURE: Buyer and Seller each acknowledge prior receipt of C.A.R. Form AD "Disclosure Regarding Real Estate Agency Relationships."

    B. POTENTIALLY COMPETING BUYERS AND SELLERS: Buyer and Seller each acknowledge receipt of a disclosure of the possibility of multiple representation by the Broker representing that principal. This disclosure may be part of a listing agreement, buyer-broker agreement or separate document (C.A.R. Form DA). Buyer understands that Broker representing Buyer may also represent other potential buyers, who may consider, make offers on or ultimately acquire the Property. Seller understands that Broker representing Seller may also represent other sellers with competing properties of interest to this Buyer.

    C. CONFIRMATION: The following agency relationships are hereby confirmed for this transaction:
Listing Agent _____ (Print Firm Name) is the agent of (check one): ☐ the Seller exclusively; or ☐ both the Buyer and Seller.
Selling Agent _____ (Print Firm Name) (if not same as Listing Agent) is the agent of (check one): ☐ the Buyer exclusively; or ☐ the Seller exclusively; or ☐ both the Buyer and Seller. Real Estate Brokers are not parties to the Agreement between Buyer and Seller.

28. JOINT ESCROW INSTRUCTIONS TO ESCROW HOLDER:

    A. The following paragraphs, or applicable portions thereof, of this Agreement constitute the joint escrow instructions of Buyer and Seller to Escrow Holder, which Escrow Holder is to use along with any related counter offers and addenda, and any additional mutual instructions to close the escrow: 1, 2, 4, 12, 13B, 14E, 18, 19, 24, 25B and C, 26, 28, 29, 32A, 33 and paragraph D of the section titled Real Estate Brokers on page 8. If a Copy of the separate compensation agreement(s) provided for in paragraph 29 or 32A, or paragraph D of the section titled Real Estate Brokers on page 8 is deposited with Escrow Holder by Broker, Escrow Holder shall accept such agreement(s) and pay out from Buyer's or Seller's funds, or both, as applicable, the Broker's compensation provided for in such agreement(s). The terms and conditions of this Agreement not set forth in the specified paragraphs are additional matters for the information of Escrow Holder, but about which Escrow Holder need not be concerned. Buyer and Seller will receive Escrow Holder's general provisions directly from Escrow Holder and will execute such provisions upon Escrow Holder's request. To the extent the general provisions are inconsistent or conflict with this Agreement, the general provisions will control as to the duties and obligations of Escrow Holder only. Buyer and Seller will execute additional instructions, documents and forms provided by Escrow Holder that are reasonably necessary to close the escrow.

    B. A Copy of this Agreement shall be delivered to Escrow Holder within **3** business days after Acceptance (or ☐ _____). Buyer and Seller authorize Escrow Holder to accept and rely on Copies and Signatures as defined in this Agreement as originals, to open escrow and for other purposes of escrow. The validity of this Agreement as between Buyer and Seller is not affected by whether or when Escrow Holder Signs this Agreement.

    C. Brokers are a party to the escrow for the sole purpose of compensation pursuant to paragraphs 29, 32A and paragraph D of the section titled Real Estate Brokers on page 8. Buyer and Seller irrevocably assign to Brokers compensation specified in paragraphs 29 and 32A, respectively, and irrevocably instruct Escrow Holder to disburse those funds to Brokers at Close Of Escrow or pursuant to any other mutually executed cancellation agreement. Compensation instructions can be amended or revoked only with the written consent of Brokers. Escrow Holder shall immediately notify Brokers: **(i)** if Buyer's initial or any additional deposit is not made pursuant to this Agreement, or is not good at time of deposit with Escrow Holder; or **(ii)** if Buyer and Seller instruct Escrow Holder to cancel escrow.

    D. A Copy of any amendment that affects any paragraph of this Agreement for which Escrow Holder is responsible shall be delivered to Escrow Holder within **2** business days after mutual execution of the amendment.

29. BROKER COMPENSATION FROM BUYER: If applicable, upon Close Of Escrow, **Buyer** agrees to pay compensation to Broker as specified in a separate written agreement between Buyer and Broker.

30. TERMS AND CONDITIONS OF OFFER:

This is an offer to purchase the Property on the above terms and conditions. All paragraphs with spaces for initials by Buyer and Seller are incorporated in this Agreement only if initialed by all parties. If at least one but not all parties initial, a counter offer is required until agreement is reached. Seller has the right to continue to offer the Property for sale and to accept any other offer at any time prior to notification of Acceptance. Buyer has read and acknowledges receipt of a Copy of the offer and agrees to the above confirmation of agency relationships. If this offer is accepted and Buyer subsequently defaults, Buyer may be responsible for payment of Brokers' compensation. This Agreement and any supplement, addendum or modification, including any Copy, may be Signed in two or more counterparts, all of which shall constitute one and the same writing.

Buyer's Initials (_____)(_____)
Seller's Initials (_____)(_____)

RPA-CA REVISED 10/02 (PAGE 7 OF 8)

Reviewed by _____ Date _____

EQUAL HOUSING OPPORTUNITY

CALIFORNIA RESIDENTIAL PURCHASE AGREEMENT (RPA-CA PAGE 7 OF 8)

FIGURE 7.1

Residential Purchase Agreement (Continued)

Property Address: _____ Date: _____

31. EXPIRATION OF OFFER: This offer shall be deemed revoked and the deposit shall be returned unless the offer is Signed by Seller and a Copy of the Signed offer is personally received by Buyer, or by _____, who is authorized to receive it by 5:00 PM on the third calendar day after this offer is signed by Buyer (or, if checked, ☐ by _____ (date), at _____ AM/PM).

Date _____   Date _____

BUYER _____   BUYER _____

_____   _____
(Print name)   **(Print name)**

_____
(Address)

32. BROKER COMPENSATION FROM SELLER:
  A. Upon Close Of Escrow, **Seller** agrees to pay compensation to Broker as specified in a separate written agreement between Seller and Broker.
  B. If escrow does not close, compensation is payable as specified in that separate written agreement.
33. ACCEPTANCE OF OFFER: Seller warrants that Seller is the owner of the Property, or has the authority to execute this Agreement. Seller accepts the above offer, agrees to sell the Property on the above terms and conditions, and agrees to the above confirmation of agency relationships. Seller has read and acknowledges receipt of a Copy of this Agreement, and authorizes Broker to deliver a Signed Copy to Buyer.
  ☐ (If checked) **SUBJECT TO ATTACHED COUNTER OFFER, DATED** _____ .

Date _____   Date _____

SELLER _____   SELLER _____

_____   _____
(Print name)   **(Print name)**

_____
(Address)

(___/___)   **CONFIRMATION OF ACCEPTANCE:** A Copy of Signed Acceptance was personally received by Buyer or Buyer's authorized
(Initials)   agent on (date) _____ at _____ AM/PM. **A binding Agreement is created when a Copy of Signed Acceptance is personally received by Buyer or Buyer's authorized agent whether or not confirmed in this document. Completion of this confirmation is not legally required in order to create a binding Agreement; it is solely intended to evidence the date that Confirmation of Acceptance has occurred.**

REAL ESTATE BROKERS:
A. Real Estate Brokers are not parties to the Agreement between Buyer and Seller.
B. Agency relationships are confirmed as stated in paragraph 27.
C. If specified in paragraph 2A, Agent who submitted the offer for Buyer acknowledges receipt of deposit.
D. **COOPERATING BROKER COMPENSATION:** Listing Broker agrees to pay Cooperating Broker (**Selling Firm**) and Cooperating Broker agrees to accept, out of Listing Broker's proceeds in escrow: **(i)** the amount specified in the MLS, provided Cooperating Broker is a Participant of the MLS in which the Property is offered for sale or a reciprocal MLS; or **(ii)** ☐ (if checked) the amount specified in a separate written agreement (C.A.R. Form CBC) between Listing Broker and Cooperating Broker.

Real Estate Broker (Selling Firm) _____
By _____   Date _____
Address _____ City _____ State _____ Zip _____
Telephone _____ Fax _____ E-mail _____

Real Estate Broker (Listing Firm) _____
By _____   Date _____
Address _____ City _____ State _____ Zip _____
Telephone _____ Fax _____ E-mail _____

ESCROW HOLDER ACKNOWLEDGMENT:
Escrow Holder acknowledges receipt of a Copy of this Agreement, (if checked, ☐ a deposit in the amount of $ _____),
counter offer numbers _____ and _____, and agrees to act as Escrow Holder subject to paragraph 28 of this Agreement, any supplemental escrow instructions and the terms of Escrow Holder's general provisions.

Escrow Holder is advised that the date of Confirmation of Acceptance of the Agreement as between Buyer and Seller is _____

Escrow Holder _____ Escrow # _____
By _____ Date _____
Address _____
Phone/Fax/E-mail _____
Escrow Holder is licensed by the California Department of ☐ Corporations, ☐ Insurance, ☐ Real Estate. License # _____

(___/___)   **REJECTION OF OFFER:** No counter offer is being made. This offer was reviewed and rejected by Seller on
(Seller's Initials)   _____ (Date)

THIS FORM HAS BEEN APPROVED BY THE CALIFORNIA ASSOCIATION OF REALTORS® (C.A.R.). NO REPRESENTATION IS MADE AS TO THE LEGAL VALIDITY OR ADEQUACY OF ANY PROVISION IN ANY SPECIFIC TRANSACTION. A REAL ESTATE BROKER IS THE PERSON QUALIFIED TO ADVISE ON REAL ESTATE TRANSACTIONS. IF YOU DESIRE LEGAL OR TAX ADVICE, CONSULT AN APPROPRIATE PROFESSIONAL.
This form is available for use by the entire real estate industry. It is not intended to identify the user as a REALTOR®. REALTOR® is a registered collective membership mark which may be used only by members of the NATIONAL ASSOCIATION OF REALTORS® who subscribe to its Code of Ethics.

SURE TRAC The System for Success™   Published by the California Association of REALTORS®

RPA-CA REVISED 10/02 (PAGE 8 OF 8)

Reviewed by _____ Date _____   EQUAL HOUSING OPPORTUNITY

CALIFORNIA RESIDENTIAL PURCHASE AGREEMENT (RPA-CA PAGE 8 OF 8)

Source: Reprinted with permission, California Association of REALTORS®. Endorsement not implied.

FIGURE 7.2

Buyer's Inspection Advisory

CALIFORNIA
ASSOCIATION
OF REALTORS®

BUYER'S INSPECTION ADVISORY
(C.A.R. Form BIA, Revised 10/02)

Property Address: _____ ("Property").

A. IMPORTANCE OF PROPERTY INVESTIGATION: The physical condition of the land and improvements being purchased is not guaranteed by either Seller or Brokers. For this reason, you should conduct thorough investigations of the Property personally and with professionals who should provide written reports of their investigations. A general physical inspection typically does not cover all aspects of the Property nor items affecting the Property that are not physically located on the Property. If the professionals recommend further investigations, including a recommendation by a pest control operator to inspect inaccessible areas of the Property, you should contact qualified experts to conduct such additional investigations.

B. BUYER RIGHTS AND DUTIES: You have an affirmative duty to exercise reasonable care to protect yourself, including discovery of the legal, practical and technical implications of disclosed facts, and the investigation and verification of information and facts that you know or that are within your diligent attention and observation. The purchase agreement gives you the right to investigate the Property. If you exercise this right, and you should, you must do so in accordance with the terms of that agreement. This is the best way for you to protect yourself. It is extremely important for you to read all written reports provided by professionals and to discuss the results of inspections with the professional who conducted the inspection. You have the right to request that Seller make repairs, corrections or take other action based upon items discovered in your investigations or disclosed by Seller. If Seller is unwilling or unable to satisfy your requests, or you do not want to purchase the Property in its disclosed and discovered condition, you have the right to cancel the agreement if you act within specific time periods. If you do not cancel the agreement in a timely and proper manner, you may be in breach of contract.

C. SELLER RIGHTS AND DUTIES: Seller is required to disclose to you material facts known to him/her that affect the value or desirability of the Property. However, Seller may not be aware of some Property defects or conditions. Seller does not have an obligation to inspect the Property for your benefit nor is Seller obligated to repair, correct or otherwise cure known defects that are disclosed to you or previously unknown defects that are discovered by you or your inspectors during escrow. The purchase agreement obligates Seller to make the Property available to you for investigations.

D. BROKER OBLIGATIONS: Brokers do not have expertise in all areas and therefore cannot advise you on many items, such as soil stability, geologic or environmental conditions, hazardous or illegal controlled substances, structural conditions of the foundation or other improvements, or the condition of the roof, plumbing, heating, air conditioning, electrical, sewer, septic, waste disposal, or other system. The only way to accurately determine the condition of the Property is through an inspection by an appropriate professional selected by you. If Broker gives you referrals to such professionals, Broker does not guarantee their performance. You may select any professional of your choosing. In sales involving residential dwellings with no more than four units, Brokers have a duty to make a diligent visual inspection of the accessible areas of the Property and to disclose the results of that inspection. However, as some Property defects or conditions may not be discoverable from a visual inspection, it is possible Brokers are not aware of them. If you have entered into a written agreement with a Broker, the specific terms of that agreement will determine the nature and extent of that Broker's duty to you. **YOU ARE STRONGLY ADVISED TO INVESTIGATE THE CONDITION AND SUITABILITY OF ALL ASPECTS OF THE PROPERTY. IF YOU DO NOT DO SO, YOU ARE ACTING AGAINST THE ADVICE OF BROKERS.**

E. YOU ARE ADVISED TO CONDUCT INVESTIGATIONS OF THE ENTIRE PROPERTY, INCLUDING, BUT NOT LIMITED TO THE FOLLOWING:
1. **GENERAL CONDITION OF THE PROPERTY, ITS SYSTEMS AND COMPONENTS:** Foundation, roof, plumbing, heating, air conditioning, electrical, mechanical, security, pool/spa, other structural and non-structural systems and components, fixtures, built-in appliances, any personal property included in the sale, and energy efficiency of the Property. (Structural engineers are best suited to determine possible design or construction defects, and whether improvements are structurally sound.)
2. **SQUARE FOOTAGE, AGE, BOUNDARIES:** Square footage, room dimensions, lot size, age of improvements and boundaries. Any numerical statements regarding these items are APPROXIMATIONS ONLY and have not been verified by Seller and cannot be verified by Brokers. Fences, hedges, walls, retaining walls and other natural or constructed barriers or markers do not necessarily identify true Property boundaries. (Professionals such as appraisers, architects, surveyors and civil engineers are best suited to determine square footage, dimensions and boundaries of the Property.)
3. **WOOD DESTROYING PESTS:** Presence of, or conditions likely to lead to the presence of wood destroying pests and organisms and other infestation or infection. Inspection reports covering these items can be separated into two sections: Section 1 identifies areas where infestation or infection is evident. Section 2 identifies areas where there are conditions likely to lead to infestation or infection. A registered structural pest control company is best suited to perform these inspections.

BIA REVISED 10/02 (PAGE 1 OF 2) Print Date

Buyer's Initials (_____)(_____)
Seller's Initials (_____)(_____)

Reviewed by _____ Date _____

EQUAL HOUSING
OPPORTUNITY

BUYER'S INSPECTION ADVISORY (BIA PAGE 1 OF 2)

Source: Reprinted with permission, California Association of REALTORS®. Endorsement not implied.

FIGURE 7.2

Buyer's Inspection Advisory (Continued)

Property Address: _____   Date: _____

4. **SOIL STABILITY:** Existence of fill or compacted soil, expansive or contracting soil, susceptibility to slippage, settling or movement, and the adequacy of drainage. (Geotechnical engineers are best suited to determine such conditions, causes and remedies.)
5. **ROOF:** Present condition, age, leaks, and remaining useful life. (Roofing contractors are best suited to determine these conditions.)
6. **POOL/SPA:** Cracks, leaks or operational problems. (Pool contractors are best suited to determine these conditions.)
7. **WASTE DISPOSAL:** Type, size, adequacy, capacity and condition of sewer and septic systems and components, connection to sewer, and applicable fees.
8. **WATER AND UTILITIES; WELL SYSTEMS AND COMPONENTS:** Water and utility availability, use restrictions and costs. Water quality, adequacy, condition, and performance of well systems and components.
9. **ENVIRONMENTAL HAZARDS:** Potential environmental hazards, including, but not limited to, asbestos, lead-based paint and other lead contamination, radon, methane, other gases, fuel oil or chemical storage tanks, contaminated soil or water, hazardous waste, waste disposal sites, electromagnetic fields, nuclear sources, and other substances, materials, products, or conditions (including mold (airborne, toxic or otherwise), fungus or similar contaminants). (For more in formation on these items, you may consult an appropriate professional or read the booklets "Environmental Hazards: A Guide for Homeowners ,Buyers, Landlords and Tenants," "Protect Your Family From Lead in Your Home" or both.)
10. **EARTHQUAKES AND FLOODING:** Susceptibility of the Property to earthquake/seismic hazards and propensity of the Property to flood. (A Geologist or Geotechnical Engineer is best suited to provide information on these conditions.)
11. **FIRE, HAZARD AND OTHER INSURANCE:** The availability and cost of necessary or desired insurance may vary. The location of the Property in a seismic, flood or fire hazard zone, and other conditions, such as the age of the Property and the claims history of the Property and Buyer, may affect the availability and need for certain types of insurance. Buyer should explore insurance options early as this information may affect other decisions, including the removal of loan and inspection contingencies. (An insurance agent is best suited to provide information on these conditions.)
12. **BUILDING PERMITS, ZONING AND GOVERNMENTAL REQUIREMENTS:** Permits, inspections, certificates, zoning, other governmental limitations, restrictions, and requirements affecting the current or future use of the Property, its development or size. (Such information is available from appropriate governmental agencies and private information providers. Brokers are not qualified to review or interpret any such information.)
13. **RENTAL PROPERTY RESTRICTIONS:** Some cities and counties impose restrictions that limit the amount of rent that can be charged, the maximum number of occupants; and the right of a landlord to terminate a tenancy. Deadbolt or other locks and security systems for doors and windows, including window bars, should be examined to determine whether they satisfy legal requirements. (Government agencies can provide information about these restrictions and other requirements.)
14. **SECURITY AND SAFETY:** State and local Law may require the installation of barriers, access alarms, self-latching mechanisms and/or other measures to decrease the risk to children and other persons of existing swimming pools and hot tubs, as well as various fire safety and other measures concerning other features of the Property. Compliance requirements differ from city to city and county to county. Unless specifically agreed, the Property may not be in compliance with these requirements. (Local government agencies can provide information about these restrictions and other requirements.)
15. **NEIGHBORHOOD, AREA, SUBDIVISION CONDITIONS; PERSONAL FACTORS:** Neighborhood or area conditions, including schools, proximity and adequacy of law enforcement, crime statistics, the proximity of registered felons or offenders, fire protection, other government services, availability, adequacy and cost of any speed-wired, wireless internet connections or other telecommunications or other technology services and installations, proximity to commercial, industrial or agricultural activities, existing and proposed transportation, construction and development that may affect noise, view, or traffic, airport noise, noise or odor from any source, wild and domestic animals, other nuisances, hazards, or circumstances, protected species, wetland properties, botanical diseases, historic or other governmentally protected sites or improvements, cemeteries, facilities and condition of common areas of common interest subdivisions, and possible lack of compliance with any governing documents or Homeowners' Association requirements, conditions and influences of significance to certain cultures and/or religions, and personal needs, requirements and preferences of Buyer.

Buyer and Seller acknowledge and agree that Broker: **(i)** Does not decide what price Buyer should pay or Seller should accept; **(ii)** Does not guarantee the condition of the Property; **(iii)** Does not guarantee the performance, adequacy or completeness of inspections, services, products or repairs provided or made by Seller or others; **(iv)** Shall not be responsible for identifying defects that are not known to Broker and **(a)** are not visually observable in reasonably accessible areas of the Property; **(b)** are in common areas; or **(c)** are off the site of the Property; **(v)** Shall not be responsible for inspecting public records or permits concerning the title or use of Property; **(vi)** Shall not be responsible for identifying the location of boundary lines or other items affecting title; **(vii)** Shall not be responsible for verifying square footage, representations of others or information contained in Investigation reports, Multiple Listing Service, advertisements, flyers or other promotional material; **(viii)** Shall not be responsible for providing legal or tax advice regarding any aspect of a transaction entered into by Buyer or Seller; and **(ix)** Shall not be responsible for providing other advice or information that exceeds the knowledge, education and experience required to perform real estate licensed activity. Buyer and Seller agree to seek legal, tax, insurance, title and other desired assistance from appropriate professionals.

By signing below, Buyer and Seller each acknowledge that they have read, understand, accept and have received a Copy of this Advisory. Buyer is encouraged to read it carefully.

_____ _____   _____ _____
Buyer Signature   Date   Buyer Signature   Date

_____ _____   _____ _____
Seller Signature   Date   Seller Signature   Date

THIS FORM HAS BEEN APPROVED BY THE CALIFORNIA ASSOCIATION OF REALTORS® (C.A.R.). NO REPRESENTATION IS MADE AS TO THE LEGAL VALIDITY OR ADEQUACY OF ANY PROVISION IN ANY SPECIFIC TRANSACTION. A REAL ESTATE BROKER IS THE PERSON QUALIFIED TO ADVISE ON REAL ESTATE TRANSACTIONS. IF YOU DESIRE LEGAL OR TAX ADVICE, CONSULT AN APPROPRIATE PROFESSIONAL.

This form is available for use by the entire real estate industry. It is not intended to identify the user as a REALTOR®. REALTOR® is a registered collective membership mark which may be used only by members of the NATIONAL ASSOCIATION OF REALTORS® who subscribe to its Code of Ethics.

SURE TRAC
The System for Success™
Published by the
California Association of REALTORS®
BIA REVISED 10/02 (PAGE 2 OF 2)

Reviewed by _____ Date _____

EQUAL HOUSING OPPORTUNITY

BUYER'S INSPECTION ADVISORY (BIA PAGE 2 OF 2)

Source: Reprinted with permission, California Association of REALTORS®. Endorsement not implied.

The broker who prepares the contract **is not allowed to give legal advice** but can explain the meaning and purpose of the contract terms to the buyer and seller. The *listing* broker, if there is one, has primary responsibility for dealing with the *seller*. If there is a different selling broker, the listing broker most often will discuss the contract terms privately with the seller after the offer has been presented by the selling broker.

Contract terms.   The purchase contract and deposit receipt shown in Figure 7.1 first requires insertion of the date on which the buyer is signing the offer and the city where it is signed, with no abbreviations. Other features of this contract are discussed below. The numbered paragraphs refer to the numbered sections of the contract.

> The property must be adequately identified.

1. **Offer.** The buyer's full name is entered. The city and county in which the property is located are provided, followed by a legal description of the property. A street address may be sufficient for city property, but a formal legal description (metes and bounds or lot and block) could be used in addition and is required for rural property. The exact acreage need not be specified, but if it is and a survey reveals a significant discrepancy (for instance, 165 acres surveyed when 185 is specified in the contract), a problem may arise later. If a lengthy legal description is needed, it is better to make a photocopy of the description from a reliable document and attach that to the contract, rather than risk an error in transcribing.

   The amount of the purchase price is supplied in both words and figures.

   The date for close of escrow (COE) is provided.

2. **Financing.** The buyer indicates how the entire purchase price is to be paid. Terms of payment usually are expressed as conditions or contingencies to the buyer's purchase. If the buyer is unable to obtain the type of loan specified (after reasonably diligent efforts), the buyer could back out of the contract.

3. **Closing and occupancy.** Will the buyer live in the residence? The date on which possession will be turned over to the buyer must be indicated. The property should be vacant at the time possession is transferred. The seller has responsibility for terminating any existing tenancy and complying with applicable rent control laws.

   If there are any assignable warranties on any item transferred as part of the sale, the seller will provide copies of the warranties to the buyer.

   All keys, electronic opening devices, security codes, or other devices will be provided to the buyer at the time of possession. If applicable, the buyer may need to make a deposit for keys to common areas.

4. **Allocation of costs.** The buyer may require the seller to provide a pest inspection and report. Allocation of the cost of property inspections as well as other costs associated with the transaction, such as transfer tax, is subject to the negotiation of the parties. In a strong buyer's market, the

seller may bear more of these costs. In a strong seller's market, the buyer may offer to pay more of these costs as an inducement to the seller. Local custom and practice also may be followed.

5. **Statutory disclosures.** All legally mandated disclosures must be made whenever applicable, including Federal Lead-Based Paint Disclosures. The first two pages of the Real Estate Transfer Disclosure Statement (shown on pages 158 and 159) must be completed by a seller of a residence of one to four units. Property located in a very high fire hazard severity zone must be identified. All written contracts for sale or lease of residential real property must contain a specified notice regarding the database maintained by law enforcement authorities that contains the locations of registered sex offenders and other related provisions.

6. **Condominium/planned unit development disclosures.** Limitations on property located in a condominium or common interest subdivision must be disclosed, including provision for vehicle parking and a copy of the most recent 12 months of minutes of meetings of the homeowners' association.

7. **Conditions affecting property.** A seller may make an "as-is" sale but still must maintain the property, disclose any known material defects, and make other disclosures required by law.

8. **Items included and excluded.** Fixtures, as defined in Chapter 2, are included in the sale of the real estate.

   Any item of personal property that will be included in the sale must be specified. Better practice is to sell such items separately so that their value is not added to the property's value for property tax purposes.

9. **Buyer's investigation of property and matters affecting property.** The buyer has the right to conduct investigations or tests of the property, including tests for lead-based paint. The buyer's inspection of the property is so important, it is the subject of a separate Buyer's Inspection Advisory form (Figure 7.2).

10. **Repairs.** Necessary property repairs must be made before closing.

11. **Buyer indemnity and seller protection for entry upon property.** The seller is not liable for any harm to the buyer and any inspectors or other workers acting on behalf of the buyer.

12. **Title and vesting.** Title insurance is the norm in California, to protect the buyer's ownership interest.

13. **Sale of buyer's property.** The contingent sale provision may be used when the buyer owns other property that must be sold before the buyer can complete this transaction.

14. **Time periods/removal of contingencies/cancellation rights.** All parties should be clear on the need to act promptly on all contract requirements.

15. **Final verification of condition.** A final walk-through inspection of the property by the buyer a day or two before closing is always advisable.

16. **Liquidated damages.** The maximum amount of **liquidated damages** (automatic damages) on the buyer's default, as set out in this section, is established by state law.

17. **Dispute resolution.** Buyer and seller agree to submit any dispute or claim stemming from this contract to mediation, before resorting to arbitration or court action. Arbitration may be agreed upon as the next step following an unsuccessful attempt at mediation. Certain legal matters (such as a mechanic's lien or probate) may require specific legal action.

18. **Prorations of property taxes and other items.** Expenses of ownership usually will be prorated so that seller and buyer pay only the amount attributable to their separate periods of ownership.

19. **Withholding taxes.** The Foreign Investment in Real Property Tax Act (FIRPTA) and California laws must be complied with.

20. **Multiple listing service (MLS).** Use of the MLS is authorized.

21. **Equal housing opportunity.** The sale must comply with all applicable fair housing or equal opportunity laws.

22. **Attorney's fees.** In a legal action, the losing party will pay the other side's legal expenses.

23. **Selection of service providers.** Brokers cannot serve as guarantors of the quality of service of any company or individual that they may be asked to name.

24. **Time of essence; entire contract; changes.** This writing supersedes all earlier written or oral agreements.

25. **Other terms and conditions.** Any addenda to the contract should be indicated.

26. **Definitions.** Clarification of terms used in the agreement.

27. **Agency.** The agency representation must be specified, even if other writings have been executed.

28. **Joint escrow instructions to escrow holder.** The terms of this agreement also serve as instructions to the escrow holder. This provision was included so that the escrow officer will not have to duplicate the language from the purchase agreement in the escrow instructions.

29. **Broker compensation from buyer.** The buyer may have an agreement to compensate the broker who will present the offer to purchase on his or her behalf.

30. **Terms and conditions of offer.** The buyer and seller must understand that the offer to purchase is not a binding agreement until it is accepted by the seller. If the buyer defaults after acceptance by the seller, the buyer may be required to compensate his or her broker.

31. **Expiration of offer.** This section specifies how long the offer will be open and how it can be accepted.

32. **Broker compensation from seller.** A paragraph providing for the seller's acceptance of the broker's **commission terms** is required by the California Business and Professions Code in the sale of a one- to four-unit residential property. If accepted, all parties having an ownership interest in the property must sign the contract as sellers.

33. **Acceptance of offer.** The seller, by signing the contract, claims to be the owner of the property or to be acting with the owner's permission.

The agreement serves as a confirmation of the agency relationships specified in it. The agreement also serves as an acknowledgment that the escrow holder has received it and agrees to serve as escrow as directed.

The **Natural Hazard Disclosure Statement** (Figure 7.3) must be provided in residential transactions of one to four dwelling units. Exceptions for spouses, co-owners, and others are found in Civil Code 1103.1. Other items may be covered in addenda to the purchase agreement. The possible presence of mold has become an important topic. The San Diego Association of REALTORS® (SDAR) has developed a mold disclosure form (Figure 7.4). SDAR has responded to comments on the mold disclosure form with its Questions and Answers on the MD: Mold Disclosure (Figure 7.5). Both pages are reprinted here with permission of the San Diego Association of REALTORS®.

> Every counteroffer rejects the offer that preceded it.

Counteroffer. If the seller changes any of the contract terms, the seller makes a **counteroffer.** Any change by the seller rejects the buyer's offer as originally written. The seller can change terms only by, in effect, creating a brand new document.

The seller attaches a counteroffer to the original offer, indicating in the counteroffer the changed or additional terms. In the contract in Figure 7.1, the seller would check the box following clause 31, the acceptance paragraph of the purchase contract, indicating that the contract is accepted "subject to attached counteroffer." The total number of pages then will include the counteroffer.

FIGURE 7.3

Natural Hazard Disclosure Statement

Client: Sample Name
Sample Company
Sample Address
Sample Address, California

Page 1

NHD WO #   **131800**
Date: **5/28/2004**

NATURAL HAZARD DISCLOSURE STATEMENT

This statement applies to the following property: **123 Any Way, Someville, California 91351**

APN# **1234-100-001**

The transferor and his or her agent(s) disclose the following information with the knowledge that even though this is not a warranty, prospective transferees may rely on this information in deciding whether and on what terms to purchase the subject property. Transferor hereby authorizes any agent(s) representing any principal(s) in this action to provide a copy of this statement to any person or entity in connection with any actual or anticipated sale of the property.

The following are representations made by the transferor and his or her agent(s) based on their knowledge and maps drawn by the state and federal governments. This information is a disclosure and is not intended to be part of any contract between the transferee and transferor.

THIS REAL PROPERTY LIES WITHIN THE FOLLOWING HAZARDOUS AREA(S): (Check the answer which applies.)

A SPECIAL FLOOD HAZARD AREA (Zone "A" or "V") designated by the Federal Emergency Management Agency.
Yes _____   No ✓_____   Do not know and information not available from local jurisdiction _____

AN AREA OF POTENTIAL FLOODING shown on a dam failure inundation map pursuant to Section 8589.5 of the Government Code.
Yes ✓_____   No _____   Do not know and information not available from local jurisdiction _____

A VERY HIGH FIRE HAZARD SEVERITY ZONE pursuant to Section 51178 or 51179 of the Government Code. The owner of this property is subject to the maintenance requirements of Section 51182 of the Government Code.
Yes ✓_____   No _____

A WILDLAND AREA THAT MAY CONTAIN SUBSTANTIAL FOREST FIRE RISKS AND HAZARDS pursuant to Section 4125 of the Public Resources Code. The owner of this property is subject to the maintenance requirements of Section 4291 of the Public Resources Code. Additionally, it is not the state's responsibility to provide fire protection services to any building or structure located within the wildlands unless the Department of Forestry and Fire Protection has entered into a cooperative agreement with a local agency for those purposes pursuant to Section 4142 of the Public Resources Code.
Yes _____   No ✓_____

AN EARTHQUAKE FAULT ZONE pursuant to Section 2622 of the Public Resources Code.
Yes _____   No ✓_____

A SEISMIC HAZARD ZONE pursuant to Section 2696 of the Public Resources Code.
Yes ✓_____   (Liquefaction Zone of Required Investigation)

No _____   Map not yet released by State _____

Yes _____   (Landslide Zone of Required Investigation)

THESE HAZARDS MAY LIMIT YOUR ABILITY TO DEVELOP THE REAL PROPERTY, TO OBTAIN INSURANCE, OR TO RECEIVE ASSISTANCE AFTER A DISASTER.
THE MAPS ON WHICH THESE DISCLOSURES ARE BASED ESTIMATE WHERE NATURAL HAZARDS EXIST. THEY ARE NOT DEFINITIVE INDICATORS OF WHETHER OR NOT A PROPERTY WILL BE AFFECTED BY A NATURAL DISASTER. TRANSFEREE(S) AND TRANSFEROR(S) MAY WISH TO OBTAIN PROFESSIONAL ADVICE REGARDING THOSE HAZARDS AND OTHER HAZARDS THAT MAY AFFECT THE PROPERTY.

> The information contained in this box is not part of the statutory form.
> ☑ **(if checked) The representations made in this form are based upon information provided by an independent third-party report provided as a substituted disclosure pursuant to California Civil Code §1102.4. Neither the seller nor the seller's agent (1) has independently verified the information contained in this form and report or (2) is personally aware of any errors or inaccuracies in the information contained on the form.**

Transferor represents that the information herein is true and correct to the best of the transferor's knowledge as of the date signed by the transferor.

Signature of Transferor(s) _____Date _____
Agent represents that the information herein is true and correct to the best of the agent's knowledge as of the date signed by the agent.

Signature of Agent _____Date _____

Signature of Agent _____Date _____

Transferee(s) represents that he or she has read and understands this document.

Signature of Transferee(s) _____Date _____

Alan Arora, President - Natural Hazards Disclosure, LLC. - A subsidiary of the California Association of REALTORS ®

Natural Hazards Disclosure, LLC certifies that this report complies with all requirements for the mandatory disclosures set forth in California Civil Code 1103.2a in form and content. Furthermore, this report qualifies as a substitute disclosure report pursuant to California Civil Code 1103.4c. As such, neither the seller nor agents shall be liable for any error, inaccuracy, or omission if not within the personal knowledge of the seller or agents. NHD, LLC maintains $20 million Errors and Omissions insurance.

16654 Soledad Canyon Road #501 • Santa Clarita, CA 91387 • Phone: 800.317.7919 • Fax: 888.999.6439 • www.naturalhazards.com

FIGURE 7.3

Natural Hazard Disclosure Statement (Continued)

Page 2a

Explanation of the Natural Hazard Disclosure Statement
by
Natural Hazards Disclosure, LLC

The State of California requires that sellers of California real estate disclose to buyers certain information of natural hazards that could have a potential adverse impact to the property. Specific format of reporting exists for residential property (Assembly Bill 248, Torlakson, 1999) The accompanying Natural Hazard Disclosure Statement prepared by Natural Hazards Disclosure, LLC (NHD, LLC) is based upon review of the following: (1) State of California Earthquake Fault Zone maps, (2) U.S. Government FEMA flood zone maps, (3) State of California Fire Responsibility Area maps, (4) State of California Very High Fire Hazard Severity Zone maps (Bates Fire maps), (5) State of California Dam Inundation Maps, and (6) State of California Seismic Hazard Zone Maps. A brief explanation of each zone designation reported is presented below. This information is general in nature but useful in evaluating some natural hazards that might influence areas of the state. *No site-specific studies have been performed by Natural Hazards Disclosure, LLC personnel, as such is beyond the scope of this data research.*

In addition to the maps reviewed by NHD, LLC there are other maps available through government agencies and private companies that might be significant to this property. There has been a requirement of geologic and/or soil engineering evaluation for development of properties in much of California over the last 20+ years. If this property was developed within that period, detailed geotechnical reports may be on file with the governing city or county. These records are generally available for review by the public. Concerns expressed in this report may have been addressed at time of development and corrections provided.
If there are disclosures contained in this report that are not understood or are of concern to the client, appropriate consultants should be contacted to provide a detailed site-specific study.

Special Flood Hazard Area (FEMA Flood Zone)
Flood Insurance Rate Maps are produced by the Federal Emergency Management Agency. The maps delineate various flood hazard zone designations for flood insurance and flood plain management purposes. The maps do not necessarily show all areas subject to flooding in the community or all planimetric features outside special flood hazard areas. Special Flood Hazard Areas (SFHAs) are areas subject to inundation by a flood having a one percent or greater probability of being equaled or exceeded during any given year. Therefore, it is possible for an SFHA to experience flooding more than once every 100 years. This flood, which is referred to as the 100-year flood (or base flood), is the national standard on which the floodplain management and insurance requirements of the National Flood Insurance Program are based. FEMA Flood Zones "A" and "V" are the principal SFHA's. Properties within an SFHA generally require FEMA flood insurance.

Area of Potential Flooding - Dam Inundation Area
Dams and/or large debris basins are used for water storage and flood control. Catastrophic failure of one of these structures from a large earthquake, foundation failure, over-flow, etc., could result in substantial loss of property and life in downstream areas. Section 8589.5 of the California Government Code requires that inundation maps and emergency response plans be prepared for certain dams and debris basins within the jurisdiction of the State. The potential inundation areas shown on Dam Inundation Hazards Maps assume catastrophic failure of a dam or basin during peak storage capacity. The inundation boundary depicted on these maps generally encompass all probable routes that may flood down stream from a failed dam or basin. The scale of the map used as the basis for this mapping is very small and, therefore, the information is considered general in nature. Areas outside of actual potential inundation areas may be included in zones depicted on the map due to the lack of sufficient detail of the base map. Also, it should be noted that there are many dams within the State for which there are no existing Dam Inundation maps available. NHD, LLC only reports on those Dam Inundation maps available from public agencies on the day that the report was prepared. *NHD recommends that a Civil Engineer or Hydrologist be retained to investigate the site if detailed flood and inundation hazard analysis is desired.*

Very High Fire Hazard Severity Zones Map (Bates Fire Zone Maps)
As a result of the Oakland Hills fire which destroyed over 3229 structures, the state adopted legislation in 1992 to produce maps of Very High Fire Hazard Severity Zones (VHFHSZ). Assemblyman Tom Bates introduced the bill adding sections 51175-51188 to the California Government Code, thus the maps are informally referred to as the "Bates Fire Maps" by the State. It is important to note that these maps identify areas of very high fire hazard <u>outside</u> of the State Fire Responsibility Areas (SRA'S discussed below). The VHFHSZ maps were produced by the State Fire Marshall through a ranking process based on fuels, topography dwelling density, and weather. Specific laws, punishable by fines, apply to property owners in the VHFHSZ'S which the buyer should be made aware of. They include brush clearance, special fire retarding roofs, keeping the roofs clear of leaves and needles, screens over chimneys, etc.

Wildland Area - State Fire Responsibility Area Fire Zone Map
State Fire Responsibility Areas (SRA) are determined by the California Department of Forestry and Fire Protection. These areas delineate land for which the State assumes primary financial responsibility for protecting natural resources from damages from fire. The system of classification is not based on the ability to protect an area from fire, but rather on the vegetative cover and natural resource values.
Public Resource Code 4126 dictates that the State Board of Forestry shall include within state responsibility areas all of the following lands:
(a) Lands covered wholly or in part by forests or by trees producing or capable of producing forest products.
(b) Lands covered wholly or in part by timber, brush, undergrowth, or grass, whether of commercial value or not, which protect the soil from excessive erosion, retard runoff of water or accelerate water percolation, if such lands are sources of water which is available for irrigation or for domestic or industrial use.
(c) Lands in areas which are principally used or useful for range or forage purposes, which are contiguous to the lands described in subdivisions (a) and (b).
The board shall not include within state responsibility areas any of the following lands:
(a) Lands owned or controlled by the federal government or any agency of the federal government.
(b) Lands within the exterior boundaries of any city, except a city and county with a population of less than 25,000 if, at the time the city and county government is established, the county contains no municipal corporations.
(c) Any other lands within the state which do not come within any of the classes which are described in Section 4126.
Public Resources Code 4136 dictates that "A seller of real property which is located within a state responsibility area determined by the board, pursuant to Section 4125, shall disclose to any prospective purchaser the fact that the property is located within a wildland area which may contain substantial forest fire risks and hazards and is subject to the requirements of Section 4291".

16654 Soledad Canyon Road #501 • Santa Clarita, CA 91387 • Phone: 800.317.7919 • Fax: 888.999.6439 • www.naturalhazards.com

Source: Reprinted with permission, California Association of REALTORS®. Endorsement not implied.

FIGURE 7.3

Natural Hazard Disclosure Statement (Continued)

Page 2b

Earthquake Fault Zone Map Search (Alquist-Priolo Zone)

The Alquist-Priolo Special Fault Studies Zone Act of 1972 directs the State of California Geological Survey (previously Division of Mines and Geology) to compile detailed maps of the surface traces of known active faults on 1:24,000 scale topographic quadrangle maps. These maps are now called Earthquake Fault Zone (or Special Studies Zone) Maps by the State. "Active Faults" are defined as faults which show evidence of movement within the past 11,000 years. Typically, the California Geological Survey plots the trace of a known or suspected "active" fault on the map and delineates a "zone" on both sides of the fault trace which is usually 1/4 mile wide. This zone is then used in real estate evaluations and/or by local Building and Safety Departments which may require that special fault studies be performed by a Registered Geologist prior to development or construction within the Alquist-Priolo zone. The studies by the geologist are performed to locate the surface trace of the fault and to provide professional judgments as to how close a proposed structure may be safely built from the fault.

It should be noted that the Earthquake Fault Zone Maps are continuously being updated as newly discovered active faults are located. Other faults which are unknown, buried, or not considered active may underlie the site. Most of Southern California lies within a region of high seismicity and the greatest seismic hazard to all buildings is moderate to strong ground shaking which will occur both within and outside established Special Studies zones. However, it is presumed that there is greater risk of ground surface rupture within the Special Studies zones. *The ability of a structure to withstand earthquake-generated ground shaking should be evaluated by a qualified structural engineer.*

Seismic Hazards Zones Map Review

The Seismic Hazards Mapping Act of 1990 (SHMA) directs the State Geologist, California Geological Survey (previously Division of Mines and Geology), to compile maps identifying various "seismic hazard zones" (California Public Resources Code Section 2690-2699.6). The purpose of the Act is to protect public safety from the effects of strong ground shaking, liquefaction, landslides, or other ground failure caused by earthquakes. Cities and Counties, or other local permitting authority must withhold the development permits for a site within a zone until a Site Investigation Report has been prepared by a Certified Engineering Geologist or Registered Civil Engineer. Liquefaction and landslide hazard zone boundaries may vary significantly from similar hazard maps contained in older County Safety Element reports. Mapping is ongoing and Official maps exist for only portions of the State at this time.

Liquefaction is the phenomenon where normally firm ground takes on a liquid-like state during a period of prolonged earthquake-induced ground shaking. This can cause the ground to settle or spread laterally and possibly cause damage to any overlying buildings or other structures. In order for liquefaction to occur, the following conditions all have to exist: 1) The water table must be within about 40 feet of the ground surface, 2) the underlying soils must fall into certain grain-size patterns, 3) the soil must be fairly "loose", and 4) the ground shaking must be prolonged.

Maps showing areas of potential liquefaction prepared by the California Geological Survey as part of the Seismic Hazards mapping program are required disclosure. These maps have had the extent of the "liquefaction potential" areas determined very conservatively by a general review of earth material types and information on depth of groundwater.

Properties mapped as being in areas of earthquake induced landsliding are typically hillside areas where landsliding may possibly occur due to 1) geologic structure within the rock, 2) rock or soil weakens, 3) steep slopes, 4) wet soil conditions or 5) a combination of the above. Natural Hazards Disclosure, LLC recommends that an independent, on-site geologic study be conducted on properties located within a landslide potential zone.

It should be noted that, historically, damages from liquefaction or earthquake induced landsliding from California earthquakes has been small when compared to the cost of damage from the ground shaking that accompanies an earthquake.

NOTICE OF CONDITIONS

Natural Hazards Disclosure, LLC (NHD, LLC) reports are based solely upon the review of databases and maps published by various local, state, and federal government agencies for public use. These maps provide a statement of general conditions and are to be used only as a "general guideline" to area conditions. However, various building departments place building restrictions and/ or special design requirements within mapped hazard zones.

Map research was performed in accordance with generally accepted current practice. No site-specific studies or site inspections have been nor will be performed by NHD, LLC NHD, LLC does not warrant or guarantee the accuracy of the maps and databases reviewed. NHD, Inc's reports are current for the day in which prepared, but it should be understood that maps and databases of natural hazard zones are subject to change by the responsible government agency without notice.

Reports are based solely upon property location provided to this office. *The client must check to make sure that the location information is correct.* Reports are for the subject property only and not for any other parcel, no matter how close to the subject site it is. *The report remains the property of NHD, LLC until paid for in full.*

NHD, LLC is responsible for the accuracy of review of the various published maps and databases that we use in our reports and the liability for NHD, Inc's services shall not be extended personally to individual employees or consultants. Most government agencies also do not assume responsibility or liability for the maps which they provide and NHD, LLC only assumes responsibility for the accurate review of these generalized hazard maps and not their contents.

Mandatory disclosure laws apply to many zone designations such as FEMA, Earthquake Fault Zones, Seismic Hazards Zones, State Fire Responsibility Areas, etc. Although NHD, LLC provides review of many hazard zones we do not warrantee that all natural hazards and/or special tax or assessment districts requiring disclosure by local or state law are reviewed.

NHD, LLC is an independent research organization, not owned or affiliated with any real estate company, bank, real estate broker, escrow or title company. We are not separately licensed or regulated, though we retain state certified engineering geologists on our staff for consultation.

16654 Soledad Canyon Road #501 • Santa Clarita, CA 91387 • Phone: 800.317.7919 • Fax: 888.999.6439 • www.naturalhazards.com

FIGURE 7.4

Mold Disclosure

MOLD DISCLOSURE

Property Address: _____

Broker(s)/Agent(s) (hereafter referred to as Broker) advise that every Buyer/Lessee should have a mold test performed by an environmental professional as either a separate test or as an addition/adjunct to their professional home inspection. Current information indicates that the presence of some types of mold may cause health problems in certain individuals. Not all molds are detectable by visual inspection conducted by Brokers or even a professional home inspector. Properties may have hidden mold problems of which the Seller/Lessor is not aware. The only way to provide reasonable assurances that the property does not have a mold or other health hazard condition is to retain the services of an environmental expert to conduct appropriate tests of the property. Normally, these tests will consist of an interior and exterior examination for airborne spores and a carpet test, but other procedures may be required. Any mold should be professionally evaluated. Failure on the part of a buyer to complete and obtain all appropriate tests, including those for mold, is against the advice of Brokers. Brokers have not and cannot verify whether or not there is any health hazard at the property. A mold evaluation is especially necessary if any of the inspection reports or disclosure documents indicate that there is evidence of past or present moisture, standing or ponding water, or water intrusion at the property, since most molds thrive on moisture. All inspections, including those to detect mold, should be completed within the inspection period established in the purchase contract.

The Environmental Hazards booklet and *Local Area Disclosures for San Diego County* booklet provide information about mold, including ways to identify it. Other sources of information about mold can be found at:

California Department of Health Services (CDHS)   U.S. Environmental Protection Agency (EPA)
Publication: *Mold in My Home: What Can I Do?*   EPA Indoor Air Quality Information
Telephone: 916-445-4171   Clearinghouse Line: 800-438-4318 or 703-356-4020
Internet: *www.dhs.ca.gov*   Internet: *www.epa.gov*

By signing this Mold Disclosure Agreement, you agree that Brokers shall have no further responsibility regarding the potential or actual existence of mold contamination at the property or any resulting injury. Nothing any sales agent may say to you can change this Agreement or the advice contained above.

The undersigned acknowledge that he or she has read and understands this Mold Disclosure.

_____   _____
Buyer/Lessee   Date

_____   _____
Buyer/Lessee   Date

**THIS DOCUMENT IS FOR USE IN SIMPLE TRANSACTIONS AND NO REPRESENTATION OR WARRANTY
IS MADE TO THE VALIDITY OR ADEQUACY OF ANY OF ITS PROVISIONS IN ANY TRANSACTION.**

Published and Distributed by:
San Diego Association of REALTORS®
4845 Ronson Court
San Diego, CA 92111-1803
Tel: 800-525-2102 Web: www.sdar.com
July 2003

**MD-11
Page 1 of 1**

┌─ OFFICE USE ONLY ─┐
Reviewed by Broker or Designee: _____
Date: _____

Source: San Diego Association of REALTORS®. Used with permission.

FIGURE 7.5

Questions and Answers on the MD: Mold Disclosure

Questions and Answers on the MD: MOLD DISCLOSURE

Q **Why do agents and brokers need to use a Mold Disclosure form?**

A By now everyone has heard the phrase "Asbestos is old, mold is gold!" What that means quite simply is that litigation concerning mold and mold-related issues is skyrocketing and producing some sizable judgments/settlements for plaintiffs. One cannot be in the real estate business in California and not be aware that mold is a huge issue, one that requires REALTORS® to be extremely vigilant in assuring that their clients are aware of both the dangers of mold itself and the dangers of being sued over mold. Further, REALTORS® need to understand that they themselves can be held accountable for failure to advise their clients regarding mold and mold-related issues, and that there are almost no insurance policies that cover mold. To assist its members in serving their clients and protecting themselves as REALTORS®, SDAR's Risk Management Committee introduced a new Mold Disclosure for use in all real estate transactions in San Diego County. While it is true that mold is covered in the Environmental Hazards and Local Area Disclosures for San Diego County (LAD) booklets, think of the new Mold Disclosure as, "You can't have too much of a good thing." Logically, the more times someone is advised of something, the more likely it is something significant. More important, the more times someone is advised of something, the less likely they will later be able to successfully argue that they were not aware of it. This is one time that redundancy is a must. It is expected that all REALTORS® use the new form, in addition to the LAD and Environmental Hazards booklet in every real estate transaction, all the time.

Q **What does the Mold Disclosure Form say and do?**

A The Mold Disclosure, a one-page, easily understood form, explains the problems with mold and the necessity of obtaining a mold inspection. The Mold Disclosure further advises the buyers that failure to obtain a mold inspection is expressly against the advice of brokers, and gives the buyers some resources to learn more about mold. Finally, the Mold Disclosure contains language that in essence relieves the broker of responsibility regarding the actual or potential existence of mold at the property, provided the form is given to and signed by the buyers.

Q **When and how should the Mold Disclosure be given to buyers?**

A The Mold Disclosure should be given to the potential buyers or lessees at the onset of the transaction. In the final analysis it doesn't matter whether a listing agent or a selling agent gives the buyer the form; however, logically (and in terms of fiduciary duty) the buyers' agent should provide the form to the buyer.

The buyers' agent should sit down with the buyers and explain the form, explain that mold is a concern for some people and can cause health problems in susceptible persons, and advise the buyers that the only way to provide reasonable assurances that the property does not have mold or other health hazard conditions is to retain the services of an environmental expert to conduct an evaluation. If there is any indication of moisture problems, visible evidence of mold, odors or ponding water at the property, this is especially true. Once the REALTOR® has presented and reviewed the form with the buyers, the buyers' signatures should be obtained on the form and a copy provided to the buyers, given to the listing agent, and retained in the buyers' agent's files.

The next step is for the buyers' REALTOR® to handwrite in "Mold Inspection" on page 4, item 11 of the Buyer's Election of Inspections (BEI). The BEI is due to be revised in the near future to contain a check-off box for Mold Inspection; hence the need for this interim method. That way, the REALTOR® has given the clients the Mold Disclosure form and then the clients are given the opportunity to elect (or not elect) to have a mold inspection done. It would be extremely difficult for a buyer to later sue over mold issues and claim that he or she was not provided any information on mold in the face of so many disclosures and so many opportunities to sign his or her name to a document relating to mold!

Q **How important is it for me to use this Mold Disclosure?**

A In the current litigious climate, REALTORS® cannot do enough to protect themselves (and their clients) from lawsuits. SDAR members are fortunate to have this new Mold Disclosure form at their disposal to help manage their risk. This form, when used in conjunction with the Environmental Hazards booklet, the Local Area Disclosures for San Diego County booklet, and the Buyer's Election of Inspections form, is an important tool in ensuring that REALTORS® are relieved of liability for mold-related claims. ■

Source: San Diego Association of REALTORS®. Used with permission.

Figure 7.6 is a typical form of counteroffer. This counteroffer form leaves room for the seller to include any change or addition to the buyer's terms that the seller wishes. This form also allows the seller to counter more than one offer by checking the second section. The form should be dated and the parties named. The seller should place a time limit on the buyer's acceptance of the counteroffer. One or two days may be sufficient. The seller signs and dates the counteroffer before giving it to the buyer.

If the terms are now acceptable to the buyer, the buyer also signs and dates the counteroffer and a binding contract is created. The buyer could instead counter the counteroffer by making a correction or addition to the terms of the counteroffer and the seller is not obligated by this new offer. This form provides for a final signature of the seller, in the event the buyer has changed the terms of the counteroffer.

Other Real Estate Contracts

Option.   The right to buy property at some time in the future at an agreed-on price is called an **option.** Some form of payment (consideration) is required for an option. The person who acquires the right to purchase (the **optionee**) pays the property owner (the **optionor**) for the privilege of holding the option. The option agreement is unique because it provides the right to exercise or not exercise the option, while preventing the property owner from canceling the option during its term. The buyer of the option is, in effect, buying time to make a decision. The option right also may be assignable.

An option is frequently combined with a lease in the expectation that the lessee will want to stay in possession of the property at the end of the lease term by exercising the option and purchasing the property.

Exchange.   In an **exchange,** owners of different properties transfer title to each other. The exchange may be a tax-deferred transaction if it involves properties held for business or investment purposes. An exchange may be accompanied by additional consideration if one property owner has a higher equity value than the other. The additional consideration, called **boot,** is taxable to the party receiving it.

Exchanges often involve loan assumptions, cash payments, and other forms of financing. Because of this—and also because of the possible tax consequences—handling an exchange can require a high level of expertise on the part of the licensee. An exchange should always be reviewed by the principal's tax preparer.

FIGURE 7.6

Counteroffer Form

CALIFORNIA ASSOCIATION OF REALTORS®

COUNTER OFFER   No. _____
For use by Seller or Buyer. May be used for Multiple Counter Offer.
(C.A.R. Form CO, Revised 10/02)

Date _____, at _____, California.
This is a counter offer to the: ☐ California Residential Purchase Agreement, ☐ Counter Offer, or ☐ Other _____ ("Offer"),
dated _____, on property known as _____ ("Property"),
between _____ ("Buyer") and _____ ("Seller").
1.   **TERMS:** The terms and conditions of the above referenced document are **accepted subject to the following:**
     **A.   Paragraphs in the Offer that require initials by all parties, but are not initialed by all parties, are excluded from the final
     agreement unless specifically referenced for inclusion in paragraph 1C of this or another Counter Offer.**
     **B.   Unless otherwise agreed in writing, down payment and loan amount(s) will be adjusted in the same proportion as in
     the original Offer.**
     C. _____
     _____
     _____
     _____
     _____
     _____
     _____
     _____
     _____
     D.   The following attached supplements are incorporated in this Counter Offer: ☐ Addendum No. _____
       ☐   ☐
2.   **RIGHT TO ACCEPT OTHER OFFERS:** Seller has the right to continue to offer the Property for sale or for other transaction, and to
     accept any other offer at any time prior to notification of acceptance, as described in paragraph 3. If this is a Seller Counter Offer,
     Seller's acceptance of another offer prior to Buyer's acceptance and communication of notification of this Counter Offer, shall revoke
     this Counter Offer.
3.   **EXPIRATION:** This Counter Offer shall be deemed revoked and the deposits, if any, shall be returned unless this Counter Offer is
     Signed by the Buyer or Seller to whom it is sent and a Copy of the Signed Counter Offer is personally received by the person making
     this Counter Offer or _____,
     who is authorized to receive it, by 5:00 PM on the third Day After this Counter Offer is made or, (if checked)
     by ☐ _____ (date), at _____ AM/PM. This Counter Offer may be executed in counterparts.
4.   ☐ **(If checked:) MULTIPLE COUNTER OFFER:** Seller is making a Counter Offer(s) to another prospective buyer(s) on terms that
     may or may not be the same as in this Counter Offer. Acceptance of this Counter Offer by Buyer shall **not** be binding unless and
     until it is subsequently re-Signed by Seller in paragraph 7 below and a Copy of the Counter Offer Signed in paragraph 7 is
     personally received by Buyer or by _____, who is authorized to receive it. Prior to
     the completion of all of these events, Buyer and Seller shall have no duties or obligations for the purchase or sale of the Property.
5.   **OFFER: BUYER OR SELLER MAKES THIS COUNTER OFFER ON THE TERMS ABOVE AND ACKNOWLEDGES RECEIPT OF A COPY.**
     _____ Date _____
     _____ Date _____
6.   **ACCEPTANCE: I/WE** accept the above Counter Offer **(If checked ☐ SUBJECT TO THE ATTACHED COUNTER OFFER)** and
     acknowledge receipt of a Copy.
     _____ Date _____ Time _____ AM/PM
     _____ Date _____ Time _____ AM/PM
7.   **MULTIPLE COUNTER OFFER SIGNATURE LINE: By signing below, Seller accepts this Multiple Counter Offer.**
     NOTE TO SELLER: Do NOT sign in this box until after Buyer signs in paragraph 6. (Paragraph 7 applies only if paragraph 4 is checked.)
     _____ Date _____ Time _____ AM/PM
     _____ Date _____ Time _____ AM/PM
8.   (_____/_____) (Initials) **Confirmation of Acceptance:** A Copy of Signed Acceptance was personally received by the maker of the Counter Offer, or
     that person's authorized agent as specified in paragraph 3 (or, if this is a Multiple Counter Offer, the Buyer or Buyer's authorized agent as specified in
     paragraph 4) on (date) _____, at _____ **AM/PM. A binding Agreement is created when a Copy of Signed
     Acceptance is personally received by the** maker of the Counter Offer, or that person's authorized agent (or, if this is a Multiple Counter
     Offer, the Buyer or Buyer's authorized agent) whether or not confirmed in this document. Completion of this confirmation is not legally
     required in order to create a binding Agreement; it is solely intended to evidence the date that Confirmation of Acceptance has occurred.

SURE TRAC
The System for Success™

Published by the
California Association of REALTORS®

Reviewed by _____ Date _____

EQUAL HOUSING OPPORTUNITY

CO REVISED 10/02 (PAGE 1 OF 1)   Print Date
COUNTER OFFER (CO PAGE 1 OF 1)

Source: Reprinted with permission, California Association of REALTORS®. Endorsement not implied.

Who Bears the Risk?

What happens if a house burns down while a sale is pending? Or what happens if a tree is knocked down in a storm and damages part of a building? Does the buyer still have to buy the property? Does the seller have to repair it?

California has answered those questions by adopting the **Uniform Vendor and Purchaser Risk Act,** which is found in the Civil Code. The answers depend on whether or not the buyer has already taken possession of the property, or taken title to it. The law states that every contract for the purchase and sale of real property will be treated as if it included the following provisions.

1. If a material part of the real property is destroyed without fault of the **buyer** (or is taken by eminent domain), and
   - neither the legal title nor possession of the property has been transferred to the buyer,
   - the **seller** (vendor) cannot enforce the contract and the buyer is entitled to recover any part of the purchase price that has already been paid.

2. If either legal title or possession has been transferred, and
   - all or part of the property is then destroyed (or taken by eminent domain) without fault of the **seller,**
   - the **buyer** must still complete the terms of the contract and is not entitled to recover any part of the purchase price already paid.

Exercise 7-3 You are to complete the Residential Purchase Agreement that appears as Figure 7.1 on pages 185 through 192, using the information that follows. The Buyers Inspection Advisory will be checked off, but is not reproduced here.

You are the broker of ABC Realty handling the listing for sale of a single-family residence belonging to Jim and Mary Ivers. The asking price for the Iverses' three-bedroom, one-bathroom home at 3840 Monroe Street, in Concord, Contra Costa County, is $323,000. The Iverses' loan balance is not assumable. On January 11, you meet Kenneth A. and Peggy M. Plummer at an open house of the Ivers residence, and the Plummers indicate they want to make an offer.

You discuss the nature of agency relationships with the Plummers and present a copy of the agency disclosure form to them. After a few minutes of private discussion, Kenneth Plummer states that they have decided to make an offer on the Ivers property, and they would like you to assist them in making the offer as their agent.

You point out the types of conflict that a dual agency representation creates, but the Plummers indicate that they still are willing to proceed on that basis.

You have a purchase agreement form with you, and go through the form with the Plummers. After completing the form as the Plummers indicate, you present it to them for their signatures.

The Plummers are offering $317,000 for the Ivers house. Peggy Plummer writes a personal check for $2,000 as the deposit. Monroe Street is not far from a branch office of First City Title Company, so the Plummers decide on First City to handle the escrow account and closing of the sale. The deposit check is made out to First City Title Company.

The Plummers will make a total cash down payment of $63,400, including the deposit. The buyers will not increase the deposit. The balance of the down payment will be deposited into the escrow account on or before closing. The remaining $253,600 will be financed by a note secured by a first deed of trust on the subject property. The agreement is contingent on both buyers and property qualifying for a loan in that amount. The buyers are to be lender-qualified within 10 calendar days for a 30-year, fixed-rate loan at an interest rate not to exceed 8 percent, with a loan fee of no more than two points plus $200.

The offer is contingent on the buyers' receipt of a property information disclosure statement from the sellers within two days after acceptance.

The buyers and sellers will deliver instructions on the closing of the sale to the escrow holder within ten calendar days from the sellers' acceptance. The closing will take place within 60 calendar days from the sellers' acceptance. The escrow fee will be paid by the buyers, as will the transfer tax.

The buyers will use the house as their primary residence. The buyers will receive possession of the property no later than 6 P.M., two days after the close of escrow.

The sellers will pay for a CLTA title report from First City Title Company and the buyers will have three days after receiving the report to disapprove it. An ALTA insurance policy from the same company will be paid by the buyers. Prorations will be made as of close of escrow. Any liens on the property are to be paid by the sellers. The buyers will take title as specified in the escrow instructions.

The sellers will install a smoke detector and water heater bracing. They must also comply with all other requirements of state and local law.

No personal property is included in the sale. The sellers warrant that the roof does not leak and all appliances and building systems are in working order. There is no septic system. No geological inspection is necessary, and the property is not in a flood hazard zone or a special studies zone. No other special property condition disclosures are necessary. Energy conservation compliance is the responsibility of the sellers. The sellers are to provide a Home Protection Plan from Home Plan, Inc., at a cost of $350.

The sellers are to pay for a pest control report of all structures, to be conducted by Pest Away, Inc., within 20 days of acceptance. The buyers have five days to review reports, disclosures, and other information provided by the sellers except for reports on lead-based paint and lead-based paint hazards, which the buyers have 20 days to review. The buyers will inspect the property and report any defects within 20 calendar days of the sellers' acceptance. The "passive removal" clause shall apply, with the sellers having a three-day response time and the buyers having a two-day right of cancellation. The buyers will have a final "walk-through" within two days before closing. The buyers agree to the provision regarding arbitration of disputes, and they also agree to the liquidated damages clause. Because the broker will be able to present the offer to the sellers on the same day it is drawn up, the buyers will expect an acceptance within two days.

Your office address is 3844 Overview Drive, Concord; your telephone number is (510) 555-6079; fax is 555-6080.

■ SUMMARY

A **contract** is a promise to do something or to refrain from doing something. A **tender** is an offer to perform a **contractual obligation.**

A contract is **executory** as long as some contract obligation remains to be performed. A contract is **executed** when the transaction has been completed. A contract may be **express** or **implied, bilateral** (if both parties are bound) or **unilateral** (if only one party is obligated). A void contract has no legal effect, and a **voidable** contract can be disavowed by its maker. A contract could also be **unenforceable.**

A contract requires an **offer** made by someone who has the **legal capacity** to enter a contract, sufficiently **definite contract terms, acceptance** by the offeree (who also must have contractual capacity), a **lawful object,** and **consideration.** An **offer** may be revoked before acceptance. A **counteroffer** rejects the previous offer and creates a new offer.

The offeree must not act under threat of harm, undue influence, mistake, or on the basis of a **fraudulent misrepresentation,** whether the fraud is **actual** or **constructive.**

The **Statute of Frauds** specifies the types of contracts that must be written to be legally enforceable.

A contract can be **discharged** by **performance, rescission, release,** or **novation.** A contract also will be terminated if performance is impossible or perhaps impractical. Performance of a contract term may be waived by the other party. A contract is modified by **reformation.** Most contracts can be **assigned** to someone else.

A **breach** of the contract terms may **discharge** the contract, but the nonbreaching party may sue for **money damages** or **specific performance.** A lawsuit must be brought within the time period set by the **Statute of Limitations.**

An **offer to purchase** may be made and accepted through a **real estate purchase contract and receipt for deposit.** Such an agreement will include any **contingencies** that, if not met, may enable one party to terminate the contract. A **counteroffer** will initiate a new offer on the proposed terms.

An **option** is a useful way to retain the right to purchase property for an extended period. An **exchange agreement** may benefit both parties and provide tax advantages.

■ IMPORTANT TERMS

Make sure you understand the following terms before you take the achievement examination.

actual fraud
affirmative fraud
assignee
assignment
assignor
bilateral contract
commercial frustration
consideration
constructive fraud
contract
contractual obligation
counteroffer
discharged contract
emancipated minor
exchange
executed contract
executory contract
express contract
fraudulent misrepresentation
implied contract

impossibility of performance
impracticability of performance
lawful object
legal capacity
minor
mutual consent
mutuality of contract
Natural Hazard Disclosure Statement
negative fraud
negligent misrepresentation
novation
offer and acceptance
offeree
offeror
option
oral contract
real estate purchase contract
    and receipt for deposit
reformation
rejection

release

rescission

revocation

specific performance

Statute of Frauds

tender

undue influence

unenforceable contract

Uniform Vendor and Purchaser
  Risk Act

unilateral contract

void contract

voidable contract

■ OPEN FOR DISCUSSION

1. Have real estate contracts gotten too long?

2. What do you suggest to improve the readability of sales contracts?

■ ACHIEVEMENT EXAMINATION 7

1. Sue is 17 years old. She can contract as an adult if she
   a. is living away from her parents.
   b. is emancipated.
   c. is an orphan.
   d. has an adult cosign with her.

2. Fred owns and runs his one-man shoe repair shop as a(n)
   a. sole proprietor.
   b. partner.
   c. executor.
   d. administrator.

3. Mary persuaded her elderly Aunt Agnes to buy a grossly overpriced condominium. Mary knew the price was too high, but she received a commission on the sale from the seller. Aunt Agnes may complain of
   a. actual fraud and undue influence.
   b. negligent misrepresentation.
   c. constructive fraud.
   d. commercial frustration.

4. The contract Haji Ababe accepted states a purchase price "as appraised on May 12, 2005, by Mike Morton, MAI." Based on this provision, the contract is
   a. void.   c. unenforceable.
   b. voidable.   d. enforceable.

5. Can Broker Bob enforce an oral listing agreement?
   a. Yes
   b. No
   c. Possibly
   d. Only if he did not have a contract form handy

6. When both parties agree to cancel a contract they effect a
   a. rescission.   c. novation.
   b. release.   d. reformation.

7. Todd Miller made an offer for the Brown residence, and the Browns accepted Todd's offer. On reconsidering, Todd decides to back out of the deal. The Browns agree to let him do so. Todd and the Browns then sign a(n)
   a. novation of the purchase contract.
   b. agreement rescinding the purchase contract.
   c. assignment of the purchase contract.
   d. agreement reforming the purchase contract.

8. Which of the following is *not* a way to terminate a contract?
   a. Rescission   c. Verification
   b. Release   d. Novation

9. Lonnie and Karen have a contract to buy the Santos house. Following a four-day rainstorm, the Santos house was pushed off its foundation by a mud slide and is now resting about halfway over a ravine. The contract probably is
   a. discharged because performance is impractical.
   b. still in effect.
   c. discharged because performance is impossible.
   d. None of the above

10. If Jane's performance of her sales contract becomes economically impractical, she should
    a. cancel the contract unilaterally.
    b. ask that the contract be terminated.
    c. claim the purchase is a mistake.
    d. tear up the contract.

11. Failure to perform a contract is a
    a. rescission.
    c. novation.
    b. breach.
    d. reformation.

12. Fred signed a contract to sell his farm to George. Fred had second thoughts and refused to sell, but the sale went through anyway. How?
    a. George threatened Fred.
    b. George received a court order for specific performance of the contract.
    c. Once signed, a contract cannot be terminated.
    d. None of the above

13. The time period in which a lawsuit can be brought is set by the
    a. equal dignities rule.
    b. Statute of Frauds.
    c. Statute of Limitations.
    d. probate court.

14. The Statute of Limitations for an action based on a written real estate contract is
    a. unlimited.
    c. four years.
    b. two years.
    d. 20 years.

15. The rule for preprinted contracts is
    a. handwriting takes precedence only over printing.
    b. printing takes precedence over typing.
    c. handwriting takes precedence over both typing and printing.
    d. All of the above

16. A property description including the words "250 acres, more or less" is
    a. fatally defective.
    b. not definite enough.
    c. sufficient if reasonably close to the exact acreage.
    d. incomplete without a metes-and-bounds description.

17. A well-drafted real estate purchase contract will include provision for
    a. the buyer's possession of the property.
    b. the financing terms.
    c. proration of property expenses.
    d. All of the above

18. Unless the seller provides the necessary documentation, part of the proceeds of a sale of real property must be withheld for federal tax purposes as provided by
    a. FHA.
    c. FIRPTA.
    b. Fannie Mae.
    d. IRS.

19. Liquidated damages paid on default by the buyer of a single-family residence who intended to occupy the dwelling cannot exceed what percentage of the purchase price?
    a. 1
    c. 7
    b. 3
    d. 10

20. Haji Ababe received an offer of $610,000 for his house. His asking price is $635,000. Haji countered with $625,000. If the buyer rejects the counteroffer, may Haji accept the $610,000?
    a. Yes
    b. No
    c. Yes, if he does so within 24 hours
    d. Only if he redrafts the original offer

CHAPTER EIGHT

FINANCING REAL ESTATE

■ PURPOSES OF FINANCING REAL ESTATE

"Affordable" financing benefits both businesses and consumers. When funds are readily available for borrowing at reasonable terms, businesses can grow and prosper. For individuals, access to financing means the dream of home ownership can become a reality. More than $2.8 trillion in home loans were originated in 2002, with 59 percent of that amount devoted to the refinancing of existing loans.

Californians benefit from a wide range of housing choices. They include single-family detached residences, town houses sharing common walls with one or more neighbors, condominiums, duplexes and other multifamily structures, cooperative apartments, houseboats, manufactured homes, and vacant parcels for custom building.

It is easy to understand why a homeowner or an investor would want to own property. Real estate has tended to grow in value over the years because of its scarcity and desirability, which make it an attractive possession.

Often the greatest financial benefit of real estate ownership is that it can be used as security for a loan. By borrowing money against the value of the property, home purchasers benefit from **present use, future appreciation** (increase in value), and **forced saving** by paying down the amount owed. There may also be **tax advantages,** as discussed in Chapter 11, "Real Estate Taxation."

Of course, the purchaser who relies on a loan to finance the purchase must have enough income to make the loan payments. But that income generally is far less than the cash that would be needed to buy most property outright. The purchaser thus uses the **leverage** of a relatively small initial cash outlay to finance purchase of a property worth many times that amount. By reducing the amount of cash that a buyer has at risk, a leveraged purchase can also help protect the buyer if market values go down.

> Most home purchases would be impossible without the use of leverage.

■ **FOR EXAMPLE:** The Sanchezes are buying a suburban house. The selling price of $500,000 is being financed by the seller. The Sanchezes will pay $100,000 cash and make a payment of $2,308.95, which includes interest and part of the principal (the balance of the loan), each month.

$100,000 Plus
$2,308.95 Per Month
for 30 Years

$500,000 House

At the end of 30 years, the Sanchezes will own their home outright and will have no further loan payments to make.

Some of the most valuable benefits of home ownership are realized when the property is sold, even if it is sold well before the end of the loan term.

■ **FOR EXAMPLE:** The Sanchezes decide to sell their home after ten years of ownership. The sales price is $880,000. By that time, they have paid down the principal of their debt by approximately $70,000 but they incur expenses of $50,000 in commission and costs on the sale. So, they net $500,000 at the close of escrow. After paying themselves back the initial $100,000 they used for their down payment, they receive a profit of $400,000. Thus, the Sanchezes have leveraged $100,000 to make $400,000.

The example above is a very simplified one, of course. It fails to take into account the year-to-year benefit of home ownership that the Sanchezes may realize thanks to the tax deductions their real estate ownership generates. They should also take into account the cost of renting comparable housing, as well as the intangible value of being owners and not renters.

■ COST OF CREDIT

A purchaser of real estate who defers part or all of the purchase price uses some form of **credit.** When the purchaser receives credit from the seller, the cost of that credit is usually the **rate of interest** charged to the purchaser. The purchaser may borrow money from another source to finance the purchase or borrow money using property already owned outright as collateral. In either case, the cost of those funds typically is expressed as interest. The cost of using money also may include loan fees or **points** paid at the time of closing, with one point equal to 1 percent of the amount borrowed.

Just as there is a market for real estate, there also is a market for the money used to finance real estate. Lenders compete for borrowers by trying to make their loans as attractive as possible. They do so by lowering interest rates and making other loan terms, such as fees and time needed for processing, as attractive as possible.

Most lenders rely on outside sources from which they receive the funds that they loan out to purchasers of real estate. If the supply of funds is diminished, or if funds become more expensive for lenders to acquire, the result will be higher interest rates and less favorable terms for borrowers.

The Money Supply

Money is a medium of exchange as well as a measure of value. In exchange for our work efforts, we earn **income** in the form of money. Income also comes from the following:

- Investments
- Rents
- Royalties
- Interest on amounts owed to us

We exchange our income for products and services, invest it, or save it. Income is taxed to provide funds for government to carry out the services it provides. Businesses also receive income and in turn make payments for taxes, salaries, and other costs of production, as well as investments.

The production of income is **cyclical.** (See Figure 8.1.) As consumer demand for goods and services increases, the elements of production flourish. Factories are built, products are made, employees are paid. These activities, in turn, pump more money into the economy.

FIGURE 8.1

Economic Cycles

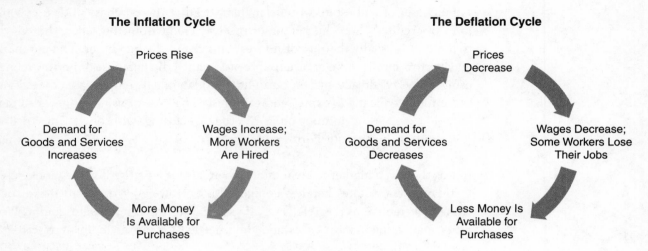

The income diverted to taxes is used to buy the goods and services that support government programs. Taxes also subsidize individuals and businesses through a variety of direct and indirect payments.

Investment funds and savings provide the capital needed for industry to grow and prosper. Savings also form the basis of the funds loaned to purchasers and developers of real estate. Savers are paid interest by lending institutions, which in turn charge a higher rate of interest to borrowers of those savings.

www.federalreserve.gov

Federal Reserve Bank System.   The Federal Reserve Bank System (the Fed) was created by Congress in 1913 to serve as the central bank of the United States. Information on the history of the Fed, as well as areas of consumer protection and links to related sites, can be found at the Web site, *www.federalreserve.gov*.

The Fed regulates the flow of money and the cost of credit to help stabilize the market fluctuations that create inflation or recession. The 12 Federal Reserve Banks follow the policies set by a seven-member Board of Governors. Members of the board are appointed by the President of the United States and confirmed by the Senate for 14-year terms. The Fed makes its own decisions but reports to Congress, and its power can be revoked by Congress. The main activities of the Fed are accomplished by

When the Chairman of the Federal Reserve Board announces a change in the Fed's interest rate, the whole world pays attention.

■ raising or lowering **reserve requirements** (cash on hand) of member banks, which decreases or increases the amount of money allowed to circulate;

■ establishing the **discount rate** (interest rate) that member banks must pay to borrow money from the Fed, which affects the **prime rate** that banks charge their most favorably rated commercial borrowers and, ultimately, the rate consumers are charged; and

■ buying and selling **government securities** to affect the amount of funds available for savings and other investment, and thus the amount available for borrowing.

Federal Home Loan Banks.   There are 12 regional Federal Home Loan Banks. Member institutions, such as federally or state-chartered savings and loan associations, are required to own capital stock in the regional Federal Home Loan Banks, which in turn lend money to member institutions.

The **Federal Home Loan Bank of San Francisco** covers the Eleventh Federal Home Loan Bank District, which includes California, Nevada, and Arizona.

Federal Deposit Insurance Corporation.   The **Federal Deposit Insurance Corporation (FDIC)** was created to insure individual accounts in participating banks and (as of 1989) savings and loan associations, up to $100,000 maximum.

Many other federal and state agencies and departments affect the availability and cost of credit. Some of them are discussed below, and others will be discussed in the next chapter. Recent legislation has had far-reaching consequences.

The Road to FIRREA

Legislation intended to place thrifts (savings and loan associations) on equal footing with commercial banks had some unfortunate consequences, including the failure of many institutions. The Depository Institutions Deregulation and Monetary Control Act of 1980 began the process by greatly expanding the ability of depository institutions to offer services and yields competitive with market rates.

With deregulation came many abuses by thrift associations that were poorly managed. Improperly documented loans, inept or falsified property appraisals, and outright theft of association funds were some abuses that led to the downfall of many institutions. Congress attempted to overhaul the thrift industry by passing the **Financial Institutions Reform, Recovery, and Enforcement Act of 1989 (FIRREA).**

FIRREA established the **Office of Thrift Supervision** and the **Housing Finance Board** to take over the savings and loan supervisory responsibilities that formerly had belonged to the Federal Home Loan Bank Board (FHLBB). FDIC was given the additional responsibility of insuring deposits in all federally chartered banks and savings institutions, as well as the bank deposits it already insured. Savings and loan deposits had previously been insured by the Federal Savings and Loan Insurance Corporation (FSLIC), which ceased operation.

Usury

Usury is the charging of an exorbitant amount or rate of interest and is the subject of both state and federal law.

State Law

In 1979 California voters passed Proposition 2, which exempted from usury laws any loan made or arranged by a real estate broker and secured by real property. California law also exempts loans made by banks and savings and loan associations. Loans of credit unions, personal finance companies, and pawnbrokers are exempt unless the loan falls in one of the statutory categories mentioned below.

1. The maximum statutory interest rate that may be charged for consumer loans (money, goods, or other things intended for personal, family, or household purposes), other than loans for the purchase, construction, or improvement of real property, is 10 percent per year.

2. Money, goods, or other things intended for the purchase, construction, or improvement of real property are subject to a maximum rate of 10 percent or the prevailing Federal Reserve Bank discount rate plus 5 percent, whichever is higher.

3. Business loans are subject to a ceiling of the Federal Reserve Bank discount rate plus 5 percent.

4. The refinancing of a loan is subject to the same maximum rate as the original loan.

Federal Law

When they cover the same subject, federal law preempts state law. Federal law exempts federally related residential first mortgage loans made after March 31, 1980, from state interest limitations. This includes loans used to finance manufactured housing (mobile homes) and the acquisition of stock in a cooperative housing corporation.

The federal act effectively limits the California usury laws to private lenders.

Seller Financing

When a seller of real property extends credit for part or all of the purchase price, it is not considered a loan for purposes of the usury laws, but merely an **extension of credit.** The seller must act in good faith, however, or the transaction can be questioned.

Appraisals. With FIRREA, the federal government also introduced minimum requirements for appraisals, as well as appraiser licensing and certification. As of January 1, 1993, a property appraisal in a **federally related transaction** (such as a loan insured or guaranteed by a federal agency or a loan sold on the secondary mortgage market) can be performed only by an appraiser licensed or certified by the state in which the property is located, as discussed in Chapter 13.

The type of property and its estimated value determine whether appraiser licensing or certification is necessary. In addition, the appraisal itself must meet or exceed certain minimum standards. Property below a stated minimum value is exempt from the requirements.

■ REAL ESTATE AS SECURITY

Why would anyone lend as much money as most real estate transactions require? Because the loan can be backed by the real property.

Real estate loans in California generally are made using two instruments.

1. The **promissory note** is the borrower's promise to pay the amount borrowed. The promissory note is evidence of the debt. It establishes the underlying obligation of the loan transaction.
2. The **security instrument** is used to identify the real estate that serves as assurance that the loan will be repaid.

With a security instrument a property owner **hypothecates** the described real estate. **Hypothecation** means the real property will be forfeited to the holder of the security instrument if the underlying debt is not paid. The process is similar to what occurs when personal property is **pledged** to secure payment of a loan. One important difference is that with a pledge, *possession* of the pledged property is turned over to the *lender* until the debt is paid. The *borrower* typically retains possession of hypothecated real property.

The security instrument is what is commonly referred to as a **mortgage.** As you will learn, however, the legal document that serves as the security instrument can take the form of either a **mortgage** or a **deed of trust,** with very different results.

Promissory Note

The **promissory note** is a promise to pay money according to specified terms. The payment may be by installments that include both interest and principal (the **amortized loan**) or by installments of interest only with the principal due in a lump sum (a **straight note**). A combination of loan types also may be used, with a lump-sum *balloon payment* due at the end of a specified term, during which only part of the principal is paid. A **balloon payment** is defined by the Real Estate Law as an installment that is at least twice the amount of the smallest installment.

Recently, interest rates have been allowed to reflect market trends by use of an **adjustable-rate note,** described later in this chapter. A loan can also call for payment of the entire amount due on demand of the holder of the note. An example of an **installment note** that specifies equal payments of both principal and interest appears in Figure 8.2.

Joint and several liability.   When more than one person signs a promissory note, there will probably be language in the note (such as the phrase "jointly and severally") indicating that each cosigner is liable for the entire financial obligation imposed by the note. This **joint and several liability** means that, if one cosigner defaults in payment on the note, the note holder can demand full payment from any other cosigner. Obviously, careful consideration should be given to any request to serve as cosigner on a note or other financial obligation.

Negotiable instrument.   To qualify as a **negotiable instrument,** a promissory note must be

- an unconditional promise made by one person to another;
- in writing;
- an agreement to pay a specified amount of money on demand or at a fixed or determinable future time;
- payable on the order of a designated person or the bearer of the note; and
- signed by its maker.

If a promissory note qualifies as a negotiable instrument, the **holder** of the note (the one to whom the money is to be paid) can sell the note, give it away, or transfer the rights it represents in some other way. With a single instrument, an obligation to pay a large sum of money can thus change hands efficiently.

> The person who receives an assignment is the assignee or transferee.

A promissory note is a contract that may be enforced by the holder of the note or anyone to whom the holder assigns or transfers the right of payment. The person to whom the assignment is made is called the **assignee** or **transferee.** If all requirements for a negotiable instrument have *not* been met, the assignee or transferee has only the rights of the original holder of the note. If a promissory note meets all the requirements of a negotiable instrument, it attains a special status. Then a transferee or an assignee may be placed in a better position than the person from whom the note was received, *if* the transferee or assignee qualifies as a **holder in due course,** as described next.

Holder in due course.   A **holder in due course** is someone who takes a negotiable instrument

- **for value,**
- **in good faith,** and

FIGURE 8.2

Installment Note—Interest Included

INSTALLMENT NOTE - INTEREST INCLUDED
(Due on Sale Clause)

$ 388,000.00   Walnut Creek, **California**   October 24 , **2---**

FOR VALUE RECEIVED, we, or either of us, promise to pay in lawful money of the United States of America, to

Local Savings and Loan Association, 7800 North Main Street,
Riverside California

or order, at place designated by payee, the principal sum of   Three hundred eighty-eight
thousand dollars . . . . (388,000.00) **dollars,**
with interest in like lawful money from   October 24 , **2---**   **at** 5¾ **per cent**
per annum the amounts of principal sum remaining unpaid from time to time.

Principal and interest payable in   180   **installments of** Three thousand two
hundred twenty-one and 99/100 dollars . . . . (3,221.99)
or more each, on the   1st   **day of each and every**   month   **beginning on the**
1st   **day of**   November   , **2--- and continuing until**   said principal
sum and interest have been paid.

The Deed of Trust securing the within note contains the following provisions:

**"In the event the herein described property or any part thereof, or any interest therein is sold, agreed to be sold, conveyed
or alienated by the Trustor, or by the operation of law or otherwise, all obligations secured by this instrument, irrespective
of the maturity dates expressed therein, at the option of the holder hereof and without demand or notice shall immediately
become due and payable."**

Each payment shall be credited first on interest then due and the remainder on principal; and interest shall
thereupon cease upon the principal so credited. Should default be made in payment of any installment of
principal or interest when due the whole sum of principal and interest shall become immediately due at the
option of the holder of this note. If action be instituted on this note I promise to pay such sum as the Court
may fix as attorney's fees. This note is secured by a Deed of Trust.

_____   _____
                                                   Charles S. Buyer

_____   _____
                                                   Marilyn H. Buyer

FTG-3012 (7/1/83)

Source: Reprinted courtesy of Founders Title Company.

■ **without notice of any defense** against its enforcement that might be made by any person.

A **defense** that a note maker could use to *prevent* enforcement of a negotiable instrument could be

■ **lack of consideration** (the note maker never received the promised funds or property in exchange for the note),

■ **prior payment** (the note already has been paid off),

■ **cancellation** (the original note holder agreed to cancel the note obligation),

■ **set-off** (the original holder owes money to the note maker that should be applied to the note debt), or

■ **fraud in the inducement** (the note maker created the note based on fraudulent representation by the payee).

Consumer Credit

The Federal Trade Commission has limited the rights of a **holder in due course** in consumer credit contracts for goods or services. Subsequent holders of such contracts are subject to all of the same defenses the maker could bring against the original holder. This provision applies to real estate only in the case of contracts for particular building improvements added after initial construction, such as siding.

The holder in due course (or anyone who acquires a negotiable instrument from a holder in due course) is not bound by the above defenses. A holder in due course can insist on collecting on the note, even if the note maker can claim one of the above defenses against the original note holder.

A holder in due course still may not be able to enforce the instrument, however, *if*

■ the note maker lacked the legal capacity to make a legal agreement,

■ the note was forged,

■ the instrument involves an illegal activity, or

■ there has been a material alteration in the terms of the note (although a subsequent holder in due course can claim payment according to the note's original terms).

■ **FOR EXAMPLE:**   Ben Phillips has purchased the Simon residence, giving a promissory note for $292,000 to his Aunt Fran, who lent him the money to buy the house. Ben promised to pay 7 percent interest on the loan. Aunt Fran gave the note to her niece Marjorie, who altered the note to read 17 percent interest. Marjorie then sold the note to an investor, who had no knowledge of the alteration. The investor informed Ben of the address to which the monthly payments should be sent. When Ben's monthly payments fell short of the 17 percent loan amount, the investor sent a reminder of the discrepancy. Does Ben have to pay the 17 percent? What does Ben have to do?

Even though the investor probably qualifies as a holder in due course, Ben can claim that the note was materially altered and refuse to pay 17 percent. Ben still must keep up the payments at the original rate of 7 percent, however.

MATH CONCEPTS

Real estate loan interest payments can be computed in two steps.

1. Principal × Rate = Annual Interest

    The **principal** is the unpaid balance of the loan. The **rate** is the percentage rate of interest paid.

2. Interest on a loan ordinarily is calculated monthly. To find interest per month, divide the annual interest by 12.

    Example: Calculate the interest to be paid for one month on a loan with a remaining balance of $176,000, when the interest rate is 6 percent.

    $$\text{Principal} \times \text{Rate} = \text{Annual Interest}$$
    $$\$176,000 \times .06 = \$10,560$$
    $$\$10,560 \div 12 = \$880 \text{ Monthly Interest}$$

To find interest for a number of days, find the daily interest by dividing the annual interest by 360 days in the year (unless the exact number of days in the year is required). Then, multiply the interest per day by the number of days for which interest is owed.

Example: Calculate the interest to be paid for 17 days on a loan with a remaining balance of $176,000, when the interest rate is 6 percent.

$$\$176,000 \times .06 = \$10,560 \text{ Annual Interest}$$
$$\$10,560 \div 360 = \$29.33 \text{ Daily Interest}$$
$$\$29.33 \times 17 = \$498.67 \text{ Interest for 17 days}$$

Another way to find daily interest is to divide the annual interest by 12, and then divide that number by 30. If you don't have a calculator, that way may be easier than dividing the annual interest by 360.

Security Instrument

The **security instrument** *hypothecates* the property that serves as the lender's assurance that the underlying debt will be repaid. The process of hypothecation, as described earlier, is similar to a pledge, but the property owner retains possession of the property.

> The security instrument usually is referred to as a mortgage, even when it is a deed of trust.

The security instrument is commonly referred to as a *mortgage*, although it may take one of several forms, only one of which technically is a mortgage. It is not commonly used in California, even though the mortgage was the first security instrument used in the state. The **deed of trust** now is the preferred security instrument in California.

Whether it takes the form of a mortgage or deed of trust, the security instrument will be recorded to provide constructive notice of the lien rights of the lender.

Mortgage. A **mortgage** is an instrument by which property is hypothecated to secure the payment of a debt or an obligation. A lien on the property is given by the **mortgagor** (borrower) to the **mortgagee** (lender). In the event of the mortgagor's default before final payment, the mortgagee's remedy is judicial (court-ordered) foreclosure. As an alternative, the mortgage instrument could contain a power-of-sale provision. A mortgage with a power of sale operates as a trust deed does when property is sold at a trustee's sale (discussed later in this chapter).

The procedure for **judicial foreclosure** changed as of July 1, 1983. Instruments that originated before that date follow the old rules, and instruments as of that date follow the new rules. If you are involved in any foreclosure matter, always consult an attorney.

In a judicial foreclosure the court orders the property sold to the highest bidder at public auction in the county where at least part of the property is located. The court appoints a commissioner or orders the sheriff to carry out the sale. Statutory notice requirements must be met.

If the bid price exceeds $5,000, the successful bidder has the option of depositing the greater of $5,000 or 10 percent of the amount bid and paying the balance within ten days of the sale. If this option is chosen, the bidder also must pay additional costs and interest that accrue between the sale and the date of payment. If full payment is not made within ten days of the sale, a new sale is conducted and the **defaulting buyer** is liable for costs of the original sale and resale, interest, attorneys' fees, and the amount of the original bid less the amount bid for the property in the subsequent sale. If no acceptable bid is received, the sale can be postponed.

The commissioner or sheriff delivers to the purchaser a **certificate of sale,** which should be recorded immediately.

The proceeds of a foreclosure are used to pay off the remaining indebtedness on the property. Any funds left over go to other lienholders in order of priority; the last recipient is the mortgagor. If the sale proceeds do not cover the indebtedness plus court costs and sale fees, the mortgagee can obtain a **deficiency judgment** for the remaining debt against the mortgagor personally, *unless*

- the mortgage was a purchase money debt (the mortgagee was the seller of the property); or
- the loan was to pay all or part of the purchase price of an owner-occupied residential dwelling of no more than four units.

Antideficiency—The Homeowner's Safety Net
California Code of Civil Procedure 580b

As long as market demand exceeds supply and prices continue to soar, California homeowners usually don't need to worry about foreclosure. Even when an individual has difficulty making mortgage payments, the sale of the property will relieve the owner of the payment burden, and most likely provide a profit over the purchase price, as well.

But what happens when the market takes a turn for the worse? And what about the worst-case scenario—the current market value of the property is less than the remaining loan balance? That's when California's antideficiency protection provides the ultimate safety net for homeowners. If a homeowner can no longer continue to make mortgage payments, the only recourse for the lender is to take back the property. *Even if the current market value of the property is less than the outstanding loan balance, the lender cannot seek a judgment against the defaulting homeowner for the difference.*

This protection is automatic, so long as the loan is the one that the owner used to purchase the property. It even extends to situations in which a chattel mortgage is given for the purchase of personal property (such as furnishings) as part of the original home acquisition. In that case, the antideficiency protection covers both loans. The protection does not apply, however, if the original home loan was refinanced. It also does not apply to any home equity loan taken out after the original purchase. The potential benefit of the law is thus greatest for homeowners who take the maximum purchase money mortgage at the time the property is first acquired.

Before a foreclosure sale, the mortgagor or anyone with a subordinate lien or encumbrance on the property may cure the default by paying all delinquencies, including court costs and fees that result from the foreclosure. The mortgage thus is placed back in effect in a process called **reinstatement.**

The least desirable aspect of judicial foreclosure is that it is time-consuming. Not only does it take many months for the sale to take place but the purchaser at a foreclosure sale receives only a certificate of sale. The purchaser does not receive possession until after the statutory **redemption period,** a period following the sale during which the judgment debtor or the judgment debtor's successor in interest can buy back the property.

The Old Rule

On sales stemming from instruments that originated before July 1, 1983, a junior lienor (such as a second-mortgage holder) also has a right of redemption. The redemption period is three months following the sale if the sale proceeds were sufficient to cover the remaining indebtedness plus interest and costs of foreclosure. Otherwise the redemption period is one year, unless the mortgagee waives or is prohibited from obtaining a deficiency judgment. The buyer at a foreclosure sale obviously must take the risk of redemption into account when deciding how much to bid for the property.

When a mortgage debt has been satisfied, the **mortgagee** must execute a **certificate of discharge,** which is recorded with the county recorder. Otherwise the mortgage lien may act as a cloud on the owner's title.

Deed of trust. It will soon become obvious, as we go over the characteristics of the deed of trust, why this is the security instrument preferred by lenders who make loans in California.

A deed of trust (or *trust deed*) is an instrument by which real property is *hypothecated* to secure *payment* of a debt or an obligation. The title to the property is transferred by the **trustor** (borrower) to the **trustee** (a neutral third party) to hold on behalf of the **beneficiary** (lender) until the debt is repaid, even though the borrower retains possession. In the event the trustor defaults on the underlying debt, the trustee is instructed to sell the property and transfer the money obtained at the sale to the beneficiary as payment of the debt. An example of a deed of trust appears in Figure 8.3.

Someone other than the borrower could place title to property in trust to secure the borrower's loan, but the trustor is usually the borrower. For example, a loan made to a business could be secured by a mortgage on the home of one of its officers.

On the trustor's **default,** the beneficiary has the option of requesting a **trustee's sale** or a **judicial foreclosure** (the same remedy available with a mortgage).

FIGURE 8.3

Short Form Deed of Trust and Assignment of Rents

RECORDING REQUESTED BY

Order No. Escrow No.

AND WHEN RECORDED MAIL TO

Name

Street Address

City & State

SPACE ABOVE THIS LINE FOR RECORDER'S USE

SHORT FORM DEED OF TRUST AND ASSIGNMENT OF RENTS
(INDIVIDUAL)

A.P.N. ______________________

This Deed of Trust, made this day of , between

, herein called **Trustor,**

whose address is ,
(number and street (city) (state) zip)

North American Title Company, a California corporation, herein called **Trustee,** and

, herein called **Beneficiary,**

Witnesseth: That Trustor IRREVOCABLY GRANTS, TRANSFERS AND ASSIGNS to TRUSTEE IN TRUST, WITH POWER OF SALE, that property in County, California, described as:

TOGETHER WITH the rents, issues and profits thereof, SUBJECT, HOWEVER, to the right, power and authority given to and conferred upon Beneficiary by paragraph (10) of the provisions incorporated herein by reference to collect and apply such rents, issues and profits.

For the Purpose of Securing: 1. Performance of each agreement of Trustor incorporated by reference or contained herein. 2. Payment of the indebtedness evidenced by one promissory note of even date herewith, and any extension or renewal thereof, in the principal sum of $ ________________ executed by Trustor in favor of Beneficiary or order. 3. Payment of such further sums as the then record owner of said property hereafter may borrow from Beneficiary, when evidenced by another note (or notes) reciting it is so secured.

T-34 (Rev. 4/94) Page 1 of 2

Source: Reprinted courtesy of the North American Title Company.

FIGURE 8.3

Short Form Deed of Trust and Assignment of Rents (Continued)

To Protect the Security of This Deed of Trust, Trustor Agrees: By the execution and delivery of this Deed of Trust and the note secured hereby, that provisions (I) to (14), inclusive, of the fictitious deed of trust recorded in Santa Barbara County and Sonoma County October 18, 1961, and in all other counties October 23, 1961, in the book and at the page of Official Records in the office of the county recorder of the county where said property is located, noted below opposite the name of the county, viz.:

COUNTY	BOOK	PAGE	COUNTY	BOOK	PAGE	COUNTY	BOOK	PAGE	COUNTY	BOOK	PAGE
Alameda	435	684	Kings	792	833	Placer	895	301	Sierra	29	335
Alpine	1	250	Lake	362	39	Plumas	151	5	Siskiyou	468	181
Amador	104	348	Lassen	171	471	Riverside	3005	523	Solano	1105	182
Butte	1145	1	Los Angeles	T2055	899	Sacramento	4331	62	Sonoma	1851	689
Calaveras	145	152	Madera	810	170	San Benito	271	383	Stanislaus	1715	456
Colusa	296	617	Marin	1508	339	San Bernardino	5567	61	Sutter	572	297
Contra Costa	3978	47	Mariposa	77	292	San Francisco	A332	905	Tehama	401	289
Del Norte	78	414	Mendocino	579	530	San Joaquin	2470	311	Trinity	93	366
El Dorado	568	456	Merced	1547	538	San Luis Obispo	1151	12	Tulare	2294	275
Fresno	4626	572	Modoc	184	851	San Mateo	4078	420	Tuolumne	135	47
Glenn	422	184	Mono	52	429	Santa Barbara	1878	860	Ventura	2062	386
Humboldt	657	527	Monterey	2194	538	Santa Clara	5336	341	Yolo	653	245
Imperial	1091	501	Napa	639	86	Santa Cruz	1431	494	Yuba	334	486
Inyo	147	598	Nevada	305	320	Shasta	684	528			
Kern	3427	60	Orange	5889	611	San Diego	Series 2 Book 1961, Page 183887				

(which provisions, identical in all counties, are printed on attached herewith) hereby are adopted and incorporated herein and made a part hereof as fully as though set forth herein at length; that he will observe and perform said provisions; and that the references to property, obligations and parties in said provisions shall be construed to refer to the property, obligations, and parties set forth in this Deed of Trust.

The undersigned Trustor requests that a copy of any Notice of Default and of any Notice of Sale hereunder be mailed to him at his address hereinbefore set forth.

STATE OF CALIFORNIA
COUNTY OF _____ } SS.

Signature of Trustor

On _____ before me, _____

_____, personally appeared _____

_____

_____

personally known to me (or proved to me on the basis of satisfactory evidence) to be the person(s) whose name(s) is/are subscribed to the within instrument and acknowledged to me that he/she/they executed the same in his/her/their authorized capacity(ies), and that by his/her/their signature(s) on the instrument the person(s), or the entity upon behalf of which the person(s) acted, executed the instrument.

WITNESS my hand and official seal.

Signature _____   (This area for official notarial seal)

FOR RECONVEYANCE SEND TO THE NEAREST OFFICE OF NORTH AMERICAN TITLE COMPANY

REQUEST FOR FULL RECONVEYANCE

To be used only when note has been paid.

Dated _____

TO NORTH AMERICAN TITLE COMPANY, Trustee:
The undersigned is the legal owner and holder of all indebtedness secured by the within Deed of Trust. All sums secured by said Deed of Trust have been fully paid and satisfied; and you are hereby requested and directed, on payment to you of any sums owing to you under the terms of said Deed of Trust, to cancel all evidences of indebtedness, secured by said Deed of Trust, delivered to you herewith together with said Deed of Trust, and to reconvey, without warranty, to the parties designated by the terms of said Deed of Trust, the estate now held by you under the same.

MAIL RECONVEYANCE TO:

_____

_____

_____   (By) _____

_____   (By) _____

**Do not lose or destroy this Deed of Trust OR THE NOTE which it secures.
Both must be delivered to the Trustee for cancellation before reconveyance will be made.**

T-34 (Rev. 4/94)   Page 2 of 2

Source: Reprinted courtesy of the North American Title Company.

Neither choice prevents the other from ultimately being used before the sale is carried out, although the four-year Statute of Limitations will be applied to a judicial foreclosure. A **trustee's sale** is made possible by the provisions of the trust instrument. On default by the trustor, the beneficiary informs the trustee of that fact by a **declaration of default,** which states the reason for the default. The beneficiary includes the original note and trust deed with the declaration.

The form of **notice of default** that appears in Figure 8.4 became effective June 1, 1985. The first statement in the notice must be printed in bold type. *The notice must be in Spanish if the trustor so requested or if the contract was negotiated in Spanish.* The beneficiary or trustee must state that the entire debt is due because of the default, or it cannot be collected at the sale.

The notice of default is sent by registered or certified mail to

- the trustor;
- any successor in interest to the trustor;
- junior lienholders;
- the State Controller (if there is a tax lien on the property); *and*
- anyone who has filed a *request for notice* with the county recorder.

If any parties other than the original trustor are involved, notice is also published in a newspaper of general circulation once a week for four weeks.

A debt under a trust deed or mortgage can be reinstated if payment of the overdue amount is made at any time after the notice of default is recorded, but no later than five business days prior to the date of sale in the subsequent recorded **notice of sale.** Some deed-of-trust forms provide for a longer period of reinstatement—if so, the longer period will apply. A junior lienholder can pay the amount in arrears, which would then be added to the debt owed under that obligation.

No less than three months after the notice of default is recorded, a **notice of trustee's sale** is given in the same manner as the notice of sale in a foreclosure. Reinstatement is possible up to five days before the sale date. Reinstatement within the five-day period preceding the sale would be at the discretion of the beneficiary and might still be allowed. The trustor always would have the opportunity to prevent the sale during that period by paying the entire debt owed, plus the costs and fees accumulated.

At the sale itself, the beneficiary lender can **credit-bid** up to the amount of the debt owed. Otherwise, payment is by cash, cashier's check from a qualified lender, or a cash equivalent designated in the notice of trustee's sale as acceptable to the trustee.

The most significant difference between a mortgage and a trust deed (or mortgage with power of sale) is that there is no **right of redemption** following a trustee's sale.

FIGURE 8.4

Notice of Default

Notice of Default and Election to Sell Under Deed of Trust
IMPORTANT NOTICE
IF YOUR PROPERTY IS IN FORECLOSURE BECAUSE YOU ARE BEHIND IN YOUR PAYMENTS, IT MAY BE SOLD WITHOUT ANY COURT ACTION, and you may have the legal right to bring your account in good standing by paying all of your past due payments plus permitted costs and expenses within the time permitted by law for reinstatement of your account, which is normally five business days prior to the date set for the sale of your property. No sale date may be set until three months from the date this notice of default may be recorded (which date of recordation appears on this notice). This amount is _____ as of _____, and will increase until your account becomes current.
(Date)

You may not have to pay the entire unpaid portion of your account, even though full payment was demanded, but you must pay the amount stated above. However, you and your beneficiary or mortgagee may mutually agree in writing prior to the time the notice of sale is posted (which may not be earlier than the end of the three-month period stated above) to, among other things, (1) provide additional time in which to cure the default by transfer of the property or otherwise: (2) establish a schedule of payments in order to cure your default; or both (1) and (2).

Following the expiration of the time period referred to in the first paragraph of this notice, unless the obligation being foreclosed upon or a separate written agreement between you and your creditor permits a longer period, you have only the legal right to stop the sale of your property by paying the entire amount demanded by your creditor.

To find the amount you must pay, or to arrange for payment to stop the foreclosure, or if your property is in foreclosure for any other reason, contact:

_____
(Name of beneficiary or mortgagee)

_____
(Mailing address)

_____
(Telephone)

If you have any questions, you should contact a lawyer or the government agency which may have insured your loan.

Notwithstanding the fact that your property is in foreclosure, you may offer your property for sale, provided the sale is concluded prior to the conclusion of the foreclosure.

Remember, **YOU MAY LOSE LEGAL RIGHTS IF YOU DO NOT TAKE PROMPT ACTION.**

NOTICE IS HEREBY GIVEN, THAT   a corporation, is duly appointed Trustee under a Deed of Trust dated   executed by
                    as Trustor, to secure certain obligations
in favor of

                    , as beneficiary,
recorded   , as instrument no.   , in book   , page   , of Official Records
                    in the Office of the
Recorder of   County, California, describing land
therein as:

including   note   for the   sum of $ said obligations

that the beneficial interest under such Deed of Trust and the obligations secured thereby, are presently held by the undersigned; that a breach of, and default in, the obligations for which such Deed of Trust is security has occurred in that payment has not been made of:

that by reason thereof, the undersigned, present beneficiary under such Deed of Trust, has executed and delivered to said duly appointed Trustee, a written Declaration of Default and Demand for Sale, and has deposited with said duly appointed Trustee, such Deed of Trust and all documents evidencing obligations secured thereby, and has declared and does hereby declare all sums secured thereby immediately due and payable and has elected and does hereby elect to cause the trust property to be sold to satisfy the obligations secured thereby.

_____

_____

Dated _____

The sale is absolutely final, and the purchaser can take possession immediately. A bidder at such a sale will understandably be willing to offer a higher price than if the sale were a judicial foreclosure.

Postponement of the Trustee's Sale

If no acceptable bid is received, or if more than one sale has been scheduled for the same time, the sale can be postponed. Postponement of the sale revives the right of reinstatement as of the date the new notice of sale is recorded, and it continues until five business days prior to the new date of sale. The same rule applies to any further postponement.

Being entitled to possession is small comfort to the purchaser if the former owner refuses to vacate the premises. An **unlawful detainer** is the legal action by which the court orders the sheriff to evict the present occupant. The purchaser at a trustee's sale must also take such an eventuality into account.

The fact that there is no right of redemption helps minimize the lender's risk, for there is a greater chance that if the borrower defaults, the debt will be repaid in full by a trustee's sale. This is true even though sale by exercise of the **power of sale** by the beneficiary or mortgagee, rather than sale by judicial foreclosure, automatically *bars* any **deficiency judgment** in the event the sale proceeds fail to cover the unpaid balance of the debt plus interest, court costs, and sale fees.

When the debt is repaid, title is deeded back to the trustor.

Following a **satisfaction** (payoff) of the debt or obligation underlying a deed of trust, the beneficiary (or assignee or transferee of the beneficiary) delivers the original note and deed to the trustee and requests a reconveyance to the trustor. The reconveyance of title to the trustor by the trustee is accomplished by the trustee's executing to the trustor a **deed of reconveyance** that is recorded in the county recorder's office. The original note and deed of trust can then be delivered to the trustor, on the trustor's written request.

On satisfaction of the debt, the beneficiary (mortgagee) is obligated to clear the trustor's (mortgagor's) title. Failure to do so can subject the beneficiary (mortgagee) to civil or criminal penalties. The trustee also can be penalized for failure to comply with statutory requirements.

Conclusion.   To summarize, the differences between mortgage and trust deed lie in the

- number of parties,
- conveyance of title,
- Statute of Limitations,
- available remedies on default,
- period of reinstatement,
- availability of redemption,
- availability of deficiency judgment, and
- procedure following satisfaction of the debt.

Most important is that the trust deed offers the lender a relatively *faster* and *cheaper* means of protecting the security interest. Sale of the encumbered property is a last resort, however, no matter what form the sale takes. The lender may very well be the only bidder at the sale, and owning the property is an alternative most lenders do not welcome.

Deed in Lieu of Foreclosure

A **deed** may be used to transfer property to the beneficiary of a trust deed with the beneficiary's consent, to prevent a forced sale. Transfer of the property to the beneficiary may be to the beneficiary's advantage if the property is worth at least the amount of the remaining debt. The trustor benefits by avoiding the publicity of a public foreclosure sale. A danger arises when the property is worth more than the outstanding debt owed to the beneficiary. In that case the beneficiary should pay the difference to the trustor, or the transfer could be challenged later in court.

Unruh Act Mortgages and Deeds of Trust

California's **Unruh Act** covers contracts for goods and services. If a **power-of-sale mortgage** or **deed of trust** on a single-family, owner-occupied residence stems from a contract that falls within the Unruh Act, even more explicit notice must be given to a trustor or mortgagor in default. Other requirements also apply.

The object of this special provision is to prevent a homeowner from unwittingly losing the home as the result of a retail installment purchase. The requirements for imposing a mortgage or deed of trust, as well as the requirements on default, can be found in the Civil Code.

**Home Equity
Sales Contracts**

The high rate of overall property appreciation in recent decades greatly increased the equity of owners of real estate throughout the state. Increased equity has made properties attractive to unscrupulous individuals seeking to take advantage of homeowners whose property is in foreclosure. By use of a **home equity sales contract,** the property owner in foreclosure may be persuaded to sell the equity in a home for far less than its true value. The problem became severe enough to warrant legislation now included in the Civil Code. The law provides the following:

- A home equity sales contract must be in letters equal to ten-point bold type.
- The contract must include notices of the equity seller's **right of cancellation.**
- The contract may be **canceled** by the equity seller at any time up to midnight of the fifth business day following the contract signing, or 8 A.M. on the day set for sale pursuant to a deed of trust, whichever comes first.

There are exceptions to these requirements for properties sold for use as a personal residence, by deed in lieu of foreclosure, trustee's sale, foreclosure sale, as authorized by statute or a court, or between blood relatives or their spouses.

> Penalties for misuse of a home equity sales contract are severe.

Penalties for violation of the law include a fine of up to $10,000 and/or imprisonment for up to one year in the county jail or state prison. The equity seller can recover damages, attorneys' fees, and costs.

Finally, any transaction involving residential real property in foreclosure in which any person initiating, entering into, negotiating, or consummating the transaction takes **unconscionable advantage** of the property owner is **voidable** and can be rescinded within two years after the sale.

Other foreclosure abuses.   The California Civil Code also covers the abuses of **mortgage foreclosure consultants.** In Section 2945(a), the legislature states that "homeowners whose residences are in foreclosure are subject to fraud, deception, harassment, and unfair dealing by foreclosure consultants…"

To combat these practices, the law specifies notice and other requirements that must be scrupulously followed by anyone (other than those exempted from the provision) who offers to

- stop or postpone a foreclosure sale;
- assist in obtaining a loan or an extension for payment; or
- perform other activities involving property in foreclosure.

Attorneys and real estate licensees are generally exempted, but readers should consult Section 2945.1 for specific requirements. Violation of the law could result in both civil and criminal penalties, including fine and/or imprisonment.

Exercise 8-1   Identify the security instrument described in each of the following situations:

1. Harvey and Helen Headstrong have purchased Whiteacre. If they default on their loan payments, they can have the loan reinstated or redeem their property if it is sold at the lender's request.

2. Bernice Babbington has purchased Blackacre. She holds title to Blackacre. If she defaults on her loan payments and Blackacre is sold at the lender's request, she cannot redeem it.

3. Mel and Millie Murphy have purchased Greenacre and are living there, even though they have conveyed title to someone else.

4. Alan Adams bought Redacre. He defaulted in his loan payments and received notice that Redacre would be sold. The day before the sale, Alan offered to pay the overdue installments and costs but was surprised when the lender demanded that the entire loan balance be paid to stop the sale.

When a Mortgage Is Really a Deed of Trust

The term **mortgage** is used generically to refer to any security device. In California, that device (instrument) most often takes the form of a **deed of trust.** The trustor (borrower), trustee (third party holding title), and beneficiary (lender) are the parties involved in a deed of trust. When we refer to a **mortgage** in the rest of this and the next chapter, however, we will mean any real property security instrument. By *mortgagor* we will mean the *borrower* under any form of security instrument, and by *mortgagee* we will mean the *lender* under any form of security instrument. In the same way, the term *foreclosure* most often means a *trustee's sale.* The use of what may appear to be the wrong terminology simply is recognition of the fact that for most of the country, those are the correct terms.

■ REAL ESTATE LENDERS—THE PRIMARY MORTGAGE MARKET

Lenders who *initiate* loans with borrowers are part of what is called the **primary mortgage market.** There are both *institutional* and *noninstitutional lenders* in the primary mortgage market.

Institutional Lenders

Institutional lenders make most of the loans used by home and business owners. *Depository institutions* include those that lend money for the purchase or refinancing of real estate or for the construction of improvements. Such institutions act as intermediaries between the borrowers and the sources of the funds the institution has available to lend. As discussed earlier, those funds are typically savings or investments.

Savings and loan associations.   Most California savings and loan associations (S&Ls) are federally chartered. All are required by state law to insure accounts through the FDIC.

There were approximately 7,900 savings and loans nationwide as of June 30, 2002. Federally chartered S&Ls (also called **thrift and loans**) are members of the Federal Home Loan Bank System. The Board of Governors of the Federal Reserve System establishes minimum reserve requirements, and the Depository Institutions Deregulation Committee determines the level of interest rates that can be paid on account deposits. In 1989, supervision of savings and loan associations was delegated by Congress to the Office of Thrift Supervision (OTS).

Loan-to-Value Ratio and PMI

The **loan-to-value ratio** is the percentage of the current appraised market value represented by the amount of the loan. In other words, what percentage of the value does the loan represent? If the loan-to-value ratio exceeds 80 percent, the borrower must obtain insurance for the loan amount over 80 percent.

Private mortgage insurance (PMI), typically added to the monthly loan payment, will automatically be discontinued after the loan has been paid down to 75 percent of the original sales price or current fair market value for all loans originated after December 31, 1990.

Loans that have been sold to Fannie Mae (Federal National Mortgage Association) or Freddie Mac (Federal Home Loan Mortgage Corporation) may be eligible to have PMI removed after the loan has been paid down to a balance of 75 percent to 80 percent of the *current appraised value,* depending on when the loan was originated. Sale of loans to Fannie Mae and Freddie Mac is discussed further in Chapter 9, "Government-Sponsored and Other Financing."

A thrift may give a loan for more than 100 percent of appraised value, but any amount over 100 percent must be given under a different investment authority of the association and treated as an unsecured loan. All thrifts (except community financial institutions, which are specifically exempt) must have at least 10 percent of all assets in residential loans.

A loan is **open-ended** if it permits the mortgagor to borrow additional money at will without further financial qualification, on the original loan terms. A **lock-in clause** in a promissory note or land contract prohibits the promissor from paying off the debt prior to the date set forth in the contract.

Home loan payment terms may be described as:

- **fully amortized** (equal payments including both interest and principal are made over the loan term),
- **partially amortized** (most of the principal remains to be paid in the last payment),
- **nonamortized** (the **straight note,** typically interest only, with the entire amount of principal due at the end of the loan term), or have
- **negative amortization** (loan payments do not cover all of the interest due, which is then added to the remaining loan balance).

Figure 8.5 summarizes important features of some of the most widely used real estate loans.

Commercial banks.   All banks must be members of the Federal Reserve System. The National Bank Act covers national banks; the California Banking Law covers state banks. Many S&Ls have been reorganized as banks.

> Banks make the greatest number of different types of loans.

Commercial banks make the broadest range of loans, including those for real estate purchase, construction, and interim financing (before a building under construction is completed), and even consumer loans for home improvements. Commercial banks also make many business and short-term credit loans, including automobile financing. Bank credit cards represent a growing portion of commercial banks' activity.

There are no restrictions on loan-to-value ratios or amortization schedules or limitations on the amount of funds that can be loaned on real estate by national banks. This is one reason why this form of institution is becoming increasingly popular. Commercial banks are supervised by the U.S. Comptroller of the Currency.

Insurance companies.   With the exception of single-family homes, insurance companies invest in most types of real estate by making mortgage loans. Insurance companies are governed by the laws of the state of their incorporation as well as by the laws of the state in which they do business. Insurance companies typically finance large commercial projects but also buy loans from mortgage companies (discussed later in this chapter) and invest in government-insured or guaranteed loans.

Mutual savings banks.   A mutual savings and loan association distributes its earnings to depositors (after providing for expenses, reserves, and other costs of

FIGURE 8.5

Common Mortgage Plans

LOANS FROM FEDERAL INSTITUTIONS ON BORROWER-OCCUPIED HOMES		
Loan Type	**Description**	**Advantages/Disadvantages**
Fixed-rate mortgage	Fixed interest rate; equal monthly payments of principal and interest until debt is paid in full	Stable, with long-term tax advantages; rarely assumable
Adjustable-rate mortgage (ARM) (also called flexible-rate or variable rate mortgage)	Interest rate changes based on index; could increase payments, term, or principal; could have rate cap or payment cap	Very popular with lenders; rate cap of no more than 5 percent advisable; with payment cap, negative amortization possible; usually assumable
Graduated payment mortgage (GPM)	Lower monthly payments rise gradually over five to ten years, then level off for remainder of term	Easier to qualify for
Graduated payment adjustable-rate mortgage (GPARM)	Same as GPM, but additional payment change possible if index changes	Easier to qualify for; could be negative amortization
Growing equity mortgage (GEM) (also called rapid payoff mortgage)	Fixed interest rate; payments vary by index or schedule	Rapid payoff as payout increases; income must also increase
Reverse annuity mortgage (RAM) (also called equity conversion mortgage)	Monthly payments are made to borrower using mortgage-free property as collateral	Provides cash to homeowner, who pays loan amount at end of term
Renegotiable-rate mortgage (RRM) (also called rollover mortgage)	Rate and payments constant for three- to five-year intervals; can change based on FHLBB index; rate cap of 5 percent over maximum 30-year term	Fair stable payments due to less-frequent changes in rate
Shared appreciation mortgage (SAM)	Below-market rate and lower payments in exchange for losing some equity	Loss of equity makes investment more expensive

Interest rate must correspond directly to change in an index, such as the rate on six-month Treasury bills, three-month Treasury notes, FHLBB's national average mortgage contract rate, or the average cost of funds of FDIC-insured institutions.

Payments may be adjusted to reflect rate change, change in loan balance, change in a national or regional cost-of-living or inflation index, or as specified by formula or schedule in the contract.

Loan balance may be adjusted to reflect interest rate change or change in a national or regional cost-of-living or inflation index.

Loan term may be adjusted only to reflect changes in interest rate, payment, or loan balance and can never exceed 40 years.

Notice of adjustment must be given at least 30 and no more than 120 days prior to adjustment and 90 to 120 days prior to maturity. No penalty for prepayment within 90 days of notice of adjustment.

operation) as dividends, rather than interest. Originally found in the New England states and relatively new to California, both mutual and stock savings and loan associations have re-formed as mutual savings banks. They can retain federal deposit insurance and follow federal regulations. They can also be state chartered.

Credit unions.   Of growing importance are the loan-making functions of credit unions, which are organized under the National Credit Union Administration, a federal agency. Credit unions receive the savings of members, frequently through payroll deductions, which they use to make loans to members. Loans may be unsecured, but more often are secured by a home, an automobile, a boat, or other asset purchased.

Credit unions typically have relatively low overhead expenses. As a result, many credit unions can offer loans at competitive interest rates while also offering interest rates on savings accounts and other investments that may be better than those offered by commercial banks and savings and loans. Participation is restricted to the defined group of prospective members, such as federal employees.

Noninstitutional Lenders

Noninstitutional lenders include

- mortgage companies,
- private individuals, and
- organizations that are not financial institutions.

Mortgage companies.   Mortgage companies, or **mortgage bankers,** make real estate loans, then sell those loans to investors. The mortgage company will service the loans it has sold on a contractual basis. Servicing a loan includes receiving payments on behalf of the investor and otherwise handling the day-to-day supervision of the investment.

Mortgage companies are a prime source of government-insured and guaranteed loan funds as well as conventional loans (loans that do not involve government cooperation). State laws regarding mortgage companies historically have been much broader than those governing banks and S&Ls. Many mortgage companies invest their own funds or borrow investment funds themselves from commercial banks.

Mortgage Bankers versus Mortgage Loan Brokers

Even though the **mortgage banker** often serves as a middleman between investor and borrower, the mortgage banker is not necessarily a mortgage broker. **Mortgage loan brokers** are licensed as real estate brokers and are governed by the California Real Estate Law. They bring borrower and lender together but typically do not invest their own funds, and they do not service loans.

Private individuals.   Nonfinancial institutions and private individuals hold one-fourth of all mortgage debt. Private individuals are the largest source of second-mortgage funds (junior loans).

When the lender is an individual, rather than a bank or mortgage company, there won't be a loan committee or arduous qualification process. In addition, an individual may offer lower loan costs and a better interest rate. When individuals make direct loans (as opposed to extending purchase-money credit), they are subject to the usury laws, unless a broker has arranged the loan.

Nonfinancial institutions.   Real estate loans make up some of the most important assets of nonfinancial institutions. These include

- pension funds,
- colleges and universities,
- trusts,
- estates,
- mortgage investment companies, and
- other groups.

As with individuals, nonfinancial institutions may make fewer demands in terms of borrower qualifications. Such investors are also unlikely to be part of the primary mortgage market for single-family homes.

Mortgage Loan Brokers

The **Real Property Loan Law** (a part of the Real Estate Law) allows a real estate broker

- to solicit borrowers or lenders or
- negotiate loans for real property.

The Real Property Loan Law applies to loans secured by equity in real property but it does not apply to purchase-money loans. Put another way, the law applies to "hard money" (cash-out) as opposed to "soft money" loans (those used to buy the property). A broker can loan his or her own funds if the borrower is informed of the source of the funds. If funds from a family member of the broker are loaned, the relationship also must be disclosed.

FIGURE 8.6

Maximum Mortgage Loan Broker Commission

Type of Security	Loan Amount	Loan Term	Maximum Commission
First deed of trust	Less than $30,000	Three years or more	10% of loan amount
		Less than three years	5%
	$30,000 or more	Any length	No limit
Second deed of trust	Less than $20,000	Three years or more	15% of loan amount
		Two to less than three years	10%
		Less than two years	5%
	$20,000 or more	Any length	No limit

FIGURE 8.7

Maximum Chargeable Mortgage Loan Broker Costs and Expenses

Loan Amount	Maximum Costs and Expenses
Up to $7,800	Actual costs or $390, whichever is less
$7,800 to $14,000	Actual costs or 5% of loan amount, whichever is less
More than $14,000	Actual costs, but not more than $700

The maximum commission that a broker can charge for negotiating or making a loan depends on

- the amount of the loan,
- the length of the loan term, and
- whether the loan is secured by a first or second deed of trust.

Maximum commission amounts are summarized in Figure 8.6.

Costs and expenses, such as appraisal fees, credit investigation fees, notary fees, and escrow fees, can be charged in addition to the commission or broker's fee. The maximum that can be charged for such costs and expenses (excluding title charges and recording fees) is shown in Figure 8.7.

If a loan is negotiated or made by a broker, a mortgage loan disclosure statement must be completed and presented to the borrower for the borrower's signature before the loan transaction is completed and the borrower becomes obligated under the terms of the agreement. This statement is separate from any other required disclosure statement.

As of January 1, 2004, the Real Estate Law allows brokers to arrange multilender loans that are secured by more than one parcel of real property. Form revisions effective as of January 2004 are RE 851A Lender/Purchaser Disclosure Statement (Loan Origination); RE 851B Lender/Purchaser Disclosure Statement (Sale of Existing Note); and RE 851D Lender/Purchaser Disclosure Statement—Multi-Property (Cross Collateralization) Addendum. All of the new forms are available at *www.dre.ca.gov*, under Mortgage Lender Brokers Forms. A sample Lender/Purchaser Disclosure Statement is shown in Figure 8.8.

www.dre.ca.gov

Advertising by a mortgage loan broker must include a statement that the broker is licensed by the Department of Real Estate.

FIGURE 8.8

Lender/Purchaser Disclosure Statement

STATE OF CALIFORNIA

DEPARTMENT OF REAL ESTATE
MORTGAGE LENDING

LENDER/PURCHASER DISCLOSURE STATEMENT
(Loan Origination)

RE 851A (Rev. 2/04)

DISCLOSURE STATEMENT SUMMARY

Note: If this is a multi-lender transaction and more than one property secures the loan, you should also refer to the attached Lender/Purchaser Disclosure Statement Multi-Property (Cross Collateralization) Addendum (RE 851D).

AMOUNT OF THIS LOAN *(SEE PART 3)*	MARKET VALUE OF PROPERTY (SEE PART 8)	TOTAL AMOUNT OF ENCUMBRANCES SENIOR TO THIS LOAN *(SEE PART 9)*
$	$	$
TOTAL AMOUNT OF ENCUMBRANCES ANTICIPATED OR EXPECTED TO BE JUNIOR TO THIS LOAN *(SEE PART 9)*	PROTECTIVE EQUITY (MARKET VALUE MINUS THIS LOAN AND TOTAL SENIOR ENCUMBRANCES)	TOTAL LOAN TO VALUE (SEE PART 10G)
$	$	%

PART 1   BROKER INFORMATION

NAME OF BROKER	REAL ESTATE LICENSE ID#
BUSINESS ADDRESS	TELEPHONE NUMBER
NAME OF BROKERS REPRESENTATIVE	

PART 2   BROKER CAPACITY IN TRANSACTION

THE BROKER IDENTIFIED IN PART 1 OF THIS STATEMENT IS ACTING IN THE FOLLOWING CAPACITY IN THIS TRANSACTION: (CHECK AS APPLIES)

☐ A. Agent in arranging a loan on behalf of another

☐ B. Principal as a borrower of funds from which broker will directly or indirectly benefit other than through the receipt of commissions, fees and costs and expenses as provided by law for services as an agent.

☐ C. Funding a portion of this loan. *(Multi-lender transactions are subject to Business and Professions Code Section 10238.)*

IF MORE THAN ONE CAPACITY HAS BEEN CHECKED, PROVIDE EXPLANATION HERE.

IF "B" HAS BEEN CHECKED, THE BROKER INTENDS TO USE FUNDS FROM THE LENDER/PURCHASER IN THIS TRANSACTION FOR:

PART 3   TRANSACTION INFORMATION

(CHECK IF APPLICABLE)

☐ THERE IS MORE THAN ONE PROPERTY SECURING THE LOAN. IF MULTI-LENDER LOAN, YOU SHOULD ALSO REFER TO ATTACHED RE 851D.

TERM OF LOAN	PRIORITY OF THIS LOAN (1ST, 2ND, ETC.)	PRINCIPAL AMOUNT $	YOUR SHARE IF MULTI-LENDER TRANS. $
INTEREST RATE % ☐ VARIABLE ☐ FIXED	(CHECK ONE) ☐ AMORTIZED ☐ PARTIALLY AMORTIZED	☐ INTEREST ONLY	***THE TRUST DEED WILL BE RECORDED.***
PAYMENT FREQUENCY ☐ MONTHLY ☐ WEEKLY	APPROXIMATE PAYMENT DUE DATE	AMOUNT OF PAYMENT $	YOUR SHARE IF MULTI-LENDER TRANS. $
BALLOON PAYMENT ☐ YES ☐ NO	APPROX. BALLOON PAYMENT DUE DATE	AMOUNT OF BALLOON PAYMENT $	YOUR SHARE IF MULTI-LENDER TRANS. $

Balloon Payment — A balloon payment is any installment payment (usually the payment due at maturity) which is greater than twice the amount of the smallest installment payment under the terms of the promissory note or sales contract.

The borrower/vendee may have to obtain a new loan or sell the property to make the balloon payment. If the effort is not successful it may be necessary for the holder of the note/contract to foreclose on the property as a means of collecting the amount owed.

There are subordination provisions. .... ☐ Yes ☐ No
        If YES, explain here or on an attachment.

FIGURE 8.8

Lender/Purchaser Disclosure Statement (Continued)

RE 851A   *Page 2 of 6*

PART 4	MULTI-LENDER TRANSACTIONS

NAME OF ESCROW HOLDER | ANTICIPATED CLOSING DATE

ADDRESS OF ESCROW HOLDER

ESTIMATED LENDER COSTS

_____ $ _____

_____ $ _____

_____ $ _____

                                    TOTAL $ _____

ESTIMATED BORROWER COSTS —
Broker will provide you a copy of the "mortgage loan disclosure statement" given to the borrower or a separate itemization of borrower's costs.

                              TOTAL $ _____

Servicing

You will be a joint beneficiary with others on this note and you should request a list of names and addresses of the beneficiaries as of the close of escrow from the broker or servicing agent. The beneficiary(ies) holding more than 50% interest in the note may govern the actions to be taken on behalf of all holders in the event of default or other matters. See Civil Code Section 2941.9.

Loan To Value

GENERALLY the aggregate principal amount of the notes or interests sold, together with the unpaid principal amount of any encumbrances upon the real property senior thereto, shall not exceed the following percentages of the current market value of the real property as determined in writing by the broker or qualified appraiser.

Single-family residence, owner-occupied 80%

Single-family residence, not owner-occupied 75%

Commercial and income-producing properties 65%

Single-family residentially zoned lot or parcel which has installed off-site improvements including drainage, curbs, gutters, sidewalks, paved roads, and utilities as mandated by the political subdivision having jurisdiction over the lot or parcel 65%

Land which has been zoned for (and if required, approved for subdivision as) commercial or Residential development 50%

Other real property 35%

The percentage amounts specified above may be exceeded when and to the extent that the broker determines that the encumbrance of the property in excess of these percentages is reasonable and prudent considering all relevant factors pertaining to the real property. However, in no event shall the aggregate principal amount of the notes or interests sold, together with the unpaid principal amount of any encumbrances upon the property senior thereto, exceed 80 percent of the current fair market value of improved real property or 50 percent of the current fair market value of unimproved real property, except in the case of a single-family residentially zoned lot or parcel as defined above, which shall not exceed 65% of current fair market value of that lot or parcel. A written statement shall be prepared by the broker that sets forth the material considerations and facts that the broker relies upon for his or her determination which shall be disclosed to the lender or note purchaser(s) and retained as a part of the broker's record of the transaction.

NOTE: If more than one property secures this loan, you should also refer to attached RE 851D.

Source: Reprinted with permission from the California Department of Real Estate.

FIGURE 8.8

Lender/Purchaser Disclosure Statement (Continued)

RE 851A   Page 3 of 6

PART 5 | **SERVICING ARRANGEMENTS**

If the loan is to be serviced by a real estate broker you must be notified within ten (10) days if the broker makes any advances on senior encumbrances to protect the security of your note. Depending on the terms and conditions of the servicing contract, you may be obligated to repay any such advances made by the broker. (Note: There must be a servicing agent on multi-lender transactions.) The broker may not guarantee or imply to guarantee, or advance any payments to you unless a securities permit is obtained from the Department of Corporations.

CHECK APPROPRIATE STATEMENTS

☐ THERE ARE NO SERVICING ARRANGEMENTS *(Does not apply to multi-lender transactions.)*   ☐ BROKER IS THE SERVICING AGENT

☐ ANOTHER QUALIFIED PARTY WILL SERVICE THE LOAN   ☐ COPY OF THE SERVICING CONTRACT IS ATTACHED

IF BROKER IS NOT SERVICING AGENT, WHAT IS THE RELATIONSHIP BETWEEN THE BROKER AND SERVICER?	COST TO LENDER FOR SERVICING ARRANGEMENTS *(EXPRESS AS DOLLAR AMOUNT OR PERCENTAGE)*
	PER ☐ MONTH ☐ YEAR PAYABLE ☐ MONTHLY ☐ ANNUALLY

NAME OF AUTHORIZED SERVICER, IF ANY

BUSINESS ADDRESS	TELEPHONE NUMBER

PART 6 | **BORROWER INFORMATION**

SOURCE OF INFORMATION

☐ BORROWER   ☐ BROKER INQUIRY   ☐ CREDIT REPORT   ☐ OTHER (DESCRIBE)

NAME	CO-BORROWER'S NAME
RESIDENCE ADDRESS	CO-BORROWER'S RESIDENCE ADDRESS
OCCUPATION OR PROFESSION	CO-BORROWER'S OCCUPATION OR PROFESSION
CURRENT EMPLOYER	CO-BORROWER'S CURRENT EMPLOYER
HOW LONG EMPLOYED? AGE	HOW LONG EMPLOYED? CO-BORROWER'S AGE

SOURCES OF GROSS INCOME *(LIST AND IDENTIFY EACH SOURCE SEPARATELY.)*	MONTHLY AMOUNT	CO-BORROWER SOURCES OF GROSS INCOME *(LIST AND IDENTIFY EACH SOURCE SEPARATELY.)*	MONTHLY AMOUNT
Gross Salary	$	Gross Salary	$
OTHER INCOME INCLUDING: Interest	$	OTHER INCOME INCLUDING: Interest	$
Dividends	$	Dividends	$
Gross Rental Income	$	Gross Rental Income	$
Miscellaneous Income	$	Miscellaneous Income	$

TOTAL EXPENSES OF ALL BORROWERS *(DO NOT COMPLETE IF BORROWER IS A CORPORATION)*

Payment of Loan being obtained	$	Spousal/Child Support	$
Rent	$	Insurance	$
Charge Account/Credit Cards	$	Vehicle Loan(s)	$
Mortgage Payments *(include taxes and property insurance)*	$	Other *(federal & state income taxes, etc.)*	$
TOTAL GROSS MONTHLY INCOME OF BORROWER(S) $		TOTAL MONTHLY EXPENSES OF BORROWER(S) $	

Source: Reprinted with permission from the California Department of Real Estate.

FIGURE 8.8

Lender/Purchaser Disclosure Statement (Continued)

RE 851A   *Page 4 of 6*

The borrower has filed for bankruptcy in the past 12 months. .... ☐ Yes   ☐ No

If YES, the bankruptcy has been discharged or dismissed. .... ☐ Yes   ☐ No

❖ *THE FOLLOWING STATEMENTS ONLY APPLY IF THE BORROWER IS A CORPORATION, PARTNERSHIP OR SOME OTHER FORM OF OPERATING BUSINESS ENTITY.*

Copies of a balance sheet of the entity and income statement covering the indicated period have been supplied by the borrower/obligor and are attached. If no, explain on addendum. .... ☐ Yes   ☐ No

If YES, Date of balance sheet .... _____

Income statement period *(from-to)* .... _____

Financial Statements have been audited by CPA or PA. .... ☐ Yes   ☐ No

Additional information is included on an attached addendum .... ☐ Yes   ☐ No

PART 7	PROPERTY INFORMATION

Identification of property which is security for note. *(If no street address, the assessor's parcel number or legal description and a means for locating the property is attached.)*

(CHECK IF APPLICABLE)
☐ THERE IS MORE THAN ONE PROPERTY SECURING THE LOAN. IF MULTI-LENDER LOAN, YOU SHOULD REFER TO ATTACHED RE 851D.

STREET ADDRESS	OWNER OCCUPIED ☐ NO ☐ YES

ANNUAL PROPERTY TAXES	ARE TAXES DELINQUENT?	IF YES, AMT. REQUIRED TO BRING CURRENT
$ ☐ ACTUAL ☐ ESTIMATED	☐ NO ☐ YES	$

SOURCE OF TAX INFORMATION

PART 8	APPRAISAL INFORMATION

Estimate of fair market value is to be determined by an independent appraisal, copy of which must be provided to you prior to you obligating funds to make the loan. Note: You may waive the requirement of an independent appraisal, in writing, on a case by case basis, in which case the broker must provide a written estimate of fair market value. The broker must provide you, the investor, with the objective data upon which the broker's estimate is based. **In the case of a construction or rehabilitation loan, an appraisal must be completed by an independent, qualified appraiser in accordance with the Uniform Standards of Professional Appraisal Practice (USPAP).**

(CHECK IF APPLICABLE)
☐ THERE IS MORE THAN ONE PROPERTY SECURING THE LOAN. IF MULTI-LENDER LOAN REFER TO ATTACHED RE 851D.

FAIR MARKET VALUE (ACCORDING TO APPRAISER) *(Place this figure or brokers estimate of fair market value on line "F" of Part 10.)*	DATE OF APPRAISAL
$	

NAME OF APPRAISER (IF KNOWN TO BROKER)	PAST AND/OR CURRENT RELATIONSHIP OF APPRAISER TO BROKER (EMPLOYEE, AGENT, INDEPENDENT CONTRACTOR, ETC.)

ADDRESS OF APPRAISER

DESCRIPTION OF PROPERTY/IMPROVEMENT	IS THERE ADDITIONAL SECURING PROPERTY? ☐ YES IF YES, SEE ADDENDUM. ☐ NO

AGE	SQUARE FEET	TYPE OF CONSTRUCTION

IF THE PROPERTY IS CURRENTLY GENERATING INCOME FOR THE BORROWER/OBLIGOR:

ESTIMATED GROSS ANNUAL INCOME	ESTIMATED NET ANNUAL INCOME
$	$

Source: Reprinted with permission from the California Department of Real Estate.

FIGURE 8.8

Lender/Purchaser Disclosure Statement (Continued)

RE 851A   *Page 5 of 6*

PART 9	ENCUMBRANCE INFORMATION

Information is being provided concerning senior encumbrances against the property, to the extent reasonably available from customary sources (excluding the note described on page 1 Part 3). **Note:** You have the option to purchase a policy of title insurance or an endorsement to an existing policy of title insurance to insure your interest. You are entitled to a copy of a written loan application and a credit report to obtain information concerning all encumbrances which constitute liens against the property. This information may help determine the financial standing and creditworthiness of the borrower.

(CHECK IF APPLICABLE)

☐ THERE IS MORE THAN ONE PROPERTY SECURING THE LOAN. IF MULTI-LENDER LOAN, YOU SHOULD REFER TO ATTACHED RE 851D.

SOURCE OF INFORMATION

☐ BROKER INQUIRY   ☐ BORROWER   ☐ OTHER *(EXPLAIN)*

Are there any encumbrances of record against the securing property at this time?....................   ☐ YES   ☐ NO

A. Over the last 12 months were any payments more than 60 days late? ....   ☐ YES   ☐ NO

B. If YES, how many? ....

C. Do any of these payments remain unpaid? ....   ☐ YES   ☐ NO

D. If YES, will the proceeds of subject loan be used to cure the delinquency? ....   ☐ YES   ☐ NO

E. If NO, source of funds to bring the loan current. ....

Encumbrances remaining and/or expected or anticipated to be placed against the property by the borrower/obligor after the close of escrow (excluding the note described on page 1).

ENCUMBRANCE(S) REMAINING (AS REPRESENTED BY THE BORROWER)

PRIORITY (1ST, 2ND, ETC.)	INTEREST RATE %	PRIORITY (1ST, 2ND, ETC.)	INTEREST RATE %
BENEFICIARY		BENEFICIARY	
ORIGINAL AMOUNT $	APPROXIMATE PRINCIPAL BALANCE $	ORIGINAL AMOUNT $	APPROXIMATE PRINCIPAL BALANCE $
MONTHLY PAYMENT $	MATURITY DATE	MONTHLY PAYMENT $	MATURITY DATE
BALLOON PAYMENT ☐ YES ☐ NO ☐ UNKNOWN	IF YES, AMOUNT $	BALLOON PAYMENT ☐ YES ☐ NO ☐ UNKNOWN	IF YES, AMOUNT $

ENCUMBRANCES EXPECTED OR ANTICIPATED (AS REPRESENTED BY THE BORROWER)

PRIORITY (1ST, 2ND, ETC.)	INTEREST RATE %	PRIORITY (1ST, 2ND, ETC.)	INTEREST RATE %
BENEFICIARY		BENEFICIARY	
ORIGINAL AMOUNT $	MATURITY DATE	ORIGINAL AMOUNT $	MATURITY DATE
MONTHLY PAYMENT $		MONTHLY PAYMENT $	
BALLOON PAYMENT ☐ YES ☐ NO ☐ UNKNOWN	IF YES, AMOUNT $	BALLOON PAYMENT ☐ YES ☐ NO ☐ UNKNOWN	IF YES, AMOUNT $

Additional remaining, expected or anticipated encumbrances are set forth in an attachment to this statement. ....   ☐ Yes   ☐ No

Source: Reprinted with permission from the California Department of Real Estate.

FIGURE 8.8

Lender/Purchaser Disclosure Statement (Continued)

RE 851A   *Page 6 of 6*

PART 10	**LOAN TO VALUE RATIO**

(CHECK IF APPLICABLE)

☐ THERE IS MORE THAN ONE PROPERTY SECURING THE LOAN. IF MULTI-LENDER LOAN, YOU SHOULD REFER TO ATTACHED RE 851D.

A. Remaining encumbrances senior to this loan *(from part 8)* .... $_____

B. Encumbrances expected or anticipated senior to this loan *(from part 9)* .... + $_____

C. Total remaining and expected or anticipated encumbrances senior to this loan .... = $_____

D. Principal amount of this loan from page 1 part 3 .... + $_____

E. Total all senior encumbrances and this loan .... = $_____

F. Fair market value from page 4 part 8 .... ÷ $_____

G. Loan to value ratio .... = _____%

Note: See Part 4 if multi-lender transaction.

BROKER VERIFICATION

The information in this statement and in the attachments hereto is true and correct to the best of my knowledge and belief.

SIGNATURE OF BROKER OR DESIGNATED REPRESENTATIVE	BROKER/CORPORATION ID#	DATE
➢		

ACKNOWLEDGMENT OF RECEIPT

The prospective lender/purchaser acknowledges receipt of a copy of this statement signed by or on behalf of the broker.

SIGNATURE OF PROSPECTIVE LENDER/PURCHASER	DATE
➢	

For licensing information, please refer to the Department of Real Estate's Web site located at www.dre.ca.gov.

or

You may call the DRE licensing information telephone number at (916) 227-0931.

Source: Reprinted with permission from the California Department of Real Estate.

■ **FOR EXAMPLE:** Mortgage loan broker Mary Miller arranges a $15,000 loan secured by a second deed of trust for a homeowner who wants extra cash to pay off some credit cards. The loan term is 15 years. Mary's commission is 10 percent of the loan amount, and loan expenses include an appraisal fee of $250, a credit report of $40, and notary fees of $15. What is the total maximum fee that Mary can charge on this loan, including brokerage commission and expenses?

Mary's commission is

$$\$15,000 \times 10\% = \$1,500$$

Expenses are

$$\$250 + \$40 + \$15 = \$305$$

Both Mary's commission and the expenses come within the limitations of the Real Property Loan Law. The total maximum fee thus is $1,500 + $305, or $1,805.

Other Restrictions on Mortgage Loan Brokers

There are other restrictions on loans made by brokers that are not greater than $30,000 for a first mortgage or $20,000 for a second mortgage. They include

■ no balloon payment (a payment more than twice the amount of the smallest payment) on an owner-occupied dwelling if the loan term is less than six years (three years for property not owner-occupied), unless the loan is taken back by the seller as part of the purchase price;

■ no borrower-paid loan servicing or loan collection fees;

■ borrower may not be required to obtain credit life or disability insurance as a loan condition; if the broker provides such insurance, only one premium may be collected, and only a borrower who might be expected to contribute to loan payments (such as a wage earner) may be insured;

■ the penalty for late payment of an installment is limited to 10 percent of the principal and interest payment; and

■ payments may be made within ten days of the date due without penalty.

On loans of any amount secured by a borrower-occupied dwelling, no prepayment penalty is allowed after seven years from the date the loan was made. In the first six years of the loan, 20 percent of the loan principal can be paid off per year without penalty. Otherwise, the maximum prepayment penalty is six months' interest on prepayments of principal that are greater than 20 percent of the unpaid principal balance.

**California
Residential Mortgage
Lending Act**

Some lending activities are conducted under the rules of the **California Residential Mortgage Lending Act.** The law applies to those involved in making or servicing mortgage loans on one- to four-family dwellings. The **Commissioner of Corporations** issues licenses for the activities covered by the law, but the following are exempt:

- **Real estate brokers** licensed in California
- Institutional and noninstitutional lenders already licensed by the state or federal government, such as banks, savings and loan associations, trust companies, and insurance companies
- An individual or company making residential mortgage loans with his, her, or its own money
- Government and pension plan employees
- Court-appointed estate or other representatives
- A trustee under a deed of trust

The law also exempts a **California finance lender** licensed under the **California Finance Lenders Law.** A **finance lender** is someone who is in the business of making consumer loans or commercial loans in which personal property may be used as collateral.

---

www.goto.com

www.yahoo.com

www.realtor.com

www.homeadvisor.com

www.realestate.com

Exercise 8-2   Loan charges usually include not only the interest rate but also a loan origination fee, points, and other costs. Make a survey of loan charges by at least three online lenders who make loans in California. Base your comparisons on both a fixed-rate and an adjustable-rate loan of $320,000, representing 80 percent of the value of a home selling for $400,000, with a down payment of 20 percent. As a further comparison, use loan terms of both 15 and 30 years. You can begin your survey by entering the search term "home loan" in one of the Internet search engines, such as *goto.com* or *yahoo.com.* You could also check out some of the online property listing services, such as *realtor.com, homeadvisor.com,* and *realestate.com.*

■ FEDERAL DISCLOSURE REQUIREMENTS

The availability of credit makes it possible for consumers of average means to indulge in the luxury of the "buy now, pay later" philosophy. The following requirements are meant to protect consumers without placing an impossible burden on their creditors.

**Truth-in-Lending
Act**

The **Truth-in-Lending Act (TILA)** is implemented by **Regulation Z** of the Federal Reserve Board. It imposes the following requirements on certain credit transactions.

TILA applies to loans made to consumers.

Creditor. A **creditor** is defined as a person who makes loans (extends credit) to consumers more than 25 times a year, or more than five times a year if the transaction involves a dwelling as security. The obligation must initially be payable by agreement to the creditor. The credit must be subject to a finance charge or payable in more than four installments by written agreement. An "arranger" of such credit is not considered a creditor, unless such a person would qualify for another reason.

Exempt transactions. Credit extended for a business, commercial, or agricultural purpose is *exempt* from Regulation Z, as is credit of more than $25,000, unless the loan is secured by real property or by personal property that is or will be used as the debtor's principal dwelling.

Credit used to acquire, improve, or maintain **rental property** that is or will be owner-occupied within a year has special rules.

- Credit to *acquire* such property of two or more units is considered credit for a business purpose.
- Credit to *improve* or *maintain* such property of four or more units is also considered as being for a business purpose.

Credit to acquire, improve, or maintain *nonowner-occupied rental property,* regardless of the number of units, is considered credit for a business purpose.

Disclosure statement. Truth-in-lending disclosures must be grouped together in a **disclosure statement,** with certain information set off by a box, a different type style, bold type, or a different color background. Regulation Z contains several model forms for different transactions.

The required disclosures must be made before the transaction is completed. In most cases that is the time of closing. Ordinarily, the disclosure statement accompanies the loan commitment information sent to the borrower by the lender after the borrower's loan application has been approved but before the transaction is closed.

Required disclosures. Regulation Z requires disclosure of relevant **finance information.** The identity of the creditor and description of the security interest to be retained must be given. Of particular importance are the **amount financed,** the **finance charge,** the **annual percentage rate (APR),** the **total (sum) of the payments,** and, in credit sales, the **total sales price.**

The borrower *must* be advised of any **prepayment penalties, rebates,** and **late-payment charges.** If any charges for credit life, disability, or similar insurance are not required as a condition of the loan, that fact must be disclosed and the borrower must separately sign or initial a request for the insurance.

The consumer in a residential mortgage transaction must be advised of whether the loan is assumable on its original terms by a subsequent purchaser of the secured property. Where applicable, pertinent sections of the loan contract should be referred to in the disclosure statement.

Right to rescind. A consumer has a three-day **right to rescind** (cancel) a credit transaction involving a security interest in the consumer's principal dwelling. The three-day period ends at midnight of the third business day following the *last* to occur of the following events:

> A **business day** is any day except Sundays and federal holidays. Some state-chartered lenders also recognize state holidays.

- Consummation of the transaction
- Delivery of the truth-in-lending disclosure statement
- Delivery of notice of the right to rescind

MATH CONCEPTS

The **annual percentage rate (APR)** is not simply the interest rate the loan carries on its face—its **nominal rate.** Instead, the APR also includes many of the financially related closing costs, including prepaid loan fees, assumption fees, finder's fees, buyer's points, and premiums for mortgage-guarantee or similar insurance.

Some closing costs, such as points paid by the seller and fees for title examination, abstract of title, title insurance, property survey, document preparation (deed or mortgage, for example), appraisal, credit report, and down payment held in escrow, are not considered finance charges, so are not calculated in the APR.

A rough rule of thumb is that a prepaid amount equal to one percentage point of the loan principal is equivalent to a ⅛ percent increase in the interest rate the loan is carrying. For example, a loan at an interest rate of 8 percent with an origination fee of one point would have an APR of about 8⅛ or 8.125 percent. The same loan with an origination fee of two points would have an APR of 8⅜, or 8¼ (8.25) percent. This is a convenient way to compare the true cost of loans that have different interest rates and origination fees.

In an emergency, the right to rescind may be waived in writing to prevent a delay in funding to the borrower.

Note: The **right to rescind** does *not* apply to

- residential purchase money, first mortgage, or trust deed loans;

- a refinancing of such a loan when no new funds are advanced by the lender; or
- a refinancing of a loan secured by property that is not occupied by the borrower.

Advertising.   The advertising requirements of the Truth-in-Lending Act and Regulation Z must be complied with by anyone advertising as a supplier of consumer credit. Ads must give the APR and all payment terms (if any are given) and specific information on the various forms of adjustable-rate loans.

Real Estate Settlement Procedures Act

The **Real Estate Settlement Procedures Act (RESPA)** requires certain disclosures by lenders in federally related mortgage loans involving the sale or transfer of residences of one to four dwelling units. A **federally related loan** is one that is

- made by a lender insured by FDIC or any other federal agency;
- financed through any federal agency, such as the Federal Housing Administration or Department of Veterans Affairs; or
- sold to Fannie Mae, Ginnie Mae, or Freddie Mac on the secondary mortgage market.

As of December 2, 1992, RESPA also includes certain transactions that had previously been exempt from the law. These include

- a refinancing transaction,
- a purchase of property for resale,
- a purchase of property of 25 or more acres,
- a purchase of a vacant lot, and
- an assumption or a novation (new agreement) involving a transfer of title subject to an existing loan.

The lender must supply every applicant for a federally related mortgage loan with

- a copy of the *Special Information Booklet* prescribed by the **Department of Housing and Urban Development (HUD)** and
- a **good-faith estimate** of the transaction closing costs.

If more than one individual applies for a loan, the information has to be given to only one of them. Both the booklet and the estimate must be mailed no later than three days after the loan application is received by the lender.

A **Uniform Settlement Statement,** also prescribed by HUD, must be prepared and presented to the borrower and seller no later than the day of closing. The borrower can waive that right. If the borrower is not present at the closing, the

Copies of HUD documents, including the Uniform Settlement Statement, can be downloaded from www.hud.gov.

statement should be delivered as soon as possible after the transaction closes. The settlement statement lists all charges of the transaction to both the borrower and the seller. The settlement statement is described in detail in Chapter 10, "Escrow and Title Insurance."

A **kickback** is an illegal fee paid by a nonlicensee (such as a loan officer) to a salesperson or broker.

The lender is not allowed to charge a fee for preparation or distribution of RESPA or Truth-in-Lending Act documents. The lender is also prohibited from paying a fee, kickback, rebate, or other thing of value to any person who does not actually provide loan services. (The same prohibitions also apply to title and escrow companies.) Examples of loan services that may be compensated include counseling the borrower, comparing borrower housing needs with available mortgage loans, and keying information into a **computerized loan origination (CLO) system.**

■ OTHER LOAN CONSIDERATIONS

Loan Assumptions and "Subject To"

When property is sold or transferred, the existing loan may be **paid off** by the seller or **assumed** by the new owner (if the loan agreement allows). Another possibility is for the property to be taken **subject to** the loan (if the loan agreement allows).

In a loan **assumption,** the new borrower is substituted for the old borrower (the seller), releasing the seller from further obligation under the note. If a property is taken **subject to** the note, the seller will technically still be liable for the remaining indebtedness. If the buyer defaults, the lender can look to the seller (the former owner) for payment.

Taking possession subject to an existing loan benefits the buyer, who cannot be held liable for any deficiency judgment that might stem from a default on the loan. Loan costs are usually lower than what would be paid to obtain a new loan.

Acceleration and Due-on-Sale Clause

Most mortgages and trust deeds contain a provision that allows the lender to declare the remaining indebtedness due and payable on the happening of certain conditions. The loan can be "called" (the lender can demand full payment) if the borrower defaults by

- missing a payment,
- failing to pay taxes,
- committing waste by failing to maintain the property that is used for security, or
- using the property for an illegal purpose.

An **acceleration clause** may also be put into effect when the borrower relinquishes possession of the secured property by sale or transfer, preventing an assumption by a new owner. Use of such an **alienation** or **due-on-sale** clause has been the subject of much case law and legislation. At present, due-on-sale clauses are enforceable. Generally, loan agreements provide that fixed-rate mortgage loans are not assumable, but variable-interest-rate loans (which allow an increase of income to lenders if market conditions warrant) are assumable.

Construction Lending

The length and expense of the housing development process has resulted in several types of specialized loans. A **construction loan** (also called an **interim loan**) is one made to finance building construction or other improvements to land. Loan funds are usually made available to the builder in increments as the construction progresses. The builder may arrange for permanent financing for the property buyer in the form of a **take-out loan** for the buyer. The proceeds of the take-out loan are used to pay off the builder's construction loan.

To ensure that funds are available for prospective purchasers of the completed properties, a mortgage banker may make a **standby commitment** to a builder, agreeing to make mortgage loans at a stated price for a future time. The builder pays a **standby fee** for this privilege.

Impound Accounts

The lender may require that an **impound account** be established for the benefit of the borrower, to accumulate reserves for future recurring costs, such as property taxes and hazard insurance. The borrower's mortgage payments will be increased to cover contributions to the impound account, which is held in trust for the borrower's benefit by the lender.

An impound account may be *required* by a lender in California as a condition of loan approval on a loan secured by a single-family, owner-occupied dwelling, only when

- the loan amount is 90 percent of property value,
- combined loan amounts exceed 80 percent of property value,
- it is required by a state or federal regulatory authority,
- the loan is made, guaranteed, or insured by a state or federal governmental lending or insuring agency, or
- the borrower has failed to pay two consecutive tax installments on the property prior to the delinquency date for the payments. *(Civil Code Section 2954)*

If both lender and borrower agree, an impound account can be established in other circumstances, as well, but cannot be made a condition of loan approval. Homeowners who make use of an impound account should verify that amounts withheld are not excessive, and also that property tax and other payments are made on time to avoid late payment penalties.

The Loan Application

A copy of the Uniform Residential Loan Application can be downloaded from www.fanniemae.com.

The **Uniform Residential Loan Application** (Form 1003) typically is used to qualify a prospective borrower purchasing a single-family residence. Form 1003 was prepared by Freddie Mac (formerly the Federal Home Loan Mortgage Corporation, or FHLMC) and Fannie Mae (FNMA, formerly the Federal National Mortgage Association), which are discussed in the next chapter.

Use of a carefully drafted form helps ensure that the federal **Equal Credit Opportunity Act** is not violated. That act prohibits discrimination based on age, sex, race, color, marital status, religion, or national origin. All applicants must be considered in light of their income, the stability of the source of that income, total assets and liabilities, and their credit rating. Several companies have created methods of analyzing a borrower's credit reports to produce a credit score. One of these companies is Fair, Isaac and Company, headquartered in San Rafael, California, which produces a credit rating commonly referred to as the **FICO score.** A borrower whose FICO score is in the highest range will be able to obtain financing at a lower interest rate than someone who has a FICO score in a lower range. Someone with a FICO score in the range of 720–850 is considered an excellent credit risk. An individual with a score below 560 is considered a poor risk and will pay a much higher interest rate, assuming a loan can be obtained. More information about credit scoring, and how a credit score can be improved, can be found at *www.myfico.com.*

www.myfico.com

If a loan is rejected, California requires that the lender provide a statement to the loan applicant within 30 days detailing the reasons for the refusal. The loan applicant also has the right to a free copy of any credit report that was considered in the loan application process. *Note: California Civil Code Section 1785 provides credit reporting protections for victims of identity theft. If a victim of identity theft provides a police report or valid DMV investigative report of the violation to a consumer credit reporting agency, the victim is entitled to receive, free of charge, up to 12 copies of his or her credit file during a consecutive 12-month period, not to exceed one copy per month.*

www.Equifax.com
www.experion.com
www.TransUnion.com

The three major credit reporting agencies are Equifax, Experian, and TransUnion.

The loan application usually follows an interview with a loan officer of the lending institution. The interview is useful in explaining the loan procedure and initially qualifying the loan applicant.

The next step is the loan officer's analysis, which includes the property being considered for purchase. An appraisal is made to ensure that the property will provide good security for the amount borrowed.

After the loan is approved, the necessary paperwork and funding are usually handled through an **escrow agent,** who makes sure that all parties have fulfilled their obligations before the transaction is closed. There is a detailed description of the obligations of buyer, seller, and escrow agent in Chapter 10.

■ SUMMARY

Buyers use the **leverage** afforded by **credit** to finance the purchase of all forms of real estate. The availability of loan funds is influenced by the cyclical nature of our economy and regulated by the **Federal Reserve Board.**

The **Office of Thrift Supervision (OTS)** regulates the savings and loan industry. **The Housing Finance Board (HFB)** oversees the **Federal Home Loan Banks,** which lend funds to member institutions. The **Financial Institutions Reform, Recovery, and Enforcement Act of 1989 (FIRREA)** provided the mechanisms for dissolution or sale of the many recently failed financial institutions.

Usury laws prohibit the charging of exorbitant rates of interest. Proposition 2 and the deregulation act exempt from the usury laws loans secured by real estate and made by most lenders.

Real estate financing is made possible by use of a **promissory note** in conjunction with a **security instrument** that **hypothecates** the real estate against which money is borrowed. Cosigners on a promissory note may have **joint and several liability.** A promissory note can be sold or transferred. If a promissory note meets the requirements for a **negotiable instrument,** a subsequent **holder in due course** can defeat most defenses to its enforcement.

The **deed of trust** is the security instrument of choice in California, although the **mortgage** also may be used. **Notice** must be given in the event of the borrower's **default.** The **judicial foreclosure** of a mortgage is a longer process than a **trustee's sale,** and there is no **right of redemption** following a trustee's sale. A **mortgage with power of sale** also will avoid a judicial foreclosure.

The **primary mortgage market** consists of both **institutional** and **noninstitutional** lenders. Institutional lenders include savings and loan associations, commercial banks, mutual savings banks, credit unions, and insurance companies. At present, a variety of loans are available from both federal and state associations, with both fixed and adjustable rates.

Noninstitutional lenders include mortgage companies and private individuals. Nonfinancial institutions, such as colleges and universities, pension funds, and trusts, also carry real estate loans, although not usually as part of the primary mortgage market.

Mortgage brokers are subject to the **Real Property Loan Law.** They must complete and deliver a **mortgage loan disclosure statement** to borrowers for signature before the transaction is completed.

The **Truth-in-Lending Act (Regulation Z)** imposes disclosure requirements on **consumer credit transactions** and restricts advertising of credit terms. The required **disclosure statement** includes all details of financing, including the **annual percentage rate (APR),** which may be much higher than the **nominal rate.** A consumer has the right to cancel a credit transaction involving a security interest in the consumer's principal dwelling within a three-day period.

The **Real Estate Settlement Procedures Act (RESPA)** requires a *Special Information Booklet* and **good faith estimate of closing costs.** A Uniform Settlement Statement must be supplied no later than the day of closing.

Some loans may be **assumed** or property may be sold **subject to** the loan. **Acceleration** or **due-on-sale clauses** are enforceable by lenders. Loan application policies must comply with the **Equal Credit Opportunity Act.**

■ IMPORTANT TERMS

Make sure you understand the following terms before you take the achievement examination.

acceleration clause
adjustable-rate mortgage (ARM)
adjustable-rate note
alienation or due-on-sale clause
amortized loan
annual percentage rate (APR)
assumption
balloon payment
beneficiary
California finance lender
California Finance Lenders Law
California Residential Mortgage
   Lending Act
certificate of discharge
computerized loan origination (CLO)
   system
construction loan

credit-bid
declaration of default
deed of reconveyance
deficiency judgment
Department of Housing and
   Urban Development (HUD)
discount rate
Equal Credit Opportunity Act
Federal Deposit Insurance Corporation
   (FDIC)
Federal Reserve Bank System
   (the Fed)
FICO score
Financial Institutions Reform,
   Recovery, and Enforcement
   act of 1989 (FIRREA)
fixed-rate mortgage

good-faith estimate

graduated payment adjustable-
rate mortgage (GPARM)

graduated payment mortgage (GPM)

growing equity mortgage (GEM)

holder in due course

home equity sales contract

Housing Finance Board

hypothecation

impound account

installment note

institutional lenders

interest

interim loan

joint and several liability

judicial foreclosure

junior lienor

kickback

leverage

loan-to-value ratio

lock-in clause

mortgage bankers

mortgagee

mortgagor

negative amortization

negotiable instrument

nominal rate

nonamortized

notice of default

notice of sale

notice of trustee's sale

open-ended mortgage

pledged

points

power of sale

power-of-sale mortgage

prime rate

principal

private mortgage insurance (PMI)

promissory note

rate

Real Estate Settlement
Procedures Act (RESPA)

Real Property Loan Law

redemption period

Regulation Z

reinstatement

renegotiable-rate mortgage
(RRM)

reverse annuity mortgage (RAM)

right of redemption

right to rescind

satisfaction

security instrument

shared appreciation mortgage (SAM)

Special Information Booklet

standby commitment

standby fee

straight note

subject to

take-out loan

trustee

trustee's sale

trustor

Truth-in-Lending Act (TILA)

unlawful detainer

Uniform Residential Loan Application

Uniform Settlement Statement

Unruh Act

usury

■ OPEN FOR DISCUSSION

When property values rose to dizzying heights in Japan, lenders began to make loans with 50-year to 100-year terms.

1. Do you see such loans in California's future?

2. In what ways can lenders help keep loan costs down?

■ ACHIEVEMENT EXAMINATION 8

1. A $450,000 house can be purchased with a $90,000 down payment using the principle of
   a. borrowed funds.
   b. leveraging.
   c. partial financing.
   d. home equity.

2. The Fed can increase or decrease the amount of money in circulation by all of the following *except*
   a. establishing the discount rate.
   b. issuing government securities.
   c. raising or lowering reserve requirements.
   d. buying and selling government securities.

3. Federal savings and loan activities are overseen by
   a. FHLMC.
   b. the Office of Thrift Supervision.
   c. the Fed.
   d. FDIC.

4. California usury laws apply primarily to
   a. financial institutions.
   b. all lenders.
   c. nonfinancial institutions.
   d. private lenders.

5. Real estate is hypothecated by use of a
   a. promissory note.
   b. negotiable instrument.
   c. security instrument.
   d. pledge.

6. To be a negotiable instrument, a promissory note must be
   a. a promise to pay money to the bearer.
   b. an oral agreement.
   c. payable at an indefinite future time.
   d. signed by the bearer.

7. A holder in due course must take a negotiable instrument
   a. within 90 days of its execution.
   b. with knowledge of all defenses against it.
   c. without notice of any defense against its enforcement.
   d. for cash.

8. In a mortgage, the lender is the
   a. mortgagor.   c. maker.
   b. mortgagee.   d. holder.

9. The highest bidder at a judicial foreclosure receives a
   a. deed.   c. title.
   b. contract.   d. certificate of sale.

10. In a deed of trust, the borrower is the
    a. trustor.   c. beneficiary.
    b. trustee.   d. holder.

11. In a deed of trust, the lender is the
    a. trustor.   c. beneficiary.
    b. trustee.   d. holder.

12. The first step in bringing about a trustee's sale is to prepare a
    a. declaration of default.
    b. notice of levy.
    c. request for notice.
    d. notice of default.

13. There is no right of redemption following a
    a. strict foreclosure.
    b. trustee's sale.
    c. judicial foreclosure.
    d. mortgage foreclosure.

14. An ARM is a
    a. graduated payment mortgage.
    b. growing equity mortgage.
    c. mortgage in which the interest rate changes periodically based on an index.
    d. reverse annuity mortgage.

15. Most adjustable-rate loans are
    a. assumable.
    b. not assumable.
    c. held by sellers.
    d. not allowed for federal institutions.

16. Interest rate and payment can change every three to five years in a
    a. graduated payment mortgage.
    b. renegotiable-rate mortgage.
    c. growing equity mortgage.
    d. reverse annuity mortgage.

17. A real estate broker who arranges loans no more than five times a year
    a. is subject to Regulation Z.
    b. is not subject to Regulation Z.
    c. does not fall within Proposition 2.
    d. has violated the Real Property Loan Law.

18. RESPA covers the
    a. listing agreement.
    b. broker's commission.
    c. Uniform Settlement Statement.
    d. loan application form.

19. John Smith bought Whiteacre, and John is making the former owner's original loan payments. If John defaults, the seller will be obligated on the loan. Which statement is true?
    a. John bought the loan.
    b. John bought the property subject to the loan.
    c. John is subject to a due-on-sale clause.
    d. John does not have title to Whiteacre.

20. A lender that discriminates against a loan applicant because of race has violated the
    a. Equal Dignities Rule.
    b. Truth-in-Lending Act.
    c. Equal Credit Opportunity Act.
    d. Lender's Law.

CHAPTER NINE

GOVERNMENT-SPONSORED AND OTHER FINANCING

■ GOVERNMENT-SPONSORED FINANCING

Loans that do *not* involve government cooperation are called **conventional loans.** Loans that are created or financed with the help of a government source are **nonconventional loans,** and they are the focus of this chapter. Both federal and state programs are discussed.

Federal Housing Administration

The **National Housing Act** was passed in 1934 in response to the numerous foreclosures brought about by the Great Depression and has been amended many times since. One of the agencies created by the National Housing Act was the **Federal Housing Administration (FHA),** a division of the **Department of Housing and Urban Development (HUD).** FHA does not make loans, but it *insures* loans made by lending institutions such as savings and loan associations, banks, life insurance companies, mortgage companies, and others. For 60 years FHA has been a major force in determining how lending practices are carried out. Information about HUD and FHA programs can be found at *www.hud.gov* or by calling 1-800-CALLFHA.

www.hud.gov

Section 203. **Section 203** of Title II of the National Housing Act specifies eligibility requirements for federal mortgage insurance for housing construction and finance. **Section 203(b)** covers mortgages on one- to four-family homes. FHA insures approximately seven million loans valued at almost $400 billion through this and its other programs.

FHA-insured loan limits. Insured loan amounts are subject to change to keep pace with market conditions. In 2004, the maximum insured loan amount ranged from $160,176 to $290,319 for a California single-family home, depending on location. The maximum is higher in counties where market values typically are higher. The maximum is $435,478 for property in Alaska, Hawaii, Guam, and the U.S. Virgin Islands. The selling price of a home can be higher than the maximum amount stated, but FHA insurance will not cover the excess. *Condominium* loan limits are approximately the same as those for single-family residences in the same county. Higher limits apply to two- to four-unit properties.

For most dwellings, the maximum loan amount is a percentage of the purchase price or FHA appraised value, whichever is less. The maximum loan-to-value percentages are shown below.

Sales Price or Appraised Value	Maximum Loan-to-Value Percentage
$50,000 or less	98.75%
Over $50,000 up to $125,000	97.65%
Over $125,000	97.15%

■ **FOR EXAMPLE:** Ruth and Bill Smith are interested in a single-family residence in San Diego County. The seller's asking price is $199,900. The Smiths intend to offer $196,000 for the property, and they make that offer contingent on getting an FHA-insured loan. What is the maximum amount FHA will insure if their offer is accepted and the property is appraised by FHA at the selling price?

In this example, the maximum loan amount is 97.15 percent of the sales price (since the property was appraised by FHA at the selling price), up to the $219,849 limit for San Diego County.

$$\$196,000 \times 97.15\% = \$190,414$$

In this case, the maximum loan amount that can be covered by FHA insurance is $190,414, which is within the ceiling set for a single-family residence in San Diego County.

Total cash investment.   The minimum cash investment made by a borrower on an FHA-insured loan must be at least 3 percent of the sales price. Any excess over the minimum down payment is applied to closing costs.

Mortgage insurance premium and monthly charge.   The FHA **mortgage insurance premium** is paid to FHA at closing. It is not considered an acquisition cost in computing down payment. The premium may be paid by the borrower or someone else, or it may be included in the loan amount. Presently, the FHA mortgage insurance premium is 1.5 percent of the loan amount, but does not apply to a loan secured by a condominium. All FHA-insured loans carry a monthly insurance charge of ½ percent.

Effective January 1, 2001, Congress provided regulations for removal of FHA mortgage insurance for all loans originated on or after that date.

Interest rate and loan term.   The interest rate may rise or fall with prevailing market rates. The **loan term** may not be longer than 35 years if the loan is approved prior to construction, or 30 years otherwise. The 30-year term has been the most popular with lenders and borrowers, but shorter-term loans are beginning to gain favor. Generally loans must be fully amortized in equal monthly payments that include both principal and interest. Monthly payments also include impounds for taxes, special assessments, and fire or other hazard insurance.

Prepayment penalty.   There are *no* prepayment penalties on FHA-insured loans.

Points.   A lender can charge **discount points** (prepaid interest) to the borrower in addition to the 1 percent loan fee. Discount points are the lender's way of increasing loan income while keeping the interest rate at a competitive level. One discount point equals one percentage point of the loan amount.

> One discount point is 1 percent of the loan amount paid up front.

Discount points are paid at closing by the borrower or someone else. Usually the seller pays discount points to increase the lender's effective yield, even though the borrower may be offered a lower-than-market interest rate. One discount point increases the overall yield on a loan by approximately ⅛ percent. Thus a loan at 7 percent and three discount points effectively earns 7⅜ percent for the lender.

■   **FOR EXAMPLE:**   Joe Dash is selling his single-family residence in Solano County. Harold Maloney and Barbara Clark have offered $159,000, contingent on their securing FHA-insured financing. Joe accepts the offer. A lender approached by Maloney and Clark is willing to make a loan of the maximum FHA-insurable amount of $151,725, to carry an interest rate of 7½ percent, with two discount points to be paid at closing, when the loan is funded. What is the amount of the discount points, and who will pay them?

The discount points are valued at $3,035 ($151,725 × 2%) and are payable as stipulated in the agreement between the buyers and Joe Dash.

Discount points are a matter for negotiation between buyer and seller. Regardless of who pays, the contract of sale should stipulate who will pay and set a limit on the number of discount points that will be paid.

Types of loans available.   In addition to the traditional fixed-rate amortized loan, FHA allows use of a **graduated payment mortgage (GPM).** The GPM is available for families who expect income to increase over the loan term and who otherwise would not qualify for a mortgage loan. Only single-family residences are eligible. With a GPM, monthly payments do *not* cover all of the interest due. The unpaid interest is added to the remaining balance of principal owed. This **negative amortization** process continues for five to ten years, depending on which of five different GPM plans is used. At that point monthly payments stay the same to the end of the loan term and are fully amortized. Because interest is paid on interest, the statute specifically preempts any state usury laws that might thus be violated.

FHA allows use of an **adjustable-rate mortgage (ARM)** for owner-occupied residences of no more than four units. The rate of interest charged is adjusted by increases in monthly payment, outstanding principal balance, loan term, or a combination of the three. Maximum loan term, however, is 40 years. Adjustment of the interest rate must correspond to a specified national interest rate index. Adjustments of no more than 1 percent of the outstanding loan balance may be made annually, with an increase of no more than 5 percent over the initial contract interest rate over the life of the loan. At the time of loan application

Buyer Qualification for an FHA Loan

The following rules are aimed at reducing the number of defaults on FHA-insured loans, in addition to preventing defaulting borrowers from acquiring more credit:

1. Total **seller** contributions, including discounts, buy-down costs, and closing costs, cannot exceed 6 percent of acquisition cost.
2. The **borrower** must be qualified at the **full note rate,** rather than the buydown rate.

The borrower's **Social Security number** must be supplied on the loan application to assist in reporting of delinquent and foreclosed loans to other federal agencies and to credit bureaus.

the borrower must be given a written explanation of the loan features as well as the possible rate and payment increases over the loan term.

FHA also allows a **shared appreciation mortgage (SAM)** for a dwelling of one to four units.

HUD Direct Endorsement Plan.

Under HUD's **Direct Endorsement Plan,** qualified lenders may process a loan without prior HUD review, except for construction projects. This program thus eliminates the lengthy processing time that is one of the major drawbacks of the federally insured loan.

Department of Veterans Affairs

The **Servicemen's Readjustment Act of 1944** (the **GI Bill of Rights**) helped ease the transition into civilian life of World War II veterans. The programs later were expanded to include veterans of later conflicts. They also include the surviving spouse of an eligible person who died as the result of a service-connected injury, and the surviving spouse of a person missing in action or listed as a prisoner of war for more than 90 days. Benefits are available as long as the surviving spouse remains unmarried.

www.va.gov

The **Department of Veterans Affairs (VA)** presently authorizes first mortgage loans as well as second mortgage loans of less than 40 percent of property value. The VA **guarantees** payment of the remaining mortgage indebtedness, up to a maximum amount. If the borrower defaults, the VA will pay the lender's net loss up to the amount of the guarantee, which is decreased proportionately as the loan amount is repaid. There is no cost to the borrower for the VA guarantee.

The VA also makes loans to veterans directly in areas where there are few mortgage lenders. Because of the abundance of financing sources in this state, there are no *direct* VA loans to veterans in California. VA-guaranteed loans are available, however.

Borrower qualifications.

VA-guaranteed loans are available to those men and women who served in the U.S. armed forces and were other than dishonorably discharged and to their spouses, as mentioned above. The period of active duty required varies, depending generally on the date of service—90 days during wartime and 181 days otherwise.

Note: As of October 28, 1992, military reservists and National Guard members who have served for six years are eligible for VA-guaranteed loans. Participation requires an upfront funding fee if the borrower makes a down payment of less than 5 percent. The fee is presently 2.4 percent.

Lending institutions are able to screen VA loan applicants for eligibility as part of the loan qualification process. Supervised lenders verify the veteran's entitlement, then process the loan as usual. There is no need for VA review and approval.

> The Certificate of Eligibility shows the veteran's entitlement.

An interested veteran should request a **Certificate of Eligibility** from the nearest VA regional office in advance of loan application. The certificate will indicate the amount of loan guarantee, called the **veteran's entitlement,** available to the veteran.

Loan guarantee amount. VA-guaranteed loans can be made for purchase, construction, repair, or improvement of a veteran's dwelling, which can be a building of one to four units or a condominium.

The *maximum* amount of the veteran's entitlement depends on the total amount of the loan. Currently, the maximum guarantee is 40 percent of the loan amount or $60,000, whichever is less. The maximum entitlement for a manufactured home loan is lower. The maximum entitlement on a cash out refinance is $36,000.

The amount of a veteran's entitlement can be restored once, if the veteran refinances a VA loan with a conventional loan.

Restoration of entitlement. The veteran's entitlement is increased to the *full* amount if

- the property has been disposed of and the VA-guaranteed loan is paid in full;
- the VA is released from liability on the original loan;
- any loss suffered by the VA has been repaid in full; or
- the property is transferred to another veteran who is entitled to VA home loan guarantee benefits.

There must be a **release** from personal liability to the government on a VA loan *prior to* an assumption of the loan by a purchaser of the property. Otherwise, the veteran remains liable under the original terms of the guarantee. *Such a release should be a condition of the sale, specified in the contract.* If the property is **foreclosed** and there has been no act of fraud, misrepresentation, or bad faith by the veteran, the VA can release the veteran from further liability.

> The CRV sets the maximum loan amount the VA will guarantee.

Certificate of Reasonable Value. The lender, using one of a panel of VA-recommended appraisers, will order a **Certificate of Reasonable Value (CRV)** for the subject property. The veteran must be given a copy of the CRV *before* signing a contract of sale, *or* the contract should include a contingency that the veteran be able to either affirm or withdraw from the transaction without penalty if the CRV value is less than the purchase price.

Types of loans available.   Veterans have had a choice of four payment plans:

1. **Fixed-term** fully amortized mortgage of no more than 30 years and 32 days.

2. **Adjustable-rate mortgage (ARM),** similar to the FHA program but based on the Treasury Securities index, on loans initiated before October 1, 1995. These loans are no longer available.

3. **Growing equity mortgage (GEM),** which is tied to an index and results in increases in payments, with the increases applied to the principal balance. The GEM is a formalized way of making additional principal payments, which increases the accumulation of equity and shortens the overall loan term.

4. **Graduated payment mortgage (GPM),** which provides for lower initial monthly payments, increasing at a rate of 7 percent annually for the first five years. From the sixth year to the end of the loan term the payments remain the same. Unlike FHA, which allows four other variations of the GPM, the VA allows only this one form of graduated payment.

Some restrictions apply on **mobile home loans.** The mobile home must be at least 40 feet long and 10 feet wide, with a minimum of 400 square feet. The maximum loan term for the purchase of a single-wide mobile home, with or without a lot, is 15 years and 32 days. The maximum loan term for the purchase of a double-wide mobile home, with or without a lot, is 20 years and 32 days.

Interest rate.   The VA now allows borrowers to negotiate the interest rate on a VA-guaranteed loan with the lender.

Down payment and closing costs.   As long as the estimate of reasonable value does not exceed the amount of the VA loan guarantee, the VA does not require a down payment, although the lender may. The VA loan guarantee can never be more than the estimate of reasonable value, but a higher purchase price may be negotiated *if* the veteran pays the difference between the reasonable value and the purchase price in cash at the closing. The cash must come from the personal resources of the veteran and not from secondary financing.

On the first use of a VA-guaranteed loan with a down payment of less than 5 percent, a funding fee of 2.15 percent of the loan amount is charged. The 2.15 percent funding fee went into effect September 30, 2004 (it was previously 2.2 percent), and will be in effect until September 30, 2011, at which time it will be reviewed. Subsequent use of a VA-guaranteed loan carries a higher funding fee, presently 3.3 percent.

The veteran can pay **discount points,** which are subject to negotiation with the lender. Veterans are permitted to finance discount points.

Refinancing.   An existing mortgage loan or other recorded lien can be **refinanced** with a VA-guaranteed **interest rate reduction refinancing loan (IRRRL).** The reasons for the refinancing, which must be acceptable to the lender, can include repairs or improvements to the property or providing the veteran with funds for educational purposes.

A veteran can refinance an existing VA loan *if* the new loan will carry a lower interest rate. The amount refinanced cannot exceed the remaining balance of the existing loan *plus* allowable closing costs (which may include discount points). The amount financed cannot be greater than the original amount guaranteed, and the overall loan term must remain the same. No additional amount will be charged against the veteran's entitlement.

Loan servicing.   The VA is available to help a veteran even after a loan is secured if the veteran is having a problem making loan payments. If a loan is delinquent three months, a **notice of default** alerts the VA to the situation. Financial counseling is provided to help the veteran pay arrearages and avoid future missed payments.

FHA versus VA Loans

At present, there are fewer distinctions between FHA-insured and VA-guaranteed loans than there have been in the past. The differences that still exist involve the following factors.

Loan purpose.   Both FHA and VA loans are available for first mortgages of owner-occupied property. VA loans also include junior liens for repairs or improvements. Although FHA technically allows some types of secondary financing, for all practical purposes the FHA market is first mortgages only.

Loan amount.   VA guarantee limits do not set the upper limit of the loan amount. FHA loan maximums are exactly that.

Interest rate.   Both VA and FHA allow lenders and borrowers to negotiate the interest rate offered, which can vary from lender to lender. Both FHA and VA allow a variety of loan types.

> Down payment and closing costs usually are lower on a VA-guaranteed loan than on an FHA-insured loan.

Down payment.   VA generally does not require a down payment, although the lender may. FHA requires a down payment of at least 1.25 to 2.85 percent of the sales price or appraised value, whichever is less, but FHA also requires a minimum cash investment of 3 percent of the sales price or appraised value, whichever is less, with the balance going toward closing costs.

Service charges.   FHA allows a service charge of 1 percent on loans involving existing buildings and 2 percent on loans for buildings to be constructed. Buyers now also can be charged discount points, which are a subject for buyer-seller negotiation. Seller contributions cannot be more than 6 percent of acquisition cost. The buyer also can be charged an FHA application fee and fees for credit report, appraisal, and other closing costs.

VA allows lenders to charge reasonable costs, including credit report, survey, title evidence, and recording fees. Other loan origination costs can be included in a flat charge that cannot exceed 1 percent of the loan amount for most properties. In certain cases, the veteran may be charged discount points. The VA funding fee ranges from .5 percent to 3 percent. depending on the down payment and origination date.

Loan prepayment.   Both agencies allow full or partial prepayment of principal at any time. The VA does require that any prepayment be at least $100 or the amount of one installment.

Refinancing to avoid default.   Both FHA and VA loans can be refinanced to avoid imminent default, so that payments may be extended beyond the initial loan term. VA loans can be refinanced only if 80 percent or more of the new loan will be paid within the original loan term limit. The FHA loan term on refinancing can be no more than three-fourths of the remaining economic life of the building.

RESPA.   Note one final similarity between FHA-insured and VA-guaranteed loans. Because both are federally related, both fall within the requirements of the **Real Estate Settlement Procedures Act (RESPA),** discussed in Chapter 8, in addition to all other disclosure requirements. A HUD settlement statement noting transaction charges for both buyer and seller appears in Chapter 10.

California Veterans Farm and Home Purchase Program

The **California Veterans Farm and Home Purchase Program** was created in 1921 to assist California veterans in acquiring home or farm property. The program is included in Division 4, Chapter 6, of the Military and Veterans Code.

www.cdva.ca.gov

Cal-Vet loans are administered by the **California Department of Veterans Affairs (CDVA),** which can be found at *www.cdva.ca.gov.* CDVA authorizes, processes, funds, and services the loans. No outside lenders are involved, because the program is totally self-supporting. Funds for Cal-Vet loans come from voter-approved State General Obligation Bonds and Revenue Bonds issued by the legislature.

CDVA buys the selected property from the seller and resells the property to the veteran on a land contract (explained later in this chapter). CDVA holds title until the veteran has repaid the amount owed, although the veteran has the right to possession of the property as his or her personal residence.

Cal-Vet loans can be used to

- purchase an existing home;
- finance a lot purchase and new construction;
- rehabilitate a home purchased "as-is"; and
- make home improvements.

> You're a California veteran if you are a veteran who currently resides in California.

Eligibility requirements. Cal-Vet loans are available only on California property and only to California veterans who have not accepted a bonus or benefit from another state. Cal-Vet loans are now available to any veteran currently living in California who served on active duty for at least 90 days (or was discharged because of a service-connected disability), received an honorable discharge or release, and served at least part of one day during one of the following periods:

World War I	April 6, 1917, through November 11, 1918
World War II	December 7, 1941, through December 31, 1946
Korean Period	June 27, 1950, through January 31, 1955
Vietnam Era	August 5, 1964, through May 7, 1975
Persian Gulf War	August 2, 1990—still open

Veterans who served entirely in peacetime are also eligible, though a different funding source may be used.

Unremarried spouses of veterans who were killed in the line of duty or who are missing in action or who are prisoners of war also are eligible.

If funds are in short supply, *preference* will be given to

- wounded or disabled veterans, then
- former prisoners of war and unremarried spouses of those missing in action or prisoners of war, then
- Vietnam-era veterans and Native American veterans applying for loans on reservation or trust land, then
- all other eligible veterans.

Loan qualifying. *Loan application* must be made before purchase. The veteran must meet ordinary standards of creditworthiness. There is no loan origination fee, though there is a $50 loan application fee.

Interest rate and loan term. The loan term typically is 30 years. The interest rate on all loans may change *annually*, depending on the cost of bonds to fund

FIGURE 9.1

Cal-Vet Loan Programs

Loan Program	Cal-Vet / VA	Cal-Vet 97	Cal-Vet 80/20
Maximum Loan	$240,000 (incl. funding fee)	$333,700	$333,700
Property/Program	New or Existing Homes (incl. VA approved Condos and PUDs)	New or Existing Homes (incl. VA approved Condos and PUDs) Construction Loans Rehabilitation Loans Mobile Homes on Land Mobile Homes in Parks	New or Existing Homes (incl. VA approved Condos and PUDs) Construction Loans Rehabilitation Loans Mobile Homes on Land Mobile Homes in Parks
		(For both programs, max. loan on Mobile Homes in Parks is $70,000 and interest rate is 1% higher)	
Down Payment	2%	3%	20%
Funding Fee	1.25%–3% Waived for vets with disability ratings of 10% or higher; May be financed	1.25%–2% Must be paid in escrow; May be financed if down payment is 5% or greater	None
Loan Origination Fee	1%	1%	1%
Other Requirements	VA Certificate of Eligibility for full entitlement		

In recognition of the wildfire tragedies in Southern California in 2003, CDVA has implemented mortgage relief assistance for veterans with Cal-Vet loans. Mortgage payments may be delayed or reduced in the case of hardship. For assistance, Cal-Vet homeowners should call 800-952-5626, or e-mail *loanserv@cdva.ca.gov*. Local Cal-Vet Home Loan offices in Ventura (805-654-6901 or *Ventura@cdva.ca.gov*), Riverside (909-774-0102 or *Riverside@cdva.ca.gov*), and San Diego (619-641-5840 or *SanDiego@cdva.ca.gov*) can also be contacted.

Except for mobile homes and condominiums, Cal-Vet home loans are covered for fire and hazard insurance. Veterans should contact GAB Robins at 800-626-1613, ext. 5.

the program. Monthly loan installments will increase to cover additional interest charges. The rate currently is 6.95 percent, and 7.95 percent for manufactured homes in an approved park.

Prepayment. Cal-Vet loans may be prepaid at any time.

Loan amount/down payment. The maximum loan amount, minimum down payment, and loan fees are shown in Figure 9.1.

Change of residence. A veteran can obtain a new Cal-Vet loan as long as the first loan is paid in full or awarded in a divorce to a nonveteran spouse.

As with all government loan programs, Cal-Vet loan requirements are subject to change at any time. Anyone interested in such a loan should contact the closest office of the California Department of Veterans Affairs. The toll-free telephone number to call within California for information on Cal-Vet loans is (800) 952-5626 (952-LOAN).

Exercise 9-1 Refer to the information discussed in this chapter to answer the following questions.

1. Could the same individual be eligible for an FHA, a VA, and a Cal-Vet loan?

2. Mary Smith is eligible for a Cal-Vet loan and would like to make the minimum down payment. What will be the maximum purchase price that the loan will cover?

3. Is a borrower's down payment likely to be lower with an FHA-insured or a VA-guaranteed loan?

■ CREATIVE FINANCING

When interest rates are high, there is an oversupply of properties for sale, or rising prices make housing less affordable, sellers frequently help to finance property purchases. Seller financing and other techniques can bring down the effective interest rate paid by buyers and make property purchases more attractive. Some of those **creative financing** techniques are discussed next.

Purchase Money Trust Deeds and Mortgages

The **purchase money trust deed** or **purchase money mortgage** is given by *buyer* to *seller* at the time of purchase to secure all or part of the purchase price. The purchase money may come from either a third party (such as an institutional lender) or in the form of credit from the seller.

Typically the seller who is willing to **take back (carry back)** a purchase-money mortgage or trust deed will set a rate lower than market interest in order to attract a greater number of qualified buyers without having to reduce the selling price drastically. The concept of seller financing certainly is not new, and it has been used to a considerable extent in California. The seller can finance a first or second mortgage or deed of trust. Without the availability of the "seller-financed second," many buyers would lack sufficient funds for the ever-increasing down payments necessitated by rising property values.

Land Contract

The **land contract,** also referred to as a **contract for deed** or **installment sales contract,** should not be confused with what we have referred to as the *contract of sale* between the parties.

A *land contract* is a form of seller financing in which the buyer takes possession of property and makes payments on its purchase but does not receive legal title to the property for **at least one year** from the date of possession. The sales contract specifies the amount of the purchase price that must be paid before legal title is conveyed. A land contract is one alternative for a buyer who does not qualify for a regular mortgage loan.

> A land contract appeals to people who don't want to deal with a bank or other institutional lender, or who may have difficulty qualifying for a loan.

A land contract usually requires little or no down payment. The buyer takes possession of the property but, because the seller retains title, it may be less risky for the seller than other forms of financing. The seller cannot automatically eliminate the buyer's interest on default, however. Courts and legislature have rejected "harsh" remedies that could prevent a defaulting buyer from realizing any buildup of equity in the property. The land contract also must follow strict notice and other requirements. *Any seller contemplating such a sale should not do so without first consulting an attorney to ensure that all legal requirements are met.*

Wraparound Mortgage or Trust Deed

The **wraparound mortgage** or **wraparound trust deed** is also called an **overriding** or an **all-inclusive trust deed (AITD).** An AITD is a way to take advantage of a seller's existing loan with a relatively low rate of interest. The existing loan is unchanged, but the buyer receives additional funds (using the property as collateral) to make the purchase, and the lender of those new funds receives payment sufficient to cover both old and new loans. The new loan "wraps around" the existing loan.

> A wraparound mortgage makes sense only when interest rates are rising.

The advantage to the buyer is that an overall less-than-market rate of interest is paid on the new loan balance. The lender benefits by receiving interest based on the entire loan balance at a rate higher than the original loan rate. The lender not only earns interest on the additional loan amount but may keep the excess earned at the new rate on the old balance as well.

A buyer could give a wraparound trust deed or mortgage to a seller, who then would make payments on the first loan. *It is important to note that a wraparound loan is possible only if the original loan documents permit such a refinancing. An acceleration clause in the original loan documents would prevent a sale under such terms. An attorney should be consulted before entering into any such transaction.*

■ **FOR EXAMPLE:** Present market interest rate on a home mortgage loan of $100,000 is 8 percent. A money market account earns 4 percent. The seller of Greenacre will hold a wraparound mortgage on his home priced at $100,000, with $20,000 down, for 20 years, at only 7 percent interest. The seller has an existing mortgage loan balance of $50,000 at 7 percent interest for 20 years. On those terms, what will be the rate of return to the seller on his remaining equity?

The seller receives $20,000 immediately, leaving an equity interest in the property of $30,000. The seller is owed yearly interest of 7 percent on $80,000, or $5,600, and owes 7 percent on $50,000, or $3,500.

The seller's yearly return is thus $2,100 ($5,600 – $3,500). That return divided by the amount "invested" ($2,100 + $30,000) indicates a rate of return of 7 percent. The buyer benefits from a lower-than-market interest rate, and the seller benefits from a return that is higher than the prevailing money market rate.

Sale-Leaseback

The **sale-leaseback,** or just **leaseback,** is a method of property transfer. It is mentioned here because it is a useful way for a financially sound but cash-poor business to gain needed capital while keeping office or other space.

By selling property it owns and uses, a business gets cash. By leasing the same space back from the buyer, the business can deduct the entire lease payment from income. Not all of the property need be sold—the land alone could be sold for the same tax reasons, but buildings on the land could be kept for depreciation deductions.

The buyer in a leaseback benefits by the typically higher payments of a lease over a mortgage and the property's appreciation (among other benefits). The lease term probably would be much longer (99 years, for instance) than the standard mortgage term (perhaps 25 years), assuring the buyer of a steady income stream.

Exercise 9-2   Identify each of the financing transactions described below.

1. Dr. Jones built a small medical clinic on her own land. After 15 years Dr. Jones sold the clinic. She still maintains her practice in the clinic building and plans to do so for many more years.

2. Ray Washington is making monthly payments on the house in which he lives with his son. Ray is buying the house but has never had legal title.

3. Debra Harold has held legal title to Blackacre for six months, since she took possession. She is making monthly payments of principal and interest to the former owner.

4. John Edwards, a veteran, pays a lower-than-market rate of interest on his home loan, which he pays directly to the government agency that funded the loan.

■ THE SECONDARY MORTGAGE MARKET

Don't confuse the secondary mortgage market with secondary financing, which is a second (junior) lien on already-mortgaged property.

The initial mortgage lender may be the borrower's only source of contact regarding the loan. The borrower may make all mortgage payments to the original lender and receive periodic statements of interest paid and remaining principal owed from the same source. Yet in today's mortgage marketplace, chances are that the initial lender has sold the promissory note that is the underlying obligation and is only servicing it for someone else.

The sale and purchase of such obligations constitutes the **secondary mortgage market.** Real estate securities are a substantial source of investment opportunities for those who otherwise might seek alternate markets. This section will review the federally originated agencies that dominate the secondary mortgage market.

Federal National Mortgage Association— "Fannie Mae"

The **Federal National Mortgage Association,** now known as **Fannie Mae** or **FNMA,** was created in 1938 as a subsidiary of the Reconstruction Finance Corporation. Information about FNMA can be found at *www.fanniemae.com.* FNMA has a 15-member Board of Directors. Ten members are elected by shareholders, and five members are appointed by the President of the United States.

www.fanniemae.com

From its original mandate to serve as a secondary market for FHA-insured and VA-guaranteed loans, FNMA's authority has been expanded to take in *conventional* mortgage loans as well. FNMA currently buys FHA and VA graduated payment mortgages, adjustable-rate mortgages, and conventional fixed-rate first and some qualifying second mortgages on dwellings of one to four units.

A conforming loan meets FNMA's criteria.

A loan that meets FNMA's underwriting criteria and dollar amount is called a **conforming loan.** Loans purchased by FNMA cannot exceed the limits established each year using the formula prescribed in the Housing and Community Development Act of 1980. For 2004, the limit was set at $333,700 for a loan on a single-family residence; $427,150 for a two-family loan; $516,300 for a three-family loan; and $614,650 for a loan secured by a four-family residence. Limits are 50 percent higher for properties in Alaska, Hawaii, the U.S. Virgin Islands, and Guam.

FNMA will buy a block (pool) of mortgages from a lender in exchange for **mortgage-backed securities** that represent undivided interests in the group of loans. The securities may be sold or kept by the lender. FNMA **guarantees** payment of all interest and principal to the holder of the securities.

In 1968 FNMA was divided into a corporation owned by private shareholders (but still called FNMA) and an organization called the **Government National Mort-**

gage Association, which is discussed in the next section of this chapter. FNMA now issues its own *common stock,* and it also obtains capital from borrowing, selling notes and debentures, selling mortgage-backed securities, and money earned from its own mortgage portfolio.

Government National Mortgage Association— "Ginnie Mae"

The **Government National Mortgage Association (GNMA),** or "Ginnie Mae," has brought many people into the residential mortgage market by offering high-yield, risk-free, guaranteed securities. These securities also have none of the servicing obligations of a regular mortgage loan portfolio. Information about GNMA can be found at *www.hud.gov/funcgnma.*

www.hud.gov/funcgnma

Unlike FNMA, GNMA does not buy securities. Instead, GNMA *guarantees* securities issued by FHA-approved home mortgage lenders. GNMA guarantees that the purchaser of privately issued securities backed by a pool of residential mortgages will receive timely payment of interest and principal, less servicing and GNMA fees. In the event of late payment by the borrower, the securities issuer advances the payment to the securities holder.

GNMA securities are backed by FHA-insured and VA-guaranteed mortgages, as well as those guaranteed by the **Farmers Home Administration (FmHA),** including single-family fixed-rate, graduated payment, growing equity, and manufactured home mortgage loans.

Federal Home Loan Mortgage Corporation— "Freddie Mac"

The **Federal Home Loan Mortgage Corporation (FHLMC),** or "Freddie Mac," was created in 1970 in direct response to the scarcity of mortgage funds. FHLMC provides a secondary market for residential conventional mortgage loans by buying such loans and reselling them to individual investors and financial institutions. Maximum loan amounts are the same as those set for FNMA.

www.freddiemac.com

FHLMC was funded initially by the sale of *nonvoting common stock* to the Federal Home Loan Banks. FHLMC now issues *preferred stock* to the general public. You can learn more about FHLMC at its Web site, *www.freddiemac.com.*

Office of Federal Housing Enterprise Oversight (OFHEO)

The **Office of Federal Housing Enterprise Oversight (OFHEO)** was created by Congress in the Federal Housing Enterprises Financial Safety and Soundness Act of 1992. OFHEO is charged with making legislative recommendations that are designed to enhance the financial safety and soundness of Fannie Mae and Freddie Mac. OFHEO does this by researching the mortgage market and conducting audits of Fannie Mae and Freddie Mac. OFHEO's Web site is *www.ofheo.gov* and has a great deal of useful information, including a house price index for all 50 states and the District of Columbia.

www.ofheo.gov

Electronic Signatures

OFHEO anticipates a growing number of loan originations accomplished via the Internet. This trend has undoubtedly benefited from the passage by Congress of the **Electronic Signatures in Global and National Commerce Act,** which took effect October 1, 2000. Many states, including California, had already adopted the Uniform Electronic Transactions Act. The new federal law gives electronic signatures and records the same legal validity as written contracts and documents in every state. The law makes it possible for a mortgage loan to be applied for, approved, and made without a single piece of paper changing hands. Not every transaction can be carried out electronically, however. The law makes exceptions for certain documents of critical nature, such as court orders, mortgage foreclosures, termination of health insurance, utility cancellations, wills, and adoptions, which will still require written documentation on paper.

Exercise 9-3   How does a secondary market for real estate mortgage loans benefit borrowers?

■ SUMMARY

Nonconventional real estate loans include those insured by the **Federal Housing Administration (FHA)** or guaranteed by the **Department of Veterans Affairs (VA).** Through a variety of loan plans, these agencies use approved lenders to make lower-interest, low-down-payment loans available for owner-occupied dwellings.

The **California Veterans Farm and Home Purchase Program** has for many years purchased and resold residences and farms to veterans. This self-supporting program is run by the **California Department of Veterans Affairs.**

In a time of expensive credit, seller financing through **purchase money mortgages** and **trust deeds** can be a boon. **Sales** or **land contracts** can be tricky but may be useful if undertaken with the proper legal advice. The **wraparound mortgage,** when allowed, can benefit both buyer and seller.

The **sale-leaseback** is a way to free up capital for a financially sound property owner.

Fannie Mae (FNMA) has encouraged the growth of a strong **secondary mortgage market** by guaranteeing payment of interest and principal to holders of the **mortgage-backed securities** it creates by buying mortgages from lenders. The **Government National Mortgage Association (GNMA)** guarantees securities issued by FHA-approved home mortgage lenders. The **Federal Home Loan Mortgage Corporation (FHLMC** or **Freddie Mac)** buys conventional residential mortgage loans for resale to investors and financial institutions. The **Office of Federal Housing Enterprise Oversight (OFHEO)** audits Fannie Mae's and Freddie Mac's activities.

■ IMPORTANT TERMS

Make sure you understand the following terms before you take the achievement examination.

all-inclusive trust deed (AITD)
California Department of Veterans
   Affairs (CDVA)
California Veterans Farm and
   Home Purchase Program
Cal-Vet loans
Certificate of Eligibility
Certificate of Reasonable Value (CRV)
conforming loan
conventional loans
creative financing
Department of Housing and
   Urban Development (HUD)
Department of Veterans Affairs (VA)
Direct Endorsement Plan
discount points
Electronic Signatures in Global
   and National Commerce Act
Fannie Mae (FNMA)
Farmers Home Administration
   (FmHA)
Federal Home Loan Mortgage
   Corporation (FHLMC),
   "Freddie Mac"

Federal Housing Administration
   (FHA)
Government National Mortgage
   Association (GNMA), "Ginnie
   Mae"
installment sales contract
interest rate reduction refinancing loan
   (IRRRL)
land contract
leaseback
mortgage-backed securities
mortgage insurance premium
National Housing Act
Office of Federal Housing
   Enterprise Oversight (OFHEO)
overriding trust deed
purchase money mortgage
purchase money trust deed
sale-leaseback
secondary mortgage market
veteran's entitlement
wraparound mortgage
wraparound trust deed

■ OPEN FOR DISCUSSION

Once property is encumbered by debt, it becomes much more difficult to transfer title. One way to simplify real estate transactions would be to have a loan stay with the borrower, with the security interest transferred to the borrower's next property (assuming that the borrower purchases property equal to or greater in value than the property sold).

What do you think of this concept?

■ ACHIEVEMENT EXAMINATION 9

1. A California veteran might have a home loan *insured* by
   a. FHA.
   c. Cal-Vet.
   b. VA.
   d. FNMA.

2. FHA appraisal value is used to set the upper limit of the
   a. purchase price.
   b. loan amount.
   c. construction cost.
   d. seller contributions.

3. In addition to a monthly charge, FHA mortgage insurance is
   a. 2.25 percent of the loan amount.
   b. variable.
   c. negotiable.
   d. determined by the lender.

4. For an existing structure, the maximum FHA mortgage loan term is
   a. 15 years and 32 days.
   b. 25 years.
   c. 30 years.
   d. 35 years.

5. One discount point will increase a lender's effective yield by approximately
   a. ¼ percent.
   c. ½ percent.
   b. ⅛ percent.
   d. 1 percent.

6. Four discount points will increase a lender's effective yield by approximately
   a. ¼ percent.
   c. ½ percent.
   b. ⅛ percent.
   d. 4 percent.

7. On FHA loans, seller contributions, including discounts and closing costs, cannot exceed
   a. $5,000.
   b. 4 percent.
   c. 5 points.
   d. 6 percent of acquisition cost.

8. Five different graduated payment mortgages are approved by
   a. FHA.
   c. Cal-Vet.
   b. VA.
   d. GNMA.

9. A veteran can have a home loan *guaranteed* by
   a. FHA.
   c. Cal-Vet.
   b. VA.
   d. FNMA.

10. The Certificate of Reasonable Value sets the upper limit of value for the
    a. purchase price.
    b. loan.
    c. guarantee.
    d. None of the above

11. Using the benefits of the GI Bill, a veteran *cannot* buy a
    a. house.
    b. condominium.
    c. farm.
    d. manufactured home.

12. A veteran can be given a home loan on property *owned* by
    a. FHA.
    c. Cal-Vet.
    b. VA.
    d. FNMA.

13. A Cal-Vet purchase loan must be applied for
    a. within one year of property purchase.
    b. before closing.
    c. before a contract of sale is signed.
    d. before talking to a property seller.

14. Cal-Vet loans are not available for
    a. single-family homes.
    b. manufactured homes.
    c. working farms.
    d. commercial property.

15. Many seller-financed purchases are examples of
    a. institutional lending.
    b. creative financing.
    c. mortgage-backed securities.
    d. blended-rate mortgages.

16. An installment sales contract also is called a
    a. GEM.
    b. GPM.
    c. land contract.
    d. contract of sale.

17. In a sale-leaseback
    a. land is never sold.
    b. buildings are always sold.
    c. both land and buildings can be sold.
    d. only a leasehold interest is sold.

18. The secondary mortgage market does *not* deal in
    a. primary mortgage market instruments.
    b. junior liens.
    c. issuing loans.
    d. mortgage-backed securities.

19. Which of the following is not a part of the primary mortgage market?
    a. FHA   c. Cal-Vet
    b. VA   d. FNMA

20. GNMA securities are *not* backed by
    a. FHA-insured loans.
    b. VA-guaranteed loans.
    c. FmHA-guaranteed loans.
    d. Cal-Vet loans.

CHAPTER TEN

ESCROW AND TITLE INSURANCE

■ ESCROW

An **escrow** is the possession by a *neutral third person* of money, a written instrument, evidence of title, or another thing of value that is received from *one party to a transaction* for delivery to the *other party to the transaction* on the performance of one or more conditions.

An escrow can involve the sale, transfer, encumbering, or leasing of *real property*, such as a house or an office building. An escrow also can help in a transaction involving *personal property*, such as a business opportunity. The emphasis in this chapter is on the use of an escrow in the sale of real estate.

The person who performs escrow duties is called an **escrow agent or escrow holder.** As an agent of both buyer and seller, the escrow holder receives and dispenses the required money or documents and carries out whatever paperwork is needed to facilitate their transfer. The escrow holder's task is not to force the parties to fulfill their obligations but to ensure that those obligations are fulfilled before the sale is closed, the funds are released, and the buyer takes title.

The escrow holder in a sale of real estate usually combines two separate functions in one transaction:

1. the sale itself, and
2. the loan that finances the sale.

The escrow holder is instructed to collect all necessary documents, properly executed and with required acknowledgments. The typical residential sales transaction may involve a dozen or more separate documents, from the promissory note and security instrument to appraisal and a preliminary report and disclosure statements.

The escrow holder's duties may include

- preparation of the necessary documents;
- calculation of the prorations, adjustments, and charges to be assessed against each party; and
- verification that all required documents and funds are on hand before the necessary transfers are made.

When all conditions to the sale have been met, the escrow agent can **close** (complete) the transaction by transferring the relevant documents and funds. At **close of escrow,** the escrow agent provides each party with a **settlement statement** that itemizes all receipts and disbursements. The closing itself may take more than one day. The parties may come to the escrow holder's office separately to sign documents while preparations are being made to record title in the name of the new owner. Local custom usually dictates the time frame. It may happen that seller and buyer never meet.

Creating an Escrow

To create a valid escrow for a real estate sale, two requirements must be met: a binding contract and conditional delivery of the necessary documents and funds.

1. Binding contract. There must be a **binding contract** between the buyer and seller. The contract can be

- a purchase contract and receipt for deposit,
- an agreement of sale,
- an option,
- an exchange agreement, or
- any other legally binding document.

Between the buyer and lender, the agreement usually is in the form of a **loan commitment** specifying the loan terms.

2. Conditional delivery.   There also must be a **conditional delivery** of the instruments of transfer to the escrow holder. Instruments of transfer include

- money,
- the deed transferring title from grantor to grantee,
- loan documents, and
- other required paperwork.

The delivery of all instruments of transfer is conditioned on the successful fulfillment of both the contract terms and any new terms imposed by the agreement establishing the escrow.

Escrow Instructions

The escrow agent is given written **escrow instructions** to carry out the terms of the contract that is the basis of the transaction. If the escrow instructions differ from the terms of the underlying agreement, such as a purchase contract, the most recent in time controls. The escrow holder must obey the escrow instructions and can be held liable for failing to do so.

Escrow instructions are called **bilateral** when they are given by both parties jointly. The escrow instructions are **unilateral** when they are given separately by each of the parties.

North versus South

In **northern California,** the general practice is to use **unilateral** escrow instructions.

In **southern California,** the general practice is to use **bilateral** escrow instructions.

After instructions to the escrow holder have been signed by the parties, neither can change the instructions unilaterally. If both parties agree, they may amend the escrow instructions at any time. It is necessary to have the agreement of both parties on every matter affecting the transaction, even if it is a condition that is to be waived by only one party.

The Escrow as Agent

A limited **agency relationship** is established between the escrow holder and the principals to the transaction, defined by the responsibilities set out in the escrow instructions. When escrow is first established, the escrow holder is the agent of both parties. As the conditions to the transaction are performed, the escrow holder acts as the agent of each party as necessary to complete the transaction.

■ **FOR EXAMPLE:** The escrow holder acts as the **agent of the grantor** when the deed is delivered to the grantee. The escrow holder acts as the **agent of the grantee** in delivering the purchase price to the grantor.

Ordinarily, the escrow holder should not be a party to the transaction. (There is an exception for licensed real estate brokers, as you will learn later in this chapter.) Unless an exception applies, the escrow holder should not give advice on any part of the transaction and should remain impartial.

Who May Be an Escrow

The California Financial Code contains the **Escrow Law.** It describes the legal requirements to act as an escrow agent. An escrow agent must be licensed by the Commissioner of Corporations, unless entitled to an exemption from licensing.

Exemptions from escrow licensing. There are *exemptions* from escrow licensing requirements for

- banks,
- savings and loan associations,
- title insurance companies,
- attorneys, and
- real estate brokers.

Note that real estate brokers who act as escrow agents are subject to special rules (discussed in the section, "The Real Estate Broker as Escrow Agent").

North versus South

In **northern California,** escrow typically is handled by the title insurance company.

In **southern California,** separately licensed escrow companies often are used, and financial institutions also perform many escrows.

General requirements. A **license** to act as an escrow agent can be held *only* by a **corporation.** An individual cannot receive such a license. The licensed corporation must be solvent and furnish a $25,000 surety bond. There are also certain liquidity and tangible net worth requirements.

An escrow agent must keep **accurate records and accounts,** which may be audited by the Commissioner of the Department of Corporations. Every fiscal year, the escrow agent (at the escrow agent's expense) must submit an independent audit prepared by a public accountant or certified public accountant.

An escrow agent is *not* allowed to do the following:

- Pay a referral fee, a commission, or any other compensation (including gifts of merchandise) to anyone other than employees of the escrow agent
- Disclose any information concerning the transaction to outside parties (Each party to the transaction may be informed of instructions of another party only when those instructions form a part of the original contract.)
- Solicit or accept escrow instructions or amendments that contain blanks to be filled in after the escrow instructions are signed
- Give advice in tax and legal matters

The Real Estate Broker as Escrow Agent

As already noted, a real estate broker need not be licensed as an escrow agent to perform the duties of an escrow. There are, however, strict requirements established by the Department of Corporations to govern brokers acting as escrows.

1. The license exemption is personal and applies only to the broker. The exemption does not apply to associates of the broker, unless they perform purely clerical functions, such as secretarial work.
2. The broker must be the selling or listing broker in the transaction or a party to the transaction.
3. Escrows must be only an incidental part of the broker's real estate business.
4. The broker may not form an association with other brokers for the purpose of conducting an escrow business.
5. The broker can advertise services as an escrow only in the context of the real estate brokerage. The broker cannot use a fictitious business name or one with the word *escrow* in the title or do anything to mislead the public as to the general nature of the brokerage.
6. All escrow funds must be kept in a trust account subject to inspection by the Commissioner of the Department of Corporations.

■ **FOR EXAMPLE:** Sally Salt, a licensed real estate broker, has decided that she can supplement her income nicely by handling escrows for other real estate brokers. Can she?

No. Unless she becomes licensed as an escrow agent, Broker Salt can act as an escrow only for transactions in which she is a party or the agent of one of the parties.

Other Principles and Prohibitions

> The escrow holder acts as an agent only in a very limited capacity.

Impartiality. The escrow holder should be **impartial** to all parties to a transaction. If the escrow holder receives conflicting instructions from the parties, neither instruction should be followed. Only written instructions signed by all parties should direct the escrow. *Oral instructions alone should never be followed.*

Interpleader. A conflict may arise between the parties as to the contract terms and resulting escrow instructions. If so, the escrow holder can bring a legal action known as **interpleader.** By this action the escrow holder forces the parties to have their rights and obligations clarified in court.

Above all, the escrow holder should *not* act as arbitrator or mediator or attempt to advise the parties on a course of action. It follows that an escrow holder should not give legal advice or speak to the parties on a matter that should be handled by the real estate broker.

Disclosure of material facts. Because of the escrow holder's position, **material facts** concerning the transaction that are unknown to the parties may come to the escrow holder's attention. If the escrow holder does receive any such information, it should be disclosed immediately to the relevant parties. On the other hand, the escrow agent is not a guarantor of the soundness of a transaction. There is no duty to conduct an independent investigation or to warn a party that a deal is not in that person's best interest.

The escrow holder should be aware of the agency relationship and treat the information in its possession accordingly. As stated earlier, there may be information to which only one principal is entitled, such as the dealings of buyer and lender. *Under no circumstances is information concerning the escrow to be released to nonparties.*

Record keeping. Accurate, up-to-date **records and accounts** are absolutely essential. Escrow files should be added to or revised daily if necessary. Likewise, an account never should be overdrawn. If documents or funds that were not part of the escrow instructions are submitted to the escrow holder, they should not be accepted.

Full and clear information. It is in the best interests of the escrow holder, as well as the parties, to make the **settlement statements** that are supplied at the conclusion of the transaction as clear and easy to follow as possible. There should never be ambiguities or missing information.

■ **FOR EXAMPLE:** Betty Buyer and Sam Seller are in escrow. Betty finds out that her loan will take longer to process than initially expected. She informs Sam, who agrees to a two-week extension of the closing of the sale. Sam phones

Reliance Escrow to relay the information. What date will the escrow holder treat as the termination date of the contract of sale?

Unless both Betty and Sam sign a written amendment to the escrow instructions (drawn up by the escrow holder), the escrow holder must treat the original termination date as still in effect.

Exercise 10-1

1. Which of the following must be a licensed escrow agent in order to act as an escrow holder in any transaction, without exception?

   Bank attorney
   Real estate broker
   Title insurance company
   Savings and loan association

2. After a much-delayed sale closing, the parties are waiting only for the proration of all of the expenses associated with the property, an apartment building. The seller, anxious to complete the sale, phones the escrow agent, telling the person handling the transaction to "just charge all expenses for this month to me, to expedite things." Can the agent do so? Why? *NO, Because both parties must agree + sign a Doc.*

3. Tom Takahashi handles escrows for Sunny Acres Title Insurance Company. Tom receives signed escrow instructions from the seller and buyer of a tract of vacant land in Sunny Acres Heights. The day before closing, Tom learns that the property has suffered severe mud slide damage. Should Tom do anything with that information? *Yes, tell both parties.*

■ ESCROW PROCEDURES

After an offer to purchase has been accepted by a seller of real estate, it is important for buyer, seller, and broker(s) to make sure that all necessary details have been covered. If there are no vague or ambiguous provisions between the parties, the escrow process will be that much smoother. *Remember that an agent is considered to be involved in a transaction even if the agent will not receive a commission or fee.*

Transaction Checklist

Both buyer and seller will be concerned that all of the points discussed in the negotiations are included in the final contract terms. The real estate agent, also, must make sure that certain information is known to the parties. Has the broker made the appropriate inspection of the property? Is the buyer fully informed of

> A checklist is a necessity to make sure all details (especially disclosures) have been covered.

all material facts concerning the property? Have the appropriate disclosures been made regarding the broker's agency relationship to seller and buyer? Have seller and buyer confirmed their understanding of the broker's role in the transaction? Have all other necessary disclosures been made? The use of a checklist, such as the one in Figure 10.1, will help ensure a successful sale closing.

Responsibilities of the Buyer

Once the requirements of the transaction are clearly established, the escrow holder knows what to expect from buyer and seller.

The **buyer** will

1. sign escrow instructions;
2. provide a copy of any contract of the buyer that will affect the escrow, such as a buyer-broker agreement;
3. review preliminary report and any encumbrances of record;
4. review all loan documents, including new loans, loans to be assumed, loans buyer is taking title "subject to," and disclosure information if seller is taking back a purchase-money mortgage;
5. obtain hazard insurance coverage;
6. review and approve all property inspection reports and arrange for final property inspection before closing;
7. examine the bill of sale covering any items of personal property to be conveyed separately at closing; and
8. deposit the cash needed to cover down payment, closing costs, and other expenses, such as revolving debt and collection accounts, if any, to be paid off at closing.

Usually, expenses may be negotiated between buyer and seller. (An exception may be a government-backed loan.) Charges typically incurred by the buyer include the

- loan fees,
- appraisal fee,
- credit report,
- lender's title insurance,
- recording fees for documents prepared on the buyer's behalf,
- notary fees for documents prepared on the buyer's behalf,
- prepayment of loan interest,
- assumption fee (if applicable),
- new fire or other hazard insurance premiums,

FIGURE 10.1

Transaction Checklist

TRANSACTION CHECKLIST

_____   Date and place of signing of contract by buyer(s).

_____   Full name, address, and marital status of each buyer. If a business, the type of business (corporation, general partnership, etc.) should be specified.

_____   Purchase price, amount of deposit, and how the deposit will be made (such as by personal check or cashier's check). The person who will hold the deposit prior to closing (the escrow holder, for instance) also should be named.

_____   Financing terms. The buyer may be required to obtain a loan commitment by a certain date. The buyer should always have the protection of a loan contingency clause in the purchase contract, such as "This offer is subject to and conditioned upon the buyer and property qualifying for and the buyer obtaining said loan within X days of opening of escrow." Without such protection, the buyer could risk forfeiting the deposit if the sale were frustrated by the buyer's or property's failure to qualify for the loan. If the buyer will assume an existing one, some provision should be made for the buyer's approval of the existing loan's terms.

_____   Encumbrances that affect title, such as restrictions and easements. These should be clarified as acceptable to the buyer, or a time period should be given in which a preliminary title report is to be received and accepted by the buyer. If the seller will retain any interest in the property, such as an easement, that interest should be specified, as should rights of any person (such as tenants) currently in possession.

_____   Required property inspections and who will pay for them. The person who will pay for necessary repairs also should be named. The buyer usually will want a final "walk-through" of the property just before closing to ensure it has been properly maintained and repaired (if necessary).

_____   Name of escrow holder, as well as who is to pay the escrow fee.

_____   Description of any other documents required from either party.

_____   Names of all real estate brokers and salespeople involved, as well as the agency role of each in the transaction, the negotiated sales commission, and who will pay the commission.

_____   Contract termination date, how long the buyer's offer is open, and when the buyer will take possession.

_____   Signatures of all parties, including broker(s). If a salesperson signs on behalf of a broker, the broker must review the contract within five days, initialing and dating it. The Real Estate Law provides for delegation of the broker's responsibility in certain instances.

■ FHA mortgage insurance, and

■ any prorated expenses the seller already has paid.

**Responsibilities
of the Seller**

The **seller** will

1. sign escrow instructions;

2. provide a copy of any contract of the seller that will affect the escrow, such as the listing agreement, and any required disclosure statement(s);

3. include seller's deed and title insurance policy and any unrecorded instruments affecting title;

4. provide information on the present status of existing loans, including consent to the submission of a beneficiary statement or demand for payoff, as required, and financing disclosure information if the seller is taking back a purchase-money mortgage;

5. provide certificates or releases on any mortgage, judgment, mechanic's lien, or other encumbrance to be paid off through escrow;

6. provide any existing hazard insurance policies to be assigned to the buyer;

7. provide any subordination agreement required by the contract;

8. provide tenant information, including their names, rent and deposit information, assignment of all leases to buyer, and the fact that tenants have been notified of the change of ownership;

9. provide executed deed on real property to the buyer;

10. provide executed bill of sale on any items of personal property, or security agreement if purchase is by installments; and

11. make available any other documents or approvals needed to close the sale.

Again, most sale expenses are open to negotiation. The seller typically will pay for the

■ title insurance,

■ structural pest control report and clearance (if needed),

■ the beneficiary statement,

■ existing loan payoff and prepayment fee (if any),

■ mortgage discount points and nonallowable fees on behalf of the buyer in FHA transactions,

■ all fees in VA transactions,

■ notary fees on documents prepared primarily on the seller's behalf, and

■ any arrearages for taxes or other prorated items.

Responsibilities of the Real Estate Agent

When a real estate agent represents a party in a transaction, there are steps the agent can take to ensure that the transaction is successfully completed. In general, a real estate agent's responsibilities are to keep informed of the progress of the escrow and assist the escrow officer when necessary. The **agent** usually will

1. deliver copies of the executed (signed) purchase contract to the parties;

2. deliver and explain the escrow instructions to the parties in the transaction, and ensure that the parties have signed and returned the instructions (it may be best to have the parties go to the escrow office for signatures);

3. provide all necessary property and transfer disclosure reports;

4. provide the escrow officer with copies of the seller's payment coupons on any loans, a property profile or copy of the grant deed indicating the present owner(s), tax information, and any other items that will assist the escrow officer;

5. advise the buyer(s) (particularly a married couple) to obtain legal advice on how to take title (agents and escrow officers, unless licensed to practice law, may not give this advice);

6. remind the seller to continue to make all payments on loans during escrow and maintain the property as required by the purchase agreement;

7. review the preliminary report as soon as it is available and explain its contents to the buyer;

8. assist the buyer in obtaining any necessary loans and place the lender in contact with the escrow officer;

9. assist the buyer in obtaining an inspection of the property and review the inspection with the buyer afterward;

10. assist the seller in ordering a timely pest control report and review the required corrective work;

11. make sure that the parties deliver the required documents and funds to escrow; and

12. provide any assistance the parties request or require that is within the agent's abilities, to ensure that the parties fulfill their obligations and are fully informed of the progress of the transaction.

The real estate broker for the seller may share the sales commission with a cooperating broker who brings the buyer to the transaction. An agreement between the two brokers will ensure that both understand the compensation that will be paid at the closing of the transaction. The Cooperating Broker Compensation Agreement and Escrow Instruction shown in Figure 10.2 can be used both to clarify the compensation that the cooperating broker will receive and to provide for payment of the compensation by the escrow holder.

FIGURE 10.2

Cooperating Broker Compensation Agreement and Escrow Instruction

---

CALIFORNIA ASSOCIATION OF REALTORS®

COOPERATING BROKER COMPENSATION AGREEMENT AND ESCROW INSTRUCTION
(C.A.R. Form CBC, Revised 10/02)

1. IDENTITY OF LISTING BROKER, PROPERTY AND SELLER:
_____ ("Listing Broker") is a real estate broker who has entered into a written agreement for the marketing and sale or lease of the real property or manufactured home described as _____, Assessor's Parcel No. _____, situated in _____, County of _____, California ("Property") for _____ ("Seller").

2. IDENTITY OF COOPERATING (SELLING) BROKER AND BUYER:
_____ ("Cooperating Broker") is a real estate broker licensed to practice real estate in California (or ☐ if checked _____) and represents _____ ("Buyer") who has offered, is contemplating making an offer, or has entered into a contract, to purchase or lease the Property.

3. LISTING BROKER COMPENSATION TO COOPERATING BROKER:
Provided that: **(i)** the transaction between the principals closes, and **(ii)** Listing Broker receives compensation for the transaction, Listing Broker agrees to pay Cooperating Broker, and Cooperating Broker agrees to accept, compensation as follows:
(check one)
  A. ☐ **Property is listed in the** _____ **Multiple Listing Service ("MLS"), Cooperating Broker is a participant in the MLS or reciprocal Multiple Listing Service and accepts the offer of compensation published in the MLS as:**
      _____% of the selling (or leasing) price or $_____.
OR B. ☐ **Property is listed in the** _____ **Multiple Listing Service ("MLS"), Cooperating Broker is a participant in the MLS or reciprocal Multiple Listing Service and accepts the offer of compensation as modified below:**
      _____% of the selling (or leasing) price or $_____.
OR C. ☐ **Property is listed in the** _____ **Multiple Listing Service ("MLS"), Cooperating Broker is NOT a Participant in the MLS or reciprocal Multiple Listing Service. Cooperating Broker compensation shall be:**
      _____% of the selling (or leasing) price or $_____.
OR D. ☐ **Property is NOT listed with any Multiple Listing Service. Cooperating Broker compensation shall be:**
      _____% of the selling (or leasing) price or $_____.

4. LISTING BROKER INSTRUCTION TO ESCROW HOLDER:
Listing Broker and Cooperating Broker instruct Escrow Holder to disburse to Cooperating Broker the amount specified in paragraph 3, out of Listing Broker's proceeds in escrow, and upon Close Of Escrow of the Property. This compensation instruction can be amended or revoked only with the written consent of both Brokers. Escrow Holder shall immediately notify Brokers if either Broker instructs Escrow Holder to change the terms of this instruction.

5. ACKNOWLEDGMENT:
By signing below, the undersigned acknowledges that each has read, understands, accepts and has received a Copy of this Agreement.

Listing Broker (Firm) _____
By (Agent) _____ Date _____
Address _____ City _____ State _____ Zip _____
Telephone _____ Fax _____ E-mail _____

Cooperating Broker (Firm) _____
By (Agent) _____ Date _____
Address _____ City _____ State _____ Zip _____
Telephone _____ Fax _____ E-mail _____

THIS FORM HAS BEEN APPROVED BY THE CALIFORNIA ASSOCIATION OF REALTORS® (C.A.R.). NO REPRESENTATION IS MADE AS TO THE LEGAL VALIDITY OR ADEQUACY OF ANY PROVISION IN ANY SPECIFIC TRANSACTION. A REAL ESTATE BROKER IS THE PERSON QUALIFIED TO ADVISE ON REAL ESTATE TRANSACTIONS. IF YOU DESIRE LEGAL OR TAX ADVICE, CONSULT AN APPROPRIATE PROFESSIONAL.

This form is available for use by the entire real estate industry. It is not intended to identify the user as a REALTOR®. REALTOR® is a registered collective membership mark which may be used only by members of the NATIONAL ASSOCIATION OF REALTORS® who subscribe to its Code of Ethics.

SURE TRAC
The System for Success™

Published by the
California Association of REALTORS®

EQUAL HOUSING OPPORTUNITY

CBC REVISED 10/02 (PAGE 1 OF 1) PRINT DATE

Reviewed by _____ Date _____

COOPERATING BROKER COMPENSATION AGREEMENT AND ESCROW INSTRUCTION (CBC PAGE 1 OF 1)

Source: Reprinted with permission, California Association of REALTORS®. Endorsement not implied.

FIGURE 10.3

The Escrow Process

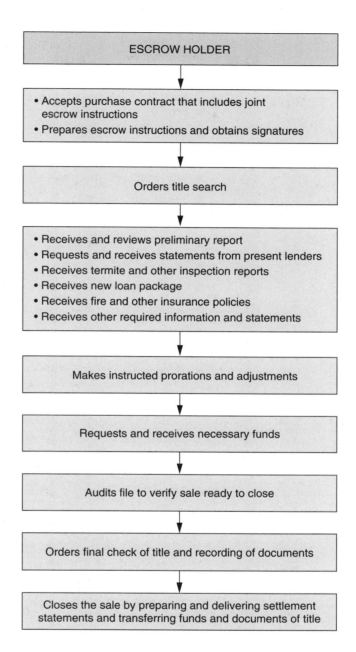

ESCROW HOLDER

- Accepts purchase contract that includes joint escrow instructions
- Prepares escrow instructions and obtains signatures

Orders title search

- Receives and reviews preliminary report
- Requests and receives statements from present lenders
- Receives termite and other inspection reports
- Receives new loan package
- Receives fire and other insurance policies
- Receives other required information and statements

Makes instructed prorations and adjustments

Requests and receives necessary funds

Audits file to verify sale ready to close

Orders final check of title and recording of documents

Closes the sale by preparing and delivering settlement statements and transferring funds and documents of title

Responsibilities of the Escrow Holder

Although local practices may vary somewhat, the duties of the **escrow holder** generally include those listed below and in the flowchart shown in Figure 10.3. Throughout this section we refer to the **escrow officer,** someone employed by an escrow company or escrow holder to handle escrow transactions. The escrow officer follows the specific procedures required by the escrow company or escrow holder, which vary from company to company and may be quite detailed.

Escrow instructions.   The escrow holder in a residential property sale typically uses a printed form of escrow instructions listing what buyer and seller must do.

Both buyer and seller *must* sign the instructions. The instructions will include such items as the

- purchase price,
- terms,
- financing provisions,
- how buyer's title is to vest,
- encumbrances that will affect the buyer's title,
- conditions affecting the transaction,
- date of closing,
- required inspections and other reports,
- expenses to be prorated,
- date on which buyer will take possession of the property,
- documents involved, and
- disbursements to be made and who will pay for them.

Since 1999 the CAR Residential Purchase Agreement (Form RPA-CA, described in Chapter 7 of this book) has included joint basic escrow instructions. Most escrow companies now send out instructions that serve as a supplement/addendum to the contract, stipulating their additional general provisions of escrow practice and providing disclosures required by federal and state laws applicable to escrow agents.

Title search.   Following a request by the escrow officer, the title company named by the parties searches the title records and provides a **preliminary report.** The preliminary report should identify the property and current owner of record, as well as any recorded liens or other encumbrances. The escrow holder reads the report to verify the legal description and to determine if there are any child support liens, taxes, or judgments for which a release will be required prior to the close of escrow. The buyer is required to review and sign acceptance of the preliminary report.

Lenders' statements.   If the property is encumbered by any loans, the escrow officer contacts all lenders. Each is asked to provide either a **demand for payoff** (if the loan is to be paid in full through escrow) or a **beneficiary statement** (if the buyer will take title subject to loans of record).

Termite and other reports.   The escrow officer receives all reports authorized by the escrow instructions and obtains the necessary *approvals* of those reports by the parties. Such reports might include a structural pest control report or a roof, an electrical, a foundation, or a soil report. If the seller has agreed to pay for indicated repairs through escrow, provision for that payment at closing must be made.

New loan package.   Most often, the buyer obtains new financing. In that case, the escrow officer receives the appropriate loan documents and instructions, obtains the buyer's signature of approval, and makes sure all conditions are met before funds are disbursed at closing.

Fire and other insurance policies.   Prudent buyers arrange to insure property they purchase, effective as soon as they take title. Lenders will insist on a policy that adequately covers the cost to repair or replace the improvements. The escrow officer must obtain, on behalf of the buyer, a copy of the **policy commitment.**

Other information and statements.   The closing may require information on property taxes, assessments for improvements such as sewers, utility payments, and other property expenses that will require an accounting at the time of closing. If the property is rented, rent payments and security deposits also may be part of the computations. Other statements, such as the FHA appraisal value required in an FHA-insured sale, are required as indicated in Chapter 9, "Government-Sponsored and Other Financing."

Prorations and adjustments.   The escrow holder, who has received all of the required information, then computes the necessary **prorations** of items charged to buyer and seller. These may include insurance, taxes, assessments, utilities, and security deposits and rents.

Tax prorations will depend on whether or not the tax has been paid. Prepaid taxes will be a credit to the seller and debit to the buyer. If current tax due has not been paid, the seller will be debited and the buyer credited the amount of tax owed up to the day of closing.

Taxes are prorated as of July 1, the first day of the tax year, or January 1, the beginning of the second half of the tax year. The escrow holder also prorates the buyer's mortgage interest as of the date funds are disbursed. Because interest payments always are made in arrears (that is, for the month just past), interest for the number of days from closing to the start of the first full month must be computed.

In most prorations, a **30-day month** is used. (In interest prorations, the lender sometimes insists on the actual number of days in the month—31, for instance.) Prorations typically assume that the buyer's rights and obligations begin on the day of closing. This means the buyer is responsible for any payments to be made for that day, such as property taxes and homeowners' association dues. It also means the buyer will receive credit for any proceeds, such as rent income, that have been received for that day.

MATH CONCEPTS

Proration is the allocation of property expenses and other charges to seller or buyer. Rents, taxes, insurance premiums, and interest on loans are only some of the expenses prorated at the time of closing a real estate transaction. Unless otherwise agreed, the standard term of 360 days per year (30 days per month) is used.

Usually, property expenses up to the day of closing are the responsibility of the seller. Depending on local custom, expenses as of the day of closing usually are the responsibility of the buyer.

■ **FOR EXAMPLE:** Ben Phillips is buying a four-unit apartment building. Monthly rents total $2,350, are due on the first day of the month, and the date of closing is October 18. What part of the October rents is Ben entitled to receive?

Using a 30-day month, rental payments are $78.33 per day ($2,350 ÷ 30). Ben will receive rents for 13 days (October 18 through October 30). Ben would thus be credited with $1,018.29 for October rents at closing ($78.33 × 13 days).

Using a 31-day month, rental payments are $75.81 ($2,350 ÷ 31) per day. Ben then would be credited with rents for 14 days, or $1,061.34 ($75.81 × 14).

If the actual number of calendar days is required, a table such as the one below can be used to calculate the number of days quickly.

| From the First Day of | To the First Day of | | | | | | | | | | | |
	Jan.	Feb.	March	April	May	June	July	Aug.	Sept.	Oct.	Nov.	Dec.
Jan.	365	31	59	90	120	151	181	212	243	273	304	334
Feb.	334	365	28	59	89	120	150	181	212	242	273	303
March	306	337	365	31	61	92	122	153	184	214	245	275
April	275	306	334	365	30	61	91	122	153	183	214	244
May	245	276	304	335	365	31	61	92	123	153	184	214
June	214	245	273	304	334	365	30	61	92	122	153	183
July	184	215	243	274	304	335	365	31	62	92	123	153
Aug.	153	184	212	243	273	304	334	365	31	61	92	122
Sept.	122	153	181	212	242	273	303	334	365	30	61	91
Oct.	92	123	151	182	212	243	273	304	335	365	31	61
Nov.	61	92	120	151	181	212	242	273	304	334	365	30
Dec.	31	62	90	121	151	182	212	243	274	304	335	365

To use the chart, add the applicable number of days in the month to the nearest full preceding month. For example, the period from June 1 to February 15 would be 260 days—245 days from June 1 to February 1, and 15 days in February. The chart does not include February 29, the extra day in the leap year every four years. In a leap year, add an extra day to all calculations that include the last day of February.

■ **FOR EXAMPLE:**   Jim and Janet Razer are buying the Landy house. The date of closing is June 16, and the key will be given to the Razers that day. The Landys have already paid both installments of the fiscal year's tax bill of $1,987.20. What amount will be charged to the Razers?

The date of closing is June 16. The Razers must pay for property taxes from June 16 to the end of the fiscal year, June 30. They thus will be charged for 15 days, or $82.80. The yearly payment of $1,987.20 is divided by 360 and that number is multiplied by 15.

Funding.   The escrow officer requests the appropriate party to deposit the required funds in the escrow account. The **lender** provides the committed percentage of the purchase price. The **buyer** (borrower) will provide whatever amount is necessary to cover the remainder of the purchase price, taking into account any deposits already made as well as additional costs of closing, such as fees and prorations.

Audit of the file.   The escrow officer *double-checks* that all conditions prior to closing have been met, including all necessary funding.

Final title review.   The escrow officer orders the title company to make a final check of the **seller's title** as of the close of business of the escrow completion date. This is done to verify that the title has not changed or been encumbered since the time of the preliminary report. If no change has occurred, the title company **records** all transaction documents.

Closing of the sale.   After the escrow officer has confirmed the recording of the transaction documents, the escrow is considered **closed**. The escrow holder will send settlements to buyer and seller, disburse funds, and deliver necessary documents as soon as possible. *Note: California law permits the lender to charge interest for no more than one day prior to the date that the loan proceeds are disbursed out of escrow or disbursed to the borrower or another party on behalf of the borrower. The law applies to notes secured by a mortgage or deed of trust on property of one to four residential units.*

Settlement statements detailing transaction costs to buyers and sellers of dwellings of one to four units are required by the **Real Estate Settlement Procedures Act (RESPA),** discussed in Chapter 8. A HUD-approved form of settlement statement (HUD-1) appears in Figure 10.4.

FIGURE 10.4

HUD-1 Settlement Statement

A. Settlement Statement | **U.S. Department of Housing and Urban Development** | OMB Approval No. 2502-0265

B. Type of Loan

1. ☐ FHA 2. ☐ FmHA 3. ☐ Conv. Unins. 4. ☐ VA 5. ☐ Conv. Ins.	6. File Number:	7. Loan Number:	8. Mortgage Insurance Case Number:

C. Note: This form is furnished to give you a statement of actual settlement costs. Amounts paid to and by the settlement agent are shown. Items marked "(p.o.c.)" were paid outside the closing; they are shown here for informational purposes and are not included in the totals.

D. Name & Address of Borrower:	E. Name & Address of Seller:	F. Name & Address of Lender:

G. Property Location:	H. Settlement Agent:	
	Place of Settlement:	I. Settlement Date:

J. Summary of Borrower's Transaction		**K. Summary of Seller's Transaction**	
100. Gross Amount Due From Borrower		**400. Gross Amount Due To Seller**	
101. Contract sales price		401. Contract sales price	
102. Personal property		402. Personal property	
103. Settlement charges to borrower (line 1400)		403.	
104.		404.	
105.		405.	
Adjustments for items paid by seller in advance		**Adjustments for items paid by seller in advance**	
106. City/town taxes to		406. City/town taxes to	
107. County taxes to		407. County taxes to	
108. Assessments to		408. Assessments to	
109.		409.	
110.		410.	
111.		411.	
112.		412.	
120. Gross Amount Due From Borrower		**420. Gross Amount Due To Seller**	
200. Amounts Paid By Or In Behalf Of Borrower		**500. Reductions In Amount Due To Seller**	
201. Deposit or earnest money		501. Excess deposit (see instructions)	
202. Principal amount of new loan(s)	502.	Settlement charges to seller (line 1400)	
203. Existing loan(s) taken subject to	503.	Existing loan(s) taken subject to	
204.		504. Payoff of first mortgage loan	
205.		505. Payoff of second mortgage loan	
206.		506.	
207.		507.	
208.		508.	
209.		509.	
Adjustments for items unpaid by seller		**Adjustments for items unpaid by seller**	
210. City/town taxes to		510. City/town taxes to	
211. County taxes to		511. County taxes to	
212. Assessments to		512. Assessments to	
213.		513.	
214.		514.	
215.		515.	
216.		516.	
217.		517.	
218.		518.	
219.		519.	
220. Total Paid By/For Borrower		**520. Total Reduction Amount Due Seller**	
300. Cash At Settlement From/To Borrower		**600. Cash At Settlement To/From Seller**	
301. Gross Amount due from borrower (line 120)		601. Gross amount due to seller (line 420)	
302. Less amounts paid by/for borrower (line 220)	( )	602. Less reductions in amt. due seller (line 520)	( )
303. Cash ☐ From ☐ To Borrower		**603. Cash ☐ To ☐ From Seller**	

Previous editions are obsolete

FIGURE 10.4

HUD-1 Settlement Statement (Continued)

L. Settlement Charges

			Paid From Borrowers Funds at Settlement	Paid From Seller's Funds at Settlement
700. Total Sales/Broker's Commission based on price $ @ % =				
Division of Commission (line 700) as follows:				
701. $	to			
702. $	to			
703. Commission paid at Settlement				
704.				
800. Items Payable In Connection With Loan				
801. Loan Origination Fee %				
802. Loan Discount %				
803. Appraisal Fee to				
804. Credit Report to				
805. Lender's Inspection Fee				
806. Mortgage Insurance Application Fee to				
807. Assumption Fee				
808.				
809.				
810.				
811.				
900. Items Required By Lender To Be Paid In Advance				
901. Interest from to @$ /day				
902. Mortgage Insurance Premium for months to				
903. Hazard Insurance Premium for years to				
904. years to				
905.				
1000. Reserves Deposited With Lender				
1001. Hazard insurance months@$ per month				
1002. Mortgage insurance months@$ per month				
1003. City property taxes months@$ per month				
1004. County property taxes months@$ per month				
1005. Annual assessments months@$ per month				
1006. months@$ per month				
1007. months@$ per month				
1008. months@$ per month				
1100. Title Charges				
1101. Settlement or closing fee to				
1102. Abstract or title search to				
1103. Title examination to				
1104. Title insurance binder to				
1105. Document preparation to				
1106. Notary fees to				
1107. Attorney's fees to				
(includes above items numbers:)				
1108. Title insurance to				
(includes above items numbers:)				
1109. Lender's coverage $				
1110. Owner's coverage $				
1111.				
1112.				
1113.				
1200. Government Recording and Transfer Charges				
1201. Recording fees: Deed $; Mortgage $; Releases $				
1202. City/county tax/stamps: Deed $; Mortgage $				
1203. State tax/stamps: Deed $; Mortgage $				
1204.				
1205.				
1300. Additional Settlement Charges				
1301. Survey to				
1302. Pest inspection to				
1303.				
1304.				
1305.				
1400. Total Settlement Charges (enter on lines 103, Section J and 502, Section K)				

Previous editions are obsolete

Exercise 10-2   Using the settlement statement form that appears in Figure 10.4, enter the details of the following residential sale transaction.

Joe and Sue Beier are purchasing the single-family house of Ed and Rita Sellar, located at 126 Courtney Place, Riverglen, California. The lender is Royal Bank. The settlement agent is California Title Company, and the place of settlement is 1234 Courtney Place, Riverglen, California. The settlement date is August 8, and the contract sale price is $749,950. No personal property is included in the sale.

Settlement charges to be paid by the borrowers total $12,472.92. Assessments (homeowners' association dues) prepaid by the sellers for the period from August 8 through September 30 total $266.13. The gross amount due from the borrowers thus is $762,689.05. The deposit is $74,995.00, and the new loan is $599,960.00. County taxes from July 1 through August 7 are $250.67. Thus $762,689.05 is due from the borrowers, and $675,205.67 has been or will be paid by the borrowers, leaving $87,483.38 to be paid by the borrowers at closing.

The sellers are credited with $216.63 for assessments from August 7 to September 30. The gross amount due the sellers thus is $750,216.13. Settlement charges to the sellers are $40,672.38. The sellers' first mortgage payoff is $186,116.51, and the second mortgage payoff is $25,390.28. On line 506 should be an express delivery fee of $10.75 incurred on the sellers' behalf; line 507 should note the $14,400 deed of trust to the buyers. County taxes of $250.67 for the period of July 1 through August 7 are credited to the sellers. Total reduction in amount due to sellers is $252,440.59. The gross amount due the sellers ($750,216.13) less total reduction ($252,440.59) thus provides $497,775.54 cash to the sellers from the closing.

The following are paid from the borrowers' funds at settlement: $6,000 loan origination fee; $47 tax service fee (line 808); $250 processing fee (line 809); $2,299.92 for 10 percent interest from August 8 to September 1 at $91.83 per day (using a 31-day month); $1,837 for a one-year hazard insurance premium to California Home Insurance; $480 for settlement or closing fee to California Title Company; $100 for document preparation to California Title Company; $20 for notary fees and $870.10 for title insurance, both paid to California Title Company. Borrower recording fees total $39 ($11 deed and $28 mortgage). The borrowers pay $125 (line 1303) as a transfer fee to the homeowners' association. Total settlement charges from the borrowers are $12,472.92.

The sellers pay $39,372.38, a 5.25 percent commission, to Frank Rice Realty and $395 for a home warranty to California Home Warranty (line 704). The sellers pay $60 for document preparation and $10 in notary fees to California Title

Company, $10 in recording fees for releases, and $825 in county deed tax stamps. Total settlement charges to the sellers are $40,672.38.

Cancellation of the Escrow.   Not every transaction reaches a successful closing. The escrow can be cancelled and the deposit returned to the buyer, only if both parties provide written instructions to the escrow holder. The Cancellation of Contract, Release of Deposit, and Joint Escrow Instructions form that appears in Figure 10.5 provides for both buyer and seller to authorize the escrow holder to cancel the escrow.

■ TITLE INSURANCE

In several earlier chapters, we have referred to the concept of **marketability of title.** Real estate has value when it can be marketed (sold). It will be easiest to sell when there are no **clouds on the title.**

Land may change hands many times over the years of documented ownership. During that time many parties may have property rights in the land, including water and mineral rights. Heirs of deceased owners may not come forward. A spouse may not join in a conveyance. How can any purchaser be sure the seller actually owns all of the rights of ownership being sold, whatever those are?

Various forms of title inspection have developed in response to the need for some guarantee that the seller actually has **good title**—title that a reasonably prudent person would accept.

Abstract of Title

In Chapter 4 we mentioned the **chain of title** from one property owner to the next. By laboriously going back through all pertinent records, including tax records and court judgments, an abstract of title can be prepared. An **abstract of title** lists every recorded change of ownership or claim on the property being examined. The abstract is accompanied by a **lawyer's opinion of title,** which comments on the present validity of any claims of lien or ownership. This way of ensuring marketability of title still is used, but it is usually a lengthy, expensive process.

Certificate of Title

When title abstractors began to perform quantities of title research, their own records became significant sources of title information. Abstract companies compiled that information into **lot books** referencing documents by property location, and **general indexes** listing names of owners alphabetically along with documents affecting their property interests. Eventually, title examiners needed to check only their company's **title plant** containing the lot books and indexes. They then

FIGURE 10.5

Cancellation of Contract, Release of Deposit, and Joint Escrow Instructions

---

CALIFORNIA ASSOCIATION OF REALTORS®

CANCELLATION OF CONTRACT, RELEASE OF DEPOSIT AND JOINT ESCROW INSTRUCTIONS
(C.A.R. Form CC, 10/03)

In accordance with the terms and conditions of the: ☐ California Residential Purchase Agreement; or ☐ Other _____ ("Agreement"), dated _____, including all amendments and related documents, on property known as _____ ("Property"), between _____ ("Buyer") and _____ ("Seller").

Paragraphs 1 and 2 below constitute escrow instructions to Escrow Holder. Release of funds (pursuant to paragraph 2) requires mutual Signed release instructions from Buyer and Seller, judicial decision or arbitration award. A party may be subject to a civil penalty of up to $1,000 for refusal to sign such instructions if no good faith dispute exists as to who is entitled to the deposited funds (Civil Code §1057.3).

1. **CANCELLATION OF CONTRACT:** ☐ Buyer or ☐ Seller cancels the Agreement and ☐ (if applicable), escrow # _____ with _____, Escrow Holder, for the following reason:

   A. ☐ Seller has failed to take the following applicable contractual action as required by the Agreement: _____
   _____.

   OR B. ☐ Seller has failed to remove the applicable contingency after being given a Notice to Seller to Perform (C.A.R. Form NSP).

   OR C. ☐ Buyer has failed to remove the applicable contingency after being given a Notice to Buyer to Perform (C.A.R. Form NBP).

   OR D. ☐ Buyer has failed to take the applicable contractual action after being given a Notice to Buyer to Perform (C.A.R. Form NBP).

   OR E. ☐ As otherwise permitted by paragraph _____ of the Agreement.

   _____ _____
   Buyer's or Seller's Signature (party cancelling the contract)   Date

   _____ _____
   Buyer's or Seller's Signature (party cancelling the contract)   Date

2. **RELEASE OF DEPOSIT**

   A. ☐ Seller authorizes release of deposit, less fees and costs, to Buyer.

   OR B. ☐ Buyer authorizes release of deposit, less fees and costs, to Seller. (☐ A liquidated damages clause was properly included as part of the Agreement, and the Property contains no more than four residential units, one of which the Buyer intended to occupy. Buyer's authorization of release of deposit to Seller is limited to no more than 3% of the purchase price. Any additional deposit to be returned to Buyer.)

   OR C. ☐ Other: _____.

   Buyer and Seller mutually release each other from all obligation to buy, sell, or exchange the Property under the Agreement, and from all claims, actions and demands that each may have against the other(s) by reason of the Agreement. Buyer and Seller intend that all rights and obligations arising out of the Agreement are null and void.

   Date _____   Date _____
   Buyer _____   Seller _____
   Buyer _____   Seller _____

The copyright laws of the United States (TITLE 17 U.S. Code) forbid the unauthorized reproduction of this form by any means, including facsimile or computerized formats. Copyright © 2003, CALIFORNIA ASSOCIATION OF REALTORS®
THIS FORM HAS BEEN APPROVED BY THE CALIFORNIA ASSOCIATION OF REALTORS® (C.A.R.). NO REPRESENTATION IS MADE AS TO THE LEGAL VALIDITY OR ADEQUACY OF ANY PROVISION IN ANY SPECIFIC TRANSACTION. A REAL ESTATE BROKER IS THE PERSON QUALIFIED TO ADVISE ON REAL ESTATE TRANSACTIONS. IF YOU DESIRE LEGAL OR TAX ADVICE, CONSULT AN APPROPRIATE PROFESSIONAL.
This form is available for use by the entire real estate industry. It is not intended to identify the user as a REALTOR®. REALTOR® is a registered collective membership mark which may be used only by members of the NATIONAL ASSOCIATION OF REALTORS® who subscribe to its Code of Ethics.

SURE TRAC
The System for Success™

Published by the
California Association of REALTORS®

CC 10/03 (PAGE 1 OF 1)   Print Date

Reviewed by _____ Date _____

CANCELLATION OF CONTRACT, RELEASE OF DEPOSIT AND JOINT ESCROW INSTRUCTIONS (CC PAGE 1 OF 1)

Source: Reprinted with permission, California Association of REALTORS®. Endorsement not implied.

could prepare a **certificate of title** stating the property's owner of record and listing any present encumbrances, usually without an attorney's opinion. The certificate of title is not often used today.

Guarantee of Title

The **guarantee of title** was next made available; it not only provided for examination of title but *guaranteed* the title as described. The title examiners using this device thus took on the responsibilities of insurers, which led to the next step in the formation of the modern title insurance industry.

Title Insurance Policies

Although the guarantee of title was useful, it was based (as were the earlier forms of title inspection) on examination of the public records. Unfortunately, there can be impediments to good title, such as forgeries or documents procured through fraud, that aren't revealed by examining public records. And not all documents may have been recorded. How, then, could the buyer be protected? The solution was the development of **title insurance**. Title insurance is available in several forms of coverage but basically insures against possible unrecorded risks.

Title insurance can be for the benefit of either *property owner* or *lender* and takes effect as of the day of closing.

Title insurance companies.   Title insurance companies in California are regulated by the state. A **title insurance company** must provide a "guarantee fund" to the Insurance Commissioner and set aside a certain amount from premiums each year as a **title insurance surplus fund.** Fee schedules must be available to the public.

Referral Fees for Title Business Are Illegal

No referral fees may be paid by any title insurer, underwritten title company or escrow company as an inducement for the placement or referral of title business. This prohibition includes both direct and indirect payments, in any form, whether or not the payment results in actual placement or referral of title business. It is part of both state law (California Insurance Code 12404) and federal law (Real Estate Settlement Procedures Act).

Standard policy.   The **standard** policy of title insurance assumes that the policyholder is able to inspect the property before purchase and determine how the land is being used and by whom. The standard policy of title insurance thus excludes

- rights or claims of persons in actual physical possession of the property (even though not shown in the public records);
- easements and liens not shown in the public records;
- any title defects known to the policyholder at the time of insurance or that would be shown by a survey;
- mining claims;
- reservations;
- water rights; or
- changes in land use dictated by zoning ordinances.

The **California Land Title Association (CLTA),** the trade association of the state's title companies, has a standard form of title insurance that its members use. Part of one of those policies, listing covered title defects as well as exceptions, appears in Figure 10.6. In practice the policy also includes a legal description of the property and lists encumbrances currently of record. If more thorough coverage than that provided in a standard policy is desired, another form of policy is available.

Extended-coverage policy.   There is an **extended-coverage** policy that is intended primarily for the benefit of **lenders.** The lender may be located some distance from the property, even out-of-state, and have no easy or inexpensive method of examining the property being encumbered. The **American Land Title Association (ALTA)** has a variety of policies, including one that extends coverage to insure property against

- rights or claims of persons in physical possession of the property (even by virtue of an unrecorded instrument);
- unrecorded easements and liens;
- rights or claims that a survey would reveal;
- mining claims;
- reservations; and
- water rights.

The property owner also can be insured by such a policy, although the ALTA extended-coverage policy will exclude any title defects actually known to the buyer at the time of purchase. Note that the ALTA extended-coverage policy, like the CLTA policy, excludes changes in land use brought about by zoning ordinances, unless there is a recorded notice of enforcement of the specified zoning.

For an additional charge, a title insurance policy will also include protection against such occurrences as post-policy issuance forgeries and forced removal of an existing structure due to prior building permit violations.

FIGURE 10.6

Policy of Title Insurance

FIGURE 10.6

Policy of Title Insurance (Continued)

EXCLUSIONS

In addition to the Exceptions in Schedule B, You are not insured against loss, costs, attorneys' fees, and expenses resulting from:

1. Governmental police power, and the existence or violation of any law or government regulation. This includes ordinances, laws and regulations concerning:

   a. building

   b. zoning

   c. land use

   d. improvements on the Land

   e. land division

   f. environmental protection

   This Exclusion does not apply to violations or the enforcement of these matters if notice of the violation or enforcement appears in the Public Records at the Policy Date.

   This Exclusion does not limit the coverage described in Covered Risk 14, 15, 16, 17 or 24.

2. The failure of Your existing structures, or any part of them, to be constructed in accordance with applicable building codes. This Exclusion does not apply to violations of building codes if notice of the violation appears in the Public Records at the Policy Date.

3. The right to take the Land by condemning it, unless:

   a. a notice of exercising the right appears in the Public Records at the Policy Date; or

   b. the taking happened before the Policy Date and is binding on You if You bought the Land without Knowing of the taking.

4. Risks:

   a. that are created, allowed, or agreed to by You, whether or not they appear in the Public Records;

   b. that are Known to You at the Policy Date, but not to Us, unless they appear in the Public Records at the Policy Date;

   c. that result in no loss to You; or

   d. that first occur after the Policy Date - this does not limit the coverage described in Covered Risk 7, 8.d, 22, 23, 24 or 25.

5. Failure to pay value for Your Title.

6. Lack of a right:

   a. to any Land outside the area specifically described and referred to in paragraph 3 of Schedule A; and

   b. in streets, alleys, or waterways that touch the Land.

   This Exclusion does not limit the coverage described in Covered Risk 11 or 18.

CONDITIONS

1. DEFINITIONS:

a. **Easement** - the right of someone else to use the Land for a special purpose.

b. **Known** - things about which You have actual knowledge. The words "Know"and "Knowing" have the same meaning as Known.

c. **Land** - the Land or condominium unit described in paragraph 3 of Schedule A and any improvements on the Land which are real property.

d. **Mortgage** - a mortgage, deed of trust, trust deed or other security instrument.

e. **Natural Person** - a human being, not a commercial or legal organization or entity. Natural Person includes a trustee of a Trust even if the trustee is not a human being.

f. **Policy Date** - the date and time shown in Schedule A. If the insured named in Schedule A first acquires the interest shown in Schedule A by an instrument recorded in the Public Records later than the date and time shown in Schedule A, the Policy Date is the date and time the instrument is recorded.

g. **Public Records** - records that give constructive notice of matters affecting Your Title, according to the state statutes where the Land is located.

h. **Title** - the ownership of Your interest in the Land, as shown in Schedule A.

i. **Trust** - a living trust established by a human being for estate planning.

j. **We/Our/Us** - First American Title Insurance Company.

k. **You/Your** - the insured named in Schedule A and also those identified in paragraph 2.b. of these Conditions.

2. CONTINUATION OF COVERAGE:

a. This Policy insures You forever, even after You no longer have Your Title. You cannot assign this Policy to anyone else.

b. This Policy also insures:

   (1) anyone who inherits Your Title because of Your death;

   (2) Your spouse who receives Your Title because of dissolution of Your marriage;

   (3) the trustee or successor trustee of a Trust to whom You transfer Your Title after the Policy Date; or

   (4) the beneficiaries of Your Trust upon Your death.

c. We may assert against the insureds identified in paragraph 2.b. any rights and defenses that We have against any previous insured under this Policy.

3. HOW TO MAKE A CLAIM

a. Prompt Notice Of Your Claim

   (1) As soon as You Know of anything that might be covered by this Policy, You must notify Us promptly in writing.

   (2) Send Your notice to First American Title Insurance Company, 114 East Fifth Street, Santa Ana, California, 92701, Attention: Claims Department. Please include the Policy number shown in Schedule A , and the county and state where the Land is located. Please enclose a copy of Your policy, if available.

   (3) If You do not give Us prompt notice, Your coverage will be reduced or ended, but only to the extent Your failure affects Our ability to resolve the claim or defend You.

b. Proof Of Your Loss

   (1) We may require You to give Us a written statement signed by You describing Your loss which includes:

   (a) the basis of Your claim;

   (b) the Covered Risks which resulted in Your loss;

   (c) the dollar amount of Your loss; and

   (d) the method You used to compute the amount of Your loss.

   (2) We may require You to make available to Us records, checks, letters, contracts, insurance policies and other papers which relate to Your claim. We may make copies of these papers.

   (3) We may require You to answer questions about Your claim under oath.

   (4) If You fail or refuse to give Us a statement of loss, answer Our questions under oath, or make available to Us the papers We request, Your coverage will be reduced or ended, but only to the extent Your failure or refusal affects Our ability to resolve the claim or defend You.

4. OUR CHOICES WHEN WE LEARN OF A CLAIM

a. After We receive Your notice, or otherwise learn, of a claim that is covered by this Policy, Our choices include one or more of the following:

   (1) Pay the claim.

   (2) Negotiate a settlement.

   (3) Bring or defend a legal action related to the claim.

   (4) Pay You the amount required by this Policy.

   (5) End the coverage of this Policy for the claim by paying You Your actual loss resulting from the Covered Risk, and those costs, attorneys' fees and expenses incurred up to that time which We are obligated to pay.

   (6) End the coverage described in Covered Risk 14, 15, 16 or 18 by paying You the amount of Your insurance then in force for the particular Covered Risk, and those costs, attorneys' fees and expenses incurred up to that time which We are obligated to pay.

   (7) End all coverage of this Policy by paying You the Policy Amount then in force and all those costs, attorneys' fees and expenses incurred up to that time which We are obligated to pay.

   (8) Take other appropriate action.

FIGURE 10.6

Policy of Title Insurance (Continued)

b. When We choose the options in paragraphs 4.a. (5), (6) or (7), all Our obligations for the claim end, including Our obligation to defend, or continue to defend, any legal action.

c. Even if We do not think that the Policy covers the claim, We may choose one or more of the options above. By doing so, We do not give up any rights.

5. HANDLING A CLAIM OR LEGAL ACTION

a. You must cooperate with Us in handling any claim or legal action and give Us all relevant information.

b. If You fail or refuse to cooperate with Us, Your coverage will be reduced or ended, but only to the extent Your failure or refusal affects Our ability to resolve the claim or defend You.

c. We are required to repay You only for those settlement costs, attorneys' fees and expenses that We approve in advance.

d. We have the right to choose the attorney when We bring or defend a legal action on Your behalf. We can appeal any decision to the highest level. We do not have to pay Your claim until the legal action is finally decided.

e. Whether or not We agree there is coverage, We can bring or defend a legal action, or take other appropriate action under this Policy. By doing so, We do not give up any rights.

6. LIMITATION OF OUR LIABILITY

a. After subtracting Your Deductible Amount if it applies, We will pay no more than the least of:

(1) Your actual loss,

(2) Our Maximum Dollar Limit of Liability then in force for the particular Covered Risk, for claims covered only under Covered Risk 14, 15, 16 or 18, or

(3) the Policy Amount then in force,

and any costs, attorneys' fees and expenses which We are obligated to pay under this Policy.

b. (1) If We remove the cause of the claim with reasonable diligence after receiving notice of it, all Our obligations for the claim end, including any obligation for loss You had while We were removing the cause of the claim.

(2) Regardless of 6.b. (1) above, if You cannot use the Land because of a claim covered by this Policy:

(a) You may rent a reasonably equivalent substitute residence and We will repay You for the actual rent You pay, until the earlier of:

(1) the cause of the claim is removed; or

(2) We pay You the amount required by this Policy. If Your claim is covered only under Covered Risk 14, 15, 16 or 18, that payment is the amount of Your insurance then in force for the particular Covered Risk.

(b) We will pay reasonable costs You pay to relocate any personal property You have the right to remove from the Land, including transportation of that personal property for up to twenty-five (25) miles from the Land, and repair of any damage to that personal property because of the relocation. The amount We will pay You under this paragraph is limited to the value of the personal property before You relocate it.

c. All payments We make under this Policy reduce the Policy Amount, except for costs, attorneys' fees and expenses. All payments we make for claims which are covered only under Covered Risk 14, 15, 16 or 18 also reduce Our Maximum Dollar Limit of Liability for the particular Covered Risk, except for costs, attorneys' fees and expenses.

d. If We issue, or have issued, a policy to the owner of a Mortgage on Your Title and We have not given You any coverage against the Mortgage, then:

(1) We have the right to pay any amount due You under this Policy to the owner of the Mortgage to reduce the amount of the Mortgage, and any amount paid shall be treated as a payment to You under this Policy, including under paragraph 4.a.of these Conditions;

(2) Any amount paid to the owner of the Mortgage shall be subtracted from the Policy Amount of this Policy; and

(3) If Your claim is covered only under Covered Risk 14, 15, 16 or 18, any amount paid to the owner of the Mortgage shall also be subtracted from Our Maximum Dollar Limit of Liability for the particular Covered Risk.

e. If You do anything to affect any right of recovery You may have against someone else, We can subtract from Our liability the amount by which You reduced the value of that right.

7. TRANSFER OF YOUR RIGHTS TO US

a. When We settle Your claim, We have all the rights You have against any person or property related to the claim. You must transfer these rights to Us when We ask, and You must not do anything to affect these rights. You must let Us use Your name in enforcing these rights.

b. We will not be liable to You if We do not pursue these rights or if We do not recover any amount that might be recoverable.

c. We will pay any money We collect from enforcing these rights in the following order

(1) to Us for the costs, attorneys' fees and expenses We paid to enforce these rights;

(2) to You for Your loss that You have not already collected;

(3) to Us for any money We paid out under this Policy on account of Your claim; and

(4) to You whatever is left.

d. If You have rights under contracts (such as indemnities, guaranties, bonds or other policies of insurance) to recover all or part of Your loss, then We have all of those rights, even if those contracts provide that those obligated have all of Your rights under this Policy.

8. ENTIRE CONTRACT

This Policy, with any endorsements, is the entire contract between You and Us. To determine the meaning of any part of this Policy, You must read the entire Policy. Any changes to this Policy must be agreed to in writing by Us. Any claim You make against Us must be made under this Policy and is subject to its terms.

9. INCREASED POLICY AMOUNT

The Policy Amount will increase by ten percent (10%) of the Policy Amount shown in Schedule A each year for the first five years following the policy date shown in Schedule A up to one hundred fifty percent (150%) of the Policy Amount shown in Schedule A. The increase each year will happen on the anniversary of the policy date shown in Schedule A.

10. SEVERABILITY

If any part of this Policy is held to be legally unenforceable, both You and We can still enforce the rest of this Policy.

11. ARBITRATION

a. If permitted in the state where the Land is located You or We may demand arbitration.

b. The arbitration shall be binding on both You and Us. The arbitration shall decide any matter in dispute between You and Us.

c. The arbitration award may be entered as a judgment in the proper court

d. The arbitration shall be under the Title Insurance Arbitration Rules of the American Arbitration Association. You may choose current Rules or Rules in existence on the Policy Date.

e. The law used in the arbitration is the law of the place where the Land is located.

f. You can get a copy of the Rules from Us.

Preliminary report.   After the title insurance policy is ordered and before the sale closes, the title insurer submits a **preliminary report** to the purchaser through the escrow holder. The preliminary report

- describes the property and names the owner of record;
- indicates any outstanding taxes, bonds, and assessments;
- identifies any conditions and restrictions on the property; and
- lists any recorded encumbrances or other items that will be exceptions to the title insurance coverage. These need to be cleared before the loan can be made, because the title insurance will not protect the lender's interest against them.

Title insurance fees.   Title insurance is paid for in a single payment. The expense of title insurance can be paid by either buyer or seller, as the parties negotiate.

- The policy fee for title insurance benefiting the *lender* typically is paid by the borrower (buyer).
- Title insurance benefiting the *buyer* could be paid for by either buyer or seller.

Local custom varies throughout the state and even from county to county.

Title companies as escrows.   Because use of title insurance is so common in California, title companies frequently serve as escrow agents.

Notice If No Title Insurance

Title insurance has become such a necessary and accepted part of real estate transactions, California law (Civil Code 1057.6) requires notice to be given if title insurance will not be provided. If title insurance will not be issued in an escrow transaction for the purchase or simultaneous exchange of real property, the purchaser or exchange parties must receive the following notice in a separate document that must be signed and acknowledged by them.

IMPORTANT: IN A PURCHASE OR EXCHANGE OF REAL PROPERTY, IT MAY BE ADVISABLE TO OBTAIN TITLE INSURANCE IN CONNECTION WITH THE CLOSE OF ESCROW SINCE THERE MAY BE PRIOR RECORDED LIENS AND ENCUMBRANCES WHICH AFFECT YOUR INTEREST IN THE PROPERTY BEING ACQUIRED. A NEW POLICY OF TITLE INSURANCE SHOULD BE OBTAINED IN ORDER TO ENSURE YOUR INTEREST IN THE PROPERTY THAT YOU ARE ACQUIRING.

Exercise 10-3   State the form of title protection that has each of the characteristics given below.

1. Statement of ownership of property, using the title company's own records
2. Statement of ownership of property, backed by the title company's guarantee
3. Title insurance excluding water rights
4. Title insurance including water rights
5. Complete documentation of all recorded rights and claims of property ownership
6. Title insurance excluding changes in land use brought about by zoning ordinances, with or without recorded notice

---

■ SUMMARY

The many steps involved in carrying out a real estate transaction proceed most efficiently when an **escrow agent** is appointed by the parties. The escrow, as an impartial third party, can collect the necessary paperwork and funds and make the required distribution only when all preconditions have been met. The interests of both buyer and seller can thus be protected.

To create a valid escrow there must be a **binding contract** and **conditional delivery** of instruments of transfer to the escrow holder. An escrow agent must be licensed by the state, with certain exceptions. If the parties cannot agree on terms, the escrow holder can bring a legal action known as **interpleader** to have a court determine the rights of the parties.

The lender of the seller will make a **demand for payoff** or submit a **beneficiary statement** if title is to be taken subject to an existing loan. The lender of the buyer will submit a loan package requiring an **appraisal** and **hazard insurance,** among other items. A **preliminary report** will indicate the current owner of record of the property and any encumbrances of record. A **structural pest control report** may indicate needed repairs. When all conditions have been met, the escrow is complete. A **settlement statement** summarizes the collection and distribution of the proceeds of the sale.

Above all, the buyer wants a **marketable title**—one a prudent person would accept. Through various forms of title examination and verification the present system of **title insurance** has been devised. A **standard policy** insures against certain risks. An **extended-coverage policy** provides more extensive coverage and is particularly useful to lenders. Referral fees for placement or referral of title business are never allowed.

If title insurance will not be issued as part of the escrow for the purchase or simultaneous exchange of real property, notice must be given to the purchaser or parties to the exchange.

■ IMPORTANT TERMS

Make sure you understand the following terms before you take the achievement examination.

abstract of title	general indexes
beneficiary statement	guarantee of title
binding contract	interpleader
certificate of title	loan commitment
close of escrow	lot books
conditional delivery	preliminary report
demand for payoff	prorations
escrow	settlement statement
escrow agent	standard policy
escrow holder	title insurance
escrow instructions	title insurance company
escrow officer	title insurance surplus fund
extended-coverage policy	title plant

■ OPEN FOR DISCUSSION

As you learned in this chapter, the details of the escrow process vary throughout the state. The number of documents produced during even a modest home purchase can be staggering.

Suggest ways in which the escrow process might be simplified.

■ ACHIEVEMENT EXAMINATION 10

1. To create an escrow there must be
   a. a binding contract.
   b. unconditional delivery.
   c. real property.
   d. All of these

2. Escrow instructions can be
   a. changed by oral agreement.
   b. only unilateral.
   c. changed only by written agreement of both parties.
   d. All of the above

3. The escrow holder acts in the capacity of
   a. mediator.
   b. agent of both parties.
   c. adviser on the transaction.
   d. surety.

4. Which of the following must be licensed as escrow agents to perform such services?
   a. Attorneys
   b. Title insurance companies
   c. Banks
   d. Escrow companies

5. In southern California, escrows are most often held by
   a. savings and loan associations.
   b. escrow companies.
   c. title insurance companies.
   d. attorneys.

6. By law a licensed escrow agent must
   a. pay a referral fee to a real estate agent.
   b. disclose information concerning the transaction to outside parties.
   c. be a corporation.
   d. have a real estate broker's license.

7. A real estate broker can serve as an escrow
   a. through associates.
   b. with other brokers.
   c. when he or she represents one of the parties to the transaction.
   d. under a fictitious business name.

8. The legal action that may be brought by an escrow holder is
   a. quiet title.
   b. interpleader.
   c. adverse possession.
   d. injunction.

9. Providing a copy of any buyer-broker agreement is the responsibility of the
   a. buyer.
   b. seller.
   c. escrow agent.
   d. real estate agent.

10. Providing tenant information is the responsibility of the
    a. buyer.
    b. seller.
    c. escrow agent.
    d. real estate agent.

11. Prorations at closing on amounts other than interest payments usually are based on
    a. a 30-day month.
    b. a 31-day month.
    c. the actual calendar number of days.
    d. the number of days indicated by the buyer.

12. If closing is on May 19, what amount will be charged to the buyers on a total property tax of $4,320 paid by the sellers for the current tax year? Remember to use the standard number of days in the month.
    a. $492
    c. $1,584
    b. $504
    d. $1,728

13. Closing is on June 15, and rent of $2,400 has been prepaid for the current month. What amount will the seller be debited at closing if the buyer receives credit for the day of closing?
    a. $1,280
    c. $1,350
    b. $1,200
    d. $2,200

14. A buyer's settlement statement includes
    a. only prorations chargeable to the buyer.
    b. the borrower's loan application.
    c. loan origination fees.
    d. all encumbrances of record.

15. The most thorough method of title check results in a(n)
    a. abstract of title.
    b. certificate of title.
    c. guarantee of title.
    d. policy of title insurance.

16. A title plant consists of
    a. all possible title records.
    b. a title company's lot books and general indexes.
    c. recorded and unrecorded title information.
    d. duplicates of county recorder's records.

17. Title insurance is paid as of the day
    a. escrow opens.
    b. the sales contract is executed.
    c. of closing.
    d. the buyer takes possession.

18. Title insurance protects a buyer against
    a. all claims from any source.
    b. all claims except those excluded by the policy.
    c. claims arising from the buyer's future actions.
    d. any claims the buyer already knows about.

19. Water rights are excluded from coverage in
    a. a standard policy of title insurance.
    b. an extended-coverage policy of title insurance.
    c. a warranty deed.
    d. all residential title insurance policies.

20. Lender's title insurance typically is paid by the
    a. buyer.
    c. lender.
    b. seller.
    d. broker.

CHAPTER ELEVEN

11

REAL ESTATE TAXATION

■ PROPERTY TAXATION

Property taxes usually are **ad valorem** taxes. They are charged in relation to the value of the property taxed. Real property provides an easily measured source of wealth for purposes of taxation. The average homeowner might not feel wealthy, but the median value of a California home is over $420,000.

Proposition 13

In 1978, California voters passed **Proposition 13,** an amendment to the California Constitution that is now Section 110.1 of the Revenue and Taxation Code. A summary of the major provisions of Proposition 13 and subsequent voter initiatives follows.

Tax rate. The *maximum* annual tax on real property set by the Board of Supervisors of each county can be no more than

- 1 percent of base year value, allowing for an annual inflation factor of no more than 2 percent, *plus*
- an additional amount to pay for indebtedness (such as transit bonds) that was already approved by voters prior to passage of Proposition 13, which generally ranges from one-quarter to one-fifth of 1 percent of property value, *and*
- bonded indebtedness approved by voters after July 1, 1978.

Property value.   The **base value** of a property is its full cash value (market value) as of February 28, 1975, or the date of a subsequent **reassessment event. Assessed value,** for property tax purposes, is the property value to which the tax rate is applied.

The rules are

- If there has been no change in the property (addition, remodeling, or other improvement) *or* its ownership since February 28, 1975, assessed value is base value as of that date *plus* an annual inflation factor of no more than 2 percent.
- If the property has been sold or has changed ownership since February 28, 1975, assessed value is the full cash value as of the date of sale or change of ownership (the base value) *plus* an inflation factor of no more than 2 percent annually in subsequent years.
- For new construction since February 28, 1975, the assessed value is the full cash value as of completion of construction (the base value) *plus* an inflation factor of no more than 2 percent annually in subsequent years.
- If existing or new property has been improved since February 28, 1975, assessed value is the base value *plus* the value of the improvement *plus* an inflation factor of no more than 2 percent annually in subsequent years.

Special rules.   Real property values have increased significantly since enactment of Proposition 13. As a result, when there is a reassessment event (property is sold or remodeled), the result in virtually all cases has been a substantial increase in the property tax base value. Taxpayers responded by passing numerous propositions to limit the effect of Proposition 13. Now the terms **purchase** and **change of ownership** do *not* include

- the transfer of real property between spouses and
- the transfer of a principal residence and the first $1 million of other real property between parents and children.

Homeowners over age 55 may be able to transfer a low assessed value to a new home.

Homeowners older than age 55 who buy or build another residence within the same county can transfer the assessed value of the previous residence to the new residence. Homeowners older than age 55 may transfer assessed value to a new residence in another county, if allowed by the new county. An application form must be submitted within three years of the purchase of the replacement property.

Severely disabled homeowners can transfer their present assessed valuation to a replacement home in the same manner available to those older than age 55. In addition, property improvements that enhance the usability of a home by a severely disabled person are not subject to reassessment.

Property Tax Collection

The **county assessor** is the elected official responsible for determining assessed values and preparing the tax roll. Anyone who acquires an interest in real property must file a **change in ownership statement** with the county recorder or assessor *within 45 days* of the date the transfer is recorded. If the transfer is not recorded, the statement must be filed within 45 days of the date of the change in ownership. The penalty for failure to file within 45 days of a written request by the assessor is $100 or 10 percent of the tax computed on the new base property value, whichever is greater. The penalty also applies if complete information is not supplied following a second request.

Taxpayer Rights

The **Morgan Property Taxpayers' Bill of Rights** requires the county assessor to allow inspection and copying of documents related to an assessed property, including an auditor's work papers.

www.boe.ca.gov

Information on property taxpayer rights can be found at the State Board of Equalization's Web site, *www.boe.ca.gov,* as well as from:

State Board of Equalization
Taxpayers' Rights Advocate's Office
P.O. Box 942879
Sacramento, CA 94279-0070
Phone: (916) 324-2798
Fax: (916) 323-3319

www.co.la.ca.us/
http://assessor.co.la.ca.us/

Tax bill information for Los Angeles County is available at *www.co.la.ca.us/.* Assessment information, including forms, can be found at the Los Angeles County Assessor Online Public Service, *http://assessor.co.la.ca.us/.*

A taxpayer who disagrees with the assessor's opinion of value may **appeal** that decision by contacting the local assessor's office or appeals board office. Time limitations apply on bringing an appeal, so the taxpayer should do so as quickly as possible and be prepared to offer **appraisal data** refuting the assessor's estimate and substantiating the taxpayer's valuation.

■ **FOR EXAMPLE:** The Smiths decide to add a few rooms to their home. They get a building permit for their planned addition of 1,500 square feet and hire a contractor. While the work is under way, an appraiser from the assessor's office comes by to look at the extent of the property improvement. When the work is finished, the appraiser comes by again, but the Smiths refuse to allow the appraiser to see the finished improvement. Judging from the outside of the property the appraiser estimates that the finished addition is 2,100 square feet. Based on that estimate, the property is reassessed and the Smiths' property tax bill increased accordingly. The Smiths then appeal the assessment, claiming that the finished addition is actually no more than 1,650 square feet and the assessment should be reduced to reflect that fact.

In this case, the court held that the assessor's estimate is the only reasonable basis on which the reassessment can be made. The Smiths' statement of the square footage of the addition is self-serving and therefore cannot serve as the basis for reassessment. The Smiths cannot complain that the estimate is inexact, because the Smiths themselves refused the assessor's appraiser access to the property.

Exemptions

The general rule is that all real property and tangible personal property (except business inventory) is taxable. Property that is **exempt** from taxation includes

- intangible property (such as stocks and promissory notes);
- personal property and household furnishings of individuals;
- property owned by a government, unless the property is outside the jurisdiction of the public entity and was taxable before acquisition, or it is new construction replacing property that was taxable when acquired;
- property used exclusively for religious, charitable, or hospital purposes; and
- property owned by nonprofit organizations, such as private schools and colleges.

In addition, many boats and seagoing vessels, as well as agricultural products (such as growing crops, fruit and nut-bearing trees less than five years old, and grapevines less than three years old) are exempt.

Homeowner's exemption. An owner-occupied residence, including a condominium or duplex unit, qualifies for a **homeowner's exemption** of the first $7,000 of full cash value. The residence must be occupied by the lien date (January 1). A form available from the county tax assessor must be completed by the owner and filed by 5 P.M. on February 15 of the tax year to receive the exemption.

If the owner's occupancy ceases, the county tax assessor must be notified, or an assessment plus 25 percent penalty will be made.

Multiply the exemption amount by four to find its full value.

Veteran's exemption. Qualified California war veterans are entitled to a $4,000 **veteran's exemption** on property not already subject to the homeowner's exemption. A veteran owning $5,000 of any type of property ($10,000 if owned by husband and wife) is ineligible. One-fourth of the value of taxable property and the full value of exempt property are included in calculating the total property owned. The $4,000 exemption also is available for the unmarried surviving spouse or pensioned father or mother of a qualified deceased veteran.

FIGURE 11.1

Important Dates in the Property Tax Year

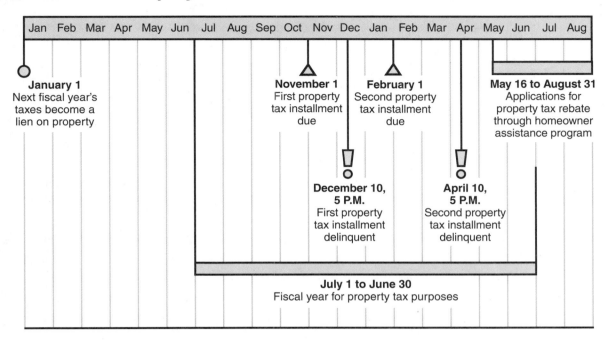

Qualified **disabled veterans** are entitled to a separate exemption. The principal residence of a veteran who is totally disabled is exempt up to $150,000, regardless of the veteran's other income or assets. An unmarried surviving spouse of a qualified veteran also is entitled to the exemption.

How to Compute the Basic Tax Rate

The **property tax year,** as shown in Figure 11.1, runs from July 1 through the following June 30. Property tax is payable in two installments due November 1 and February 1. The November payment is delinquent after 5 P.M. on December 10, and the February payment is delinquent after 5 P.M. on April 10. If those dates fall on a weekend or legal holiday, the deadline is 5 P.M. of the next business day.

A 10 percent **penalty** is added to delinquent installments. After the second delinquent installment, a $10 fee is charged for adding the property to the delinquent roll.

■ **FOR EXAMPLE:** Carol and Bill Waters have owned their home in Valley Meadow since 1974. The assessor's appraised value of the Waters home at the time Proposition 13 went into effect was $62,000, and the Waters receive a homeowner's exemption. There are no additional assessments, although there has been an annual increase of 2 percent in assessed valuation due to inflation. The current assessed value of the Waters' home is thus $110,200. What tax do the Waters currently pay? What amount is due in the first installment? What amount will be due if that installment is paid after December 10?

Assessor's appraised value	$110,200.00
Less homeowner's exemption	7,000.00
Taxable amount	$103,200.00
Tax rate (.01)	.01
Tax	$ 1,032.00
Installment	$ 516.00
Delinquent payment	$ 567.60

The impact of Proposition 13 is apparent when comparing its effect on similar properties when one has undergone a reassessment event and the other has not.

■ **FOR EXAMPLE:** John and Mildred Marsh, neighbors of Carol and Bill Waters, moved to their home in Valley Meadow in 1996. The purchase price of their home was $308,000. With the 2 percent inflation factor applied each year since, the assessed value of the Marsh home is now $340,056.88. The Marshes receive a homeowner's exemption. What is the Marshes' total tax? The first installment? The delinquent payment on the first installment?

Base value	$340,056.88
Less homeowner's exemption	7,000.00
Taxable amount	$333,056.88
Tax rate	.01
Tax	$ 3,330.57
Installment	$ 1,665.29
Delinquent payment	$ 1,831.82

Exercise 11-1   Mark Jones, single, purchased a home in Valley Meadow on July 1, 2000. The purchase price was $395,000, and Mark is entitled to a homeowner's exemption. Compute Mark's first year property tax bill, the amount of each installment, and the amount of the delinquent payment.

Supplemental Assessments

Few people take possession of real estate on July 1, the first day of the tax year. For the first few years after Proposition 13 took effect, reassessments following property purchase, transfer, construction, or improvement were made only on the next January 1, even if the reassessment event occurred earlier.

As of July 1, 1983, new procedures were put into effect to make sure property is reassessed as quickly as possible. Now if the reassessment event takes place between January 1 and May 31, there are two **supplemental assessments** to adjust for any increase in tax liability. If the reassessment event takes place between June 1 and the last day of December, there is one supplemental assessment. A Notice of Supplemental Assessment may be appealed within 60 days of issuance of the notice.

Tax Lien

When a lien is created.   On January 1, when the assessment roll takes effect for the next tax year, a **lien** is placed on all assessed real property in the amount of the tax due.

> Real property can also serve as security for personal property taxes.

Taxes on personal property also may be liens on secured real property if they are listed with or cross-referenced to real property on the secured assessment roll. The assessor determines whether the real property is sufficient security for the personal property tax. At the taxpayer's request, real property owned by the taxpayer elsewhere in the county also may secure the personal property tax lien. Before the lien date the assessor issues and records a certificate to that effect. The real and personal property are cross-referenced in the tax rolls.

Priority of property tax lien.   The **property tax lien** takes priority over all others, with some exceptions. The exceptions are for the following:

- Holders of a security interest or mechanic's lien
- Someone who bought the property or took title to it without knowledge of the lien
- A judgment lien creditor who acquired a right, title, or interest, prior to the recording of the property tax lien

Redemption

On June 8 of the tax year, the delinquent tax list is published in a local newspaper of general circulation. **Unpaid taxes** are subject to delinquency payments. Over time, the amount owed also is increased by additional costs, interest, and redemption penalties. If a taxpayer begins making currently due payments, such arrearages may be paid in five annual installments. At the time all past due amounts have been paid, the county tax collector issues a **certificate of redemption.**

Tax Sale

If property is not redeemed by the owner within **five years** it may be sold. If the property is damaged by a disaster and is located in an area declared to be a disaster area by local, state, or federal officials, the five-year period begins running from the date of the damage. After the applicable five-year period, the tax collector has two years in which to sell the property. The former owner's right to redeem the property is in effect until the close of business on the last business day before a sale occurs.

The tax collector can sell the property to a taxing agency, revenue district, or certain nonprofit organizations. A nonprofit organization purchasing residential property must rehabilitate the property and sell it to low-income persons. If the property is vacant, the organization can dedicate it to public use or construct housing for low-income purchasers.

The tax collector also can sell the property to the highest bidder at **public auction.** The County Board of Supervisors approves the minimum bid. The sale price at auction must equal at least 50 percent of the property's fair market value as determined by the county assessor within one year prior to the auction date. The high bid must be paid in cash or negotiable paper, or a combination of the two, as the tax collector decides.

The purchaser at a tax sale receives a **tax deed.**

Tax Relief for Renters

Renters pay property taxes, in effect, when they pay rent. In recognition of this fact, there is a state income tax credit available to qualified renters meeting income limits. The credit was first available in the 1998 tax year. Details of the income qualifications are in Assembly Bill 2797 (Cardoza).

Property Tax Postponement and Homeowner Assistance

The state recognizes that many older people on fixed incomes are property owners but have little funds to set aside for taxes. The **Property Tax Postponement Law** allows a senior citizen (person aged 62 or older) to postpone payment of taxes on his or her personal residence. Postponement also may be made by persons who are blind or disabled, as defined in the law. If the applicant is married, only one spouse need qualify. The individual applying for postponement must

> A senior citizen is aged 62 or older.

- own, occupy, and have at least a 20 percent equity interest in the property, based on its assessed value, and
- have an annual total household income of no more than $24,000.

The deferral of property tax creates a lien on the property in favor of the state. Interest on the amount of tax postponed is charged at the rate earned by California's Pooled Money Investment Fund. There is no time limit on the deferral amount and interest, which are recovered by the state when

- the property is *sold,*
- the claimant *no longer occupies* the property, or
- the claimant *no longer qualifies.*

www.sco.ca.gov

Information and claim forms can be obtained from the State Controller's Office, Box 942005, Sacramento, 94250-2005, by calling 1-800-952-5661, or by visiting the Web site of the State Controller at *www.sco.ca.gov.*

Older taxpayers also may qualify for a rebate (refund) of property tax already paid through the **Homeowner Assistance Program.** This program is available to senior citizens and to blind or disabled citizens of any age, provided the taxpayer has a household income of no more than $12,000. The taxpayer must file an application with the Franchise Tax Board between May 16 and August 31 to be entitled to the reimbursement for that fiscal year. The exact amount of the reimbursement is determined by the Franchise Tax Board.

An eligible taxpayer may apply for both property tax postponement and the Homeowner Assistance Program. The amount of any rebate granted will be applied against the lien created by the postponement.

Special Assessments

A **special assessment** is imposed on real property for a specific local purpose, such as sewer or street construction or repair. A special assessment will appear as a separate entry on the property tax bill. Special assessments are made on an ***ad valorem*** basis (according to property value) and also are liens on the property until paid.

Special assessments require approval of **two-thirds of voters.** Assessments are proposed by a local governing body or by an improvement district created by a city or county, as provided by state law. An assessment for a particular project can be made in one tax period or spread out over a number of years.

Improvement districts also secure financing by issuing **bonds** that are repaid by assessments.

Benefit Assessments

A **benefit assessment** also may be called a **local assessment, levy based on other than assessed value, special benefit assessment,** or **special assessment.** It is different in form and effect from a true special assessment, however.

A benefit assessment differs from a special assessment in that its tax base is only the properties benefited. Also, a benefit assessment is *not* a deductible tax for federal and state income tax purposes. A benefit assessment is considered a nondeductible assessment to finance a property improvement, rather than a deductible assessment to finance maintenance.

Benefit assessments have been specifically authorized by the state through various measures since 1885. An **improvement area** is created to assess only the property benefited by the improvement. Examples of improvements include grading and finishing of streets, construction of sewers, and acquisition of public utilities. As with special assessments, bonds may be issued for benefit assessments and repaid by tax levy.

Mello-Roos and Other Disclosures

A special form of property assessment is that created by the **Mello-Roos Community Facilities Act.** This law expanded the type of facilities and services that could be provided by improvement bonds and also eliminated the requirement that improvements specifically benefit individual properties. Mello-Roos assessments still are a lien on property, but amounts owed are billed and collected separately from other property taxes.

Because of confusion over the nature of Mello-Roos assessments and the fact that they do not appear on the property tax bill, a seller of a one- to four-unit dwelling subject to a Mello-Roos assessment must **disclose** that fact to a prospective purchaser.

Disclosure must also be made if there are any fixed lien assessments on the property to pay bonds issued under the Improvement Bond Act of 1915 (Streets and Highways Code 8500 and following). Until December 31, 2004, this disclosure requirement can be satisfied by providing the buyer with a copy of the most recent year's property tax bill or an itemization of current assessment amounts applicable to the property. Assessments may also be made under the Street Improvement Act of 1911.

Documentary Transfer Tax

California allows a city or county to impose a **documentary transfer tax** on all transfers of real property located in the jurisdiction. Notice of payment of the documentary transfer tax usually appears on the face of the deed transferring title, but it also can appear on a separate paper filed with the deed.

If a **county** has adopted a transfer tax, a **city** within the county may adopt a similar ordinance.

> Transfer tax is $.55 per $500 of new money changing hands. It does not include any loan being assumed.

The **tax rate** is 55 cents per $500 or fraction of $500 of the consideration (price) paid for the property. There is no tax if the total consideration is $100 or less (such as the "love and affection" stated as consideration in a gift deed). In computing transfer tax, the consideration paid for the property excludes any preexisting liens or encumbrances that were not removed by the sale (such as an assumed loan). If a portion of the sales price is not subject to the documentary transfer tax, that information must be provided on the deed or a separate paper filed with the deed. The declaration of the amount of tax due must state whether the property consideration or value was or was not exclusive of the value of any remaining lien or encumbrance.

■ **FOR EXAMPLE:**   The 1200 Via Loca house is sold for $687,575. An existing first trust deed of $524,000 is assumed by the purchaser. What amount of documentary transfer tax may be charged?

$$\$687,575 - 524,000 = \$163,575$$
$$\$163,575 \div 500 = \$327.15, \text{ rounded up to } 328$$
$$\$328 \times .55 = \$180.40 \text{ transfer tax}$$

Cities sometimes impose documentary transfer tax far in excess of the minimum charged by most counties. For example, the following cities have passed ordinances imposing the indicated transfer tax per $1,000 of value transferred:

Alameda County		Los Angeles County	
Alameda	$5.40	Culver City	$4.50
Berkeley	$15.00	Los Angeles	$4.50
Piedmont	$13.00	Pomona	$2.20
Oakland	$15.00	Redondo Beach	$2.20
Hayward	$4.50	Santa Monica	$3.00

■ **FOR EXAMPLE:**   The 1200 Via Loca house in the last example is located in Los Angeles. If the sales price and assumed loan amount are the same, what is the total amount of documentary transfer tax that will be charged?

$$\$163,575 \div 1,000 = \$163.575, \text{ rounded to } 164$$
$$\$164 \times 4.50 = \$738$$
$$\$738 + 180.40 = \$918.40 \text{ transfer tax}$$

Taxation of Manufactured Homes

http://housing.hcd.ca.gov

Manufactured (mobile) homes can be either personal property or real property. As **personal property,** a manufactured home is subject to vehicle license fee status. Vehicle license fee status means that title to the manufactured home is registered with the Department of Housing and Community Development (HCD). HCD's Web site can be found at *http://housing.hcd.ca.gov*. If treated as **real property,** a manufactured home is subject to local real property taxation.

Qualification as real property.   A manufactured home qualifies as **real** property under the Health and Safety Code if

- a building permit is obtained,
- the home is attached to a foundation,
- a certificate of occupancy is obtained, and
- a document stating that the home is attached to a foundation is recorded.

The manufactured home is then treated as a fixture or an improvement to the real estate. HCD cancels its title registration, and title is registered with the county recorder where the manufactured home is located.

There are specific conditions for *removal* of a manufactured home from its foundation. All property owners must give written consent, supplied to HCD, and the local assessor must be notified by 30 days in advance of the move. A transportation permit or mobile-home registration is issued by HCD, as appropriate.

After removal from its foundation, a manufactured home becomes personal property until it again qualifies as real property.

Other State Taxes

Sales tax and use tax. Information concerning sales tax and use tax is available from the local office of the State Board of Equalization.

California Sales Tax

The current *minimum* sales tax charged in California is 7.25 percent of gross receipts. In the past the state has received 6 percent, the counties .25 percent, and the local taxing authorities 1 percent.

In addition to the minimum sales tax rate, individual counties can add charges and typically do so to cover transportation or water district costs. San Francisco has an 8.5 percent sales tax rate; Los Angeles has an 8.25 percent sales tax rate. A complete list of counties and sales tax rates is available at the State Board of Equalization's Web site, *www.boe.ca.gov.*

---

www.boe.ca.gov

State **sales tax** is owed by retailers of tangible personal property regardless of whether or not the tax was paid by a customer. There are exceptions. Sales of food, for instance, are *not* taxed. The retailer can add sales tax to the product price paid by the customer or pay the tax separately. Buildings removed from land by a seller may be subject to sales tax. Buildings removed by a buyer as part of a transaction are not subject to sales tax. When a business is sold, *fixtures* are subject to sales tax, but *inventory* is not.

Use tax is charged to the purchaser for storage, use, or other consumption of certain purchased or leased tangible personal property. The purchaser is not liable for the tax if the tax was paid to a retailer who has a **seller's permit** to collect it.

If a business requiring a seller's permit is sold, the buyer may be liable for tax owed by the seller. The sale of any business that requires a seller's permit should include provision for an amount to be held in escrow until the State Board of Equalization provides a **tax clearance.**

Broker sales of manufactured homes.   A real estate broker selling manufactured homes as a **retailer** must obtain a seller's permit and report applicable sales or use tax.

New manufactured homes sold as dwellings on or after July 1, 1980, are subject to sales tax on 75 percent of selling price, in addition to property tax. Unattached furnishings are subject to the regular full retail sales tax. Used manufactured homes subject to property tax are exempt from sales tax (except for unattached furnishings). Sales tax applies to manufactured homes that are subject to license fees.

A real estate broker may act as an agent in the sale of a manufactured home, rather than as a dealer. As an agent, the broker should be aware that the sale of a manufactured home that is subject to *property tax* will involve neither sales nor use tax. The purchaser of a manufactured home that is *not* subject to property tax will be charged use tax on the purchase price.

State Inheritance, Gift, and Estate Taxes

To take advantage of federal inheritance tax credits, the California **inheritance tax** and **gift tax** were repealed by voters on June 8, 1982, and no longer apply to estates of decedents who died or to gifts made after that date.

Proposition 6, which repealed the California inheritance and gift taxes, brought into effect the California **estate tax.** The estate tax payable is the maximum amount allowed as a credit on federal estate taxes for death taxes paid to the state. There is no increase in the total tax due, but some of the tax paid is shifted to the state rather than going to the federal government.

A **California estate tax return** must be filed and tax paid, if any is due, within nine months after the date of death, if a federal estate tax return is required. There is a late filing penalty of 5 percent of tax due per month or fraction of a month, to a maximum of 25 percent, which can be waived for good cause. An extension will be granted if an extension has been granted for filing of the federal tax return. Interest is charged after the initial nine-month filing period.

Federal Gift Tax

A **gift** is a voluntary transfer by an individual of any type of property for less than full consideration. The giver is the **donor;** the recipient of the gift is the **donee.** No gift tax return need be made on a gift to one donee, in one year, of a *present interest* valued at $11,000 or less. (A married couple could give $11,000 each, for a total of $22,000 to one donee in one year.) If the gift is a *future interest*, a return always must be made.

As of 1982, payments made on behalf of someone else as tuition to an educational organization or to a person who provides medical care are *not* considered gifts, no matter what the amount.

Federal gift tax returns must be filed by April 15 of the year following the gift. Even though a return must be filed, there may be a *credit* or an *exemption* available to reduce or eliminate any tax liability. Transfers between spouses, for instance, are not taxed.

Federal Estate Tax

The Economic Growth and Tax Relief Reconciliation Act of 2001 provides for a gradual phase-out of federal estate tax. In 2004, the gross estate of a deceased person had to be more than $1,500,000 before any federal estate tax was due. This amount will continue to increase through 2009, as shown in the table below. The federal estate tax will be repealed as of 2010.

Amount	Year
$1,500,000	2004
$1,500,000	2005
$1,500,000	2006
$2,000,000	2007
$2,000,000	2008
$3,500,000	2009

www.irs.gov

There is no limit on the amount of property that can be left to a spouse. For estates of decedents dying after 1997, the executor can elect to exclude the adjusted value of a qualified family-owned business interest, up to a limited amount, as set out in Section 2033A of the Internal Revenue Code. A **federal estate tax return** must be filed within nine months of death, even if there is no tax due. The **Internal Revenue Service (IRS)** makes pamphlets available that explain the applicable rules.

Federal Tax Liens

Under the Internal Revenue Code, unpaid federal taxes become a **lien** on all property and rights to property belonging to the taxpayer during the lien period, even if acquired *after* the lien arises. **Notice** of a lien against **real property** must be filed in the county recorder's office where the property is located for the lien to be effective against purchasers, mortgagees of any type, mechanics' lienors, and judgment lien creditors.

An **estate tax lien,** which is not recorded, attaches to all of the deceased's property at the moment of death. Even though unrecorded, the estate tax lien is valid against later purchasers. Two kinds of recorded estate tax liens are used when tax payments are made in installments or when real property is used in a closely held family business.

A **gift tax lien** is unrecorded. A lien in the amount of the tax is imposed on all gifts made during the year. Gift tax unpaid by the donor becomes a personal liability of the donee.

■ FEDERAL INCOME TAXES

A **federal income tax return** must be filed by April 15 for the preceding calendar year if adjusted gross income is high enough or federal income tax has been withheld and a refund is due. Both individuals and corporations are taxed, but the discussion that follows deals primarily with individuals.

The amount of **gross income** required before a tax is imposed on an individual depends on

- whether the income earner is married or single (including the divorced or legally separated),
- whether there are any dependent children, and
- if there is a spouse, whether the income earner is living with the spouse and whether income earner and spouse are filing jointly or separately.

The tax law revisions and clarifications passed by Congress in 1986, 1990, 1993, 1997, 1998, 1999, and 2001, which will be referred to here, have been phased in gradually. Bear in mind that future tax law revisions are inevitable. Your local Internal Revenue Service office has complete details on the current law.

Awareness of issues of concern does not mean that one becomes a tax adviser.

The real estate licensee should not serve as a tax adviser. But it may be in a real estate broker's or salesperson's best interest to be as familiar as possible with the tax ramifications of real estate transactions. Virtually all important decisions affecting tax liability must be made *before* a transaction is negotiated. The terms of sale will have serious implications for most taxpayers, for whom the purchase of a home is the most important investment of a lifetime. For the investor the transaction becomes even more complex. Unless a real estate licensee is qualified as an income tax or investment counselor, advice on tax and economic factors should be left to the client's tax preparer or adviser.

Tax Terms

The following is only a partial list of the many tax concepts covered by the Internal Revenue Code, but it will serve as a general introduction.

Adjusted gross income. **Adjusted gross income** is the taxpayer's total income. Not all income is taxable.

Child support payments are nontaxable income, for example, while alimony payments are considered taxable income in the year received.

Taxable income. A taxpayer's **taxable income** is found by taking allowed deductions from **adjusted gross income.** Taxpayers choose to take the standard deduction or to itemize deductions separately using the required form. Homeowners may find that the home mortgage interest and property taxes they pay, in addition to charitable and other allowed deductions, provide a greater reduction of taxable income than the standard deduction.

Tax bracket. The **tax bracket** is the tax rate applicable to a taxpayer's taxable income. The higher the taxable income, the higher the rate. At present, income up to a certain level is taxed at 10 percent, with income above that level taxed at a higher percentage. At very high income levels (more than $319,100), individual taxpayers not only are taxed at a 35 percent rate, other effects of the tax law make the highest effective tax rate 51 percent.

Ordinary income. **Ordinary income** is included in gross income for tax purposes and includes wages, business income, profits, interest, dividends, rents, and royalties, among other items.

Capital asset. A **capital asset** is all property except business inventory or other property held for sale in the ordinary course of one's business. Capital assets include a personal residence, land held for investment, stocks, bonds, and machinery and equipment used in business.

Basis. The **basis** of property generally is its cost when acquired, also known as **book value.** Certain business property can be **depreciated**—that is, its cost can be deducted from income, spread out over a number of years. The property's basis is reduced by the amount of depreciation already claimed, but it also can be increased by the cost of any improvements made. The result is an **adjusted cost basis.**

Capital gain. **Capital gain** is the difference between the sale price of a capital asset less selling costs and its adjusted cost basis.

The holding period for capital gains tax treatment is 12 months. Gains on investment real estate are taxed generally at 10 percent to 20 percent (8 percent to 18 percent for property held for at least five years). There is a depreciation recapture rate (tax on prior depreciation deductions) of 25 percent.

Depreciation. **Depreciation** is a deduction from income for the loss in value through wear and tear of property used in a trade or business or held for the production of income. In effect, depreciation allows the cost of property to be spread over its useful life. An owner-occupied residence, even though purchased for its appreciation potential, is *not* considered a depreciable investment. The cost of improvements to qualified real property can be depreciated over a certain number of years. Land is not depreciable. Later in this chapter we discuss one of the ways in which depreciation is determined.

Tax Considerations for the Homeowner

Improvements to real estate owned as a personal residence, whether house, condominium, or stock in a cooperative apartment, cannot be depreciated. **Homeowners** receive other forms of preferential treatment, however. As of August 5, 1997, homeowners are allowed an exemption from federal income taxation of up to $250,000 (for single taxpayers) or $500,000 (for a couple who are married at the time of sale) of the profit on the sale of the principal residence. The exemption will be allowed if the home was owned and occupied for two of the last five years prior to the sale.

The full $250,000 single/$500,000 married exemption is available every two years. Under certain circumstances, if qualified property is owned for less than two years, a proportionate share of the exemption can be taken. (If a residence is occupied for only one year, then sold as a result of a qualifying job relocation, 50 percent of the applicable exemption can be used.)

■ **FOR EXAMPLE:** Penelope Pilot owns her home, for which she paid $172,000, and has occupied it as her principal residence for seven years. If Penelope sells her home for $395,000, purchasing a new one a few months later for $445,000, must she pay any federal income tax on her profit?

No. Penelope's profit of $223,000 (which will be even lower after it is reduced by expenses of sale, such as a real estate commission) is less than the $250,000 profit she is allowed to receive free from federal income tax.

Deductions. **Mortgage interest payments** on first and second homes are **deductible** from taxable income on loan amounts up to $1,000,000. Interest on loans secured by a personal residence, but not used to purchase the residence (home equity loans), is deductible on loan amounts up to $100,000. Local property taxes are also deductible. For most homebuyers, such **deductions** make the difference between an affordable home payment and one that is not.

Tax credits. A **tax credit** is a direct deduction, not from income but from tax owed. Credits for home solar energy system installations, as well as energy and water conservation measures, have been available in the past. Whether they will be available again depends on whether conservation and development of alternative sources of energy are again viewed as desirable goals to be pursued, even at the expense of a loss in tax revenue.

Tax Considerations for the Investor

An **investor** is someone who buys property for its appreciation or income potential and who does not plan to occupy it personally. An investor *cannot* take advantage of the homeowner's exemption from federal income taxation, but receives other benefits of property ownership.

Mortgage interest and property taxes are deductible from property income. Property income also can be reduced by expenses of operation, such as maintenance, utilities, and property management.

Depreciation. One of the most important tax benefits for the real estate investor involves the **depreciation** of property improvements.

Property that can be depreciated, which includes buildings used in business or for rental or other income-producing activities, is called **recovery property.** The cost of real estate (after subtracting nondepreciating land value) is recovered through deductions from taxable income over a certain number of years. The 1986 tax reform law provided for the depreciable value of real estate owned as of January 1, 1987, to be deducted over 27½ years (residential rental property) or 31½ years (most other real property), in equal amounts each year. This is called the **straight-line method** of computing depreciation. The 1993 tax law revisions increased the depreciation period for commercial (nonresidential) property from 31½ to 39 years.

■ **FOR EXAMPLE:** Richard Rembrandt purchased an apartment complex for $750,000. The land is valued at $125,000 and the improvements are valued at $625,000. What is the amount of the yearly depreciation deduction available to Richard?

The depreciation deduction is $22,727 per year ($625,000 ÷ 27.5).

Investors in a real estate partnership may take allowable deductions, but only up to the amount at risk. Losses from partnership investments cannot be used to offset wages and other income.

> Those in the real estate business can deduct rental property losses from other income without limitation.

A person **actively** involved in managing rental real estate and earning less than $100,000 per year can offset up to $25,000 of losses against that income per year. The allowable deduction is phased out as income rises, and there is no deduction when income is $150,000 or more. **As of January 1, 1994, a taxpayer whose primary business is real estate (and spouse, if filing a joint return) can deduct rental property losses from "active" income, including real estate commissions, without limitation.**

The longer depreciation term currently in effect has forced many would-be investors to carefully examine the **cash-flow** (income-producing) potential of investment property. With the tax advantages of property ownership of somewhat less importance, the property buyer must consider the traditional goal of investment—the ability to generate profit through income or long-term appreciation.

Tax-Deferred Exchanges   Property held for productive use in a trade or business or for investment may be exchanged between owners and qualify for deferral of taxation. To be a **tax-deferred exchange,** as defined in **Section 1031 of the Internal Revenue Code,** the properties exchanged must be of *like kind* in nature or character. Most real property can be exchanged for other real property, such as an office building for vacant land, but property held for personal use cannot be exchanged for investment property. For example, a personal residence cannot be exchanged for a house that will be rented.

The *Starker* case set the precedent for delayed (nonsimultaneous) exchanges. Property is sold, with the proceeds held by a third party until a new property is identified (within 45 days) and purchased (within 180 days). In a reverse-Starker, the replacement property is purchased before the relinquished property is sold. *Caution:* Strict legal requirements mean that adequate counsel should be involved in planning and execution of an exchange.

The property received in an exchange will have the same **cost basis** for the recipient as the property transferred, provided that no money or other additional consideration accompanies the transfer. Additional consideration, or **boot,** will result in reportable gain for tax purposes in the amount of the cash value of the boot received.

■ **FOR EXAMPLE:**   Barbara Krause exchanged her eight-unit apartment building for a four-store strip shopping center owned by Tom Doyle. Both properties were owned free and clear, but Barbara paid $100,000 in cash in addition to turning over the deed to the apartment building. Disregarding any commission or other expenses of sale, what is the tax impact of the transaction for each party?

Barbara's tax basis in her new property is the tax basis of her old property, plus $100,000. She owes no tax on the transaction.

Tom's tax basis in his new property is the tax basis of his old property, less $100,000. In addition, Tom will be taxed on the $100,000 in boot that he received as part of the transaction.

Calculation of gain becomes more difficult when there is a mortgage on one or both properties. The taxpayer then is considered to have received income equal to the relief from indebtedness on the property transferred (the amount of the mortgage). Such **mortgage relief** is offset, however, by any indebtedness on the property received.

A real estate dealer may not make a tax-deferred exchange of property held for sale to customers and may not immediately sell property received in an exchange.

Installment Sales

In an **installment sale,** a taxpayer sells property and receives payments over a term that extends beyond the present tax year. The taxpayer can elect to report any profit on the transaction at the time of sale *or* as installment payments are received. The taxpayer's basis in the property plus costs of sale are totaled and deducted from the purchase price (if reported in the year of sale) or deducted proportionately from each tax year's installment payments, with the remainder reported as taxable income. Interest income is always taxable.

Spreading out the reporting of income usually favors the taxpayer/seller, who may avoid a step up to a higher tax bracket or who may not be able to pay the required tax in the year of sale. Investment property probably will have been depreciated by the taxpayer, however, and the taxpayer's cost basis in the property reduced accordingly. To the extent that the installment contract price exceeds the property's reduced basis, it must be reported as gain in the year of sale (for installment sales after June 6, 1984).

■ **FOR EXAMPLE:** Angela is about to close on the sale of her home. After paying sale expenses, she will receive $50,000 in cash from the equity in her home. If Angela takes the $50,000 cash and places the funds in a five-year U.S. treasury note, she will receive 6.5 percent annual interest on her money, or $3,250, which will be compounded (added to principal each year). Instead, Angela may decide to lend the buyers of her home the $50,000 by taking a second trust deed and accepting payments that include interest of 8 percent, the same rate the buyers are paying to the lender on the first deed of trust. If Angela accepts payments of interest only, she will receive interest income of $4,000 per year ($50,000 × 8%), or $333.33 per month ($4,000 ÷ 12). If she chooses, Angela can place the interest income in a savings or money market account and receive future interest on that money, as well.

■ STATE INCOME TAX

In general, California income tax law conforms to the federal tax law because both use the same basic computational methods. Information on both individual and business taxes, including tax forms, can be obtained at the **California Franchise Tax Board's** Web site, *www.ftb.ca.gov.* You will also find information about

www.ftb.ca.gov

the **Taxpayer Advocate's Office,** as well as the text of the **California Taxpayers' Bill of Rights.**

Who Must File

Generally a **state income tax return** must be filed by persons who have been residents of California for the entire year if

- they are single or a head of household with gross income of more than $12,346; or
- they are married with a combined gross income of more than $24,692.

Persons who are nonresidents for part of the year and have income from sources in California file a nonresident or part-year resident tax return regardless of sources of income.

Estates, trusts, and partnerships report income as under federal law. **Corporations** incorporated in or doing business in California are subject to the **California franchise tax.**

Tax Withholding

Unless an exemption applies, a buyer of California real property must withhold and remit to the Franchise Tax Board funds equal to 3⅓ percent of the property's sales price, if the seller is an individual (not a trust, estate, corporation, limited liability company, or partnership). Exemptions apply to

- the sale of property for less than $100,000,
- the sale of a principal residence,
- an Internal Revenue Code Section 1031 tax-deferred exchange,
- an involuntary conversion under IRC Section 1033, and
- the sale of property at a loss for California income tax purposes.

Exercise 11-2   Matt and Irene Clock are considering purchasing the Folsom house as their principal residence. They never have owned a home and are not sure they can afford one. Their combined gross income is $9,800 per month. They have saved $145,000 and have no outstanding debts. The rent on their present two-bedroom, two-bath apartment is $1,875 per month, and they pay utility bills of $186 per month, averaged over the year. They anticipate yearly rent increases of 5 percent. Their landlord is holding their security deposit of $1,655.

The three-bedroom, two-bathroom Folsom house could be purchased for $575,000, requiring a down payment of $115,000 and monthly principal and interest payments of $2,757.93 on a loan of $460,000, with a 6 percent fixed interest rate and a 30-year term. During the first year of the loan, only $5,648.85 in principal would be paid; in the fifth year, $7,176.81 in principal would be paid. The yearly property tax bill would be $5,865, and annual fire insurance would be $1,400. The Folsoms have paid utility bills averaging $225 per month and the Clocks use that figure.

1. What are the Clocks' present and anticipated total apartment rental expenses before taxes? After taxes, assuming a 28 percent tax rate? In five years?

2. What would be the Clocks' total monthly expenses as homeowners, before taxes? After taxes, assuming a 28 percent tax rate? In five years?

3. What other factors should the Clocks take into account in determining the financial advantages and disadvantages of home ownership?

■ SUMMARY

Proposition 13, approved by California voters, amended the California Constitution to limit the state's ability to increase property tax assessments over 1975 base values. Now there must be a **reassessment event**—transfer of title, new construction, or a property improvement—or assessed valuation may be raised only by an inflation factor of no more than 2 percent annually.

The **property tax year** runs from July 1 through the following June 30, with tax due in two installments on November 1 (delinquent after 5 P.M. on December 10) and February 1 (delinquent after 5 P.M. on April 10). A state tax lien that will take priority over most creditors takes effect on January 1 of the tax year.

Property not **redeemed** by a **delinquent taxpayer** after five years may be sold at public auction.

The **Property Tax Postponement Law** allows some property owners age 62 or older, or blind or disabled, to defer payment of property tax and interest. **Homeowner Assistance** also may provide a cash rebate of tax paid for a qualified individual.

Special assessments and **benefit assessments** are additional means by which local governing bodies or improvement districts can increase property taxes for a specific purpose. A **documentary transfer tax** (with notice of payment usually shown on the face of a deed) may be required by a city or county.

Manufactured (mobile) homes are subject to either **vehicle license fee** status or **real property taxation.** The form of taxation depends on how title is registered and whether the home is permanently attached to a foundation. A real estate broker selling manufactured homes as a retailer must obtain a seller's permit.

Sales tax paid on retail purchases benefits both the state and individual counties. **Use tax** is charged on storage, use, or other consumption of certain purchased or leased tangible personal property.

California imposes an **estate tax** that is the maximum amount allowed as a credit for state taxes against federal estate taxes. **Federal gift tax** is imposed on gifts of more than $11,000 to one recipient in one year. **Federal estate tax** is imposed on estates of more than the amount set for the tax year.

Unpaid federal taxes become a **lien** on all property of the taxpayer, even if acquired after the lien arises. Notice of a lien against real property must be recorded, but estate and gift tax liens need not be recorded.

Homeowners now can take advantage of the tax **exclusion** of up to $250,000 in profit on the sale of the principal residence if single, or $500,000 in profit if married.

The **tax-deferred exchange** may postpone recognition of taxable gain. An **installment sale** may enable a taxpayer to report gain only when actually received.

California **state income tax** is paid by individuals. Corporations in California pay **franchise tax.**

■ IMPORTANT TERMS

Make sure you understand the following terms before you take the achievement examination.

ad valorem	homeowner's exemption
adjusted cost basis	inheritance tax
adjusted gross income	installment sale
assessed value	Mello-Roos Community Facilities Act
base value	Morgan Property Taxpayers' Bill
basis	of Rights
benefit assessment	ordinary income
boot	Property Tax Postponement Law
California Franchise Tax Board	property tax year
capital asset	Proposition 13
capital gain	reassessment event
certificate of redemption	recovery property
change in ownership statement	sales tax
county assessor	special assessment
deductions	straight-line method
depreciation	supplemental assessment
documentary transfer tax	taxable income
donee	tax bracket
donor	tax credit
estate tax	tax-deferred exchange
franchise tax	Taxpayer Advocate's Office
gift	tax rate
gift tax	use tax
Homeowner Assistance Program	veteran's exemption

■ OPEN FOR DISCUSSION

The United States is an unusual country in that it provides generous tax incentives for home ownership, such as allowing interest payments on home loans to be deducted from taxable income.

1. Make an argument for continuing this practice.

2. Make an argument for discontinuing this practice.

■ ACHIEVEMENT EXAMINATION 11

1. Property taxes are *ad valorem* taxes, which means that they are
   a. charged in relation to the value of the property taxed.
   b. charged once at the time of a property transfer.
   c. use taxes.
   d. sales taxes.

2. The Smiths' sale of their residence is a
   a. release of equity.
   b. reassessment event.
   c. local assessment.
   d. notice of change of ownership.

3. The property tax year runs from
   a. January 1 through December 30.
   b. April 10 through December 10.
   c. July 1 through June 30.
   d. December 10 through December 9.

4. A lien in the amount of tax due is placed on all assessed real property on
   a. April 15.   c. January 1.
   b. December 10.   d. July 1.

5. When all past-due property taxes are paid, the county tax collector issues a
   a. receipt for unpaid taxes.
   b. letter of credit.
   c. certificate of redemption.
   d. release of equity.

6. The buyer of property at an auction by the tax collector receives a
   a. certificate of sale.
   b. release of equity.
   c. quitclaim deed.
   d. tax deed.

7. Property tax postponement may be available to persons
   a. of any age but limited income.
   b. who are blind or disabled.
   c. who are renters.
   d. who have at least a 10 percent equity interest in the property.

8. The Homeowner Assistance Program may be available to persons
   a. of any age but limited income.
   b. who are blind or disabled.
   c. who are renters.
   d. who file an application with the State Board of Equalization.

9. A deed may show on its face that which of the following taxes was paid?
   a. Release of equity
   b. Gift tax
   c. Deed tax
   d. Documentary transfer tax

10. Sales and use taxes are the responsibility of the
    a. Internal Revenue Service.
    b. Franchise Tax Board.
    c. State Board of Equalization.
    d. Department of Housing and Community Development.

11. In California there is a state sales tax on
    a. food.
    b. buildings to be removed from land by the buyer as part of a transaction.
    c. fixtures sold as part of a business.
    d. inventory sold as part of a business.

12. The state of California collects
    a. federal income tax.
    b. gift tax.
    c. estate tax.
    d. inheritance tax.

13. A gift is made
    a. by a donor to a beneficiary.
    b. when an individual voluntarily transfers property for anything less than full consideration.
    c. any time property is transferred between parent and child.
    d. when like-kind property is exchanged.

14. Gift tax is payable when the total value of gifts to an individual in one year is more than
    a. $8,000.   c. $15,000.
    b. $11,000.   d. $28,000.

15. Sam gave his friend Joe $15,000 for his tuition at Old Ivy, sending the money directly to the school. Must a gift tax return be filed?
    a. Yes, because this is a gift
    b. No, because this gift has an exemption
    c. Yes, so that the exemption can be claimed
    d. No, because this is not considered a gift

16. Mario died in 2004, leaving only his separate property estate valued at $500,000. Must an estate tax return be filed?
    a. Yes
    b. No
    c. Only if Mario was a widower
    d. Only if the estate is probated

17. The rate of federal income tax paid depends on the taxpayer's
    a. tax bracket.
    b. state income tax paid.
    c. location.
    d. source of income.

18. Property that can be depreciated for income tax purposes is called
    a. recovery property.
    b. tax basis.
    c. boot.
    d. like-kind property.

19. With respect to investment property, an investor can make use of
    a. the residence replacement rule.
    b. exclusion from taxation.
    c. property tax postponement.
    d. mortgage interest deductions from property income.

20. Who of the following is *not* required to file a state income tax return?
    a. A single person earning $18,000 per year
    b. A married couple with a combined income of more than $25,000
    c. A widower earning $20,000
    d. A single person with an income of $10,000

12

LANDLORD AND TENANT

■ THE LEASEHOLD

A **lease** is a contract that conveys an interest in real property from one person to another. Any form of real estate ownership can be leased. Most frequently, a lease transfers the **use** of property without transferring outright ownership. The use can be occupancy only, or it can include the right to remove such property assets as oil, gas, or other minerals from the surface or subsurface of the land. The California Civil Code, beginning at Section 1940, governs situations in which a person "hires" real property. **Tenants, lessees, boarders, lodgers,** and others (but not guests at hotels) are included in those provisions, which will be mentioned throughout this chapter.

The owner of a **leasehold** has **exclusive** right of possession of the real estate (land and/or buildings) during the lease term. The lease is the instrument that sets the conditions of the occupancy.

- The **lessor (landlord)** is someone who owns an interest in real property.
- The **lessee (tenant)** is someone who acquires use and possession of the property for a fixed period of time.
- **Rent** is the consideration paid by the tenant to the landlord in exchange for use of the property.

(Because they are more familiar to most people, the terms *landlord* and *tenant* will be used throughout the rest of this chapter, instead of the terms *lessor* and *lessee*.)

The Leasehold as Property

Historically, a leasehold estate was considered **personal property.** Even though a leasehold estate conveyed possession of real estate, it was a personal property right rather than a real property right. This meant that important protections available to real property owners, such as that provided by what is referred to as the "antideficiency law," were not available to holders of a leasehold estate.

California law now provides that an estate for years (leasehold) generally is treated as **real property** in

- giving constructive notice of the existence of a leasehold by **recording;**
- determining the **priority** of lien claimants;
- determining the legal **rights** and **remedies** of the parties when an estate for years is hypothecated by a mortgage or trust deed;
- applying the **antideficiency** law.

Types of Leasehold Estates

Estate for years.   An **estate for years** is a leasehold created by landlord and tenant for a particular period of time. The period of time could be a fixed number of years, months, weeks, or even days. An estate for years always will have a definite termination date that the parties agree to before the lease begins. No termination notice is required.

> A lease for six months still qualifies as an estate for years.

Estate from period to period.   An **estate from period to period** is also called a **periodic tenancy.** At the end of the lease term, if the tenant offers an additional rent payment and the landlord accepts the payment, the lease is renewed for an identical period. The lease continues from period to period until one of the parties gives notice of termination.

Periodic tenancies usually have month-to-month terms. If no lease term has been specified by landlord and tenant, a month-to-month tenancy will be presumed for most real property. Exceptions are lodgings and dwelling houses, if there is no local custom as to lease term. Other exceptions are agricultural or grazing land, where a one-year term is presumed.

Estate at will.   In the early days of the common law, an **estate at will** was one that could be terminated by either landlord or tenant at any time, without the consent of the other party. California and other states now have statutory notice requirements that must be met by either landlord or tenant to terminate a tenancy. In addition, the landlord's acceptance of rent creates a periodic tenancy. For these reasons, a true tenancy at will now is uncommon.

Estate at sufferance. An **estate at sufferance** is created when a tenant remains in possession at the end of the agreed-on lease term, without consent of the landlord. An estate at sufferance is also created when a tenant gives notice of intent to vacate but stays on after the date specified in the notice, again, without prior consent of the landlord. Unless the tenant pays rent that is accepted by the landlord, creating a periodic tenancy, the landlord can give notice of termination under an estate at sufferance at any time. For this reason, the estate at sufferance is considered the lowest (least valuable) estate of tenancy.

Creating a Leasehold

An *agreement* to create a leasehold estate that is to terminate **more than one year following the date of the agreement** must be *in writing*. A written lease is required if the lease is to terminate more than a year in the future, even if the lease term is for less than one year.

Practically speaking, both landlord and tenant benefit from a written lease agreement, no matter how long the term. Even though only the landlord need sign the lease (the tenant can accept the lease terms by occupying the property), both parties should sign to avoid misunderstandings. As the landlord's agent, a property manager will probably sign the lease on the landlord's behalf.

www.ca-apartment.org

A typical form of *residential* lease, prepared by the California Association of REALTORS®, appears in Figure 12.1 on pages 344–349. A variety of lease and other forms are available to members of the California Apartment Association through its Web site, *www.ca-apartment.org.* It is important to remember the following characteristics of every lease:

■ A lease, whether oral or written, is a **contract.** As such it must follow the contract formalities outlined in Chapter 7.

■ Parties to the contract must have **legal capacity,** and there must be an **offer** by one party that is **accepted** by the other.

■ The contract must have **definite terms** and a **lawful object** and must be supported by sufficient **consideration.**

■ If the contract is written, it cannot be changed by oral agreement of the parties. A contract **modification** does take place, however, if both parties **perform** in accordance with orally agreed-on changes.

A carefully drawn lease agreement covers the subjects discussed next. You can remember them as the four *P's:*

1. Parties
2. Property
3. Period of time
4. Payment

Parties.   The lease should **identify** the landlord and tenant, as well as any other persons expected to occupy the leased premises.

Property.   The property should be adequately **described** and its allowable **use** specified.

Clause 10 of the lease form, shown in Figure 12.1, concerns neighborhood conditions. As of July 1, 1999, all written leases and rental agreements and contracts for sale of residential real property must contain a specified notice regarding the database maintained by law enforcement authorities that contains the locations of registered sex offenders and other related provisions.

Period of time (lease term).   The **date** on which the lease is to commence and the **length** of the lease term always should be mentioned. By law, property located in a city or town *cannot* have a lease term longer than 99 years. The 99-year limitation also applies to land leased for the production of oil, gas, or other hydrocarbons. Lands used for agricultural or horticultural purposes cannot be leased for longer than 51 years. The probate court determines the maximum lease term for property belonging to a minor or an incompetent person.

If no lease term is specified for a dwelling, the length of time for which rent is paid is considered the lease term. A weekly rent payment implies a weekly term. If there is no specified time to which the rent applies, a month-to-month tenancy is presumed.

The tenant must receive a copy of the lease or rental agreement within 15 days of executing the agreement. Annually after that, the landlord must provide the tenant with a copy of the lease or rental agreement within 15 days of the tenant's request. If the rental agreement is oral, the landlord must provide the tenant with a written statement setting forth the information required under the new law.

Payment.   Rent is the usual consideration paid for possession and use of leased property. A tenant is obligated to pay rent after taking possession or after the period of the lease term begins. Rent can be made payable in advance of the actual possession or beginning of the lease term, or at any other agreed-on time. If the parties fail to stipulate when rent is due, California law provides that it shall be payable at the *end* of the lease term if the term is one year or less (or as local custom dictates).

All residential leases and rental agreements must include the name, telephone number, and address of the person or entity to whom rent payments are to be made, and if rent may be paid personally, the usual days and hours the person will be available to receive rent payments. The landlord can choose not to include this information, but only if the landlord expressly includes in the lease or rental agreement specific information that will allow the tenant to pay by direct deposit into the landlord's account or by electronic funds transfer. The lease or rental agreement must also include the form by which rent payments are to be made.

If the address provided by the landlord does not allow for personal delivery, it is conclusively presumed that the landlord received the rent on the date posted, if the tenant provides proof of mailing to the name and address provided by the landlord.

Security deposit.   A **security deposit** is an amount paid at the *start* of the lease term and retained by the landlord until the tenant vacates the premises. All or part of the security deposit may be kept by the landlord at the end of the lease term to cover costs of any *default in rent payments* by the tenant or *reasonable costs of repairs or cleaning* necessitated by the tenant's use of the premises.

The security required for a rental of residential property includes any charges imposed at the beginning of the tenancy, including costs associated with processing a new tenant and costs associated with cleaning the property. Application screening fees are not included. The landlord must notify the tenant in writing of the tenant's option to request an initial inspection on termination of the tenancy, and the tenant's right to be present at the inspection. If the tenant requests an initial inspection, the landlord must make that inspection prior to a final inspection, after the tenant vacates, and provide the tenant with an itemized list of potential deductions from the security. The tenant must have the opportunity to remedy identified deficiencies during the period from the initial inspection until the end of the tenancy. The maximum amount of a security deposit is

- two months' rent for an **unfurnished** residential property or
- three months' rent for a **furnished** residential property.

Within **three weeks** after the tenant has vacated the premises, the landlord must give the tenant a written itemized statement of the basis for the disposition of the security deposit and return any remaining amount.

If the landlord's interest in the property is *transferred*, the security deposit also is transferred. The tenant is notified by personal delivery or certified mail of the transfer, any claims against the security deposit, and the transferee's name, address, and telephone number. *Alternatively*, the remaining security deposit can be returned to the tenant along with an itemized statement of the basis for the disposition of any amount not returned.

A landlord retaining any amount of the security deposit in bad faith is subject to damages of twice the amount of the security, in addition to the actual loss suffered by the tenant.

FIGURE 12.1

Residential Lease or Month-to-Month Rental Agreement

CALIFORNIA ASSOCIATION OF REALTORS®

RESIDENTIAL LEASE OR MONTH-TO-MONTH RENTAL AGREEMENT
(C.A.R. Form LR, Revised 1/04)

_____ ("Landlord") and
_____ ("Tenant") agree as follows:

1. **PROPERTY:**
   A. Landlord rents to Tenant and Tenant rents from Landlord, the real property and improvements described as: _____ ("Premises").
   B. The Premises are for the sole use as a personal residence by the following named person(s) **only**: _____.
   C. The following personal property, maintained pursuant to paragraph 11, is included: _____ or ☐ (if checked) the personal property on the attached addendum.

2. **TERM:** The term begins on (date) _____ ("Commencement Date"), **(Check A or B):**
   ☐ **A. Month-to-Month:** and continues as a month-to-month tenancy. Tenant may terminate the tenancy by giving written notice at least 30 days prior to the intended termination date. Landlord may terminate the tenancy by giving written notice as provided by law. Such notices may be given on any date.
   ☐ **B. Lease:** and shall terminate on (date) _____ at _____ ☐ AM/☐ PM. Tenant shall vacate the Premises upon termination of the Agreement, unless: **(i)** Landlord and Tenant have in writing extended this agreement or signed a new agreement; **(ii)** mandated by local rent control law; or **(iii)** Landlord accepts Rent from Tenant (other than past due Rent), in which case a month-to-month tenancy shall be created which either party may terminate as specified in paragraph 2A. Rent shall be at a rate agreed to by Landlord and Tenant, or as allowed by law. All other terms and conditions of this Agreement shall remain in full force and effect.

3. **RENT:** "Rent" shall mean all monetary obligations of Tenant to Landlord under the terms of the Agreement, except security deposit.
   A. Tenant agrees to pay $ _____ per month for the term of the Agreement.
   B. Rent is payable in advance on the **1st (or ☐** _____ **) day** of each calendar month, and is delinquent on the next day.
   C. If Commencement Date falls on any day other than the day Rent is payable under paragraph 3B, and Tenant has paid one full month's Rent in advance of Commencement Date, Rent for the second calendar month shall be prorated based on a 30-day period.
   D. **PAYMENT:** Rent shall be paid by ☐ cash, ☐ personal check, ☐ money order, ☐ cashier check, ☐ other _____, to (name) _____ (phone) _____ at (address) _____, (or at any other location specified by Landlord in writing to Tenant) between the hours of _____ and _____ on the following days _____. If any payment is returned for non-sufficient funds ("NSF") or other reason then all future Rent shall be paid by ☐ cash, ☐ money order, ☐ cashier check.

4. **SECURITY DEPOSIT:**
   A. Tenant agrees to pay $ _____ as a security deposit. Security deposit will be ☐ transferred to and held by the Owner of the Premises, or ☐ held in Owner's Broker's trust account.
   B. All or any portion of the security deposit may be used, as reasonably necessary, to: **(i)** cure Tenant's default in payment of Rent (which includes Late Charges, NSF fees or other sums due); **(ii)** repair damage, excluding ordinary wear and tear, caused by Tenant or by a guest or licensee of Tenant; **(iii)** clean Premises, if necessary, upon termination of the tenancy; and **(iv)** replace or return personal property or appurtenances. **SECURITY DEPOSIT SHALL NOT BE USED BY TENANT IN LIEU OF PAYMENT OF LAST MONTH'S RENT.** If all or any portion of the security deposit is used during the tenancy, Tenant agrees to reinstate the total security deposit within five days after written notice is delivered to Tenant. Within 21 days after Tenant vacates the Premises, Landlord shall: **(1)** furnish Tenant an itemized statement indicating the amount of any security deposit received and the basis for its disposition and supporting documentation as required by California Civil Code § 1950.5(g); and **(2)** return any remaining portion of the security deposit to Tenant.
   C. **Security deposit will not be returned until all Tenants have vacated the Premises. Any security deposit returned by check shall be made out to all Tenants named on this Agreement, or as subsequently modified.**
   D. No interest will be paid on security deposit unless required by local law.
   E. If the security deposit is held by Owner, Tenant agrees not to hold Broker responsible for its return. If the security deposit is held in Owner's Broker's trust account, **and** Broker's authority is terminated before expiration of this Agreement, **and** security deposit is released to someone other than Tenant, **then** Broker shall notify Tenant, in writing, where and to whom security deposit has been released. Once Tenant has been provided such notice, Tenant agrees not to hold Broker responsible for the security deposit.

5. **MOVE-IN COSTS RECEIVED/DUE:** Move-in funds made payable to _____ shall be paid by ☐ cash, ☐ personal check, ☐ money order, ☐ cashier check.

Category	Total Due	Payment Received	Balance Due	Date Due
Rent from _____ to _____ (date)				
*Security Deposit				
Other _____				
Other _____				
Total				

*The maximum amount Landlord may receive as security deposit, however designated, cannot exceed two months' Rent for unfurnished premises, or three months' Rent for furnished premises.

LR REVISED 1/04 (PAGE 1 OF 6) Print Date

Tenant's Initials (_____)(_____)
Landlord's Initials (_____)(_____)
Reviewed by _____ Date _____

EQUAL HOUSING OPPORTUNITY

RESIDENTIAL LEASE OR MONTH-TO-MONTH RENTAL AGREEMENT (LR PAGE 1 OF 6)

Source: Reprinted with permission, California Association of REALTORS®. Endorsement not implied.

FIGURE 12.1

Residential Lease or Month-to-Month Rental Agreement (Continued)

Premises: _____   Date: _____

6. LATE CHARGE;RETURNED CHECKS:
   A. Tenant acknowledges either late payment of Rent or issuance of a returned check may cause Landlord to incur costs and expenses, the exact amounts of which are extremely difficult and impractical to determine. These costs may include, but are not limited to, processing, enforcement and accounting expenses, and late charges imposed on Landlord. If any installment of Rent due from Tenant is not received by Landlord within **5 (or ☐ _____) calendar days** after the date due, or if a check is returned, Tenant shall pay to Landlord, respectively, an additional sum of $ _____ or _____% of the Rent due as a Late Charge and $25.00 as a NSF fee for the first returned check and $35.00 as a NSF fee for each additional returned check, either or both of which shall be deemed additional Rent.
   B. Landlord and Tenant agree that these charges represent a fair and reasonable estimate of the costs Landlord may incur by reason of Tenant's late or NSF payment. Any Late Charge or NSF fee due shall be paid with the current installment of Rent. Landlord's acceptance of any Late Charge or NSF fee shall not constitute a waiver as to any default of Tenant. Landlord's right to collect a Late Charge or NSF fee shall not be deemed an extension of the date Rent is due under paragraph 3 or prevent Landlord from exercising any other rights and remedies under this Agreement and as provided by law.

7. PARKING: (Check A or B)
   ☐ **A.** Parking is permitted as follows: _____
   The right to parking ☐ is ☐ is not included in the Rent charged pursuant to paragraph 3. If not included in the Rent, the parking rental fee shall be an additional $ _____ per month. Parking space(s) are to be used for parking properly licensed and operable motor vehicles, except for trailers, boats, campers, buses or trucks (other than pick-up trucks). Tenant shall park in assigned space(s) only. Parking space(s) are to be kept clean. Vehicles leaking oil, gas or other motor vehicle fluids shall not be parked on the Premises. Mechanical work or storage of inoperable vehicles is not permitted in parking space(s) or elsewhere on the Premises.
   OR ☐ **B.** Parking is not permitted on the Premises.

8. STORAGE: (Check A or B)
   ☐ **A.** Storage is permitted as follows: _____
   The right to storage space ☐ is, ☐ is not, included in the Rent charged pursuant to paragraph 3. If not included in the Rent, storage space fee shall be an additional $ _____ per month. Tenant shall store only personal property Tenant owns, and shall not store property claimed by another or in which another has any right, title or interest. Tenant shall not store any improperly packaged food or perishable goods, flammable materials, explosives, hazardous waste or other inherently dangerous material, or illegal substances.
   OR ☐ **B.** Storage is not permitted on the Premises.

9. UTILITIES: Tenant agrees to pay for all utilities and services, and the following charges: _____ except _____, which shall be paid for by Landlord. If any utilities are not separately metered, Tenant shall pay Tenant's proportional share, as reasonably determined and directed by Landlord. If utilities are separately metered, Tenant shall place utilities in Tenant's name as of the Commencement Date. Landlord is only responsible for installing and maintaining one usable telephone jack and one telephone line to the Premises. Tenant shall pay any cost for conversion from existing utilities service provider.

10. CONDITION OF PREMISES: Tenant has examined Premises and, if any, all furniture, furnishings, appliances, landscaping and fixtures, including smoke detector(s).
   (Check all that apply:)
   ☐ **A.** Tenant acknowledges these items are clean and in operable condition, with the following exceptions: _____
       _____.
   ☐ **B.** Tenant's acknowledgment of the condition of these items is contained in an attached statement of condition (C.A.R. Form MIMO).
   ☐ **C.** Tenant will provide Landlord a list of items that are damaged or not in operable condition within **3 (or ☐ _____) days** after Commencement Date, not as a contingency of this Agreement but rather as an acknowledgment of the condition of the Premises.
   ☐ **D.** Other: _____.

11. MAINTENANCE:
   A. Tenant shall properly use, operate and safeguard Premises, including if applicable, any landscaping, furniture, furnishings and appliances, and all mechanical, electrical, gas and plumbing fixtures, and keep them and the Premises clean, sanitary and well ventilated. Tenant shall be responsible for checking and maintaining all smoke detectors and any additional phone lines beyond the one line and jack that Landlord shall provide and maintain. Tenant shall immediately notify Landlord, in writing, of any problem, malfunction or damage. Tenant shall be charged for all repairs or replacements caused by Tenant, pets, guests or licensees of Tenant, excluding ordinary wear and tear. Tenant shall be charged for all damage to Premises as a result of failure to report a problem in a timely manner. Tenant shall be charged for repair of drain blockages or stoppages, unless caused by defective plumbing parts or tree roots invading sewer lines.
   B. ☐ Landlord ☐ Tenant shall water the garden, landscaping, trees and shrubs, except: _____
       _____.
   C. ☐ Landlord ☐ Tenant shall maintain the garden, landscaping, trees and shrubs, except: _____
       _____.
   D. ☐ Landlord ☐ Tenant shall maintain _____.
   E. Tenant's failure to maintain any item for which Tenant is responsible shall give Landlord the right to hire someone to perform such maintenance and charge Tenant to cover the cost of such maintenance.
   F. The following items of personal property are included in the Premises without warranty and Landlord will not maintain, repair or replace them: _____

Tenant's Initials   (_____)(_____)
Landlord's Initials (_____)(_____)

LR REVISED 1/04 (PAGE 2 OF 6)

Reviewed by _____ Date _____

EQUAL HOUSING OPPORTUNITY

RESIDENTIAL LEASE OR MONTH-TO-MONTH RENTAL AGREEMENT   (LR PAGE 2 OF 6)

Source: Reprinted with permission, California Association of REALTORS®. Endorsement not implied.

FIGURE 12.1

Residential Lease or Month-to-Month Rental Agreement (Continued)

Premises: _____   Date: _____

12. **NEIGHBORHOOD CONDITIONS:** Tenant is advised to satisfy him or herself as to neighborhood or area conditions, including schools, proximity and adequacy of law enforcement, crime statistics, proximity of registered felons or offenders, fire protection, other governmental services, availability, adequacy and cost of any speed-wired, wireless internet connections or other telecommunications or other technology services and installations, proximity to commercial, industrial or agricultural activities, existing and proposed transportation, construction and development that may affect noise, view, or traffic, airport noise, noise or odor from any source, wild and domestic animals, other nuisances, hazards, or circumstances, cemeteries, facilities and condition of common areas, conditions and influences of significance to certain cultures and/or religions, and personal needs, requirements and preferences of Tenant.

13. **PETS:** Unless otherwise provided in California Civil Code § 54.2, no animal or pet shall be kept on or about the Premises without Landlord's prior written consent, except: _____.

14. **RULES/REGULATIONS:**
   A. Tenant agrees to comply with all Landlord rules and regulations that are at any time posted on the Premises or delivered to Tenant. Tenant shall not, and shall ensure that guests and licensees of Tenant shall not, disturb, annoy, endanger or interfere with other tenants of the building or neighbors, or use the Premises for any unlawful purposes, including, but not limited to, using, manufacturing, selling, storing or transporting illicit drugs or other contraband, or violate any law or ordinance, or commit a waste or nuisance on or about the Premises.
   B. (If applicable, check one)
   ☐ **1.** Landlord shall provide Tenant with a copy of the rules and regulations within _____ days or _____.
   OR ☐ **2.** Tenant has been provided with, and acknowledges receipt of, a copy of the rules and regulations.

15. ☐ **(If checked) CONDOMINIUM;PLANNED UNIT DEVELOPMENT:**
   A. The Premises is a unit in a condominium, planned unit development, common interest subdivision or other development governed by a homeowners' association ("HOA"). The name of the HOA is _____. Tenant agrees to comply with all HOA covenants, conditions and restrictions, bylaws, rules and regulations and decisions. Landlord shall provide Tenant copies of rules and regulations, if any. Tenant shall reimburse Landlord for any fines or charges imposed by HOA or other authorities, due to any violation by Tenant, or the guests or licensees of Tenant.
   B. (Check one)
   ☐ **1.** Landlord shall provide Tenant with a copy of the HOA rules and regulations within _____ days or _____.
   OR ☐ **2.** Tenant has been provided with, and acknowledges receipt of, a copy of the HOA rules and regulations.

16. **ALTERATIONS;REPAIRS:** Unless otherwise specified by law or paragraph 27C, without Landlord's prior written consent, **(i)** Tenant shall not make any repairs, alterations or improvements in or about the Premises including: painting, wallpapering, adding or changing locks, installing antenna or satellite dish(es), placing signs, displays or exhibits, or using screws, fastening devices, large nails or adhesive materials; **(ii)** Landlord shall not be responsible for the costs of alterations or repairs made by Tenant; **(iii)** Tenant shall not deduct from Rent the costs of any repairs, alterations or improvements; and **(iv)** any deduction made by Tenant shall be considered unpaid Rent.

17. **KEYS;LOCKS:**
   A. Tenant acknowledges receipt of (or Tenant will receive ☐ prior to the Commencement Date, or ☐ _____):
   ☐ _____ key(s) to Premises,   ☐ _____ remote control device(s) for garage door/gate opener(s),
   ☐ _____ key(s) to mailbox,   ☐ _____,
   ☐ _____ key(s) to common area(s),   ☐ _____.
   B. Tenant acknowledges that locks to the Premises ☐ have, ☐ have not, been re-keyed.
   C. If Tenant re-keys existing locks or opening devices, Tenant shall immediately deliver copies of all keys to Landlord. Tenant shall pay all costs and charges related to loss of any keys or opening devices. Tenant may not remove locks, even if installed by Tenant.

18. **ENTRY:**
   A. Tenant shall make Premises available to Landlord or Landlord's representative for the purpose of entering to make necessary or agreed repairs, decorations, alterations, or improvements, or to supply necessary or agreed services, or to show Premises to prospective or actual purchasers, tenants, mortgagees, lenders, appraisers, or contractors.
   B. Landlord and Tenant agree that 24-hour written notice shall be reasonable and sufficient notice, except as follows. 48-hour written notice is required to conduct an inspection of the Premises prior to the Tenant moving out, unless the Tenant waives the right to such notice. Notice may be given orally to show the Premises to actual or prospective purchasers provided Tenant has been notified in writing within 120 days preceding the oral notice that the Premises are for sale and that oral notice may be given to show the Premises. No notice is required to **(i)** enter in case of an emergency; **(ii)** if the Tenant is present and consents at the time of entry or **(iii)** the Tenant has abandoned or surrendered the Premises. No written notice is required if Landlord and Tenant orally agree to an entry for agreed services or repairs if the date and time of entry are within one week of the oral agreement.
   C. (If checked) ☐ Tenant authorizes the use of a keysafe/lockbox to allow entry into the Premises and agrees to sign a keysafe/lockbox addendum (C.A.R. Form KLA).

19. **SIGNS:** Tenant authorizes Landlord to place FOR SALE/LEASE signs on the Premises.

20. **ASSIGNMENT;SUBLETTING:** Tenant shall not sublet all or any part of Premises, or assign or transfer this Agreement or any interest in it, without Landlord's prior written consent. Unless such consent is obtained, any assignment, transfer or subletting of Premises or this Agreement or tenancy, by voluntary act of Tenant, operation of law or otherwise, shall be null and void and, at the option of Landlord, terminate this Agreement. Any proposed assignee, transferee or sublessee shall submit to Landlord an application and credit information for Landlord's approval and, if approved, sign a separate written agreement with Landlord and Tenant. Landlord's consent to any one assignment, transfer or sublease, shall not be construed as consent to any subsequent assignment, transfer or sublease and does not release Tenant of Tenant's obligations under this Agreement.

21. **JOINT AND INDIVIDUAL OBLIGATIONS:** If there is more than one Tenant, each one shall be individually and completely responsible for the performance of all obligations of Tenant under this Agreement, jointly with every other Tenant, and individually, whether or not in possession.

Tenant's Initials (_____)(_____)
Landlord's Initials (_____)(_____)

Copyright © 1994-2003, CALIFORNIA ASSOCIATION OF REALTORS®, INC.
LR REVISED 1/04 (PAGE 3 OF 6)

| Reviewed by _____ Date _____ |

RESIDENTIAL LEASE OR MONTH-TO-MONTH RENTAL AGREEMENT (LR PAGE 3 OF 6)

EQUAL HOUSING OPPORTUNITY

Source: Reprinted with permission, California Association of REALTORS®. Endorsement not implied.

FIGURE 12.1

Residential Lease or Month-to-Month Rental Agreement (Continued)

Premises: _____   Date: _____

22. ☐ **LEAD-BASED PAINT (If checked):** Premises was constructed prior to 1978. In accordance with federal law, Landlord gives and Tenant acknowledges receipt of the disclosures on the attached form (C.A.R. Form FLD) and a federally approved lead pamphlet.

23. ☐ **MILITARY ORDNANCE DISCLOSURE:** (If applicable and known to Landlord) Premises is located within one mile of an area once used for military training, and may contain potentially explosive munitions.

24. ☐ **PERIODIC PEST CONTROL:** Landlord has entered into a contract for periodic pest control treatment of the Premises and shall give Tenant a copy of the notice originally given to Landlord by the pest control company.

25. **DATABASE DISCLOSURE:** NOTICE: The California Department of Justice, sheriff's departments, police departments serving jurisdictions of 200,000 or more, and many other local law enforcement authorities maintain for public access a database of the locations of persons required to register pursuant to paragraph (1) of subdivision (a) of Section 290.4 of the Penal Code. The data base is updated on a quarterly basis and a source of information about the presence of these individuals in any neighborhood. The Department of Justice also maintains a Sex Offender Identification Line through which inquiries about individuals may be made. This is a "900" telephone service. Callers must have specific information about individuals they are checking. Information regarding neighborhoods is not available through the "900" telephone service.

26. **POSSESSION:** If Landlord is unable to deliver possession of Premises on Commencement Date, such Date shall be extended to the date on which possession is made available to Tenant. If Landlord is unable to deliver possession within **5 (or ☐ _____) calendar days** after agreed Commencement Date, Tenant may terminate this Agreement by giving written notice to Landlord, and shall be refunded all Rent and security deposit paid. Possession is deemed terminated when Tenant has returned all keys to the Premises to Landlord. ☐ Tenant is already in possession of the Premises.

27. **TENANT'S OBLIGATIONS UPON VACATING PREMISES:**
   A. Upon termination of the Agreement, Tenant shall: **(i)** give Landlord all copies of all keys or opening devices to Premises, including any common areas; **(ii)** vacate and surrender Premises to Landlord, empty of all persons; **(iii)** vacate any/all parking and/or storage space; **(iv)** clean and deliver Premises, as specified in paragraph C below, to Landlord in the same condition as referenced in paragraph 10; **(v)** remove all debris; **(vi)** give written notice to Landlord of Tenant's forwarding address; and **(vii)** _____.
   B. All alterations/improvements made by or caused to be made by Tenant, with or without Landlord's consent, become the property of Landlord upon termination. Landlord may charge Tenant for restoration of the Premises to the condition it was in prior to any alterations/improvements.
   C. **Right to Pre-Move Out Inspection and Repairs as follows: (i)** After giving or receiving notice of termination of a tenancy (C.A.R. Form NTT), or before the end of a lease, Tenant has the right to request that an inspection of the Premises take place prior to termination of the lease or rental (C.A.R. Form NRI). If Tenant requests such an inspection, Tenant shall be given an opportunity to remedy identified deficiencies prior to termination, consistent with the terms of this Agreement. **(ii)** Any repairs or alterations made to the Premises as a result of this inspection (collectively, "Repairs") shall be made at Tenant's expense. Repairs may be performed by Tenant or through others, who have adequate insurance and licenses and are approved by Landlord. The work shall comply with applicable law, including governmental permit, inspection and approval requirements. Repairs shall be performed in a good, skillful manner with materials of quality and appearance comparable to existing materials. It is understood that exact restoration of appearance or cosmetic items following all Repairs may not be possible. **(iii)** Tenant shall: **(a)** obtain receipts for Repairs performed by others; **(b)** prepare a written statement indicating the Repairs performed by Tenant and the date of such Repairs; and **(c)** provide copies of receipts and statements to Landlord prior to termination. Paragraph 27C does not apply when the tenancy is terminated pursuant to California Code of Civil Procedure § 1161(2), (3) or (4).

28. **BREACH OF CONTRACT;EARLY TERMINATION:** In addition to any obligations established by paragraph 27, in the event of termination by Tenant prior to completion of the original term of the Agreement, Tenant shall also be responsible for lost Rent, rental commissions, advertising expenses and painting costs necessary to ready Premises for re-rental. Landlord may withhold any such amounts from Tenant's security deposit.

29. **TEMPORARY RELOCATION:** Subject to local law, Tenant agrees, upon demand of Landlord, to temporarily vacate Premises for a reasonable period, to allow for fumigation (or other methods) to control wood destroying pests or organisms, or other repairs to Premises. Tenant agrees to comply with all instructions and requirements necessary to prepare Premises to accommodate pest control, fumigation or other work, including bagging or storage of food and medicine, and removal of perishables and valuables. Tenant shall only be entitled to a credit of Rent equal to the per diem Rent for the period of time Tenant is required to vacate Premises.

30. **DAMAGE TO PREMISES:** If, by no fault of Tenant, Premises are totally or partially damaged or destroyed by fire, earthquake, accident or other casualty that render Premises totally or partially uninhabitable, either Landlord or Tenant may terminate the Agreement by giving the other written notice. Rent shall be abated as of the date Premises become totally or partially uninhabitable. The abated amount shall be the current monthly Rent prorated on a 30-day period. If the Agreement is not terminated, Landlord shall promptly repair the damage, and Rent shall be reduced based on the extent to which the damage interferes with Tenant's reasonable use of Premises. If damage occurs as a result of an act of Tenant or Tenant's guests, only Landlord shall have the right of termination, and no reduction in Rent shall be made.

31. **INSURANCE:** Tenant's or guest's personal property and vehicles are not insured by Landlord, manager or, if applicable, HOA, against loss or damage due to fire, theft, vandalism, rain, water, criminal or negligent acts of others, or any other cause. **Tenant is advised to carry Tenant's own insurance (renter's insurance) to protect Tenant from any such loss or damage.** Tenant shall comply with any requirement imposed on Tenant by Landlord's insurer to avoid: **(i)** an increase in Landlord's insurance premium (or Tenant shall pay for the increase in premium); or **(ii)** loss of insurance.

32. **WATERBEDS:** Tenant shall not use or have waterbeds on the Premises unless: **(i)** Tenant obtains a valid waterbed insurance policy; **(ii)** Tenant increases the security deposit in an amount equal to one-half of one month's Rent; and **(iii)** the bed conforms to the floor load capacity of Premises.

Tenant's Initials (_____)(_____)
Landlord's Initials (_____)(_____)

LR REVISED 1/04 (PAGE 4 OF 6)

Reviewed by _____ Date _____   EQUAL HOUSING OPPORTUNITY

RESIDENTIAL LEASE OR MONTH-TO-MONTH RENTAL AGREEMENT (LR PAGE 4 OF 6)

Source: Reprinted with permission, California Association of REALTORS®. Endorsement not implied.

FIGURE 12.1

Residential Lease or Month-to-Month Rental Agreement (Continued)

Premises: _____ Date: _____

33. WAIVER: The waiver of any breach shall not be construed as a continuing waiver of the same or any subsequent breach.

34. NOTICE: Notices may be served at the following address, or at any other location subsequently designated:

Landlord: _____ Tenant: _____

_____ _____

_____ _____

35. TENANT ESTOPPEL CERTIFICATE: Tenant shall execute and return a tenant estoppel certificate delivered to Tenant by Landlord or Landlord's agent within 3 days after its receipt. Failure to comply with this requirement shall be deemed Tenant's acknowledgment that the tenant estoppel certificate is true and correct, and may be relied upon by a lender or purchaser.

36. TENANT REPRESENTATIONS; CREDIT: Tenant warrants that all statements in Tenant's rental application are accurate. Tenant authorizes Landlord and Broker(s) to obtain Tenant's credit report periodically during the tenancy in connection with the modification or enforcement of this Agreement. Landlord may cancel this Agreement: **(i)** before occupancy begins; **(ii)** upon disapproval of the credit report(s); or **(iii)** at any time, upon discovering that information in Tenant's application is false. A negative credit report reflecting on Tenant's record may be submitted to a credit reporting agency if Tenant fails to fulfill the terms of payment and other obligations under this Agreement.

37. MEDIATION:
A. Consistent with paragraphs B and C below, Landlord and Tenant agree to mediate any dispute or claim arising between them out of this Agreement, or any resulting transaction, before resorting to court action. Mediation fees, if any, shall be divided equally among the parties involved. If, for any dispute or claim to which this paragraph applies, any party commences an action without first attempting to resolve the matter through mediation, or refuses to mediate after a request has been made, then that party shall not be entitled to recover attorney fees, even if they would otherwise be available to that party in any such action.
B. The following matters are excluded from mediation: **(i)** an unlawful detainer action; **(ii)** the filing or enforcement of a mechanic's lien; and **(iii)** any matter within the jurisdiction of a probate, small claims or bankruptcy court. The filing of a court action to enable the recording of a notice of pending action, for order of attachment, receivership, injunction, or other provisional remedies, shall not constitute a waiver of the mediation provision.
C. Landlord and Tenant agree to mediate disputes or claims involving Listing Agent, Leasing Agent or property manager ("Broker"), provided Broker shall have agreed to such mediation prior to, or within a reasonable time after, the dispute or claim is presented to such Broker. Any election by Broker to participate in mediation shall not result in Broker being deemed a party to the Agreement.

38. ATTORNEY FEES: In any action or proceeding arising out of this Agreement, the prevailing party between Landlord and Tenant shall be entitled to reasonable attorney fees and costs, except as provided in paragraph 37A.

39. CAR FORM: C.A.R. Form means the specific form referenced or another comparable form.

40. OTHER TERMS AND CONDITIONS;SUPPLEMENTS: _____

_____

The following ATTACHED supplements are incorporated in this Agreement: ☐ Keysafe/Lockbox Addendum (C.A.R. Form KLA); ☐ Interpreter/Translator Agreement (C.A.R. Form ITA); ☐ Lead-Based Paint and Lead-Based Paint Hazards Disclosure (C.A.R. Form FLD)

41. TIME OF ESSENCE; ENTIRE CONTRACT; CHANGES: Time is of the essence. All understandings between the parties are incorporated in the Agreement. Its terms are intended by the parties as a final, complete and exclusive expression of their Agreement with respect to its subject matter, and may not be contradicted by evidence of any prior agreement or contemporaneous oral agreement. If any provision of the Agreement is held to be ineffective or invalid, the remaining provisions will nevertheless be given full force and effect. Neither this Agreement nor any provision in it may be extended, amended, modified, altered or changed except in writing. The Agreement and any supplement, addendum or modification, including any copy, may be signed in two or more counterparts, all of which shall constitute one and the same writing.

42. AGENCY:
A. CONFIRMATION: The following agency relationship(s) are hereby confirmed for this transaction:
Listing Agent: (Print firm name) _____
is the agent of (check one): ☐ the Landlord exclusively; or ☐ both the Landlord and Tenant.
Leasing Agent: (Print firm name) _____
(if not same as Listing Agent) is the agent of (check one): ☐ the Tenant exclusively; or ☐ the Landlord exclusively; or ☐ both the Tenant and Landlord.
B. DISCLOSURE: ☐ (If checked): The term of this lease exceeds one year. A disclosure regarding real estate agency relationships (C.A.R. Form AD) has been provided to Landlord and Tenant, who each acknowledge its receipt.

43. ☐ TENANT COMPENSATION TO BROKER: Upon execution of this Agreement, Tenant agrees to pay compensation to Broker as specified in a separate written agreement between Tenant and Broker.

44. ☐ INTERPRETER/TRANSLATOR: The terms of this Agreement have been interpreted/translated for Tenant into the following language: _____. Landlord and Tenant acknowledge receipt of the attached interpretation/translation agreement (C.A.R. Form ITA).

45. FOREIGN LANGUAGE NEGOTIATION: If this Agreement has been negotiated primarily in Spanish, Tenant has been provided a Spanish language translation of this Agreement pursuant to the California Civil Code.

Tenant's Initials (_____)(_____)
Landlord's Initials (_____)(_____)

Copyright © 1994-2003, CALIFORNIA ASSOCIATION OF REALTORS®, INC.
LR REVISED 1/04 (PAGE 5 OF 6)

Reviewed by _____ Date _____

EQUAL HOUSING OPPORTUNITY

RESIDENTIAL LEASE OR MONTH-TO-MONTH RENTAL AGREEMENT (LR PAGE 5 OF 6)

Source: Reprinted with permission, California Association of REALTORS®. Endorsement not implied.

FIGURE 12.1

Residential Lease or Month-to-Month Rental Agreement (Continued)

Premises: _____   Date: _____

> Landlord and Tenant acknowledge and agree Brokers: **(a)** do not guarantee the condition of the Premises; **(b)** cannot verify representations made by others; **(c)** cannot provide legal or tax advice; **(d)** will not provide other advice or information that exceeds the knowledge, education or experience required to obtain a real estate license. Furthermore, if Brokers are not also acting as Landlord in this Agreement, Brokers: **(e)** do not decide what rental rate a Tenant should pay or Landlord should accept; and **(f)** do not decide upon the length or other terms of tenancy. Landlord and Tenant agree that they will seek legal, tax, insurance and other desired assistance from appropriate professionals.

Tenant _____   Date _____
Address _____ City _____ State _____ Zip _____
Telephone _____ Fax _____ E-mail _____

Tenant _____   Date _____
Address _____ City _____ State _____ Zip _____
Telephone _____ Fax _____ E-mail _____

46. ☐ **GUARANTEE:** In consideration of the execution of the Agreement by and between Landlord and Tenant and for valuable consideration, receipt of which is hereby acknowledged, the undersigned ("Guarantor") does hereby: **(i)** guarantee unconditionally to Landlord and Landlord's agents, successors and assigns, the prompt payment of Rent or other sums that become due pursuant to this Agreement, including any and all court costs and attorney fees included in enforcing the Agreement; **(ii)** consent to any changes, modifications or alterations of any term in this Agreement agreed to by Landlord and Tenant; and **(iii)** waive any right to require Landlord and/or Landlord's agents to proceed against Tenant for any default occurring under this Agreement before seeking to enforce this Guarantee.

Guarantor (Print Name) _____
Guarantor _____   Date _____
Address _____ City _____ State _____ Zip _____
Telephone _____ Fax _____ E-mail _____

47. OWNER COMPENSATION TO BROKER: Upon execution of this Agreement, Owner agrees to pay compensation to Broker as specified in a separate written agreement between Owner and Broker (C.A.R. Form LCA).
48. RECEIPT: If specified in paragraph 5, Landlord or Broker, acknowledges receipt of move-in funds.

Landlord _____   Date _____
(Owner or Agent with authority to enter into this Agreement)
Landlord _____   Date _____
(Owner or Agent with authority to enter into this Agreement)
Landlord Address _____ City _____ State _____ Zip _____
Telephone _____ Fax _____ E-mail _____

> **REAL ESTATE BROKERS:**
> **A.**   Real estate brokers who are not also Landlord under the Agreement are not parties to the Agreement between Landlord and Tenant.
> **B.**   Agency relationships are confirmed in paragraph 42.
> **C.**   **COOPERATING BROKER COMPENSATION:** Listing Broker agrees to pay Cooperating Broker **(Leasing Firm)** and Cooperating Broker agrees to accept: **(i)** the amount specified in the MLS, provided Cooperating Broker is a Participant of the MLS in which the Property is offered for sale or a reciprocal MLS; or **(ii)** ☐ (if checked) the amount specified in a separate written agreement between Listing Broker and Cooperating Broker.

Real Estate Broker (Leasing Firm) _____
By (Agent) _____   Date _____
Address _____ City _____ State _____ Zip _____
Telephone _____ Fax _____ E-mail _____
Real Estate Broker (Listing Firm) _____
By (Agent) _____   Date _____
Address _____ City _____ State _____ Zip _____
Telephone _____ Fax _____ E-mail _____

THIS FORM HAS BEEN APPROVED BY THE CALIFORNIA ASSOCIATION OF REALTORS® (C.A.R.). NO REPRESENTATION IS MADE AS TO THE LEGAL VALIDITY OR ADEQUACY OF ANY PROVISION IN ANY SPECIFIC TRANSACTION. A REAL ESTATE BROKER IS THE PERSON QUALIFIED TO ADVISE ON REAL ESTATE TRANSACTIONS. IF YOU DESIRE LEGAL OR TAX ADVICE, CONSULT AN APPROPRIATE PROFESSIONAL.
This form is available for use by the entire real estate industry. It is not intended to identify the user as a REALTOR®. REALTOR® is a registered collective membership mark which may be used only by members of the NATIONAL ASSOCIATION OF REALTORS® who subscribe to its Code of Ethics.

Published and Distributed by:
REAL ESTATE BUSINESS SERVICES, INC.
a subsidiary of the California Association of REALTORS®
525 South Virgil Avenue, Los Angeles, California 90020

SURE TRAC
The System for Success®
LR REVISED 1/04 (PAGE 6 OF 6)

Reviewed by _____ Date _____

EQUAL HOUSING OPPORTUNITY

RESIDENTIAL LEASE OR MONTH-TO-MONTH RENTAL AGREEMENT (LR PAGE 6 OF 6)

Source: Reprinted with permission, California Association of REALTORS®. Endorsement not implied.

> A security deposit on residential property cannot be nonrefundable.

If any question arises about the validity of a claim, the law presumes that the tenant is entitled to the return of the entire security deposit. The landlord has the burden of proving the reasonableness of the amounts claimed. In fact, the California Civil Code provides that in a lease or rental of **residential property,** a security deposit can *never* be labeled "nonrefundable."

Similar provisions apply in the case of nonresidential property, but

- the amount of the required security deposit is *not* limited,
- the landlord has up to 60 *days* to return the deposit after deductions for repairs or cleaning, and
- no written itemization is necessary.

The security deposit often is a substantial amount of money. It is in the tenant's best interest to inspect the premises being leased carefully at the time of first taking possession by completing a **statement of property condition.** If the tenant provides such a statement to the landlord at both the beginning and the end of the lease term, there should be fewer disputes later about repairs properly charged against the tenant's security deposit.

Possession by the tenant.   The tenant's right to possession is ensured by the **covenant of quiet enjoyment** made by the landlord, which is implied by law. The covenant refers not to noise but to interference by the landlord in the tenant's possession or use of the property. The landlord could interfere with the tenant's possession by removing the tenant from the property by the eviction process discussed later in this chapter.

The landlord also could bring about a **constructive eviction** of the tenant by

- failing to make necessary repairs, after notice from the tenant;
- interfering with the tenant's legitimate use of the property;
- threatening to remove the tenant;
- making unwarranted alterations to the property; or
- attempting to lease the property to someone else.

Landlord's right of entry.   The landlord has the right to enter the premises if necessary. The California Civil Code permits such **right of entry** in the following cases:

- an *emergency*;
- when the tenant has *abandoned* the premises;
- pursuant to a *court order*;

- so that the landlord can make necessary or agreed-on *repairs* or perform other required *services*; and
- so that the landlord can *show* the property to prospective tenants, mortgagees, purchasers, workers, or contractors.

The landlord must give the tenant **notice** of the intended entry unless there is an emergency (and then must notify the tenant immediately afterward), or the tenant has abandoned the premises, or it is impractical to do so. Notice of *at least 24 hours* is presumed to be sufficient.

Tenant improvements.   A residential lease usually requires prior approval by the landlord before the tenant makes any alterations to the premises. Subject to negotiation, a commercial lease is likely to require that the tenant make property alterations, called "tenant improvements," and also may require that the tenant return the property to its original condition on termination.

What If a Tenant Has Installed a Fixture?

If the lease mentions fixtures installed by the tenant, then the lease terms apply.

If no prior agreement was made regarding fixtures installed by the tenant and removal of a fixture would damage the property, the tenant may not remove the fixture, even at the conclusion of the lease term.

If there is no prior agreement regarding fixtures and the fixture can be removed without injury to the property, the tenant may do so if the fixture was installed by the tenant for the purpose of trade, manufacture, ornamental, or domestic use.

The best way to avoid conflict is to clarify the status of such items before they are brought onto the property.

Transferability.   The tenant may need to vacate the premises before the end of the lease term. The landlord may agree to **terminate** the lease (to increase the rent paid by a new tenant, for instance).

A tenant also can transfer possession of leased property by **sublease** or **assignment,** unless prohibited from doing so by the lease terms. The lease could require landlord approval before a sublease or an assignment. The landlord's decision on approval must be *reasonable*.

In a **sublease** the tenant transfers possession of the property to another party for only part of the remaining lease term. The original tenant then has a reversion, which is the right to possess the property when it is vacated by the sublessee. The original tenant's interest is also called a **sandwich lease.** *Primary responsibility for payment of rent remains with the original tenant.*

Alternatively, the tenant can make a **lease assignment** of the entire remaining lease term to another party. In an assignment, the first tenant retains no interest in the property but is secondarily liable for lease obligations, unless the landlord agrees to release the first tenant from further liability.

Renewal of the lease. The lease usually specifies the procedure for its renewal. It is preferable to have a new lease drawn up for the new term, although the old lease could be extended on the original terms.

A lease could provide for an **automatic renewal** or extension of the lease term if the tenant were to remain in possession after the termination date. All such provisions in leases are now *voidable* by the party who did not prepare the lease unless

- the automatic renewal clause is printed in at least eight-point *boldface type*; and
- the existence of the automatic renewal provision is noted *directly above* the space provided for the tenant's signature, again in at least eight-point *boldface type*.

Exercise 12-1

1. Sue Parker rents a one-bedroom apartment in Walnut Grove for $450 per month. Sue's rent probably will increase in three months, when her lease term ends. What kind of leasehold estate does Sue have?

2. The lease on Jim Smith's apartment ended last month. The landlord has not offered to renew the lease, and Jim has not made another rent payment. What kind of leasehold estate does Jim have?

3. When must a lease agreement be in writing?

4. Jim Smith rented an office in which to conduct his bookmaking operation from his good friend Sam, who liked the convenience of placing bets in his own building. Jim was arrested before the lease term expired and will not be returning for some time. Can Sam collect the remaining rent payments?

5. Sue Parker is considering a move to a new one-bedroom unfurnished apartment. The monthly rent is $650, and the landlord expects a security deposit of $2,000. That amount seems excessive to Sue. Is she right?

6. Sue decided to take over the apartment of a friend who is going abroad. Sue will rent the apartment for nine months, then return it to her friend. What will Sue have?

7. While Sue was at work, her landlord went into her apartment without her knowledge to turn off the gas line, which was leaking somewhere in the building. Should Sue object?

Landlord's Obligations

As a minimum the landlord must follow all applicable housing or building standards. Even if there is no express provision in a lease agreement, there is a legally implied **warranty of habitability.** The California legislature has specified in the Civil Code the conditions under which a dwelling will be considered **untenantable.** They are listed in the box on the next page.

Covenant to repair.   In most lease agreements the landlord expressly covenants (promises) to make necessary repairs to the premises. If there is no express promise to repair, a court may find an implied **covenant to repair,** depending on the nature of the work required.

■ **FOR EXAMPLE:**   The Jolly Arms apartment complex has a tennis court for the exclusive use of residents. The tennis court is not mentioned in the lease that the apartment management firm uses, however. Part of the tennis court is destroyed in a small mud slide and the tennis court is fenced off and not repaired. The tenants bring suit against the owner of the complex and the management firm, claiming breach of the covenant to repair. Will they be successful?

Unless repairs to the tennis court are specifically mentioned in the lease, a tennis court may not be considered an element of habitability that automatically will impose an implied covenant to repair.

Residential tenant's remedies.   To whom can a tenant complain? The local Building Inspection Department, Health Department, or Fire Department will receive tenant complaints on applicable violations of state or local building, fire and safety, and other standards. The tenant's complaint will be investigated, and the landlord will be required to make necessary repairs.

If a residential landlord won't make repairs that are necessary to make the property **tenantable** (livable), the tenant is allowed to make repairs to the property. The tenant must give written or oral notice of the needed repairs to the landlord or the landlord's agent, then wait a reasonable time (30 days, for example, depending on the circumstances) for the landlord to act. After that time, if the landlord has not acted, the tenant can spend up to one month's rent on repairs. The tenant may not **repair and deduct** more than twice in any 12-month period.

An Untenantable Dwelling

California law defines an **untenantable dwelling** as one that substantially lacks any of the following:

■ Adequate weatherproofing, including unbroken windows and doors

■ Plumbing or gas lines that conformed to local building codes when installed and have been maintained in good working order

■ Hot and cold running water, with fixtures and sewage disposal system approved under applicable law

■ Heating facilities that conformed to applicable law when installed and have been maintained in good working order

■ Electrical lighting, with equipment and wiring that conformed to local building codes when installed and have been maintained in good working order

■ Building and grounds clean, sanitary, and free of debris, rubbish, rodents, and vermin at the time the lease term begins, with areas under the control of the landlord to be so maintained during the lease term

■ Adequate trash receptacles, provided in clean condition and good repair and so maintained by the landlord when under the landlord's control

■ Floors, stairways, and railings maintained in good repair

> A landlord is not allowed to retaliate against a tenant who complains.

A landlord is not allowed to penalize a tenant who complains to an appropriate agency about the condition of the premises or who uses rent money for repairs. Actions considered "penalties" include retaliatory eviction, increasing rent, or decreasing services. If the landlord does retaliate against the tenant and the tenant is not in default in payment of rent, the landlord may *not* recover possession of the premises, cause the tenant to quit the premises, increase rent, or decrease services, for *180 days* from notice of the complaint or needed repair.

If the landlord fails to make a necessary repair, the tenant also may sue the landlord for **breach of the warranty of habitability.** Or the tenant could simply **abandon** the premises with no further obligation to pay rent or otherwise comply with the lease terms. The tenant should seek competent professional advice before taking either action, however.

Commercial tenant's remedies. There are important exceptions to a commercial tenant's remedies, for a commercial tenant is regarded as being in a better bargaining position than a residential tenant.

At present the courts generally do *not* allow a commercial tenant to **repair and deduct.** A commercial tenant can bring a **lawsuit** against the landlord for breach of warranty, rather than use the breach as a reason for nonpayment of rent. The commercial tenant also may treat the breach as a **constructive eviction,** vacate the premises, and sue for damages.

Tenant's Obligations

In addition to paying rent, the **tenant** must care for the leased property and use it appropriately. The tenant's duties are specified in the California Civil Code.

- The tenant must keep the premises as clean and sanitary as conditions permit. Rubbish and other waste must be disposed of in a clean and sanitary manner. (The landlord could agree in writing to undertake the duties of maintenance and waste disposal.)
- The tenant must use all electrical, gas, and plumbing fixtures properly and keep them as clean and sanitary as conditions permit.
- Neither the tenant nor any person on the premises with the tenant's permission may deface, impair, or remove any part of the structure or its equipment.
- With regard to a dwelling place, different portions of the property may be used by the tenant only for the purposes for which they were designed and intended. For instance, only the kitchen may be used for cooking.

Landlord's remedies. If a tenant is in substantial violation of his or her obligation to use **ordinary care** to maintain the premises, a residential landlord has no duty to make resulting necessary repairs. The lease could give the tenant the **duty to repair,** but if such repairs are not reasonable the landlord will be unable to sue for damages if the repairs are not made.

Breach of lease terms also may give the landlord grounds for terminating the lease and evicting the tenant if necessary.

Liability of Landlord and Tenant

A guest in a leased building trips on a piece of loose tile flooring, falls, and breaks his arm. Who is liable for damages arising from the **defective condition** of the premises?

Under certain conditions, *landlord and/or tenant* could be liable for injuries suffered on the premises by anyone, whether tenant, an invited guest, someone permitted on the premises (such as a meter reader), or even a trespasser.

The **landlord** of *residential* property may be liable under a negligence theory for injuries to tenants that result from the defective condition of the premises at the time the tenant takes possession, if the landlord failed to correct the defect. The landlord's liability generally extends to damages that arise from injuries caused by *defective conditions* in the leased real estate that the landlord knew or should, with reasonable diligence, have known about. Even after the tenant takes possession, the landlord must repair defects that are brought to the landlord's attention. The landlord also is charged with the condition of public areas or areas over which the landlord retains control, such as hallways, stairways, and elevators.

■ **FOR EXAMPLE:** An apartment tenant suffered serious injuries after falling in a slippery bathtub. Is the landlord liable for the tenant's injuries?

In this case, yes, because the landlord should have treated the bathtub to make it safer for residents.

> The tenant should notify the landlord of a dangerous condition.

The landlord is not allowed to hide a defect in the property or simply post a warning sign. On the other hand, if the tenant is *aware* of a property defect that arises after taking possession and fails to notify the landlord, the landlord will *not* be liable for any subsequent injury.

The landlord is *not* liable to a **trespasser** who is injured on the property if the landlord did not know and could not be expected to know of an unsafe condition.

The **tenant's** liability extends to injuries on the premises as a result of the tenant's lack of ordinary care in maintaining the premises.

■ **FOR EXAMPLE:** A trespasser entered the premises of an automobile paint stripping company through a hole in a fence. The trespasser noticed a vat of a smelly liquid next to a business building. The vat was partially covered with a piece of plywood. The trespasser climbed onto the plywood to look through one of the building's windows. The plywood broke, and the trespasser fell into the vat, which contained highly corrosive acid used in stripping paint from cars. The landlord did not know of the hole in the fence, which was not there when the property was originally leased. The landlord was aware of the purpose for which the property had been leased, however. Is the landlord liable for the severe burns suffered by the trespasser?

No, the landlord is not liable for the trespasser's injuries. The property was used for its expected ordinary business purpose, and the landlord was unaware of the hole in the fence. The tenant may be liable to the trespasser if the tenant knew, or should have known, about the hole in the fence.

Exercise 12-2   Who usually bears responsibility for each of the following in a residential apartment building?

1. Termite infestation *landlord*

2. Hole in plaster wall made by guest of tenant *tenant*

3. Injury suffered by guest who trips over tenant's coffee table

tenant

4. Insufficient lighting in common hallway *landlord*
5. Broken main entry door to building *landlord*
6. Window broken by present tenant *tenant*
7. Window broken by previous tenant *landlord*
8. Trash pickup from outside receptacles *landlord*
9. Removing trash from premises *tenant*
10. Injuries to trespasser who falls through floorboard weakened by tenant's bathtub overflow that was never reported to the landlord *tenant*

Discriminatory Acts

The **Unruh Civil Rights Act,** found in the California Civil Code, forbids discrimination as to age, sex, race, color, religion, ancestry, national origin, disability, or medical condition in *accommodations* and *business establishments*. Under this law there can be no arbitrary eviction, rent increase, or withholding of services by virtually any landlord, including the owner of a nonowner-occupied single-family dwelling that is sold or leased for income or gain. An exception to the prohibition of discrimination based on age is made for housing designed to meet the physical and social needs of senior citizens.

■ **FOR EXAMPLE:** Len Lessor brings an action to evict Adam Lessee from one of his rental properties because Adam has numerous tattoos, receives public assistance, and is a student.

Len will not be successful because all of those "reasons" are arbitrary and fail to establish good cause for an eviction.

California's **Fair Employment and Housing Act (FEHA),** found in the Government Code, prohibits housing discrimination based on marital status as well as race, color, religion, sex, marital status, national origin, ancestry, familial status, or disability. The **Department of Fair Employment and Housing** enforces the law, which is based on the former Rumford Fair Housing Act.

■ **FOR EXAMPLE:** Some years ago Len Lessor tried to evict Alice Tenant because Alice, an unmarried woman, was living with an unrelated adult male. Len was unsuccessful because his intended action violated what was then the Rumford Act. Len recently decided to require that each member of an unrelated couple living together in one of his apartments meet his rental financial requirements, even though married couples can aggregate their income to meet the financial requirements. Can Len do that?

No. The Fair Employment and Housing Act bans discrimination based on marital status.

Since 1968, **federal law** has expressly prohibited public and private discrimination based on race, religion, or national origin or ancestry in the sale, rental, or lease of housing. Discrimination based on sex was prohibited in 1974. With the passage of the **Fair Housing Amendments Act of 1988,** discrimination on the basis of handicap or familial status (age) is also prohibited. These and other federal prohibitions against discrimination in housing will be covered further in Chapter 15, "Government Control of Land Use."

Note: "Discrimination" under FEHA does *not* include refusal to rent part of a single-family, owner-occupied dwelling to only one individual. All notices and advertisements must comply with FEHA, except for those expressing a preference for applicants of one sex for the sharing of living areas in a single dwelling unit.

Termination of the Lease

There are various ways by which a lease may be terminated, both with and without the consent of both parties.

Expiration of the lease term.   The lease itself should specify a termination date or the length of any notice to be given to the other party before termination.

A **lease for a definite term** terminates at the end of that term, even without notice.

> Landlord and tenant are free to agree on a termination date.

A **periodic tenancy** may be terminated on notice equal to the lease period but no more than 60 days. If a tenant fails to give adequate notice of termination, additional rent may be owed even if the premises are vacated as of the end of the lease term. If both parties agree, notice to vacate may be shorter than 60 days.

■ **FOR EXAMPLE:**   Jane Dough rented an apartment on a month-to-month basis as of the first of each month. On April 15 she notified her landlord that she would vacate the apartment on April 30. Jane Dough is liable for rent up to May 15. If Jane gives notice on April 15 of her intent to vacate on May 15, she still will owe rent only through May 15.

A **tenancy at will** always requires at least 60 days' written notice of termination to a tenant. A **tenant at sufferance** need not be given advance notice. The *death* of landlord or tenant automatically terminates a tenancy at will or tenancy at sufferance. It does not terminate a tenancy for a definite term unless the lease provides otherwise.

Surrender of the leasehold estate.   The lease interest can be given up by a **surrender** of the leasehold. This will happen if both parties consent to it, or if one of them acts in a manner inconsistent with the existence of the lease (such as the landlord leasing the property to someone else).

Grounds for unilateral termination. Either landlord or tenant may have grounds for **termination** of the lease without the other's consent.

A lease may be terminated by a **tenant** when

- the landlord has violated the tenant's right to *quiet enjoyment* (possession),
- the landlord has violated the *duty to repair*,
- the landlord otherwise has failed to keep the premises *habitable*,
- the landlord *evicts* the tenant,
- the landlord *breaches* a condition of the lease,
- the premises are *destroyed* and there is no covenant to repair, or
- the property is taken by *eminent domain*. (If only part of the property is taken, the lease will be effective as to the rest unless a court determines the remaining property is unsuitable for its leased purpose.)

A lease may be terminated by a **landlord** when

- the tenant uses the premises for an *unauthorized purpose*,
- the tenant *abandons* the premises,
- the tenant *breaches* a condition of the lease, or
- the premises are *destroyed* and there is no covenant to repair.

Request for demolition. California requires the owner of a residential dwelling unit (or the owner's agent) who applies to any public agency for a permit to demolish the unit to give written notice of the request to current tenants prior to applying for the permit. Notice of the request must be given to prospective tenants prior to entering into or initiating a rental agreement. The notice must include the earliest possible approximate date the owner expects the demolition to occur as well as the approximate date the owner will terminate the tenancy. If a landlord fails to provide the required notice, a court may award a tenant actual damages and moving expenses, in addition to a civil penalty not to exceed $2,500 and reasonable attorney's fees.

Abandonment. **Abandonment** is the tenant's voluntary relinquishment of the premises without the landlord's express or implied consent and with no intention to perform future lease obligations. (The landlord's express or implied consent would make the relinquishment a surrender rather than an abandonment.)

If rent is owed for at least 14 days and the landlord reasonably believes the tenant has abandoned the premises, the landlord can establish the fact of abandonment by giving *written notice* of that belief. The tenant must respond in writing within 15 days after personal service of the notice, or 18 days after receiving a mailed notice, denying any intent to abandon the property and giving the landlord a forwarding address where he or she can be reached. Notice is not strictly necessary, but it is a wise precaution that will protect the landlord if the tenant shows up later.

The abandonment notice can be given in addition to any other notice and may prove to be the fastest way to establish the landlord's right to retake possession of the property.

Eviction

Eviction is the process by which a tenant can be removed from the leased premises. The landlord must first *notify* the tenant of the breach of the lease or other unfulfilled obligation.

Notice. If the tenant has not paid the required rent, the lessor must first give three days' written **notice to pay or quit,** requesting compliance with the lease terms or property relinquishment. An example of such a notice appears in Figure 12.2. Similar notice is given if the tenant has breached some other lease provision.

If notice to terminate is given as discussed earlier, the notice period will be the period specified in the lease, the period of tenancy, or 30 days. In a periodic tenancy the notice period is 30 days, unless the lease specifies a shorter period, which must be at least seven days. Even when a tenant has breached such a lease (by not paying rent, for instance), the landlord may choose to use the 30-day notice to prevent the tenant from paying the rent and curing the breach. The landlord also could give both forms of notice.

Notice must be *written* and *personally served* on the other party or, in the tenant's absence, on a suitable person at the tenant's residence or place of business. If served on a third party, notice also must be mailed to the tenant at the tenant's residence address. If no residence or business address is known, notice must be placed in a conspicuous place on the leased property and also mailed to the tenant at the property location.

Government Owned or Subsidized Housing

Special notice requirements apply for rental housing owned or subsidized by a government agency. An action to evict such a tenant usually cannot be brought without first holding an administrative hearing. At the hearing, the tenant can be represented by an attorney, inspect all relevant documents, cross-examine the landlord's witnesses, and present contrary evidence, including witnesses, on the tenant's behalf. The tenant also has the right to have the hearing conducted in private.

FIGURE 12.2

Notice to Pay Rent or Quit

CALIFORNIA
ASSOCIATION
OF REALTORS®

THREE-DAY NOTICE TO PAY RENT OR QUIT
(C.A.R. Form PRQ, Revised 10/01)

To: _____

and all subtenants and any other occupants in possession of the premises located at (Street Address) _____

_____ (Unit/Apartment #) _____

(City) _____ (State) _____ (Zip Code) _____, ("Premises").

WITHIN THREE DAYS from service of this Notice you are required to either: **(i)** pay rent for the Premises in the following

amount, which is past due, to (Name) _____

(Phone)_____ at (Address)_____

_____

between the hours of _____ on the following days: _____.

Past Due Rent: $ _____ for the period _____ to _____

$ _____ for the period _____ to _____

$ _____ for the period _____ to _____

Total Due: $_____ .

OR (ii) vacate the Premises and surrender possession.

If you do not pay the past due amount or give up possession, a legal action will be filed seeking not only damages and

possession, but also a statutory damage penalty for an additional $600.00. Landlord declares a forfeiture of the lease if

past due rent is not paid and you continue to occupy the Premises. As required by law, you are hereby notified that a

negative credit report reflecting on your credit record may be submitted to a credit reporting agency if you fail to pay your

rent.

Landlord (Owner or Agent) _____ Date _____

(Keep a copy for your records.)

RIEBSNC   Published and Distributed by:
REAL ESTATE BUSINESS SERVICES, INC.
a subsidiary of the CALIFORNIA ASSOCIATION OF REALTORS®
525 South Virgil Avenue, Los Angeles, California 90020

OFFICE USE ONLY
Reviewed by Broker
or Designee _____
Date _____

EQUAL HOUSING
OPPORTUNITY

PRQ-11 REVISED 10/01 (PAGE 1 OF 1)   Print Date

THREE-DAY NOTICE TO PAY RENT OR QUIT (PRQ-11 PAGE 1 OF 1)

Unlawful detainer. If the tenant fails to comply after notice to pay or quit has been given, the landlord can **sue** for rent owed (which does not terminate the lease). The landlord also can request an **order of eviction** from the court by a legal proceeding called **unlawful detainer.** If the court decides in favor of the landlord and if the notice to the tenant stated the landlord's intention to declare a forfeiture of the lease, the lease will be forfeited.

The tenant will be liable for damages (such as rent owed) up to the date of the court's judgment or the date the landlord retakes possession of the premises. If the landlord failed to include a statement of intention to declare a forfeiture in the notice, the tenant's liability for damages is up to the court's determination.

A landlord of residential property may not cause disruption or termination of the tenant's utility service, even if the right of eviction has been granted.

Tenant's response. The tenant can defeat the unlawful detainer action if

- proper notice was not given;
- the landlord's action is retaliatory;
- the alleged facts are not true;
- the landlord's action is arbitrary (without good cause); or
- there is some other legal barrier to the eviction, such as a violation of the Unruh Act.

A tenant may *willfully* and *maliciously* remain in possession of leased premises after the expiration or termination of the lease term, in what is called a **holdover tenancy.** In that case, the tenant is liable to the landlord for *three times* the amount of rent and any damages due, as punitive damages.

> An unlawful detainer action is given priority over all other civil cases.

An unlawful detainer is not the only legal action that can be brought by a landlord against a tenant, but it may be the *quickest* way to regain possession of leased premises. Courts must give unlawful detainer suits precedence over all other cases—except criminal cases—in setting a court date.

Lessor and lessee frequently settle their differences before a trial. The landlord may forgive part or all of the rent owed, or even pay the tenant's moving expenses, in exchange for a prompt vacancy. If the tenant has proof of some breach by the landlord, it is more likely that concessions will be made.

Writ of possession. The landlord who succeeds in an unlawful detainer suit can be awarded **rent arrearages, damages** caused by the unlawful detention, and **possession** of the leased premises. If possession is granted, the clerk of the court issues a **writ of possession** that directs the sheriff or marshal to take all legal steps necessary to remove the tenant(s) from the premises.

The sheriff or marshal executes the writ by *serving* it on one occupant of the property. Service is accomplished by leaving a copy of the writ with the occupant or an employee or agent of the occupant or a suitable member of the occupant's household. If that is not possible, a copy of the writ is *posted* in a conspicuous place on the premises, and another copy is served *personally* or *by mail* to the judgment debtor.

Five days after the service, the sheriff or marshal may remove any occupant still on the premises, *unless* the occupant

- is *not* named in the writ and
- claims possession or a right to possession that stems from *before* the time at which the unlawful detainer action was filed with the court.

Stay of execution.

The tenant may receive a **stay of execution** of a judgment in favor of the landlord for *five days* in order to pay back rent and have legal possession restored *if*

- the reason for the eviction is nonpayment of rent,
- the lease would not have expired otherwise, and
- the termination notice did not declare the forfeiture of the tenant's lease rights.

The trial court also can stay execution of the judgment under its own authority.

Tenant's personal possessions.

An **inventory** must be made of any of the tenant's personal possessions left behind when the tenant vacates the premises. The inventory is made or verified by the sheriff or marshal. The landlord must store the possessions for 30 days (on or off the premises), during which time they can be reclaimed on payment of reasonable storage fees. If unclaimed, they may be sold at public auction and the proceeds applied to storage and sale costs. Any remaining sale proceeds and security or other deposits must be returned to the tenant.

- **FOR EXAMPLE:** Marvin Leach was evicted from an apartment at the Jolly Arms. Marvin never responded to any of the notices that were sent. When the property manager took possession of the apartment, a sheriff's deputy was present to inventory the clothing and furnishings Marvin had left behind. The items then were stored in a locked basement area inaccessible to tenants. The landlord also changed the locks to the apartment. One week later, Marvin showed up and demanded the key to his apartment. He said he had been called out of the country on a very important assignment and had simply been too busy to send word back to the property manager. Does Marvin have the right to reclaim his apartment?

No. It was Marvin's responsibility to make sure that his absence was understood and not misinterpreted as an abandonment of the apartment. By failing to contact the property manager, Marvin forfeited his right to the apartment. He can reclaim the belongings he left in the apartment, but he must pay any reasonable storage fees. He also will receive any part of his security deposit to which he is entitled.

■ MOBILE-HOME TENANCIES

Laws applying to mobile homes appear in many California code sections. Some of the most important provisions are mentioned here.

Mobilehome Residency Law

The **Mobilehome Residency Law (MRL)** (Civil Code Sections 798–799.6) regulates manufactured (mobile) home rental agreements, charges, grounds for eviction, and eviction procedures.

The MRL defines a *mobile home*, *mobile home park*, *homeowner*, *resident*, and *tenancy* to which the law is applicable. General landlord-tenant laws apply to manufactured housing, except where they are preempted by specific laws regarding such homes.

Applicability. The MRL applies to agreements between (1) mobile home park management and the resident of an owner-occupied home and (2) mobile home park management and a nonresident owner who rents a home to someone else. In the latter case, the agreement could include provision for subletting.

Agreements between park management and the resident of a park owned home are not included in the MRL, although for the sake of uniformity similar provisions should be used.

Parks are subject to the same provisions against discrimination that apply to other residential landlords, although the type and size of homes within a park can be controlled.

Fees. The *prescribed lease form* includes any fees to be paid by the tenant, although an additional fee can be imposed after 60 days' written notice. Fees are *limited* to rent, utilities, and incidental reasonable service charges.

Termination. The MRL states the following as the *only* permitted reasons for termination of a lease by mobile home park management:

- Nonpayment of rent, utility charges, or reasonable incidental service charges
- Failure to comply with reasonable park rules or regulations as set out in the rental agreement or amendments
- Conduct by the homeowner or resident on park premises that is a "substantial annoyance" to other homeowners or residents
- Failure of homeowner or resident to comply with applicable laws and ordinances within a reasonable time
- Condemnation of the park
- Change of use of the park

Notice.   If a tenant has not paid rent, utility bills, or other fees for at least five days from their due date, termination proceedings may begin. A written **notice to pay or quit** must be made, allowing *three days* for payment to be made. Written **notice of termination** must be given *60 days* before the termination date. A copy of the notice must be sent to the registered mobile-home owner and junior lienholders within ten days of service on the homeowner.

> A notice of termination can be defeated by payment, but only twice in a 12-month period.

Notice of termination can be given at the same time as notice to pay or quit, but payment within the three-day period will satisfy both. The registered homeowner (if not the same as the resident), the legal owner (if there is a deed of trust on the property), and any junior lienholders have *30 days* after the notice of termination is mailed in which to cure the default but may do so no more than twice during a 12-month period.

If the homeowner or resident has not complied with reasonable park rules, a *seven-day* written *notice to comply* must precede the 60-day notice of termination, *unless* three such notices already have been given within a 12-month period.

Other notice provisions apply if the termination is due to a change of use of the park in which the home is located.

Exercise 12-3   What is the minimum notice or other time requirement for each of the following?

1. Notice to terminate a tenancy at will   30
2. Tenant's denial of abandonment of premises   15 or 18 days mailed
3. Notice to pay or quit   3
4. Enforcement of writ of possession   5
5. Storage of tenant's personal belongings after eviction   30
6. Notice to pay or quit under MRL   3
7. Notice to terminate under MRL   60

■ OTHER LEASE ARRANGEMENTS

Lease Option

A lease can serve many purposes. A **lease option,** unlike an option alone, conveys the **right of possession** as well as the option right. In residential transactions especially, the lease option can be a way to ensure a subsequent purchase, particularly if part of each lease payment is applied to the eventual down payment.

■ **FOR EXAMPLE:** Joan Nest would like to purchase a home, but she has only $9,000, not enough for an adequate down payment on the kind of house she would like to buy. Al Hast agrees to give Joan a one-year lease with option to purchase on his single-family residence. Joan will make a monthly payment of $2,000 in consideration for the lease and option. This is somewhat more than the average rental in the area of $1,400 for a comparable home, but $600 of every payment will be credited to Joan in the event she chooses to buy the property at the end of the lease term at an agreed purchase price of $170,000.

At the end of the lease term Joan will have a credit of $7,200, which, added to her savings of $9,000 (plus interest), will give her enough for the down payment she wants to make. If the property appreciates in value over the term of the lease, Joan also will benefit from the already agreed-on purchase price. Al, who has seen other property in his area take many months to sell and needs to move to take a new job, is happy to have the house rented for the time being at a higher-than-market payment. He also is reasonably confident Joan will buy the house at the end of the lease term.

Commercial Leases

In the typical **gross lease** the tenant pays a fixed amount for rent over the lease term. In turn, the landlord pays all expenses of ownership, such as taxes, assessments, and insurance.

An **escalator clause** in a lease may provide for an increase in payments based on an increase in an index such as the **consumer price index (CPI)** or the **wholesale price index (WPI).** This type of lease is called a **graduated lease.**

> With a percentage lease, both landlord and tenant share in the success of the tenant's business.

Commercial lease rent payments also may be based on the income earned on the leased premises. In a **percentage lease,** the rent is a percentage of the tenant's **gross income,** usually with a minimum base amount. As income increases, the percentage typically decreases.

■ **FOR EXAMPLE:** Pam's Pins and Needles Shop pays a base monthly rent of $1,000 plus 4 percent of gross income over $20,000 per month and 2 percent of gross income over $40,000 per month. If proceeds for February are $32,000, what is the required rent payment for that month?

The required payment is $1,480, which is the base rent of $1,000 plus 4 percent of $12,000 ($32,000 − $20,000).

With a **net lease,** the landlord is guaranteed a specific (net) income because the tenant pays that amount plus some or all of the operating and other expenses, such as taxes, insurance, assessments, maintenance, and other charges. The tenant's obligations are stipulated in the lease agreement. A net lease is also called a **triple net lease** or **3N lease.**

Other lease terms.   New contract issues involving commercial properties have arisen as a result of the terrorist attacks of September 11, 2001. Issues that are now of concern, particularly with well-known buildings, include access control and security, including admittance to the building, parking, and mail and other deliveries. They are subject to negotiation between landlord and tenant, but should be covered.

■ PROPERTY MANAGEMENT

An increasingly important area of real estate investment is **property management.** Having a local property manager enables property owners to make profitable use of income-producing property they may never see. Even for local owners, a qualified property manager can take on many of the burdens of being a landlord.

Any type of property, from a single-family residence to a 1,000-unit office building, can be managed by an agent of the owner. The size of modern structures and widespread holdings of some investors have made property management a necessary specialty in the real estate field.

The Resident Property Manager

In California, every building with 16 or more dwelling units must have a **resident apartment manager.** By living on the premises, the resident manager helps ensure that tenant complaints are handled promptly.

Duties of the Property Manager

An on-site resident property manager, or professional management firm or individual with a real estate broker's license, can act as the owner's agent to

- lease units,
- collect rents,
- maintain communication with tenants, and
- conduct all day-to-day business necessary to maintain the property.

The property manager ordinarily earns a fee based on the income the property produces in rents. The property manager also may receive a separate fee for such activities as supervising alterations or remodeling. A typical form of **property management agreement** is shown in Figure 12.3. It details the expected duties of the property manager.

FIGURE 12.3

Property Management Agreement

CALIFORNIA ASSOCIATION OF REALTORS®

PROPERTY MANAGEMENT AGREEMENT
(C.A.R. Form PMA, Revised 4/03)

_____ ("Owner"), and
_____ ("Broker"), agree as follows:

1. **APPOINTMENT OF BROKER:** Owner hereby appoints and grants Broker the exclusive right to rent, lease, operate and manage the property(ies) known as _____
_____ and any additional property that may later be added to this Agreement ("Property"), upon the terms below, for the period beginning (date) _____ and ending (date) _____, at 11:59 PM.
(If checked:) ☐ Either party may terminate this Property Management Agreement ("Agreement") on at least 30 days written notice _____ months after the original commencement date of this Agreement. After the exclusive term expires, this Agreement shall continue as a non-exclusive agreement that either party may terminate by giving at least 30 days written notice to the other.

2. **BROKER ACCEPTANCE:** Broker accepts the appointment and grant, and agrees to:
   A. Use due diligence in the performance of this Agreement.
   B. Furnish the services of its firm for the rental, leasing, operation and management of the Property.

3. **AUTHORITY AND POWERS:** Owner grants Broker the authority and power, at Owner's expense, to:
   A. **ADVERTISING:** Display FOR RENT/LEASE and similar signs on the Property and advertise the availability of the Property, or any part thereof, for rental or lease.
   B. **RENTAL;LEASING:** Initiate, sign, renew, modify or cancel rental agreements and leases for the Property, or any part thereof; collect and give receipts for rents, other fees, charges and security deposits. Any lease or rental agreement executed by Broker for Owner shall not exceed _____ year(s) or ☐ shall be month-to-month. Unless Owner authorizes a lower amount, rent shall be: ☐ at market rate; OR ☐ a minimum of $ _____ per _____; OR ☐ see attachment.
   C. **TENANCY TERMINATION:** Sign and serve in Owner's name notices that are required or appropriate; commence and prosecute actions to evict tenants; recover possession of the Property in Owner's name; recover rents and other sums due; and, when expedient, settle, compromise and release claims, actions and suits and/or reinstate tenancies.
   D. **REPAIR;MAINTENANCE:** Make, cause to be made, and/or supervise repairs, improvements, alterations and decorations to the Property; purchase, and pay bills for, services and supplies. Broker shall obtain prior approval of Owner for all expenditures over $ _____ for any one item. Prior approval shall not be required for monthly or recurring operating charges or, if in Broker's opinion, emergency expenditures over the maximum are needed to protect the Property or other property(ies) from damage, prevent injury to persons, avoid suspension of necessary services, avoid penalties or fines, or suspension of services to tenants required by a lease or rental agreement or by law, including, but not limited to, maintaining the Property in a condition fit for human habitation as required by Civil Code §§ 1941 and 1941.1 and Health and Safety Code §§ 17920.3 and 17920.10.
   E. **REPORTS, NOTICES AND SIGNS:** Comply with federal, state or local law requiring delivery of reports or notices and/or posting of signs or notices.
   F. **CONTRACTS;SERVICES:** Contract, hire, supervise and/or discharge firms and persons, including utilities, required for the operation and maintenance of the Property. Broker may perform any of Broker's duties through attorneys, agents, employees, or independent contractors and, except for persons working in Broker's firm, shall not be responsible for their acts, omissions, defaults, negligence and/or costs of same.
   G. **EXPENSE PAYMENTS:** Pay expenses and costs for the Property from Owner's funds held by Broker, unless otherwise directed by Owner. Expenses and costs may include, but are not limited to, property management compensation, fees and charges, expenses for goods and services, property taxes and other taxes, Owner's Association dues, assessments, loan payments and insurance premiums.
   H. **SECURITY DEPOSITS:** Receive security deposits from tenants, which deposits shall be ☐ given to Owner, or ☐ placed in Broker's trust account and, if held in Broker's trust account, pay from Owner's funds all interest on tenants' security deposits if required by local law or ordinance. Owner shall be responsible to tenants for return of security deposits and all interest due on security deposits held by Owner.
   I. **TRUST FUNDS:** Deposit all receipts collected for Owner, less any sums properly deducted or disbursed, in a financial institution whose deposits are insured by an agency of the United States government. The funds shall be held in a trust account separate from Broker's personal accounts. Broker shall not be liable in event of bankruptcy or failure of a financial institution.
   J. **RESERVES:** Maintain a reserve in Broker's trust account of $ _____.
   K. **DISBURSEMENTS:** Disburse Owner's funds held in Broker's trust account in the following order:
      (1) Compensation due Broker under paragraph 6.
      (2) All other operating expenses, costs and disbursements payable from Owner's funds held by Broker.
      (3) Reserves and security deposits held by Broker.
      (4) Balance to Owner.
   L. **OWNER DISTRIBUTION:** Remit funds, if any are available, monthly (or ☐ _____), to Owner.
   M. **OWNER STATEMENTS:** Render monthly (or ☐ _____), statements of receipts, expenses and charges for each Property.
   N. **BROKER FUNDS:** Broker shall not advance Broker's own funds in connection with the Property or this Agreement.
   O. ☐ (If checked) Owner authorizes the use of a keysafe/lockbox to allow entry into the Propery and agrees to sign a keysafe/lockbox addendum (C.A.R. Form KLA).

Owner's Initials (_____)(_____)
Broker's Initials (_____)(_____)

Reviewed by _____ Date _____

EQUAL HOUSING OPPORTUNITY

PMA REVISED 4/03 (PAGE 1 OF 3) Print Date

PROPERTY MANAGEMENT AGREEMENT (PMA PAGE 1 OF 3)

Source: Reprinted with permission, California Association of REALTORS®. Endorsement not implied.

FIGURE 12.3

Property Management Agreement (Continued)

Owner Name: _____   Date: _____

4. **OWNER RESPONSIBILITIES:** Owner shall:
   A. Provide all documentation, records and disclosures as required by law or required by Broker to manage and operate the Property, and immediately notify Broker if Owner becomes aware of any change in such documentation, records or disclosures, or any matter affecting the habitability of the Property.
   B. Indemnify, defend and hold harmless Broker, and all persons in Broker's firm, regardless of responsibility, from all costs, expenses, suits, liabilities, damages, attorney fees and claims of every type, including but not limited to those arising out of injury or death of any person, or damage to any real or personal property of any person, including Owner, for: **(i)** any repairs performed by Owner or by others hired directly by Owner; or **(ii)** those relating to the management, leasing, rental, security deposits, or operation of the Property by Broker, or any person in Broker's firm, or the performance or exercise of any of the duties, powers or authorities granted to Broker.
   C. Maintain the Property in a condition fit for human habitation as required by Civil Code §§ 1941 and 1941.1 and Health and Safety Code §§ 17920.3 and 17920.10 and other applicable law.
   D. Pay all interest on tenants' security deposits if required by local law or ordinance.
   E. Carry and pay for: **(i)** public and premises liability insurance in an amount of no less than $1,000,000; and **(ii)** property damage and worker's compensation insurance adequate to protect the interests of Owner and Broker. Broker shall be, and Owner authorizes Broker to be, named as an additional insured party on Owner's policies.
   F. Pay any late charges, penalties and/or interest imposed by lenders or other parties for failure to make payment to those parties, if the failure is due to insufficient funds in Broker's trust account available for such payment.
   G. Immediately replace any funds required if there are insufficient funds in Broker's trust account to cover Owner's responsibilities.
5. **LEAD-BASED PAINT DISCLOSURE:**
   A. ☐ The Property was constructed on or after January 1, 1978.
   OR B. ☐ The Property was constructed prior to 1978.
      (1) Owner has no knowledge of lead-based paint or lead-based paint hazards in the housing except: _____
      _____
      (2) Owner has no reports or records pertaining to lead-based paint or lead-based paint hazards in the housing, except the following, which Owner shall provide to Broker: _____.
6. **COMPENSATION:**
   A. Owner agrees to pay Broker fees in the amounts indicated below for:
      (1) Management: _____.
      (2) Renting or Leasing: _____.
      (3) Evictions: _____.
      (4) Preparing Property for rental or lease: _____.
      (5) Managing Property during extended periods of vacancy: _____.
      (6) An overhead and service fee added to the cost of all work performed by, or at the direction of, Broker: _____.
      (7) Other: _____.
   B. This Agreement does not include providing on-site management services, property sales, refinancing, preparing Property for sale or refinancing, modernization, fire or major damage restoration, rehabilitation, obtaining income tax, accounting or legal advice, representation before public agencies, advising on proposed new construction, debt collection, counseling, attending Owner's Association meetings or _____
      _____.
      If Owner requests Broker to perform services not included in this Agreement, a fee shall be agreed upon before these services are performed.
   C. Broker may divide compensation, fees and charges due under this Agreement in any manner acceptable to Broker.
   D. Owner further agrees that:
      (1) Broker may receive and keep fees and charges from tenants for: **(i)** requesting an assignment of lease or sublease of the Property; **(ii)** processing credit applications; **(iii)** any returned checks and/or (☐ if checked) late payments; and **(iv)** any other services that are not in conflict with this Agreement.
      (2) Broker may perform any of Broker's duties, and obtain necessary products and services, through affiliated companies or organizations in which Broker may own an interest. Broker may receive fees, commissions and/or profits from these affiliated companies or organizations. Broker has an ownership interest in the following affiliated companies or organizations: _____
      _____
      Broker shall disclose to Owner any other such relationships as they occur. Broker shall not receive any fees, commissions or profits from unaffiliated companies or organizations in the performance of this Agreement, without prior disclosure to Owner.
      (3) Other: _____
7. **AGENCY RELATIONSHIPS:** Broker shall act, and Owner hereby consents to Broker acting, as dual agent for Owner and tenant(s) in any resulting transaction. If the Property includes residential property with one-to-four dwelling units and this Agreement permits a tenancy in excess of one year, Owner acknowledges receipt of the "Disclosure Regarding Agency Relationships" (C.A.R. Form AD). Owner understands that Broker may have or obtain property management agreements on other property, and that potential tenants may consider, make offers on, or lease through Broker, property the same as or similar to Owner's Property. Owner consents to Broker's representation of other owners' properties before, during and after the expiration of this Agreement.
8. **NOTICES:** Any written notice to Owner or Broker required under this Agreement shall be served by sending such notice by first class mail or other agreed-to delivery method to that party at the address below, or at any different address the parties may later designate for this purpose. Notice shall be deemed received three (3) calendar days after deposit into the United States mail OR ☐ _____.

Owner's Initials (_____)(_____)
Broker's Initials (_____)(_____)

PMA REVISED 4/03 (PAGE 2 OF 3)

Reviewed by _____ Date _____

EQUAL HOUSING
OPPORTUNITY

PROPERTY MANAGEMENT AGREEMENT (PMA PAGE 2 OF 3)

FIGURE 12.3

Property Management Agreement (Continued)

Owner Name: _____ Date: _____

9. DISPUTE RESOLUTION

A. MEDIATION: Owner and Broker agree to mediate any dispute or claim arising between them out of this Agreement, or any resulting transaction before resorting to arbitration or court action, subject to paragraph 9B(2) below. Paragraph 9B(2) below applies whether or not the arbitration provision is initialed. Mediation fees, if any, shall be divided equally among the parties involved. If, for any dispute or claim to which this paragraph applies, any party commences an action based on a dispute or claim to which this paragraph applies, without first attempting to resolve the matter through mediation, or refuses to mediate after a request has been made, then that party shall not be entitled to recover attorney fees, even if they would otherwise be available to that party in any such action. THIS MEDIATION PROVISION APPLIES WHETHER OR NOT THE ARBITRATION PROVISION IS INITIALED.

B. ARBITRATION OF DISPUTES: (1) Owner and Broker agree that any dispute or claim in law or equity arising between them regarding the obligation to pay compensation under this agreement, which is not settled through mediation, shall be decided by neutral, binding arbitration, including and subject to paragraph 9B(2) below. The arbitrator shall be a retired judge or justice, or an attorney with at least 5 years of residential real estate law experience, unless the parties mutually agree to a different arbitrator, who shall render an award in accordance with substantive California Law. The parties shall have the right to discovery in accordance with Code of Civil Procedure § 1283.05. In all other respects, the arbitration shall be conducted in accordance with Title 9 of Part III of the California Code of Civil Procedure. Judgment upon the award of the arbitrator(s) may be entered in any court having jurisdiction. Interpretation of this agreement to arbitrate shall be governed by the Federal Arbitration Act.

(2) EXCLUSIONS FROM MEDIATION AND ARBITRATION: The following matters are excluded from mediation and arbitration hereunder: **(i)** a judicial or non-judicial foreclosure or other action or proceeding to enforce a deed of trust, mortgage, or installment land sale contract as defined in Civil Code § 2985; **(ii)** an unlawful detainer action; **(iii)** the filing or enforcement of a mechanic's lien; and **(iv)** any matter that is within the jurisdiction of a probate, small claims, or bankruptcy court. The filing of a court action to enable the recording of a notice of pending action, for order of attachment, receivership, injunction, or other provisional remedies, shall not constitute a waiver of the mediation and arbitration provisions.

"NOTICE: BY INITIALING IN THE SPACE BELOW YOU ARE AGREEING TO HAVE ANY DISPUTE ARISING OUT OF THE MATTERS INCLUDED IN THE 'ARBITRATION OF DISPUTES' PROVISION DECIDED BY NEUTRAL ARBITRATION AS PROVIDED BY CALIFORNIA LAW AND YOU ARE GIVING UP ANY RIGHTS YOU MIGHT POSSESS TO HAVE THE DISPUTE LITIGATED IN A COURT OR JURY TRIAL. BY INITIALING IN THE SPACE BELOW YOU ARE GIVING UP YOUR JUDICIAL RIGHTS TO DISCOVERY AND APPEAL, UNLESS THOSE RIGHTS ARE SPECIFICALLY INCLUDED IN THE 'ARBITRATION OF DISPUTES' PROVISION. IF YOU REFUSE TO SUBMIT TO ARBITRATION AFTER AGREEING TO THIS PROVISION, YOU MAY BE COMPELLED TO ARBITRATE UNDER THE AUTHORITY OF THE CALIFORNIA CODE OF CIVIL PROCEDURE. YOUR AGREEMENT TO THIS ARBITRATION PROVISION IS VOLUNTARY."

"WE HAVE READ AND UNDERSTAND THE FOREGOING AND AGREE TO SUBMIT DISPUTES ARISING OUT OF THE MATTERS INCLUDED IN THE 'ARBITRATION OF DISPUTES' PROVISION TO NEUTRAL ARBITRATION."

Owner's Initials _____ / _____   Broker's Initials _____ / _____

10. EQUAL HOUSING OPPORTUNITY: The Property is offered in compliance with federal, state and local anti-discrimination laws.

11. ATTORNEY FEES: In any action, proceeding or arbitration between Owner and Broker regarding the obligation to pay compensation under this Agreement, the prevailing Owner or Broker shall be entitled to reasonable attorney fees and costs from the non-prevailing Owner or Broker, except as provided in paragraph 9A.

12. ADDITIONAL TERMS: ☐ Keysafe/Lockbox Addendum (C.A.R. Form KLA); ☐ Lead-Based Paint and Lead-Based Paint Hazards Disclosure (C.A.R. Form FLD) _____

13. TIME OF ESSENCE; ENTIRE CONTRACT; CHANGES: Time is of the essence. All understandings between the parties are incorporated in this Agreement. Its terms are intended by the parties as a final, complete and exclusive expression of their Agreement with respect to its subject matter, and may not be contradicted by evidence of any prior agreement or contemporaneous oral agreement. If any provision of this Agreement is held to be ineffective or invalid, the remaining provisions will nevertheless be given full force and effect. Neither this Agreement nor any provision in it may be extended, amended, modified, altered or changed except in writing. This Agreement and any supplement, addendum or modification, including any copy, may be signed in two or more counterparts, all of which shall constitute one and the same writing.

Owner warrants that Owner is the owner of the Property or has the authority to execute this contract. Owner acknowledges Owner has read, understands, accepts and has received a copy of the Agreement.

Owner _____ Date _____
Owner _____
    Print Name   Social Security/Tax ID # (for tax reporting purposes)
Address _____ City _____ State _____ Zip _____
Telephone _____ Fax _____ E-mail _____

Owner _____ Date _____
Owner _____
    Print Name   Social Security/Tax ID # (for tax reporting purposes)
Address _____ City _____ State _____ Zip _____
Telephone _____ Fax _____ E-mail _____

Real Estate Broker (Firm) _____ Date _____
By (Agent) _____
Address _____ City _____ State _____ Zip _____
Telephone _____ Fax _____ E-mail _____

THIS FORM HAS BEEN APPROVED BY THE CALIFORNIA ASSOCIATION OF REALTORS® (C.A.R.). NO REPRESENTATION IS MADE AS TO THE LEGAL VALIDITY OR ADEQUACY OF ANY PROVISION IN ANY SPECIFIC TRANSACTION. A REAL ESTATE BROKER IS THE PERSON QUALIFIED TO ADVISE ON REAL ESTATE TRANSACTIONS. IF YOU DESIRE LEGAL OR TAX ADVICE, CONSULT AN APPROPRIATE PROFESSIONAL.

This form is available for use by the entire real estate industry. It is not intended to identify the user as a REALTOR®. REALTOR® is a registered collective membership mark which may be used only by members of the NATIONAL ASSOCIATION OF REALTORS® who subscribe to its Code of Ethics.

SURE•TRAC
The System for Success™

Published by the
California Association of REALTORS®

Reviewed by _____ Date _____

PMA REVISED 4/03 (PAGE 3 OF 3)

PROPERTY MANAGEMENT AGREEMENT (PMA PAGE 3 OF 3)

Source: Reprinted with permission, California Association of REALTORS®. Endorsement not implied.

Qualifications of the Property Manager

Real estate brokers can be property managers, but sound business practice as well as ethical considerations require that they be adequately prepared before offering their services as property managers.

Knowledge of contracts, lease requirements, building operation, maintenance, and other aspects of property management, including the "people skills" necessary to deal with tenants, must be learned by training, study, or experience. Large commercial projects may require the services of multiple agents, separately skilled in marketing, accounting, public relations, and other property management abilities.

■ RENT CONTROL

A **rent control ordinance** is imposed by a local governing body to protect tenants from relatively high rent increases over the occupancy period of a lease. In the past, as many as one-quarter of California's residential units were subject to some form of rent control.

Types of Rent Control

There are two types of rent control in California, based on whether a new tenant benefits from existing rent protection. There is also a state law that eliminates rent control on new units, single-family homes, and other properties.

Ordinances with vacancy decontrol. If an ordinance contains a vacancy decontrol provision, when a unit becomes vacant there is no restriction on the rent set for a new tenant. After the premises have been leased again, the new rent becomes the new base amount and is again subject to controls. Los Angeles, Oakland, San Francisco, and San Jose have this type of ordinance.

Ordinances without vacancy decontrol. Ordinances *without* a vacancy decontrol provision limit rent increases for new tenants as well as for existing ones. Berkeley, Cotati, East Palo Alto, Palm Springs, and Santa Monica all have this type of ordinance.

State Law

The **Costa-Hawkins Rental Housing Act** preempts local rent control laws on

- new units with a certificate of occupancy issued after February 1, 1995;
- single-family dwellings; and
- multiunit dwellings in areas with vacancy control, except where the tenancy is terminated by the landlord's service of a termination notice or a change in the tenancy's terms.

> State law has greatly reduced the impact of rent control.

From January 1, 1996, through December 31, 1998, after a voluntary vacancy, abandonment, or eviction based on nonpayment of rent on one of these units, landlords were allowed to increase rents by the greater of 15 percent or up to 70 percent of the prevailing market rate for a comparable unit. Two rent increases were allowed during the initial three-year period.

As of January 1, 1999, there are no limits on allowable rent increases for new tenancies *and* tenancies created on or after January 1, 1996.

http://pen.ci.santa-monica.
ca.us/cm/index.htm

Information on how the new law has affected one community can be found at the City of Santa Monica's Web site, *http://pen.ci.santa-monica.ca.us /cm/index.htm.*

Exercise 12-4   Carl Jones wants to lease a storefront for his new business, Carl's Computers. In addition to selling computers, he will also be conducting classes in computer and Internet use.

Percentage lease —   *lease percentage*

Carl approaches Barbara Krause, who has a vacant unit in a small strip shopping center in a high-traffic area near a community college. Barbara is impressed by Carl's business plan and agrees to lease space to him. She is interested in helping him become established, and also in benefiting from the expected growth of his business.

What kind of lease would best accomplish the aims of both Carl and Barbara?

■ SUMMARY

A **lease** is a form of contract transferring a less-than-freehold estate—the right to property possession and use but not ownership. The **lessor (landlord)** conveys the leased premises to the **lessee (tenant).** The tenant pays **rent** in consideration for the lease. A **security deposit** may also be required. If rent is unpaid, the landlord has the ultimate remedy of **eviction.**

A written lease agreement may be required by law, and it always is preferable. A lease follows the same formalities as any other contract. A statement of property condition at the time the lease begins will help when the tenant vacates the premises.

If the tenant's **right to quiet enjoyment** of the premises is interfered with by the landlord, the tenant may complain of being **constructively evicted.** The landlord has only a limited **right to enter** the leased premises and usually must give notice to the tenant first.

The tenant may be able to **sublease** or **assign** the right of possession granted by the lease. There are strict requirements for **automatic renewal** of leases.

The landlord makes an **implied warranty of habitability** and an **express** or **implied covenant to repair** the premises. Certain minimal requirements must be met or a dwelling is considered **untenantable.** If the landlord fails to meet those responsibilities, the tenant can complain to the appropriate authorities, withhold rent to make necessary repairs the landlord has not made, sue the landlord, or abandon the premises.

The tenant must also maintain the premises and cannot expect repairs from the landlord for damage resulting from the tenant's own **negligence.**

Both landlord and tenant may be liable to persons injured on the premises if the premises are under their control and they fail to exercise **ordinary care.** A landlord may be liable for injuries to a tenant of residential property caused by the **defective condition** of the premises.

Discrimination in accommodations and business establishments is forbidden by the **Unruh Civil Rights Act.** Discrimination in housing is forbidden by the **California Fair Employment and Housing Act.** Federal prohibitions against housing discrimination also apply.

Notice may be required to **terminate** a lease. The leasehold estate could be surrendered by agreement of the parties. There are specific grounds for termination before the end of the lease term, and the tenant could simply abandon the premises.

Eviction can be carried out only by a prescribed procedure, including notice to the tenant. An **unlawful detainer** is the legal action that can result in a **writ of possession** directing the sheriff or marshal to remove the tenant(s) from the premises.

Manufactured home rentals have certain unique requirements, although they basically follow general landlord-tenant law. Other types of leases can range from the **lease option** to the **net lease** used in commercial transactions.

Property management is an important and growing area of real estate professionalism. **Rent control** in several forms exists in communities throughout the state. Legal counsel must be consulted for particular requirements of individual ordinances as well as state law.

■ IMPORTANT TERMS

Make sure you understand the following terms before you take the achievement examination.

abandonment

constructive eviction

Costa-Hawkins Rental Housing Act

covenant of quiet enjoyment

covenant to repair

escalator clause

estate at sufferance

estate at will

estate for years

estate from period to period

eviction

Fair Employment and Housing
Act (FEHA)

Fair Housing Amendments Act
of 1988

gross lease

holdover tenancy

landlord

lease

lease assignment

leasehold

lease option

lessee

lessor

Mobilehome Residency Law
(MRL)

net lease

notice to pay or quit

percentage lease

periodic tenancy

property management

rent

rent control

resident apartment manager

right of entry

sandwich lease

security deposit

tenant

unlawful detainer

Unruh Civil Rights Act

untenantable dwelling

warranty of habitability

■ OPEN FOR DISCUSSION

Lack of affordable housing continues to be a problem in California and is a deterrent to business entry and growth.

Suggest ways in which decent housing can be provided for all citizens, particularly the "working poor."

■ ACHIEVEMENT EXAMINATION 12

1. An apartment in San Francisco can be leased for a term of no more than
   a. 150 years.
   b. a reasonable time.
   c. 99 years.
   d. 51 years.

2. An office in Los Angeles can be leased for a term of no more than
   a. 150 years.
   b. a reasonable time.
   c. 99 years.
   d. 51 years.

3. Agricultural land can be leased for a term of no more than
   a. 150 years.
   b. a reasonable time.
   c. 99 years.
   d. 51 years.

4. A security deposit on furnished residential property can be no more than
   a. two months' rent.
   b. three months' rent.
   c. a reasonable amount.
   d. $2,000.

5. If a question arises as to the validity of a landlord's claim against a tenant's security deposit
   a. the landlord is presumed to be entitled to the security deposit.
   b. the tenant is presumed to be entitled to the security deposit.
   c. the security deposit is forfeited to the state.
   d. there is no presumption regarding ownership of the security deposit.

6. Lulu Landlord wants to give Tom Tenant's apartment to her nephew Ken. Lulu tries to drive Tom out by constantly phoning him, visiting him, and insisting that his apartment be used to show prospective tenants for other units what the building is like. Lulu is violating Tom's
   a. right to use the property without interference.
   b. covenant to repair.
   c. covenant of quiet enjoyment.
   d. warranty of habitability.

7. A landlord has a right of entry
   a. in an emergency.
   b. only to show the premises to prospective tenants.
   c. only when the tenant agrees.
   d. any time.

8. Transfer of all of a tenant's rights under a lease is a(n)
   a. assignment.   c. freehold estate.
   b. sublease.   d. estate at will.

9. A lease may be renewed automatically only if
   a. the landlord prepared the lease.
   b. the tenant and landlord are unable to agree on any other term.
   c. the automatic renewal provision is noted in a separate document referenced in the lease.
   d. all of the statutory requirements are met.

10. A dwelling is untenantable if it substantially lacks
    a. a heating unit.
    b. windows in every room.
    c. a trash compactor.
    d. freeway access.

11. Because a tenant complains about the condition of the building, the landlord may
    a. evict the tenant.
    b. raise the tenant's rent.
    c. shut off the tenant's utilities.
    d. investigate the complaint.

12. Which of the following may be considered in choosing a tenant?
    a. Marital status
    b. National ancestry
    c. Whether the prospective tenant is on welfare
    d. Tenant's income

13. On May 15, Jacquie Jones notified her landlord that she would be vacating her retail store location on June 30. Jacquie has a month-to-month periodic tenancy. Until what date will she incur rent?
    a. June 15
    b. June 30
    c. July 15
    d. July 30

14. A landlord must follow the legal requirements for an eviction
    a. from leased premises.
    b. but can shorten the notice required if the tenant agrees.
    c. unless the tenant can be physically removed.
    d. unless the housing is government subsidized.

15. A landlord may begin eviction proceedings with a(n)
    a. notice of termination.
    b. notice of abandonment.
    c. notice to pay or quit.
    d. order of eviction.

16. The sheriff or marshal can forcibly remove a tenant by a
    a. judgment of eviction.
    b. writ of possession.
    c. notice of eviction.
    d. notice to pay or quit.

17. Harry's Haberdashery has a percentage lease based on 5 percent of gross income of up to $25,000 per month and 2½ percent of gross income above that amount. The minimum Harry must pay is $1,000 per month. For a month in which Harry has a gross income of $47,000, what will be his rent payment?
    a. $1,800   c. $2,800
    b. $4,675   d. $3,675

18. The owner of 417 Main, an office building, receives a guaranteed monthly income from her tenants and pays no expenses. She has a
    a. gross lease.   c. percentage lease.
    b. trust lease.   d. net lease.

19. A property manager
    a. must be a real estate broker.
    b. is the property owner's agent.
    c. is the tenant's agent.
    d. is not an agent.

20. James moved out of his apartment at the end of the lease term. The landlord will be allowed to increase the rent for a new tenant to reflect the current market value because the local rent control ordinance
    a. provides for vacancy control.
    b. provides for vacancy decontrol.
    c. is based on an index.
    d. is favorable to the tenant.

CHAPTER THIRTEEN

13

REAL ESTATE APPRAISING

■ APPRAISER LICENSING

Perhaps the most important step in selling real estate is pricing it right. This means that the asking price must reflect what buyers in the marketplace are willing to pay for property of that type. And that is where a property appraisal—an estimate of a property's market value—comes in.

The importance of the appraisal was newly recognized in the 1980s. The failure of many lending institutions in that decade was blamed in part on faulty appraisals of property that served as collateral for loans. When borrowers could no longer make loan payments and defaulted, lenders were left with property that was worth considerably less than the remaining loan balances. At that point, the industry was almost entirely unregulated, except through the efforts of trade associations. Congress took action in response to the crisis.

The Financial Institutions Reform, Recovery, and Enforcement Act of 1989 (FIRREA) requires that as of January 1, 1993, all property appraisals that are part of **federally related transactions** be performed only by appraisers licensed or certified by the state in which the property is located. Individual federal agencies are allowed to set a minimum property value. Appraiser licensing or certification is not required below that value.

State qualifications for a licensed or certified appraiser and a licensing or certifying examination must meet or exceed those produced by the Appraiser Qualification Board of the Appraisal Foundation. In addition, each state must set standards for an acceptable appraisal report that meet or exceed those developed by the Appraisal Standards Board of the Appraisal Foundation. The Appraisal Foundation is a nonprofit association of trade groups, including appraisers, lenders, educators, and others, located in Washington, D.C.

This chapter covers

- the requirements to become licensed or certified as an appraiser in California;
- what an appraisal is and how an appraisal may be used;
- the basic economic principles that affect market value;
- how a competitive market analysis can assist a seller or buyer in estimating market value;
- the three basic methods of appraising real estate;
- how the appraiser reconciles the estimates received by each of the appraisal approaches; and
- the ways in which the appraiser's conclusion of market value is reported.

Federally Related Transactions

A **federally related transaction** is any real estate–related financial transaction involving or identified as such by a federal institution's regulatory agency. Because this definition includes all loans made by federally chartered banks and savings and loans, it includes most residential mortgage loans.

California Law

California's appraiser regulations went into effect November 1, 1992. Enforcement was made the responsibility of the newly created **Office of Real Estate Appraisers (OREA),** which was made part of the Business, Transportation, and Housing Agency. As of January 1, 1998, four categories of appraiser credentials are issued:

1. **Trainee license** (requiring 90 classroom hours of instruction but no experience in appraising) allows a prospective appraiser to work under the technical supervision of a licensed appraiser in order to gain the experience necessary to qualify for a residential license;

2. **Residential license** (requiring 90 classroom hours of instruction and 2,000 hours of acceptable appraisal experience), for appraisals of noncomplex one-unit to four-unit residential property up to a transaction value of $1 million, and nonresidential property up to a transaction value of $250,000;

3. **Certified residential** (requiring 120 classroom hours of instruction and a minimum of 2,500 hours and two and one-half years of acceptable appraisal experience), for appraisals of all residential property, and nonresidential property up to a transaction value of $250,000; and

4. **Certified general** (requiring 180 classroom hours of instruction and a minimum of 3,000 hours and two and one-half years of acceptable appraisal experience, with at least 1,500 hours of the experience in nonresidential properties), for appraisals of all real estate.

Effective January 1, 2003, all applicants must complete the 15-hour national USPAP (Uniform Standards of Professional Appraisal Practice) course.

In addition to education requirements, applicants for licensing or certification must pass the appropriate examination. A license or certification is valid for four years, and continuing education requirements (14 hours for each calendar year in which the license is valid for six months or more) must be met to qualify for renewal. Information on appraiser licensing and certification requirements can be obtained from OREA at (916) 322-2500 or *www.orea.ca.gov*.

www.orea.ca.gov

The largest trade association of appraisal professionals in the United States is the Appraisal Institute. Its Web site, *www.appraisalinstitute.org,* has a directory of appraisers and links to an extensive list of real estate-related Web sites. The site also provides access to the Appraisal Institute's Lum Library of publications, which provides search and copying services free of charge to members and for a fee to nonmembers.

www.appraisalinstitute.org

■ WHAT IS A REAL ESTATE APPRAISAL?

Most often, a **real estate appraisal** is the appraiser's estimate of a property's monetary value on the open market. An appraisal can also be made for a variety of other purposes, however, such as to find insurance or investment value. An appraisal also can indicate a property's type and condition, its utility for a given purpose, or its *highest and best use* (a concept that will be discussed in this chapter). The term **appraisal** is used to refer to both

■ the **process** by which the appraiser arrives at an estimate of value and

■ the **written report** in which the appraiser explains how the estimate was made.

Any of the property interests discussed in Chapter 3, such as a life estate or remainder, can be appraised. Usually, though, the property interest being appraised is a **fee simple estate.**

The appraiser

- *inspects* the property,
- compiles a variety of *data,* and
- considers *market forces* and *local market conditions* to arrive at an estimate of the property's value.

The data and factors considered will vary somewhat, depending on the method of appraisal used.

The appraiser's **final value conclusion** will be a dollar value. Most often, the value conclusion is the appraiser's estimate of the property's market value as of the date of the property inspection. An appraisal can provide an estimate of value as of some other date, however, such as the date property was taken in a condemnation proceeding.

Market Value

The value of an item can be defined as the amount of money or goods or services that will be accepted in exchange for it. This **value in exchange** is not the only type of value, however. Real estate is described as having a **value in use,** which refers to its value when used for a particular purpose. This value is subjective because it depends on the needs of a unique user.

> Market value is an estimate of what a typical buyer would pay.

When real estate is appraised, the value most often being sought is **market value.** The **market value** of real estate is the most probable price it would bring in an **arm's-length transaction** under normal conditions on the open market. This value is *objective*, because it is not based on the requirements of a particular owner. In an arm's-length transaction

- *neither* buyer nor seller is acting under duress;
- the real estate has been on the market a *reasonable* length of time for property of its type;
- both buyer and seller are acting with *full knowledge* of the property's assets and defects;
- *no unusual circumstances* exist, such as a sale involving related parties; and
- the price represents the *normal consideration* for the property sold, unaffected by creative financing or sales concessions granted by anyone associated with the sale.

Elements of Market Value

Four basic elements (that you can remember by the word *DUST*) must be present before any product has a market value. A market exists only when **demand** has been created by a product's **utility,** or usefulness, coupled with its relative **scarcity.** The product must also have the quality of **transferability;** that is, there must be no impediment to its sale. In the case of real estate, a fifth element also is usually necessary. The buyer must be able to secure suitable **financing.**

The market for real estate, then, is determined by

- the property's possible uses,
- the availability of similar property and suitable financing,
- the number of potential purchasers, and
- the ability of the seller to convey good title to the buyer.

Basic Value Principles

It is the appraiser's task to recognize the factors that influence market value as early and as thoroughly as possible. As you study the basic value principles defined in this section, keep in mind that new buzzwords and concepts are constantly making an appearance. For example, many inner-city neighborhoods are now undergoing what is termed **gentrification** as relatively well-off young professionals buy older buildings in declining areas and invest money and labor in restoring their purchases.

Highest and best use.   The **highest and best use** of real estate is its

- **most profitable,**
- **physically possible,** and
- **legally permissible** use.

A **highest and best use study** can be made of a vacant site or a site to be redeveloped. If a structure exists on the property, the cost of renovating or demolishing that structure must be considered.

Balance.   In general, a **balance** of varying land uses results in the highest property values overall. For example, housing should benefit from its proximity to business office and shopping areas.

Supply and demand.   The principle of **supply and demand** reflects the relationship between the number of properties on the market at a given time and the number of potential buyers. All other factors being equal, prices tend to rise if demand is greater than supply. Prices tend to fall if supply exceeds demand.

Real estate markets tend to be most stable when there is a moderate oversupply of properties on the market relative to demand. To some extent this reflects the fact that the marketplace usually includes sellers who can "wait out" a slow market or take their properties off the market for a time (rather than lower the asking price).

Conformity.   Buildings exhibit **conformity** when they are similar in design, construction, and age. Particularly in residential neighborhoods, all property owners usually will benefit when there is consistency in the quality of design and construction.

Progression and regression.   The value of a building is enhanced if buildings around it have a higher value, either because they are better maintained or better designed, or both. This is an example of the principle of **progression.**

According to the principle of **regression,** a building's value declines if the buildings around it have a lower value. For example, no matter how beautiful or extravagant a house is, it will not realize its full market potential if it is in a neighborhood of smaller, less luxurious (and thus less valuable) houses.

> An improvement adds value only if it is what buyers want.

Contribution.   A property improvement may or may not increase the property's overall market value, regardless of the cost of the improvement. In an appraisal, a property improvement is valued at only its **contribution** to the property's market value. The addition of a second bathroom, for instance, probably will contribute more of its cost to the market value of a house than a kitchen remodeling will.

Competition.   Commercial properties are affected by **competition,** both positively and negatively. As businesses are attracted to a particular area, interest in the area generally increases. At a certain point, however, the market will become saturated and some businesses will suffer. In Silicon Valley, for example, office construction at present is well behind market demand. Competition has brought attention to the benefits offered by the area (such as a skilled work force) and enabled property owners to profit. In the current market climate it may be difficult to remember that, only a few years ago, there were many "see-throughs" (vacant office buildings) in Los Angeles as well as the Bay Area.

Change.   As residents of California are well aware, real estate—land—is subject to a wide range of natural and other influences. Real estate undergoes constant **change** from

- **physical,**
- **economic,**
- **social,** and
- **political** forces.

A change may be subtle or catastrophic. Physical changes include the gradual accretion of soil along a riverbank that increases a property's size, as well as the earthquake that demolishes a structure within seconds. Economic forces include the availability of jobs, transportation, and credit. Social forces include subjective factors that influence our decisions on lifestyles, family planning, education, leisure, and retirement. Zoning, building codes, rent control, and other restrictions on property use are political forces that can be used as growth or antigrowth initiatives.

Life cycle.   Both buildings and neighborhoods go through **life cycles.** As they are developed, they achieve **growth,** attain a period of **equilibrium** (or stability) in which little change is evident, then **decline** as properties deteriorate. By the time the first three stages of the cycle have been completed, the properties involved will show the effects of wear and tear, even when they have been adequately maintained. If otherwise well located, they will attract the investment needed to keep up increased maintenance and undergo a fourth stage, **revitalization,** before they begin another cycle of gradual deterioration.

Anticipation.   Real estate is purchased for its expected future benefits. Because real estate values historically have increased, the expectation or **anticipation** of purchasers usually is that values will continue to rise. Purchases based on that anticipation add to market demand, which helps fulfill the expectation.

Substitution.   The principle of **substitution** is that value tends to be decided by the cost of acquiring an equally desirable property. This principle provides the basis of most residential real estate appraisals. The appraiser determines the value of a property that is **comparable** to the one being appraised and applies that value to the subject property. If there are two comparable properties, the one with the lower price will attract the greatest demand.

Exercise 13-1   Which basic value principle(s) does each of the following case examples illustrate?

1. Jeff Powell has finally remodeled his extra bedroom as the den of his dreams. The rosewood wainscoting is set off by hand-painted reproduction antique wallpaper and by light fixtures that Jeff salvaged from the wreck of a yacht. The den was expensive, but Jeff is philosophical, believing that he will always be able to recoup his expenses if he has to sell his house.

2. Dr. Baez began her dentistry practice in a small office building in a tiny farm community many miles from the city, surrounded by nothing but flat, unproductive farmland, and three major freeways. Dr. Baez now owns that building, several apartment complexes, a strip shopping center, and a condo on Maui.

3. Papa Joe has owned his corner grocery store for 40 years. He grew up only a few blocks from the store, in a house that is still his home. He remembers the way the neighborhood looked when he was a boy and there were still many open spaces to explore. When he took over the store

a vacant lot was hard to find. Papa Joe was happy with his business, even when his friends began moving to the suburbs and he had fewer customers. The neighborhood got pretty seedy, and he was robbed a few times. Lately though, he has noticed quite a few young people moving in and working hard to fix up their houses. New businesses are also opening. Papa Joe has decided to stay and has even put in a gourmet takeout deli counter.

4. The Blairs own a five-bedroom, three-bathroom house in a well-kept but modest section of town. The Blairs' house is the largest in their neighborhood. They have decided to sell their home and have asked Dave Dollar, a real estate agent, for his estimate of what sales price they can expect. Dave knows that a house very similar to the Blairs' was sold a few weeks ago, but that house is about a mile away and only a block from an elementary school. Dave goes over his figures very carefully before he explains to the Blairs why he thinks their house should sell for somewhat less than the other house.

■ THE APPRAISAL PROCESS

The flowchart in Figure 13.1 shows the steps an appraiser takes in gathering, recording, and analyzing the many types of data that contribute to the final estimate of value.

Forms itemizing the specific information sought are very useful. The examples in Figure 13.2 show parts of a **neighborhood data** form, a **site data** form, and a **building data** form.

The appraiser first becomes familiar with the national, regional, city, and neighborhood factors that affect the subject property (the property being appraised). Then, the appraiser's focus shifts to the subject itself.

What effect does the location of the property have? Is the subject property located in the direction of growth of the city in which it is located or of a nearby city? Will building restrictions and zoning ordinances impede or aid its value? Is the property's size an optimum one for its highest and best use? Does the topography of the area lend itself to that use? Is the property located on a major thoroughfare that will help or hinder its desirability? These are only some of the concerns the appraiser will have in mind.

The right data forms the basis of an accurate appraisal.

After a thorough description of the subject property, and in light of all the other information compiled, the appraiser is ready to gather the data needed for the specific **appraisal techniques.** You can remember them by the three C's—comparison, cost, and capitalization.

FIGURE 13.1

The Appraisal Process

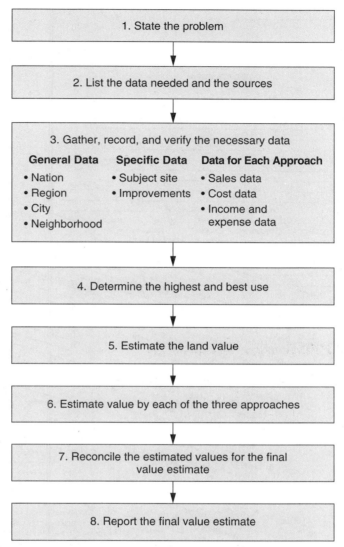

Source: *Fundamentals of Real Estate Appraisal,* 8th Edition, by William L. Ventolo, Jr., and Martha R. Williams. © 2001 by Dearborn Financial Publishing, Inc. All subsequent references to this title will use only the title and edition number.

■ The **sales comparison approach** requires descriptions of comparable properties that have sold recently.

■ The **cost approach** requires building cost data.

■ The **income capitalization approach** requires income and expense data on the subject and/or comparable properties.

Although we have provided only the briefest coverage of the data collection process, we must stress that the appraiser's thorough knowledge of the subject, market area, and other pertinent facts provides the substance of an accurate

FIGURE 13.2

Data Forms

SITE DATA FORM

ADDRESS: _____
LEGAL DESCRIPTION: _____
_____
_____
_____
_____
_____

DIMENSIONS: _____
SHAPE: _____ SQUARE FEET: _____
TOPOGRAPHY: _____ VIEW: _____
NATURAL HAZARDS: _____
☐ INSIDE LOT   ☐ CORNER LOT   ☐ FRONTAGE: _____
ZONING: _____ ADJACENT AREAS: _____
UTILITIES: ☐ ELECTRICITY ☐ TELEPHONE ☐ CABLE TV   ABOVE/BELOW ___
☐ WATER ☐ GAS ☐ SANITARY SEWERS ☐ STORM S___
IMPROVEMENTS: ☐ SIDEWALKS ☐ CURBS ☐ ALLEY ☐ ___
☐ DRIVEWAY (PAVING: ___
LANDSCAPING: _____
TOPSOIL: _____
EASEMENTS: _____
DEED RESTRICTION___
COMMON AREAS: ___
SITE PLAT: ___

BUILDING DATA FORM

ORIENTATION: N S E W
SQUARE FEET: _____
GOOD AVERAGE FAIR POOR

NO. OF STORIES: _____
AGE: _____

ADDRESS: _____
NO. OF UNITS: _____ DESIGN: _____
TYPE: _____
GENERAL CONDITION OF EXTERIOR _____
FOUNDATION TYPE ___ BSMT./CRAWL SP./SLAB
EXTERIOR WALLS: BRICK/BLOCK/VENEER/STUCCO/
WOOD/ALUMINUM/VINYL
WINDOW FRAMES: METAL/WOOD   SCREENS: _____
STORM WINDOWS: _____
ATTACHED/DETACHED
NUMBER OF CARS: ☐ SHED
GARAGE: _____ ☐ PATIO
☐ DECK
☐ PORCH
OTHER
GENERAL CONDITION OF INTERIOR
INTERIOR WALLS: DRY WALL/PLASTER/WOOD
CEILINGS: _____
FLOORS: WOOD/CONCRETE/TILE/CARPET
ELECTRICAL WIRING AND SERVICE: _____
HEATING PLANT: _____ AGE: _____
GAS/OIL/WOOD/ELECTRIC
CENTRAL AIR-CONDITIONING: _____ TY___
NUMBER OF FIREPLACES: _____
OTHER _____ F___
BATHROOM: FLOOR___WALLS___F
BATHROOM: FLOOR___WALLS___F
BATHROOM: FLOOR___WALLS___
BATHROOM: FLOOR___WALLS___
KITCHEN: _____ FIXTURES _____

ROOM SIZES | LIVING ROOM | DIN___
BASEMENT
1ST FLOOR
2ND FLOOR
ATTIC
DEPRECIATION (DESCRIBE)
PHYSICAL DETERIORATI___
FUNCTIONAL OBSOLES___
EXTERNAL OBSOLESC___

NEIGHBORHOOD DATA FORM

BOUNDARIES: ADJACENT TO:
NORTH _____
SOUTH _____
EAST _____
WEST _____
TOPOGRAPHY: _____ ☐ URBAN ☐ SUBURBAN ☐ RURAL
STAGE OF LIFE CYCLE OF NEIGHBORHOOD: ☐ GROWTH ☐ EQUILIBRIUM ☐ DECLINE
% BUILT UP: _____ GROWTH RATE: ☐ RAPID ☐ SLOW ☐ STEADY
AVERAGE MARKETING TIME: _____ PROPERTY VALUES: ☐ INCREASING ☐ DECREASING ☐ STABLE
SUPPLY/DEMAND: ☐ OVERSUPPLY ☐ UNDERSUPPLY ☐ BALANCED
CHANGE IN PRESENT LAND USE: _____
POPULATION: ☐ INCREASING ☐ DECREASING ☐ STABLE   AVERAGE FAMILY SIZE: _____
AVERAGE FAMILY INCOME: _____ INCOME LEVEL: ☐ INCREASING ☐ DECREASING
PREDOMINANT OCCUPATIONS: _____

TYPICAL PROPERTIES:	% OF	AGE	PRICE RANGE	% OWNER OCCUPIED	% RENTALS
VACANT LOTS					
SINGLE-FAMILY RESIDENCES					
2-6-UNIT APARTMENTS					
OVER 6-UNIT APARTMENTS					
NONRESIDENTIAL PROPERTIES					

TAX RATE: _____ ☐ HIGHER ☐ LOWER ☐ SAME AS COMPETING AREAS
SPECIAL ASSESSMENTS OUTSTANDING: _____ EXPECTED: _____
SERVICES: ☐ POLICE ☐ FIRE ☐ GARBAGE COLLECTION   OTHER: _____
DISTANCE AND DIRECTION FROM
BUSINESS AREA: _____
COMMERCIAL AREA: _____
PUBLIC ELEMENTARY AND HIGH SCHOOLS: _____
PRIVATE ELEMENTARY AND HIGH SCHOOLS: _____
RECREATIONAL AND CULTURAL AREAS: _____
CHURCHES AND SYNAGOGUES: _____
EXPRESSWAY INTERCHANGE: _____
PUBLIC TRANSPORTATION: _____
TIME TO REACH BUSINESS AREA: _____ COMMERCIAL AREA: _____
GENERAL TRAFFIC CONDITIONS: _____
PROXIMITY TO HAZARDS (AIRPORT, CHEMICAL STORAGE, ETC.): _____
PROXIMITY TO NUISANCES (SMOKE, NOISE, ETC.): _____

appraisal. **The most valuable component of an appraisal is the competence and experience of the appraiser.**

All three appraisal methods may not be used in every appraisal. The appraiser uses the most appropriate method(s), then selects the value that (in the appraiser's opinion) is the most reliable indicator of value. The final value selection process is called **reconciliation,** and will be discussed later in this chapter.

■ SALES COMPARISON APPROACH

The method that usually is the most significant in appraising residential property is the **sales comparison approach.** In addition, it is the easiest to learn of the three approaches and the reasoning behind it is easy to understand. The sales comparison approach is also called the **market data approach** or **market comparison approach** or **paired sales approach.**

- The appraiser finds three to five (or more) recently sold properties that are similar (comparable) in basic characteristics to the property that is the subject of the appraisal. The sales should have occurred within the last six months. Each comparable property should offer *amenities* (special features, such as a swimming pool) similar to those offered by the subject property.
- The appraiser analyzes each sale and notes significant *differences* between the comparable properties and the subject property.
- The appraiser then **adjusts** the sales price of each comparable property to more accurately reflect the features of the subject property. The appraiser can also make an adjustment to compensate for a sale that occurred earlier than six months before the date of the appraisal.
- The appraiser's final step is to analyze the resulting figures and choose the one that best represents the value of the subject property.

This process can be expressed as a formula:

$$\text{Sales price of comparable property} \quad \pm \quad \text{Adjustments} \quad = \quad \text{Indicated value of subject property}$$

The appraiser **adds** to the sales price of the comparable property the value of any feature that is present in the subject property but not in the comparable property. The appraiser **subtracts** from the sales price of the comparable property the value of any feature that is present in the comparable property but not in the subject property.

■ **FOR EXAMPLE:** House *A* is being appraised. House *B* is comparable to house *A*. House *B*, which has a three-car garage, sold for $196,000. House *A* has only a two-car garage. The extra garage space is valued by the appraiser at $5,500, based on recent sales.

Using the formula for the market comparison approach, the value of the extra garage space is subtracted from the price of house *B*, as shown below.

$$\$196,000 - \$5,500 = \$190,500$$

The adjusted price of house *B* is $190,500. This adjusted price will be compared to that of other properties to estimate a market value for house *A*.

Comparable properties ideally should be located in the same neighborhood as the subject property. They also should be substantially similar to the subject property in style, age, number and type of rooms, size of lot and building, type of construction, and general condition. The financing terms under which the property was sold should be typical of financing in the area, without special consideration for either buyer or seller. The sales should be fairly recent, ideally no more than three to six months before the date of appraisal, or an adjustment will have to be made. Current listings should be examined to reveal any downward trend in seller expectations.

> A forced sale usually places the seller at a disadvantage and the transaction will not be a good comparable.

Any variation in the above specifications would be treated as an adjustment to the sales price of the comparable property. The one variable that would be difficult, if not impossible, to treat as an adjustment would be a sale that was not an arm's-length transaction. Perhaps the seller acted under the duress of an impending foreclosure, divorce action, or immediate job transfer. In such a case the property probably should be disqualified as a comparable.

Real estate agents who perform market analyses for prospective clients and customers have ready sources of sales information—their own files. They also can obtain sales information from multiple-listing services and can exchange data on transactions that have closed with other agents. Once a transaction has been recorded in the county clerk's office, the county assessor also is a source of sales information.

Exercise 13-2 takes you through a very simplified version of an appraisal of a single-family residence using the sales comparison approach. Read all of the information given, then supply the necessary calculations in the chart. When you have finished, decide which of the indicated values appears to come closest to the market value of the subject property. Isolate the high and low figures and find the value that most closely represents the entire range of values.

Exercise 13-2   You are to find the current market value of house *X*.

House *X* is a one-story, single-family residence with wood siding. It has a living room, a formal dining room, a kitchen, a family room with fireplace, four bedrooms, two bathrooms, and an attached two-car garage.

Appliances are in good condition, and the seller will pay for a home warranty to cover repairs to major mechanical systems for one year.

House *X* is in a neighborhood of similar homes, all landscaped and well maintained, and presents an attractive streetside appearance.

House *A* is comparable to house *X* but has an extra half-bath off the family room.

House *B* is comparable to house *X* but has no fireplace.

House *C* is comparable to house *X*, but no home warranty was provided by the seller. House *C* is also on a corner lot at a major cross street through the subdivision.

House *A* sold for $215,250, house *B* sold for $208,000, and house *C* sold for $199,000.

In this price range, an extra half-bath is valued at $4,000, a fireplace is valued at $3,200, a home warranty costs $350, and a location on a busy and noisy cross street will affect total value by $12,000.

Complete the following chart, using the figures above.

	Comparables		
	A	**B**	**C**
Sales price	215,250	208,000	199,000
Adjustment variables			
Extra half-bath	-4000		
No fireplace		+3200	
No home warranty			+350
Poor location			+12,000
Total adjustments	211,250	211,200	211,350
Adjusted value			

Competitive Market Analysis

Many real estate agents who are not appraisers will supply the information necessary for a **competitive market analysis (CMA),** also called a **comparable market analysis.** The agent's purpose is to assist the seller or buyer in determining the property's fair market value. A CMA ordinarily is more limited in scope than an appraisal and does not include an opinion of value by the agent.

The most frequently used source of data for a CMA is the bank of properties handled through the agent's **multiple-listing service.** Sales and/or asking prices and length of time on the market will be examined for three categories of property in a defined area:

1. Property that was sold recently;
2. Property that is for sale now; and
3. Property that was previously listed for sale, but the listing has expired or the property was withdrawn from the market.

Properties that failed to sell may reveal more than properties that sold.

The sales and/or asking prices, when examined together, indicate to the **seller** a range of values that includes the listing or asking price as well as the likely sales price of the subject property. Such data also indicate the number of days the property may be expected to be on the market before it sells.

For the **buyer,** the market analysis suggests a price range from which to select an offer to purchase and the maximum price that should be paid.

■ COST APPROACH

In the **cost approach** for establishing value, the appraiser determines what it would cost to duplicate the subject property.

- The appraiser begins with the **present cost** of improvements on the subject property,
- **subtracts** the amount by which those improvements have depreciated, then
- **adds** in the value of the land to arrive at an indicated value.

The formula for the cost approach is

$$
\begin{array}{c} \text{Reproduction or} \\ \text{replacement cost} \\ \text{of improvement(s)} \end{array} - \begin{array}{c} \text{Accrued} \\ \text{depreciation} \end{array} + \begin{array}{c} \text{Site} \\ \text{value} \end{array} = \begin{array}{c} \text{Property} \\ \text{value} \end{array}
$$

Reproduction cost is the cost of a new building of exactly the same design and materials as the subject property. **Replacement cost** is the cost of a new building using modern methods, design, and materials and having the same use as the subject property but without the identical specifications. The replacement cost of a building is used, rather than its reproduction cost, when its design or construction is not *economically feasible* to reproduce today. Certain design features could be impossible to duplicate at any price. Because skilled craftspeople may not be available to produce special building features, such as ornate cornices, moldings, or ceilings, the closest modern substitutes are evaluated instead.

Site value is determined by the sales comparison approach or other appropriate method. The records of the county tax assessor show a land-to-improvements ratio that can be useful in evaluating comparable properties to derive land value alone. Many lenders making government-backed loans do not accept other valuation sources for their appraisals.

> Local labor costs are probably the biggest construction cost variable.

The cost approach has the drawback of relying on construction cost estimates that differ greatly from region to region, even within a state. Builders' costs vary and often depend on the number of units under construction. Construction techniques also affect cost. For instance, prefabricated roof trusses may cut on-site labor costs.

There are national and regional **cost manuals** that the appraiser can use to keep cost estimates up to date. Such manuals are revised frequently, and the better ones have computerized update services that reflect price changes on a weekly or even daily basis.

Finally, the cost approach assumes that the building(s) already on the site represents its highest and best use. As mentioned earlier in this chapter, the **value in use** of a property is its value to its present owner and, thus, is a **subjective** value. **Market value,** on the other hand, should be an **objective** determination. A property with no utility to anyone but its present owner will not be evaluated fairly by the cost approach. In the same way, a property that is not put to its highest and best use is not an appropriate subject for the cost approach. For example, an ornate but little-used movie theater may have great sentimental value but probably would be better appraised for the redevelopment value of its site rather than as a structure maintaining its present use.

The cost approach method is ideal for special purpose properties—those that have no comparables in the area or which produce no income. Examples are museums, schools, and churches.

Finding Reproduction or Replacement Cost

The appraiser can use any one or more of four methods to find the reproduction or replacement cost of property improvements. They are the

1. **square-foot method;**
2. **unit-in-place method;**
3. **quantity survey method;** and
4. **index method.**

1. Square-foot method.   Using this method, the appraiser multiplies the current cost per square foot of a comparable building by the number of square feet in the subject building. This is the method most frequently used by appraisers. A similar approach is the **cubic-foot method,** most commonly used for nonresidential properties such as warehouses. An updated cost manual can be used to find the cost per square or cubic foot of a property with the same specifications as the subject building.

2. Unit-in-place method.   This method makes use of the construction cost per unit of measure of each of the component parts of the subject property, such as walls, plumbing units, heating units, and so on. Each unit cost includes material, labor, overhead, and builder's profit. The cost per unit is multiplied by the number of units of each component part, and the individual unit costs are then totaled. Most measurements will be in square feet, although mechanical and plumbing systems will be estimated as complete units.

3. Quantity survey method.   This method requires a thorough itemization of all construction costs, both direct (materials and labor) and indirect (permits, taxes, profits, insurance, and other overhead). Every material, labor, and indirect cost is estimated separately, and the individual costs are totaled. The quantity survey method can be used only by someone familiar with all facets of building construction. It is very accurate, but time consuming.

4. Index method.   In this method, the appraiser multiplies the original cost of the subject property by a factor that represents the percentage increase (or decrease) of construction costs generally from the time of construction to the present time. Cost reporting or indexing services provide information on cost changes over time as well as from area to area.

If the original cost of the subject structure is known, the index method is the simplest way to estimate present cost. It is a very imprecise method, however, and for that reason it should be used only as a check on the estimate arrived at by one of the other methods.

Depreciation

Tax depreciation is not the same as appraisal depreciation.

Depreciation is a loss in value from any cause. Note that depreciation for appraisal purposes is *not* the depreciation that Uncle Sam allows investors to deduct from income in computing taxes. Depreciation for tax purposes is meant to encourage investment, and it may have absolutely no relation to the loss in value to a structure brought about by physical deterioration and other causes. The appraiser's job is to estimate the *actual* loss in value from depreciation and reduce the replacement cost of the subject property accordingly.

There are three main types of depreciation. Some forms of depreciation are considered **curable** because they can be remedied by a repair or an addition to the property at relatively low cost. In other words, the property's value after the repair or improvement is increased by an amount greater than the cost to do the work. Other forms of depreciation are considered **incurable** because there is no easy or economical way to remedy them.

The three forms of depreciation are

1. **physical deterioration;**
2. **functional obsolescence;** and
3. **external obsolescence.**

1. Physical deterioration.   **Physical deterioration** includes damage or destruction to a building as well as the more subtle effects of ordinary wear and tear. Examples of physical deterioration include windows destroyed by vandals, roof damage caused by a violent storm, and wood siding that has cracked and separated over time.

2. Functional obsolescence.   **Functional obsolescence** occurs when a building's design, layout, or utility is no longer desirable. Functional obsolescence reflects the changing requirements of the marketplace and may be observed in both houses and commercial structures. The suburban house with only one bathroom and the gas station forced out of business because the owner cannot afford to upgrade the underground holding tanks, as required by law, are both examples of functional obsolescence. The selling price of the house will suffer. The gas station will remain vacant until another use for the property is found or it is sold for the value of its site.

3. External obsolescence.   **External obsolescence,** also called **environmental obsolescence** or **economic obsolescence,** is the loss in a property's value due to *outside* causes. Changes in nearby land use through development, rezoning, or transfer of ownership may bring about a loss in value. Ironically, rezoning may increase the value of the rezoned property while decreasing the value of adjacent property. Property on a residential street rezoned to allow commercial uses most likely will *increase* in value. Adjacent property, which must remain residential, probably will *decline* in value due to greater noise and traffic.

Economic factors tend to have a ripple effect and eventually affect property values. For example, if a major employer moves to a distant location, there may be more homes on the market as transferred employees move to the new location, which will lower prices. As the population decreases and unemployment rises, both the housing market and businesses dependent on consumer spending will suffer.

Computing Depreciation

The two most widely used direct methods of computing depreciation are the **straight-line method** and **observed condition method.**

Straight-line method.   The **straight-line method** of computing depreciation is the easiest to understand and the least complicated to use. Every building has an **economic life,** which is the period of years in which it may be used for its originally intended purpose.

If the value of the building is divided by the number of years of its estimated economic (useful) life, the resulting figure is the amount by which the building can be expected to depreciate every year. If property is well maintained, however, its rate of depreciation may be slowed. In that case, its **effective age** will be less than its age in actual calendar years.

■   **FOR EXAMPLE:**   A storage warehouse is constructed at a cost of $325,000 and has an estimated economic life of 50 years. After 30 years of good mainte-nance, the building has an effective age of only 20 years. By how much will the building have depreciated?

$$\frac{\$325,000}{50} = \$6,500 \text{ depreciation each year}$$

Or $6,500 \times 20 = \$130,000 \text{ total depreciation}$

$$\frac{100\%}{50} = 2\% \text{ depreciation per year}$$

The straight-line method is one that the Internal Revenue Service uses. The number of years prescribed by the IRS is not necessarily the number of years the appraiser will use, however.

Observed condition method.   The **observed condition method** of computing depreciation is also called the **breakdown method.** It requires the appraiser to estimate the loss in value caused by every individual item of depreciation, whether curable or incurable.

Curable items are those that can be economically remedied, considering the remaining useful life of the building and cost of repair. All other items are considered incurable. Many buildings damaged by earthquakes or mud slides could be repaired, but at too great an expense to make the repairs feasible as a practical matter.

External obsolescence generally is *incurable,* because by definition it is caused by outside forces.

The appraiser determines the effect on value of each item in every category of depreciation (physical deterioration, functional obsolescence, and external obsolescence). The appraiser then deducts the loss in value in each category from the reproduction cost of the subject building. Computing depreciation in a very old building by the breakdown method might be an overwhelming task, and another approach would be advisable.

■ **FOR EXAMPLE:**   The reproduction cost of a building is $670,000. Its depreciation is estimated as follows:

Physical deterioration	
Curable	$ 84,000
Incurable	67,000
Functional obsolescence	
Curable	43,000
Incurable	0
External obsolescence	
Curable	0
Incurable	0
Total	$ 194,000

Depreciated building cost is reproduction cost less depreciation:

$$\$670,000 - \$194,000 = \$476,000$$

Land value would be added to the depreciated building cost to find total property value.

Remember that a cost estimate of value usually determines the upper limit of a property's value. A buyer ordinarily does not want to pay more for an existing building than it would cost to build a new one.

Exercise 13-3   Find the current market value of house *X* using the square-foot method of estimating value by the cost approach.

House *X* has a living area of 25 feet by 60 feet, with an attached garage of 25 feet by 25 feet. Current cost per square foot of a residence with the specifications of house *X* is $55 per square foot of living area and $35 per square foot of garage space. House *X* had an original useful life of 40 years and is now four years old.

A few lots are still available in house *X*'s subdivision. A lot comparable to the one on which house *X* is built is valued at $26,000.

Living area   = _____ square feet   @ _____   per square foot = _____

Garage area   = _____ square feet   @ _____   per square foot = _____

Total reproduction cost = _____

$$\frac{\text{Total reproduction cost}}{\text{Years of useful life}} = \$\_\_\_\_\_ \text{ Yearly depreciation}$$

Yearly depreciation × _____ years = $_____ Total depreciation

Reproduction cost − Total depreciation + Land value = _____

The estimate of value of house *X* by the cost approach is _____.

■ INCOME CAPITALIZATION APPROACH

In estimating value by the **income capitalization approach,** the appraiser first determines the property's potential gross income. **Potential gross income** is a property's maximum income from all sources. An office or apartment building might produce income from vending machines or a laundry room in addition to rental income. A single-family residence probably would have only a base monthly rent.

> The "going rate" for a property is its market rent.

The appraiser estimates what is called the property's **market rent** or **economic rent.** **Market rent** is an estimate of the property's rent potential—what it could rent for if available for rental on today's market. The rent received by the current property owner is called the property's **contract rent** or **scheduled rent. Contract rent** may be higher or lower than **market rent.**

The appraiser next makes an allowance for **vacancy and collection losses.** Not every unit in the building will be continuously occupied, and sometimes a tenant is delinquent in rent payments. The appraiser estimates and then subtracts these anticipated losses from gross income to derive **effective gross income.**

Yearly **operating expenses** are then subtracted from effective gross income to arrive at **net operating income.** By applying a **capitalization rate** to net operating income, the appraiser arrives at an estimate of market value.

The **capitalization ("cap") rate** is the property owner's annual expected rate of return. The capitalization rate can be expressed as the relationship between the net operating income the property produces and its market value. As an equation,

$$\frac{\textbf{Net operating income}}{\textbf{Value}} = \textbf{Capitalization rate}$$

We can also derive two corollaries from that equation:

$$\textbf{Capitalization rate} \times \textbf{Value} = \textbf{Net operating income}$$

$$\frac{\textbf{Net operating income}}{\textbf{Capitalization rate}} = \textbf{Value}$$

The capitalization rate can be developed by analyzing net income and sales prices of comparable properties.

■ **FOR EXAMPLE:** Building *Y* produces a yearly net operating income of $32,000. What is the market value of building *Y*?

Building *D* has a net operating income of $35,000 per year, and it sold two months ago for $389,000. Building *E* has a net operating income of $31,000 per year, and it sold last week for $345,000.

Building *D* and building *E* are otherwise comparable to building *Y*. They are in the same area and are also six-unit apartment buildings of the same age and general physical condition as building *Y*. Using the equation for the capitalization rate:

$$\frac{\$35,000}{\$389,000} = 9\% \qquad\qquad \frac{\$31,000}{\$345,000} = 9\%$$

The capitalization rates for building *D* and building *E* support the assigning of a capitalization rate of 9 percent to building *Y*. Using the equation for value:

$$\frac{\$32,000}{.09} = \$355,555.56$$

The indicated market value of building *Y*, rounded to the nearest hundred dollars, is $355,600.

Note: Financing costs have not been included in this discussion of net operating income. Financing costs will vary, depending on the individual property buyer's financial position and negotiating power with a lender. Thus, interest and principal payments are considered costs associated with a particular buyer rather than with operating expenses of the property being appraised. In short, how a property is financed does not affect its value. All property is treated as if it is held free and clear.

Gross Income Multipliers   Many properties, including single-family residences, are not purchased primarily for their income-producing potential. For those properties a simpler method of determining value based on income may be used. Begin by dividing the **sales**

price of a rented, comparable property by the **gross income** the property produces to arrive at a factor called the **gross income multiplier (GIM).** As an equation,

$$\frac{\text{Sales price}}{\text{Gross income}} = \text{GIM}$$

The gross income multiplier is sometimes referred to as the "gross multiplier."

An **annual GIM** is more likely to be used for industrial or commercial property. A **monthly GIM** generally is used for residential property. Because its income is generally limited to rent, the multiplier for a single-family residence is usually termed a **gross rent multiplier (GRM).**

■ **FOR EXAMPLE:** A commercial building with an annual gross income of $48,000 sold two months ago for $535,000. What is that building's gross income multiplier? Using the equation:

$$\frac{\$535,000}{\$48,000} = 11.1$$

The building's gross income multiplier is 11.1, rounding to the nearest tenth.

The appraiser compares the GIM of at least four comparable properties to determine the multiplier most applicable to the subject property. The GIM selected for the subject property then is multiplied by the actual or projected rental of the subject to find its market value. As an equation,

Gross income × GIM = Market value

■ **FOR EXAMPLE:** Building *Y* has an annual gross income of $63,000. What is its market value, using the gross income multiplier method?

Of four comparable properties, one has a GIM of 10.0, one has a GIM of 8.5, and the other two each have a GIM of 9.5.

Discounting the high and low figures, we arrive at a gross income multiplier for the subject property of 9.5. Applying the equation:

$$\$63,000 \times 9.5 = \$598,500$$

Building *Y* has a market value of $598,500.

The gross income multiplier method is not accurate enough to serve as the sole means of determining market value. It fails to take into account the many property variables that contribute to gross income. It also fails to consider the many property expenses that can reduce effective net income. Because it is relatively easy to use, however, it may be a useful check of the market value estimate reached by another appraisal method.

Exercise 13-4   You are appraising a single-family residence that may be purchased as a rental property. Complete the following chart to determine the property's gross income multiplier. Then estimate its market value.

Sale No.	Market Value	Monthly Gross Income	Gross Income Multiplier
1	$385,000	$1,825	211.0
2	382,000	1,810	211.0
3	370,000	1,775	208.5
4	365,000	1,775	205.6
5	368,000	1,700	216.5
Subject	_____	1,800	_____

■ RECONCILIATION AND THE APPRAISAL REPORT

The appraiser begins the final step in the appraisal process with as many as three different value estimates, depending on the number of approaches used—sales comparison, cost, and/or income capitalization. To determine the most appropriate estimate of value for the subject property, the appraiser now reconsiders each of the value estimates in light of

- ■ the type of property being appraised,
- ■ the purpose of the appraisal, and
- ■ other factors that may be unique to the appraisal.

The process of weighing the differing value estimates in light of their relevance to the appraisal problem is called **reconciliation,** or *correlation.* The goal of the analysis is to select the value estimate that is *most likely* to be an accurate reflection of market value. The appraiser's final estimate of value is presented and explained in the report to the client.

To comply with the **Uniform Standards of Professional Appraisal Practice (USPAP),** the appraiser must identify an appraisal report as a

- ■ **self-contained report;**
- ■ **summary report;** or
- ■ **restricted report.**

A **self-contained report** will have all of the elements necessary for a full appraisal, including a full description of all data considered and all techniques used in the appraisal process.

A **summary report** will provide the most important details of the appraiser's analysis, including a brief version of pertinent data and a shortened discussion of the appraisal techniques utilized.

A **restricted report** will be limited in either the method of valuation used or the property interests valued. Any such limitation must be stated in the appraisal.

Self-Contained Report

The **self-contained report,** also called a **narrative report,** is the most comprehensive report the appraiser can make. It includes a complete statement of the appraiser's credentials. It provides a thorough description of the property being appraised, the purpose of the appraisal, and a summary of the background data supporting each estimate of value.

The self-contained report provides an overview of the subject property's region, city, and neighborhood. It may total 30 pages or more, even for a single-family residence. It is used most often in a legal proceeding, such as the probate of an estate, a divorce settlement, litigation, or a condemnation action where extensive detail is necessary.

The contents of a self-contained appraisal report are listed on page 401.

Summary Form Report

www.fanniemae.com

A **summary report** is commonly used by government agencies and the lenders with which they do business, typically by means of a standardized form. The type of property and the purpose of the appraisal dictate the exact form used. The **Uniform Residential Appraisal Report (URAR),** Form 1004, used by Fannie Mae, Freddie Mac, and many other agencies, appears in Figure 13.3.

The Self-Contained Appraisal Report

A typical self-contained appraisal includes:

- title page;
- appraiser's estimate of value;
- table of contents;
- purpose of the appraisal;
- definition of value sought;
- property right being appraised;
- highest and best use;
- summary of important conclusions;
- city or village data;
- neighborhood data;
- financing available;
- site data and utilities;
- zoning;
- amenities, such as schools, shopping, recreation, transportation;
- description of improvements;
- sales comparison approach analysis;
- cost approach analysis;
- income capitalization approach analysis;
- reconciliation of values reached by each of the three approaches;
- underlying assumptions and limiting conditions to which the appraisal is subject, such as the existence of no unseen geologic problems;
- certificate of appraisal;
- qualifications of appraiser; and
- appendixes with photographs of subject property, plot plan, metropolitan area map, and local street map showing proximity of comparable sales used in the appraisal.

FIGURE 13.3

Uniform Residential Appraisal Report

UNIFORM RESIDENTIAL APPRAISAL REPORT File No.

Property Description

SUBJECT		
Property Address	4807 Catalpa Road	City Woodview State CA Zip Code 90000
Legal Description	Attached	County Delta
Assessor's Parcel No. 6412-028-007		Tax Year XXXX R.E. Taxes $ Prop.13 Special Assessments $ 465
Borrower	Current Owner	Occupant [ ] Owner [ ] Tenant [ ] Vacant
Property rights appraised [X] Fee Simple [ ] Leasehold	Project Type [ ] PUD [ ] Condominium (HUD/VA only)	HOA$ /Mo.
Neighborhood or Project Name Forest Glen	Map Reference	Census Tract
Sales Price $	Date of Sale	Description and $ amount of loan charges/concessions to be paid by seller
Lender/Client	Address	
Appraiser	Address	

NEIGHBORHOOD

Location	[ ] Urban [X] Suburban [ ] Rural	Predominant occupancy	Single family housing	Present land use %	Land use change
Built up	[X] Over 75% [ ] 25-75% [ ] Under 25%		PRICE $ (000) / AGE (yrs)	One family 100%	[X] Not likely [ ] Likely
Growth rate	[ ] Rapid [X] Stable [ ] Slow	[X] Owner	90 Low 7	2-4 family	[ ] In process
Property values	[X] Increasing [ ] Stable [ ] Declining	[ ] Tenant	120 High 7	Multi-family	To:
Demand/supply	[X] Shortage [ ] In balance [ ] Over supply	[ ] Vacant (0-5%)	Predominant	Commercial	
Marketing time	[X] Under 3 mos. [ ] 3-6 mos. [ ] Over 6 mos.	[ ] Vacant (over 5%)	110 7	( )	

Note: Race and the racial composition of the neighborhood are not appraisal factors.

Neighborhood boundaries and characteristics: The Forest Glen neighborhood is bounded on the east by the Village of Willow; south, 40th Street; west, Grand Street; north, Park District land.

Factors that affect the marketability of the properties in the neighborhood (proximity to employment and amenities, employment stability, appeal to market, etc.): The City of Woodview has remained attractive to newcomers from in-state and out-of-state because of its proximity to Bay City and diversity of employment opportunities. Houses in the price range offered by Forest Glen have benefitted from their relative affordability in the greater metropolitan area.

Market conditions in the subject neighborhood (including support for the above conclusions related to the trend of property values, demand/supply, and marketing time -- such as data on competitive properties for sale in the neighborhood, description of the prevalence of sales and financing concessions, etc.): The market is stable, with property values slowly but steadily increasing. Typical financing is the conventional mortgage, at interest rates from 7 to 8-1/4%, with as much as 95% of purchase price financed. Financing concessions are unusual.

PUD

Project Information for PUDs (If applicable) -- Is the developer/builder in control of the Home Owners' Association (HOA)? [ ] Yes [ ] No
Approximate total number of units in the subject project _____. Approximate total number of units for sale in the subject project _____.
Describe common elements and recreational facilities:

SITE

Dimensions 65' x 130'		Topography	Level
Site area 8,450 sq. ft.	Corner Lot [ ] Yes [X] No	Size	8,450 SF/Typical
Specific zoning classification and description R-2, Single-family residential		Shape	Rectangular
Zoning compliance [X] Legal [ ] Legal nonconforming (Grandfathered use) [ ] Illegal [ ] No zoning		Drainage	Appears adequate
Highest & best use as improved [X] Present use [ ] Other use (explain)		View	Neighborhood
		Landscaping	Average

Utilities	Public	Other	Off-site Improvements	Type	Public	Private		
Electricity	X		Street	Asphalt	X		Driveway Surface	Asphalt
Gas	X		Curb/gutter	Concrete	X		Apparent easements	Utilities
Water	X		Sidewalk	Concrete	X		FEMA Special Flood Hazard Area [ ] Yes [X] No	
Sanitary sewer	X		Street lights		X		FEMA Zone Map Date	
Storm sewer	X		Alley				FEMA Map No.	

Comments (apparent adverse easements, encroachments, special assessments, slide areas, illegal or legal nonconforming zoning use, etc.): Underground electric and telephone lines; no other easements or encroachments evident.

DESCRIPTION OF IMPROVEMENTS

GENERAL DESCRIPTION	EXTERIOR DESCRIPTION	FOUNDATION	BASEMENT	INSULATION
No. of Units 1	Foundation Concrete	Slab	Area Sq. Ft.	Roof
No. of Stories 1	Exterior Walls Stucco	Crawl Space Conc. walls	% Finished	Ceiling 6" [X]
Type (Det./Att.) Detached	Roof Surface Asph. Shingle	Basement	Ceiling	Walls 6" [X]
Design (Style) Ranch	Gutters & Dwnspts. Galv./paint	Sump Pump	Walls	Floor
Existing/Proposed Existing	Window Type Aluminum	Dampness	Floor	None
Age (Yrs.) 7	Storm/Screens Aluminum	Settlement	Outside Entry	Unknown
Effective Age (Yrs.)	Manufactured House	Infestation		

ROOMS	Foyer	Living	Dining	Kitchen	Den	Family Rm.	Rec. Rm.	Bedrooms	# Baths	Laundry	Other	Area Sq. Ft.
Basement												
Level 1		1	1	1		1		3	2		6 clos.	
Level 2												

Finished area above grade contains: 7 Rooms; 3 Bedroom(s); 2 Bath(s); 1,950 Square Feet of Gross Living Area

INTERIOR	Materials/Condition	HEATING	KITCHEN EQUIP.	ATTIC	AMENITIES	CAR STORAGE:
Floors	Vinyl/cpt/oak/Avg.	Type FA	Refrigerator [X]	None	Fireplace(s) # 1 [X]	None
Walls	Dryw/paint/paper/Ag.	Fuel Gas	Range/Oven [X]	Stairs	Patio	Garage # of cars
Trim/Finish	Pine/Avg.	Condition Very go	Disposal [X]	Drop Stair [X]	Deck	Attached
Bath Floor	Ceramic/Avg.	COOLING	Dishwasher [X]	Scuttle	Porch	Detached 2
Bath Wainscot	Ceramic/Ave.	Central Yes	Fan/Hood [X]	Floor	Fence Rear [X]	Built-in
Doors		Other	Microwave	Heated	Pool	Carport
		Condition Good	Washer/Dryer	Finished		Driveway Asphalt

COMMENTS

Additional features (special energy efficient items, etc.): 6" insulation above ceiling and behind drywall.

Condition of the improvements, depreciation (physical, functional, and external), repairs needed, quality of construction, remodeling/additions, etc.: The subject shows evidence of normal wear and tear only. Physical deterioration is estimated at 10%, with no sign of functional or external obsolescence. Overall property condition is good.

Adverse environmental conditions (such as, but not limited to, hazardous wastes, toxic substances, etc.) present in the improvements, on the site, or in the immediate vicinity of the subject property: No adverse conditions on or near the property were noted by the appraiser during a routine property inspection.

Freddie Mac Form 70 6-93   10 CH.   PAGE 1 OF 2   Fannie Mae Form 1004 6-93

FIGURE 13.3

Uniform Residential Appraisal Report (Continued)

	UNIFORM RESIDENTIAL APPRAISAL REPORT File No.

Valuation Section

COST APPROACH

ESTIMATED SITE VALUE	= $ 30,000	Comments on Cost Approach (such as, source of cost estimate, site value, square foot calculation and, for HUD, VA and FmHA, the estimated remaining economic life of the property):
ESTIMATED REPRODUCTION COST-NEW OF IMPROVEMENTS:		
Dwelling 1,950 Sq. Ft @ $ 52 = $101,400		
Sq. Ft @ $ =		
Fence, extra insul. = 1,300		
Garage/Carport 500 Sq. Ft @ $ 15 = 7,500		
Total Estimated Cost-New = $ 110,200		
Less Physical | Functional | External		
Depreciation 10% = $ 11,020		
Depreciated Value of Improvements = $ 99,180		
"As-is" Value of Site Improvements = $ 3,400		
INDICATED VALUE BY COST APPROACH = $ 132,580		

SALES COMPARISON ANALYSIS

ITEM	SUBJECT	COMPARABLE NO. 1		COMPARABLE NO. 2		COMPARABLE NO. 3	
Address	4807 Catalpa	(C)		(D)		(E)	
Proximity to Subject							
Sales Price	$ N/A		$128,000		$ 129,500		$137,250
Price/Gross Liv. Area	$	☑	$ 64.81	☑	$ 66.41	☑	$ 70.75 ☑
Data and/or							
Verification Sources							
VALUE ADJUSTMENTS	DESCRIPTION	DESCRIPTION	+ (-) $ Adjustment	DESCRIPTION	+ (-) $ Adjustment	DESCRIPTION	+ (-) $ Adjustment
Sales or Financing Concessions		Conv. mort.		Conv. mort.		Conv. mort.	
Date of Sale/Time		Current		Current		Current	
Location	Resid./Gd.	Resid./Equal		Resid./Equal		Resid./Equal	
Leasehold/Fee Simple	Fee simple	Fee simple		Fee simple		Fee simple	
Site	8,450 SF/Avg.	8,450 SF/Eq.		8,450 SF/Eq.		8,450 SF/Eq.	
View	Nbhd./Avg.	Nbhd./Equal		Nbhd./Equal		Nbhd./Equal	
Design and Appeal	Ranch/Good	Ranch/Equal		Ranch/Equal		Ranch/Equal	
Quality of Construction	Average	Equal		Equal		Equal	
Age	7 Yrs.	7 Yrs.		7 Yrs.		7 Yrs.	
Condition	Good	Good		Good		Good	
Above Grade	Total Bdrms Baths	Total Bdrms Baths		Total Bdrms Baths		Total Bdrms Baths	
Room Count	7 | 3 | 2	7 | 3 | 2		7 | 3 | 2		7 | 3 | 2	
Gross Living Area	1,950 Sq. Ft.	1,975 Sq. Ft.		1,950 Sq. Ft.		1,940 Sq. Ft.	
Basement & Finished Rooms Below Grade	Crawlspace	Crawlspace		Crawlspace		Finished Basement	- 7,000
Functional Utility	Good	Good		Good		Good	
Heating/Cooling	Central	Central		Central		Central	
Energy Efficient Items	Extra insul.	Extra insul.		Extra insul.		Extra insul.	
Garage/Carport	2-Car det.	2-Car det.		2-Car det.		2-car det.	
Porch, Patio, Deck, Fireplace(s), etc.	Patio, firepl.	Patio	+ 2,000	Patio, firepl.		Patio, firepl.	
Fence, Pool, etc.	Fence	Fence		Fence		Fence	
Net Adj. (total)		X + - $	2,000	+ - $	-0-	+ X - $	7,000
Adjusted Sales Price of Comparable			$130,000		$ 129,500		$ 130,250

Comments on Sales Comparison (including the subject property's compatibility to the neighborhood, etc.): The subject property conforms to the condition and quality of other property in the subject neighborhood.

ITEM	SUBJECT	COMPARABLE NO. 1	COMPARABLE NO. 2	COMPARABLE NO. 3
Date, Price and Data Source for prior sales within year of appraisal	N/A			

Analysis of any current agreement of sale, option, or listing of the subject property and analysis of any prior sales of subject and comparables within one year of the date of appraisal:

RECONCILIATION

INDICATED VALUE BY SALES COMPARISON APPROACH = $130,000

INDICATED VALUE BY INCOME APPROACH (If Applicable) Estimated Market Rent $ 975 /Mo. x Gross Rent Multiplier 130 = $126,750

This appraisal is made [X] "as is" [ ] subject to the repairs, alterations, inspections, or conditions listed below [ ] subject to completion per plans and specifications.

Conditions of Appraisal: _____

Final Reconciliation: Income approach value low since rents usually cover mortgage loan amount only. While reproduction cost is higher, prevailing market prices are best indicator of value.

The purpose of this appraisal is to estimate the market value of the real property that is the subject of this report, based on the above conditions and the certification, contingent and limiting conditions, and market value definition that are stated in the attached Freddie Mac Form 439/Fannie Mae Form 1004B (Revised 6/93).

I (WE) ESTIMATE THE MARKET VALUE, AS DEFINED, OF THE REAL PROPERTY THAT IS THE SUBJECT OF THIS REPORT, AS OF _____ (WHICH IS THE DATE OF INSPECTION AND THE EFFECTIVE DATE OF THIS REPORT) TO BE $ 130,000

APPRAISER:	SUPERVISORY APPRAISER (ONLY IF REQUIRED):	
Signature Aria Appraiser	Signature	[ ] Did [ ] Did Not
Name ARIA APPRAISER	Name	Inspect Property
Date Report Signed 12-17-XXXX	Date Report Signed	
State Certification #	State	State Certification #	State
Or State License #	State	Or State License #	State

Freddie Mac Form 70 6-93   10 CH.   PAGE 2 OF 2   Fannie Mae Form 1004 6-93

U.S. Forms, Inc. 1-800-225-9583   USF# 00110

■ SUMMARY

An accurate **appraisal** is a necessary and very important part of any real estate transaction. An **appraisal** is also useful for many other purposes, from acquiring insurance to determining a property's **highest and best use.**

An appraised value can be determined as of the date on which the **appraiser** inspects the subject property or any time in the past. The value most often sought is **market value,** which is a result of **demand, utility, scarcity, transferability,** and the availability of suitable financing.

The **appraiser** follows certain valuation principles that provide a way to define and examine forces at work in the marketplace, such as **competition, growth, anticipation,** and **supply and demand.**

Using the **sales comparison approach,** the **appraiser** analyzes data regarding the subject property and comparable properties to determine **market value.** The **appraiser** must know the marketplace to judge whether properties are comparable to the subject property.

Using the **cost approach,** the **appraiser** estimates what it would cost to construct a new building having the same utility as the subject property. The value of the site without improvements is added to the **reproduction** or **replacement cost** of the improvements, less the amount by which they have **depreciated.** Computing **reproduction cost** requires knowledge of current construction methods and costs, particularly if the **unit-in-place** or **quantity survey method** is used.

Depreciation can be **physical, functional,** or **external.** Items of **curable depreciation** can be corrected economically. Items of **incurable depreciation** cannot be corrected economically.

Using the **income capitalization approach,** the appraiser develops the appropriate **capitalization rate** for the subject property. The **appraiser** then applies that rate to the property's **net operating income** to find property value. For some properties a better approach is to use a **gross income multiplier.**

All three approaches to value may be used in an **appraisal.** The **appraiser** will choose the value most appropriate for the property being appraised. In this process, called **reconciliation,** the **appraiser** uses the other values to support the conclusion of value or explain variances.

The **sales comparison approach** usually is the best indicator of value for residential property. The **cost approach** is the most reliable indicator for newly constructed property. The **income capitalization approach** is the best indicator of value for commercial/industrial property and apartment buildings of five units or more.

■ IMPORTANT TERMS

Make sure you understand the following terms before you take the achievement examination.

anticipation
appraisal
arm's-length transaction
balance
capitalization ("cap") rate
change
competition
competitive market analysis
    (CMA)
conformity
contract rent
contribution
cost approach
decline
demand
depreciation
effective gross income
equilibrium
external obsolescence
federally related transaction
functional obsolescence
gentrification
gross income multiplier (GIM)
growth
highest and best use
income capitalization approach
index method
market rent
market value
net operating income

observed condition method
Office of Real Estate Appraisers
    (OREA)
physical deterioration
potential gross income
progression
quantity survey method
reconciliation
regression
replacement cost
reproduction cost
restricted report
revitalization
sales comparison approach
scarcity
self-contained report
site value
square-foot method
straight-line method
substitution
summary report
supply and demand
transferability
Uniform Residential Appraisal Report
    (URAR)
unit-in-place method
utility
value in exchange
value in use

■ OPEN FOR DISCUSSION

Organizations such as the Appraisal Institute are creating national databases of property information, including sales and appraisal data.

1. Do you think such databases will eventually replace the work of professional appraisers?

2. What are some of the reasons why the appraiser will still be a necessary part of the transaction?

■ ACHIEVEMENT EXAMINATION 13

1. A house is appraised at $123,000, even though it cost $135,000 to build three years earlier. Which factor below could *not* have contributed to the loss in value?
   a. Regression
   b. Gentrification
   c. Functional obsolescence
   d. Supply and demand

2. Ed Wilson owns a vacant lot and employs an appraiser to determine the property's
   a. growth.
   b. reproduction cost.
   c. replacement cost.
   d. highest and best use.

3. Since the Peterson factory closed down, houses in Sunny Acres are taking longer to sell, and prices have gone down. This is a result of
   a. highest and best use.
   b. supply and demand.
   c. contribution.
   d. conformity.

4. A house that benefits from the splendor of its neighbors is an example of the principle of
   a. balance.   c. progression.
   b. contribution.   d. regression.

5. Charlie Addison has a deluxe five-bedroom house in a neighborhood of modest three-bedroom houses. The value of Charlie's house will be affected in an example of
   a. substitution.   c. progression.
   b. scarcity.   d. regression.

6. An improvement to a house may or may not create a corresponding increase in the house's market value. This is an example of
   a. balance.   c. contribution.
   b. progression.   d. regression.

7. Carla and Jose are looking forward to eventually retiring on the profit they will make from selling their house. Their attitude is an example of
   a. progression.   c. acquisition.
   b. growth.   d. anticipation.

8. House A sold for $167,000 and is comparable to the house being appraised, but it has an extra half-bath valued at $3,300. What is the adjusted value of house A?
   a. $170,300   c. $163,700
   b. $172,000   d. $164,700

9. To find a cost approach estimate of a 19th-century San Francisco Victorian-style mansion, you probably would use
   a. reproduction cost.
   b. replacement cost.
   c. historical building cost.
   d. cost averaging.

10. The cubic-foot method of estimating construction cost is best used for
    a. single-family residences.
    b. manufactured homes.
    c. industrial properties.
    d. multifamily residential properties.

11. Appraiser Hansen estimated all direct and indirect construction costs of the Harley Building separately, then totaled them. She used the
    a. unit-in-place method.
    b. index method.
    c. quantity survey method.
    d. cost averaging method.

12. A single-family residence with a one-car garage may be an example of
    a. external obsolescence.
    b. functional obsolescence.
    c. economic obsolescence.
    d. environmental obsolescence.

13. Houses adjacent to a new highway will probably suffer from
    a. curable external obsolescence.
    b. incurable functional obsolescence.
    c. curable functional obsolescence.
    d. incurable external obsolescence.

14. Which of the following is *not* a form of depreciation?
    a. Physical deterioration
    b. Straight-line method
    c. Economic obsolescence
    d. Functional obsolescence

15. The upper limit of a property's value usually is determined by the
    a. market comparison approach.
    b. cost approach.
    c. income approach.
    d. sales comparison approach.

16. Vacancy and collection losses are subtracted from potential gross income to derive
    a. net operating income.
    b. gross operating income.
    c. effective gross income.
    d. capitalization rate.

17. An office building with an annual gross income of $70,175 sold for $800,000. What is the building's gross income multiplier?
    a. 11.4   c. .0877
    b. 1.147   d. 12

18. The gross rent multiplier for most single-family residences in Sally Murphy's neighborhood is 168. What is the market value of Sally's house using that GRM, if the house rents for $1,975 per month?
    a. $371,300   c. $331,800
    b. $117,559   d. $33,180

19. The step in which the appraiser arrives at a final estimate of value is called
    a. equilibrium.   c. substitution.
    b. reconciliation.   d. equalization.

20. The most comprehensive method of conveying the result of an appraisal is the
    a. self-contained report.
    b. form report.
    c. restricted report.
    d. summary report.

CHAPTER FOURTEEN

RESIDENTIAL DESIGN AND CONSTRUCTION

■ BUILDING CONSTRUCTION STANDARDS

Federal, state, and local standards of design and construction help ensure safe dwellings and workplaces. This section describes the standards that apply to housing in California. The emphasis is on the wood-frame structure, the most commonly used form of residential building.

Federal Regulations

On the national level, federally insured (FHA) or guaranteed (VA) loans require inspection and compliance with **minimum property requirements (MPRs)** first established in 1934. Since 1986, FHA has permitted local **building codes** to set the standard for most property specifications. Property that fails to meet the minimum requirements may have to undergo corrective work. Approval of the property (and loan) will be withheld until satisfactory completion of all necessary repairs or additions.

The term *manufactured home* is used by the federal government to describe a house constructed in a factory to comply with the Department of Housing and Urban Development (HUD) building code. Manufactured homes must meet the National Manufactured Home Construction and Safety Standards. The standards for "HUD-code" homes include design and construction, minimum room sizes, durability, fire resistance, insulation, weatherproofing, and energy efficiency. Buyers must be given a *homeowner's manual* that covers general maintenance, safety, and information on state agencies enforcing the federal standards.

State Regulations

The State of California regulates the building industry through building codes and by requiring building contractors to be licensed.

State Housing Law. The **Housing Law** sets minimum construction and occupancy requirements for all dwellings, including apartment houses and hotels. It is under the administration of the Codes and Standards Division of the **Department of Housing and Community Development.** Compliance with construction standards is the responsibility of the local building official and inspectors. Occupancy and sanitation standards are enforced by local health officers.

The **Commission of Housing and Community Development** is required by the legislature to adopt regulations that comply with the **uniform codes** that set construction standards for the industry. Local building codes must comply with state regulations.

All three major code organizations in the United States (including the former International Conference of Building Officials (ICBO) in Whittier, Calif.) merged in 2000 to create the International Code Council (ICC). The International Building Code and the International Residential Building Code were adopted by ICC, revised in 2003, and are scheduled for revision every three years. They are now the standards being adopted across the country. The former ICBO office in Whittier is now a branch office of ICC, found at *www.iccsafe.org*.

www.iccsafe.org

Building codes are enforced by the appropriate municipal or county governing authority. A **building permit** must be obtained before construction is allowed to begin. Application for a permit is made to the local building official, who also is supplied with plot plan and building plans and specifications for the proposed structure. Problem areas are pointed out and can be revised. The permit is issued only when the application is finally approved.

Periodic inspections during the construction process help ensure that code requirements are met. In addition, a completed building cannot be placed into service until the local building department issues a **certificate of occupancy (CO).** A **temporary CO** may be issued to allow occupancy while minor features of the work are still under way. All construction must be successfully completed by the date stated in the temporary certificate.

The **California Department of Health Services,** acting through the local health officer required in every county and city, may halt construction if contamination of the water supply, the drainage system, or proper sewage disposal is threatened.

In addition, California's *Mobilehome Accommodation Structures Law* regulates buildings and other structures used with manufactured homes at grade level. The *Mobilehome Parks Act* regulates construction and operation of parks for manufactured homes as well as parks for recreational vehicles. Both laws are part of the Health and Safety Code.

Contractors' License Law.   Under the **Contractors' License Law,** the **Contractors' State License Board** licenses all building contractors working within the state. The current license status of all California contractors can be checked at *www.cslb.ca.gov*.

www.cslb.ca.gov

Criminal charges can be brought against any unlicensed individual who does the work of a contractor and is not exempt from the licensing law.

No contractor's license is needed for

■ work (including labor and materials) costing less than $500 (but the worker must disclose the lack of a contractor's license to the customer),

■ owner-performed work (unless the owner intends to offer the property for sale),

■ certain construction for agricultural purposes,

■ oil and gas operations, and

■ work performed by public entities and public utilities.

To be licensed, a contractor must meet both experience and knowledge qualifications. Various private schools throughout the state specialize in preparing students for the contractors' licensing exam. If the requirements are met, the applicant for a contractor's license must post a *bond* or *cash deposit* with the state. This fund is for the benefit of persons who might be damaged or defrauded by the contractor in the conduct of his or her business.

A contractor's license can be *suspended* or *revoked* for

■ failing to follow plans and specifications,

■ abandoning a project,

■ diverting funds,

■ violating building laws or work safety regulations, or

■ breaching the construction contract in a material respect.

Local Regulations

Since 1970, local building codes have been required to follow the uniform codes adopted by the Commission of Housing and Community Development. Local variations necessitated by local conditions must be specifically approved. Local

FIGURE 14.1

Roof Designs

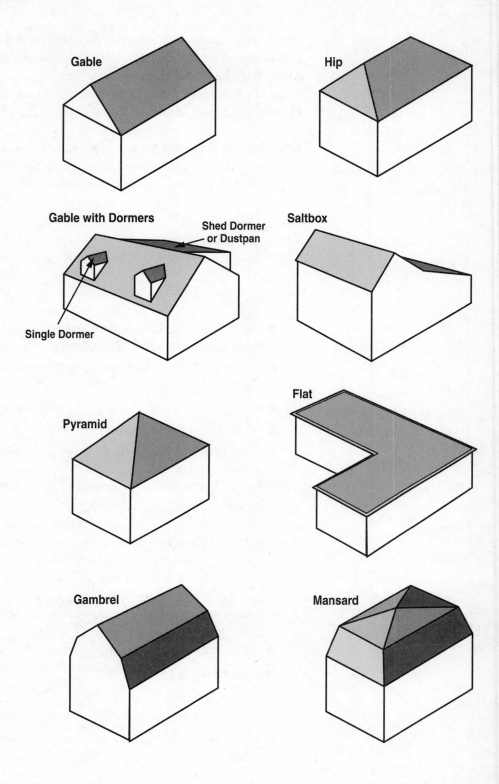

codes also may prohibit undesirable practices otherwise allowed by the uniform codes. An example is the "piggybacking" of copper wiring to a system with aluminum wiring.

Local codes do not apply to the *construction* of HUD-code (manufactured) homes, but do apply to site improvements, such as grading, foundation work, and installation of utilities as well as placement and anchoring of the home on the site.

Local governments also initiate regulations regarding land use, fire safety, sanitation, density, building setbacks, and property line requirements. These are covered in Chapter 15, "Government Control of Land Use."

Exercise 14-1   Broker Bob wants to sell the Gray house, one of his listings, but knows that it needs some foundation repair work. With the Grays' approval, and for a small fee, Broker Bob hires a work crew that places new support jacks under the Gray house and rebuilds some of the foundation walls. Broker Bob supervises the entire job. Do you see any problems with this arrangement?

■ ARCHITECTURE

Present-day architects and builders may borrow parts of one or more of the classic designs. Design features are adapted, using modern materials and techniques, to make the resulting concept a workable one for current tastes and living patterns.

Roof Styles

The roof styles illustrated in Figure 14.1 are referred to in the descriptions of architectural styles that follow. The variations are based on the direction, degree of pitch (steepness), and number of roof planes.

Architectural Styles

The architectural styles described and illustrated on pages 414–417 typically have most, if not all, of the features listed.

Colonial American or Cape Cod

- Wood siding with shutters
- One to two or more stories
- Steep-pitched, wood-shingled roof
- Shed addition
- Dormer windows
- Multipaned glass windows, usually placed symmetrically in relation to front door

Southern Colonial

- Large, with two or more stories
- Tall wood columns
- Exterior finish of wood, painted white
- Exterior occasionally brick

Dutch Colonial

- One and one-half or two and one-half stories
- Distinctive gambrel roof
- Dormers

Victorian

- Wood, with elaborate decoration
- More than one story
- All white, pastel, or deep colors used at the turn of the 19th century, or (especially in contemporary models) with siding and trim in contrasting colors
- High-ceilinged rooms
- Leaded and stained-glass windows
- Front porch, sometimes wrapping around side of house

Town House or Row House

- Adjoins or shares a common (party) wall with neighboring house
- Found in cities or as part of a suburban development
- Exterior style variations possible, limited to front expanse and roofline

English Tudor

- Brick or stone and stucco with exposed wood timbers
- Large, usually two stories
- Diamond-paned windows
- Elaborate interior wood paneling or molding

French Provincial

- Large, with white brick or brick and stucco exterior
- Hip roof
- Two stories, possibly with dormers

Spanish

- White or pastel stucco exterior
- One story (two-story Santa Barbara or Monterey style)
- Brown or orange tile roof
- Courtyard
- Wrought-iron trim and fencing

California Ranch

■ One story

■ Wood or masonry exterior

■ Built on concrete slab or shallow crawlspace

■ Attached garage on concrete slab

Contemporary

■ One or more stories

■ Wood, stucco, or masonry exterior finish

■ Roof low-pitched or flat

■ Minimal decoration

■ Open floor plan

Within the described range of styles, differences in floor level can affect both design and layout. The split-level house, illustrated below, can be useful both in conserving expensive foundation costs and in taking advantage of a sloping lot.

An extreme slope, whether uphill or downhill from the building site, also calls for special consideration. For very steep sites, a contemporary design often is most attractive.

The most common style of **manufactured home** is the ranch, as shown below. Some types of modular factory-built housing allow virtually unlimited design and size specifications and are indistinguishable from their site-built counterparts.

Exercise 14-2 Describe the architectural style and features of the house pictured below.

■ DESIGN AND FUNCTION

The design of a home includes all of the elements of the floor plan: number of rooms, their size, and their relation to one another. Design is influenced by aesthetic and functional concerns, as well as external factors such as placement of a house on its site to allow maximum sunlight and/or view.

Orientation on the Site

The placement of a house on a site is called its **orientation.** Orientation is generally best when the greatest window expanse faces south. With a deep enough roof overhang, south-facing windows allow the winter sunlight in, yet are shielded from the summer sun. This is particularly important in desert communities. Figure 14.2 shows this principle at work. During the winter

FIGURE 14.2

Solar Angles and Overhang

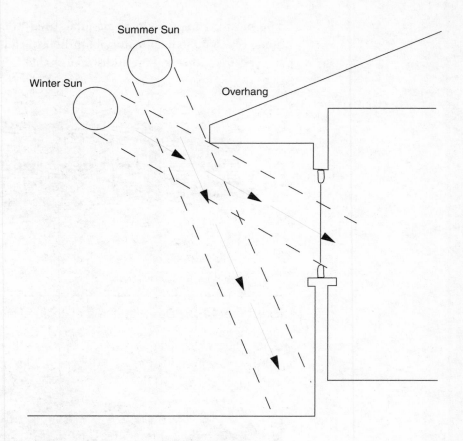

months the sun's arc is much lower in the sky than it is in the summer months, allowing maximum use of the natural heating power of sunlight. In the summer the sun's higher arc permits a roof overhang to block much or all of the sunlight from the interior of the structure.

In a region that has relatively mild winters, a southern exposure to the rear of the house may be desirable. Such an orientation allows maximum use of outdoor facilities, such as a patio or swimming pool.

Especially on a hillside lot, the view may be the primary consideration in orienting the house. Because contemporary designs do not require rigid placement of front entry and windows, those features can be placed to take maximum advantage of the site. Often a fence-enclosed outside patio can turn a part of the house with a poor view into an attractive oasis.

Many subdivisions are designed to allow homes to take maximum advantage of a common area. The common area may include a park, walkway, golf course, swimming pool, or clubhouse. The benefit of being near or adjacent to a common area must be balanced against any resulting loss of privacy, increased noise, or actual danger. Errant golf balls can be more than just a nuisance, and there must be adequate fencing to safeguard small children from hazards such as ponds.

Floor Plan

The floor plan of a house should provide for both easy **circulation** and convenient **access** to living areas. The old "railroad" concept of all rooms in a line, with entry from one to the next, is highly undesirable. Each bedroom should have a separate entry, and the most luxurious plan gives each bedroom its own adjoining bathroom. As much as possible, bedrooms should be isolated from living areas.

The "great room" combining kitchen and family/living areas has become more popular than separate kitchen and family room, visually expanding the floor area of both spaces. Telecommuting and home computer use have created demand for a separate office space, with a separate outside entrance a useful feature. Traditional exterior styles often belie the open, high-ceilinged spaces within. Even the one-story ranch-style houses built throughout California by the thousands after World War II have proven their versatility. They are still in demand as expandable starter homes as well as homes that suit the needs of the growing number of seniors. Some, such as the distinctive homes built by Joseph Eichler, are valued even more highly today for their innovative use of glass and easy flow of indoor and outdoor spaces.

Most California single-family dwellings do not have **basements**—that is, rooms that are partly or entirely below ground level. Houses in some city areas, such as San Francisco, have what are called basements, but these are actually ground-level garage and storage spaces. Such buildings typically have outside stairway access to the main entrance on the second level of the building.

A house without a basement loses storage space but saves on the cost of the increased concrete needed for the deeper foundation walls and floor. Because there are few exceptionally cold areas in the state, the insulation value of a basement is not usually a factor. Hillside houses often make use of a lower level that is properly a basement but may have one or more walls above the surface of the slope. Such basement space may be counted in the home's living area, if typical of homes in the community.

Exercise 14-3   Label each space in the floor plan below according to its most likely best use.

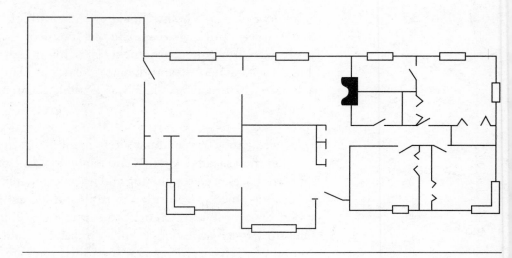

■ CONSTRUCTION STAGES

You should be familiar with the names of the various construction stages and components of a house, particularly if you are taking the real estate licensing examination. Refer to the diagrams as you read through this section.

Site Preparation

Preparing a parcel of land for building requires much more than simply leveling it with a bulldozer. Before a building permit will be issued, the contractor will have to comply with all local, national, and federal requirements regarding site utilization. A soil engineer's report, **perc test** of the ability of water to drain (percolate) through the soil, seismic analysis, environmental impact report, and other studies may be necessary. The previous use of the site might dictate removal and replacement of soil if hazardous materials were stored or present on the property in the past. Sites identified as **brownfields** by the Environmental Protection Agency require extensive remediation.

Hillside locations, found throughout California, have their own unique requirements. Grading might require construction of retaining walls to prevent earth movement above or below the site. Seasonal water flow might necessitate extensive drainage systems and extraordinarily deep foundation supports, and make a site uneconomical for building.

Often, the lack of vacant building sites results in the "tear-down" phenomenon in which an older home is purchased for the value of the underlying land, then

FIGURE 14.3

Foundation

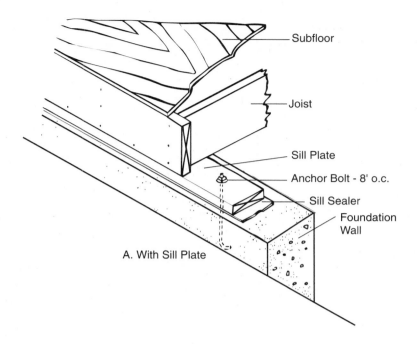

Subfloor

Joist

Sill Plate

Anchor Bolt - 8' o.c.

Sill Sealer

Foundation Wall

A. With Sill Plate

Foundation

torn down so that a new home can be built. The tendency to build huge new homes on such sites has not been well received in some communities, with the result that the approval process in such cases has become much more difficult.

The wood-frame house typically rests on **foundation walls** of poured concrete. The site is excavated, the foundation walls are poured into wood forms, the wood forms are removed after the concrete has cured, and dirt (**backfill**) is moved back against the walls. The floor of the house also may be concrete, poured either at the same time as the foundation walls or after. More commonly used is the wood floor on concrete foundation walls, usually plywood panels over wood beams called **girders** and **joists.** This design leaves a **crawl space** beneath the home for ventilation and protection against termites. It is illustrated in Figure 14.3. Instead of continuous concrete foundation walls, some older homes have concrete or stone supports called **footings.**

Insect infestation is possible wherever wood comes into contact with earth. Termites also can build their earth tunnels from the ground to the wood structure along cement foundation walls or supports. The foundation itself should be chemically treated to poison termites, and any wood that must be in even indirect contact with earth, such as a fence post or deck support, also should be chemically treated and inspected regularly. As a general rule there should be no direct contact of wood with earth.

The **sill** is the wood member that is placed directly on the foundation wall. Since 1931 California building codes have required the use of **anchor bolts** through the

FIGURE 14.4

Wall Framing with Platform Construction

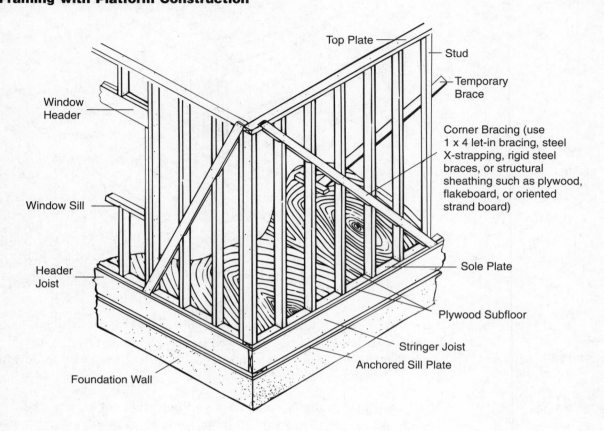

sill and into the foundation wall as an earthquake safety measure. Nevertheless, the California legislature has estimated that *1.2 million* homes in the state have foundations that are not adequately secured (Government Code 8897).

Framework

After the foundation has been prepared, the house frame is erected. The **frame** is the skeleton to which the exterior and interior walls are attached. The frame consists of vertical supports called **studs,** which local building codes require to be *no more than 16 inches apart.* Short, horizontal pieces of wood are placed between the studs at intervals to act as **fire stops** by blocking air drafts.

In **platform frame** construction the frame of a multistory house is built one story at a time, with each story supporting the next. Figure 14.4 shows the components of a platform frame system. The **post-and-beam frame,** used less frequently than the platform frame, allows great design flexibility. Ceiling boards are supported on beams that rest on posts placed within the house. Because the wall frame studs do not have to bear the full weight of the ceiling and roof, they can be spaced farther apart, allowing for greater room area.

As California earthquakes have demonstrated many times, ground movement can create tremendous forces that buildings withstand only if they are properly anchored and braced.

Exterior Walls

Insulating **sheathing** of plywood or drywall is applied to exterior walls, which are then ready for **siding,** whether wood, aluminum, brick, stone, or other material. **Stucco,** a type of plaster, requires wood furring strips to be nailed to the plywood, with metal lathing stretched over the wood strips as a base for the stucco.

> Plywood sheathing provides bracing needed for a building to ride out an earthquake.

Plywood sheathing is an excellent way to provide the **bracing** needed to protect a building in an earthquake. A sheet of plywood securely fastened to wall studs serves the same purpose as an X-shaped wall bracing system. Plywood sheathing allows a building to move with the movement of the earth, yet keeps the structure intact so that it returns to its original shape.

Masonry, which refers to any use of brick or stone, is either solid or veneer. If veneer, it is a decorative finish and does not support the roof structure. The thickness of the walls is one way to tell whether masonry is veneer. With masonry veneer, the depth of the walls generally is eight to ten inches or less.

Unreinforced masonry is very susceptible to earthquake damage. The Government Code requires an owner who has actual or constructive knowledge that such a building is located in a Seismic Zone 4 to post a prescribed notice at the building's entrance. The notice is not required if the walls are nonloadbearing and have steel or concrete frames. If the building's buyer receives the required notice and fails to bring the building into code compliance within five years, the buyer cannot receive any state earthquake repair payment until all other applicants have been paid.

Government Code Section 8875.6 requires the transferor (or the transferor's agent) of any unreinforced masonry building with wood frame floors or roofs that was built before January 1, 1975, to deliver to the purchaser as soon as practicable before a sale, transfer, or exchange, a copy of the *Commercial Property Owner's Guide to Earthquake Safety* described in Section 10147 of the Code. This requirement does not apply to transfers between spouses or co-owners, from an estate or trust administrator, from mortgagor to mortgagee, or pursuant to a court order.

Insulation

In the days of (relatively) cheap oil and gas energy, **insulation** of walls and ceiling was of less importance than it is today. The effectiveness of various kinds of insulation is expressed by their **R-value.** When more than one layer of insulation is used, the R-values of the individual layers are added to each other to find the total R-value of all the layers. Thus if insulation of R-9 is placed over insulation of R-11, the two layers provide a total insulation value of R-20. An R-1 value is equivalent to about 1½ inches of insulation.

Any hardware store customer has probably seen the bulky aluminum-foil-clad rolls of fiberglass or rockwool insulation that are sized to fit between wall studs. Such products are easy to install in a home with an exposed ceiling frame accessible through an attic. Unless walls are insulated before interior walls are finished, they require the services of a professional. Insulation can be blown into wall cavities, for instance, using the proper equipment. *Protective clothing, including mask and gloves, is necessary during any handling of insulation materials.*

> Putting an insulating blanket on a water heater can save energy and money.

Other building components also can be insulated. A fiberglass "blanket" can be purchased for a water heater and installed by the homeowner. Water pipes can be wrapped to help prevent heat loss. Water pipes wrapped with insulation will be less likely to suffer from the effects of a sudden freeze, which could cause them to burst.

The California State Energy Resources Conservation and Development Commission has established a statewide **home energy rating program.** The residential dwelling seller (or agent) must provide a copy of an information booklet on the program to the buyer.

Until the mid-1970s **asbestos** was frequently used in walls and sprayed on ceilings and other building components. Asbestos fibers, released when the material is handled or as it deteriorates, now are believed to be a potential cause of cancer if inhaled. Use of **urea formaldehyde** is prohibited in most parts of the United States. Toxic fumes from this product may cause nausea and other adverse reactions. Urea formaldehyde frequently is found in older manufactured homes, where its effects may be amplified by poor ventilation. The hazards stemming from use of lead-based paint are mentioned on page 426. Any building suspected

FIGURE 14.5

Rafter Framing

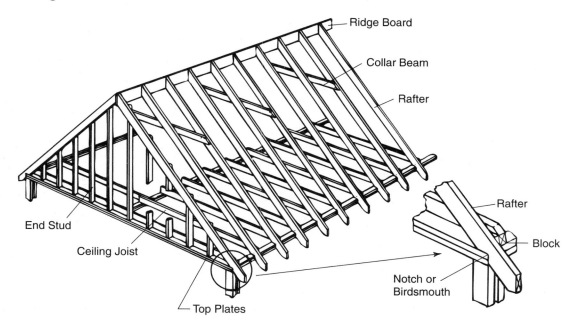

of having lead-based paint, asbestos, or urea formaldehyde in its construction should be inspected by a competent professional.

Roof

Basic roof styles were illustrated in Figure 14.1. The roof structure is shown in Figure 14.5. Roofs are formed by **rafters,** sheathing, and a finishing material. The rafters meet at the **ridge board,** the highest point of construction of a frame building. Sheathing is usually plywood. Spaced sheathing of one-inch by four-inch boards is used for a wood shake or shingle roof to allow better air circulation. A heavy waterproof paper called **building paper** goes over the sheathing first.

Roof finishes can range from wood shakes or shingles to mineral fiber shingles, tile, or slate. Sheet metal, called **flashing,** surrounds openings cut in the roof for chimneys and vents. A flat roof, the hardest to waterproof because it allows water and snow to collect, is covered with tar, which must be renewed periodically.

Wood-look, mineral-based shingles and shakes are now being made to simulate the attractiveness of wood yet provide the protection of a long-wearing, fireproof material. *Increasingly, the fire hazard posed by wood roof coverings has resulted in ordinances prohibiting their use either for new construction or to replace an existing roof.*

Wood roof coverings are prohibited in many parts of the state.

Lead-Based Paint

The presence of lead in paint used in housing is a major health concern. Deteriorating paint releases lead; renovations can release large amounts of lead into the home as well as the surrounding soil.

The danger of lead exposure to adults includes high blood pressure, memory and concentration problems, and difficulty during pregnancy. The danger to children includes damage to the brain and nervous system, behavior and learning problems, slowed growth, and hearing loss.

Encapsulation using special paints that prevent lead from leaching through to the surface may be the best preventative.

Since 1978, the use of **lead-based paint** in housing has been prohibited by the federal government. It has been estimated that 83 percent of homes built before 1978 (about 64 million homes) contain lead-based paint.

The **Residential Lead-Based Paint Hazard Reduction Act of 1992,** a federal law, requires disclosure of the possible presence of lead-based paint in homes built before 1978. Sellers and landlords of rental units must also comply with the law. The enforcement body is the **Environmental Protection Agency (EPA).**

www.epa.gov
www.epa.gov/lead/nlic.htm

Information on legal requirements is available from the **National Lead Information Center (NLIC),** (202) 659-1192, as well as EPA branches and state health departments. The EPA has a Web site at *www.epa.gov.* NLIC can be found at *www.epa.gov/lead/nlic.htm.*

The law does not require a seller or landlord to conduct any testing or hazard reduction. The seller or landlord must disclose any known presence of lead and provide copies of available lead hazard evaluations and reports.

The prospective buyer or renter must

- receive an EPA disclosure pamphlet (or state-approved alternative);
- have ten days in which to arrange a property inspection; and
- sign a lead warning statement and acknowledgment.

Real estate agents must

The CAR lead-based paint disclosure and acknowledgment form (FLD-11) was released in April 1999.

- inform the seller or landlord of the requirements;
- make sure that the buyer or renter has received the necessary documentation; and
- retain the signed disclosure/acknowledgment statement for three years.

FIGURE 14.6

Types of Windows

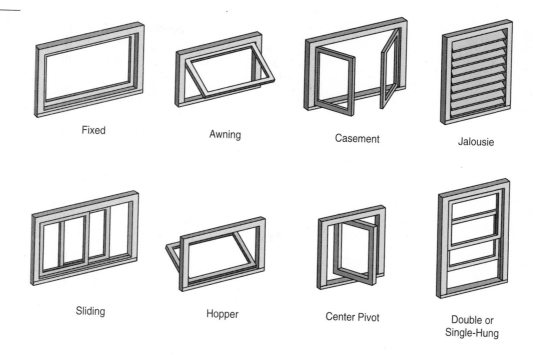

Fixed Awning Casement Jalousie

Sliding Hopper Center Pivot Double or
Single-Hung

The roof **eave** is the part of a pitched roof that extends beyond the outer wall of the house. It may be enclosed by a **soffit** or left open. A better-quality house has a **gutter** along the eave to direct rain runoff through a **downspout.**

Windows

Windows are available in many styles and materials. Aluminum framing has replaced wood for most construction, but the more expensive wood windows are also popular, particularly in remodeling. Some of the common window styles are pictured in Figure 14.6. The fixed type does not open, and some windows have both fixed and opening sections. Casement windows are unusual in that they open outward.

Doors

There usually are three exterior doors to a house—the main entrance, the service door leading to garage or rear area, and the patio door leading to patio, deck, or garden. Although exterior doors usually are—or should be—made of solid wood, plywood, or wood filler, interior doors are often hollow core. Patio doors are most often sliding glass doors, although multipaned glass doors (called French doors) are popular. Some single-pane glass doors use removable wood panes to simulate a French door.

Interior Walls

Interior walls can be finished with **plasterboard,** also referred to as **drywall, wallboard,** or **sheetrock.** Plasterboard is a preformed layer of plaster sandwiched between layers of paper and cut into sheets that are typically four feet by eight feet. Its weight makes plasterboard difficult to handle, but it can be cut, if necessary, to fit around door and window openings, and it covers large areas quickly.

The seams between sections of plasterboard are covered with a special tape. As a last step, plasterboard can be covered with a texturing material, usually rolled on, to give the appearance of hand-applied plaster.

Most plaster finishes can be painted, and smooth finishes can be wallpapered. **Plasterboard** is a much cheaper alternative to the **lath and plaster** technique in which wet plaster is applied directly to the wall against a backing of wood and wire.

Interior walls also can be paneled with wood, either in boards or in lightweight sheets of wood veneer plywood, usually four feet by eight feet. There also are wood-look and marble-look panels.

Floor

Plywood floor **underlayment** or **subflooring** can be finished with wood boards, tile (wood parquet, ceramic, vinyl, or asphalt), or carpeting.

Utilities

In new homes, **telephone wiring** that allows installation of two separate lines is becoming standard. Urban areas now offer the advantages of fiber optic cable connections to take maximum advantage of Internet services.

Although 110-volt **electrical service** was once the norm, the electrical system of any house built today should be wired for 240-volt service, to allow use of the widest range of appliances. Wiring in the average house also should be able to carry at least 100 amperes (amps) of electricity at the required voltage. Because of the steadily increasing number of household appliances, many contractors recommend a minimum of 150 amps.

Both heating and air-conditioning units are found in many homes in California. An air-conditioning unit can be rated in terms of its energy consumption. The **energy-efficiency ratio (EER)** is found by dividing the unit's capacity measured in British Thermal Units (BTUs) by the number of watts of electricity needed to run it. For example, a 36,000-BTU (three-ton) air conditioner that needs 6,000 watts to run has an EER of 6.0. A unit of the same capacity that needs 5,000 watts to run has an EER of 7.2. A higher EER means that less energy is consumed and the unit is more efficient. A household water heater should have at least a 40-gallon capacity.

Solar heating of both room air and water supply has enjoyed some popularity, although initial installation expense may make a solar unit more a luxury than a practical addition to an existing building. The simplest form of solar heat, of course, is the sunlight coming through a window. If water-filled tanks are placed inside the house at a place where the sun can shine on them, they absorb the heat of the sunlight and will help warm the house at night when that heat is dispersed. To some degree any heat-absorbing material, such as ceramic tile flooring, will produce the same effect. Such a solar-heating system is called *passive*, because it has no mechanical parts.

The Health and Safety Code provides that any city or county may permit windows required for light and ventilation of habitable rooms in dwellings to open into areas provided with natural light and ventilation that are designed and built to act as passive solar energy collectors. This provision would allow the addition to a house of a greenhouse-style room with water-filled heat collectors, or a stone or tile floor serving the same purpose, designed to receive maximum sunlight during the day to retain heat to be released into the interior of the house (through window openings) at night.

There are also *active* solar-heating systems. Typically, a water-filled panel, or "collector," is placed on a surface facing the sun, usually the building roof. The water warmed by the sun flows to a storage tank in the house, and colder water is returned to the collector. A small pump operates the system. The warm water can be used directly, such as for bathing, and also warms the air as it passes through the pipes. A backup conventional heating system can be used on cloudy days. The house shown in Figure 14.7 has a typical active rooftop installation. An active system may be a cost-effective way to heat a swimming pool.

Fixtures

Kitchen and bathroom.   The kitchen requires special attention. **Cabinets,** usually of wood, can be custom-made on-site or prefabricated. Some **appliances** may be built-in, including dishwasher, range top, wall oven, and trash compactor. There may be a separate counter "island" in the kitchen with chopping block, sink, and self-exhausting broiler/range top. Ceramic tile has historically been a desirable counter and wall finish around fixtures in kitchen and bathroom, although many other possibilities now are available, including natural granite and marble, wood, Formica™, and synthetic granite and marble.

Plumbing fixtures—bathtubs, toilets, and sinks—can range from standard grade cast iron or pressed steel coated with enamel to molded fiberglass. Many home-owners consider the stainless-steel sink attractive, and it also is easier to maintain. A double-basin sink is desirable for the kitchen. The newest trend is the so-called gourmet sink, with a deep basin alongside a shallow basin containing a garbage disposal unit.

Smoke detectors.   California law requires that any single-family house (including factory-built houses) sold on or after January 1, 1986, have an operable smoke detector. A battery-operated unit is sufficient in most counties,

FIGURE 14.7

**Active Solar Heat
System Panel**

but some (such as San Francisco) require a smoke detector to be wired to the home's electrical system to avoid the danger of an inoperable battery.

The seller of the house is responsible for smoke-detector installation and must give the buyer a written statement indicating compliance with the law. If the seller does not do so, the buyer cannot rescind the contract of sale, but the seller may be liable for damages of $100 plus attorney's fees and court costs.

Water heater bracing.   To help reduce earthquake-caused damage to dwellings, as of January 1, 1996, California law requires that all water heaters be braced, anchored, or strapped to resist falling or horizontal displacement. The seller of real property must certify to the buyer that the law has been complied with.

■ MANUFACTURED HOMES

Manufactured homes now account for one-third of all new single-family home purchases in the United States.

California's Business and Professions Code defines what it still terms a "mobile home" as a "structure transportable in one or more sections, designed and equipped to contain not more than two dwelling units to be used with or without a foundation system." The definition of a mobile home does not include recreational vehicles, commercial coaches, or modular housing. The code defines a mobile-home park as "any area or tract of land where two or more mobilehome lots are rented or leased or held out for rent or lease."

Advantages of Manufactured/ Mobile Homes

Mass production of building components and assembly in factories make it possible for builders to ignore inclement weather. This results in homes that are constructed without exposure to the elements, avoiding delays and dangerous working conditions. They are also significantly cheaper than houses constructed on-site. The need to transport a manufactured/mobile home limits the maximum size of a single construction unit, but two or more units can be combined on-site, allowing a degree of flexibility in design.

California's mobile-home parks are often tailored to specific recreational or residential lifestyles (such as those of senior citizens). A well-planned mobile-home park with adequate space between units, limited access, and reduced speed limits contributes to the value of its homes.

Exercise 14-4   Using the diagrams and definitions in this chapter, label the indicated parts of the house shown below.

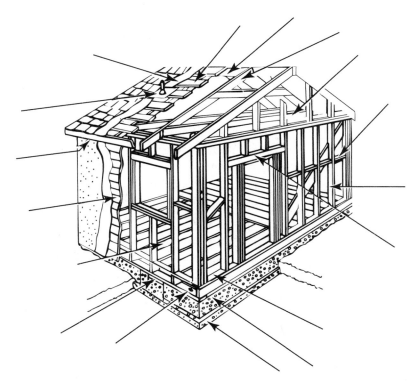

■ SUMMARY

Residential construction makes use of designs and techniques that have been available for many years. New concepts for both site-built and manufactured housing have made homebuilding more efficient, economical, and responsive to contemporary needs. Some innovations, such as smoke detectors, present low-cost ways to improve the safety of the home environment. Other innovations, such as solar-heating systems, promote the goal of making the best possible use of our natural resources.

Real estate is a dynamic industry—one that requires knowledge of where we are, as well as where we are going. Technological advances and design trends both shape and mirror consumer desires. Federal, state, and local law-making bodies dictate requirements for acceptable housing. Awareness of how those desires and requirements are changing benefits consumers, as well as real estate brokers and salespeople, who in turn can do the best possible job for every client.

■ IMPORTANT TERMS

Make sure you understand the following terms before you take the achievement examination.

anchor bolts
asbestos
backfill
bracing
brownfields
building paper
building codes
building permit
California Department of Health
   Services
certificate of occupancy (CO)
Contractors' State License Board
crawl space
Department of Housing and
   Community Development
downspout
drywall
eave
energy-efficiency ratio (EER)
fire stops
flashing

foundation
frame
home energy rating program
girders
gutter
insulation
joists
lath and plaster
lead-based paint
manufactured home
masonry
minimum property requirements (MPRs)
orientation
perc test
plasterboard
platform frame
post-and-beam frame
R-value
rafters
ridge board
sheathing

sheetrock
siding
sill
soffit
solar heating

stucco
studs
uniform codes
urea formaldehyde
wallboard

■ OPEN FOR DISCUSSION

Manufactured housing generally is perceived by the public as less desirable than site-built housing.

1. What are some of the reasons for this perception?

2. What can be done to change it?

■ ACHIEVEMENT EXAMINATION 14

1. In contracting for any work on someone else's property, a contractor's license is not needed
    a. by an attorney.
    b. by a real estate broker.
    c. by a real estate salesperson.
    d. if the work costs less than $500.

2. A contractor's license can be suspended or revoked for
    a. abandoning a project.
    b. violating building laws.
    c. breaching a construction contract.
    d. Any of the above

3. A type of roof with two steeply pitched planes is called a
    a. gambrel roof.   c. gable roof.
    b. flat roof.   d. saltbox roof.

4. A Dutch colonial house is distinguished by a
    a. hip roof.   c. gable roof.
    b. shed roof.   d. gambrel roof.

5. Ornate exterior woodwork is usually found on a(n)
    a. Colonial American house.
    b. Victorian house.
    c. English Tudor house.
    d. California ranch house.

6. An architectural style in which homes share a common wall is called
    a. Colonial American.
    b. Victorian.
    c. Spanish.
    d. a town house.

7. The location of a house on its site is called its
    a. view.   c. orientation.
    b. architecture.   d. floor plan.

8. The sun's arc in the sky is highest in
    a. summer.   c. winter.
    b. fall.   d. spring.

9. A good floor plan has
    a. the kitchen near the garage.
    b. bedrooms near living areas.
    c. one bathroom for every three bedrooms.
    d. no closets in the bedrooms, to conserve space.

10. Earthquake protection is provided by
    a. anchor bolts.
    b. cross-bracing.
    c. plywood sheathing.
    d. All of these

11. A two-story platform house is built
    a. with studs that extend from the first floor to the ceiling of the second story.
    b. one story at a time.
    c. with posts within the house that support beams.
    d. with no interior supporting walls.

12. The vertical supports in a wood frame house are called
    a. studs.   c. joists.
    b. plates.   d. beams.

13. A post-and-beam frame house is built
    a. with studs that extend from the first floor to the ceiling of the second story.
    b. one story at a time.
    c. with posts within the house that support beams.
    d. with interior supporting walls.

14. A brick or stone exterior finish is called
    a. glazing.   c. veneer.
    b. paneling.   d. tile.

15. The main roof supports are the
    a. soffits.   c. gutters.
    b. rafters.   d. eaves.

16. A window that opens out is called a
    a. double-hung window.
    b. horizontal sliding window.
    c. casement window.
    d. fixed window.

17. A relatively inexpensive and easy-to-install interior wall finishing is
    a. plasterboard.
    b. drywall.
    c. wallboard.
    d. All of the above

18. Heat from sunlight reaching water-filled containers is used in
    a. active solar-heating systems only.
    b. passive solar-heating systems.
    c. most homes.
    d. air-conditioning systems.

19. Every house sold on or after January 1, 1986, must have at least
    a. three bedrooms.
    b. two bathrooms.
    c. one smoke detector.
    d. one garage.

20. As of January 1, 1996, all water heaters must be
    a. cemented in place.
    b. braced, anchored, or strapped.
    c. at least 80 gallons in capacity.
    d. warranted by the state.

CHAPTER FIFTEEN

GOVERNMENT CONTROL OF LAND USE

■ LAND-USE REGULATIONS

Police Power and Eminent Domain

Public safety laws do not require compensation to property owners.

Land-use controls are possible because of the government's **police power.** This power enables government bodies to regulate private activity by enacting laws that benefit the public health, safety, and general welfare. As a general rule, the owner of property is not compensated for any loss in property value that results from the government's exercise of its police power.

Some of the ways in which the use of real estate is regulated were included in earlier chapters. Chapter 14, "Residential Design and Construction," discussed building codes and other criteria that establish standards for safe housing. Additional government controls of the *use* of real estate are covered in this chapter.

www.cacities.org
www.sannet.gov

Links to Web sites of many California cities can be found at City Link 2000, the site of the League of California Cities, *www.cacities.org.* The most useful sites, such as that of the City of San Diego (*www.sannet.gov*), provide the city's charter, Municipal Code, agendas, and other information.

Government also may take all or some of the rights of *ownership* from private individuals by exercising its power of **eminent domain.** The government does compensate individuals when property is "taken" through the process called **condemnation,** as when buildings are torn down to make way for highway expansion.

The **fair market value** of the real estate is paid to compensate the willing or unwilling former owner. When only part of a property is taken, compensation generally is based on the difference between the value of the entire parcel before the taking and the value of the remaining part.

> Taking a property by condemnation does require compensation to the property owner.

■ **FOR EXAMPLE:** Agricultural land zoned for residential use is purchased for development. The purchase price is much greater than it would be for land zoned for strictly agricultural use. The land then is rezoned to strictly agricultural use before the development begins. Should the landowner be compensated for the loss in market value caused by the change in zoning classification?

At present the answer to that question is "No," unless the property owner is denied all reasonable use of the property. The United States Supreme Court is called on to consider such cases frequently, however, and eventually may decide that loss in land value resulting from any change in use is a *taking* and must be compensated.

Just compensation on the taking of all or part of a property may include not just the fair market value of the property but also

- ■ moving costs,
- ■ mortgage prepayment penalties, and even a
- ■ "going out of business" payment.

Assistance in finding new housing is required when residential property is condemned. Tenants who must relocate also are entitled to relocation payments and services. These protections are the result of the **Uniform Relocation Assistance and Real Property Acquisition Policies Act of 1970.** The act applies to all federal agencies and those agencies using federal funds for property acquisition. This covers a great number of condemnation actions because it includes property taken as part of federally financed road improvements, such as a freeway.

Inverse condemnation is a proceeding brought by a landowner when government puts nearby land to a use that diminishes the value of the owner's property. The Tucker Act of 1887, another federal law, allows a landowner to bring such a suit against the federal government.

■ **FOR EXAMPLE:** A roadway is dredged for a canal, and the owner of adjacent property is deprived of reasonable access to his land. The property owner has a claim for damages based on inverse condemnation.

City Planning

When an area is first settled, there usually is abundant land for all purposes. Planning for the use of the land may be considered an unnecessary burden on development. At a certain point, however, there is demand from all sectors of society on ever-scarcer land and resources. **City planning** then becomes a useful tool to help ensure orderly, sensible growth and development.

Early city plans in California include that of the city of Paso Robles in San Luis Obispo County, which was planned in the late 1860s by Drury Woodson James. A modern example is the City of Irvine, in Orange County, created on what was the 53,000-acre Irvine Ranch. Since the 1960s the Irvine Company has developed residential and business areas within the city and has even donated land for what is now the campus of the University of California at Irvine. More recently, development of the inland valleys has seen the creation of many new planned communities.

Community development goals are set out in the General Plan.

The General Plan.   Every city and county within California now is required by state law to adopt a comprehensive, long-term **General Plan** for development within its jurisdiction.

The General Plan, also referred to as the **master plan,** is both a statement of policy and a means to enact that policy. It usually includes background information on the area economy, its development, population growth, and existing land uses. It states the goals and policies determining future development and gives one or more maps showing population distribution and designated land-use areas and density. In addition, the General Plan presents a program designed to implement the stated policy.

The local **planning commission,** required by state law for counties but optional for cities, formulates the General Plan, which then is adopted by resolution of the legislative body.

Form-Based Planning

Assembly Bill 1268, signed into law in July 2004, is an outgrowth of the *White Paper on Smart Growth Policy in California*, prepared for the Governor's Office of Planning and Research in February 2003. The new law expands on the traditional system of planning to allow a concept called **form-based planning.** In traditional planning, different specialists working apart from one another design separate components of the urban landscape, often leading to isolated land-use areas and "sprawl." Form-based planning provides for a mix of land uses, while taking into account the relationship of buildings and public areas, resulting in a much more "pedestrian-friendly" urban environment.

The General Plan

The Government Code requires that every General Plan include provision for

- **land use,** including standards of population density and building intensity;
- **circulation**, including distribution of transportation facilities and public utilities;
- **housing** at all income levels;
- **conservation** of natural resources;
- **open space** to preserve natural resources in light of recreational needs and public health and safety;
- **noise** problems, both existing and foreseeable; and
- **safety** from fire, seismic (earthquake), and geological hazards.

Where applicable the general plan also provides for **coastal development,** protection of **mineral and forestry resources,** and development within **seismic zones.** The plan also may include local areas of concern, such as **historic preservation.**

Since 1982 counties have been required to have a **solid waste management plan** consistent with the county's General Plan.

Finally, every county with a public airport served by a certified air carrier has an airport land-use commission that must prepare an airport land-use plan that is consistent with the general plan, unless a specific exception is allowed.

Procedure for adoption. The Government Code outlines the procedure for adoption of a General Plan or an amendment to the General Plan. If the jurisdiction has a planning commission, a public hearing is held before that group, and a majority of planning commissioners must vote in favor of the plan. Then another public hearing is held by the local governing body (city council or county board of supervisors), which can adopt the plan or amendment by resolution.

The specific plan. A specific plan can be formulated after a General Plan has been adopted. The specific plan may be so detailed that no further land-use regulations (such as zoning) are required. In the specific plan, further attention is given to population growth as well as environmental, economic, and other considerations in particular areas. Locations of streets and utilities, projected population density, building construction requirements, and topographical information (terrain and physical features) can be provided.

Zoning

Zoning is the dividing of a city into areas, or **zones,** limited to certain land uses and/or building requirements. Zoning is the primary device for controlling land use and the principal tool for implementing the General Plan.

Zoning is authorized by the California Constitution as an exercise of a city's **police power.** It must be consistent with the policies and long-range goals of the General Plan. If there is a conflict, the General Plan takes precedence over zoning. The state has established a procedure for citizen complaints regarding noncompliance with the General Plan.

Zoning is the primary method of regulating property use.

Zoning specifications.   **Zoning ordinances** typically cover

- permitted uses,
- minimum parcel size,
- building height limitations,
- lot coverage limitations,
- required setbacks, and
- maximum density.

A zoning ordinance also typically provides for a **conditional use permit** that allows a **nonconforming use,** such as a church in a residential zone.

Figure 15.1 shows part of one city's zoning regulations. Note that both the property classifications and letter and number designations vary widely throughout the state. There is no uniform system of zone classification. An extensive listing of municipal codes, including zoning ordinances, for cities throughout the Untied States, can be found at the Web site of the Seattle Public Library, *www.spl.lib.wa.us//govpubs/municode.html.*

www.spl.lib.wa.us// govpubs/municode.html

Zoning changes.   The overall designated land use may be changed in the process called **rezoning.**

A **zoning variance** permits a change in the specifications required by the zoning ordinance, if a property owner is placed at a disadvantage by the prescribed zoning specifications. State law permits a zoning variance where "the strict application of the zoning ordinance deprives such property of privileges enjoyed by other property in the vicinity and under identical zoning classification." To expedite routine applications for permits, variances, and appeals, many jurisdictions have a **zoning administrator, zoning board,** or **board of zoning adjustment.**

- **FOR EXAMPLE:**   The Long family owns a home in Hundred Oaks, and would like to build a backyard deck behind their home. Because of the unusual configuration of their hillside lot, their home is closer to the rear property line than other homes in the subdivision. A deck similar in size to the ones built by their neighbors would violate the local zoning ordinance by being too close to the rear boundary line. What can the Longs do?

FIGURE 15.1

Summary of Zoning Regulations

GENERALIZED SUMMARY OF ZONING REGULATIONS
CITY OF LOS ANGELES

NOTE: THIS SUMMARY IS ONLY INTENDED TO BE A GUIDE; DEFINITIVE INFORMATION SHOULD OBTAINED FROM THE DEPARTMENT OF BUILDING AND SAFETY.

ZONE	USE	MAXIMUM HEIGHT STORIES	FEET	REQUIRED YARDS FRONT	SIDE	REAR	MINIMUM PER LOT	AREA PER DWELLING UNIT	MINIMUM LOT WIDTH	PARKING REQUIRED
AGRICULTURAL										
A1	AGRICULTURAL One-Family Dwellings-Parks Playgrounds Community Centers Golf Courses-Truck Gardening- Extensive Agricultural Uses			20% lot depth 25 Ft. max.	25 Ft. Maximum 10% Lot Width 3 Ft. minimum	25% lot depth 25 Ft. max.	5 Acres	2½ Acres	300 Ft.	Two Spaces Per Dwelling Unit
A2	AGRICULTURAL A1 Uses	3	45 Ft.				2 Acres	1 Acre	150 Ft.	
RA	SUBURBAN Limited Agricultural Uses One-Family Dwellings	•			10 Ft.- plus 1 Ft.- 3 Stories- less than 70 Ft. width 10% lot width 3 Ft. min.		17,500 Sq. Ft. (1)	17,500 Sq. Ft. (1)	70 Ft. (1)	Two Covered Spaces Per Dwelling Unit
ONE FAMILY RESIDENTIAL										
RE40	RESIDENTIAL ESTATE One-Family Dwellings Parks Playgrounds Community Centers Truck Gardening	3	45 Ft.	20% lot depth 25 Ft. Max.	10 Ft. min. plus 1 Ft.- 3 stories 10 Ft. max. 10% Lot Width 5 Ft. min.- plus 1 Ft. 3 stories	25% lot depth 25 Ft. Max.	40,000 Sq. Ft (1)	40,000 Sq. Ft. (1)	80 Ft. (1)	Two Covered Spaces Per Dwelling Unit
RE20							20,000 Sq. Ft. (1)	20,000 Sq. Ft. (1)	80 Ft. (1)	
RE15							15,000 Sq. Ft. (1)	15,000 Sq. Ft. (1)	80 Ft. (1)	
RE11					5 Ft., less than 50 Ft. width 3 Ft. Min.		11,000 Sq.Ft. (1)	11,000 Sq.Ft. (1)	70 Ft. (1)	
RE9							9,000 Sq.Ft. (1)	9,000 Sq.Ft. (1)	65 Ft. (1)	
RS	SUBURBAN One-Family Dwellings- Parks- Playgrounds- Truck Gardening			20% lot depth 25 Ft. Max.	5 Ft., less than 50 Ft. 10% Lot Width 3 Ft. Minimum Plus 1 Ft. 3 stories	20 Ft. Min.	7,500 Sq. Ft.	7,500 Sq. Ft.	60 Ft.	
R1	ONE-FAMILY DWELLING RS Uses	3	45	20% lot depth 20 Ft. Max.		15 Ft. Min.	5,000 Sq. Ft.	5,000 Sq. Ft.	50 Ft.	
RZ 2.5	RESIDENTIAL ZERO SIDE YARD			10 Ft. Min.	None(3) or 3 Ft. plus 1 Ft.- 3 stories	None(3) or 15 Ft.	2,500 Sq. Ft.	2,500 Sq. Ft.	30 Ft. with driveway, 25 Ft. w/o driveway	Two covered spaces per dwelling unit
RZ 3	Dwelling across not more than five lots (2)						3,000 Sq. Ft.	3,000 Sq. Ft.	20 Ft.- flag curved or cul-de-sac	
RZ 4	Parks- Playgrounds						4,000 Sq. Ft.	4,000 Sq. Ft.		
RZ 5							5,000 Sq. Ft.	5,000 Sq. Ft.		
RW1	ONE-FAMILY RESIDENTIAL WATERWAYS ZONE	2	30 Ft.	10 Ft. min.	10% width 3 Ft. Minimum	15 Ft. Min.	2,300 Sq. Ft.	2,300 Sq. Ft.	28 Ft.	

(1) "H" Hillside or Mountainous Area designation may alter these requirements in the RA-H or RE-H Zones, subdivisions may be approved with smaller lots, providing larger lots are also included. Each lot may be used for only one single-family dwelling. See minimum width and area requirements below.

ZONE COMBINATION	MINIMUM TO WHICH NET AREA MAY BE REDUCED	MINIMUM TO WHICH LOT WIDTH MAY BE REDUCED
RA-H	14,000 Sq. Ft.	63 Ft.
RE9-H	7,200 Sq. Ft.	60 Ft.
RE11-H	8,800 Sq. Ft.	63 Ft.
RE15-H	12,000 Sq. Ft.	72 Ft.
RE20-H	16,000 Sq. Ft.	72 Ft.
RE40-H	32,000 Sq. Ft.	No Reduction

(2) See Section 12.08 B 1 of the Zone Code.
(3) See Section 12.08 C4 of the Zone Code.

CP-7150 (5/86)

Source: Los Angeles City Planning Department.

FIGURE 15.1

Summary of Zoning Regulations (Continued)

GENERALIZED SUMMARY OF ZONING REGULATIONS
CITY OF LOS ANGELES

COMMERCIAL

ZONE	USE	MAXIMUM HEIGHT STORIES	FEET	REQUIRED YARDS FRONT	SIDE	REAR	MINIMUM AREA PER LOT/UNIT	MINIMUM LOT WIDTH	LOADING SPACE	PARKING REQUIRED
CR	LIMITED COMMERCIAL Banks, Clubs, Hotels, Churches, Schools, Business and Professional child care, parking areas, R4 uses	6	75 Ft.		10 Ft. 10 % lot width, 5-ft. min. for corner lots; same as R4 for residential uses or adjoining an "A" or "R" Zone	15 Ft. plus 1 Ft. each story above 3rd	Same as R4 for Residential purposes Otherwise None	40 Ft. Comm. use; 50 Ft. residential use	Hotels, Institutions, and with every building where lot abuts an alley Minimum Loading Space 400 Sq. Ft.	One space per 500 Sq. Ft. of floor area within all buildings on any lot.
C1	LIMITED COMMERCIAL Local retail stores Offices or Businesses, Hotels, hospitals and/or Clinics, Parking Areas- CR uses except churches, schools and museums R3 Uses	Unlimited (6)		10 Ft. min.	Same as R3 for corner lots, or residential uses or adjoining an "A" "R" Zone	15 Ft. plus 1 Ft. each story above 3rd, 20 Ft. max. Residential Use or abutting an "A" or "R" Zone.	Same as R3 for Residential purposes, except 5,000 Sq.Ft. per unit in C1-H Zones Otherwise None		Additional Space Required for Buildings containing more than 50,000 Sq. Ft. of floor area. None required for apartment buildings 30 Units or Less.	One space per 200 Sq. Ft. of total floor area of medical service facilities.
C1.5	LIMITED COMMERCIAL C1 Uses-Department Stores, Theatres, Broadcasting Studios, Parking Buildings, Parks and Playgrounds R4 uses.					Yards provided at lowest residential story. Otherwise None	Same as R4 for Residential purposes Otherwise None			

ZONE	USE	MAXIMUM HEIGHT STORIES	FEET	REQUIRED YARDS FRONT	SIDE	REAR	MINIMUM AREA PER LOT/UNIT	MINIMUM LOT WIDTH	LOADING SPACE	PARKING REQUIRED
C2	COMMERCIAL C1.5 Uses-Retail Businesses with Limited Manufacturing, Auto Services Station and Garage, Retail Contractors Businesses, Churches, Schools, R4 uses.				None for Commercial buildings Residential uses- same as in R4 Zone Yards provided at lowest residential story.		Same as R4 for Residential purposes Otherwise None	40 Ft. Comm. Use; 50 Ft. residential use	Hospitals, Hotels, Institutions, and with every building where lot abuts an alley Minimum Loading Space 400 Sq. Ft. Additional Space Required for Buildings containing more than 50,000 Sq. Ft. of floor area. None required for buildings 30 units or less.	One space per 500 sq. Ft. of floor area within all buildings on any lot. One space per 200 Sq. Ft. of total floor area or medical service facilities.
C4	COMMERCIAL C2 Uses- (With Exceptions, such as Auto Service Stations, Amusement Enterprises, Hospitals Second-Hand Businesses) R4 Uses	Unlimited (6)								
C5	COMMERCIAL C2 Uses-Limited Floor Areas for Light Manufacturing of the CM-Zone Type, R4 Uses									
CM	COMMERCIAL MANUFACTURING Wholesale Business, Storage Buildings, clinics, Limited manufacturing, C2 Uses-Except Hospitals, Schools, Churches, R3 Uses				None for Industrial or Commercial buildings Residential Uses-same as in R4 Zone		Same as R3 for Residential purposes Otherwise None			

Source: Los Angeles City Planning Department.

The Longs can seek a variance to the zoning ordinance to allow their backyard deck to be built closer to the rear lot line than the minimum setback stated in the ordinance. Because they are asking only to be allowed to enjoy their property in the same way that neighboring property owners are able to enjoy theirs, the Longs most likely will be allowed a variance.

Planned development. The **planned development,** or **planned unit development (PUD),** is both a type of development and a zoning classification. A PUD usually allows individually owned residential property together with shared common areas. A PUD also may include commercial and/or industrial uses.

Redevelopment

The deteriorating condition of some urban neighborhoods has served as the impetus for local redevelopment efforts. California's **Community Redevelopment Law** (found in the Health and Safety Code) allows the formation of a **Community Redevelopment Agency (CRA).** CRAs work to rehabilitate existing structures or bring in new development both to provide low- and moderate-income housing and to employ low-income persons.

The governing board of a CRA often is composed of city council members. The redevelopment proposed must conform to the General Plan but need not conform to zoning ordinances. Instead, the redevelopment plan must contain its own building use limitations. The CRA can use the power of **eminent domain** to acquire parcels, it can borrow money from any source to finance purchase and construction, and generally it can act as a developer would.

Funding for CRA activities can come from a variety of bond programs, some of which require voter approval. Repayment can be through **tax increment funding,** using the additional taxes produced by the redevelopment property. Repayment also can be through the issuing of tax-exempt **mortgage revenue bonds.** In 1979 the state legislature also gave cities and counties the authority to levy special assessments on property within the redevelopment area to pay indebtedness, thus avoiding the limitations of Proposition 13 (described in Chapter 11, "Real Estate Taxation").

Exercise 15-1 Why should the following factors be taken into account in formulating a general plan for a newly incorporated suburban city?

Proximity (20 miles) to city of 2 million population

County plan encouraging commercial development

No-growth initiative passed by voters of a neighboring city

Generally hilly terrain with past mud slide problems

■ SUBDIVISIONS

Most land development involves the **subdividing** of a parcel of land for the purpose of sale, lease, or financing. Controlled land development is important, and subdivisions often involve sales to consumers. For these reasons there are two laws that specifically govern planning, design, site preparation, construction of improvements, and sales of subdivision land. They are the

1. **Subdivided Lands Law** and
2. **Subdivision Map Act.**

Subdivided Lands Law

The **Subdivided Lands Law** (found in the Business and Professions Code) describes the forms of ownership allowed in a subdivision of *five or more parcels* on up to 160 acres of land.

The Subdivided Lands Law also regulates the marketing and financing of the subdivision. For purposes of this law, the different parcels do not need to be adjacent or contiguous (touching).

The Subdivided Lands Law is administered by the Real Estate Commissioner. Its objective is to protect purchasers of property in new subdivisions from fraud, misrepresentation, or deceit in the marketing of the property.

Details of any subdivision offered for sale in California must be submitted to the Real Estate Commissioner, who prepares and issues a subdivision public report describing the property. Before issuing the report, the commissioner also receives information on the project's financial status. This is primarily to make sure that improvements to the land will be made as promised to purchasers.

Types of Subdivisions

The three basic types of subdivisions are the

1. **standard subdivision,**
2. **common interest subdivision,** and
3. **undivided interest subdivision.**

Standard subdivision. In the **standard subdivision** the owners of separate parcels have no shared interest in any part of the subdivided land. Subdivision lots can be sold unimproved—but with utilities installed—to individual owners or developers for building purposes. Subdivision lots also can be fully improved with completed homes and offered with or without seller-arranged financing.

If land is divided into parcels of 160 acres or more, it is not considered a subdivision as defined by the law. There is an exception to this general rule, however. If land is divided for sale for oil and gas purposes, it will be considered a subdivision no matter how large the individual parcels are.

Common interest subdivision. In the **common interest subdivision** a separate ownership or leasehold interest in a parcel is accompanied by a shared interest in what are called the **common areas** of the subdivision. The common areas usually are governed by a **homeowners' association.** Examples of common interest subdivisions are planned developments and condominiums. Some of the different forms of common interest subdivisions are summarized below.

Common Interest Subdivisions

Planned development. A planned development consists of individually owned parcels or lots as well as areas owned in common.

Community apartment project. A community apartment project is one in which the owner has an individual interest in the land and exclusive right of occupancy of an apartment on the land. All owners are tenants in common. The project will receive one tax bill and any loan will be on the entire project and the responsibility of all tenants.

Condominium project. The owner of a condominium has an exclusive ownership interest in the airspace of a particular portion of real property, as well as an interest in common in the land and structure. The condominium form of ownership has been used for apartments, offices, stores, and industrial space. A condominium can be purchased and financed like any other real property.

Stock cooperative project. Most stock cooperatives are apartment buildings. Each owner in a stock cooperative project is a shareholder in a corporation that holds title to the property, and the individual shareholders receive a right of exclusive occupancy of a portion of the property.

Limited equity housing cooperative. A limited equity housing cooperative is a stock cooperative financed by the California Housing Finance Agency.

Time-share project. The latest type of primarily vacation use property is the time-share. In a time-share project a purchaser receives the right to exclusive use of a portion of the property for a particular period of time each year, in perpetuity or for a certain number of years. There must be 12 or more separate interests before the project will be subject to DRE regulation.

A time-share estate includes an estate interest in the property, but a **time-share use** does not. Time-share properties range from city apartments to campground spaces. There is a *three-day right to rescind* an offer to purchase a time-share.

Undivided interest subdivision. In an **undivided interest subdivision** each owner is a tenant in common with all other owners. Each has the nonexclusive right to the use and occupancy of the property. An example of a common interest subdivision is a campground with shared facilities.

The Subdivision Public Report

Subdivisions must meet the requirements of the Subdivided Lands Law before the Real Estate Commissioner will issue the necessary **public report.** All prospective purchasers must be given a copy of the report and be allowed to read it.

In general a notice of intention, a questionnaire, and an application must be filed. After a notice of intention has been filed or a public report has been made, any *material change* involving the subdivision must be reported to the commissioner. Examples of material changes include changes to lot size, deed restrictions, or financing terms.

The report requirements are stricter for common interest subdivisions (such as condominiums) than for standard subdivisions. The public report for a standard residential subdivision usually discloses

- project name, location, and size;
- subdivider's name;
- interest to be acquired by purchaser or lessee;
- procedure for handling all payments, taxes, and assessments;
- extraordinary expenses at closing or expected in the future;
- hazards or adverse environmental factors;
- all conditions or restrictions on use of the property;
- unusual easements, rights-of-way, or setbacks; and
- special building permit requirements.

> False or misleading advertising is always prohibited.

Guidelines for advertising or promoting a subdivision are provided in the Commissioner's Regulations. False or misleading advertising of any type is prohibited, regardless of whether it is specifically mentioned in the regulations.

Because the public report may take months to compile, the subdivider may begin taking reservations for future purchases on the basis of an approved **conditional public report** (called the "pink report"). No sales can be closed or transactions completed, however, until the **final public report** (called the "white report") is received. All persons who make a property reservation agreement based on a conditional report *or* who make an offer to purchase based on a final public report must indicate in writing that they have received and read the applicable report.

The signed receipt for the public report must be in the form required by the Commissioner's Regulations. The subdivider must keep the receipt and make it available for inspection by the commissioner for three years from the date it is signed.

> ## Right to Negotiate Property Inspections
>
> The public report for a residential subdivision must disclose that a prospective buyer has the right to negotiate with the seller to permit inspections of the property by the buyer (or someone designated by the buyer) under terms mutually agreeable to buyer and seller. (Business and Professions Code 11010.11)

Renewal.   If all parcels have not been sold within five years of issuance of a final public report, it can be renewed for an additional five years.

Filing fees.   The Subdivided Lands Law sets maximum filing fees, but the commissioner can charge less if administrative costs warrant it.

Subdivision Map Act

The **Subdivision Map Act** (found in the Government Code) establishes a statewide procedure for filing a subdivision plan when property is divided into two or more parcels. The different parcels generally must be contiguous (touching).

The Subdivision Map Act is an **enabling act.** This means that it authorizes cities and counties to establish subdivision requirements by local ordinance. Its purpose is to give local governments direct control of all physical aspects of a subdivision, such as lot design, placement of streets and sewers, and so on. Although the act makes some procedural and other requirements, much of the content of the subdivision map will be dictated by the local authority.

The objectives of the Subdivision Map Act are

1. to coordinate subdivision design, including streets and utilities, with the General Plan; and
2. to ensure that areas of a subdivision dedicated to public use, such as public streets, will be properly improved initially.

The Subdivision Map

The **subdivision map** must take into account much more than just parcel division lines and street locations. The Subdivision Map Act provides for tentative, final, and parcel maps for most subdivisions.

Tentative map. The initial map is called the **tentative subdivision map.** It does not need to be based on a final, detailed survey of the property to be subdivided, unless that is required by local ordinance. A survey prepared by a registered civil engineer or licensed surveyor is always useful, however.

The tentative map typically is required by local ordinance to include

- legal description, including property boundaries of land and all parcels;
- widths and names of all existing streets;
- proposed street widths and grades and public areas;
- existing and proposed road, drainage, sewer, and other utility easements;
- source of water supply;
- storm water overflow and direction and flow of all watercourses; and
- proposed property use.

The developer (subdivider) is generally responsible for installing streets, curbs, and public utilities, and the government is responsible for maintaining them. From the developer's perspective, the most important consideration is the land remaining after accounting for streets, sidewalks, curbs, and so on. A **commercial acre** is the portion of an acre remaining after deducting the area required for streets and other improvements.

> Both state and local rules must be followed in preparing a subdivision map.

Final map. Requirements specified by local ordinance must be met in preparing the **final map.** In addition, the Subdivision Map Act specifies certain requirements for a final subdivision map, beginning with the color of ink (black) and size of paper (18 by 26 inches) to be used.

Each parcel must be numbered, each block must be numbered or lettered, and each street must be named. The exact boundaries of the land must be shown. All soils reports are to be made part of the public record. If the subdivision will interfere with full and complete use of rights-of-way, easements, or other interests held by a public entity or public utility, the public entity or utility must be notified of the subdivision formation and given a chance to object to it.

A **dedication** or offer to dedicate any part of the land for public purposes must be made by a certificate signed by all parties having an interest of record in the land. Compliance with state law creates a **statutory dedication**. The clerk of each approving legislative body signs a **certificate of execution** indicating the acceptance or rejection of such dedicated property. The engineer or surveyor responsible for the map also signs a certificate that the survey is true and complete as shown.

Other certificates also may be required. If the property is within an unincorporated area, the county surveyor and, if applicable, the city engineer must certify that the map is technically correct and conforms to both the law and the tentative map.

Parcel map. Preparation of a **parcel map** may be waived by local ordinance. If not, the parcel map must meet both state and local requirements. The paper and ink specifications noted above also apply to parcel maps. Each parcel must be designated and all property boundaries shown. The subdivider must sign and acknowledge the parcel map by certificate. The engineer or surveyor conducting the field survey and preparing the map must certify its accuracy.

Procedure for Subdivision Map Approval

Approval of the subdivision map is the responsibility of the advisory agency designated by the city or county. Typically, this is the planning commission, but it could be any other official or official body so designated, such as the city council or a committee of city officials.

There are *notice, hearing, time limitation,* and other requirements involved in the subdivision map approval process. Notice and opportunity for hearing are *required* only when a map approval would constitute a *significant* deprivation of other landowners' property rights. The better practice, however, is to give notice and an opportunity for hearing before any subdivision approval.

Approval of the **tentative map** requires that it conform to the general or specific plan, as well as to local ordinances or actions regarding housing needs. It also must meet requirements for future passive or natural heating or cooling opportunities. The site must be physically suitable for the proposed use and not likely to cause substantial environmental damage or serious public health problems.

The **final map** must be filed before the tentative map expires, which is two years after its approval or conditional approval (three years for maps approved before May 16, 1996), plus any extension granted, with the total time not to exceed five years. The final map must be in substantial compliance with the tentative map. Local ordinances determine the approval procedure, but notice and an opportunity for hearing must be given to adjoining property owners if the subdivision will result in significant deprivation of their property rights.

Figure 15.2 shows the basic differences between the Subdivided Lands Law and the Subdivision Map Act.

Other Subdivision Requirements

Environmental impact report. An **environmental impact report (EIR),** authorized by the **California Environmental Quality Act of 1970 (CEQA),** may be required before subdivision approval.

FIGURE 15.2

Comparison of Subdivision Laws

	Subdivision Map Act	Subdivided Lands Law
Number of Parcels	Two or more	Five or more
Size of Parcels	Any size	Exempt if 160 acres or larger, as surveyed
Residential Subdivisions within City Limits	Included	Exempt
Parcels Contiguous	Yes	No
"Proposed Division"	Not included	Included
Condominiums	Included	Included
Community Apartments	Included	Included
Stock Cooperatives	Included only if five or more dwelling units converted	Included
Limited Equity Housing Cooperatives	Not included	May be exempt
Time-Shares	Not included	Included if 12 or more
Agricultural Leases	Not included	Included
Zoned Industrial or Commercial Subdivisions	Included	Exempt
Long-Term Leasing of Spaces in Mobile-Home Parks or Trailer Parks	Not included	Included
Leasing of Space in Apartment, Industrial, or Commercial Building	Not included	Not included
Out-of-State Subdivisions	Not included	Included

CEQA requires an EIR or negative declaration.

CEQA requires any government agency that must approve a project (which may include the Real Estate Commissioner as well as a local governing body) to prepare an EIR if the project will have a *significant effect* on the environment. Subdivision approval must be denied if the design of either the project or its improvements is likely to

■ *cause substantial environmental damage or*
■ *substantially injure fish or wildlife or their habitat.*

It is in the best interest of a subdivision developer to determine whether an EIR is necessary even before a tentative subdivision map is prepared. The government agency is authorized to issue a **negative declaration** (a statement that there will be no impact on the environment significant enough to warrant preparation of an EIR) if that is the case.

Alquist-Priolo Earthquake Fault Zoning Act. The **Alquist-Priolo Earthquake Fault Zoning Act** (formerly called the Alquist-Priolo Special Studies Zones Act) regulates development in earthquake fault areas. It is concerned solely with possible damage from fault ruptures, rather than from seismic (shaking) effects.

A geologic report must be obtained by local government for any new project initiated after May 4, 1975, involving improvements or structures in an **earthquake fault zone,** typically within a quarter of a mile or more of an active fault. If there are no undue hazards, the city or county can waive the report if the state geologist approves.

Any agent—or a seller acting without an agent—of real estate located within an earthquake fault zone identified as such in a reasonably available map must disclose that fact to any prospective buyer.

www.consrv.ca.gov/dmg/ index.htm

Maps of earthquake fault zones can be obtained from the California Department of Conservation, Division of Mines and Geology, which has offices in Los Angeles, Pleasant Hill, and Sacramento. Maps can be ordered or downloaded from *www.consrv.ca.gov/dmg/index.htm.*

The **Seismic Hazards Mapping Act** requires the same type of disclosure for property located in a **seismic hazards zone,** if a map of the property's area is reasonably available. A map of the San Francisco area was released in 1995, with maps covering the rest of the state due for release over the next several years.

http://quake.wr.usgs.gov/

The United States Geologic Service provides information on earthquake preparation and recent earthquake activity at *http://quake.wr.usgs.gov/.*

Coastal Zone Conservation Act. The Coastal Zone Conservation Act defines **coastal zones,** which generally run the length of the state from the sea inland 1,000 or more yards, depending on terrain. The act authorizes local governments to make policies providing for coastal conservation and to require permits from developers of such property or owners seeking to improve it.

Rangeland, Grazing Land, and Grassland Protection Act. The Rangeland, Grazing Land, and Grassland Protection Act has established a program that provides grants for acquisition of conservation easements to protect, restore, or enhance California's rangeland, grazing land, and grasslands. Procedures and criteria for awarding of grants can be found in Division 10.4 of the California Public Resources Code.

Exercise 15-2

1. Ernest Holmes is subdividing the Eagle Ranch property. Ernest's subdivision map was approved and a notice of intention was filed with the Real Estate Commissioner. Ernest then decided to change the deeds to include more CC&Rs. Must Ernest notify the commissioner?

2. Describe the differences between the Subdivision Map Act and Subdivided Lands Law in the following areas:

	Subdivision Map Act	Subdivided Lands Law
Number of subdivision units or parcels		
Inclusion of undivided interests		
Inclusion of time-shares		
Inclusion of stock cooperatives		
Opportunity for notice and hearing		

■ FAIR HOUSING LAWS

Over the past 30 years, both the federal and the state governments have passed legislation to prohibit housing discrimination. This issue is so important, it is a mandatory subject for real estate license renewal.

Discrimination in Housing

Owners of housing are not to discriminate in the sale, rental, or lease of their property. **Real estate brokers** should not accept the listing of any property where such discrimination is attempted. Real estate property owners, brokers, salespeople, lenders, landlords, and hotel keepers are held to the same standard of conduct expected of all ethical citizens and professionals. Arbitrary discrimination, particularly in supplying housing, is strictly forbidden by both federal and state law.

Federal law. The **1866 Civil Rights Act** prohibits racial discrimination in every property transaction. Although long ignored, the 1866 Civil Rights Act was upheld in 1968 by the U.S. Supreme Court in the case of **Jones v. Mayer.** The Court found a constitutional basis for the 1866 Act in the 13th Amendment to the U.S. Constitution prohibiting slavery. A private individual may file a lawsuit in federal court alleging discrimination under the 1866 Civil Rights Act.

Shortly before the Supreme Court decision in *Jones v. Mayer,* Congress enacted the **Federal Fair Housing Act** (Title VIII of the Civil Rights Act of 1968), based on the goal of "fair housing throughout the United States." As since amended, it prohibits discrimination based on

- race,
- color,
- religion,
- sex,
- national origin,
- ancestry,
- handicap, or
- familial status.

The Federal Fair Housing Act applies to a sale or lease of residential property, as well as to advertising, lending, real estate brokerage activities, and other services related to residential transactions. It is enforceable by individuals, the Department of Housing and Urban Development (HUD), and the U.S. Attorney General. An individual has one year in which to file a complaint alleging discrimination with HUD's Office of Equal Opportunity (OEO), or two years in which to file a lawsuit in federal or state court. Both steps also could be taken, within the separate deadlines.

Some properties are **exempt** from the prohibitions against discrimination based on familial status (households with children under the age of 18). The act exempts **adult communities,** provided that

- *all* residents are older than age 62 or
- at least 80 percent of the units are occupied by people older than age 55 and special services are offered for the elderly, such as recreation areas.

Some **transactions** exempt from the Federal Fair Housing Act include those involving

- preference to members of religious organizations or societies or affiliated nonprofit organizations, when dealing with their own property, and as long as membership is not restricted on the basis of race, color, or national origin; and
- preference or limitation to members of private clubs with lodgings that are not open to the public and are not operated for a commercial purpose.

No one is exempt from the 1866 Civil Rights Act that forbids racial discrimination.

Also exempt are transactions involving a single-family home sold or rented by its owner (if the owner owns no more than three such homes) or the rental of a room or unit in an owner-occupied dwelling of up to four units. Despite these exemptions, the property owner still would be subject to the 1866 Civil Rights Act. Also, being exempt from the Federal Fair Housing Act does not serve as an exemption from state law.

State law.   California's prohibitions against discrimination generally have been broader than the federal government's. In addition, local jurisdictions have passed a variety of antidiscrimination ordinances aimed at offering the widest housing choice to every resident of the state.

The **Unruh Civil Rights Act** prohibits discrimination based on age, sex, race, color, religion, ancestry, or national origin in accommodations and business establishments.

California's **Fair Employment and Housing Act** (formerly the Rumford Fair Housing Act) prohibits discrimination based on race, color, religion, sex, marital status, national origin, or ancestry. It applies to anyone supplying housing accommodations, including the sale, rental, lease, or financing of virtually all types of housing.

Examples of discrimination include refusal to show property and arbitrary financing requirements. An individual may file a complaint alleging discrimination with the state **Department of Fair Employment and Housing.**

In addition to the above laws, Sections 54–55.1 of the California Civil Code prohibit discrimination in the rental, leasing, or sale of housing accommodations to persons who are blind, visually handicapped, deaf, or otherwise physically disabled.

Discrimination in Lending

In addition to federal requirements, state-licensed savings and loan associations are subject to state regulations and guidelines adopted in 1976 that prohibit redlining. **Redlining** is the practice of rejecting real estate loan applications because of the location of the property involved. Redlining, which focused on low-income areas, undoubtedly hastened the decay of many inner-city neighborhoods. The state prohibition applies to *all* loans for the financing of dwellings of one to four units, including conventional, FHA-insured, and VA-guaranteed loans.

As of January 1, 1978, California's **Housing Financial Discrimination Act** (the **Holden Act**) prohibits all financial institutions from discriminating in real estate loan decisions based on the geographic location, the neighborhood, or another characteristic of the property, unless such a decision can be shown to be based on sound business practice. *All* loans on owner-occupied dwellings of one to four units, whether for purchase, construction, repair, remodeling, or refinancing, are included. The law also applies to secured home improvement loans from a financial institution, even if the property is not to be owner-occupied. There may be no consideration of

- race,
- color,
- religion,
- sex,
- marital status,
- national origin,
- ancestry, or
- conditions, characteristics, or trends in the neighborhood or geographic area surrounding the subject property.

Complaints of violations of the Housing Financial Discrimination Act may be brought to the **Secretary for Business and Transportation,** who has 30 days to act on the complaint.

Various remedies are available in the event discrimination is found, including granting of the loan, granting of more favorable loan terms, or requiring payment of damages of up to $1,000. Decisions of the secretary may be appealed to the Office of Administrative Hearings, and from that body to a court.

Lenders must notify loan applicants of both the existence of the law and the complaint procedure.

Exercise 15-3   The Smiths are selling their house without an agent. What forms of discrimination are acceptable in their consideration of prospective purchasers?

■ SUMMARY

Using its power of **eminent domain,** a government can procure property by **condemnation** in exchange for the property's **fair market value.** Federal involvement requires relocation assistance for displaced property owners and tenants.

In an **inverse condemnation** action, a property owner complains that the value of property is impaired by the government's use of other property.

The power of eminent domain involves a "taking" of property. A government can use its **police power** to regulate property use and is not required to compensate the owner for any resulting loss in value.

The **General Plan,** or **master plan,** establishes the development policies and goals of a city or county. The **specific plan** goes even further in defining desired population density and building intensity.

Zoning is the primary form of land-use regulation. A **conditional use permit** or **zoning variance** may be sought if a **nonconforming use** is desired.

A **Community Redevelopment Agency** can act as a developer would in refurbishing and rebuilding dilapidated residential buildings. Financing may be repaid through **tax increment funding** or **mortgage revenue bonds.**

The **Subdivided Lands Law** provides for issuance by the Real Estate Commissioner of a **public report** on the **subdivision** and available financing. A **conditional public report** allows property reservations even before a **final public report** is issued by the commissioner.

The **Subdivision Map Act** establishes minimum subdivision approval standards, which are elaborated on by local ordinances. Besides the **subdivision map,** an **environmental impact report** may be necessary. Special consideration will be given to property in an **earthquake fault zone, seismic hazards zone,** or **coastal zone.**

Discrimination in housing and business establishments is strictly prohibited by both federal and state law. Financing cannot be based on discriminatory practices such as the **redlining** of certain areas as unsuitable for loans.

■ IMPORTANT TERMS

Make sure you understand the following terms before you take the achievement examination.

city planning	1866 Civil Rights Act
coastal zone	eminent domain
commercial acre	environmental impact report (EIR)
common interest subdivision	Fair Employment and Housing Act
community apartment project	Federal Fair Housing Act
Community Redevelopment Agency	form-based planning
condemnation	General Plan
conditional use permit	Housing Financial Discrimination Act
condominium project	inverse condemnation
Department of Fair Employment and Housing	*Jones v. Mayer*
	limited equity housing cooperative
earthquake fault zone	master plan

mortgage revenue bonds

negative declaration

nonconforming use

parcel map

planned development

planned unit development (PUD)

police power

public report

redlining

rezoning

seismic hazards zone

standard subdivision

stock cooperative project

Subdivided Lands Law

subdivision map

Subdivision Map Act

tax increment funding

time-share project

undivided interest subdivision

Unruh Civil Rights Act

zones

zoning

zoning ordinances

zoning variance

■ OPEN FOR DISCUSSION

1. If you could eliminate one regulation affecting land use, what would it be?

2. If you had to create one new regulation affecting land use, what would it be?

■ ACHIEVEMENT EXAMINATION 15

1. Land-use policies and goals are established through the
    a. general plan.
    b. subdivision report.
    c. preliminary report.
    d. notice of intention.

2. The general plan must consider
    a. housing at current market rates.
    b. only present land uses and hazards.
    c. the needs of all applicants for development permits.
    d. housing at all income levels.

3. Planning for future development does not include consideration of
    a. solid waste management.
    b. conservation of natural resources.
    c. safety.
    d. Contractors' License Law.

4. Zoning ordinances are an exercise of a government's
    a. power of eminent domain.
    b. power of condemnation.
    c. police power.
    d. judicial power.

5. Funding for a CRA project can be repaid through
    a. eminent domain.
    b. tax increment funding.
    c. only Proposition 13-allowed assessments.
    d. special assessments on property outside the redevelopment area.

6. Land may be subdivided for purposes of
    a. sale.   c. financing.
    b. lease.   d. All of these

7. The Subdivided Lands Law applies to subdivisions of land into
    a. 2 or more parcels.
    b. 5 or more parcels.
    c. 12 or more parcels.
    d. 25 or more parcels.

8. An out-of-state subdivider of California land
    a. must procure a public report.
    b. need not procure a public report.
    c. can decide whether to procure a public report.
    d. needs a public report only to finance a California subdivision.

9. A standard subdivision includes
    a. single-family residences and condominiums.
    b. no common interests.
    c. only residential property.
    d. no irregularly shaped parcels.

10. A subdivision consisting of individually owned lots as well as areas owned in common is a
    a. planned development.
    b. community apartment project.
    c. condominium project.
    d. stock cooperative project.

11. A subdivision consisting of individual owner-ship of airspace and areas owned in common is a
    a. planned development.
    b. community apartment project.
    c. condominium project.
    d. stock cooperative project.

12. A corporation holds title to property and share-holders having a right of occupancy to part of the property own the corporation in a
    a. planned development.
    b. community apartment project.
    c. condominium project.
    d. stock cooperative project.

13. The subdivision public report is issued by the
    a. advisory agency.
    b. planning commission.
    c. Real Estate Commissioner.
    d. Department of Real Estate.

14. A final subdivision public report has an initial term of
    a. one year.   c. four years.
    b. two years.   d. five years.

15. The Subdivision Map Act allows
    a. the state to have a say in how property is subdivided.
    b. local jurisdictions to determine whether a subdivision is desirable.
    c. developers to dictate how subdivision will take place.
    d. neighboring landowners to petition to have land subdivided.

16. A "proposed subdivision" is covered by the
    a. Subdivision Map Act.
    b. Subdivided Lands Law.
    c. Contractors' License Law.
    d. Contractors' State License Board.

17. Disclosure of the fact that property is located in a special studies zone must be made by the
    a. city council or board of supervisors.
    b. property buyer.
    c. real estate agent who represents the seller.
    d. seller, in addition to the real estate agent.

18. Discrimination in housing is prohibited by
    a. federal law.
    b. state law.
    c. Both a and b
    d. Neither a nor b

19. A homeowner whose property is exempt from the requirements of the Federal Fair Housing Act will still be subject to the
    a. 1866 Civil Rights Act.
    b. Housing Financial Discrimination Act.
    c. Subdivision Map Act.
    d. Subdivided Lands Law.

20. The broadest prohibition against all forms of discrimination in the sale of residential real estate is found in
    a. the Federal Fair Housing Act.
    b. *Jones v. Mayer.*
    c. California law.
    d. the Civil Rights Act of 1968.

I

MATH APPENDIX

Every real estate transaction involves arithmetic. A real estate agent must know the principles of basic mathematics to determine square footage, loan payment amounts, closing costs, and other necessary parts of a transaction. Consumers and investors should understand how the computations that will affect their sale or purchase are being carried out.

If you plan to take a real estate licensing exam, you will be allowed to use a simple calculator (no tape printout or beeping sounds). Make sure you understand how your calculator works. Will you be able to *chain* steps of a problem in sequence by entering all of the information without stopping for a subtotal? For example, if you enter 15 + 5 × 7, will the answer be 140 (15 + 5 = 20 and 20 × 7 = 140)? The directions that come with your calculator will explain how to enter information. But a calculator won't help you unless you have a basic understanding of the mathematics involved in the problems you are given.

■ DOLLARS AND DECIMALS

Some of the most important real estate calculations involve dollars and cents. What will be the asking price? What will be the offer? Which closing expenses will be prorated? What will be the commission—to the listing broker and the selling broker? You'll need to be comfortable working with decimals and percentages throughout a transaction.

A dollar contains 100 cents.

one cent = one-hundredth (⅟₁₀₀) of a dollar = $.01

The decimal point divides the dollars and cents. We indicate one dollar and fifteen cents by $1.15. One hundred dollars and fifteen cents is $100.15. Every number to the *left* of the decimal point is *increased* by a factor of ten.

ten dollars = $10.00
one hundred dollars = $100.00
one thousand dollars = $1,000.00

Every number to the *right* of the decimal point is *decreased* by a factor of ten.

ten cents = one-tenth (⅒) of a dollar = $.10
one cent = one-hundredth (¹⁄₁₀₀) of a dollar = $.01
one mill = one-thousandth (¹⁄₁₀₀₀) of a dollar = $.001

Decimals aren't used only for money calculations. They are also used to indicate percentages.

Percentages

One percent is one hundredth or .01.

A *percentage* is another way of expressing a number that has been carried out to two decimal places. The number .02, which is the same as ²⁄₁₀₀, may also be written as 2%. The number .38, ³⁸⁄₁₀₀ is also 38%. A number carried out to more than two decimal places can also be expressed as a percentage. Thus .698 can be written 69.8%. The important point to remember is that the percent sign has the effect of moving the decimal point two places to the *right*.

■ **FOR EXAMPLE:** The Barlows intend to subdivide their suburban lot, keeping ⅝ of the lot for their own use. What percentage of their land will they keep?

$$⅝ = 8\overline{)5.000} = .625 = 62.5\%$$

The Barlows will keep 62.5 percent of their land.

Some fractions are commonly expressed as their decimal equivalents, and vice versa.

⅒ = .100	= 10%		½ = .50	= 50%
⅛ = .125	= 12.5% or 12½%		⅗ = .60	= 60%
⅙ = .167	= 16.7% or 16⅔%		⅝ = .625	= 62.5% or 62½%
⅕ = .20	= 20%		⅔ = .667	= 66.7% or 66⅔%
¼ = .25	= 25%		¾ = .75	= 75%
⅓ = .333	= 33.3% or 33⅓%		⅘ = .80	= 80%
⅜ = .375	= 37.5% or 37½%		⅞ = .875	= 87.5% or 87½%
⅖ = .40	= 40%			

When converting a percentage to its decimal equivalent, move the decimal point two places to the *left* and remove the percent sign. Thus 82% becomes .82, and 67.6% becomes .676.

Percentages are used in problem solving to express the relationship (**percentage rate,** or simply **rate**) between part of something (**part**) and all of that thing (**whole**). The rate, part, and whole can be expressed in formulas:

Whole   ×   Rate   =   Part
Part   ÷   Whole   =   Rate
Part   ÷   Rate   =   Whole

As a memory aid, the formulas can be illustrated as follows:

$$\frac{\text{Part}}{\text{Whole} \mid \text{Rate}}$$

The horizontal line indicates a division and the vertical line indicates a multiplication.

■ **FOR EXAMPLE:** A house and lot are priced at $88,000. The lot alone is valued at $17,600. What percentage of the total asking price is attributable to the value of the lot?

Because we are looking for the rate, we will use the formula

Part ÷ Whole = Rate

$$\begin{array}{r} .20 \\ \$88,000 \overline{)\ \$17,600.00.} \end{array} = 20\%$$

The value of the lot represents 20 percent of the property's total asking price.

■ **FOR EXAMPLE:** If the broker's commission is 6 percent of the selling price, what will the commission be on the sale of property for $144,000?

Here we know the rate and the whole and we are looking for the part, so we use the formula

Whole   ×   Rate   =   Part
$144,000   ×   6%   = $8,640

The broker's commission for this sale is $8,640.

■ **FOR EXAMPLE:** The commission for the sale of Whiteacre was $14,400. The broker's commission rate was 6 percent. What was the selling price of Whiteacre?

Because we know the part paid to the broker and the rate, we use the formula

Part ÷ Rate = Whole

$$\begin{array}{r} 240000. \\ .06. \overline{)\ \$14,400.00.} \end{array} = \$240,000$$

Whiteacre's selling price was $240,000.

■ INTEREST AND LOAN FINANCE PROBLEMS

The formula for computing real estate loan interest payments is:

$$\text{Principal} \times \text{Rate} \times \text{Time} = \text{Interest}$$
$$PRT = I$$

The **principal** is the unpaid balance of the loan. The **rate** is the percentage rate of interest to be paid. The **time** is the length of the period for which interest is to be paid.

Ordinarily time is expressed in years or parts of a year. A year is considered to have 360 days and a month 30 days, unless the exact number of days in the year or month is required.

> Use a 360-day year unless a problem specifies a calendar year.

If interest is to be calculated for a number of days, time is expressed as a fraction in which the numerator is the number of days and the denominator is 360. Interest for 65 days thus becomes $^{65}/_{360}$. If interest is being computed for a number of months, the fractional part of a year may be used; for example, four months is $^{4}/_{12}$ or $^{1}/_{3}$ of a year.

■ **FOR EXAMPLE:** Calculate the interest to be paid for one month on a loan with a remaining balance of $92,000 when the interest rate is 6 percent.

$$\text{Principal} \times \text{Rate} \times \text{Time} = \text{Interest}$$
$$\$92{,}000 \times .06 \times \tfrac{1}{12} = \text{Interest}$$
$$\$5{,}520 \times \tfrac{1}{12} = \text{Interest}$$
$$\$460 = \text{Interest}$$

The formula for interest can also be used to find principal, rate, or time. So,

$$PRT = I$$
$$P = \frac{I}{RT}$$
$$R = \frac{I}{PT}$$
$$T = \frac{I}{PR}$$

Use the formulas to solve the following example problems. Note that all the problems deal with simple interest.

■ **FOR EXAMPLE:** Sam Jones paid $840 as one month's interest at 7 ½ percent on the outstanding balance of his loan. What is the current outstanding principal balance of Sam's loan?

Because principal is being computed, use the formula as follows:

$$\text{Principal} = \frac{\text{Interest}}{\text{Rate} \times \text{Time}}$$

$$\text{Principal} = \frac{\$840}{7\frac{1}{2}\% \times \frac{1}{12}}$$

$$\text{Principal} = \frac{\$840}{.075 \times \frac{1}{12}}$$

$$\text{Principal} = \frac{\$840}{.00625}$$

$$\text{Principal} = \$134,400$$

■ **FOR EXAMPLE:** What rate would be paid if an interest payment of $6,800 was made on a loan amount of $85,000 for one year?

$$\text{Rate} = \frac{\text{Interest}}{\text{Principal} \times \text{Time}}$$

$$\text{Rate} = \frac{\$6,800}{\$85,000}$$

$$\text{Rate} = 8\%$$

■ **FOR EXAMPLE:** Joan Wood just made an interest-only payment of $2,760 on her remaining home equity loan balance of $92,000. Joan's interest rate is 9 percent. What period of time does her interest payment cover?

$$\text{Time} = \frac{\text{Interest}}{\text{Principal} \times \text{Rate}}$$

$$\text{Time} = \frac{\$2,760}{\$92,000 \times 9\%}$$

$$\text{Time} = \frac{\$2,760}{\$8,280}$$

$$\text{Time} = .333 = \frac{1}{3} \text{ year} = 4 \text{ month}$$

Interest rate tables, such as the one in Table A.1, can be used to shortcut some of the steps involved in computing monthly payments of principal and interest. Such tables can be used to determine interest payments. They also can be used to tell the potential investor how much of the principal balance must be paid to pay down the loan balance over a given number of payments, referred to as **amortization.**

■ **FOR EXAMPLE:** What will be the monthly payment on a loan of $60,000 for 15 years at 8 percent interest if the loan is to be fully amortized by the end of that time?

Using Table A.1, we see that a loan of $1,000 at 8 percent for 15 years requires a payment of $9.56 per month to be completely paid in that time. The monthly payment on a $60,000 loan is, thus,

$$\$9.56 \times 60 = \$573.60$$

A monthly payment of $573.60 will fully amortize a $60,000 loan payable at 8 percent for 15 years.

Prorations

The mathematics involved in computing prorations were mentioned in the "Escrow Procedures" section of Chapter 10, "Escrow and Title Insurance." **Prorations,** which indicate the allocation to seller and buyer of the expenses incurred during their relative periods of ownership, are usually handled as part of the escrow process.

We assume that all expenses up to the day of closing are the responsibility of the seller. Expenses as of the day of closing are the responsibility of the buyer. The standard term of 360 days per year (30 days per month) is used. If the strict number of calendar days is required, a table such as the one found in the "MATH CONCEPTS" example on page 296 may be used to calculate the number of days quickly.

The standard 30-day month formulation may favor either seller or buyer in a transaction, depending on whether it is a 31-day month and whether income or expense is being prorated.

■ **AREA**

The real estate professional often needs to determine the floor or ground area of property.

Square footage is floor ground area.

The **perimeter** of a building or parcel is the sum of the length of all of its sides. **Area,** or **square footage,** is a measurement of the floor or ground space within the perimeter. Square footage is arrived at by multiplying the length and width

TABLE A.1

Monthly Payments to Amortize a $1,000 Loan

Term of Years	Interest Rate														
	5%	5½%	6%	6½%	7%	7½%	8%	8½%	9%	9½%	10	10½%	11%	11½%	12%
1	85.61	85.84	86.07	86.30	86.53	86.76	86.99	87.22	87.46	87.69	87.92	88.15	88.38	88.62	88.85
2	43.88	44.10	44.33	44.55	44.78	45.00	45.23	45.46	45.69	45.92	46.14	46.38	46.61	46.84	47.07
3	29.98	30.20	30.43	30.65	30.88	31.11	31.34	31.57	31.80	32.04	32.27	32.50	32.74	32.98	32.21
4	23.03	23.26	23.49	23.72	23.95	24.18	24.42	24.65	24.89	25.13	25.36	25.60	25.85	26.09	26.33
5	18.88	19.11	19.34	19.57	19.81	20.04	20.28	20.52	20.76	21.01	21.25	21.50	21.75	22.00	22.25
6	16.11	16.34	16.58	16.81	17.05	17.30	17.54	17.78	18.03	18.28	18.53	18.78	19.04	19.30	19.56
7	14.14	14.38	14.61	14.85	15.10	15.34	15.59	15.84	16.09	16.35	16.61	16.87	17.13	17.39	17.66
8	12.66	12.90	13.15	13.39	13.64	13.89	14.14	14.40	14.66	14.92	15.18	15.45	15.71	15.98	16.26
9	11.52	11.76	12.01	12.26	12.51	12.77	13.02	13.28	13.55	13.81	14.08	14.36	14.63	14.91	15.19
10	10.61	10.86	11.11	11.36	11.62	11.88	12.14	12.40	12.67	12.94	13.22	13.50	13.78	14.06	14.35
11	9.87	10.12	10.37	10.63	10.89	11.15	11.42	11.69	11.97	12.24	12.52	12.81	13.10	13.39	13.68
12	9.25	9.51	9.76	10.02	10.29	10.56	10.83	11.11	11.39	11.67	11.96	12.25	12.54	12.84	13.14
13	8.74	8.99	9.25	9.52	9.79	10.06	10.34	10.62	10.90	11.19	11.48	11.78	12.08	12.38	12.69
14	8.29	8.55	8.82	9.09	9.36	9.64	9.92	10.20	10.49	10.79	11.09	11.39	11.70	12.01	12.32
15	7.91	8.17	8.44	8.72	8.99	9.28	9.56	9.85	10.15	10.45	10.75	11.06	11.37	11.69	12.01
16	7.58	7.85	8.12	8.40	8.68	8.96	9.25	9.55	9.85	10.15	10.46	10.78	11.10	11.42	11.74
17	7.29	7.56	7.84	8.12	8.40	8.69	8.99	9.29	9.59	9.90	10.22	10.54	10.86	11.19	11.52
18	7.04	7.31	7.59	7.87	8.16	8.45	8.75	9.06	9.37	9.68	10.00	10.33	10.66	10.99	11.32
19	6.81	7.08	7.37	7.65	7.95	8.25	8.55	8.86	9.17	9.49	9.82	10.15	10.48	10.82	11.16
20	6.60	6.88	7.17	7.46	7.76	8.06	8.37	8.68	9.00	9.33	9.66	9.99	10.33	10.67	11.02
25	5.85	6.15	6.45	6.76	7.07	7.39	7.72	8.06	8.40	8.74	9.09	9.45	9.81	10.17	10.54
30	5.37	5.68	6.00	6.33	6.66	7.00	7.34	7.69	8.05	8.41	8.78	9.15	9.53	9.91	10.29
35	5.05	5.38	5.71	6.05	6.39	6.75	7.11	7.47	7.84	8.22	8.60	8.99	9.37	9.77	10.16
40	4.83	5.16	5.51	5.86	6.22	6.59	6.96	7.34	7.72	8.11	8.49	8.89	9.28	9.68	10.08

of a rectangular area or taking one-half of the base multiplied by the height of a triangular area.

A **rectangle** is a four-sided figure with all sides touching at a 90-degree angle (one-fourth of a circle, which has 360 degrees). If any sides meet at an angle greater or less than 90 degrees, another method of computing area must be used.

Area of rectangle = Length × Width
$$A = L \times W$$

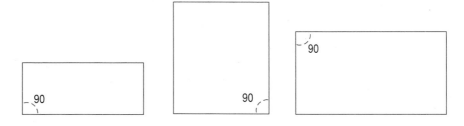

The area of a rectangle is found by multiplying its length by its width. Only units of like measure can be multiplied by each other in deriving area, and the answer will always be in square units of that measure. For example, if feet are multiplied by feet, the resulting area will be in square feet.

■ **FOR EXAMPLE:**   Find the area of the following rectangle.

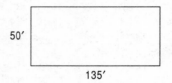

A = L × W
A = 50 feet × 135 feet
A = 6,750 square feet

■ **FOR EXAMPLE:**   Harvey Rand is selling a small house that measures 25 feet by 40 feet. What is the square footage of the house?

A = L × W
A = 25 feet × 40 feet
A = 1,000 square feet

The house has 1,000 square feet.

A **triangle** is simply a three-sided figure. We find the area of a triangle by taking one-half of its base multiplied by its height.

■ **FOR EXAMPLE:**   Find the area of a triangle having a base of 80 feet and a height of 40 feet.

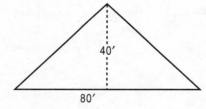

Area =   ½(Base × Height)
A =   ½(*BH*)
A =   ½(80 feet × 40 feet)
A =   1,600 square feet

Remember that all units of measure of a given figure must be of the same kind—that is, inches, feet, yards, or whatever unit is used. The answer will always be given in *square* units.

■ **FOR EXAMPLE:** Gladstone Realty is selling a triangular lot with a road frontage of 90 feet and a maximum depth of 600 feet. What is the area of the lot?

$$A = \tfrac{1}{2}(BH)$$
$$A = \tfrac{1}{2}(90 \text{ feet} \times 600 \text{ feet})$$
$$A = 27{,}000 \text{ square feet}$$

Irregularly shaped property can be measured easily by a nonsurveyor only if its dimensions can be translated into rectangles and triangles.

■ **FOR EXAMPLE:** George Gladstone of Gladstone Realty is appraising the Newsome house. The following diagram shows the measurements of the house. What is its square footage, exclusive of the garage space? What is the square footage of the garage space?

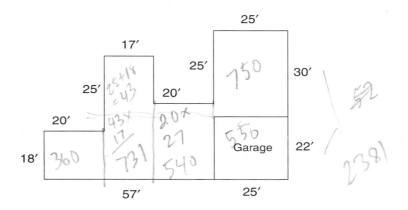

The Newsome house is actually a group of rectangles; the square footage of each of those rectangles can be found, then totaled to find the total square footage of the house.

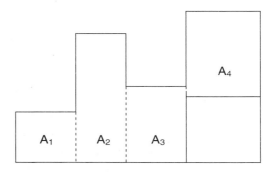

$$A = L \times W$$
$$A_1 = 18 \text{ feet} \times 20 \text{ feet}$$
$$A_2 = 17 \text{ feet} \times 43 \text{ feet}$$
$$A_3 = 20 \text{ feet} \times 27 \text{ feet}$$
$$A_4 = 25 \text{ feet} \times 30 \text{ feet}$$
$$A = (360 + 731 + 540 + 750) \text{ square feet}$$
$$A = 2{,}381 \text{ square feet excluding garage}$$
$$\text{Garage Area} = 22 \text{ feet} \times 25 \text{ feet}$$
$$\text{Garage Area} = 550 \text{ square feet}$$

Computing Construction Costs

As you learned in Chapter 13, there are several different ways to estimate building construction costs. The most basic is the *square-foot method*, using the type of calculations that were covered in the last section.

Ordinary homes and commercial buildings have a certain *cost per square foot*, depending on the quality of construction materials used. That cost may vary from region to region within the state and country, but experience and industry averages can give a fairly accurate figure to use.

■ **FOR EXAMPLE:** Dave Murphy, a building contractor, has been asked to estimate the cost to build a new house having the dimensions and quality of the Newsome house described in the last example. Dave knows that this type of structure will cost approximately $62 per square foot, including labor and overhead. The garage area can be built for less, $35 per square foot if the ceiling and interior walls are left unfinished. Based on those figures, what is the cost of constructing a new house to the specifications of the Newsome house?

$$\text{Living Area} = 2{,}381 \text{ square feet}$$
$$2{,}381 \times \$62 = \$147{,}622$$
$$\text{Garage Area} = 550 \text{ square feet}$$
$$550 \times \$35 = \$19{,}250$$
$$\text{Total Cost} = \$166{,}872$$

■ SUMMARY

The mathematical calculations required in the average real estate transaction are not complicated, but they do require familiarity with a few basic concepts and formulas. After you have become comfortable working with percentages, interest, amortization, prorations, and finding area, you will have the groundwork for handling most of the necessary computations.

Handwritten notes at top:

756,000 × 2.5% = 18,900
18,900 × 70% = 13,230

780,000
× 20% =
156,000
- 156,000
= 624,000

using chart

624 × 8.17 = 5098.08
624 × 6.33 = 3949.92

■ MATH ACHIEVEMENT EXAMINATION

1. Sales associate Brian Lee found a buyer for the property located at 611 Prince Edward Road, listed with another firm. Brian worked as the buyer's agent in exchange for a commission to his brokerage firm of 2.5% of the sales price. Brian's share of any commissions he earns is 70%. If the property sold for $756,000, what did Brian earn?

2. Bob and Beverly are refinancing their home loan. Their new loan of $175,000 will be at a fixed interest rate of 6.625% for 30 years. The monthly payment is $1,120.54. How much of the first payment will be interest? How much will be principal?

   Handwritten: 175,000 × 6.625% = 11593.75 ÷ 12
   = 966.15 - (1120.54 - 966.15) = 154.39

3. Using the table on page 467, compute the monthly payment on a loan of $260,000 at an interest rate of 7% for 15 years. Then, find the monthly payment on the same loan for a term of 30 years.

   Handwritten: 8.99 × 260 = 2337.40
   6.66 × 260 = 1731.60

4. A parcel of land on the Old Sonoma Highway is for sale. The parcel is 1,150 feet by 2,400 feet. How many square feet does the parcel contain? How many acres is that?

   Handwritten: 2,760,000 SQ FT ÷ (43,560) 63.36 Acres

5. Lois Lovely, a movie star, is building a house in Palm Springs. The house will have 7,200 square feet, and construction is estimated at $265 per square foot. What is the estimated construction cost of the house?

   Handwritten: 7200
   × 265.
   $1,908,000

6. Amir is shopping for a home mortgage loan on the condominium he is purchasing in Long Beach. The purchase price is $780,000 and Amir will make a 20% down payment. He must choose either a 30-year loan at an interest rate of 6½% or a 15-year loan at an interest rate of 5½%. Which loan will require the smallest monthly payment? What will that payment be?

7. Property in Sunny Glen has appreciated at an average rate of 8% per year for the last four years. If Trevor and Jessica bought a house for $230,000 four years ago, and it appreciated at the average rate, how much is it worth today?

   Handwritten: 248,400
   268,272
   289,7376
   3129/2.46

8. Using the facts in problem 7, if Trevor and Jessica made a 10% down payment on their home, and have paid down their mortgage by $8,000, how much equity do they have in their home?

   Handwritten: 230,000
   - 23,000
   207,000
   - 8000
   199,000
   312,913
   - 199,000
   113,913

9. The owner of Saguaro Saddles, a horse ranch, is planning to enlarge her facility by purchasing an adjoining parcel. The parcel is listed as "20 acres more or less" and is described as the East ½ of the Northwest ¼ of the Southeast ¼ of Section 15. Do the two descriptions match? If the parcel is priced at $16,500 per acre, what is the total asking price?

   Handwritten: 330,000

10. Spurgeon Vineyard in Temecula was sold for $1,325,000. The total commission on the sale was $66,250. What percentage of the sales price did this represent?

   Handwritten: 5%

INTERNET APPENDIX

The following list contains Internet resources that have been mentioned in this book and others that may be of interest to readers. You are encouraged to explore other resources, including the numerous online property listing services and lenders.

Appraisal Institute
www.appraisalinstitute.org

Association of Real Estate License Law Officials
www.arello.org

California Apartment Association
www.ca-apartment.org

California Association of Business Brokers
www.cabb.org

California Association of Community Managers
www.cacm.org

California Association of Mortgage Brokers
www.cambweb.org

California Association of REALTORS® (CAR)
Information on courses to obtain the GRI (Graduate, REALTOR® Institute) designation in California is available at *www.eDesignations.com.*
www.car.org

California bills and statutes
www.leginfo.ca.gov

California Building Industry Association
www.cbia.org

California Department of Conservation, Division of Mines, and Geology
www.consrv.ca.gov/dmg/index.htm

California Department of Finance
www.dof.ca.gov

California Department of Housing and Community Development
http://housing.hcd.ca.gov

California Department of Real Estate (DRE)
www.dre.ca.gov

California Department of Veterans Affairs (CDVA)
www.cdva.ca.gov

California Environmental Protection Agency
www.calgold.ca.gov

California Mortgage Association
www.californiamortgageassociation.com

California Mortgage Bankers Association
www.cmba.com

California Real Estate Education Association
www.creea.org

City of San Diego
www.sannet.gov

City of Santa Monica
http://pen.ci.santa-monica.ca.us/cm/index.htm

Contractors' State License Board
www.cslb.ca.gov

Department of Housing and Urban Development (HUD)
www.hud.gov

Department of Veterans Affairs (VA)
www.va.gov

Environmental Protection Agency (EPA)
www.epa.gov

Equifax
www.Equifax.com

Executive Council of Homeowners
www.echo-ca.org

Experian
www.experian.com

Fannie Mae (FNMA)
www.fanniemae.com

Federal Home Loan Mortgage Corporation (FHLMC)
www.freddiemac.com

Federal Reserve Bank System (the Fed)
www.federalreserve.gov

Franchise Tax Board
www.ftb.ca.gov

Government National Mortgage Association (GNMA)
www.hud.gov/funcgnma

Inman Real Estate News Service
www.inman.com

Internal Revenue Service (IRS)
vwww.irs.gov

International Code Council (ICC)
www.iccsafe.org

League of California Cities
www.cacities.org

Los Angeles County
www.co.la.ca.us/

Los Angeles County Assessor Online Public Service
http://assessor.co.la.ca.us/

National Association of Real Estate Brokers, Inc. (NAREB)
www.nareb.com

National Association of Real Estate Investment Trusts
www.nareit.com

National Association of REALTORS® (NAR)
www.realtor.com
www.realtor.org

National Lead Information Center (NLIC)
www.epa.gov/lead/nlic.htm

Office of Federal Housing Enterprise Oversight (OFHEO)
www.ofheo.gov

Office of Real Estate Appraisers (OREA)
www.orea.ca.gov

Professional Publishing, Inc.
www.profpub.com

Real Estate Educators Association
www.reea.org

Realty
www.realtytimes.com

Seattle Public Library
www.spl.lib.wa.us//govpubs/municode.html

Secretary of State Business Service Center
www.ss.ca.gov/business/business.htm

Small Business Administration
www.sba.gov

State Bar of California
www.calbar.org

State Board of Equalization
www.boe.ca.gov

State Controller's Office
www.sco.ca.gov

State of California
www.ca.gov

United States Geologic Service
http://quake.wr.usgs.gov/

GLOSSARY

abandonment. Giving up possession or ownership of property by nonuse, usually accompanied by some affirmative act, such as removing one's belongings from an apartment.

abstract of judgment. Document stipulating the outcome of a legal action, which can be filed in any county where the judgment debtor has property.

abstract of title. A summary or digest of all recorded transfers, conveyances, legal proceedings, and any other facts relied on as evidence of title to show continuity of ownership and indicate any possible impairments to title.

acceleration clause. A provision in a real estate financing instrument that allows the lender to declare the remaining indebtedness due and payable on the happening of certain conditions, such as the sale of the property or the borrower's default in payment.

acceptance. Indication by the person to whom an offer is made (the *offeree*) of agreement to the terms of the offer. If the offer requires a writing, the acceptance must also be in writing.

accession. The process of manufactured or natural improvement or addition to property.

accretion. Accession by natural forces, such as alluvion.

acknowledgment. A formal declaration made before an authorized person by a person who has executed a written instrument, stating that the execution of the instrument is the person's own act.

acquisition cost. For FHA-insured loans, the price to procure property, including purchase price and all nonrecurring closing costs, including discount points, FHA application fee, service charge and credit report, FHA appraisal, escrow, document preparation, title insurance, termite inspection, reconveyance, and recording fees.

acre. A measure of land equaling 160 square rods, 4,840 square yards, or 43,560 square feet, or a tract about 208.71 feet square.

action for declaratory relief. Legal proceeding brought to determine the respective rights of the parties before a controversy arises.

action to quiet title. A court proceeding brought to establish title to real property.

actual age. The number of years since completion of a building; also called *historical* or *chronological* age.

actual authority. The authority an agent has because it is specified in the agency agreement, or that the agent believes he or she has because of an unintentional or a careless act of the principal.

adjustable rate mortgage. Finance instrument whose interest rate will vary according to the change in an identified index or rate, such as the 11th District Cost of Funds.

adjusted cost basis. Purchase price of property plus cost of specified improvements, less any depreciation deductions taken on the property.

adjusted gross income. Income from all sources less deductions for taxes, depreciation, and other allowable deductions.

administrator. Personal representative of the estate of a decedent, appointed by the probate court. See also **executor.**

ad valorem. A Latin phrase meaning "according to value," used to describe a tax charged in relation to the value of the property taxed.

adverse possession. A method of acquiring title to real property by occupying the property against the interests of the true owner and fulfilling other statutory requirements.

after-acquired title. If title is acquired by a grantor only after a conveyance to a grantee, the deed to the grantee becomes effective at the time the grantor actually receives title.

agency. The relationship between a principal and the agent of the principal that arises out of a contract, whether express or implied, written or oral, by which the agent is employed by the principal to do certain acts dealing with a third party.

agent. One who acts for and with authority from another person, called the *principal*; a *special* agent is appointed to carry out a particular act or transaction, and any other agent is a *general* agent.

air rights. The real property right to the reasonable use of the airspace above the surface of the land.

alienation. The transferring of property to another; an involuntary transfer of title.

alienation clause. See **due-on-sale clause.**

all-inclusive trust deed. See **wraparound mortgage or trust deed.**

alluvion. Alluvium; the increase of soil along the bank of a body of water by natural forces.

amortization. The payment of a financial obligation in installments; recovery over a period of time of cost or value. A loan has negative amortization when the loan payments do not cover all of the interest due, which then is added to the remaining loan balance.

annual percentage rate (APR). The relative cost of credit as determined in accordance with Regulation Z of the Board of Governors of the Federal Reserve System for implementing the federal Truth-in-Lending Act.

anticipation, principle of. Expectation that property will offer future benefits, which tends to increase present value.

apparent authority. Authority to act as an agent that someone appears to have but does not actually have, which will place no obligation on the party the agent claims to represent if that party is in no way responsible for the representation.

appraisal. An estimate of a property's monetary value on the open market; an estimate of a property's type and condition, its utility for a given purpose, or its highest and best use.

appropriation, right of. See **right of appropriation.**

appurtenance. Anything affixed (attached) to or used with land for its benefit that is transferred with the land.

APR. See **annual percentage rate.**

area. Measure of the floor or ground space within the perimeter of a building or land parcel.

arm's-length transaction. A transaction in which neither party acts under duress and both have full knowledge of the property's assets and defects, the property involved has been on the market a reasonable length of time, there are no unusual circumstances, and the price represents the normal consideration for the property sold, without unusual financing terms.

assessed valuation. A valuation placed on a piece of property by a public authority as a basis for levying taxes on that property.

assessor. The official responsible for determining assessed values.

assignee. Party to whom an assignment of rights is made.

assignment. Transfer of rights from one party to another, usually for compensation.

assignor. Party making an assignment of rights to someone else.

assumption. An undertaking or adoption of a debt or an obligation resting primarily on another person.

attachment. The process by which real or personal property of a party to a lawsuit is seized and retained in the custody of the court.

attorney-at-law. Someone licensed by the state to practice law.

attorney-in-fact. An agent who has been granted a power of attorney by a principal.

avulsion. The tearing or washing away of land along the bank of a body of water by natural forces.

balance, principle of. The combination of land uses that results in the highest property values overall.

balloon payment. An installment payment on a promissory note—usually the final payment—that is significantly larger than the other installment payments.

bankruptcy. A federal court proceeding in which the court takes possession of the assets of an insolvent debtor and sells the nonexempt assets to pay off creditors on a pro rata basis; title to the debtor's assets is held by a *trustee in bankruptcy*.

baselines. Imaginary lines that run east-west and intersect meridians that run north-south to form the starting point for land measurement using the rectangular survey system of land description.

basis. Cost basis is the dollar amount assigned to property at the time of acquisition under provisions of the Internal Revenue Code for the purpose of determining gain, loss, and depreciation in calculating the income tax to be paid upon the sale or exchange of the property; adjusted cost basis is derived after the application of certain additions, such as for improvements, and deductions, such as for depreciation.

beneficiary. One on whose behalf a trustee holds property conveyed by a trustor; the lender under a deed of trust.

benefit assessment. Amount owed by owners of property that is enhanced by the construction or renovation of improvements.

bequest. Transfer of property, particularly personal property, called a legacy, by will. See also **devise**.

bill of sale. Written instrument that conveys title to personal property.

blind ad. Ad in which the name of the person placing the ad is not mentioned.

blockbusting. The practice on the part of unscrupulous speculators or real estate agents of inducing panic selling of homes at prices below market value, especially by exploiting the prejudices of property owners in neighborhoods in which the racial makeup is changing or appears to be on the verge of changing.

bond. An obligation; a real estate bond is a written obligation issued on security of a mortgage or trust deed.

book value. The current value for accounting purposes of an asset expressed as original cost plus capital additions minus accumulated depreciation.

boot. Cash received in an exchange of property in addition to the property.

breach. The failure of a duty imposed by law or by contract, either by omission or commission.

building code. Standards for building, planning, and construction established by state law and local ordinance.

bundle of rights. The legal rights of ownership of real property, including the rights of possession, use, disposition, and exclusion of others from the property.

business opportunity. The assets of an existing business enterprise, including its goodwill.

Cal-Vet loan. Home or farm loan procured through the California Veterans Farm and Home Purchase Program.

capital assets. Assets of a permanent nature used in the production of income, such as land, buildings, machinery, and equipment; usually distinguishable under income tax law from "inventory," assets held for sale to customers in the ordinary course of the taxpayer's trade or business.

capital gain. The amount by which the net resale proceeds of a capital item exceed the adjusted cost basis of the item.

capitalization rate. The rate of interest that is considered a reasonable return on an investment, used in the process of determining value based on net operating income; the yield necessary to attract investment.

capitalization recapture. The return of an investment; an amortization rate based on the right of the investor to get back the purchase price at the end of the term of ownership or over the productive life of the improvements.

cash flow. The net income generated by a property before depreciation and other noncash expenses.

caveat emptor. Latin phrase meaning "Let the buyer beware."

CC&Rs. Covenants, conditions, and restrictions; limitations on land use imposed by deed, usually when land is subdivided, as a means of regulating building construction, density, and use for the benefit of other property owners; may be referred to simply as *restrictions*.

certificate of reasonable value. Property appraisal required for a VA-guaranteed loan.

certificate of redemption. Issued by the county tax collector when all past due amounts have been paid.

certificate of sale. Document received by the buyer at an execution or a judicial foreclosure sale; replaced by a sheriff's deed if the debtor fails to redeem the property during the statutory redemption period.

certificate of title. Statement of a property's owner of record as well as any existing encumbrances.

chain of title. The history of the conveyances and encumbrances affecting the present owner's title to property, as far back as records are available.

change, principle of. Effect on property value of constantly varying physical, economic, social, and political forces.

chattel mortgage. Use of personal property to secure or guarantee a promissory note.

chattel real. An estate related to real estate, such as a lease of real property.

chattels. Personal property; any property that is not real property.

city planning. Land-use recommendations adopted by local jurisdiction, determined by use of demographic, geographic, economic, and other data.

civil law. Legal system based on laws and regulations, without the influence of judicial decisions as in the common law system.

closing. The completion of a real estate transaction, at which point required documents are transmitted and funds are transferred.

cloud on the title. Any claim, condition, or encumbrance that impairs title to real property.

coastal zone. An area of about 1,800 square miles that runs the length of the state from the sea inland about 1,000 yards, with wider spots in coastal estuarine, habitat, and recreational areas; any development or improvement of land within the coastal zone must meet local requirements for coastal conservation and preservation of resources, as authorized by the Coastal Zone Conservation Act.

codes. Bound volumes of laws and regulations.

codicil. Written amendment to a will, made with the same legal formalities.

color of title. A claim of possession to real property based on a document erroneously appearing to convey title to the claimant.

commercial acre. That portion of an acre of newly subdivided land remaining after dedication for streets, sidewalks, parks, and so on.

commingling. Placing funds in an inappropriate financial account, such as depositing a deposit check in a broker's business account instead of a trust account.

commission. An agent's compensation for performing the duties of the agency; in real estate practice, typically a percentage of the selling price of property, rentals, or other property value.

common interest subdivision. An area of land divided into separate parcels but with some of the land set aside for shared ownership by all of the owners of the separate parcels.

common law. The body of law from England based on custom, usage, and court decisions.

community apartment project. A form of subdivision in which the owner has an individual interest in the land and exclusive right of occupancy of an apartment on the land.

community property. All property acquired by husband and wife during marriage except that qualifying as separate property.

community redevelopment agency (CRA). An agency authorized by state law but formed by a local governing body to provide low- and moderate-income housing and employ low-income persons by rehabilitating existing structures and/or bringing new development.

competition, principle of. Business profits encourage competition, which ultimately may reduce profits for any one business.

competitive market analysis. Informal estimate of market value performed by a real estate agent for either seller or buyer, utilizing the sales history of nearby properties; usually expressed as a range of values that includes the probable market value of the subject property.

compound interest. Interest paid on original principal and also on the accrued and unpaid interest that has accumulated as the debt matures.

concurrent ownership. Ownership of property by more than one person, not necessarily in equal shares.

condemnation. See **eminent domain.**

condition. A qualification of an estate granted that can be imposed only in a conveyance; it can be a condition precedent or a condition subsequent. See also **CC&Rs.**

conditional license. License that is issued to a salesperson who has not completed all of the required education courses, contingent on all education requirements being met.

conditional use permit. Authorization for a land use that would otherwise not be permitted by zoning ordinances.

condition precedent. A qualification of a contract or transfer of property providing that unless and until the performance of a certain act, the contract or transfer will not take effect.

condition subsequent. A stipulation in a contract or transfer of property that already has taken effect that will extinguish the contract or defeat the property transfer.

condominium. A subdivision providing an exclusive ownership (fee) interest in the airspace of a particular portion of real property, as well as an interest in common in a portion of that property.

conforming loan. A loan that meets the requirements established for purchase by Fannie Mae.

conformity, principle of. Holds that property values are maximized when buildings are similar in design, construction, and age, particularly in residential neighborhoods.

consideration. Anything of value given or promised by a party to induce another to enter into a contract; may be a benefit conferred on one party or a detriment suffered by the other.

construction loan. See **interim loan.**

constructive eviction. Interference by the landlord in a tenant's legitimate use of leased property, such as by making unwarranted alterations to the property.

contract. A written or an oral agreement to do or not to do certain things. There may be an *express* agreement of the parties or a contract may be *implied* by their conduct. A *unilateral* contract imposes an obligation on only one of the parties, whereas both parties to a *bilateral* contract have an obligation to perform. A contract is *executory* when a contract obligation is to be performed in the future, and *executed* when all obligations have been performed and the contract transaction has been completed. A real estate contract must be a signed writing made by competent parties, for valuable consideration, with an offer by one party that is accepted by the other.

contract rent. The rent agreed to by lessor and lessee.

contribution, principle of. A component part of a property is valued in proportion to its contribution to the value of the entire property, regardless of its separate actual cost.

conventional loan. A loan secured by a mortgage or trust deed that is made without governmental underwriting (FHA-insured or VA-guaranteed).

cooperating broker. The broker who finds a buyer for property listed for sale by another broker.

cooperating split. Sharing of the compensation (usually, a commission) received by the listing broker with the broker who brings the buyer to the transaction.

cooperative apartment. See **stock cooperative.**

corporation. A legal entity that acts through its board of directors and officers, generally without liability on the part of the person or persons owning it. A domestic corporation is one chartered in California—any other corporation is a foreign corporation in California.

correction lines. Guide meridians running every 24 miles east and west of a meridian, and standard parallels running every 24 miles north and south of a base line, used to correct inaccuracies in the rectangular survey system of land description caused by the earth's curvature.

cost approach. Appraisal method in which site value is added to the present reproduction or replacement cost of all property improvements, less depreciation, to determine market value.

counteroffer. Any change to the terms of an offer, made in response to it.

covenant. An agreement or a promise to do or not to do a particular act, usually imposed by deed. See also **CC&Rs.**

covenant of quiet enjoyment. Promise of a landlord, implied by law, not to interfere in the possession or use of leased property by the tenant.

covenant to repair. Express or legally implied obligation of the landlord to make necessary repairs to leased premises.

declaration of homestead. See **homestead.**

dedication. The giving of land by its owner for a public use, and the acceptance of the land for such use by the appropriate government officials.

deed. Written instrument that, when properly executed and delivered, conveys title to real property from a grantor to a grantee.

deed in lieu of foreclosure. A deed to real property accepted by a lender from a defaulting borrower to avoid the necessity of foreclosure proceedings by the lender.

deed of trust. See **trust deed.**

defendant. A person against whom legal action is initiated for the purpose of obtaining criminal sanctions (in a case involving violation of a penal statute) or damages or other appropriate judicial relief (in a civil case).

deficiency judgment. A judgment given by a court when the value of security pledged for a loan is insufficient to pay off the debt of the defaulting borrower.

Department of Real Estate. California agency that administers the Real Estate Law, including the licensing of real estate brokers and salespeople.

depreciation. Decrease in value of an asset that is allowed in computing property value for tax purposes; in appraising, a loss in the value of a property improvement from any cause; depreciation is *curable* when it can be remedied by a repair or an addition to the property, and it is *incurable* when there is no easy or economic way to cure the loss. See also **physical deterioration, functional obsolescence,** and **external obsolescence.**

devise. Transfer of title to property by will. See also **bequest.**

devisee. Person receiving title to property by will. See also **legatee.**

devisor. One who wills property to another.

discount points. See **points.**

discount rate. Interest rate charged member banks by Federal Reserve Banks.

documentary transfer tax. A tax applied on all transfers of real property located in a county that the county is authorized by the state to collect; notice of payment is entered on the face of the deed or on a separate paper filed with the deed.

dominant tenement. See **easement.**

donee. One who receives a gift.

donor. One who makes a gift.

dual agency. An agency relationship in which the agent represents two principals in their dealings with each other.

due diligence. Acting with the appropriate degree of skill and care in fulfilling one's responsibilities under an agency or other contractual relationship.

due-on-sale clause. An acceleration clause in a real estate financing instrument granting the lender the right to demand full payment of the remaining indebtedness upon a sale of the property.

earthquake fault zone. As defined by the state geologist, the area in such close proximity to an earthquake fault that movement of the fault presents a property hazard; location within an earthquake fault zone must be disclosed to a prospective purchaser by the seller (or seller's agent, if there is one).

easement. The right to a specific use of or the right to travel over the land of another. The land being used or traveled over is the *servient tenement;* the land that is benefited by the use is the *dominant* *tenement.* An *easement appurtenant* is a property interest that belongs to the owner of the dominant tenement and is transferred with the land; an *easement in gross* is a personal right that usually is not transferable by its owner.

easement by prescription. Acquiring a specific use of or the right to travel over the land of another by statutory requirements similar to those for adverse possession.

economic life. The period of time over which an improved property will yield a return on investment over and above the return attributable solely to the land.

economic obsolescence. See **external obsolescence.**

economic rent. The reasonable rental expectancy if the property were available for renting at the time of its valuation.

effective gross income. Property income from all sources, less allowance for vacancy and collection losses.

emblements. Crops produced annually by labor and industry as distinguished from crops that grow naturally on the land.

eminent domain. The right of the government to acquire title to property for public use by condemnation; the property owner receives compensation—generally fair market value. See also **inverse condemnation.**

encroachment. The unlawful intrusion of a property improvement onto adjacent property.

encumbrance. Anything that affects or limits the fee simple title to or affects the condition or use of real estate.

environmental impact report (EIR). Evaluation of effects on the environment of a proposed development; may be required by local government.

environmental obsolescence. See **external obsolescence.**

equal dignities rule. Requires a writing if an agreement (such as a listing agreement) involves a transaction (such as the sale of real estate) that requires a writing.

equity. Difference between current market value and the remaining indebtedness on a property; free-and-clear property value.

equity of redemption. The right to redeem property during the foreclosure period, or during a statutorily prescribed time following a foreclosure sale.

escalator clause. Provision in a lease agreement for an increase in payments based on an increase in an index such as the consumer price index.

escheat. The reverting of property to the state when there are no heirs capable of inheriting.

escrow. The deposit of instruments and/or funds (with instructions) with a neutral third party to carry out the provisions of an agreement or a contract.

escrow agent. Escrow holder; the neutral third party holding funds or something of value in trust for another or others.

estate. The interest held by the owner of property.

estate at sufferance. The occupancy of a tenant after the lease term expires.

estate at will. A tenancy in which the tenant's time of possession is indefinite.

estate for years. A tenancy for a fixed term.

estate from period to period. Periodic tenancy; a tenancy for a fixed term, automatically renewed for the same term unless owner or tenant gives the other written notice of intention to terminate the tenancy.

estoppel. A bar against future conduct. By acting as if an agency relationship exists, a principal is prevented by estoppel from denying it in future.

eviction. Dispossession by process of law.

exchange. A means of trading equities in two or more real properties, treated as a single transaction through a single escrow.

exclusive agency listing. A listing agreement employing a broker as sole agent for a seller of real property under the terms of which the broker is entitled to compensation if the property is sold through any other broker, but not if a sale is negotiated by the owner without the services of an agent.

exclusive authorization and right-to-sell listing. A listing agreement employing a broker as agent for a seller of real property under the terms of which the broker is entitled to compensation if the listed property is sold during the duration of the listing, whether by the listing agent, another agent, or the owner acting without the services of an agent.

executor. Personal representative of the estate of a decedent, named in the decedent's will. See also **administrator.**

express agreement. An agreement established by written or oral communication of the parties that both parties acknowledge as their intention.

external obsolescence. Economic or environmental obsolescence; loss in value due to outside causes, such as changes in nearby land use.

federally related transaction. Transaction that involves a federally chartered or insured lender.

fee simple absolute. A fee simple estate with no restrictions on its use.

fee simple defeasible. An interest in land, such as a fee simple conditional or fee simple with special limitation, that may result in the estate of ownership being defeated.

fee simple estate. The greatest interest in real property one can own, including the right to use the property at present and for an indeterminate period of time in the future.

fee simple qualified. A fee simple estate with some restrictions on the right of possession.

fiduciary. A person in a position of trust and confidence who owes a certain loyalty to another, such as an agent to a principal.

final subdivision map. See tentative subdivision map.

fiscal year. A business or an accounting year as distinguished from a calendar year.

fixture. Anything permanently attached to land or improvements so as to become real property.

foreclosure. Sale of real property by mortgagee, trustee, or other lienholder on default by the borrower. See also **judicial foreclosure action.**

form appraisal report. A short report, typically two pages plus addenda, using a preprinted form to summarize the data contributing to an appraiser's conclusion of value.

franchise. A contract or agreement between the franchisor (grantor) and the franchisee (grantee).

franchise tax. California tax on corporations.

fraud. The intentional and successful use of any cunning, deception, collusion, or artifice to circumvent, cheat, or deceive another person, so that the other person acts on it to the loss of property and legal injury; *actual fraud* is a deliberate misrepresentation or a representation made in reckless disregard of its truth or falsity, the suppression of truth, a promise made without the intention to perform it, or any other act intended to deceive; *constructive fraud* is any misrepresentation made without fraudulent intent (the deliberate intent to deceive). Fraud is *affirmative* when it is a deliberate statement of a material fact that the speaker knows to be false and on which the speaker intends another person to rely, to his or her detriment. Fraud is *negative* when it is a deliberate concealment of something that should be revealed.

freehold estate. An estate in land in which ownership is for an indeterminate length of time, as in a fee simple or life estate.

front foot. Property measured by the front linear foot on its street line, each front foot extending the depth of the lot.

fructus industriales. Plant growth that is the result of cultivation.

fructus naturales. Plant growth that does not require cultivation, such as natural trees, grasses, and shrubbery.

functional obsolescence. Loss in value due to adverse factors within a structure that affect its marketability, such as its design, layout, or utility.

general partnership. An association of two or more persons to carry on a business as co-owners for profit.

general plan. Master plan; includes a statement of policy of the development and land uses within a city or county and a program to implement that policy.

gift deed. A deed for which the only consideration is "love and affection."

goodwill. An intangible but a salable asset of a business derived from the expectation of continued public patronage.

graduated payment mortgage. Financing instrument in which payments are increased during the first five years of the loan term, and then remain fixed for the remainder of the term.

grant deed. A limited warranty deed using a granting clause—the word "grant" or words to that effect—assuring the grantee that the estate being conveyed is free from encumbrances placed on the property by the present owner (the grantor), and that the grantor has not previously conveyed the property to anyone else.

grantee. A person to whom property is transferred by grant.

grantor. A person conveying property to another by grant.

gross income. Total property income from all sources before any expenses are deducted.

gross income multiplier. Gross rent multiplier; a number derived by dividing the sales price of a comparable property by the income it produces, which then is multiplied by the gross income produced by the subject property to derive an estimate of value.

gross lease. Provides for the tenant to pay a fixed rental over the lease term, with the landlord paying all expenses of ownership, such as taxes, assessments, and insurance.

ground lease. An agreement for the use of land only, sometimes secured by improvements placed on the land by the user.

ground rent. Earnings of improved property credited to earnings of the ground itself after allowance is made for earnings of improvements.

growing equity mortgage. Financing instrument in which payments of principal are increased based on the movement of a stated index, thereby decreasing the loan term.

guarantee of title. Guarantee of title as determined from examination of the public records and described in the guarantee document.

guide meridians. See **correction lines.**

highest and best use. In appraising real estate, the most profitable, physically possible, and legally permissible use for the property under consideration.

holder in due course. Someone who takes a negotiable instrument for value, in good faith, and without notice of any defense against its enforcement that might be made by any person.

holdover tenancy. Possession of property by a tenant who remains in possession after the expiration or termination of the lease term.

holographic will. A will written entirely in the testator's handwriting, signed, and dated by the testator.

homestead. A statutory exemption of real property used as a home from the claims of certain creditors and judgments up to a specified amount.

hypothecation. Use of real property as collateral for a debt.

implied agency. Action of a principal that causes a third party to rely on the representation of an agency relationship.

implied warranties. Warranties by grantor to grantee that will be implied by law, even if not mentioned in the deed; the grantor warrants that he or she has not already conveyed the property, and that there are no encumbrances on the property brought about by the grantor or any person who might claim title from the grantor.

impound account. A trust account established by a lender for accumulation of borrower funds to pay taxes and other recurring costs.

income capitalization approach. Appraisal method in which the actual or likely net operating income of property is divided by its expected rate of return (capitalization rate) to arrive at an estimate of market value. See also **capitalization rate.**

independent contractor. A person employed by another who has almost complete freedom to accomplish the purposes of the employment.

index method. Way of estimating building reproduction cost by multiplying the original cost of the subject building by a factor that represents the percentage change in construction costs generally from the time of construction to the time of valuation.

inherent authority. The authority of an agent to perform activities that are not specifically mentioned in the agency agreement but are necessary or customary to carry out an authorized act.

injunction. A writ or an order issued by a court to restrain one or more parties to a suit or proceeding from doing an act deemed to be inequitable or unjust in regard to the rights of some other party or parties in the suit or proceeding.

installment sales contract. See **sales contract.**

institutional lenders. A financial intermediary or depository, such as a savings and loan association, commercial bank, or life insurance company, that pools the money of its depositors and then invests funds in various ways, including trust deeds and mortgage loans.

interest. A portion, share, or right in something; partial ownership; the charge in dollars for the use of money for a period of time.

interest rate. The percentage of a sum of money borrowed that is charged for its use.

interim loan. A short-term temporary loan used until permanent financing is available, typically during building construction.

interim use. The use to which a site or improved property may be put until ready for the more productive highest and best use.

Internet. Worldwide network of computers, originally created for military and university communications, making use of telephone lines or microwave links.

interpleader. A court proceeding that may be brought by someone, such as an escrow agent, who holds property for another, for the purpose of deciding who among the claimants is legally entitled to the property.

intestate succession. Statutory method of distribution of property that belonged to someone who died intestate (without having made a valid will).

inverse condemnation. A legal action brought by the owner of land when government puts nearby land to a use that diminishes the value of the owner's property.

joint and several liability. Obligation of all cosigners of a promissory note to repay the entire note, even if one defaults.

joint tenancy. Ownership of property by two or more co-owners, each of whom has an equal share and the right of survivorship.

joint venture. Two or more individuals or firms joining together on a single project as partners, typically with a lender contributing the necessary funds and the other partner(s) contributing his or her expertise.

judgment. The final determination of a court of competent jurisdiction of a matter presented to it; may include an award of money damages.

judicial foreclosure action. Proceeding in which a mortgagee, a trustee, or another lienholder on property requests a court-supervised sale of the property to cover the unpaid balance of a delinquent debt.

kickback. An illegal fee paid by a nonlicensee to a salesperson or bank.

land. The earth's surface, including substances beneath the surface extending downward to the center of the earth and the airspace above the surface for an indefinite distance upward.

land contract. See **sales contract.**

landlord. Lessor; one who leases his or her property to another.

lateral support. The support that the soil of an adjoining owner gives to a neighbor's land.

lease. A contract between a property owner, called *lessor* or *landlord,* and another, called *lessee* or *tenant,* conveying and setting forth the conditions of occupancy and use of the property by the tenant.

leaseback. See **sale-leaseback.**

leasehold. Interest of one who leases property.

leasehold estate. A tenant's right to occupy real estate during the term of the lease; a personal property interest.

lease option. A lease accompanied by the right to purchase the leased property within a specified period for a specified or determinable price.

legacy. Property, usually personal property, transferred by will.

legal description. A land description used to define a parcel of land to the exclusion of all others that is acceptable by a court of law.

legatee. Person who receives property, called a legacy, by bequest. See also **devisee.**

lessee. One who leases property owned by someone else.

lessor. Property owner; landlord.

letter of opinion. A letter from appraiser to client presenting only the appraiser's conclusion of value, with no supporting data.

leverage. Use of debt financing to purchase an investment, thus maximizing the return per dollar of equity invested; enables a purchaser to obtain possession for little or no initial cash outlay and relatively small periodic payments on the debt incurred.

lien. An encumbrance that makes property security for the payment of a debt or discharge of an obligation; a *voluntary lien* is one agreed to by the property owner, such as a deed of trust; an *involuntary lien* exists by operation of law to create a burden on property for certain unpaid debts, such as a tax lien.

life estate. An interest in real property conveying the right to possession and use for a term measured by the life or lives of one or more persons, most often the holder of the life estate.

limited equity housing cooperative. A stock cooperative financed by the California Housing Finance Agency.

limited partnership. Partnership of one or more general partners, who run the business and are liable as partners, and limited partners, investors who do not run the business and are liable only up to the amount invested.

liquidated damages. An amount agreed on by the parties to be full damages if a certain event occurs.

listing agreement. Authorization by the owner of property, acting as principal, for a real estate broker to act as the agent of the principal in finding a person to buy, lease, or rent property; may be used to employ a real estate broker to act as agent for a person seeking property to buy, lease, or rent.

littoral rights. Right to use of water from a lake or other body of still water by adjoining property owners.

lock-in clause. Provision in a promissory note or land contract that prohibits the promissor from paying off the debt prior to the date set forth in the contract.

lot and block system. Subdivision system; method of legal description of land using parcel maps identified by tract, block, and lot numbers.

manufactured home. A structure transportable in one or more sections, designed and equipped to contain not more than two dwelling units, and to comply with HUD building specifications.

marker. See metes and bounds.

marketable title. Title that a reasonably prudent purchaser, acting with full knowledge of the facts and their legal significance, would be willing and ought to accept.

market comparison approach. See sales comparison approach.

market data approach. See sales comparison approach.

market rent. The rent that could be charged for property at the present time, based on demand and the number of available properties.

market value. The most probable price property would bring in an arm's-length transaction under normal conditions on the open market. See also arm's-length transaction.

master plan. The General Plan; the comprehensive, long-term land-use plan for a jurisdiction.

material fact. A fact that would be likely to affect the judgment of a person to whom it is known, such as information concerning the poor physical condition of a building that is for sale.

mechanic's lien. A statutory lien against real property in favor of persons who have performed work or furnished materials for the improvement of the property.

meridians. Imaginary lines that run north to south and intersect base lines that run east to west to form the starting point for land measurement using the rectangular survey system of land description.

metes and bounds. Method of legal description of land using distances (called *metes*) measured from a point of beginning and using natural or artificial boundaries (called *bounds*) as well as single objects (called *monuments* or *markers*) as points of reference.

minor. A person younger than 18 years of age.

mobile home. See **manufactured home.**

mobile-home park. Any area or tract of land where two or more mobile-home lots are rented or leased or held out for rent or lease.

monument. See **metes and bounds.**

mortgage. A legal instrument by which property is pledged by a borrower, the *mortgagor*, as security for the payment of a debt or an obligation owed to a lender, the *mortgagee*.

mortgage insurance. Private mortgage insurance, required by lenders when mortgage indebtedness exceeds 80 percent of property value; also refers to a term life insurance policy that may be purchased by a borrower in an amount equal to the remaining mortgage indebtedness.

mortgage loan disclosure statement. The statement on a form approved by the Real Estate Commissioner that is required by law to be furnished by a mortgage loan broker to the prospective borrower of a loan of a statutorily prescribed amount before the borrower becomes obligated to complete the loan.

mortgage revenue bonds. Method of financing community redevelopment projects through issuance of bonds that are repaid by property assessments.

multiple-listing clause. Clause in a listing agreement, usually part of an exclusive authorization and right-to-sell listing, taken by a member of a multiple-listing service (MLS), providing that the property will be made available through the MLS, in accordance with the MLS rules.

multiple-listing service (MLS). An organization of real estate agents providing for a pooling of listings and the sharing of commissions on transactions involving more than one agent.

narrative appraisal report. The longest and most thorough appraisal report, containing a summary of all factual materials, techniques, and appraisal methods used in setting forth the appraiser's conclusion of value.

negative declaration. Statement that a proposed property use is not expected to have a significant impact on the environment and therefore does not require preparation of an environmental impact report.

negotiable instrument. An instrument, such as a promissory note, that is capable of being assigned or transferred in the ordinary course of business.

net listing. A listing agreement providing that the agent may retain as compensation for his or her services all sums received over and above a net price to the owner.

net, net, net lease. See **triple net lease.**

net operating income. Profit; the money remaining after expenses are deducted from income.

nominal rate. The stated interest rate of a loan before taking into account loan fees, points, and other costs that make up the annual percentage rate (APR).

nonconforming use. A property use that is not allowed by the current zoning ordinance.

nonexclusive listing. See **open listing.**

notice. Knowledge of a fact; *actual notice* is express or implied knowledge of a fact; *constructive notice* is knowledge of a fact that is imputed to a person by law because of the person's actual notice of circumstances and the inquiry that a prudent person would have been expected to make; *legal notice* is information required to be given by law.

novation. The substitution or exchange of a new obligation or contract for an old one by mutual agreement of the parties.

null and void. Of no legal validity or effect.

observed condition method. Breakdown method; depreciation computed by estimating the loss in value caused by every item of depreciation, whether curable or incurable.

offeree. The party to whom an offer is made.

offeror. The party who makes an offer.

open listing. Nonexclusive listing; the nonexclusive right to secure a purchaser, given by a property owner to a real estate agent; more than one agent may be given such authorization, and only the first to procure a ready, willing, and able buyer—or an offer acceptable to the seller—will be entitled to compensation.

opinion of title. An attorney's written evaluation of the condition of the title to a parcel of land after examination of the abstract of title.

option. A right given for a consideration to purchase or lease property on specified terms within a specified time, with no obligation on the part of the person receiving the right to exercise it.

ordinance. Law established by the governing body of a municipal or county jurisdiction.

ordinary income. Income that does not qualify for capital gains treatment.

ostensible agency. Holding out an agency relationship on which another relies.

overriding trust deed. See **wraparound mortgage or trust deed.**

ownership in severalty. Separate ownership; ownership of property by one person only.

parcel map. Map that shows all property boundaries within a subdivision.

partition action. Court proceeding by which co-owners may force a division of the property or its sale, with co-owners reimbursed for their individual shares.

partnership. See **general partnership.**

percentage lease. Provides for rent as a percentage of the tenant's gross income, usually with a minimum base amount; the percentage may decrease as the tenant's income increases.

periodic tenancy. See **estate from period to period.**

personal property. All property that is not real property.

physical deterioration. Loss in value brought about by wear and tear, disintegration, use, and action of the elements.

plaintiff. The person who sues in a court action.

planned development. See **planned unit development.**

planned unit development (PUD). A land-use design that provides intensive utilization of the land through a combination of private and common areas with prearranged sharing of responsibilities for the common areas; individual lots are owned in fee with joint ownership of open areas; primarily residential but may include commercial and/or industrial uses.

planning commission. An agency of local government charged with planning the development, redevelopment, or preservation of an area.

plottage. Assemblage; an appraisal term for the increased value of two or more adjoining lots when they are placed under single ownership and available for use as a larger single lot.

points. One point represents one percentage point of a loan amount; may be charged by lenders at the time of loan funding to increase the loan's effective interest rate.

police power. The right of government to enact laws and enforce them to benefit the public health, safety, and general welfare.

potential gross income. The maximum income that property is capable of producing.

power of attorney. A written instrument authorizing an agent to act in the capacity of the principal; a *general power of attorney* provides authority to carry out all of the business dealings of the principal; a *special power of attorney* provides authority to carry out a specific act or acts.

power of sale. The power that may be given by a promissory note to a trustee, a mortgagee, or another lienholder to sell secured property without judicial proceedings if the borrower defaults.

preliminary report. Title company's initial review of the status of a property's title; i.e., the existence of liens or other encumbrances that could affect its marketability.

primary mortgage market. Composed of lenders that deal directly with borrowers. See also **secondary mortgage market.**

prime rate. Interest rate banks charge their most favorably rated commercial borrowers.

principal. The employer of an agent; one of the parties to a transaction; the amount of money borrowed.

private mortgage insurance (PMI). Mortgage guaranty insurance available to conventional lenders on the high-risk portion of a loan, with payment included in the borrower's loan installments.

probate. Court proceeding by which the property of a decedent is distributed according to the decedent's will or, if the decedent died intestate (without a will), according to the state law of intestate succession.

procuring cause. The cause originating a series of events that lead directly to the intended objective; in a real estate transaction the procuring cause is the real estate agent who first procures a ready, willing, and able buyer.

progression, principle of. The worth of a less-valuable building tends to be enhanced by proximity to buildings of greater value.

promissory note. A written promise to repay a loan under stipulated terms; establishes personal liability for payment by the person making the note.

property management. A branch of the real estate business involving the marketing, operation, maintenance, and other day-to-day requirements of rental properties by an individual or a firm acting as agent of the owner.

proration. Adjustment of interest, taxes, insurance, and other costs of property ownership on a pro rata basis as of the closing or agreed-on date; usually apportions those costs based on seller's and buyer's respective periods of ownership.

public report. Real Estate Commissioner's report on a subdivision, including plans for improvements.

puffing. Exaggerated comments or opinions that paint an overly optimistic picture of property attributes; may lead to a claim of misrepresentation.

purchase-money mortgage or trust deed. A trust deed or mortgage given as part or all of the purchase consideration for real property.

quantity survey method. Way of estimating building reproduction cost by making a thorough itemization of all construction costs, both direct (material and labor) and indirect (permits, overhead, profit), then totaling those costs.

quiet title. See **action to quiet title.**

quitclaim deed. A deed that conveys any interest the grantor may have in the property at the time of the execution of the deed, without any warranty of title or interest.

ranges. In the rectangular survey system of land description, townships running east and west of a meridian.

ratification. The adoption or approval of an act by the person on whose behalf it was performed, as when a principal ratifies conduct of an agent that was not previously authorized.

ready, willing, and able buyer. A buyer who wants and is prepared to purchase property, including being able to finance the purchase, at the agreed-on price and terms.

real estate. Real property; land; includes the surface of the earth, the substances beneath the surface, the airspace above the surface, fixtures, and anything incidental or appurtenant to the land.

real estate board. A local organization whose members consist primarily of real estate brokers and salespeople.

real estate broker. A person employed for a fee by another to carry on any of the activities listed in the Real Estate Law definition of a broker.

Real Estate Education and Research Fund. California fund financed by a fixed portion of real estate license fees, designed to encourage research in land use and real estate development.

real estate investment trust (REIT). Way for investors to pool funds for investments in real estate and mortgages, with profits taxed to individual investors, rather than the corporation.

real estate salesperson. A person licensed under the provisions of the Real Estate Law to act under the control and supervision of a real estate broker in carrying on any of the activities listed in the license law.

real estate syndicate. An organization of real estate investors, typically in the form of a limited partnership.

real property. See **real estate**.

reassessment event. Sale or other transaction, such as addition of improvements, that triggers a revaluation of property for tax purposes.

reconciliation. In appraising, the final step, in which the estimates of value reached by each of the three appraisal approaches (sales comparison, cost, and income capitalization) are weighed in light of the type of property being appraised, the purpose of the appraisal, and other factors, to arrive at a final conclusion of value.

reconveyance deed. Instrument by which the trustee returns title to the trustor after the debt underlying a deed of trust is paid.

Recovery Account. State fund financed by real estate license fees and intended to help compensate victims of real estate licensee fraud, misrepresentation, deceit, or conversion of trust funds, when a court-ordered judgment cannot be collected.

recovery property. Property that can be depreciated for income tax purposes, with the cost of the property deducted from income over a stated period.

rectangular survey system. Section and township system; U.S. government survey system; method of legal description of land using areas called *townships* measured from meridians and baselines.

redlining. An illegal lending policy of denying real estate loans on properties in certain areas because of alleged higher lending risks, without due consideration of the individual loan applicant.

reformation. An action to correct a mistake in a contract, deed, or another document.

regression, principle of. A building's value will decline if the buildings around it have a lower value.

release. Removal of part of a contract obligation, for consideration, by the party to whom the obligation is owed; removal of part of a property from a lien on payment of part of the debt owed.

reliction. The increase of a landowner's property by the receding of an adjacent body of water.

remainder. The right of future possession and use that will go to someone other than the grantor upon termination of a life estate.

renegotiable rate mortgage. A financing instrument in which the interest rate is adjusted after an agreed-to period following origination, such as three or five years.

rent. The consideration paid for possession and use of leased property.

rent control. A regulation imposed by a local governing body as a means of protecting tenants from relatively high rent increases over the occupancy period of a lease.

repair and deduct. Tenant's remedy when landlord is on notice of and fails to make necessary repairs to leased premises.

replacement cost. The cost of a new building using modern construction techniques, design, and materials but having the same utility as the subject property.

reproduction cost. The cost of a new building of exactly the same design and materials as the subject property.

rescission. The cancellation of a contract and restoration of the parties to the same position they held before the contract was formed.

resident apartment manager. Apartment manager who resides in one of the units; required of every California apartment building having at least 16 units.

restraint on alienation. An illegal condition that would prohibit a property owner from transferring title to real estate.

restricted license. Real estate license on which one or more conditions are imposed by the Real Estate Commissioner as the result of a disciplinary action.

restriction. A limitation on the use of real property; public restrictions imposed by government include zoning ordinances; private restrictions imposed by deed may require the grantee to do or refrain from doing something. See also **CC&Rs.**

reverse annuity mortgage. Finance instrument that creates an increasing amount of debt secured by the borrower's residence, based on the amount paid out to the borrower, typically monthly.

reversion. The right of future possession and use retained by the grantor of a life estate.

rezoning. Change in the land use designation of an area.

right of appropriation. Right of government to take, impound, or divert water flowing on the public domain from its natural course for some beneficial purpose.

right of entry. Right of the landlord to enter leased premises in certain circumstances.

right of survivorship. The right of surviving cotenants to share equally in the interest of a deceased cotenant; the last surviving cotenant is sole owner of the property.

riparian rights. The right of a landowner whose property borders a lake, river, or stream to the use and enjoyment of the water adjacent to or flowing over the property, provided the use does not injure other riparian landowners.

safety clause. Provision that protects a listing broker's commission in the event that property is sold within a stated period to someone who was first brought to the property during the term of the listing.

sale-leaseback. A transaction in which at the time of sale the seller retains occupancy by concurrently agreeing to lease the property from the purchaser.

sales comparison approach. Market comparison approach; market data approach; appraisal method in which the sales prices of properties that are comparable in construction and location to the subject property are analyzed and adjusted to reflect differences between the comparables and the subject.

sales contract. Land contract; installment sales contract; a contract used in a sale of real property whereby the seller retains title to the property until all or a prescribed part of the purchase price has been paid, but no earlier than one year from the date of possession.

salvage value. In computing depreciation for tax purposes under all but the declining balance method, the reasonably anticipated fair market value of the property at the end of its useful life.

sandwich lease. A leasehold interest between the primary lease and the operating lease.

satisfaction. Discharge of an obligation before the end of its term by payment of the total debt owed.

secondary financing. A loan secured by a second (or subsequent) mortgage or trust deed on real property.

secondary mortgage market. Investment opportunities involving real property securities, other than direct loans from lender to borrower; loans may be bought, sold, or pooled to form the basis for mortgage-backed securities.

section. A standard land area of one mile square, containing 640 acres, used in the rectangular survey system of land description.

section and township system. See **rectangular survey system.**

security deposit. An amount paid at the start of a lease term and retained by the landlord until the tenant vacates the premises, all or part of which may be kept by the landlord at that time to cover costs of any default in rent payments or reasonable costs of repairs or cleaning necessitated by the tenant's use of the premises.

security instrument. A written document executed by a debtor by which the described property is made security for the underlying debt.

seismic hazards zone. Area specified by the California Department of Geology as being at high risk of severe earth movement.

separate property. Property owned by a married person other than community property, including property owned before marriage, property acquired by gift or inheritance, income from separate property, and property acquired with the proceeds of separate property.

servient tenement. See easement.

set-back ordinance. An ordinance requiring improvements built on property to be a specified distance from the property line, street, or curb.

settlement statement. HUD-1; document provided to buyer and seller at closing that indicates all of the income and expenses of the transaction.

severalty, ownership in. See ownership in severalty.

shared equity mortgage. A financing instrument that provides for the lender to share in the property's appreciation.

sheriff's deed. Deed given to the purchaser at a court-ordered sale to satisfy a judgment, without warranties.

short rate. Increased premium charged by insurance company upon early cancellation of policy to compensate insurer for the fact that the original rate was calculated on the full term of the policy.

simple interest. Interest computed on the principal amount of a loan only. See also compound interest.

single agency. Representation of only one party to a transaction; e.g., a seller's agent or buyer's agent.

sinking fund. Fund set aside from the income from property that, with accrued interest, eventually will pay for replacement of the improvements.

sole proprietor. Only owner of a business.

special assessment. Appropriation in the form of a tax on property that is enhanced by the addition or renovation of improvements, such as a light-rail line.

special limitation. A limiting condition specified in a transfer of fee simple ownership that, if not complied with, will immediately and automatically extinguish the estate and return title to the grantor.

special studies zone. One of the areas, typically within a quarter-mile or more of an active earthquake fault, requiring a geologic report for any new project involving improvements or structures initiated after May 4, 1975; the report may be waived by city or county if the state geologist approves.

special warranty deed. A deed in which the grantor warrants or guarantees the title only against defects arising during the grantor's ownership of the property and not against defects existing before the time of the grantor's ownership.

specific performance. An action to compel a breaching party to adhere to a contract obligation, such as an action to compel the sale of land as an alternative to money damages.

specific plan. Formulated after adoption of a general plan by a city or county to give further details of community development, including projected population density and building construction requirements.

square-foot method. Way of finding reproduction cost by multiplying the current cost per square foot of a comparable building by the number of square feet in the subject building.

standard parallels. See correction lines.

standard subdivision. Area of land divided into parcels intended for separate ownership, with no common (shared) ownership by all of the owners of any of the land.

standby commitment. Mortgage banker's promise, for which builder pays a standby fee, to make loans available to prospective purchasers on stated terms.

Statute of Frauds. A state law requiring certain contracts to be in writing and signed before they will be enforceable, such as a contract for the sale of real estate.

Statute of Limitations. Law that stipulates the specific time period during which a legal action must be brought following the act that gives rise to it.

statutory warranty deed. A short-term warranty deed that warrants by inference that the seller is the undisputed owner, has the right to convey the property, and will defend the title if necessary; if the seller does not do so, the new owner can defend against said claims and sue the former owner.

steering. The illegal act of directing prospective homebuyers to or from a particular residential area on the basis of the homebuyer's race or national origin.

stock cooperative. A form of subdivision, typically of an apartment building, in which each owner in the stock cooperative is a shareholder in a corporation that holds title to the property, each shareholder being entitled to use, rent, or sell a specific apartment unit. See also **limited equity housing cooperative.**

straight-line method. Depreciation computed at a constant rate over the estimated useful life of the improvement.

straight note. A note in which a borrower repays the principal in a lump sum at maturity, with interest due in installments or at maturity.

subdivision. The division of real property into separate parcels or lots for the purpose of sale, lease, or financing.

subdivision map. Document showing division of land into two or more parcels, required before subdivision approval.

subdivision public report. Issued by the Real Estate Commissioner after a subdivision developer has met the requirements of the Subdivided Lands Law; provides details of the project and financing, and a copy must be given to all prospective purchasers.

subject to. When a grantee takes title to real property "subject to" a mortgage or trust deed, the grantee is not responsible to the holder of the promissory note for the payment of the amount due, and the original maker of the note retains primary responsibility for the underlying debt.

sublease. A lease given by a lessee (tenant).

subordination agreement. An agreement by the holder of an encumbrance against real property to permit that claim to take an inferior position to other encumbrances against the property.

substitution, principle of. Market value tends to be set by the present or recent cost of acquiring an equally desirable and valuable property, comparable in construction and/or utility.

supply and demand, principle of. Takes into account the effect on market value of the relationship between the number of properties on the market at a given time and the number of potential buyers.

survey. The process by which a parcel of land is measured and its area determined.

syndicate, real estate. See **real estate syndicate.**

tack. Adding together successive periods of adverse possession.

take-out loan. The loan arranged by the owner or builder/developer for a buyer; the permanent financing that pays off and replaces the interim loan used during construction.

tax deed. Deed issued by the county tax collector when property is sold at public auction because of nonpayment of taxes.

tax increment funding. Payments on bonds through collection of increased taxes on improvements financed by the bonds.

taxable gross income. Income from all sources, less certain payments, such as contributions to a qualified retirement plan.

tenancy in common. Co-ownership of property in equal or unequal shares by two or more persons, each holding an undivided interest without right of survivorship.

tenancy in partnership. Ownership by two or more persons, acting as partners, of property held for partnership purposes.

tenant. Lessee under a lease; one who has the legal right to possession and use of property belonging to another.

tender. An offer to perform a contracted obligation.

tentative subdivision map. The initial or tentative map required of subdividers by the Subdivision Map Act, submitted to the local planning commission, which notes its approval or disapproval; a final map embodying any changes requested by the planning commission also must be submitted.

testator. A person who makes a will.

tiers. In the rectangular survey system of land description, townships running north and south of a baseline.

time-share estate. A right of occupancy in a time-share project (subdivision) coupled with an estate in the real property.

time-share project. A form of subdivision of real property into rights to the recurrent, exclusive use or occupancy of a lot or unit of the property on an annual or other periodic basis, for a specified period of time.

time-share use. A license or contractual or membership right of occupancy in a time-share project that is not coupled with an estate in the real property.

title insurance. Insurance to protect a real property owner or lender up to a specified amount against certain types of loss affecting title or marketability.

tort. Any wrongful act, other than a breach of contract, for which a civil action may be brought by the person wronged.

township. A standard land area of six miles square, divided into 36 sections of one mile square each, used in the rectangular survey system of land description.

trade fixtures. Articles of personal property that are attached by a business tenant to real property that are necessary to the carrying on of a trade and are removable by the tenant.

triple net lease. Guarantees a specified net income to the landlord, with the tenant paying that amount plus all operating and other property expenses, such as taxes, assessments, and insurance.

trust account. An account separate from a broker's own funds (business and personal) in which the broker is required by law to deposit all funds collected for clients before disbursement.

trust deed. A deed issued by a borrower of funds (the trustor) conveying title to a trustee on behalf of a lender, the beneficiary of the trust; the trust deed authorizes the trustee to sell the property to pay the remaining indebtedness to the beneficiary if the trustor defaults on the underlying obligation.

trustee. One who holds property conveyed by a trustor on behalf of (in trust for) the beneficiary, to secure the performance of an obligation.

trustee in bankruptcy. See **bankruptcy.**

trustee's deed. Deed given to the purchaser at a foreclosure sale by the trustee acting under a deed of trust.

trustor. One who conveys property to a trustee to hold on behalf of (in trust for) a beneficiary to secure the performance of an obligation; borrower under a deed of trust.

undivided interest subdivision. An area of land divided into parcels where each owner is a tenant in common with all other owners; for example, a campground with shared facilities.

undue influence. Use of a fiduciary or confidential relationship to obtain a fraudulent or an unfair advantage over another's weakness of mind, distress, or necessity.

Uniform Commercial Code. Establishes a unified and comprehensive method for regulation of security transactions in personal property.

unit-in-place method. Way of estimating building reproduction cost by adding the construction cost per unit of measure of each of the component parts of the subject property; each unit cost includes material, labor, overhead, and builder's profit.

unlawful detainer. Legal action that may be brought to evict a tenant who is in unlawful possession of leased premises.

untenantable. Property lacking one or more necessary utilities, such as water, or in such poor condition that it falls below minimum property standards; uninhabitable.

URL. Uniform resource locator, the address of a site on the World Wide Web, such as *www.dre.ca.gov.*

useful life. The period of years in which a property improvement may be used for its originally intended purpose.

U.S. government survey system. See **rectangular survey system.**

usury. The charging of a rate of interest on a loan that is greater than the rate permitted by law.

vacancy decontrol. See **rent control.**

vacancy factor. The percentage of a building's space that is unrented over a given period.

value in exchange. The value of property expressed as the kind and amount of other property that would be acceptable in a transfer of ownership.

value in use. The subjective value of property to its present owner, as opposed to market value, which should be objective.

void. To have no force or effect; that which is unenforceable.

voidable. That which can be adjudged void but is not void unless action is taken to make it so.

waiver. The giving up of a right or privilege voluntarily.

warranties, implied. See **implied warranties.**

warranty deed. A deed that expressly warrants that the grantor has good title; the grantor thus agrees to defend the premises against the lawful claims of third persons.

warranty of habitability. Legally implied obligation of a landlord to meet minimal housing and building standards.

will. A written, legal declaration of a person called a *testator*, expressing the testator's desires for the disposition of his or her property after death.

World Wide Web. Interconnected computer sites accessed by modem.

wraparound mortgage or trust deed. Overriding or all-inclusive trust deed; a financing device in which a lender assumes payments on an existing debt and takes from the borrower a junior lien with a face value in an amount equal to the amount outstanding on the old instrument and the additional amount of money borrowed.

writ of execution. A court order directing the sheriff or another officer to satisfy a money judgment out of the debtor's property, including real estate not exempt from execution.

writ of possession. Order issued by the court directing the sheriff or marshal to take all legal steps necessary to remove the occupant(s) from the specified premises.

yield. Profit; return; the interest earned by an investor on an investment or by a bank on the money it has loaned.

zones. Defined land areas with designated land uses and building specifications.

zoning. An act of city or county government specifying the possible uses of property in a particular area.

zoning ordinances. Local laws, regulations, and codes requiring compliance with designated land uses.

zoning variance. An exception to a requirement of a zoning ordinance to permit a use of the land that is reasonable in light of neighboring land uses.

ANSWER KEY

Chapter 1
The Business of Real Estate

Exercise 1-1, Page 6
No. The broker cannot delegate primary responsibility for all brokerage activities, which must be lawfully authorized.

Exercise 1-2, Page 25
Salesperson Sally has, arguably, engaged in a dishonest business practice that could result in suspension or revocation of her real estate license. Broker Bob should have reviewed the newsletter before allowing Sally to print and distribute it, particularly because she is a new, inexperienced salesperson. Broker Bob thus shares in Sally's conduct.

Achievement Examination 1, Page 32

1. b	6. c	11. d	16. d
2. b	7. b	12. d	17. d
3. a	8. c	13. b	18. c
4. d	9. d	14. c	19. d
5. a	10. d	15. d	20. a

Chapter 2
The Nature of Real Property

Exercise 2-1, Page 45
A house is a fixture because it is permanently attached to land.

A room air conditioner is personal property if it is not installed in such a way that there is an alteration to the building.

A motor home is personal property because it is intended to be readily moved and is not attached to land.

A space heater that is a free-standing appliance is personal property. A wall-mounted space heater is a fixture.

A brick patio is a fixture because it is permanently attached.

A fireplace is a fixture.

Patio furnishings are personal property because they are not attached to the land.

Wall-to-wall carpeting is a fixture because it is attached to a building in such a way that it cannot be readily removed.

A wood deck on piers sunk into the ground is a fixture.

A room-size rug is personal property because it is not attached.

A hot tub may or may not be a fixture, depending on its installation. A hot tub built into the ground or a deck is a fixture, but a portable hot tub requiring no physical alteration of land or building in order to be installed is personal property.

A chandelier is a fixture, for it is a permanent attachment.

Achievement Examination 2, Page 57

1. c	6. d	11. d	16. a
2. c	7. a	12. a	17. d
3. d	8. b	13. a	18. c
4. a	9. b	14. c	19. c
5. c	10. b	15. d	20. b

Chapter 3
Ownership of Real Property

Exercise 3-1, Page 62
1. life estate
2. fee simple estate subject to a condition subsequent
3. fee simple estate subject to a condition subsequent
4. estate of tenancy
5. Simon has a life estate. Yvonne has a remainder. If Simon dies before Annette, his heirs acquire the life estate until Annette's death.

Exercise 3-2, Page 68
1. joint tenancy
2. community property
3. tenancy in common
4. tenancy in partnership
5. separate property held in sole ownership

Exercise 3-3, Page 72
1. corporation
2. sole proprietorship
3. syndicate held as a limited partnership
4. trust

Achievement Examination 3, Page 75
1. a	6. a	11. d	16. d
2. c	7. c	12. c	17. a
3. c	8. b	13. b	18. a
4. d	9. d	14. d	19. c
5. d	10. a	15. b	20. c

Chapter 4
Transferring Real Estate

Exercise 4-1, Page 88
1. Helen owns the condominium as separate property.
2. George and Helen own the house as community property.
3. Yes, by the power of eminent domain.
4. Perhaps not. George and Helen are entitled to the fair market value of their home, which may have appreciated from its initial purchase price.

5. Yes. Community property may be willed by its owner.
6. No, because the "squatters" have perfected title to the "back 40" after five years of adverse possession.
7. Tim can bring a foreclosure action to force the sale of the property.
8. Henry died intestate. The law of intestate succession will be enforced through the legal process known as probate.
9. The other 70 feet of the property were lost in the flood by a process called avulsion.

Exercise 4-2, Page 90
1. No. No valid deed can be created and title conveyed, unless and until the grantor signs the deed.
2. Aunt Nellie still owns the condo, for she was incapable of making a valid deed.
3. There has been no conveyance. A deed must be in writing.
4. Diego has a problem. Because the property description is not specific enough, a valid deed has not been created.
5. Perhaps, but title to the estate will pass through Uncle Anthony's will, if he has one, or by the laws of intestate succession, and not by the deed he prepared. The deed is invalid because it never was delivered to the grantee.

Exercise 4-3, Page 96
1. grant deed
2. quitclaim deed
3. trust deed
4. gift deed or grant deed
5. reconveyance deed
6. sheriff's deed

Achievement Examination 4, Page 99
1. b	6. c	11. c	16. c
2. a	7. d	12. b	17. a
3. b	8. a	13. a	18. b
4. d	9. c	14. d	19. b
5. a	10. d	15. b	20. c

Chapter 5
Encumbrances

Exercise 5-1, Page 106

C. L. Drake has 90 days to file a mechanic's lien claim and 90 days after that to begin a foreclosure action, if necessary. These deadlines are in effect because work was stopped 60 days ago and neither a notice of completion nor a notice of cessation was filed.

Exercise 5-2, Page 113

The power company could put up its line if it already owned an easement over Harvey's property, or if that part of Harvey's property was condemned for that purpose. Of course Harvey would have to be sent a notice of any condemnation proceeding, but it is up to Harvey to make sure that his mail is forwarded so that he receives any such notice.

The owner of the little house may have acquired an easement by prescription across Harvey's land, if he has used the new road continuously for five years and fulfilled all of the other requirements for such an easement.

Exercise 5-3, Page 117

1. Herb could make the upkeep of the property a condition of the deed he gives his grantee (the buyer). He also could impose a covenant or restriction to that effect, but the condition, covenant, or restriction would terminate when the grantee conveyed the property. Practically speaking, Herb might have a difficult time finding a buyer willing to accept such an encumbrance.

2. Mary cannot impose such a condition on her nephew's ownership of the property because it is a restraint on his free alienation of the property—that is, his right to sell it.

Exercise 5-4, Page 121

1. So long as the houseboat is their principal dwelling and place of residence, it can qualify as Harold's and Cynthia's homestead.

2. Because the equity the Potters have in their houseboat does not exceed the total amount of their mortgage balance and the $75,000 homestead exemption, creditors probably will not succeed in forcing a sale of their home.

Achievement Examination 5, Page 124

1. d	6. b	11. b	16. c
2. a	7. c	12. b	17. b
3. c	8. d	13. a	18. a
4. d	9. a	14. c	19. c
5. a	10. b	15. d	20. d

Chapter 6
The Law of Agency

Exercise 6-1, Page 136

1. There is no listing to take. Glenda has no control over the ranch, since title is held in trust for her. Even if Glenda did have title, because she is an unemancipated minor she does not have the legal capacity to enter into a contract for the sale of real estate.

2. The salespeople of ABC Real Estate are independent contractors.

3. Certainly, Sam can sign a listing agreement on behalf of his broker for any property that he feels his firm is qualified to handle. If Sam does list the Nelson property, by showing the property to the Patels he would be acting in a dual agency capacity. Sam's broker then would be an agent for both the Patels and Jim Nelson. Sam should undertake such a representation only after fully informing Jim Nelson of the existence of his agreement with the Patels, informing the Patels of his agreement with Jim Nelson, and discussing the matter with his broker.

Exercise 6-2, Page 139

a. No. There is no written agreement between the Simpsons and Broker Bonita.

b. No. There is no written agreement between the Simpsons and Broker Bonita.

c. Yes. Now there is a written document, signed by both the Simpsons and Broker Bonita, designating Broker Bonita as sales agent. Because a selling price and commission rate had been discussed earlier, unless a different arrangement was specified in the contract, the earlier terms will apply. The Simpsons have ratified Broker Bonita's conduct in bringing a prospective buyer to them.

Exercise 6-3, Page 142

1. No. Although Frank can delegate some of the responsibility of the listing agreement, he cannot turn over complete authority to someone else without the express consent of his principal. Frank's personal efforts and supervision of others in carrying out the terms of the listing agreement are what the seller bargained for, and Frank cannot transfer those responsibilities to someone else.

2. Because the offer is to be presented the next day, Frank should hold on to the check. If the offer is not accepted, he can simply return the check to the buyer. If the offer is accepted, he then can deposit the check in an escrow account. He should take precautions to safeguard the check while it is in his possession, as he could be liable for its loss.

3. No. Broker Rice has commingled his customer's funds with his own. Broker Rice is subject to sanctions by the Real Estate Commissioner. Depending on when he noticed the error, Broker Rice should have returned the check to the buyer or placed it in his trust account or an escrow depository if one already was stipulated.

Exercise 6-4, Page 161

Broker Carroll, in agreeing to act in the future for a buyer, has breached her fiduciary duty to Mrs. Meyer. At the very least she owes Mrs. Meyer the duty of full disclosure of her dealings with the buyer. She should have informed Mrs. Meyer of both her relationship with the buyer and the intent of the buyer in making an offer. By actively working against Mrs. Meyer's best interest in persuading her to accept the investor's offer, Broker Carroll may be liable for fraud.

Achievement Examination 6, Page 166

1. a	6. b	11. b	16. c
2. b	7. a	12. c	17. c
3. b	8. b	13. d	18. c
4. a	9. d	14. a	19. c
5. b	10. d	15. c	20. d

Chapter 7
Contracts

Exercise 7-1, Page 179

1. After Sally's first phone call to Clive, they do not have an agreement because they have no writing. If Clive accepts an offer that does not mention a commission for Sally, she still has no written agreement, and Clive is not obligated to pay her a commission. If the purchase offer accepted by Clive had stipulated a commission for Sally, she could have used that as the basis for her claim for a commission from Clive.

2. No, because no purchase price was specified.

3. No, because the identity of the house's designer, which would have a significant impact on the purchase price in this case, was misrepresented to him.

4. The oral lease for a term expiring more than one year from the date of agreement is unenforceable.

Exercise 7-2, Page 183

1. The Turners can ask Ted Markham to agree to rescind the contract. If he refuses, they can ask him to release them from their contract obligation on payment of some consideration, perhaps the earnest money deposit. The Turners also could refuse to go ahead with the sale, claiming impracticability of performance; if they succeed, they may be liable for damages.

2. The Wilsons can agree to rescind the contract if their deposit is returned. The Wilsons could sue for specific performance. Alternatively, they could sue for any damages they may have incurred as a result of the sale being canceled.

Exercise 7-3, Page 206

See the completed Real Estate Purchase Contract and Receipt for Deposit on pages 502–509.

Achievement Examination 7, Page 211

1. b	6. a	11. b	16. c
2. a	7. b	12. b	17. d
3. a	8. c	13. c	18. c
4. d	9. c	14. c	19. b
5. b	10. b	15. c	20. b

Chapter 8
Financing Real Estate

Exercise 8-1, Page 234

1. mortgage
2. mortgage with power of sale
3. trust deed
4. trust deed

Exercise 8-2, Page 248

You generally will find that interest rates on fixed-rate loans are higher than those initially set on adjustable-rate loans and that a longer loan term will have a higher interest rate than a shorter loan term.

Achievement Examination 8, Page 259

1. b	6. a	11. c	16. b
2. b	7. c	12. a	17. b
3. b	8. b	13. b	18. c
4. d	9. d	14. c	19. b
5. c	10. a	15. a	20. c

Chapter 9
Government-Sponsored and Other Financing

Exercise 9-1, Page 272

1. Yes, if the individual was a qualified California veteran.
2. Maximum sales price would be $339,684.
3. The borrower's initial expenditure can be lowest with a VA-guaranteed loan, which need not involve a down payment, generally does not include discount points, and has a limit on closing costs.

Exercise 9-2, Page 274

1. sale-leaseback
2. sales contract
3. purchase money mortgage
4. Cal-Vet loan

Exercise 9-3, Page 277

The secondary market for real estate mortgage loans benefits borrowers by providing lenders with a source of funds from which to make additional loans.

Achievement Examination 9, Page 279

1. a	6. c	11. c	16. c
2. b	7. d	12. c	17. c
3. a	8. a	13. c	18. c
4. c	9. b	14. d	19. d
5. b	10. c	15. b	20. d

Chapter 10
Escrow and Title Insurance

Exercise 10-1, Page 287

1. Only a real estate broker must be licensed as an escrow agent, and only if the broker serves as escrow holder in a transaction in which he or she is neither a party nor the selling or listing broker.
2. No, unless both parties agree in writing to any changes in escrow instructions. The escrow agent is bound by the latest written instructions only.
3. Tom should immediately inform both seller and buyer of what he has learned, as the mud slide damage could have a serious impact on any potential use of the land.

Exercise 10-2, Page 300

See the completed settlement statement on pages 510 and 511.

Exercise 7-3

CALIFORNIA ASSOCIATION OF REALTORS®	**CALIFORNIA** **RESIDENTIAL PURCHASE AGREEMENT** **AND JOINT ESCROW INSTRUCTIONS** For Use With Single Family Residential Property — Attached or Detached (C.A.R. Form RPA-CA, Revised 10/02)

Date ___1/11/xx___, at ___Concord_____, California.

1. **OFFER:**
   A. **THIS IS AN OFFER FROM** __Kenneth A. Plummer and Peggy M. Plummer_____ ("Buyer").
   B. **THE REAL PROPERTY TO BE ACQUIRED** is described as _____
      _All real estate at 3840 Monroe Street_____, Assessor's Parcel No. _____, situated in
      _____, County of __Contra Costa_____, California, ("Property").
   C. **THE PURCHASE PRICE** offered is ___Three hundred seventeen thousand_____
      _____ Dollars $ ___317,000____.
   D. **CLOSE OF ESCROW** shall occur on _____ (date)(or ☑ __60__ **Days** After Acceptance).
2. **FINANCE TERMS:** Obtaining the loans below **is a contingency** of this Agreement unless: **(i)** either 2K or 2L is checked below; or **(ii)** otherwise agreed in writing. Buyer shall act diligently and in good faith to obtain the designated loans. Obtaining deposit, down payment and closing costs **is not a contingency.** Buyer represents that funds will be good when deposited with Escrow Holder.
   A. **INITIAL DEPOSIT:** Buyer has given a deposit in the amount of . . . .$ _2,000.00___
      to the agent submitting the offer (or to ❑ _____), by personal check
      (or ❑ _____), made payable to __First City Title Company_____,
      which shall be held uncashed until Acceptance and then deposited within **3** business days after
      Acceptance (or ❑ _____), with
      Escrow Holder, (or ❑ into Broker's trust account).
   B. **INCREASED DEPOSIT:** Buyer shall deposit with Escrow Holder an increased deposit in the amount of . . .$ _____
      within ____ **Days** After Acceptance, or ❑ _____
   C. **FIRST LOAN IN THE AMOUNT OF** . . . .$ _253,600.00_
      (1) NEW First Deed of Trust in favor of lender, encumbering the Property, securing a note payable at
      maximum interest of _____% fixed rate, or _____% initial adjustable rate with a maximum
      interest rate of _____%, balance due in _____ years, amortized over __30___ years. Buyer
      shall pay loan fees/points not to exceed _two___ (These terms apply whether the designated loan
      is conventional, FHA or VA.) $250.__
      (2) ❑ FHA ❑ VA: (The following terms only apply to the FHA or VA loan that is checked.)
      Seller shall pay _____% discount points. Seller shall pay other fees not allowed to be paid by
      Buyer, ❑ not to exceed $_____. Seller shall pay the cost of lender required Repairs
      (including those for wood destroying pest) not otherwise provided for in this Agreement, ❑ not to
      exceed $ _____. (Actual loan amount may increase if mortgage insurance premiums,
      funding fees or closing costs are financed.)
   D. **ADDITIONAL FINANCING TERMS:** __Seller financing, (C.A.R. Form SFA); ❑secondary financing, ...$ _____
      (C.A.R. Form PAA, paragraph 4A); ❑assumed financing (C.A.R. Form PAA, paragraph 4B)
      _____
      _____
   E. **BALANCE OF PURCHASE PRICE** (not including costs of obtaining loans and other closing costs) in the amount of . . .$ _61,400.00_
      to be deposited with Escrow Holder within sufficient time to close escrow.
   F. **PURCHASE PRICE (TOTAL):** . . . .$ _____
   G. **LOAN APPLICATIONS:** Within **7 (or** ❑ _____**) Days** After Acceptance, Buyer shall provide Seller a letter from lender or mortgage loan broker stating that, based on a review of Buyer's written application and credit report, Buyer is prequalified or preapproved for the NEW loan specified in 2C above.
   H. **VERIFICATION OF DOWN PAYMENT AND CLOSING COSTS:** Buyer (or Buyer's lender or loan broker pursuant to 2G) shall, within **7 (or** ❑ _____**) Days** After Acceptance, provide Seller written verification of Buyer's down payment and closing costs.
   I. **LOAN CONTINGENCY REMOVAL: (i)** Within **17 (or** ☑ __10__**) Days** After Acceptance, Buyer shall, as specified in paragraph 14, remove the loan contingency or cancel this Agreement; **OR (ii)** (if checked) ❑ the loan contingency shall remain in effect until the designated loans are funded.
   J. **APPRAISAL CONTINGENCY AND REMOVAL:** This Agreement is **(OR,** if checked, ❑ is NOT) contingent upon the Property appraising at no less than the specified purchase price. If there is a loan contingency, at the time the loan contingency is removed (or, if checked, ❑ within **17 (or** ____**) Days** After Acceptance), Buyer shall, as specified in paragraph 14B(3), remove the appraisal contingency or cancel this Agreement. If there is no loan contingency, Buyer shall, as specified in paragraph 14B(3), remove the appraisal contingency within **17 (or** ____**) Days** After Acceptance.
   K. ❑ **NO LOAN CONTINGENCY** (If checked): Obtaining any loan in paragraphs 2C, 2D or elsewhere in this Agreement is NOT a contingency of this Agreement. If Buyer does not obtain the loan and as a result Buyer does not purchase the Property, Seller may be entitled to Buyer's deposit or other legal remedies.
   L. ❑ **ALL CASH OFFER** (If checked): No loan is needed to purchase the Property. Buyer shall, within **7 (or** ❑ ____**) Days** After Acceptance, provide Seller written verification of sufficient funds to close this transaction.
3. **CLOSING AND OCCUPANCY:**
   A. Buyer intends (or ❑ does not intend) to occupy the Property as Buyer's primary residence.
   B. **Seller-occupied or vacant property:** Occupancy shall be delivered to Buyer at _____ AM/PM, ❑ on the date of Close Of Escrow; ❑ on _____; or ❑ no later than _____ **Days** After Close Of Escrow. (C.A.R. Form PAA, paragraph 2.) If transfer of title and occupancy do not occur at the same time, Buyer and Seller are advised to: **(i)** enter into a written occupancy agreement; and **(ii)** consult with their insurance and legal advisors.

<table>
<tr><td>The copyright laws of the United States (Title 17 U.S. Code) forbid the unauthorized reproduction of this form, or any portion thereof, by photocopy machine or any other means, including facsimile or computerized formats. Copyright © 1991-2003, CALIFORNIA ASSOCIATION OF REALTORS®, INC. ALL RIGHTS RESERVED.
RPA-CA REVISED 10/02 (PAGE 1 OF 8) Print Date</td><td>Buyer's Initials (___RAP___)(___GMP___)
Seller's Initials (_____)(_____)
Reviewed by _____ Date _____ </td></tr>
</table>

CALIFORNIA RESIDENTIAL PURCHASE AGREEMENT (RPA-CA PAGE 1 OF 8)

Source: Reprinted with permission, California Association of REALTORS®. Endorsement not implied.

Exercise 7-3 (Continued)

Property Address: __3840 Monroe Street, Concord, California__   Date: __1/11/xx__

C. **Tenant-occupied property: (i) Property shall be vacant** at least **5 (or** ❑ _____ **) Days** Prior to Close Of Escrow, unless otherwise agreed in writing. **Note to Seller: If you are unable to deliver Property vacant in accordance with rent control and other applicable Law, you may be in breach of this Agreement.**

OR (ii) (if checked) ❑ **Tenant to remain in possession.** The attached addendum is incorporated into this Agreement (C.A.R. Form PAA, paragraph 3.);

OR (iii) (if checked) ❑ **This Agreement is contingent** upon Buyer and Seller entering into a written agreement regarding occupancy of the Property within the time specified in paragraph 14B(1). If no written agreement is reached within this time, either Buyer or Seller may cancel this Agreement in writing.

D. At Close Of Escrow, Seller assigns to Buyer any assignable warranty rights for items included in the sale and shall provide any available Copies of such warranties. Brokers cannot and will not determine the assignability of any warranties.

E. At Close Of Escrow, unless otherwise agreed in writing, Seller shall provide keys and/or means to operate all locks, mailboxes, security systems, alarms and garage door openers. If Property is a condominium or located in a common interest subdivision, Buyer may be required to pay a deposit to the Homeowners' Association ("HOA") to obtain keys to accessible HOA facilities.

4. ALLOCATION OF COSTS (If checked): Unless otherwise specified here, this paragraph only determines who is to pay for the report, inspection, test or service mentioned. If not specified here or elsewhere in this Agreement, the determination of who is to pay for any work recommended or identified by any such report, inspection, test or service shall be by the method specified in paragraph 14B(2).

   A. WOOD DESTROYING PEST INSPECTION:

     (1) ❑ Buyer ❑ Seller shall pay for an inspection and report for wood destroying pests and organisms ("Report") which shall be prepared by ____Pest Away, Inc._____, a registered structural pest control company. The Report shall cover the accessible areas of the main building and attached structures and, if checked: ❑detached garages and carports, ❑detached decks, ❑the following other structures or areas _____. The Report shall not include roof coverings. If Property is a condominium or located in a common interest subdivision, the Report shall include only the separate interest and any exclusive-use areas being transferred and shall not include common areas, unless otherwise agreed. Water tests of shower pans on upper level units may not be performed without consent of the owners of property below the shower.

     OR (2) ❑ **(If checked)** The attached addendum (C.A.R. Form WPA) regarding wood destroying pest inspection and allocation of cost is incorporated into this Agreement.

   B. OTHER INSPECTIONS AND REPORTS:

     (1) ❑ Buyer ❑ Seller shall pay to have septic or private sewage disposal systems inspected _____.

     (2) ❑ Buyer ❑ Seller shall pay to have domestic wells tested for water potability and productivity _____.

     (3) ❑ Buyer ❑ Seller shall pay for a natural hazard zone disclosure report prepared by _____.

     (4) ❑ Buyer ❑ Seller shall pay for the following inspection or report _____.

     (5) ❑ Buyer ❑ Seller shall pay for the following inspection or report _____.

   C. GOVERNMENT REQUIREMENTS AND RETROFIT:

     (1) ❑ Buyer ❑ Seller shall pay for smoke detector installation and/or water heater bracing, if required by Law. Prior to Close Of Escrow, Seller shall provide Buyer a written statement of compliance in accordance with state and local Law, unless exempt.

     (2) ❑ Buyer ❑ Seller shall pay the cost of compliance with any other minimum mandatory government retrofit standards, inspections and reports if required as a condition of closing escrow under any Law. _____.

   D. ESCROW AND TITLE:

     (1) ☑ Buyer ❑ Seller shall pay escrow fee _____.

       Escrow Holder shall be ___First City Title Company_____.

     (2) ❑ Buyer ☑ Seller shall pay for **owner's** title insurance policy specified in paragraph 12E _____.

       Owner's title policy to be issued by ___First City Title Company_____.

       (Buyer shall pay for any title insurance policy insuring Buyer's **lender**, unless otherwise agreed in writing.)

E. OTHER COSTS:

     (1) ☑ Buyer ❑ Seller shall pay County transfer tax or transfer fee _____.

     (2) ☑ Buyer ❑ Seller shall pay City transfer tax or transfer fee _____.

     (3) ❑ Buyer ❑ Seller shall pay HOA transfer fee _____.

     (4) ❑ Buyer ❑ Seller shall pay HOA document preparation fees _____.

     (5) ❑ Buyer ☑ Seller shall pay the cost, not to exceed $ _350.00_____, of a one-year home warranty plan, issued by ___Home Plan, Inc._____, with the following optional coverage: _None_____.

     (6) ❑ Buyer ❑ Seller shall pay for_____.

     (7) ❑ Buyer ❑ Seller shall pay for_____.

5. STATUTORY DISCLOSURES (INCLUDING LEAD-BASED PAINT HAZARD DISCLOSURES) AND CANCELLATION RIGHTS:

   A. (1) Seller shall, within the time specified in paragraph 14A, deliver to Buyer, if required by Law: **(i)** Federal Lead-Based Paint Disclosures and pamphlet ("Lead Disclosures"); and **(ii)** disclosures or notices required by sections 1102 et. seq. and 1103 et. seq. of the California Civil Code ("Statutory Disclosures"). Statutory Disclosures include, but are not limited to, a Real Estate Transfer Disclosure Statement ("TDS"), Natural Hazard Disclosure Statement ("NHD"), notice or actual knowledge of release of illegal controlled substance, notice of special tax and/or assessments (or, if allowed, substantially equivalent notice regarding the Mello-Roos Community Facilities Act and Improvement Bond Act of 1915) and, if Seller has actual knowledge, an industrial use and military ordnance location disclosure (C.A.R. Form SSD).

     (2) Buyer shall, within the time specified in paragraph 14B(1), return Signed Copies of the Statutory and Lead Disclosures to Seller.

     (3) In the event Seller, prior to Close Of Escrow, becomes aware of adverse conditions materially affecting the Property, or any material inaccuracy in disclosures, information or representations previously provided to Buyer of which Buyer is otherwise unaware, Seller shall promptly provide a subsequent or amended disclosure or notice, in writing, covering those items. **However, a subsequent or amended disclosure shall not be required for conditions and material inaccuracies disclosed in reports ordered and paid for by Buyer.**

Buyer's Initials (___RAP___)(___GMP___)
Seller's Initials (_____)(_____)

RPA-CA REVISED 10/02 (PAGE 2 OF 8)

Reviewed by _____ Date _____

EQUAL HOUSING OPPORTUNITY

CALIFORNIA RESIDENTIAL PURCHASE AGREEMENT (RPA-CA PAGE 2 OF 8)

Source: Reprinted with permission, California Association of REALTORS®. Endorsement not implied.

Exercise 7-3 (Continued)

Property Address: __3840 Monroe Street, Concord, California__ Date: __1/11/xx__

(4) If any disclosure or notice specified in 5A(1), or subsequent or amended disclosure or notice is delivered to Buyer after the offer is Signed, Buyer shall have the right to cancel this Agreement within **3 Days** After delivery in person, or **5 Days** After delivery by deposit in the mail, by giving written notice of cancellation to Seller or Seller's agent. (Lead Disclosures sent by mail must be sent certified mail or better.)

(5) Note to Buyer and Seller: Waiver of Statutory and Lead Disclosures is prohibited by Law.

B. NATURAL AND ENVIRONMENTAL HAZARDS: Within the time specified in paragraph 14A, Seller shall, if required by Law: **(i)** deliver to Buyer earthquake guides (and questionnaire) and environmental hazards booklet; **(ii)** even if exempt from the obligation to provide a NHD, disclose if the Property is located in a Special Flood Hazard Area; Potential Flooding (Inundation) Area; Very High Fire Hazard Zone; State Fire Responsibility Area; Earthquake Fault Zone; Seismic Hazard Zone; and **(iii)** disclose any other zone as required by Law and provide any other information required for those zones.

C. DATA BASE DISCLOSURE: NOTICE: The California Department of Justice, sheriff's departments, police departments serving jurisdictions of 200,000 or more and many other local law enforcement authorities maintain for public access a data base of the locations of persons required to register pursuant to paragraph (1) of subdivision (a) of Section 290.4 of the Penal Code. The data base is updated on a quarterly basis and a source of information about the presence of these individuals in any neighborhood. The Department of Justice also maintains a Sex Offender Identification Line through which inquiries about individuals may be made. This is a "900" telephone service. Callers must have specific information about individuals they are checking. Information regarding neighborhoods is not available through the "900" telephone service.

6. CONDOMINIUM/PLANNED UNIT DEVELOPMENT DISCLOSURES:

A. SELLER HAS: 7 (or ☐ _____) Days After Acceptance to disclose to Buyer whether the Property is a condominium, or is located in a planned unit development or other common interest subdivision (C.A.R. Form SSD).

B. If the Property is a condominium or is located in a planned unit development or other common interest subdivision, Seller has **3 (or ☐ _____) Days** After Acceptance to request from the HOA (C.A.R. Form HOA): **(i)** Copies of any documents required by Law; **(ii)** disclosure of any pending or anticipated claim or litigation by or against the HOA; **(iii)** a statement containing the location and number of designated parking and storage spaces; **(iv)** Copies of the most recent 12 months of HOA minutes for regular and special meetings; and **(v)** the names and contact information of all HOAs governing the Property (collectively, "CI Disclosures"). Seller shall itemize and deliver to Buyer all CI Disclosures received from the HOA and any CI Disclosures in Seller's possession. Buyer's approval of CI Disclosures is a contingency of this Agreement as specified in paragraph 14B(3).

7. CONDITIONS AFFECTING PROPERTY:

A. Unless otherwise agreed: **(i) the Property is sold (a) in its PRESENT physical condition as of the date of Acceptance and (b) subject to Buyer's Investigation rights; (ii)** the Property, including pool, spa, landscaping and grounds, is to be maintained in substantially the same condition as on the date of Acceptance; and **(iii)** all debris and personal property not included in the sale shall be removed by Close Of Escrow.

B. SELLER SHALL, within the time specified in paragraph 14A, **DISCLOSE KNOWN MATERIAL FACTS AND DEFECTS affecting the Property, including known insurance claims within the past five years, AND MAKE OTHER DISCLOSURES REQUIRED BY LAW (C.A.R. Form SSD).**

C. NOTE TO BUYER: You are strongly advised to conduct investigations of the entire Property in order to determine its present condition since Seller may not be aware of all defects affecting the Property or other factors that you consider important. Property improvements may not be built according to code, in compliance with current Law, or have had permits issued.

D. NOTE TO SELLER: Buyer has the right to inspect the Property and, as specified in paragraph 14B, based upon information discovered in those inspections: **(i)** cancel this Agreement; or **(ii)** request that you make Repairs or take other action.

8. ITEMS INCLUDED AND EXCLUDED:

A. NOTE TO BUYER AND SELLER: Items listed as included or excluded in the MLS, flyers or marketing materials are **not** included in the purchase price or excluded from the sale unless specified in 8B or C.

B. ITEMS INCLUDED IN SALE:

(1) All EXISTING fixtures and fittings that are attached to the Property;

(2) Existing electrical, mechanical, lighting, plumbing and heating fixtures, ceiling fans, fireplace inserts, gas logs and grates, solar systems, built-in appliances, window and door screens, awnings, shutters, window coverings, attached floor coverings, television antennas, satellite dishes, private integrated telephone systems, air coolers/conditioners, pool/spa equipment, garage door openers/remote controls, mailbox, in-ground landscaping, trees/shrubs, water softeners, water purifiers, security systems/alarms; and

(3) The following items: __None__

_____.

(4) Seller represents that all items included in the purchase price, unless otherwise specified, are owned by Seller.

(5) All items included shall be transferred free of liens and without Seller warranty.

C. ITEMS EXCLUDED FROM SALE: __None__

9. BUYER'S INVESTIGATION OF PROPERTY AND MATTERS AFFECTING PROPERTY:

A. Buyer's acceptance of the condition of, and any other matter affecting the Property, is a contingency of this Agreement as specified in this paragraph and paragraph 14B. Within the time specified in paragraph 14B(1), Buyer shall have the right, at Buyer's expense unless otherwise agreed, to conduct inspections, investigations, tests, surveys and other studies ("Buyer Investigations"), including, but not limited to, the right to: **(i)** inspect for lead-based paint and other lead-based paint hazards; **(ii)** inspect for wood destroying pests and organisms; **(iii)** review the registered sex offender database; **(iv)** confirm the insurability of Buyer and the Property; and **(v)** satisfy Buyer as to any matter specified in the attached Buyer's Inspection Advisory (C.A.R. Form BIA). Without Seller's prior written consent, Buyer shall neither make nor cause to be made: **(i)** invasive or destructive Buyer Investigations; or **(ii)** inspections by any governmental building or zoning inspector or government employee, unless required by Law.

B. Buyer shall complete Buyer Investigations and, as specified in paragraph 14B, remove the contingency or cancel this Agreement. Buyer shall give Seller, at no cost, complete Copies of all Buyer Investigation reports obtained by Buyer. Seller shall make the Property available for all Buyer Investigations. Seller shall have water, gas, electricity and all operable pilot lights on for Buyer's Investigations and through the date possession is made available to Buyer.

Buyer's Initials (__RAP__)(__GMP__)
Seller's Initials (_____)(_____)

RPA-CA REVISED 10/02 (PAGE 3 OF 8)

Reviewed by _____ Date _____

EQUAL HOUSING OPPORTUNITY

CALIFORNIA RESIDENTIAL PURCHASE AGREEMENT (RPA-CA PAGE 3 OF 8)

Source: Reprinted with permission, California Association of REALTORS®. Endorsement not implied.

Exercise 7-3 (Continued)

Property Address: _3840 Monroe Street, Concord, California_   Date: _1/11/xx_

10. **REPAIRS:** Repairs shall be completed prior to final verification of condition unless otherwise agreed in writing. Repairs to be performed at Seller's expense may be performed by Seller or through others, provided that the work complies with applicable Law, including governmental permit, inspection and approval requirements. Repairs shall be performed in a good, skillful manner with materials of quality and appearance comparable to existing materials. It is understood that exact restoration of appearance or cosmetic items following all Repairs may not be possible. Seller shall: **(i)** obtain receipts for Repairs performed by others; **(ii)** prepare a written statement indicating the Repairs performed by Seller and the date of such Repairs; and **(iii)** provide Copies of receipts and statements to Buyer prior to final verification of condition.

11. **BUYER INDEMNITY AND SELLER PROTECTION FOR ENTRY UPON PROPERTY:** Buyer shall: **(i)** keep the Property free and clear of liens; **(ii)** Repair all damage arising from Buyer Investigations; and **(iii)** indemnify and hold Seller harmless from all resulting liability, claims, demands, damages and costs. Buyer shall carry, or Buyer shall require anyone acting on Buyer's behalf to carry, policies of liability, workers' compensation and other applicable insurance, defending and protecting Seller from liability for any injuries to persons or property occurring during any Buyer Investigations or work done on the Property at Buyer's direction prior to Close Of Escrow. Seller is advised that certain protections may be afforded Seller by recording a "Notice of Non-responsibility" (C.A.R. Form NNR) for Buyer Investigations and work done on the Property at Buyer's direction. Buyer's obligations under this paragraph shall survive the termination of this Agreement.

12. **TITLE AND VESTING:**
    A. Within the time specified in paragraph 14, Buyer shall be provided a current preliminary (title) report, which is only an offer by the title insurer to issue a policy of title insurance and may not contain every item affecting title. Buyer's review of the preliminary report and any other matters which may affect title are a contingency of this Agreement as specified in paragraph 14B.
    B. Title is taken in its present condition subject to all encumbrances, easements, covenants, conditions, restrictions, rights and other matters, whether of record or not, as of the date of Acceptance except: **(i)** monetary liens of record unless Buyer is assuming those obligations or taking the Property subject to those obligations; and **(ii)** those matters which Seller has agreed to remove in writing.
    C. Within the time specified in paragraph 14A, Seller has a duty to disclose to Buyer all matters known to Seller affecting title, whether of record or not.
    D. At Close Of Escrow, Buyer shall receive a grant deed conveying title (or, for stock cooperative or long-term lease, an assignment of stock certificate or of Seller's leasehold interest), including oil, mineral and water rights if currently owned by Seller. Title shall vest as designated in Buyer's supplemental escrow instructions. THE MANNER OF TAKING TITLE MAY HAVE SIGNIFICANT LEGAL AND TAX CONSEQUENCES. CONSULT AN APPROPRIATE PROFESSIONAL.
    E. Buyer shall receive a CLTA/ALTA Homeowner's Policy of Title Insurance. A title company, at Buyer's request, can provide information about the availability, desirability, coverage, and cost of various title insurance coverages and endorsements. If Buyer desires title coverage other than that required by this paragraph, Buyer shall instruct Escrow Holder in writing and pay any increase in cost.

13. **SALE OF BUYER'S PROPERTY:**
    A. This Agreement is NOT contingent upon the sale of any property owned by Buyer.
    OR B. ☐ (If checked): The attached addendum (C.A.R. Form COP) regarding the contingency for the sale of property owned by Buyer is incorporated into this Agreement.

14. **TIME PERIODS; REMOVAL OF CONTINGENCIES; CANCELLATION RIGHTS: The following time periods may only be extended, altered, modified or changed by mutual written agreement. Any removal of contingencies or cancellation under this paragraph must be in writing (C.A.R. Form CR).**
    A. **SELLER HAS: 7 (or ☐ _2_) Days** After Acceptance to deliver to Buyer all reports, disclosures and information for which Seller is responsible under paragraphs 4, 5A and B, 6A, 7B and 12.
    B. **(1) BUYER HAS: 17 (or ☐ _20_) Days** After Acceptance, unless otherwise agreed in writing, to:
        (i) complete all Buyer Investigations; approve all disclosures, reports and other applicable information, which Buyer receives from Seller; and approve all matters affecting the Property (including lead-based paint and lead-based paint hazards as well as other information specified in paragraph 5 and insurability of Buyer and the Property); and
        (ii) return to Seller Signed Copies of Statutory and Lead Disclosures delivered by Seller in accordance with paragraph 5A.
        (2) Within the time specified in 14B(1), Buyer may request that Seller make repairs or take any other action regarding the Property (C.A.R. Form RR). Seller has no obligation to agree to or respond to Buyer's requests.
        (3) By the end of the time specified in 14B(1) (or 2I for loan contingency or 2J for appraisal contingency), Buyer shall, in writing, remove the applicable contingency (C.A.R. Form CR) or cancel this Agreement. However, if the following inspections, reports or disclosures are not made within the time specified in 14A, then Buyer has **5 (or ☐ _3_) Days** after receipt of any such items, or the time specified in 14B(1), whichever is later, to remove the applicable contingency or cancel this Agreement in writing: **(i)** government-mandated inspections or reports required as a condition of closing; or **(ii)** Common Interest Disclosures pursuant to paragraph 6B.
    C. **CONTINUATION OF CONTINGENCY OR CONTRACTUAL OBLIGATION; SELLER RIGHT TO CANCEL:**
        (1) Seller right to Cancel; Buyer Contingencies: Seller, after first giving Buyer a Notice to Buyer to Perform (as specified below), may cancel this Agreement in writing and authorize return of Buyer's deposit if, by the time specified in this Agreement, Buyer does not remove in writing the applicable contingency or cancel this Agreement. Once all contingencies have been removed, failure of either Buyer or Seller to close escrow on time may be a breach of this Agreement.
        (2) Continuation of Contingency: Even after the expiration of the time specified in 14B(1), Buyer retains the right to make requests to Seller, remove in writing the applicable contingency or cancel this Agreement until Seller cancels pursuant to 14C(1). Once Seller receives Buyer's written removal of all contingencies, Seller may not cancel this Agreement pursuant to 14C(1).
        (3) Seller right to Cancel; Buyer Contract Obligations: Seller, after first giving Buyer a Notice to Buyer to Perform (as specified below), may cancel this Agreement in writing and authorize return of Buyer's deposit for any of the following reasons: **(i)** if Buyer fails to deposit funds as required by 2A or 2B; **(ii)** if the funds deposited pursuant to 2A or 2B are not good when deposited; **(iii)** if Buyer fails to provide a letter as required by 2G; **(iv)** if Buyer fails to provide verification as required by 2H or 2L; **(v)** if Seller reasonably disapproves of the verification provided by 2H or 2L; **(vi)** if Buyer fails to return Statutory and Lead Disclosures as required by paragraph 5A(2); or **(vii)** if Buyer fails to sign or initial a separate liquidated damage form for an increased deposit as required by paragraph 16. **Seller is not required to give Buyer a Notice to Perform regarding Close of Escrow.**
        (4) Notice To Buyer To Perform: The Notice to Buyer to Perform (C.A.R. Form NBP) shall: **(i)** be in writing; **(ii)** be signed by Seller; and **(iii)** give Buyer at least **24 (or ☐ _____)** hours (or until the time specified in the applicable paragraph, whichever occurs last) to take the applicable action. A Notice to Buyer to Perform may not be given any earlier than **2 Days** Prior to the expiration of the applicable time for Buyer to remove a contingency or cancel this Agreement or meet a 14C(3) obligation.

Buyer's Initials (_RAP_)(_GMP_)
Seller's Initials (_____)(_____)

Reviewed by _____ Date _____

EQUAL HOUSING OPPORTUNITY

CALIFORNIA RESIDENTIAL PURCHASE AGREEMENT (RPA-CA PAGE 4 OF 8)

Source: Reprinted with permission, California Association of REALTORS®. Endorsement not implied.

Exercise 7-3 (Continued)

Property Address: 3840 Monroe Street, Concord, California   Date: 1/11/xx

D. EFFECT OF BUYER'S REMOVAL OF CONTINGENCIES : If Buyer removes, in writing, any contingency or cancellation rights, unless otherwise specified in a separate written agreement between Buyer and Seller, Buyer shall conclusively be deemed to have: **(i)** completed all Buyer Investigations, and review of reports and other applicable information and disclosures pertaining to that contingency or cancellation right; **(ii)** elected to proceed with the transaction; and **(iii)** assumed all liability, responsibility and expense for Repairs or corrections pertaining to that contingency or cancellation right, or for inability to obtain financing.

E. EFFECT OF CANCELLATION ON DEPOSITS: If Buyer or Seller gives written notice of cancellation pursuant to rights duly exercised under the terms of this Agreement, Buyer and Seller agree to Sign mutual instructions to cancel the sale and escrow and release deposits, less fees and costs, to the party entitled to the funds. Fees and costs may be payable to service providers and vendors for services and products provided during escrow. **Release of funds will require mutual Signed release instructions from Buyer and Seller, judicial decision or arbitration award. A party may be subject to a civil penalty of up to $1,000 for refusal to sign such instructions if no good faith dispute exists as to who is entitled to the deposited funds (Civil Code §1057.3).**

15. FINAL VERIFICATION OF CONDITION: Buyer shall have the right to make a final inspection of the Property within **5 (or ____2____) Days** Prior to Close Of Escrow, NOT AS A CONTINGENCY OF THE SALE, but solely to confirm: **(i)** the Property is maintained pursuant to paragraph 7A; **(ii)** Repairs have been completed as agreed; and **(iii)** Seller has complied with Seller's other obligations under this Agreement.

16. LIQUIDATED DAMAGES: If Buyer fails to complete this purchase because of Buyer's default, Seller shall retain, as liquidated damages, the deposit actually paid. If the Property is a dwelling with no more than four units, one of which Buyer intends to occupy, then the amount retained shall be no more than 3% of the purchase price. Any excess shall be returned to Buyer. Release of funds will require mutual, Signed release instructions from both Buyer and Seller, judicial decision or arbitration award.
BUYER AND SELLER SHALL SIGN A SEPARATE LIQUIDATED DAMAGES PROVISION FOR ANY INCREASED DEPOSIT. (C.A.R. FORM RID)

Buyer's Initials _RAP_ / _GMP_	Seller's Initials _____ / _____

17. DISPUTE RESOLUTION:

A. MEDIATION: Buyer and Seller agree to mediate any dispute or claim arising between them out of this Agreement, or any resulting transaction, before resorting to arbitration or court action. Paragraphs 17B(2) and (3) below apply whether or not the Arbitration provision is initialed. Mediation fees, if any, shall be divided equally among the parties involved. If, for any dispute or claim to which this paragraph applies, any party commences an action without first attempting to resolve the matter through mediation, or refuses to mediate after a request has been made, then that party shall not be entitled to recover attorney fees, even if they would otherwise be available to that party in any such action. THIS MEDIATION PROVISION APPLIES WHETHER OR NOT THE ARBITRATION PROVISION IS INITIALED.

B. ARBITRATION OF DISPUTES: (1) Buyer and Seller agree that any dispute or claim in Law or equity arising between them out of this Agreement or any resulting transaction, which is not settled through mediation, shall be decided by neutral, binding arbitration, including and subject to paragraphs 17B(2) and (3) below. The arbitrator shall be a retired judge or justice, or an attorney with at least 5 years of residential real estate Law experience, unless the parties mutually agree to a different arbitrator, who shall render an award in accordance with substantive California Law. The parties shall have the right to discovery in accordance with California Code of Civil Procedure §1283.05. In all other respects, the arbitration shall be conducted in accordance with Title 9 of Part III of the California Code of Civil Procedure. Judgment upon the award of the arbitrator(s) may be entered into any court having jurisdiction. Interpretation of this agreement to arbitrate shall be governed by the Federal Arbitration Act.

(2) EXCLUSIONS FROM MEDIATION AND ARBITRATION: The following matters are excluded from mediation and arbitration: (i) a judicial or non-judicial foreclosure or other action or proceeding to enforce a deed of trust, mortgage or installment land sale contract as defined in California Civil Code §2985; (ii) an unlawful detainer action; (iii) the filing or enforcement of a mechanic's lien; and (iv) any matter that is within the jurisdiction of a probate, small claims or bankruptcy court. The filing of a court action to enable the recording of a notice of pending action, for order of attachment, receivership, injunction, or other provisional remedies, shall not constitute a waiver of the mediation and arbitration provisions.

(3) BROKERS: Buyer and Seller agree to mediate and arbitrate disputes or claims involving either or both Brokers, consistent with 17A and B, provided either or both Brokers shall have agreed to such mediation or arbitration prior to, or within a reasonable time after, the dispute or claim is presented to Brokers. Any election by either or both Brokers to participate in mediation or arbitration shall not result in Brokers being deemed parties to the Agreement.

"NOTICE: BY INITIALING IN THE SPACE BELOW YOU ARE AGREEING TO HAVE ANY DISPUTE ARISING OUT OF THE MATTERS INCLUDED IN THE 'ARBITRATION OF DISPUTES' PROVISION DECIDED BY NEUTRAL ARBITRATION AS PROVIDED BY CALIFORNIA LAW AND YOU ARE GIVING UP ANY RIGHTS YOU MIGHT POSSESS TO HAVE THE DISPUTE LITIGATED IN A COURT OR JURY TRIAL. BY INITIALING IN THE SPACE BELOW YOU ARE GIVING UP YOUR JUDICIAL RIGHTS TO DISCOVERY AND APPEAL, UNLESS THOSE RIGHTS ARE SPECIFICALLY INCLUDED IN THE 'ARBITRATION OF DISPUTES' PROVISION. IF YOU REFUSE TO SUBMIT TO ARBITRATION AFTER AGREEING TO THIS PROVISION, YOU MAY BE COMPELLED TO ARBITRATE UNDER THE AUTHORITY OF THE CALIFORNIA CODE OF CIVIL PROCEDURE. YOUR AGREEMENT TO THIS ARBITRATION PROVISION IS VOLUNTARY."

"WE HAVE READ AND UNDERSTAND THE FOREGOING AND AGREE TO SUBMIT DISPUTES ARISING OUT OF THE MATTERS INCLUDED IN THE 'ARBITRATION OF DISPUTES' PROVISION TO NEUTRAL ARBITRATION."

Buyer's Initials _RAP_ / _GMP_	Seller's Initials _____ / _____

Buyer's Initials (_____)(_____)
Seller's Initials (_____)(_____)

Reviewed by _____ Date _____

CALIFORNIA RESIDENTIAL PURCHASE AGREEMENT (RPA-CA PAGE 5 OF 8)

Source: Reprinted with permission, California Association of REALTORS®. Endorsement not implied.

Exercise 7-3 (Continued)

Property Address: __3840 Monroe Street, Concord, California__   Date: __1/11/xx__

18. **PRORATIONS OF PROPERTY TAXES AND OTHER ITEMS:** Unless otherwise agreed in writing, the following items shall be PAID CURRENT and prorated between Buyer and Seller as of Close Of Escrow: real property taxes and assessments, interest, rents, HOA regular, special, and emergency dues and assessments imposed prior to Close Of Escrow, premiums on insurance assumed by Buyer, payments on bonds and assessments assumed by Buyer, and payments on Mello-Roos and other Special Assessment District bonds and assessments that are now a lien. The following items shall be assumed by Buyer WITHOUT CREDIT toward the purchase price: prorated payments on Mello-Roos and other Special Assessment District bonds and assessments and HOA special assessments that are now a lien but not yet due. Property will be reassessed upon change of ownership. Any supplemental tax bills shall be paid as follows: **(i)** for periods after Close Of Escrow, by Buyer; and **(ii)** for periods prior to Close Of Escrow, by Seller. TAX BILLS ISSUED AFTER CLOSE OF ESCROW SHALL BE HANDLED DIRECTLY BETWEEN BUYER AND SELLER. Prorations shall be made based on a 30-day month.
19. **WITHHOLDING TAXES:** Seller and Buyer agree to execute any instrument, affidavit, statement or instruction reasonably necessary to comply with federal (FIRPTA) and California withholding Law, if required (C.A.R. Forms AS and AB).
20. **MULTIPLE LISTING SERVICE ("MLS"):** Brokers are authorized to report to the MLS a pending sale and, upon Close Of Escrow, the terms of this transaction to be published and disseminated to persons and entities authorized to use the information on terms approved by the MLS.
21. **EQUAL HOUSING OPPORTUNITY:** The Property is sold in compliance with federal, state and local anti-discrimination Laws.
22. **ATTORNEY FEES:** In any action, proceeding, or arbitration between Buyer and Seller arising out of this Agreement, the prevailing Buyer or Seller shall be entitled to reasonable attorney fees and costs from the non-prevailing Buyer or Seller, except as provided in paragraph 17A.
23. **SELECTION OF SERVICE PROVIDERS:** If Brokers refer Buyer or Seller to persons, vendors, or service or product providers ("Providers"), Brokers do not guarantee the performance of any Providers. Buyer and Seller may select ANY Providers of their own choosing.
24. **TIME OF ESSENCE; ENTIRE CONTRACT; CHANGES:** Time is of the essence. All understandings between the parties are incorporated in this Agreement. Its terms are intended by the parties as a final, complete and exclusive expression of their Agreement with respect to its subject matter, and may not be contradicted by evidence of any prior agreement or contemporaneous oral agreement. If any provision of this Agreement is held to be ineffective or invalid, the remaining provisions will nevertheless be given full force and effect. **Neither this Agreement nor any provision in it may be extended, amended, modified, altered or changed, except in writing Signed by Buyer and Seller.**
25. **OTHER TERMS AND CONDITIONS,** including attached supplements:
    A. ✓ Buyer's Inspection Advisory (C.A.R. Form BIA)
    B. ___ Purchase Agreement Addendum (C.A.R. Form PAA paragraph numbers: _____)
    C. _____
    _____
    _____

26. **DEFINITIONS:** As used in this Agreement:
    A. **"Acceptance"** means the time the offer or final counter offer is accepted in writing by a party and is delivered to and personally received by the other party or that party's authorized agent in accordance with the terms of this offer or a final counter offer.
    B. **"Agreement"** means the terms and conditions of this accepted California Residential Purchase Agreement and any accepted counter offers and addenda.
    C. **"C.A.R. Form"** means the specific form referenced or another comparable form agreed to by the parties.
    D. **"Close Of Escrow"** means the date the grant deed, or other evidence of transfer of title, is recorded. If the scheduled close of escrow falls on a Saturday, Sunday or legal holiday, then close of escrow shall be the next business day after the scheduled close of escrow date.
    E. **"Copy"** means copy by any means including photocopy, NCR, facsimile and electronic.
    F. **"Days"** means calendar days, unless otherwise required by Law.
    G. **"Days After"** means the specified number of calendar days after the occurrence of the event specified, not counting the calendar date on which the specified event occurs, and ending at 11:59PM on the final day.
    H. **"Days Prior"** means the specified number of calendar days before the occurrence of the event specified, not counting the calendar date on which the specified event is scheduled to occur.
    I. **"Electronic Copy" or "Electronic Signature"** means, as applicable, an electronic copy or signature complying with California Law. Buyer and Seller agree that electronic means will not be used by either party to modify or alter the content or integrity of this Agreement without the knowledge and consent of the other.
    J. **"Law"** means any law, code, statute, ordinance, regulation, rule or order, which is adopted by a controlling city, county, state or federal legislative, judicial or executive body or agency.
    K. **"Notice to Buyer to Perform"** means a document (C.A.R. Form NBP), which shall be in writing and Signed by Seller and shall give Buyer at least 24 hours **(or as otherwise specified in paragraph 14C(4))** to remove a contingency or perform as applicable.
    L. **"Repairs"** means any repairs (including pest control), alterations, replacements, modifications or retrofitting of the Property provided for under this Agreement.
    M. **"Signed"** means either a handwritten or electronic signature on an original document, Copy or any counterpart.
    N. **Singular and Plural** terms each include the other, when appropriate.

Buyer's Initials (___*RAP*___)(___*GMP*___)
Seller's Initials (_____)(_____)

RPA-CA REVISED 10/02 (PAGE 6 OF 8)

Reviewed by _____ Date _____

EQUAL HOUSING OPPORTUNITY

CALIFORNIA RESIDENTIAL PURCHASE AGREEMENT (RPA-CA PAGE 6 OF 8)

Exercise 7-3 (Continued)

Property Address: __3840 Monroe Street, Concord, California_____   Date: __1/11/xx_____

27. AGENCY:
   A. DISCLOSURE: Buyer and Seller each acknowledge prior receipt of C.A.R. Form AD "Disclosure Regarding Real Estate Agency Relationships."
   B. POTENTIALLY COMPETING BUYERS AND SELLERS: Buyer and Seller each acknowledge receipt of a disclosure of the possibility of multiple representation by the Broker representing that principal. This disclosure may be part of a listing agreement, buyer-broker agreement or separate document (C.A.R. Form DA). Buyer understands that Broker representing Buyer may also represent other potential buyers, who may consider, make offers on or ultimately acquire the Property. Seller understands that Broker representing Seller may also represent other sellers with competing properties of interest to this Buyer.
   C. CONFIRMATION: The following agency relationships are hereby confirmed for this transaction:
   Listing Agent _____ABC Realty_____ (Print Firm Name) is the agent of (check one): ☐ the Seller exclusively; or ☑ both the Buyer and Seller.
   Selling Agent _____(Print Firm Name) (if not same as Listing Agent) is the agent of (check one): ☐ the Buyer exclusively; or ☐ the Seller exclusively; or ☐ both the Buyer and Seller. Real Estate Brokers are not parties to the Agreement between Buyer and Seller.

28. JOINT ESCROW INSTRUCTIONS TO ESCROW HOLDER:
   A. The following paragraphs, or applicable portions thereof, of this Agreement constitute the joint escrow instructions of Buyer and Seller to Escrow Holder, which Escrow Holder is to use along with any related counter offers and addenda, and any additional mutual instructions to close the escrow: 1, 2, 4, 12, 13B, 14E, 18, 19, 24, 25B and C, 26, 28, 29, 32A, 33 and paragraph D of the section titled Real Estate Brokers on page 8. If a Copy of the separate compensation agreement(s) provided for in paragraph 29 or 32A, or paragraph D of the section titled Real Estate Brokers on page 8 is deposited with Escrow Holder by Broker, Escrow Holder shall accept such agreement(s) and pay out from Buyer's or Seller's funds, or both, as applicable, the Broker's compensation provided for in such agreement(s). The terms and conditions of this Agreement not set forth in the specified paragraphs are additional matters for the information of Escrow Holder, but about which Escrow Holder need not be concerned. Buyer and Seller will receive Escrow Holder's general provisions directly from Escrow Holder and will execute such provisions upon Escrow Holder's request. To the extent the general provisions are inconsistent or conflict with this Agreement, the general provisions will control as to the duties and obligations of Escrow Holder only. Buyer and Seller will execute additional instructions, documents and forms provided by Escrow Holder that are reasonably necessary to close the escrow.
   B. A Copy of this Agreement shall be delivered to Escrow Holder within **3** business days after Acceptance (or ☑ __10 Calendar Days_____). Buyer and Seller authorize Escrow Holder to accept and rely on Copies and Signatures as defined in this Agreement as originals, to open escrow and for other purposes of escrow. The validity of this Agreement as between Buyer and Seller is not affected by whether or when Escrow Holder Signs this Agreement.
   C. Brokers are a party to the escrow for the sole purpose of compensation pursuant to paragraphs 29, 32A and paragraph D of the section titled Real Estate Brokers on page 8. Buyer and Seller irrevocably assign to Brokers compensation specified in paragraphs 29 and 32A, respectively, and irrevocably instruct Escrow Holder to disburse those funds to Brokers at Close Of Escrow or pursuant to any other mutually executed cancellation agreement. Compensation instructions can be amended or revoked only with the written consent of Brokers. Escrow Holder shall immediately notify Brokers: **(i)** if Buyer's initial or any additional deposit is not made pursuant to this Agreement, or is not good at time of deposit with Escrow Holder; or **(ii)** if Buyer and Seller instruct Escrow Holder to cancel escrow.
   D. A Copy of any amendment that affects any paragraph of this Agreement for which Escrow Holder is responsible shall be delivered to Escrow Holder within **2** business days after mutual execution of the amendment.

29. BROKER COMPENSATION FROM BUYER: If applicable, upon Close Of Escrow, **Buyer** agrees to pay compensation to Broker as specified in a separate written agreement between Buyer and Broker.

30. TERMS AND CONDITIONS OF OFFER:
   This is an offer to purchase the Property on the above terms and conditions. All paragraphs with spaces for initials by Buyer and Seller are incorporated in this Agreement only if initialed by all parties. If at least one but not all parties initial, a counter offer is required until agreement is reached. Seller has the right to continue to offer the Property for sale and to accept any other offer at any time prior to notification of Acceptance. Buyer has read and acknowledges receipt of a Copy of the offer and agrees to the above confirmation of agency relationships. If this offer is accepted and Buyer subsequently defaults, Buyer may be responsible for payment of Brokers' compensation. This Agreement and any supplement, addendum or modification, including any Copy, may be Signed in two or more counterparts, all of which shall constitute one and the same writing.

Buyer's Initials (___RAP___)(___GMP___)
Seller's Initials (_____)(_____)

RPA-CA REVISED 10/02 (PAGE 7 OF 8)

Reviewed by _____ Date _____

EQUAL HOUSING OPPORTUNITY

CALIFORNIA RESIDENTIAL PURCHASE AGREEMENT (RPA-CA PAGE 7 OF 8)

Source: Reprinted with permission, California Association of REALTORS®. Endorsement not implied.

Exercise 7-3 (Continued)

Property Address: __3840 Monroe Street, Concord, California__   Date: __1/11/xx__

31. EXPIRATION OF OFFER: This offer shall be deemed revoked and the deposit shall be returned unless the offer is Signed by Seller and a Copy of the Signed offer is personally received by Buyer, or by ____(Broker)_____, who is authorized to receive it by 5:00 PM on the third calendar day after this offer is signed by Buyer (or, if checked, ❑ by __1/13/xx_____ (date), at _____ AM/PM).

Date __1/11/xx_____   Date __1/11/xx_____

BUYER __*Kenneth A. Plummer*_____   BUYER __*Peggy M. Plummer*_____
_____Kenneth A. Plummer_____   _____Peggy M. Plummer_____
(Print name)   **(Print name)**

_____
(Address)

32. BROKER COMPENSATION FROM SELLER:
    A. Upon Close Of Escrow, **Seller** agrees to pay compensation to Broker as specified in a separate written agreement between Seller and Broker.
    B. If escrow does not close, compensation is payable as specified in that separate written agreement.
33. ACCEPTANCE OF OFFER: Seller warrants that Seller is the owner of the Property, or has the authority to execute this Agreement. Seller accepts the above offer, agrees to sell the Property on the above terms and conditions, and agrees to the above confirmation of agency relationships. Seller has read and acknowledges receipt of a Copy of this Agreement, and authorizes Broker to deliver a Signed Copy to Buyer.
    ❑ (If checked) **SUBJECT TO ATTACHED COUNTER OFFER, DATED** _____.

Date _____   Date _____

SELLER _____   SELLER _____

_____   _____
(Print name)   **(Print name)**

(Address)

(____/____)   **CONFIRMATION OF ACCEPTANCE:** A Copy of Signed Acceptance was personally received by Buyer or Buyer's authorized
(Initials)   agent on (date) _____ at _____ AM/PM. **A binding Agreement is created when a Copy of Signed Acceptance is personally received by Buyer or Buyer's authorized agent whether or not confirmed in this document. Completion of this confirmation is not legally required in order to create a binding Agreement; it is solely intended to evidence the date that Confirmation of Acceptance has occurred.**

REAL ESTATE BROKERS:
A.   **Real Estate Brokers are not parties to the Agreement between Buyer and Seller.**
B.   Agency relationships are confirmed as stated in paragraph 27.
C.   If specified in paragraph 2A, Agent who submitted the offer for Buyer acknowledges receipt of deposit.
D.   **COOPERATING BROKER COMPENSATION:** Listing Broker agrees to pay Cooperating Broker **(Selling Firm)** and Cooperating Broker agrees to accept, out of Listing Broker's proceeds in escrow: **(i)** the amount specified in the MLS, provided Cooperating Broker is a Participant of the MLS in which the Property is offered for sale or a reciprocal MLS; or **(ii)** ❑ (if checked) the amount specified in a separate written agreement (C.A.R. Form CBC) between Listing Broker and Cooperating Broker.

Real Estate Broker (Selling Firm) _____
By _____   Date _____
Address _____ City _____ State _____ Zip _____
Telephone _____ Fax _____ E-mail _____

Real Estate Broker (Listing Firm) _____
By _____   Date _____
Address _____ City _____ State _____ Zip _____
Telephone _____ Fax _____ E-mail _____

ESCROW HOLDER ACKNOWLEDGMENT:
Escrow Holder acknowledges receipt of a Copy of this Agreement, (if checked, ❑ a deposit in the amount of $ _____), counter offer numbers _____ and _____, and agrees to act as Escrow Holder subject to paragraph 28 of this Agreement, any supplemental escrow instructions and the terms of Escrow Holder's general provisions.

Escrow Holder is advised that the date of Confirmation of Acceptance of the Agreement as between Buyer and Seller is _____

Escrow Holder _____   Escrow # _____
By _____   Date _____
Address _____
Phone/Fax/E-mail _____
Escrow Holder is licensed by the California Department of ❑ Corporations, ❑ Insurance, ❑ Real Estate. License # _____

(____/____)   **REJECTION OF OFFER:** No counter offer is being made. This offer was reviewed and rejected by Seller on
(Seller's Initials) _____ (Date)

THIS FORM HAS BEEN APPROVED BY THE CALIFORNIA ASSOCIATION OF REALTORS® (C.A.R.). NO REPRESENTATION IS MADE AS TO THE LEGAL VALIDITY OR ADEQUACY OF ANY PROVISION IN ANY SPECIFIC TRANSACTION. A REAL ESTATE BROKER IS THE PERSON QUALIFIED TO ADVISE ON REAL ESTATE TRANSACTIONS. IF YOU DESIRE LEGAL OR TAX ADVICE, CONSULT AN APPROPRIATE PROFESSIONAL.
This form is available for use by the entire real estate industry. It is not intended to identify the user as a REALTOR®. REALTOR® is a registered collective membership mark which may be used only by members of the NATIONAL ASSOCIATION OF REALTORS® who subscribe to its Code of Ethics.

SURE TRAC
The System for Success™
Published by the
California Association of REALTORS®

Reviewed by _____ Date _____

EQUAL HOUSING OPPORTUNITY

RPA-CA REVISED 10/02 (PAGE 8 OF 8)
CALIFORNIA RESIDENTIAL PURCHASE AGREEMENT   (RPA-CA PAGE 8 OF 8)

Source: Reprinted with permission, California Association of REALTORS®. Endorsement not implied.

Exercise 10-2

A. **Settlement Statement**	U.S. Department of Housing and Urban Development		OMB Approval No. 2502-0265

B. Type of Loan

1. ☐ FHA 2. ☐ FmHA 3. ☐ Conv. Unins.	6. File Number:	7. Loan Number:	8. Mortgage Insurance Case Number:
4. ☐ VA 5. ☐ Conv. Ins.			

C. Note: This form is furnished to give you a statement of actual settlement costs. Amounts paid to and by the settlement agent are shown. Items marked "(p.o.c.)" were paid outside the closing; they are shown here for informational purposes and are not included in the totals.

D. Name & Address of Borrower:	E. Name & Address of Seller:	F. Name & Address of Lender:
Joe Beier and Sue Beier	Ed Sellar and Rita Sellar	Royal Bank

G. Property Location:	H. Settlement Agent: California Title Company	
126 Courtney Place River Glen, California	Place of Settlement: 126 Courtney Place River Glen, California	I. Settlement Date: 8/8/xx

J. Summary of Borrower's Transaction		K. Summary of Seller's Transaction	
100. Gross Amount Due From Borrower		**400. Gross Amount Due To Seller**	
101. Contract sales price	749,950.00	401. Contract sales price	749,950.00
102. Personal property		402. Personal property	
103. Settlement charges to borrower (line 1400)	12,472.92	403.	
104.		404.	
105.		405.	
Adjustments for items paid by seller in advance		**Adjustments for items paid by seller in advance**	
106. City/town taxes to		406. City/town taxes to	
107. County taxes to		407. County taxes to	
108. Assessments 8/8/xx to 9/30/xx	266.13	408. Assessments 8/8/xx to 9/30/xx	266.13
109.		409.	
110.		410.	
111.		411.	
112.		412.	
120. Gross Amount Due From Borrower	762,689.05	**420. Gross Amount Due To Seller**	750,216.13
200. Amounts Paid By Or In Behalf Of Borrower		**500. Reductions In Amount Due To Seller**	
201. Deposit or earnest money	74,995.00	501. Excess deposit (see instructions)	
202. Principal amount of new loan(s)	599,960.00	502. Settlement charges to seller (line 1400)	40,672.38
203. Existing loan(s) taken subject to		503. Existing loan(s) taken subject to	
204.		504. Payoff of first mortgage loan	186,116.51
205.		505. Payoff of second mortgage loan	25,390.28
206.		506. Express Delivery Fee	10.75
207.		507.	
208.		508.	
209.		509.	
Adjustments for items unpaid by seller		**Adjustments for items unpaid by seller**	
210. City/town taxes to		510. City/town taxes to	
211. County taxes 7/1/xx to 8/7/xx	250.67	511. County taxes 7/1/xx to 8/7/xx	250.67
212. Assessments to		512. Assessments to	
213.		513.	
214.		514.	
215.		515.	
216.		516.	
217.		517.	
218.		518.	
219.		519.	
220. Total Paid By/For Borrower	675,205.67	**520. Total Reduction Amount Due Seller**	252,440.59
300. Cash At Settlement From/To Borrower		**600. Cash At Settlement To/From Seller**	
301. Gross Amount due from borrower (line 120)	762,689.05	601. Gross amount due to seller (line 420)	750,216.13
302. Less amounts paid by/for borrower (line 220)	(675,205.67)	602. Less reductions in amt. due seller (line 520)	(252,440.59)
303. Cash ☑ From ☐ To Borrower	87,483.38	**603. Cash** ☑ To ☐ From Seller	497,775.54

Previous editions are obsolete

Exercise 10-2 (Continued)

L. Settlement Charges

		Paid From Borrowers Funds at Settlement	Paid From Seller's Funds at Settlement
700. Total Sales/Broker's Commission based on price $ 749,950 @ 5.25 % = $39,372.38			
Division of Commission (line 700) as follows:			
701. $ 39,372.38 to Frank Rice Realty			
702. $ to			
703. Commission paid at Settlement			39,372.38
704. **Home Warranty from California Home Warranty**			395.00
800. Items Payable In Connection With Loan			
801. Loan Origination Fee %		6,000.00	
802. Loan Discount %			
803. Appraisal Fee to			
804. Credit Report to			
805. Lender's Inspection Fee			
806. Mortgage Insurance Application Fee to			
807. Assumption Fee			
808. Tax Service Fee		47.00	
809. Processing Fee		250.00	
810.			
811.			
900. Items Required By Lender To Be Paid In Advance			
901. Interest from 8/8/xx to 9/1/xx @$ 95.83 /day		2,299.92	
902. Mortgage Insurance Premium for months to			
903. Hazard Insurance Premium for One years to California Home Ins.		1,837.00	
904. years to			
905.			
1000. Reserves Deposited With Lender			
1001. Hazard insurance months@$ per month			
1002. Mortgage insurance months@$ per month			
1003. City property taxes months@$ per month			
1004. County property taxes months@$ per month			
1005. Annual assessments months@$ per month			
1006. months@$ per month			
1007. months@$ per month			
1008. months@$ per month			
1100. Title Charges			
1101. Settlement or closing fee to California Title Company		480.00	
1102. Abstract or title search to			
1103. Title examination to			
1104. Title insurance binder to			
1105. Document preparation to California Title Company		100.00	60.00
1106. Notary fees to California Title Company		20.00	10.00
1107. Attorney's fees to			
(includes above items numbers:)			
1108. Title insurance to California Title Company		1,275.00	
(includes above items numbers:)			
1109. Lender's coverage $			
1110. Owner's coverage $			
1111.			
1112.			
1113.			
1200. Government Recording and Transfer Charges			
1201. Recording fees: Deed $ 11.00 ; Mortgage $ 28.00 ; Releases $ 10.00		39.00	10.00
1202. City/county tax/stamps: Deed $ 825.00 ; Mortgage $			825.00
1203. State tax/stamps: Deed $; Mortgage $			
1204.			
1205.			
1300. Additional Settlement Charges			
1301. Survey to			
1302. Pest inspection to			
1303. Transfer Fee to Homeowner's Association		125.00	
1304.			
1305.			
1400. Total Settlement Charges (enter on lines 103, Section J and 502, Section K)		$12,472.92	$40,672.38

Previous editions are obsolete

Exercise 10-3, Page 309

1. certificate of title
2. guarantee of title
3. CLTA standard policy of title insurance
4. ALTA extended-coverage policy of title insurance
5. abstract of title
6. CLTA standard policy of title insurance

Achievement Examination 10, Page 311

1. a	6. c	11. a	16. b
2. c	7. c	12. b	17. c
3. b	8. b	13. a	18. b
4. d	9. a	14. c	19. a
5. b	10. b	15. a	20. a

Chapter 11
Real Estate Taxation

Exercise 11-1, Page 318

Assessor's appraised value	$ 395,000
Less homeowner's exemption	7,000
Taxable amount	388,000
Tax rate	.01
Tax	$ 3,880
Installment	$ 1,940
Delinquent payment	$ 2,134

Exercise 11-2, Page 333

1. The Clocks' present rental expenses are $2,061 per month ($1,875 rent plus $186 utilities). In the fifth year they will be paying $2,465.07, assuming a 5 percent increase per year and no increase in utility payments, and will start the sixth year at $2,579.02 per month. They will receive no tax break on the rental expenses.

2. As homeowners, the Clocks will have monthly expenses of $3,588.35 ($2,757.93 mortgage payment plus $488.75 as one month's share of the property tax plus $116.67 as one month's share of fire insurance plus $225 for utilities) before taxes. After taxes, taking into account that they will be paying $27,446.31 in interest and $5,865 in property tax the first year, their payment is effectively $1,019.93 ($27,446.31 interest + $5,865 property tax = $33,311.31 tax deductions; $33,311.31 × 28% tax rate = $9,327.17 by which the Clocks' taxes will be reduced; $9,327.17 ÷ 12 = $777.26 monthly tax benefit; $3,588.35 − $777.26 = $2,811.09 effective monthly housing expense). In five years, when a greater share of the Clocks' mortgage payment is principal, they will have monthly expenses of $3,588.35 before taxes, and $2,846.74 after taxes.

3. The Clocks also should take into account any reduction in their state income tax resulting from mortgage interest and property tax deductions, the possibility that they will move into a higher tax bracket and have a greater benefit from the allowable deductions, the condition of the house (Will it need major repairs in the near future?), the loss of income from the $115,000 used as a down payment, the equity buildup in the house over the loan term, the appreciation (or depreciation) of real estate, the fact that they may not qualify for the loan they want, the fact that as homeowners they will have to cut back on other expenses in the first years of ownership to cover their housing bills, the size of their family and their likely needs in the future, and the housing amenities that they have come to expect or would prefer to have.

Achievement Examination 11, Page 337

1. a	6. d	11. c	16. a
2. b	7. b	12. c	17. a
3. c	8. b	13. b	18. a
4. c	9. d	14. b	19. d
5. c	10. c	15. d	20. d

Chapter 12
Landlord and Tenant

Exercise 12-1, Page 352

1. estate for years
2. estate at sufferance

3. A lease agreement must be written when the lease term will end more than one year from the date of the agreement.

4. No. The lease contract did not have a lawful object.

5. Yes. The landlord can demand a security deposit of no more than two months' rent for an unfurnished apartment—in this case, $1,300.

6. Sue will have a sublease.

7. No. The landlord has the right to enter the premises in an emergency.

Exercise 12-2, Page 356

1. landlord
2. tenant
3. tenant
4. landlord
5. landlord
6. tenant
7. landlord
8. landlord
9. tenant
10. tenant

Exercise 12-3, Page 365

1. 30 days
2. 15 days after personal service or 18 days after mailed notice of landlord's belief of abandonment
3. 3 days
4. 5 days
5. 30 days
6. 3 days
7. 60 days

Exercise 12-4, Page 372

A percentage lease would be useful in this situation. It would allow for a base rent affordable for a new business and also provide for rent increases as the business grows.

Achievement Examination 12, Page 375

1. c	6. c	11. d	16. b
2. c	7. a	12. d	17. a
3. d	8. a	13. b	18. d
4. b	9. d	14. a	19. b
5. b	10. a	15. c	20. b

Chapter 13
Real Estate Appraising

Exercise 13-1, Page 383

1. contribution
2. supply and demand, change, growth, anticipation
3. growth, equilibrium, decline, change, supply and demand, competition, gentrification
4. supply and demand, conformity, regression

Exercise 13-2, Page 388

See the completed chart on page 514.

Exercise 13-3, Page 395

Living area = 1,500 square feet @ $55 per square foot	=	$ 82,500
Garage area = 625 square feet @ $35 per square foot	=	$ 21,875
Total reproduction cost	=	$104,375
Yearly depreciation	=	$ 2,609
Total depreciation	=	$ 10,436

Reproduction cost – Total depreciation + Land value = $119,939

Estimate of value of house X by the cost approach is $119,939.

Exercise 13-4, Page 399

Subject's gross income multiplier = 211

Subject's market value = $1,800 × 211 = $379,000

Achievement Examination 13, Page 406

1. b	6. b	11. c	16. c
2. d	7. d	12. b	17. a
3. b	8. c	13. d	18. c
4. c	9. b	14. b	19. b
5. d	10. c	15. b	20. a

Chapter 14
Residential Design and Construction

Exercise 14-1, Page 413

Broker Bob may be charged with contracting without a license. Such extensive repairs surely cost more than $200; Broker Bob does not qualify for any exception from the Contractors' License Law.

Exercise 13-2

	Comparables		
	A	**B**	**C**
Sales price	$215,250	$208,000	$199,000
Adjustment variables			
Extra half-bath	–4,000		
No fireplace		+3,200	
No home warranty			+350
Poor location			+12,000
Total adjustments	–4,000	+3,200	+12,350
Adjusted value	$211,250	$211,200	$211,350

Exercise 14-3

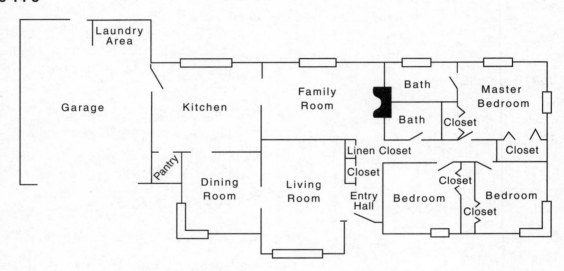

Exercise 14-2, Page 417

The photograph shows a one-story, ranch-style house with attached two–car garage. The house has wood siding, brick trim, a brick chimney, stucco end wall, and wood shake roof.

Exercise 14-3, Page 420

See the completed figure above.

Exercise 14-4, Page 431

(Clockwise, from top center) sheathing, ridge board, rafter, joist, firestop, stud, header, plate, foundation, footing, anchor bolt, crawl space, joist, sheathing, eave, flashing, building paper

Achievement Examination 14, Page 434

1. d	6. d	11. b	16. c
2. d	7. c	12. a	17. d
3. c	8. a	13. c	18. b
4. d	9. a	14. c	19. c
5. b	10. d	15. b	20. b

Chapter 15
Government Control of Land Use

Exercise 15-1, Page 444

A city of 2 million would influence the expected population, commercial development, and property uses of a nearby suburban community. Increasing housing demand in the city would make surrounding property more desirable, just as the expense of commercial development in the city would bring business to outlying communities. The result would be greater demand for city and consumer services in the affected communities.

A county plan encouraging commercial development would increase the predictability of the above conditions.

If a community limits development, greater demand for both residential and commercial uses may be placed on nearby communities.

Development always will be limited by geologic features that prevent safe construction or require the imposition of strict controls.

Exercise 15-2, Page 453
1. Yes, because inclusion of more property restrictions is a material change in the subdivision offering.
2. See the completed chart below.

Exercise 15-3, Page 456
The Smiths are prohibited from all forms of unlawful discrimination in the sale of their house.

Achievement Examination 15, Page 459

1. a	6. d	11. c	16. b
2. d	7. b	12. d	17. c
3. d	8. a	13. c	18. c
4. c	9. b	14. d	19. a
5. b	10. a	15. b	20. c

Appendix 1
Math Appendix

Math Achievement Examination, Page 471
1. $756,000 × 2.5% = $18,900 buyer's broker's commission
   $18,900 × 70% = $13,230 sales associate's commission
2. $175,000 × 6.625% = $11,593.75 annual interest
   $11,593.75 ÷ 12 = $966.15 first month's interest
   $1,120.54 − $966.15 = $154.39 first month's principal
3. $260,000 ÷ 1,000 = 260
   $8.99 × 260 = $2,337.40 monthly payment for 15 years
   $6.66 × 260 = $1,731.60 monthly payment for 30 years
4. 1,150 feet × 2,400 feet = 2,760,000 square feet
   2,760,000 ÷ 43,560 = 63.36 acres

Exercise 15-2

	Subdivision Map Act	Subdivided Lands Law
Number of subdivision units or parcels	two or more	five or more
Inclusion of undivided interests	no	yes
Inclusion of time-shares	no	yes
Inclusion of stock cooperatives	only if five or more units are converted	yes
Opportunity for notice and hearing	only if significant deprivation of other landowner's property rights is involved	no

5. 7,200 square feet × $265 = $1,908,000 construction cost

6. $780,000 × 80% = $624,000 loan amount

   624 × 6.33 = $3,949.92 monthly payment on 30-year loan at 6.5%

   624 × 8.17 = $5,098.08 monthly payment on 15-year loan at 5.5%

7. $230,000 × 108% = $248,400 appreciated value at end of year 1

   $248,400 × 108% = $268,272 appreciated value at end of year 2

   $268,272 × 108% = $289,734 appreciated value at end of year 3

   $289,734 × 108% = $312,913 appreciated value at end of year 4

8. $230,000 × 90% = $207,000 original loan amount

   $207,000 − $8,000 = $199,000 remaining loan amount

   $312,913 − $199,000 = $113,913 equity in the home

9. ½ × ¼ × ¼ × 640 = ¹⁄₃₂ × 640 = 20 acres, so the descriptions match

   $16,600 × 20 = $330,000

10. $66,250
   $1,325,000 │ Rate

   $66,250 ÷ $1,325,000 = 0.5 = 5%

INDEX

Power of eminent domain. *See* Eminent domain
Power of sale, 86, 231
Power-of-sale mortgage, 232
Preliminary notice, 104
Preliminary report, 294, 303
Prepaid rental listing service (PRLS), 14
Prepayment, 263, 271
Presidios, 36
Price, 177
Primary mortgage market, 234-48
Prime rate, 216-17
Principal
    agent relationship with, 128
    definition of, 223, 464
    duties, 155-56
    liability, 161
Priority, 340
Priority of claims, 121
Prior payment defense, 222
Private grant, 84
Private individuals, 238-39
Private land, 85
Private mortgage insurance (PMI), 235
PRLS. *See* Prepaid rental listing service
Probate, 80-81
Probate Code, 81
Procuring cause, 154
Professional associations, 29-30
Progression, 382
Promissory note, 219-20
Property
    buyer's investigation of, 196
    conditions affecting, 196
    description, 342
    maintenance standards, 116
    management, 367-71
    statement of condition, 350
    value, 314
Property management agreement, 367-70
Property taxation
    benefit assessments, 321-22
    computations, 317-18
    documentary transfer tax, 322-23
    exemptions, 316-17
    homeowner assistance, 320-21
    manufactured homes, 323-24
    penalty, 317
    Proposition 13, 313-14
    redemption, 319
    renter relief, 320
    special assessments, 321
    supplemental assessments, 318-19
    tax collection, 315-16
    tax lien, 319
    tax sale, 319-20
Property Tax Postponement Law, 320
Property tax year, 317
Proposition 2, 218
Proposition 6, 325
Proposition 13, 313-14

Prorations
    computation, 296-97, 466
    escrow holder duties, 295
    definition of, 296
    purchase agreement provisions, 197
Prospective economic advantage, 155-56
Public auction, 320
Public dedication, 85
Public grant, 84-85
Public land, 84
Public report, 447-48
PUD. *See* Planned unit development
Pueblos, 37
Purchase agreement
    broker duties, 184, 195
    buyer's inspection advisory, 193-94
    contract terms, 195-98
    counteroffer, 205
    mold disclosure, 202-3
    natural hazard disclosure statement, 199-201
    sample, 185-192
Purchase money mortgage, 272
Purchase money trust deed, 272

Q

Quantity survey method, 392
Quasi-community property, 67
Quitclaim deed, 93, 95, 111-12

R

Rafter, 425
RAM. *See* Reverse annuity mortgage
Rancho grants, 37, 39
Range, 48
Rangeland, Grazing Land, and Grassland Protection Act, 452
Rapid payoff mortgage, 237
Rate, 223, 464
Ratification, 138
Ready, willing, and able buyer, 154
Real estate, 39
    appraisal. *See* Appraisal
    broker. *See* Broker
    brokerage. *See* Brokerage
    definition of, 59
    listing agreement. *See* Listing agreement
    purchase contract, 169
    purchase contract and receipt for deposit, 184-208
    salesperson. *See* Salesperson
    syndicate, 71
Real Estate Act of 1919, 1
Real Estate Advisory Commission, 3
Real Estate Commissioner
    Department of Real Estate, 2
    license law enforcement, 21-24
    Regulations, 2, 6
    responsibilities of, 3, 4
    selection of, 2-3

Real Estate Education and Research Fund, 25
Real Estate Fraud Prosecution Trust Fund, 92
Real estate investment trust (REIT), 72
Real Estate Law
    broker activities, 6, 10-11
    broker-salesperson relationship, 5-6
    Department of Real Estate, 2-3
    enforcement of, 21-24
    licensed activities, 6, 10-11
    mortgage loan broker, 240
    provisions, 1-3
Real Estate Settlement Procedures Act (RESPA), 251-52, 269, 297
Real Estate Transfer Disclosure Statement, 157, 158-60
Real property
    bundle of rights, 39
    definition of, 39-42, 59
    distinction of, 44-45
    historical perspective, 35-38
    land description, 45-54
    leasehold as, 340
    manufactured (mobile) home as, 323-24
    notice of tax lien, 326
    ownership issues, 44, 45, 66
    personal property and, 40-45
    sale of, 44-45
    title transfer, 44
    transactions, 10
Real Property Loan Law, 239
Realtist, 29
REALTOR®, 29
REALTOR®-ASSOCIATE, 29
Reasonable care and skill, 154
Reassessment event, 314
Reconciliation, 399-400
Reconveyance deed, 96
Recording, 92-93, 340
Record keeping, 286
Recovery Account, 25, 28, 161
Recovery property, 330
Rectangle, 467-68
Rectangular survey system, 47-52
Redemption period, 226
Redlining, 455
Refinance, 268, 269
Reformation, 181
Regression, 382
Regulations of Real Estate Commissioner, 2, 5
Regulation Z, 248-51
Reinstatement, 225
REIT. *See* Real estate investment trust
Rejection, 174
Release, 107, 181
Reliction, 82
Remainder, 61-62
Remainderman, 61-62
Remedies, 340
Renegotiable-rate mortgage (RRM), 237

Rent, 339, 342-43, 362
Rental property, 249
Rent control ordinance, 371-72
Renter, 320
Repairs, 196
Replacement cost, 390-92
Reproduction cost, 390-92
Request for reconveyance, 96
Rescission, 181
Reserve requirements, 216
Resident apartment manager, 367
Residential Lead-Based Paint Hazard
    Reduction Act, 426
Residential lease, 341, 344-49
Residential license, 378
RESPA. *See* Real Estate Settlement
    Procedures Act
Restraint on alienation, 115
Restricted license, 21, 23
Restricted report, 400
Restrictions, 114-18
Retaliation, 354
Reverse annuity mortgage (RAM), 237
Reversion, 61-62
Revitalization, 383
Revocation, 21, 174-75
Rezoning, 441
Ridge board, 425
Right of appropriation, 41
Right of cancellation, 233
Right of entry, 350-51
Right of possession, 366
Right to rescind, 250-51
Right of redemption, 229
Rights, 340
Right of survivorship, 65, 67
Riparian rights, 41
Rollover mortgage, 237
Roof, 412, 413, 425, 427
RRM. *See* Renegotiable-rate mortgage
Rumford Fair Housing Act, 357, 455
R-value, 424

S

Safety, 440
Safety clause, 144
Sale, 143, 154, 297
Sales associate, 3
Sales comparison approach, 385, 387-90
Salesperson, 3
    activities of, 6, 10-11
    broker relationship, 5-6
    conduct, 25
    definition of, 6
    discharge of, 5
    employment change, 5
    license examination, 19
    license requirements, 17-18
    license term/renewal, 20

negligent supervision of, 23
    unlawful conduct, 26-28
Sales tax, 324-25
SAM. *See* Shared appreciation mortgage
San Diego Association of REALTORS®
    (SDAR), 198
Sandwich lease, 352
Satisfaction, 107, 231
Savings and loan association (S&L), 235-36
SBA. *See* Small Business Administration
Scarcity, 380
Scheduled rent, 396
S corporation, 70
SDAR. *See* San Diego Association of
    REALTORS®
Secondary mortgage market, 275-77
Secret profit, 22, 153
Secretary for Business and Transportation, 456
Secretary of State Business Service Center, 71
Section, 49
Section and township system, 47-52
Security deposit, 343, 350
Security instrument, 219, 224-32
Seismic Hazards Mapping Act, 452
Seismic zones, 440, 452
Self-contained report, 400, 401
Seller
    disclosure, 157
    FHA provisions, 264
    financing, 272
    responsibilities of, 290
Seller's title, 297
Separate ownership, 63
Separate property, 66
Service charges, 268-69
Servicemen's Readjustment Act of 1944, 265
Service providers, 197
Servient tenement, 108-13
Set-off defense, 222
Settlement statement, 282, 286, 297, 298-99
Shared appreciation mortgage (SAM), 237, 265
Shareholders, 69
Sheathing, 423
Sheetrock, 427-28
Sheriff's deed, 87, 96
Siding, 423
Sill, 421
Single agency, 132
Site preparation, 420-21
Site value, 391
Six-month rule, 119
S&L. *See* Savings and loan association
Small Business Administration (SBA), 12
Smoke detectors, 429-30
Social forces, 382-83
Social Security number, 16, 264
Soffit, 427
Solar heating, 428-29, 430
Sole proprietorship, 4, 63, 69, 173

Solid waste management plan, 440
Spanish language contracts, 172
Special agent, 128-29
Special assessment, 321
Special benefit assessment, 321
Special Information Booklet, 251
Special power of attorney, 133
Specific lien, 102
Specific performance, 182
Specific plan, 440
Square footage, 466
Square-foot method, 391-92, 470
Standard subdivision, 445-46
Standard title insurance policy, 303-4
Standby commitment, 253
Standby fee, 253
Starting time, 104
State Board of Equalization, 324
Statement of property condition, 350
Statute of Frauds, 137-38, 179
Statute of limitations, 183
Statutory dedication, 85, 449
Statutory disclosures, 196
Statutory language, 6
Stay of execution, 363
Stock cooperative project, 446
Straight-line method, 330, 394
Straight note, 219, 236
Stucco, 423
Studs, 422
Subagent, 129, 154
Subdivided Lands Law, 2, 445, 448
Subdivision
    laws, 451
    map, 46, 448-50
    public report, 447-48
    system, 46-47
    types of, 445-47
Subdivision Map Act, 448-49
Subflooring, 428
Subject to, 252
Sublease, 351-52
Subsidized housing, 360
Substitution, 383
Succession, 78
Summary report, 400
Supplemental assessment, 318-19
Supply and demand, 381
Surrender, 358-59
Suspension, 21
Syndicate, 71, 73

T

Tack, 83
Take back financing, 272
Take-out loan, 253
Tax
    bracket, 328
    clearance, 324